Hungary

written and researched by

Charles Hebbert, Norm Longley and Dan Richardson

with additional contributions by

Emma Rees

NEW YORK • LONDON • DELHI

www.roughguides.com

Contents

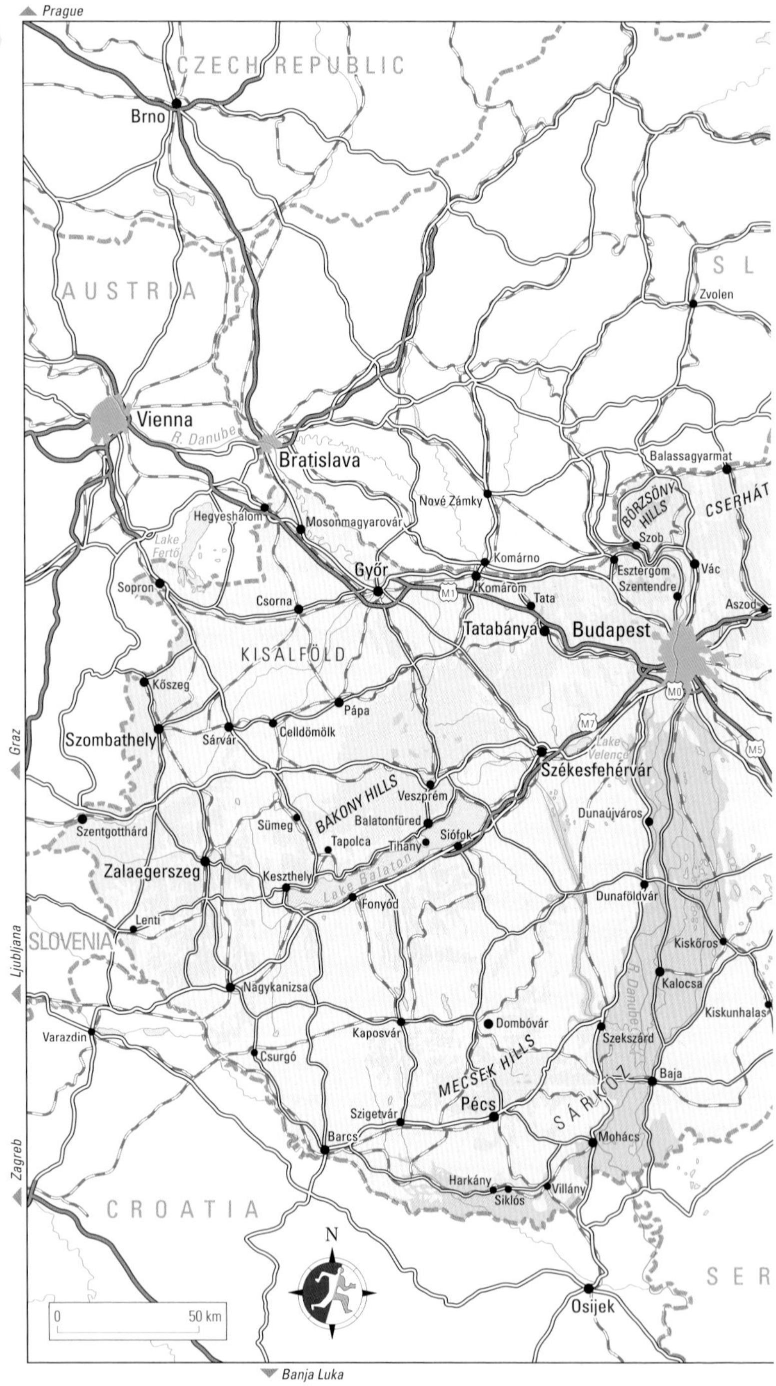
Prague
CZECH REPUBLIC
Brno
AUSTRIA
Vienna
R. Danube
Bratislava
Hegyeshalom
Mosonmagyaróvár
Lake Fertő
Sopron
Csorna
Győr
M1
Nové Zámky
Komárno
Komárom
Tata
Tatabánya
Budapest
KISALFÖLD
Kőszeg
Szombathely
Sárvár
Celldömölk
Pápa
Graz
Szentgotthárd
Sümeg
BAKONY HILLS
Veszprém
Balatonfüred
Tapolca
Tihány
Siófok
Zalaegerszeg
Keszthely
Lake Balaton
Fonyód
Lenti
SLOVENIA
Ljubljana
Nagykanizsa
Varazdin
Kaposvár
Dombóvár
Csurgó
MECSEK HILLS
Pécs
Szigetvár
Barcs
Zagreb
Harkány
Siklós
Villány
CROATIA
N
0
50 km
Osijek
Banja Luka
S L
Zvolen
Balassagyarmat
BÖRZSÖNY HILLS
CSERHÁT
Szob
Esztergom
Vác
Szentendre
Aszod
M0
M7
M5
Lake Velence
Székesfehérvár
Dunaújváros
Dunaföldvár
Kiskőrös
R. Danube
Kalocsa
Kiskunhalas
Szekszárd
Baja
SÁRKÖZ
Mohács
SER

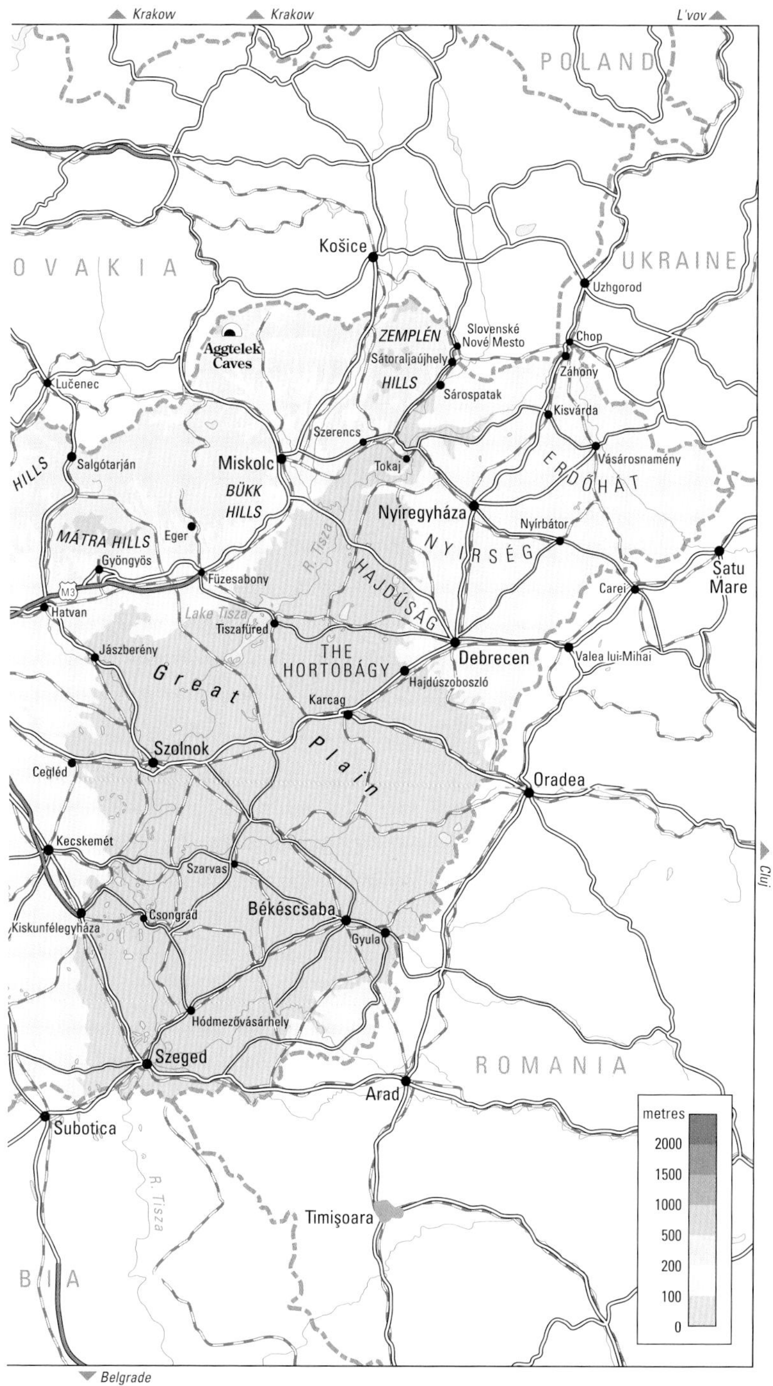

Krakow
Krakow
L'vov
POLAND
SLOVAKIA
UKRAINE
Košice
Uzhgorod
Aggtelek Caves
ZEMPLÉN HILLS
Slovenské Nové Mesto
Sátoraljaújhely
Sárospatak
Chop
Záhony
Lučenec
Kisvárda
Szerencs
Tokaj
Vásárosnamény
Salgótarján
Miskolc
HILLS
BÜKK HILLS
ERDŐHÁT
Nyíregyháza
Nyírbátor
Eger
MÁTRA HILLS
NYÍRSÉG
HAJDÚSÁG
R. Tisza
Gyöngyös
Füzesabony
Satu Mare
Carei
M3
Hatvan
Lake Tisza
Tiszafüred
Debrecen
Valea lui Mihai
Jászberény
THE HORTOBÁGY
Hajdúszoboszló
Great Plain
Karcag
Szolnok
Cegléd
Oradea
Kecskemét
Cluj
Szarvas
Békéscsaba
Csongrád
Kiskunfélegyháza
Gyula
Hódmezővásárhely
Szeged
ROMANIA
Arad
Subotica
metres
2000
1500
1000
500
200
100
0
R. Tisza
Timişoara
SERBIA
Belgrade

Introduction to Hungary

A relatively small, landlocked nation of just over ten million people, Hungary boasts much more beyond its beautiful, and very hip, capital city, Budapest. Gorgeous Baroque towns stand cheek by jowl with ancient castles and fortresses, while nature asserts itself spectacularly in the form of Lake Balaton, one of Europe's largest lakes. Equally stunning are the thickly forested Northern Uplands, and the beguiling landscape of the vast Great Plain, not to mention one of the grandest stretches of the great Danube River. Aside from the country's extraordinary concentration of thermal spas, there is also a wealth of other activities available, including a range of watersports, horse-riding, cycling and hiking, while nearly two dozen wine regions offer the chance to sample a range of quality wines little known beyond its own borders.

Right at the heart of Europe, Hungary was likened by the poet Ady to a "river ferry, continually travelling between East and West, with always the sensation of not going anywhere but of being on the way back from the other bank"; this seems especially evident in the Hungarians' strong identification with the West, and simultaneous display of fierce pride in themselves as Magyars – a race that transplanted itself from Central Asia. After some forty years of Communist rule, the country embarked on reforming state socialism long before Gorbachev, making the transition to multi-party democracy without a shot being fired, while the removal of

Hungary boasts much more beyond its beautiful, and very hip, capital city, Budapest

the Iron Curtain along its border set in motion the events leading to the fall of the Berlin Wall. The ensuing spread of glossy Western capitalism, particularly in the capital, has brought very mixed blessings indeed for Hungarians – many of whom saw their living standards fall sharply. Following the country's accession to the EU in 2004 – which was broadly favoured by most Hungarians – there is a fresh sense of optimism, though what benefits membership will bring, only time will tell.

Where to go

The capital, **Budapest**, dominates the country in every sense – administratively, commercially and culturally. Divided into two distinct parts by the River Danube – the historical Buda district on the elevated west bank, and the grittier but more dynamic Pest district on the eastern side – the city boasts a welter of fine museums and churches, coffee houses, Turkish baths and Roman

▼ Cifra Palace, Kecskemét

Fact file

- Hungary, covering an **area** of 93,000 square kilometres, lies in the Carpathian basin in the heart of Europe. Two-thirds of the country is flatland, the greatest single area being the Great Plain, or *puszta*, which sprawls across the eastern half of the country. The remainder is undulating terrain, with only one mountain, Mount Kékes in the Northern Uplands, topping 1000m. There are nine **national parks** spread around the country, the largest of which is the Hortobágy on the Great Plain. Hungary has Central Europe's largest and warmest **lake**, the Balaton, two major rivers – the Danube and the Tisza – and over a thousand natural springs.
- On October 23, 1989, Hungary became an **independent republic** once again. The 1989 constitution set in place a parliamentary system of government, elected every four years, with the prime minister at its head. The head of state, the president, is elected every five years. Having been admitted to NATO in 1999, Hungary finally achieved its greatest political goal in 2004 when the country joined the **European Union**.
- With few natural resources, Hungary's **economy** is driven largely by its manufacturing industry. Foreign investment is amongst the highest of the former Communist countries.
- The **population** of the country currently stands at just over ten million, one fifth of whom live in the capital Budapest. It is estimated that over five million Hungarians live outside the country, a large number in Transylvania, Romania.

Hungarian wine

Wine making – first introduced by the Romans over two thousand years ago – has long played a large part in the lives of Hungarians. Today the industry is undergoing something of a renaissance, but it hasn't always been such a success story: production ceased completely during the 150 years of Ottoman rule, while decades of low-quality mass output under Communism did little to enhance the reputation of Hungarian vintages. It's only really in the last few years that the industry has been well and truly revitalized, with a growing number of small-scale, family-owned wineries opening up and foreign firms queuing to get a slice of the action. Of Hungary's 22 wine-growing regions, the most celebrated are the Tokaj-Hegyalja – whose wines are perhaps the most well-known abroad, notably the sweet dessert wine, Aszú – and Villány-Siklós, Hungary's first wine road, which consistently yields both fine-quality reds and whites; the Cabernet Sauvignon and Cabernet Franc are particularly treasured. Beyond these two regions, consider sampling the reds of Szekszárd, in southern Transdanubia, and the whites of Lake Balaton, particularly around Badacsony and Balatonboglár. Wine cellars (*borpince*) abound in all these regions and are by far the best places to enjoy a drink, although you could always head to a wine bar (*borozo*) instead; most restaurants have a good stock too. See p.44 for more on Hungarian wine.

ruins, as well as some splendid architecture and a diversity of entertainment unmatched in many Central or Eastern European cities.

The most obvious attraction after Budapest is the magnificent **Danube Bend**, one of the most spectacular stretches of this immense river. Sweeping its way north out of the capital, the river passes through the delightful town of Szentendre on the west bank – a popular day-trip from the capital – before moving serenely on through historic Visegrád and up to Esztergom, the centre of Hungarian Catholicism. Southwest of Budapest, **Lake Balaton**, with its string of brash resorts, styles itself as "the Nation's Playground", and contains Europe's largest thermal bath at Héviz, and some splendid wine regions, notably around the Badacsony Hills on the north shore and Balatonboglár on the southern shore.

Encircling Balaton and encompassing the area west of the Danube, **Transdanubia** has the country's most varied topography, from the flat, rather monotonous landscape of the northern Kisalföld to the verdant, forested Orség in the southwest. The region also claims some of the country's finest towns and cities, most notably Sopron with its atmospheric Belváros (inner town), and the vibrant city of Pécs, notable for its superb museums and Islamic architecture. Further south, the vineyards around Villány and Siklós – Hungary's first wine road – yield some of the country's finest wines.

The mildly hilly mountain ranges of the **Northern Uplands**, spreading eastwards from Budapest, offer Hungary's best opportunities for leisurely pursuits, including hiking, cycling and even skiing. The region is also home to the country's most fantastic natural wonder, the Aggtelek Caves, whilst the more sparsely populated northwestern region, the Zemplén range, will appeal to castle enthusiasts and those seeking to get off the beaten track. The Uplands are also famed for their wine centres, the most renowned being Eger – an enchanting town in its own right, showcasing some marvellous Baroque architecture – and Tokaj.

The area south of the Uplands is dominated by the vast, flat swathe of land known as the **Great Plain**, bisected in two by Hungary's other great river, the Tisza. Covering almost fifty percent of the country, the Plain doesn't have the clear-cut attractions of other regions, but it can be a rewarding place to visit. Szeged, close to the Serbian border, is the area's most appealing centre, with some delightful architecture and perhaps the country's most beautiful synagogue. Further east, its rival city Debrecen serves as the jumping-off point for the archaic Erdőhát region and the mirage-haunted Hortobágy *puszta*, home to a fantastic array of wildlife.

Thermal baths

They say drill anywhere in Hungary and you'll find a thermal spring – a boast that's not too far off the mark. Throughout the country, countless hot springs and wells lurk beneath the relatively thin surface of the Carpathian basin, providing a plentiful supply of superheated, mineral-rich water for the country's numerous baths. The first springs were discovered some two thousand years ago in the Roman town of Aquincum (meaning "abundant water") in north Budapest, but it wasn't until the Turkish occupation of the sixteenth and seventeenth centuries that a bathing culture really developed. The end of the nineteenth century witnessed the discovery of more springs – and the construction of more baths – and today Hungary boasts over eighty towns and settlements accommodating more than 120 baths. The largest and best-known of these is at Hévíz, at the western end of Lake Balaton, but it is in Budapest that some of the grandest baths in Europe can be found, often Art Nouveau halls with elegant Roman-style columns topped with a vaulted glass roof. Taking a dip in one of these opulent-looking affairs is an experience not to be missed – see p.98 for more.

Popular areas can be mobbed in summer, but rural areas receive few visitors, even during the high season.

When to go

Most visitors come in the summer, when nine or ten hours of sunshine can be relied on most days, sometimes interspersed with short, violent storms. The humidity that causes these is really only uncomfortable in Budapest, where the crowds don't help; elsewhere the climate is agreeable. Budapest, with its spring and autumn festivals, sights and culinary delights, is a standing invitation to come out of season. But other parts of Hungary have little to offer during the winter, and the weather doesn't become appealing until late spring. May, warm but showery, is the time to see the Danube Bend, Tihany or Sopron before everyone else arrives; June is hotter and drier, a pattern reinforced throughout July, August and September. There's little variation in temperatures across the country: the Great Plain is drier, and the highlands are wetter, during summer, but that's about as far as climatic changes go. The number of tourists varies more – popular areas such as Szentendre and Tihany can be mobbed in summer, but rural areas receive few visitors, even during the high season.

Average daytime temperatures

	Jan		Mar		May		July		Sept		Nov	
	°F	°C	°F	°C	°F	°C	°F	°C	°F	°C	°F	°C
Budapest	29	-2	42	6	61	16	72	22	63	17	42	6
Debrecen	27	-3	41	5	60	16	70	21	61	16	41	5
Miskolc	27	-3	37	3	57	14	68	20	63	17	37	3
Szeged	31	-1	42	6	61	16	70	21	64	18	41	5

things not to miss

It's not possible to see everything that Hungary has to offer in one trip – and we don't suggest you try. What follows is a selective taste of the country's highlights: outstanding buildings, natural wonders and colourful festivals. They're arranged in five colour-coded categories, which you can browse through to find the very best things to see, and experience. All highlights have a page reference to take you straight into the guide, where you can find out more.

01 **Hollókő** Page **330** • Nestling in the heart of the Cserhát Hills, a visit to this exquisitely preserved village – a World Heritage Site – is a must for its architecture and folk customs.

02 Thermal baths Page **98** • There's no better way to relax than in one of Budapest's magnificent Turkish baths.

03 The Badacsony Page **223** • Hike to the top of this extraordinary volcanic outcrop on Balaton's north shore for fantastic views of the lake.

04 Pécs Page **297** • Vital and absorbing, the city of Pécs has one of the most significant collections of Turkish buildings in this part of Europe.

05 Tihany Peninsula Page **213** • The picturesque village of Tihany, overlooked by a Benedictine abbey, is the jewel in Lake Balaton's crown.

06 Aggtelek Caves Page **355** • Take a tour through the largest, and one of the most amazing, stalactite cave systems in Europe.

07 Szentendre Page **157** • This once thriving artists' colony, just 19km from Budapest, is now a delightful town boasting some magical museums, great art and a rich Serbian legacy.

08 Statue Park Page **100** • Communism isn't quite dead in this extraordinary Budapest park housing a collection of monumental statues from the old regime.

09 Watersports on Lake Balaton Pages **205 & 226** • Siófok and Keszthely are just two of the resorts where you can sail, windsurf or, of course, swim.

10 Wine cellars Pages **309 & 361** • You shouldn't leave Hungary without visiting one of its famous wine cellars, the best of which are located on the Villány-Siklós wine road and in the Tokaj-Hegyalja region.

11 Eger Page **337** • Atmospheric Uplands town strewn with gorgeous Baroque architecture and famed for its local red wine, "Bull's Blood".

12 Paprika Page **381** • The foodstuff most commonly associated with Hungary is not quite the fiery stuff of legend but it is an integral part of the Magyar kitchen.

13 Esterházy Palace Page **274** • Once one of the most opulent palaces in Europe, this eighteenth-century Baroque and Rococo masterpiece is still the most beautiful in the country.

14 Hortobágy National Park Page **426** • You'll find blue-skirted cowboys, rodeo shows and a diverse collection of wildlife – water buffalo, corkscrew-horned sheep and wild boar – in Hungary's largest national park; there's also excellent bird-watching.

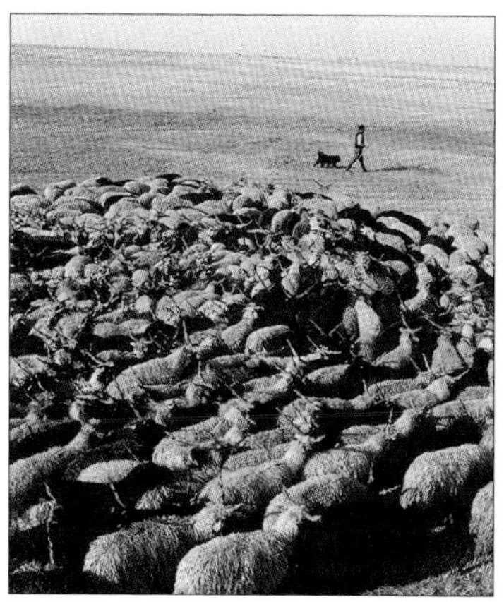

15 Budapest Spring Festival Page **138** • The capital's premier annual arts festival hosts a matchless line up of music, theatre and film, as well as a grand parade.

16 Pannonhalma Monastery Page **260** • The grand-looking Benedictine abbey, designed in an unusual amalgamation of architectural styles, is Hungary's most impressive monastery.

17 Sopron Page **265** • Pretty town, close to the Austrian border, featuring a spectacular Belváros brimming with absorbing museums and architecture.

18 The Vár, Budapest Page **85** • Historic Castle Hill is the capital's defining feature, a long, elevated plateau spotted with bastions, churches and some fine museums.

19 Busójárás Carnival Page **311** • Masked "*busó*" figures dressed in animal hides parade through the town and in boats across the Danube in this awesome spectacle.

21 Hiking in the Bükk Hills Page **336** • These lovely, beech-covered hills in the Northern Uplands are Hungary's prime hiking region, with trails to suit walkers of all abilities.

20 Danube Bend Page **171** • One of the most enchanting stretches of the River Danube sweeps its way up from Budapest before twisting dramatically through a forested valley towards Slovakia – the views are best appreciated from atop Visegrád Citadel.

22 Folk and Gypsy music Page **472** • Don't pass up the chance to experience the ubiquitous, irrepressible sounds of Hungarian folk and Gypsy music.

Basics

Basics

Getting there

Flying is the easiest way to reach Hungary, with several airlines now flying direct from airports in the UK and Ireland, as well as direct flights from the US and Canada. Flights from Australasia, however, still require a change of planes. Travelling overland from the UK takes around a day by train and a day and a half by bus, although with an Inter-Rail or Eurail pass you can take in Hungary as part of a wider European trip. Another option is to drive, a journey of over 1700km, best covered over a couple of days.

Airfares always depend on the **season**, with the highest fares from June to August, when the weather is best; fares drop during the "shoulder" seasons (March–May & Sept–Oct); and you'll get the best prices during the low season, November to February (excluding Christmas and New Year when prices are hiked up and seats are at a premium).

You can often cut costs by going through a **specialist flight agent** – either a consolidator, who buys up blocks of tickets from the airlines and sells them at a discount, or a **discount agent**, who in addition to dealing with discounted flights may also offer special student and youth fares and a range of other travel-related services such as travel insurance, rail passes, car rentals, tours and the like. Some agents specialize in **charter flights**, which may be cheaper than anything available on a scheduled flight, but again departure dates are fixed and withdrawal penalties are high.

Booking flights online

Many airlines and discount travel websites give you the opportunity to book your tickets, hotels and holiday packages **online**, cutting out the costs of agents and middlemen; these are worth going for, as long as you don't mind the inflexibility of non-refundable, non-changeable deals that many offer. There are some bargains to be had on **auction sites** too, if you're prepared to bid keenly. Almost all airlines have their own websites, offering flight tickets that can sometimes be just as cheap, and are often more flexible.

Online booking agents and general travel sites

Ⓦ **www.cheapflights.co.uk** (UK & Ireland), Ⓦ **www.cheapflights.com** (US), Ⓦ **www.cheapflights.ca** (Canada)
Ⓦ **www.cheapflights.com.au** (Australia & NZ) Flight deals, travel agents, plus links to other travel sites.
Ⓦ **www.cheaptickets.com** (US) Discount flight specialists. Also on Ⓣ 1-888/922-8849.
Ⓦ **www.ebookers.com** (UK) Efficient, easy-to-use flight finder, with competitive fares.
Ⓦ **www.etn.nl/discount** A hub of consolidator and discount agent links, maintained by the nonprofit European Travel Network.
Ⓦ **www.expedia.co.uk** (UK)
Ⓦ **www.expedia.com** (US)
Ⓦ **www.expedia.ca** (Canada) Discount airfares, all-airline search engine and daily deals.
Ⓦ **www.flyaow.com** "Airlines of the Web" – online air travel info and reservations.
Ⓦ **www.gaytravel.com** (US) Gay travel agent offering accommodation, cruises, tours and more. Also on Ⓣ 1-800/GAY-TRAVEL.
Ⓦ **www.geocities.com/thavery2000** An extensive list of airline websites and US toll-free numbers.
Ⓦ **www.kelkoo.co.uk** (UK) Useful price-comparison site, checking several sources of low-cost flights (and other goods & services) according to specific criteria.
Ⓦ **www.lastminute.com** (UK)
Ⓦ **www.au.lastminute.com** (Australia)
Ⓦ **www.lastminute.co.nz** (NZ) Comprehensive site with last-minute offers for flights, accommodation and car hire.
Ⓦ **www.opodo.co.uk** (UK) Popular and reliable source of low airfares. Owned by, and run in conjunction with, nine major European airlines.

Ⓦ **www.priceline.co.uk** (UK)
Ⓦ **www.priceline.com** (US) Name-your-own-price website that has deals at around forty percent off standard fares.
Ⓦ **www.skyauction.com** (US) Bookings from the US only. Auctions tickets and travel packages to destinations worldwide.
Ⓦ **www.travelocity.co.uk** (UK)
Ⓦ **www.travelocity.com** (US)
Ⓦ **www.travelocity.ca** (Canada) City breaks, flights and hotels.
Ⓦ **www.travel.yahoo.com** Incorporates some Rough Guides material in its coverage of destination countries and cities across the world, with information about places to eat and sleep.
Ⓦ **www.zuji.com.au** (Australia) Destination guides, hot fares and great deals for car rental, accommodation and lodging.

From the UK and Ireland

Flying to Budapest has never been easier or cheaper. Getting to Hungary by **train** is an attractive, albeit more expensive option, but worth considering if part of a wider European trip, as is travelling by **car**. By way of contrast, the **bus** journey is an incredibly arduous one.

By air

A number of low-cost airlines, in addition to the established carriers, British Airways (BA) and the Hungarian national airline Malév, fly to Budapest from several **UK** airports. **BA** run two daily direct scheduled flights from London Heathrow to Budapest, as well as five weekly scheduled flights from London Gatwick during the summer, while **Malév** offer two daily flights from London Heathrow, and two flights, five days a week, from Stansted. **Fares** vary widely depending on time of year and length of stay; economy-class return fares with both start from around £180 in high season and £100 in low season. There are currently three **low-cost airlines** flying from the UK to Budapest: **easyJet**, whose schedule includes two daily flights from Luton and one from London Gatwick, as well as one daily flight from Bristol and Newcastle; **SkyEurope**, operating one to two daily flights from Stansted; and Polish-based **Wizz Air**, operating two to three daily flights from Luton and three weekly flights from Liverpool. These flights do fill up quickly, and you should think about booking a couple of months ahead for the summer; moreover, the earlier you book, the cheaper the flight is likely to be. **Tickets** with all three airlines can be obtained for as little as £50 return, including tax.

Travelling from **Ireland**, **Malév** offer daily direct flights from **Dublin** to Budapest, and **Aer Lingus** run four weekly flights on the same route; **fares** with both start from around £140 return. From **Belfast**, **British Midland** operate daily flights to Heathrow, with the onward journey to Budapest with BA, the combined through ticket costing around £250.

Airlines

Aer Lingus UK ⓣ0845 084 4444, Republic of Ireland ⓣ0818/365 000, Ⓦwww.aerlingus.ie.
British Airways UK ⓣ0870 850 9850, Republic of Ireland ⓣ1800 626 747, Ⓦwww.ba.com.
bmi UK ⓣ0870/607 0555, Ⓦwww.flybmi.com.
easyJet UK ⓣ0871 750 0100, Ⓦwww.easyjet.com.
Malév Hungarian Airlines UK ⓣ0870 909 0577, Republic of Ireland ⓣ01/844 4303, Ⓦwww.malev.hu.
SkyEurope UK ⓣ020/7365 0365, Ⓦwww.skyeurope.com.
Wizz Air ⓣ0048/22500 9499, Ⓦwww.wizzair.com.

Travel agents

Co-op Travel Care UK ⓣ0870 112 0085, Ⓦ**www.travelcareonline.com**. Flights and holidays from the UK's largest independent travel agent. Nonpartisan and informed advice.
Flightcentre UK ⓣ0870/890 8099, Ⓦ**www.flightcentre.co.uk**. Rock-bottom fares.
Flights4Less UK ⓣ0871 222 3423, Ⓦ**www.flights4less.co.uk**. Good discount airfares. Part of lastminute.com.
Holidays4Less UK ⓣ0871 222 3423, Ⓦ**www.holidays4less.co.uk**. Discounted package deals. Part of lastminute.com.
Joe Walsh Tours Republic of Ireland ⓣ01/676 0991, Ⓦ**www.joewalshtours.ie**. Long-established general budget fares and holidays agent.
McCarthys Travel Republic of Ireland ⓣ021/427 0127, Ⓦ**www.mccarthystravel.ie**. Established Irish travel agent now part of the Worldchoice chain of travel shops. Featuring flights, short breaks and group holidays.
North South Travel UK ⓣ01245/608 291, Ⓦ**www.northsouthtravel.co.uk**. Friendly, competitive travel agency, offering discounted fares. Profits are

used to support projects in the developing world, especially the promotion of sustainable tourism.

Premier Travel UK ⓣ028/7126 3333, ⓦwww.premiertravel.uk.com. Discount flight specialists.

STA Travel UK ⓣ0870 160 0599, ⓦwww.statravel.co.uk. Specialists in low-cost flights, overland and holiday deals. Good discounts for students and under-26s.

Top Deck UK ⓣ020/7244 8000, ⓦwww.topdecktravel.co.uk. Long-established agent dealing in discount flights and tours.

Trailfinders UK ⓣ020/7938 3939, ⓦwww.trailfinders.com, Republic of Ireland ⓣ01/677 7888, ⓦwww.trailfinders.ie. One of the best-informed and most efficient agents for independent travellers.

Travel Bag UK ⓣ0870 890 1456, ⓦwww.travelbag.co.uk. Discount deals on flights, accommodation and car rental.

Travel Care UK ⓣ0870 112 0085, ⓦwww.travelcare.co.uk. Flights, holiday deals and city breaks.

USIT Northern Ireland ⓣ028/9032 7111, ⓦwww.usitnow.com, Republic of Ireland ⓣ0818/200 020, ⓦwww.usit.ie. Specialists in student, youth and independent travel – flights, trains, study tours, TEFL, visas and more.

Tours

Budapest is now an extremely popular **city-break** destination and this is reflected in the growing number of operators offering the city as a destination in itself or as part of a two- or three-centre trip. Compare the various deals carefully, since season and type of accommodation can affect prices offered by the various companies. In addition, more specialized package tours to the city and other parts of the country are also available.

Tour operators

CME Travel ⓣ0870 128 0636, ⓦwww.cmefortravel.co.uk. Hungarian specialists offering Budapest city breaks, spa and therapy packages, and an extensive range of tailor-made tours such as bird-watching, fishing, horse-riding and gastronomic trips, as well as fly/drive holidays.

Cycle Rides Ltd ⓣ0800 389 3384. ⓦwww.cycle-rides.co.uk. Well-run cycling tours throughout Europe, including a two-week Krakow to Budapest tour in August, which incorporates 11 nights' camping (£820 including flights).

Bridgewater Travel ⓣ0161/703 3000, ⓦwww.bridgewater-travel.co.uk. Packages – Budapest city breaks and accommodation – and flight-only deals from London.

Exodus ⓣ0870 240 5550, ⓦwww.exodus.co.uk. Range of tours including self-guided cycling trips from Vienna to Budapest (8 days £470/15 days £825), and multi-country (Czech Republic/Poland/Slovakia) tours with some walking (11 days £610/15 days £850).

Explore Worldwide ⓣ01252/760 000, ⓦwww.explore.co.uk. Two-week guided hiking tours of Hungary, Czech Republic and Slovakia from around £760. The Hungary leg includes a visit to Budapest and moderate walking in the Northern Uplands.

HF Holidays ⓣ020/8905 9556, ⓦwww.hfholidays.co.uk. Hungarian cycling tours, featuring Vienna to Budapest via Lake Balaton (£730), and wildlife and spas on the Great Plain (£600).

Martin Randall Travel ⓣ020/8742 3355, ⓦwww.martinrandall.com. Upmarket art, architecture and music tours on specific dates with expert guides and speakers. Trips include the Budapest Spring Festival from £1180 and the Austro-Hungarian Music Festival from £2150.

Prospect Tours ⓣ020/7486 5704, ⓦwww.prospecttours.com. Eight-day Danube River cruises from Vienna to Durnstein, taking in Esztergom and Budapest (from £1560), and a four-night Christmas break in a five-star hotel (£925).

Regent Holidays ⓣ0117/921 1711, ⓦwww.regent-holidays.co.uk. Eastern European specialists offering Budapest city breaks (£260), tailor-made touring itineraries, and flights only.

Saga Holidays ⓣ0800 414525, ⓦwww.saga.co.uk. Ten-day tour from Budapest to Salzburg via Vienna, part of which is a cruise along the Danube (from £849); caters to senior travellers.

St Albans Travel Service ⓣ01727 840244, ⓦwww.theatrebreaks.com. Two-night opera breaks in Budapest for £185, plus tailor-made breaks. Prices do not include flights, although the company can arrange these separately.

Thermalia Travel ⓣ020/7586 7725, ⓦwww.thermalia.co.uk. Spa holiday specialists offering stays at four-star thermal resorts in Budapest, Hévíz and Bükk from around £720 for seven nights, plus beauty, fitness and slimming courses, tennis for beginners, golf and sailing.

By rail

Although it's an attractive option, travelling by **train** is likely to be considerably more expensive than flying, and the shortest journey from London's Victoria Station to Budapest takes around 25 hours. However, stopovers on the way are possible and prices are more attractive if you're a student, under 26 or over 60. If you have an Inter-Rail or Eurail train pass, you can take in Hungary as part of a wider rail trip around Europe (see p.33 for details of rail passes).

A standard second-class London to Budapest **return ticket**, incorporating Eurostar, costs around £300. Tickets have two to three months' return validity, and stopovers are allowed as long as you stick to the prescribed route. Arriving in Paris, you can continue the journey to Budapest (one daily train from Gare de l'Est) via Munich or Vienna, both of which take around 19 hours.

To vary things a little you could get a **hydrofoil** from Vienna to Budapest – a journey that takes around four and a half hours. The hydrofoils, jointly operated by Blue Danube (Ⓦwww.ddsg-blue-danube.at) and Mahart Passnave (Ⓦwww.mahartpassnave.hu), depart at 9am daily in low season (April & Sept–Oct), at 8am daily from May to July, and at 8am and 1pm daily in August. A one-way ticket costs about €75, and a return around €100.

Rail agents

Eurostar UK Ⓣ0870 160 6600, Ⓦwww.eurostar.com. Trains to Paris Gare du Nord (2hr 40min) or Brussels-Midi/Zuid (2hr 20min). Up to 24 trains a day to Paris; up to 10 a day to Brussels. Some trains additionally stop at Ashford in Kent (40min from London), Calais (1hr 20min) and/or Lille (1hr 40min). If taking a bike you should register it a day in advance (£20 per cycle per journey). Inter-Rail, Eurail and Eurodomino passes give discounts on Eurostar trains.

International Rail UK Ⓣ0870 751 5000, Ⓦwww.international-rail.com. Offers a wide variety of rail options, including Eurostar, all European passes and tickets, international sleepers, ferry crossings and more.

Rail Europe UK Ⓣ0870 584 8848, Ⓦwww.raileurope.co.uk. Broad range of mainstream rail options, including Eurostar, and tickets for major destinations in Europe. Also Inter-Rail and Eurodomino passes.

Trainseurope UK Ⓣ0900 195 0101 (60p/min, refundable against a booking), Ⓦwww.trainseurope.co.uk. Useful selection of rail options, for travel all across Europe (including many parts of Eastern Europe). Point-to-point tickets, passes, Eurotunnel, Inter-Rail, Eurodomino, and more.

By bus

The **bus** journey to Budapest from London (around 27hr) is extremely hard-going, and can often work out more expensive than flying. A standard return fare costs around £110 (valid for six months), but regular promotional offers can bring this down to as low as £70.

Eurolines UK Ⓣ08705 808 808, Ⓦwww.eurolines.co.uk, Republic of Ireland Ⓣ01/836 6111, Ⓦwww.eurolines.ie. Five buses a week (daily in July and August) from Victoria Coach Station direct to Győr and Budapest. In the UK, book through National Express (Ⓣ0870 580 8080, Ⓦwww.nationalexpress.com) and from Eurolines agents nationwide.

Busabout UK Ⓣ020/7950 1661, Ⓦwww.busabout.com. Hop-on, hop-off bus network, operating throughout Europe in summer (April–Oct). Although there are no direct buses from London to Budapest, you can get an add-on connection (the "Budapest Link") from Vienna.

By car

If you have the time and inclination, **driving to Hungary** can be a pleasant proposition. However, it's really only worth considering if you are going to travel in Hungary for an extended period, or want to take advantage of various stopovers en route. Once across the channel (see below), the most direct **route** to Budapest is from Ostend, travelling via Brussels, Aachen, Cologne, Frankfurt, Nürnberg, Linz and Vienna. It's a distance of 1500km, which, driving nonstop, can be covered in 24 hours, but you shouldn't bank on driving it in under 36. To avoid the long queues at Hegyeshalom and other main **border crossings** over summer, consider entering Hungary from Deutsch-Kreutz, just south of Eisenstadt, instead. Detailed printouts of the route can be obtained from the AA (Ⓦwww.theaa.com), or RAC (Ⓦwww.rac.co.uk). See p.35 for information about licences, insurance and driving in Hungary.

The most common cross-Channel options for the majority of travellers are the **ferry and hoverspeed** links between Dover and Calais or Ostend. The much quicker Hoverspeed, with its Seacat Catamarans, operates on both these routes, whilst a number of ferry companies operate more regular services between Dover and Calais. Further ferry services operate out of Folkestone, Ramsgate, Newhaven and Portsmouth to France; Felixstowe to Zeebrugge; Harwich to Holland; and Hull to Zeebrugge and Rotterdam. Ferry prices vary dramatically according to the time of year, time of day, length of stay and, for motorists, the size of your car, though there are usually a host of special offers going on throughout the year. Whilst the Hoverspeed is more expensive, the journey time is half that of the ferry.

You could also travel via the Eurotunnel (ⓣ0870/535 3535, ⓦwww.eurotunnel.com), which operates drive-on, drive-off shuttle trains for vehicles and their passengers only. Trains run continuously between Folkestone and Coquelles, near Calais. There are up to four departures per hour (only one per hour midnight–6am) with a journey time of 35min (45min for some night departure times). It is possible to turn up and buy your ticket at the tollbooths, though at busy times booking is advisable; if you've booked, you must arrive at least 30min before your scheduled departure. Fares depend on the time of year, time of day and length of stay; it's cheaper to travel between 10pm and 6am, while the highest fares apply on weekends and in July and August. **Bikes** are carried on a specially adapted carriage that makes the crossing twice a day.

Ferry companies

Hoverspeed UK ⓣ0870 240 8070, ⓦwww.hoverspeed.co.uk. Dover to Calais.
P&O Ferries UK ⓣ0870 520 2020, ⓦwww.poferries.com. Dover to Calais.
SeaFrance UK ⓣ0870 571 1711, ⓦwww.seafrance.com. Dover to Calais.
Stena Line Britain ⓣ0870 570 7070, Northern Ireland ⓣ028/9074 7747, ⓦwww.stenaline.co.uk, Republic of Ireland ⓣ01/204 7777, ⓦwww.stenaline.ie. Harwich to Hook of Holland.

From the US and Canada

Malév are the only airline to offer direct flights from **North America** to Hungary. They operate daily from **New York**'s JFK airport to Budapest during high season (June–Aug) and two weekly flights in the low season (Nov–Feb), with **fares** from around US$800 high season and US$550 low season. With other airlines you may fly on a one- or two-stop flight via London, Paris or Frankfurt. Apex fares on nondirect flights are virtually identical on all carriers; Lufthansa, for example, offer low-season midweek return fares to Budapest (via Frankfurt) from around US$550 from New York and US$850 from West Coast cities, rising to US$950 and US$1250 respectively during high season. You can sometimes cut the cost of high-season travel by buying a ticket from travel agencies specializing in Eastern Europe. Full-time students and anyone under 26 can take advantage of the excellent deals offered by **student/youth travel agencies**, which also have an added advantage with their flexibility: there are low penalties for changes or cancellations, and the tickets are valid for six months to a year. Those who don't meet the student/youth requirements can still save some money by buying tickets through **travel agencies** such as those listed below.

From **Canada**, Malév operates five weekly direct flights from **Toronto** in high season and two weekly flights during low season, with **fares** from around C$1300 high season and C$900 low season. Otherwise, a major European carrier like Lufthansa (via Frankfurt) offers return fares from around C$1600 high season and C$1250 low season.

If you're planning to see Hungary as part of a wider European **rail** tour, you should consider buying a Eurail pass before you leave home (see p.33).

Airlines

Air Canada ⓣ1-888/247-2262, ⓦwww.aircanada.com.
Air France US ⓣ1-800/237-2747, Canada ⓣ1-800/667-2747, ⓦwww.airfrance.com.
American Airlines ⓣ1-800/624-6262, ⓦwww.aa.com.
Austrian Airlines ⓣ1-800/843-0002, ⓦwww.aua.com.
British Airways ⓣ1-800/AIRWAYS, ⓦwww.ba.com.
Northwest/KLM International ⓣ1-800/447-4747, ⓦwww.nwa.com, ⓦwww.klm.com.
Lufthansa US ⓣ1-800/645-3880, Canada ⓣ1-800/563-5954, ⓦwww.lufthansa.com.
Malév Hungarian Airlines ⓣ1-800/223-6884 or 212/566-9944, ⓦwww.malev.hu.
United Airlines ⓣ1-800/538-2929, ⓦwww.united.com.

Travel agents

Airtech ⓣ212/219-7000, ⓦwww.airtech.com. Standby seat broker; also deals in consolidator fares.

Educational Travel Center ⓣ1-800/747-5551 or 608/256-5551, ⓦwww.edtrav.com. Low-cost fares worldwide, student/youth discount offers, and Eurail passes, car rental and tours.

Flightcentre US ⓣ1-866/WORLD-51, ⓦwww.flightcentre.us, Canada ⓣ1-888/WORLD-55, ⓦwww.flightcentre.ca. Rock-bottom fares worldwide.

New Frontiers US ⓣ1-800/677-0720, ⓦwww.newfrontiers.com. Discount firm, specializing in travel from the US to Europe, with hotels and package deals.

STA Travel US ⓣ1-800/329-9537, Canada ⓣ1-888/427-5639, ⓦwww.statravel.com. Worldwide specialists in independent travel; also student IDs, travel insurance, car rental, rail passes, and more.

Student Flights ⓣ1-800/255-8000 or 480/951-1177, ⓦwww.isecard.com/studentflights. Student/youth fares, plus student IDs and European rail and bus passes.

TFI Tours ⓣ1-800/745-8000 or 212/736-1140, ⓦwww.lowestairprice.com. Well-established consolidator with a wide variety of global fares.

Travel Avenue ⓣ1-800/333-3335, ⓦwww.travelavenue.com. Full-service travel agent that offers discounts in the form of rebates.

Travel Cuts US ⓣ1-800/592-CUTS, Canada ⓣ1-888/246-9762, ⓦwww.travelcuts.com. Popular, long-established student-travel organization, with worldwide offers.

Travelers Advantage ⓣ1-877/259-2691, ⓦwww.travelersadvantage.com. Discount travel club, with cash-back deals and discounted car rental. Membership required ($1 for 3 months' trial).

Travelosophy US ⓣ1-800/332-2687, ⓦwww.itravelosophy.com. Good range of discounted and student fares worldwide.

Worldtek Travel ⓣ1-800/243-1723, ⓦwww.worldtek.com. Discount travel agency for worldwide travel.

Tour operators

Adventures Abroad ⓣ1-800/665-3998 or 604/303-1099, ⓦwww.adventures-abroad.com. Adventure specialists. Numerous Budapest and countrywide tours as well as longer, multi-country (eg Czech/Slovak republics, Romania, Bulgaria) and multi-city (eg Prague and Vienna) tours.

Classic Journeys ⓣ1-800/200-3887, ⓦwww.classicjourneys.com. Eight-day, two-city tours, starting in Prague and finishing in Budapest, from around US$2895.

Contiki Tours ⓣ1-888/CONTIKI, ⓦwww.contiki.com. 18- to 35-year-olds-only tour operator. Extensive European tours, many of which incorporate Budapest in the itinerary.

Elderhostel ⓣ877/426-8056, ⓦwww.elderhostel.org. Specialists in educational and activity programmes for senior travellers. Hungary is offered as part of several multi-country (eg Czech Republic, Austria, Poland and Slovenia) tours (including a Jewish Heritage tour), as well as a two-week food and wine trip (US$2427).

Forum International Travel ⓣ1-800/252-4475, ⓦwww.foruminternational.com. Easy seven-day self-guided cycling tours from Vienna to Budapest staying in family pensions and hotels (from $655 including bicycle rental), and Danube Bike and River Cruise (Passau–Vienna–Budapest – from US$630). April/May to September.

Saga Holidays ⓣ1-877/265-6862, ⓦwww.sagaholidays.com. Group and educational travel for senior travellers. Budapest city breaks, Danube Cruises and multi-country tours.

Wilderness Travel ⓣ1-800/368-2794, ⓦwww.wildernesstravel.com. Thirteen-day hiking trips from Budapest to Krakow, incorporating the capital, Eger and the Bükk Hills on the Hungary leg (US$2895).

From Australia and New Zealand

There are **no direct flights** to Hungary from Australia or New Zealand so you'll have to change airlines, either in Asia or Europe, although the best option is to fly to a Western European gateway and get a connecting flight from there. A standard return fare from eastern **Australia** to Budapest, via London, with the Australian carrier Qantas, is around A$2800 high season and A$2000 low season. Most flights typically require a stop in London, Paris or Frankfurt, continuing onwards from there.

The same routings apply for flights from **New Zealand**, with a standard return fare with Air New Zealand from around NZ$2800 high season, and NZ$2200 low season. You'll possibly be better off buying a discounted fare to Australia and proceeding from there.

Airlines

Aeroflot Australia ⓣ02/9262 2233, ⓦwww.aeroflot.com.au.

Air France Australia ⓣ1300 361 400, New Zealand ⓣ09/308 3352, ⓦwww.airfrance.com.

Air New Zealand Australia ⓣ13 24 76, ⓦwww.airnz.com.au, New Zealand ⓣ0800 737 000, ⓦwww.airnz.co.nz.

Austrian Airlines Australia ⓣ1800 642 438

or 02/9251 6155, New Zealand ⓣ09/522 5948, ⓦwww.aua.com.
British Airways Australia ⓣ1300 767 177, New Zealand ⓣ0800 274 847, ⓦwww.ba.com.
Lufthansa Australia ⓣ1300 655 727, New Zealand ⓣ0800 945 220, ⓦwww.lufthansa.com.
Qantas Australia ⓣ13 13 13, New Zealand ⓣ0800 808 767 or 09/357 8900, ⓦwww.qantas.com.

Travel agents

Flight Centre Australia ⓣ13 31 33, ⓦwww.flightcentre.com.au, New Zealand ⓣ0800 243 544, ⓦwww.flightcentre.co.nz. Rock-bottom fares worldwide.
Holiday Shoppe New Zealand ⓣ0800 808 480, ⓦwww.holidayshoppe.co.nz. Great deals on flights, hotels and holidays.
STA Travel Australia ⓣ1300 733 035, New Zealand ⓣ0508/782 872, ⓦwww.statravel.com. Worldwide specialists in low-cost flights, overlands and holiday deals. Good discounts for students and under-26s.
Trailfinders Australia ⓣ02/9247 7666, ⓦwww.trailfinders.com.au. One of the best-informed and most efficient agents for independent travellers.
travel.com.au and **travel.co.nz** Australia ⓣ1300/130 482 or 02/9249 5444, ⓦwww.travel.com.au, New Zealand ⓣ0800/468 332, ⓦwww.travel.co.nz. Comprehensive online travel company, with discounted fares.

Tour operators

Danube Travel Australia ⓣ03/9530 0888. Danube river cruises and specialist tours.
Eastern Eurotours Australia ⓣ1800 242 353 or 07/ 5526 2855. ⓦwww.easterneurotours.com.au. Package tours to Budapest and multi-city tours including Vienna and Prague.
Explore Holidays Australia ⓣ1300/731 000 or 02/9857 6200, ⓦwww.exploreholidays.com.au. Accommodation and package tours to Budapest.

Red tape and visas

Citizens of the EU, US, Canada, Australia and New Zealand, and most other European countries, can enter Hungary with just a passport and may stay in the country for up to ninety days. Many European countries (though not the UK or Ireland) require only an identity card.

Hungarian embassies and consulates

Australia Embassy: 17 Beale Crescent, Deakin, Canberra, ACT 2600 ⓣ02/6282 3226 or 6285 3484; consulate: Suite 405 Edgecliffe Centre, 203–233 New South Head Rd, Edgecliffe, Sydney, NSW 2027 ⓣ02/9328 7859 or 9328 7860.
Britain 35b Eaton Place, London SW1X 8BY ⓣ020/7235 2664. Mon–Fri 9.30am–noon.
Canada Embassy: 299 Waverley St, Ottawa, Ontario, K2P 0V9 ⓣ613/230-2717; consulates: 1200 McGill College Ave, Suite 2040, Montréal, Québec H3B 4G7 ⓣ514/393-3302; 121 Bloor St, East Suite 1115, Toronto ⓣ416/923-8981.
Ireland Embassy: 2 Fitzwilliam Place, Dublin 2 ⓣ01/661 2902.
New Zealand Consulate: PO Box 29-039, Wellington 6030 ⓣ04/973 7507.
US Embassy: 3910 Shoemakers St NW, Washington DC 20008 ⓣ202/362-6730; visa enquiries ⓣ202/362-6737; 223 East 52nd St, New York, NY 10022 ⓣ212/752-0669; consulate: 11766 Wilshire Blvd, Suite 410, Los Angeles, CA 90025 ⓣ310/473-9344.

Lost passports

Lost passports must be reported to the local police station. You then take the police report to your consulate, who can sort out your papers to leave the country or issue a new passport. You may need to go back to the police for an exit stamp in order to leave the country. Your consulate should be notified by the police if your passport is found.

Customs

Even though Hungary is a member of the EU, special customs restrictions apply to what you are allowed to export from the country. Visitors are allowed to take home 200 cigarettes (or 250g of tobacco or 50 cigars), one litre of wine and one litre of spirits. Customs regulations change fairly frequently so it's worth checking the latest rules at a Hungarian consulate or tourist office before leaving home.

Information, websites and maps

A large number of free brochures, maps and special-interest leaflets are produced by the Hungarian National Tourist Office, and distributed by their offices abroad and by Tourinform – the extensive network of tourist information centres within Hungary. As well as the booklets on hotels and campsites, there are also useful brochures on cultural events and festivals, gastronomy and wine, health tourism, riding, cycling and activity holidays.

Within Hungary, **Tourinform** has an office in just about every town and city, and in some villages too. Invariably, they have an abundance of information on accommodation (although most do not book rooms), restaurants and activities, and many can also supply you with a free map. In addition to Tourinform you'll find local **tourist agencies** in most towns, many of which are regionally based and have a few branches in towns of close proximity; for example, Balatontourist, one of the biggest, have offices all around Lake Balaton. These are primarily useful for booking **accommodation** in private rooms and apartments, although most branches of the nationwide agency, **Ibusz** (detailed throughout the Guide), are able to arrange somewhere to sleep.

Information offices abroad

Britain Hungarian National Tourist Office, 46 Eaton Place, London SW1X 8AL ⓣ020/7823 1032. ⓦwww.hungarywelcomesbritain.com.

US Hungarian National Tourist Office, c/o Embassy of the Republic of Hungary, Commercial Counsellor's Office, 150 E 58th St, 33rd Floor, New York, NY 10155-3398 ⓣ212/355-0240, ⓦwww.gotohungary.com.

Governmental travel advisories

Australian Department of Foreign Affairs ⓦwww.dfat.gov.au.

British Foreign & Commonwealth Office ⓦwww.fco.gov.uk.

Canadian Department of Foreign Affairs ⓦwww.dfait-maeci.gc.ca.

Irish Department of Foreign Affairs ⓦwww.irlgov.ie/iveagh.

New Zealand Ministry of Foreign Affairs ⓦwww.mft.govt.nz.

US State Department ⓦtravel.state.gov.

Useful websites

ⓦ**www.access-hungary.hu** Business and politics in Hungary with daily news updates.

ⓦ**www.budapestinfo.com** The best site for information on the capital, as well as online hotel and services bookings.

Ⓦ **www.budapestsun.com** Online version of the daily English-language newspaper.
Ⓦ **www.budapestweek.com** Arts and entertainment weekly for Budapest with a useful classifieds section.
Ⓦ **www.festivalcity.hu** Complete programme listings and ticket-ordering service for the Budapest Spring Festival.
Ⓦ **www.gayguide.net/Europe/Hungary/Budapest** Excellent site for the gay community; travel information for Budapest and other towns as well as advice and contacts.
Ⓦ **www.hotels.hu** Site listing most of Hungary's hotels and pensions.
Ⓦ **www.hungarytourism.hu** Official site of the Hungarian National Tourist Office with information on all aspects of travel within the country.
Ⓦ **www.insidehungary.com** Comprehensive national news site.
Ⓦ **www.met.hu** Daily weather bulletins and forecasts.
Ⓦ **www.tourinform.hu** Information on all Tourinform offices throughout the country, plus a hotline and events calendar.
Ⓦ **www.travelport.hu** Excellent general Hungarian site, including online accommodation booking service.
Ⓦ **www.winesofhungary.com** Interesting site with information on Hungarian wine and wine regions, with links to dozens of wineries.

Maps

You may want to supplement the maps in this book with Hungarian **town plans** (*városi-térkép*), which also detail main sights and tram and bus routes. These maps cost between 300Ft and 400Ft and are available from Tourinform offices, local tourist agencies or bookshops (*könyvesbolt*). If you're travelling by car, the *Magyar Auto Atlasz* is a must. Available from bookshops, it contains **road maps** and plans of most towns (though some of the street names may be out of date). Tourinform also issues a variety of useful, free road maps, including one showing Budapest's one-way streets and bypasses. Many Tourinform offices, as well as bookshops, stock **hiking maps** (*turistatérkép*) covering the highland regions, which should be purchased in advance wherever possible, as they may not be available on the spot; see p.51 for more on hiking. If you want to buy Hungarian maps in advance of your trip, try one of the specialist map suppliers listed below.

Map outlets

In the UK and Ireland

Blackwell's Map Centre 50 Broad St, Oxford OX1 3BQ Ⓣ01865/793 550, Ⓦwww.maps.blackwell.co.uk. Branches in Bristol, Cambridge, Cardiff, Leeds, Liverpool, Newcastle, Reading and Sheffield.
The Map Shop 30a Belvoir St, Leicester LE1 6QH Ⓣ0116/247 1400, Ⓦwww.mapshopleicester.co.uk.
National Map Centre 22–24 Caxton St, London SW1H 0QU Ⓣ020/7222 2466, Ⓦwww.mapsnmc.co.uk.
National Map Centre Ireland 34 Aungier St, Dublin Ⓣ01/476 0471, Ⓦwww.mapcentre.ie.
Stanfords 12–14 Long Acre, London WC2E 9LP Ⓣ020/7836 1321, Ⓦwww.stanfords.co.uk. Also at 39 Spring Gardens, Manchester Ⓣ0161/831 0250, and 29 Corn St, Bristol Ⓣ0117/929 9966.
The Travel Bookshop 13–15 Blenheim Crescent, London W11 2EE Ⓣ020/7229 5260, Ⓦwww.thetravelbookshop.co.uk.
Traveller 55 Grey St, Newcastle-upon-Tyne NE1 6EF Ⓣ0191/261 5622, Ⓦwww.newtraveller.com.

In the US and Canada

110 North Latitude US Ⓣ336/369-4171, Ⓦwww.110nlatitude.com.
Book Passage 51 Tamal Vista Blvd, Corte Madera, CA 94925 and in the San Francisco Ferry Building Ⓣ1-800/999-7909 or Ⓣ415/927-0960, Ⓦwww.bookpassage.com.
Distant Lands 56 S Raymond Ave, Pasadena, CA 91105 Ⓣ1-800/310-3220, Ⓦwww.distantlands.com.
Globe Corner Bookstore 28 Church St, Cambridge, MA 02138 Ⓣ1-800/358-6013, Ⓦwww.globecorner.com.
Longitude Books 115 W 30th St #1206, New York, NY 10001 Ⓣ1-800/342-2164, Ⓦwww.longitudebooks.com.
Map Town 400 5 Ave SW #100, Calgary, AB, T2P 0L6 Ⓣ1-877/921-6277 or Ⓣ403/266-2241, Ⓦwww.maptown.com.
Travel Bug Bookstore 3065 W Broadway, Vancouver, BC, V6K 2G9 Ⓣ604/737-1122, Ⓦwww.travelbugbooks.ca.
World of Maps 1235 Wellington St, Ottawa, ON, K1Y 3A3 Ⓣ1-800/214-8524 or Ⓣ613/724-6776, Ⓦwww.worldofmaps.com.

In Australia and New Zealand

Mapland 372 Little Bourke St, Melbourne, VC Ⓣ03/9670 4383, Ⓦwww.mapland.com.au.
Map Shop 6–10 Peel St, Adelaide, SA Ⓣ08/8231

2033, Ⓦwww.mapshop.net.au.
Map World 371 Pitt St, Sydney, NSW ⓣ02/9261 3601, Ⓦwww.mapworld.net.au. Also at 900 Hay St, Perth, WA ⓣ08/9322 5733, Jolimont Centre, Canberra, ACT ⓣ02/6230 4097 and 1981 Logan Road, Brisbane, QLD ⓣ07/3349 6633.
Map World 173 Gloucester St, Christchurch ⓣ0800/627 967, Ⓦwww.mapworld.co.nz.

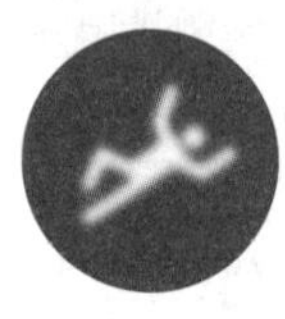

Insurance

Even though EU health-care privileges apply in Hungary, you'd do well to take out an insurance policy before travelling to cover against theft, loss and illness or injury. Before paying for a new policy, however, it's worth checking whether you are already covered: some all-risks home insurance policies may cover your possessions when overseas, and many private medical schemes include cover when abroad. In Canada, provincial health plans usually provide partial cover for medical mishaps overseas, while holders of official student/teacher/youth cards in Canada and the US are entitled to meagre accident coverage and hospital in-patient benefits. Students will often find that their student health coverage extends during the vacations and for one term beyond the date of last enrolment.

After checking out the possibilities above, you might want to contact a specialist travel insurance company, or consider the travel insurance deal we offer (see box below). A typical travel insurance policy usually provides cover for the loss of baggage, tickets and – up to a certain limit – cash or cheques, as well as cancellation or curtailment of your journey. Most of them exclude so-called dangerous sports unless an extra premium is paid: in Hungary this could mean, for example, windsurfing or hiking. Many policies can be chopped and changed to exclude coverage you don't need; for example, sickness and accident benefits can often be excluded or included at will. If you do take medical coverage, ascertain whether benefits will be paid as treatment proceeds or only after you return home, and if there is a 24-hour medical emergency number. When securing baggage cover, make sure that the per-article limit – typically under £500/$750/

Rough Guides travel insurance

Rough Guides has teamed up with Columbus Direct to offer you travel insurance that can be tailored to suit your needs.

Readers can choose from many different travel insurance products, including a **low-cost backpacker** option for long stays; a **short break** option for city getaways; a **typical holiday** package option; and many others. There are also **annual multi-trip** policies for those who travel regularly, with variable levels of cover available. Different sports and activities (trekking, skiing, etc) can be covered if required on most policies.

Rough Guides travel insurance is available to the residents of 36 different countries with different language options to choose from via our website Ⓦwww.roughguides.com - where you can also purchase the insurance.

Alternatively, UK residents should call 0800 083 9507; US citizens should call ⓣ1-800 749-4922; Australians should call ⓣ1 300 669 999. All other nationalities should call ⓣ+44 870 890 2843.

C$1235/A$1260 and sometimes as little as £250/$400/C$610/A$630 – will cover your most valuable possession. If you need to make a claim, you should keep receipts for medicines and medical treatment, and in the event you have anything stolen, you must obtain an official statement from the police (*rendőrseg*).

Health

No inoculations are required for Hungary, and standards of public health are good. Tap water is safe everywhere, while potable springs (*forrás*) and streams are designated on maps, and with signs, as *ivóvíz*. The national health service (OTBF) will provide free emergency treatment in any hospital or doctor's office for citizens of the EU and most other European countries, but there is a charge for drugs and non-emergency care.

You shouldn't have too much to get alarmed about travelling around Hungary. Sunburn (*napszúrás*) and insect bites (*rovarcsípés*) are the most common **minor complaints**: suntan lotion is sold in supermarkets, and pharmacists stock *Vietnámi balzsam* (Vietnamese-made "Tiger Balm" – the best bug-repellent going) and bite ointment. Mosquitoes are pesky, but the bug to beware of in forests is the *kullancs*, which bites and then burrows into human skin, causing inflammation of the brain. The risk is fairly small, but if you get a bite which seems particularly painful, or are suffering from a high temperature and stiff neck following a bite, it's worth having it checked out as quickly as possible.

All towns and some villages have a **pharmacy** (*gyógyszertár* or *patika*), with staff (who are most likely to understand German) authorized to issue a wide range of drugs. However, pharmaceutical products are mainly of East European origin, so anyone requiring specific medication should bring a supply with them. Opening hours are normally Monday–Friday 9am–6pm, Saturday 9am–noon or 1pm; signs in the window give the location or telephone number of the nearest all-night (*éjjeli* or *ügyeleti szolgálat*) pharmacy.

In more serious cases, provincial tourist offices can direct you to local **medical centres** or doctors' offices (*orvosi rendelő*), while your embassy in Budapest will have the addresses of foreign-language-speaking **doctors** and **dentists**, who will probably be in private (*magán*) practice. Private medicine is much cheaper than in the West, as attested to by the thousands of Austrians who come here for treatment. (See the hospitals and dentistry listings at the end of the Budapest chapter for details of some private clinics in the capital.) For muscular, skin or gynaecological complaints, doctors often prescribe a soak at one of Hungary's numerous **medicinal baths** (*gyógyfürdő*).

In **emergencies**, dial ⓣ104 for the *Mentők* ambulance service, or catch a taxi to the nearest hospital (*Kórház*). The standard of **hospitals** varies enormously, but low morale and shortages of beds testify to poor wages and the general underfunding of the health service. Depending on local conditions, Westerners might get the best available treatment, or be cold-shouldered.

There is an **AIDS Advisory Service** in Budapest at Budapest VIII, Joszef út 46 (Mon–Thurs 8am–4pm, Fri 8am–noon; ⓣ1/303-4490), and an information line (Mon–Thurs 8am–4pm, Fri 8am–1pm; ⓣ1/338-2419). There is another AIDS helpline in Sopron, at Magyar utca 14 (ⓣ99/333 399).

Costs, money and banks

Although Hungary is not quite the bargain destination it once was, it's still extremely good value on the whole, compared to costs in the UK and the US, with the exception of Budapest and some of the Lake Balaton resorts. Prices in some hotels are often quoted in euros, but you pay in forint – Hungary is unlikely to convert to the euro any time before 2007.

Average costs

As with most destinations, your biggest expenditure will be **accommodation**; outside Budapest and the Balaton, the average three-star hotel charges anywhere between £30–40 (€42–56/US$54–72) for a double room with shower, a pension marginally less, while a private room costs about £10/€14/US$18. Eating out remains extremely affordable: a three-course meal with wine in a decent **restaurant** costs around £10–15/€14–21/US$18–27. **Public transport** is very cheap: as a rule, there's little difference between train and bus fares, and you should expect to pay around £4/€5.60/US$7.20 for a journey of 100km. **Museum** admission charges vary from around 50p to £2 (€0.70–2.80/US$0.90–3.60), though many of the state-run museums in Budapest now offer free entry. Some places have free admission on certain days, and in a few towns it is possible to purchase an all-in-one ticket giving you access to all the town's museums – these are identified in the book where relevant.

Discounts

If you're planning to stay in Hungary for any length of time, you could invest in the **Hungary Card** (€30), available from all Tourinform offices, which offers a good range of countrywide discounts, including reductions on certain hotels and restaurants, museum entrances, public transport and special events. The **Budapest Card** (see p.71) offers similar discounts in the capital.

Full-time students are eligible for the **International Student ID Card** (ISIC; Ⓦwww.isiccard.com), which entitles the bearer to special air, rail and bus fares, and discounts at museums, theatres and other attractions. For Americans there's also a health benefit, providing up to $3000 in emergency medical coverage and $100 a day for sixty days in the hospital, plus a 24-hour hotline to call in the event of a medical, legal or financial emergency. The card costs $22 in the US; C$16 in Canada; A$18 in Australia; NZ$20 in New Zealand; £7 in the UK; and €13 in the Republic of Ireland.

You have to be 26 or younger to qualify for the **International Youth Travel Card**, which costs £7/US$22/C$16/A$18/NZ$20 and carries the same benefits. Teachers qualify for the **International Teacher Card**, offering similar discounts and costing £7/US$22/C$16/€13/A$18/NZ$20. All these cards are available in the US from Council Travel, STA, Travel CUTS and, in Canada, Hostelling International (see p.40 for addresses); in Australia and New Zealand from STA or Campus Travel; in Ireland from USIT or STA and in the UK from STA. Several other travel organizations and accommodation groups also sell their own cards, good for various discounts.

Currency and exchange rates

Hungary's unit of **currency** is the **forint** (Ft or HUF), which comprises 100 fillér. The forint comes in **notes** of 200, 500, 1000, 2000, 5000, 10,000 and 20,000 Ft, with 1, 2, 5, 10, 20, 50 and 100 Ft coins. The **exchange rate** is currently around 350Ft to the pound sterling and around 200Ft to the US dollar; if you want to check the latest rate, check out the websites Ⓦwww.xe.net/currency or Ⓦwww.oanda.com/converter.

Banks and changing money

As a rule you're best off changing money in **banks**, which you can find in all but the smallest towns and which are generally open Monday to Friday between 9am and 3 or 4pm. Otherwise, you can change money at private exchange offices, also found in most towns, or at tourist agencies, such as Ibusz. Very few places charge commission. Changing **travellers' cheques** is a relatively painless operation, and can be done at any bank or regional tourist office, or at the majority of large hotels and campsites. Note that banks often close quite early, however, before 3pm on weekdays and even earlier on Fridays. There are also an increasing number of **Automatic Currency Exchange Machines**, where you insert your foreign currency in return for Forints, a convenient method if there is nowhere open. The exchange rate is usually the same as that offered in banks. The advantages of changing money on the illegal **black market** are negligible and, in any case, scalpers are skilled at cheating. Make sure you get rid of any **unwanted forints** before you leave the country, as it's unlikely you'll be able to change them once outside Hungary.

Cash and travellers' cheques

If taking **cash**, a modest amount of low-denomination euros is advisable, though dollars and pound sterling are also accepted in most places. If carrying **travellers' cheques**, then by far the most recognised are American Express, either sterling or dollars. The usual fee for travellers' cheque sales is one or two percent, though this fee may be waived if you buy the cheques through a bank where you have an account. It pays to get a selection of denominations. Make sure to keep the purchase agreement and a record of cheque serial numbers safe and separate from the cheques themselves. In the event that cheques are lost or stolen, report the loss forthwith to the issuing company's office in Hungary.The American Express office is at Deák Ferenc utca 10 (Mon–Fri 9am–5.30pm, Sat 9am–2pm; ⓣ1/235-4330); lost or stolen cheques can usually be replaced within 24 hours.

Credit and debit cards

Credit cards can be used either in ATMs or over the counter. Mastercard, Visa and American Express are accepted just about everywhere, but other cards may not be recognized in Hungary. Remember that all cash advances are treated as loans, with interest accruing daily from the date of withdrawal; there may be a transaction fee on top of this. However, you should probably be able to make withdrawals from ATMs in Hungary using your **debit card** and the flat transaction fee is usually quite small – your bank will be able to advise on this. Make sure you have a personal identification number (PIN) that's designed to work overseas. **Cash machines** (ATMs) can be found in even the smallest towns.

A compromise between travellers' cheques and plastic is **Visa TravelMoney**, a disposable pre-paid debit card with a PIN which works in all ATMs that take Visa cards. You load up your account with funds before leaving home, and when they run out you simply throw the card away. You can buy up to nine cards to access the same funds – useful for couples or families travelling together – and it's a good idea to buy at least one extra as a backup in case of loss or theft. There is also a 24-hour toll-free customer assistance number (ⓣ06/800 11272) and a number to call collect: ⓣ410/581-9994. The card is available in most countries from branches of Travelex and AAA. For more information, check the Visa website at ⓦinternational.visa.com/ps/products/vtravelmoney.

Wiring money

Having money **wired** from home using one of the companies listed below is never convenient or cheap, and should be considered a last resort. It's also possible to have money wired directly from a bank in your home country to a bank in Hungary, although this is somewhat less reliable because it involves two separate institutions. If you go this route, your home bank will need the address of the branch bank where you want to pick up the money and the address and telex number of the Budapest head office, which will act as the clearing house; money wired this way normally takes two working days to arrive, and costs around £25/US$40/C$54/A$52/NZ$59 per transaction.

Money-wiring companies

Travelers Express/MoneyGram US ⓣ1-800/444-3010, Canada ⓣ1-800/933-3278, UK, Ireland and New Zealand ⓣ0800 6663 9472, Australia ⓣ1800 6663 9472, ⓦwww.moneygram.com.

Western Union US and Canada ⓣ1-800/CALL-CASH, Australia ⓣ1800 501 500, New Zealand ⓣ0800 005 253, UK ⓣ0800 833 833, Republic of Ireland ⓣ66/947 5603, ⓦwww.westernunion.com (customers in the US and Canada can send money online).

Getting around

Although it doesn't break any speed records, public transport in Hungary is, on the whole, clean, cheap and reliable. The country's predominantly flat landscape is ideal for driving and cycling. Regional transport schedules are summarized under "Travel details" at the end of each chapter.

By rail

The centralization of the **MÁV** rail network means that many cross-country journeys are easier if you travel via Budapest rather than on branch lines where services are slower and less frequent. **Timetables** displayed in stations are in yellow (for departures) or white (for arrivals), with the different types of fast trains picked out in red. By far the fastest are the **InterCity** ("IC" on the timetable) trains, which run express services between Budapest and all the larger towns; don't be misled by **Express** trains (marked "Ex" on timetables) – although they stop at major centres only, and cost ten percent more than *gyorsvonat* and *sebesvonat* services, which stop more regularly, they are still pretty slow. The slowest trains (**személyvonat**) halt at every hamlet along the way, and since the fare is the same as on a *gyorsvonat*, you might as well opt for the latter. It's not worth using international trains for journeys within Hungary, since they are expensive and not always faster.

Hungarian transport terms

Finding out travel information (*információ*) can be your biggest problem, since transport staff rarely speak anything but Hungarian, which is also the only language used for notices and announcements (except around Lake Balaton, where German is widely spoken). The following should be useful for **deciphering timetables**. *Érkező járatok* (or *érkezés*) means "**arrivals**", and *induló járatok* (or *indulás*) "**departures**".

Trains or buses **to** (*hova*) a particular destination leave from a designated **platform** (for example *vágány 1*) or **bus-stand** (*kocsiállás*); and the point of arrival for services **from** (*honnan*) a place may also be indicated.

Some services run (*közlekedik*, *köz.* for short) *munkaszüneti napok kivételével naponta köz* – **daily, except on holidays**, meaning Sunday and public holidays; *munkanapkon (hetfőtől-péntekig) köz* – **weekdays, Monday to Friday**; *munkaszüneti napokon köz* – **on holidays**; or *09.30-tól délig vasárnap köz* – **on Sunday 9.30am–noon**. *Átszállás* means "**change**"; *át* "**via**"; and *kivételével* "**except**".

Most trains have first- and second-class sections, and many also feature a buffet car (indicated on timetables). **Second-class** trains have PVC seats and can be uncomfortable and crowded. **First class** offers slightly more comfort. International services routed through Budapest have **sleeping cars** and **couchettes** (*hálókocsi* and *kusett*), for which tickets can be bought at MÁV offices in advance, or sometimes on the train itself. **Bicycles** (*bicikli*) can be carried on most passenger trains (you have to buy a separate bicycle ticket, which is around 25 percent of the full ticket price); look for the bicycle pictogram on the timetable. Some trains have special carriages with stands for bikes; otherwise, you must go to the first or last carriage.

If you're planning to travel extensively by rail, it's worth investing in the chunky **timetable** (*Hivatalos Menetrend*; 850Ft; note that the larger format version has no extra information), which also has details of the narrow-gauge lines. It is available from the MÁV office in Budapest at VI, Andrássy út 35 (Ⓣ1/322-8082) and most of the larger train stations. You can also check train information, in English, on Ⓦwww.elvira.hu.

Tickets

Tickets (*jegy*) for domestic train services can be bought at the station (*pályaudvar* or *vasútállomás*) on the day of departure, although it's possible to reserve them up to sixty days in advance. You can break your journey once between the point of departure and the final destination, but must get your ticket validated within an hour of arrival at the interim station. **Fares** are calculated by distance travelled, although the type of train travelled on will also be reflected in the price; to give you some idea, a journey of 100km, travelling second-class on an Express train, will cost around 1300Ft. A **one-way ticket** is *egy útra*, and a **return**, *retur* or *oda-vissza*. If you're found travelling without a ticket you will incur a **fine** of 2000Ft, on top of the fare itself.

Seat bookings (*helyjegy*), in the form of a separate numbered bit of card, are obligatory for services marked ® on timetables (mostly international or Express trains), and optional on those designated by an R. It is advisable to book a seat on InterCity trains, especially those going to Lake Balaton in the summer, but otherwise it is not necessary. Bookings can be made up to two months in advance at any MÁV office. It's best to buy tickets for **international trains** (*nemzetközi gyorsvonat*) at least 36 hours in advance, since demand can be high. The central MÁV ticket office in Budapest, which handles bookings, gets very crowded during summer so be prepared for a long wait.

Concessionary fares on domestic services are available for children under 6 (free) if they don't occupy a separate seat – and for children aged between 6 and 14 (66 percent discount). BIJ/Eurodomino ticket holders get 25 to 50 percent off, and women over 55 and men over 60 get a 20 percent reduction if they show a passport.

Rail passes

There are a number of **rail passes** available which cover travelling in Hungary, although given how cheap train travel is here, none is particularly good value if you're planning to use them just for one country. Passes are issued by Rail Europe (see p.34), the umbrella company for all national and international rail purchases – its comprehensive website is the most useful source of information on which rail passes are available; it also gives all current prices. Those presently available for travel within Hungary are the Eurail, InterRail and Eurodomino passes.

Eurail passes

The **Eurail Pass**, which must be purchased before arrival in Europe, allows unlimited free first-class travel around the country and sixteen other countries, and is available in increments of 15 days, 21 days, 1 month, 2 months and 3 months. If you're under 26 you can opt for the **Eurail Youthpass**, which is valid for second-class travel or, if you're travelling with one to four companions, a joint **Eurail Saverpass**, both of which are available in the same increments as the Eurail Pass and work out cheaper. You stand a better chance of getting your money's worth out of a **Eurail Flexipass**, which is good for 10 or 15 days' travel within a 2-month period. This, too, comes in first-class, under 26/

second-class (**Eurail Youth Flexipass**) and group (**Eurail Saver Flexipass**) versions. The **Hungarian Flexipass** allows unlimited free first-class train travel in Hungary on any 5 days within 15, or 10 days within 1 month. The **Eurail Romania-Hungary Pass** allows unlimited free first-class train travel on 5, 6, 8 or 10 days within 2 months within these two countries, while the **Eurail Romania-Hungary Youthpass** allows for the same travel facility but in second class.

Eurail must normally be bought outside Europe, but people resident outside the EU can go to Rail Europe's central **London office** and buy a Eurail pass over the counter, on production of a non-EU passport.

Inter-Rail passes

These passes are only available to **European residents**, and you will be asked to provide proof of residency before being allowed to purchase one. They come in over-26 and (cheaper) under-26 versions, and cover 28 European countries (including Turkey and Morocco) grouped together in zones. Hungary falls within zone D, which also includes the Czech and Slovak republics, Poland and Croatia.

Passes are available for one zone for 16 days (£159/€222 for under-26s or £223/€312 for over-26s), two zones in 22 days (£215/€300 or £303/€425), or a global pass covering all zones for travel in one month (£295/€413 or £415/€580). The Inter-Rail website (Ⓦwww.raileurope.co.uk/inter-rail) has the most up-to-date information and prices. Inter-Rail passes do not include travel between Britain and the Continent, although Inter-Rail Pass holders are eligible for discounts on rail travel in Britain and Northern Ireland and cross-Channel ferries, free travel on the Brindisi–Patras ferry between Italy and Greece, plus discounts on other shipping services around the Mediterranean, Scandinavia and the Balearics. The Inter-Rail Pass also gives a discount on the London–Paris Eurostar service.

Eurodomino passes

Only available to European residents of six months or longer, the range of individual country passes available from **Eurodomino** (Ⓦ www.raileurope.co.uk/railpasses/eurodomino/htm) provide unlimited travel in 28 European and North African countries. The passes are available for first or second class for between three and eight days' travel within a one-month period; prices vary depending on the country, but include most high-speed train supplements. You can buy as many separate country passes as you want. There is a discounted price for under-26s and children aged 4–11.

Rail contacts

In the UK and Ireland

Rail Europe UK Ⓣ0870 5848 848, Ⓦwww.raileurope.co.uk. Discounted rail fares for under-26s on a variety of European routes; also agents for Inter-Rail, Eurostar and Eurodomino.

In the US and Canada

CIT Rail US Ⓣ1-800/CIT-TOUR, Ⓦwww.cit-rail.com.
DER Travel US Ⓣ1-800/283-2424, Ⓦwww.der.com/rail.
Europrail International Canada Ⓣ1-888/667-9734, Ⓦwww.europrail.net.

Useful timetable publications

The **Thomas Cook European Timetable** details schedules of over 50,000 trains in Europe, as well as timings of over 200 ferry routes and rail-connecting bus services. It's updated and issued every month; main changes are in the June edition (published in May), which has details of the summer European schedules, and the October one (published in Sept), which includes winter schedules. Some years' editions include advance summer/winter timings also. The book can be purchased online (which gets you a ten percent discount) at Ⓦwww.thomascookpublishing.com or from branches of Thomas Cook (see Ⓦwww.thomascook.co.uk for your nearest branch), and costs £10.50. Their useful **Rail Map of Europe** can also be purchased online with 25 percent off the normal retail price of £7.95.

Rail Europe US ⓣ1-877/257-2887, Canada ⓣ1-800/361-RAIL, ⓦwww.raileurope.com/us.
ScanTours US ⓣ1-800/223-7226 or 310/636-4656, ⓦwww.scantours.com.

In Australia and New Zealand

CIT World Travel Australia ⓣ02/9267 1255 or 03/9650 5510, ⓦwww.cittravel.com.au.
Rail Plus Australia ⓣ1300 555 003 or 03/9642 8644, ⓦwww.railplus.com.au.
Trailfinders Australia ⓣ02/9247 7666 or ⓣ03/9600 3022, ⓦwww.trailfinder.com.au.

By bus

Buses from Budapest are generally comfortable, though the stock in the rest of the country can be quite ropey. Regional **Volán** companies run the bulk of Hungary's **buses**, which are called *busz* (pronounced "boose" as in "loose", *not* "bus", which means "fuck" in Hungarian). **Fares** are calculated by distance travelled; to give you some idea, a 100km trip costs around 1200Ft. Schedules are clearly displayed in bus stations (*autóbuszállomás* or *autóbusz pályaudvar*) in every Hungarian town. Arrive early to confirm the departure bay (*kocsiállás*) and to be sure of getting a seat. For long-distance services originating in Budapest or major towns, you can buy tickets with a seat booking up to half an hour before departure; after that you get them from the driver, but you risk standing throughout the journey. You can also reserve seats up to sixty days in advance at the station. Services **in rural areas** may be limited to one or two a day, and tickets are only available on board the bus. As on trains, children under 6 travel free unless they occupy a separate seat, and there is a 33 percent discount for children up to the age of 10; otherwise there are no concessions.

By boat

Between April and October the Mahart company (ⓦwww.mahartpassnave.hu) operates domestic and international **passenger boats** on the section of the Danube running through the capital, between Budapest and Esztergom (via Szentendre and Visegrád), while Balaton Shipping (ⓦwww.balatonihajozas.hu) operates ferry services on Lake Balaton (where there is also a car ferry between Szántód and Tihanyrév operating March–Nov).

By car and motorbike

Although road traffic has increased significantly in recent years and many minor roads are still in poor condition, **driving** in Hungary is fairly hassle-free. Motorways and dual carriageways are generally in good condition, as are most single-lane roads, although country roads tend to be busy and much less pleasant. Hungarians, however, are some of the most aggressive drivers on the Continent, and have an unnerving tendency to overtake at absurdly dangerous moments. To drive in Hungary you'll need your **driving licence** and **third-party insurance**. The only potential drawback to **motorcycling** is that obtaining spare parts may be a problem should you have a breakdown. Motorcyclists must be over 18, wear a helmet, and have a log book or other registration document, plus insurance. The rules of the road (and speed limits) are the same as for cars.

Roads and services

Hungary's roads fall into four categories. Hungary's small **motorway** network, which is still being extended, consists of the M1 to the border with Austria at Hegyeshalom; the M3 towards Miskolc, which currently stops after about 170km at Polgár, near Tiszaújváros; the M5 to Kecskemét and Kiskunfélegyháza; and the M7 to Balaton, which currently goes as far as Siófok. The M0 is the ring motorway around the capital, of which the stretch between the M5 and the M1 is complete. To travel on all the motorways (except the M0) you will need to purchase a **vignette** (*Matrica*), available from most petrol stations and currently costing 1270Ft for four days, 2000Ft for ten days and 3400Ft for a month. A system of mobile patrols and electronic number-plate readers enforces the scheme, and there are steep fines for those travelling on a motorway without one. Most rental car companies do not provide the vignette.

Lesser **highways** (numbered with a single digit from one to eight) radiate from Budapest like spokes in a wheel, linked by **secondary roads** identified by two or three digits (the first one indicates the highway which the road joins; for example, roads 82 and 811 both meet Route 8 at some point). Lastly, there are unnumbered, bumpy

back-country roads, which tourists seldom use. **Pedestrian zones** (found in many towns and shaded light blue on maps) are indicated by "Restricted Access" signs – *kivéve célforgalom*. **Petrol stations** (*benzinkút*), many of which are now open 24 hours, can be found everywhere, even in the most rural backwaters. Lead-free (*ólómmentes benzin*) petrol is by far the most widely used, although, at around 250Ft per litre, it's not particularly cheap. Typical **parking** costs are around 120Ft for one hour, though in Budapest and in some of the resorts around Balaton you can expect to pay double this amount. Information on nationwide **driving conditions**, albeit in Hungarian or German only, can be obtained from ÚTINFORM (☎1/322-7643); conditions in Budapest are monitored by FŐVINFORM (☎1/317-1173).

Rules and regulations

Speed limits for vehicles are 130kph on motorways, 110kph on highways, 90kph on other roads and 50kph in built-up areas. Besides driving on the right, the most important **rules** are the prohibitions against repeatedly switching from lane to lane on highways, using a hand-held mobile phone whilst driving, and sounding the horn in built-up areas unless to avert an accident. It is also compulsory for driver and passengers to wear seatbelts, to use dipped headlights during the day when driving outside built-up areas, and to keep a triangular breakdown sign, spare bulbs and a first-aid box in the car. Children under the age of 12 are forbidden to travel in the front seat. At crossroads, vehicles coming from the right have right of way, unless otherwise indicated by signs, and pedestrians have priority over cars turning onto the road. Remember that trams *always* have right of way, and that some traffic islands serve as bus or tram stops. On highways and secondary roads it's illegal to reverse, make U-turns, or stop at islands.

Drinking and driving is totally prohibited. The police are no longer empowered to levy on-the-spot fines, so should you find yourself in receipt of a penalty, this must be paid at the post office. Be particularly wary of wagons, cyclists, livestock and pedestrians in rural areas, especially at night. **Pedestrians**, meanwhile, should never assume that a car will stop for them on a pedestrian crossing; drivers in Hungary will often do anything to avoid having to slow down and make way for pedestrians, swerving around them instead or screeching to a sudden halt.

Accidents and emergencies

Accidents should be reported to the Hungária Biztosító international motoring department at Budapest XI, Hamzsabégi út 60 (☎1/466-8800; Mon–Fri 8am–4pm) within 24 hours; if someone is injured the police must also be notified (☎107). For breakdowns call the Autóklub Segélyhívó **24-hour breakdown service** (☎188) anywhere in the country, run by the **Hungarian Automobile Club** (Magyar Autóklub or MAK). Their headquarters is at Budapest II, Rómer Floris utca 4A (☎1/345-1800), but they have several **repair shops** in the capital including Boldizsár utca 2 in the XI district (☎1/310-2958), and Nefelejcs utca 4 in the VII district (☎1/295-0074).

Motoring organizations

In the UK and Ireland

AA UK ☎0870 600 0371, Ⓦwww.theaa.com.
AA Ireland Dublin ☎01/617 9999, Ⓦwww.aaireland.ie.
RAC UK ☎0800 550 055, Ⓦwww.rac.co.uk.

In the US and Canada

AAA ☎1-800/AAA-HELP, Ⓦwww.aaa.com.
CAA ☎613/247-0117, Ⓦwww.caa.ca.

In Australia and New Zealand

AAA Australia ☎02/6247 7311, Ⓦwww.aaa.asn.au; NZ ☎0800 500 444, Ⓦwww.nzaa.co.nz.

Car rental

Renting a car is easy provided you're 21 or older, and hold a valid national driving licence that's at least one year old. You can order a car through rental agencies in your own country, which sometimes works out cheaper, particularly if you book online. In Hungary, most of the major companies have an outlet in Budapest (see "Listings" in the Budapest chapter), including the airport, as well as in some of the major cities.

Car rental **costs** are not particularly cheap; expect to pay around £35/€50/US$64 upwards for a day's hire (unlimited mileage) and £220/€300/US$390 for a week, though, as anywhere, it becomes cheaper the longer the rental period. There's little difference in price amongst the major companies, but you might find that local companies, such as Recent Car in Budapest, offer better deals. Credit cards are usually required for a deposit. Before signing, check on any mileage limits or other restrictions or extras, as well as what you're covered for in the event of an accident. You may be able to take the car into neighbouring countries, although most companies charge extra for this.

Car rental agencies

In Britain

Avis ⓣ0870 606 0100, ⓦwww.avis.co.uk.
Budget ⓣ01442/276 266, ⓦwww.budget.co.uk.
Europcar ⓣ0870 607 5000, ⓦwww.europcar.co.uk.
National ⓣ0870 536 5365, ⓦwww.nationalcar.co.uk.
Hertz ⓣ0870 844 8844, ⓦwww.hertz.co.uk.
Holiday Autos ⓣ0870 400 0099, ⓦwww.holidayautos.co.uk.
Suncars ⓣ0870 500 5566, ⓦwww.suncars.com.

In Ireland

Avis Northern Ireland ⓣ028/9024 0404, Republic of Ireland ⓣ021/428 1111, ⓦwww.avis.ie.
Budget Republic of Ireland ⓣ09/0662 7711, ⓦwww.budget.ie.
Europcar Northern Ireland ⓣ028/9442 3444, Republic of Ireland ⓣ01/614 2888, ⓦwww.europcar.ie.
Hertz Republic of Ireland ⓣ01/676 7476, ⓦwww.hertz.ie.
Holiday Autos Republic of Ireland ⓣ01/872 9366, ⓦwww.holidayautos.ie.

In the US and Canada

Auto Europe US and Canada ⓣ1-888/223-5555, ⓦwww.autoeurope.com.
Avis US ⓣ1-800/230-4898, Canada ⓣ1-800/272-5871, ⓦwww.avis.com.
Budget US ⓣ1-800/527-0700, Canada ⓣ1-800/472-3325, ⓦwww.budget.com.
Europcar US & Canada ⓣ1-877/940 6900, ⓦwww.europcar.com.
Hertz US ⓣ1-800/654-3131, Canada ⓣ1-800/263-0600, ⓦwww.hertz.com.
National ⓣ1-800/962-7070, ⓦwww.nationalcar.com.
Thrifty US and Canada ⓣ1-800/847-4389, ⓦwww.thrifty.com.

In Australia

Avis ⓣ13 63 33 or 02/9353 9000, ⓦwww.avis.com.au.
Budget ⓣ1300 362 848, ⓦwww.budget.com.au.
Hertz ⓣ13 30 39 or 03/9698 2555, ⓦwww.hertz.com.au.
Holiday Autos ⓣ1300 554 432, ⓦwww.holidayautos.com.au.
National ⓣ13 10 45, ⓦwww.nationalcar.com.au.

In New Zealand

Avis ⓣ09/526 2847 or 0800 655 111, ⓦwww.avis.co.nz.
Budget ⓣ09/976 2222 or ⓣ0800 652-227, ⓦwww.budget.co.nz.
Hertz ⓣ0800 654 321, ⓦwww.hertz.co.nz.
Holiday Autos ⓣ0800 144 040, ⓦwww.holidayautos.co.nz.
National ⓣ0800 800 115 or ⓣ03/366-5574, ⓦwww.nationalcar.co.nz.

Hitchhiking

Hitchhiking (*autostop*) is widely practised by young Magyars, and is considered pretty safe. However, as anywhere, it's a potentially risky business and if you do decide to travel this way, you should take all sensible precautions.

Cycling

Given the generally flat terrain, and the light winds and low rainfall from July until the end of September, **cycling** is a good way to get around Hungary. There's a growing number of cycle paths in the country, indicating an increasing awareness of the cycling community. However, there are several caveats for cyclists: they are not allowed on main roads (with single-digit numbers) or on some secondary roads in "peak hours" (7–9.30am and 4–6pm). In towns, there are sunken tramlines and slippery cobbled streets to contend with.

There is a series of very enjoyable touring routes, ranging from the serene calm of Lake Balaton to the more rugged and demanding Bükk Hills range, which is more suited to mountain-bikers. However, the 290-kilometre route along Hungary's western border, from Lake Fertő in the north down to the Őrség region, is regarded as one of the most scenic and varied. Generally speaking, May and September – when the weather is at its most appealing and the roads are free from the tourist hordes – are the ideal cycling months.

If you wish to transport your bike by train, look out for the bicycle or luggage symbols in the timetable; you'll have to pay a small charge. See p.50 for more cycling information.

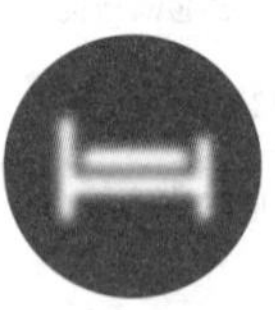

Accommodation

The range of places to stay in Hungary has increased radically in recent years. Competitively priced, high-quality pensions and guesthouses are appearing on a regular basis, often offering better value for money than hotels. For those with less cash to spend, there are enough private rooms, hostels and college dormitories to go around, even in high season. All in all, it shouldn't prove difficult to find somewhere that suits your tastes and budget.

Most towns have several hotels, pensions and private lodgings, and quite often a campsite or hostel within close proximity to the centre. Even so, the cheapest places tend to fill up quickly during high season (June–Aug), so it's wise to make **reservations** if you're on a tight budget or bound for somewhere with limited possibilities. **Bookings** for the largest nationwide hotel chain, Danubius, are handled through its head office at Szent István tér 11, Budapest (ⓣ1/374-7200, ⓦwww.danubiusgroup.com). Other hotels and pensions can be reserved direct or through local tourist agencies, whilst nearly all branches of Ibusz deal in private accommodation. Details of all Hungary's hotels and campsites can be found in free booklets available from the Hungarian Tourist Board.

Hotels and pensions

Hungarian **hotels** (*szálló* or *szállóda*) are classified according to a **five-star grading system**, although this gives only a vague idea of prices, which can vary dramatically according to the locality and the time of year. Moreover, the ratings are not always the best guide to standards, as some places officially meet the basic criteria in terms of facilities, but are in fact poor. Prices in Budapest and the Balaton region are on average around 15–25 percent higher than in other areas, though rates can drop by as much as thirty percent in those hotels on Balaton that open over the **winter**. **Breakfast** is usually, but not always, included in the price.

Five-star establishments, of which there are

Accommodation price codes

Accommodation in this guide is graded according to the price bands given below. Note that prices refer to the **cheapest available double room in high season**. Out of season rates can fall by as much as thirty percent. For dormitories in hostels, the price per bed has been given. Note that many places now post current room rates in **euros**, even though you pay in forints.

❶ Under 3000Ft	❹ 7000–10,000Ft	❼ 18,000–25,000Ft
❷ 3000–5000Ft	❺ 10,000–14,000Ft	❽ 25,000–40,000Ft
❸ 5000–7000Ft	❻ 14,000–18,000Ft	❾ over 40,000Ft

very few outside Budapest, have all the facilities you'd expect from a luxury hotel, whilst four-star establishments are reliably comfortable, with pristine bathrooms, satellite TV, minibar and Internet access all standard features. Many also house a fitness suite, sauna and other leisure facilities. Three-star places are, generally speaking, reliable with perfectly adequate facilities, though, compared to some of the pensions about, many do not represent decent value for money. Further down the ladder, you're in hit-or-miss territory when it comes to two-star hotels, whilst you're definitely better off forsaking a one-star for private accommodation or a hostel/dormitory. More often than not, one- and two-star hotels are soulless, tatty looking places with limited facilities; many won't have private bathrooms, although they do usually have a sink in the room. Single rooms are more difficult to come by, particularly in high season, and **solo travellers** are likely to end up paying for a double.

Private (often family-owned) **pensions** are appearing in ever greater numbers in towns and villages throughout Hungary, where they often undercut hotels with the same star rating. While some are purpose-built, with a restaurant on the premises, others are simply someone's house with a TV in the living room and a few rooms upstairs. There's no correlation between their appearance and title – some style themselves *panzió* (or *penzió*), others as *fogadó*. Places that describe themselves as **motels** are usually on the edge of town, or further out along the highway. Some coexist with bungalows and a campsite to form a tourist complex, and quite a few are near a thermal bath or swimming pool, with restaurants and sports facilities, too.

Private rooms

Hostels aside, taking a **private room** is often the cheapest option available, particularly if two of you are sharing; expect to pay around £10/€14/US$18 for a double room and £8/€11/US$14 for a single, though, as with hotels, prices are rather inflated in Budapest and around Lake Balaton. The common practice is to charge thirty percent extra if you stay fewer than three nights, while a general lack of single rooms means that **solo travellers** often have to pay for the price of a double. This type of accommodation (termed *Fiz*, short for *fizetővendégszolgálat*) can be arranged by Ibusz or local tourist agencies, or simply by knocking on the door of places displaying *szoba kiadó* or *Zimmer frei* signs, which abound along the west bank of the Danube Bend, both shores of Lake Balaton, and in thermal spas throughout Hungary.

Although tourist offices rent sight unseen, you can still exercise judgement when choosing a room by rejecting dubious-sounding locations. As a rule of thumb, a town's Belváros (inner sector) is likely to hold spacious apartments with parquet floors, high ceilings and a balcony overlooking a courtyard, whereas in the outlying zones you'll probably be housed in a charmless, high-rise modern development. **Breakfast** is not usually included in the price, although some owners will provide breakfast for a fee whilst others might greet you in the morning with a cup of coffee. By offering a small amount of money, you may also be able to use the washing machine. It's also possible to rent whole **apartments** in some towns and resorts, also bookable through agencies such as Ibusz.

Village homestays

Village tourism (*falusi turizmus*) – farmhouse-style accommodation in villages – is a thriving sector in Hungary, and something many smaller villages are being encouraged to partake in. Currently, the most popular areas for village tourism are in the Northern Uplands and the Őrség and Tisza regions. While the scheme offers the opportunity to stay and socialize with a Hungarian family, the downside is that the majority of places are in extremely remote areas and, unless you have your own transport, often very difficult to reach. Accommodation is **graded** according to a sunflower classification system; four sunflowers, the highest grade, denotes a house where rooms have private bathroom or shower/toilet. The majority of places, however, offer shared bathrooms and toilets, either with other guests and/or the hosts. Expect to **pay** around £8–12/€11–17/US$14–21 for a double bed per night; meals are not usually included in the price but many households are willing to cook a meal on request. Tourinform and local tourist agencies can provide details, or you can contact the **Hungarian Federation of Rural Tourism** in Budapest at Király utca 93 (Ⓣ1/352-9804), who produce a brochure listing all homestay accommodation in the country.

Hostels and dormitories

Hungary has a reasonable number of **youth hostels** (*Ifjúsági Szálló*), which still provide some of the cheapest accommodation around, typically £5/€7/US$7 for a dorm bed in Budapest, slightly less elsewhere. Some are official IYHF hostels, for which you'll need a membership card issued by the national hostel organization in your own country (see below), though, in practice, many hostels in Hungary don't insist on one. Most hostels, except some of those in Budapest, are open during the summer only and **reservations** for any hostel in the country can be made through the Hungarian Youth Hostels Association Travel Section (Ⓦwww.youthhostels.hu). They also produce a handbook listing all hostels around the country.

There are two other kinds of official **tourist hostels**: *túristaszálló*, generally found in provincial towns, and *túristaház*, located in highland areas favoured by hikers. Both are graded "A" or "B" depending on the availability of hot water and the number of beds per room. *Túristaszálló* rates range from £2/€2.80/US$3.60 to £8/€11/US$14 – the former for a bed, the latter for a double or triple room. In *túristaház*, which rarely have separate rooms, a dormitory bed goes for £2–3/€2.80–4.20/US$3.60–5.40. It's generally advisable to make bookings for tourist hostels through the regional tourist office.

In many towns, you can also stay in vacant **college dormitories** for about £5/€7/US$9 a night. Generally, these accept tourists over the whole of the summer vacation (roughly July to mid-August) and in some cases at weekends throughout the year. It is usually possible to make bookings through Ibusz or other tourist agencies, but otherwise you can just turn up at the designated college (*kollégium*) and ask if there are any beds available.

Youth hostel associations

In England and Wales

Youth Hostel Association (YHA) Ⓣ0870 770 8868, Ⓦwww.yha.org.uk. Annual membership £14; under-18s £7; lifetime £200 (or five annual payments of £41).

In Scotland

Scottish Youth Hostel Association Ⓣ0870 155 3255, Ⓦwww.syha.org.uk. Annual membership £6, for under-18s £2.50.

In Northern Ireland

Hostelling International Northern Ireland Ⓣ028/9032 4733, Ⓦwww.hini.org.uk. Adult membership £13; under-18s £6; family £25; life £75.

In Ireland

Irish Youth Hostel Association Ⓣ01/830 4555, Ⓦwww.irelandyha.org. Annual membership €20; under-18s €10; family €40; lifetime €100.

In the US

Hostelling International-American Youth Hostels Ⓣ301/495-1240, Ⓦwww.hiayh.org. Annual membership for adults (18–55) is $28, for seniors (55 or over) is $18, and for under-18s and groups of ten or more, is free. Life memberships are $250.

In Canada

Hostelling International Canada Ⓣ1-800/663 5777 or 613/237 7884, Ⓦwww.hihostels.ca. Rather than sell the traditional 1- or 2-year memberships, the association now sells one Individual Adult membership with a 28- to 16-month term. The length of the term depends on when the membership is sold, but a member can receive up to 28 months of membership for just C$35+tax. Membership is free for under-18s and you can become a lifetime member for C$175.

In Australia

Australia Youth Hostels Association Ⓣ02/9261 1111, Ⓦwww.yha.com.au. Adult membership rate A$52 (under-18s A$19) for the first twelve months and then A$37 each year after.

In New Zealand

Youth Hostelling Association New Zealand Ⓣ0800 278 299 or 03/379 9970, Ⓦwww.yha.co.nz. Adult membership NZ$40 for one year, NZ$60 for two and NZ$80 for three; under-18s free; lifetime NZ$300.

Campsites and chalets

There's a good spread of **campsites** (*kemping*) throughout Hungary, with by far the greatest concentration around Lake Balaton. These range across the spectrum of "de luxe" to third class. The better places usually have an on-site restaurant and shops, whilst quite a few boast sporting facilities such as a swimming pool and tennis courts; second- or third-class sites often have a nicer ambience, with lots of old trees rather than a manicured lawn and acres of campers and trailers. Expect to pay at least £2/€2.80/US$3.60, twice that around Lake Balaton, which has some of the most expensive sites in Hungary. **Fees** are calculated on a basic ground rent, plus a charge per person and a charge for any vehicle, and, for non-students, an obligatory local tax (*kurtaxe*). There are **reductions** of 25–30 percent during "low" season (Oct–May), and during the high season for those with an international camping carnet (see below). Children up to the age of 14 also qualify for 50 percent reductions. The majority of sites are open from April or May to September or October, with a few open all year round; it's advisable to ring ahead at the more popular sites, such as those around Balaton. While a few resorts and towns have semi-official **free campsites** (*szabad kemping*), **camping rough** is illegal, although young Hungarians sometimes do it in highland areas where there are "rain shelters" (*esőház*).

If you're planning to do a lot of camping, an **international camping carnet** is a good investment. The carnet gives discounts at member sites and serves as useful identification. Many campsites will take it instead of making you surrender your passport during your stay, and it covers you for third-party insurance when camping. In the **UK and Ireland**, the carnet costs £4.50/€10, and is available to members of the AA or the RAC (see p.36), or for members of the **Camping and Caravanning Club** (Ⓣ024/7669 4995, Ⓦwww.campingandcaravanningclub.co.uk; annual membership £29 plus £5 joining fee), the **CTC** (Ⓣ0870 873 0061, Ⓦwww.ctc.org.uk, annual membership £30.50), or the foreign touring arm of the same company, the **Carefree Travel Service** (Ⓣ024/7642 2024), which provides the carnet free if you take out insurance with them; this last organization also books ferry crossings and inspects camping sites in Europe. In the **US and Canada**, the carnet is available from home motoring organizations (see p.36), or from **Family Campers and RVers** (FCRV; Ⓣ1-800/245-9755 or Ⓣ716/668-6242, Ⓦwww.fcrv.org). FCRV annual membership costs US$25, and the carnet an additional US$10.

Rates for renting **chalets** or *faház*, literally "wooden houses", are around £4–15/€5.60–21/US$7.20–27, depending on amenities and size (they usually sleep 2–4 people). The first-class chalets – with well-equipped kitchens, hot water and a sitting room or terrace – are excellent, while the most primitive at least have clean bedding and don't leak. An alternative source of accommodation is **holiday homes** or **workers' hostels** (*üdülőház*), which proliferate around resorts. Traditionally, these buildings were reserved for trade-union members, and even today many still reserve a large proportion of their rooms for workers. Standards are similar to those of a two-star hotel, though can vary from the grim to the respectable; some operate as fully functioning hotels, some have just a handful of rooms available, whilst others do not accept tourists at all.

Eating and drinking

Even under Communism, Hungary was renowned for its abundance of food: material proof of the "goulash socialism" that amazed visitors from Romania and the Soviet Union. Nowadays, there is more choice than ever, particularly in Budapest, where almost every world cuisine is available.

For foreigners the archetypal Magyar dish is "goulash" – historically the basis of much **Hungarian cooking**. The ancient Magyars relished cauldrons of *gulyás* (pronounced "gou-yash"), a soup made of potatoes and whatever meat was available, which was later flavoured with paprika and beefed up into a variety of stews, modified over the centuries by various foreign influences. Hungary's Slav neighbours probably introduced native cooks to yogurt and sour cream – vital ingredients in many dishes – while the influence of the Turks, Austrians and Germans is apparent in a variety of sticky pastries and strudels, as well as recipes featuring sauerkraut or dumplings. Another influence was that of France, which revolutionized Hungarian cooking in the Middle Ages and again in the nineteenth century. For a **glossary** of food and drink terms see p.482.

Breakfast, snacks and sandwiches

As a nation of early risers, Hungarians like to have a calorific **breakfast** (*reggeli*). Commonly, this includes cheese, eggs or salami together with bread and jam, and in rural areas is often accompanied by a shot of *pálinka* (brandy) to "clear the palate" or "aid digestion".

A whole range of places purveys **snacks**, notably *csemege* or **delicatessens**, which display a tempting spread of salads, open sandwiches, pickles and cold meats; in a few, you can eat on the premises. For other sit-down nibbles, people patronize either *bisztró*, which tend to offer a couple of hot dishes besides the inevitable salami rolls; *snackbár*, which are superior versions of the same, with leanings in the direction of being a patisserie; or *büfé*. These last are found in department stores and stations, and are sometimes open around the clock. The food on offer, though, is often limited to sausages – including those comprising parts of the lung or liver (*hurka*), and the greasier version filled with rice (*kolbász*).

On the streets, according to season, vendors preside over tables of *kukorica* (corn on the cob) or trays of *gesztenye* (roasted chestnuts). Fried-fish (*sült hal*) shops are common in towns near rivers or lakes. *Szendvics* (sandwich), *hamburger* and *gofri* (waffle) stands are mushrooming in many towns, as are Chinese fast-food and Turkish kebab joints, which offer further cheap alternatives. Another popular munch is *lángos*: the native, mega-size equivalent of doughnuts, often sold with a sprinkling of cheese and soured cream. For fresh fruit and produce, head to the local outdoor **market** (*piac*) or market hall (*vásárcsarnok*), where people select their fish fresh from glass tanks, and their mushrooms from a staggering array of *gomba*, which are displayed alongside toxic fungi in a "mushroom parade" to enable shoppers to recognize the difference.

No list of snacks is complete without mentioning **bread** (*kenyér*), which is so popular that "Hungarians will even eat bread with bread", as the old saying has it. White bread remains the staple of the nation, but in many supermarkets, especially in Budapest, you can usually get a range of brown (*barna*) and rye (*rozs*) breads.

Restaurants and meals

Hungarians have a variety of words for their finely distinguished **restaurants**. In theory an **étterem** is a proper restaurant, while a **vendéglő** approximates to the Western notion of a bistro, though in practice the terms are often used interchangeably. The old word for an inn, **csárda**, now applies to posh places specializing in certain dishes (for example, a "Fishermen's inn", or **halászcsárda**, serves fish), restaurants alongside roads or with rustic pretensions, as well as to the humbler rural establishments that the name originally signified.

Traditionally, Hungarians take their main meal at **lunchtime**, although the old tendency for restaurants to have fewer dishes available in the evenings has now disappeared. However, it is worth remembering that many places still close early, around 10pm, especially outside the capital. You'll find many restaurants, at least those in the more touristy areas, with bands of musicians playing at lunchtime and in the evening, their violin airs and melodic plonkings of the cimbalom (see p.472) an essential element of the "scene". While some restaurants offer a bargain set menu (*napi menü*) of basic dishes, the majority of places are strictly *à la carte*. You'll probably be asked if you want a **starter** (*előételek*) – generally a soup or salad, though nobody will mind if you just have one of the dishes offered as the **main course** (*főételek*) or, alternatively, order just a soup and a starter. Bread is supplied almost automatically, on the grounds that "a meal without bread is no meal". **Drinks** are normally listed on the menu under the heading *italok*. For a three-course meal with wine, expect to pay around £5–10/€7–14/US$9–18 in an average restaurant, twice that in downtown Budapest.

Most places have **menus** in German (and less frequently, English), a language of which most waiters and waitresses have a smattering. However, look out for those places, particularly in Budapest, that give you a menu without prices, a sure sign that they're expensive, or plan to rip you off – get the waiter to bring you a menu with the prices listed, or leave. **Overcharging** is common, so check that bill assiduously. A service charge is rarely included in the bill and so the staff depend on customers **tipping** (ten percent of the total is customary, if you think it's merited). Be warned that if you say "thank you" as you hand the money over, this implies that they can keep the change. Unfortunately, standards of service still leave much to be desired, even in many Budapest restaurants, with a certain lethargy afflicting many waiting staff.

Vegetarian food

Despite the emergence of *vegetarianus* restaurants in Budapest, and a growing understanding of the concept, **vegetarians** are still poorly catered for. Although an increasing number of restaurants offer vegetarian dishes, many of these are depressingly predictable, and it's only in the more upmarket places that the choices become anything like tempting. You can find yourself on a diet of vegetables or cheese fried in breadcrumbs; these are known as *rántott gomba* (mushrooms), *rántott karfiol* (cauliflower), or *rántott sajt* (cheese), and – if you are lucky – *padlizsán* (aubergine), *zukkini* (courgette), or *tök* (pumpkin). *Gomba paprikás* (mushroom paprika stew) is also OK if it is cooked in oil rather than in fat. Alternatively, there are eggs – fried (literally "mirror" – *tükörtojás*), soft-boiled (*lágy tojás*), scrambled (*tojásrántotta*), or in mayonnaise (*kaszínótojás*) – or salads, though in winter these are often of the pickled vegetable variety. Even innocuous vegetable soups may contain meat stock, and the pervasive use of sour cream and animal fat in cooking means that avoiding animal products or by-products is difficult. However, greengrocers (*zöldségbolt*) and markets sell excellent produce which, combined with judicious shopping in supermarkets (for pulses, grains, etc), should see you through.

Coffee houses and patisseries

Many Hungarians like to kick-start the day with **coffee**, followed by further intakes at various intervals throughout the day, usually in the form of tiny glasses of *kávé*: superstrong, served black and sweetened to taste, this is a brew that can double your heartbeat. **Coffee houses** were once the centres of Budapest's cultural and political life – hotbeds of gossip where penurious writers got credit and the clientele dawdled for hours over the free newspapers. Sadly this is no longer the case, but you'll find plenty of unpretentious *kávéház* serving the beverage with milk (*tejeskávé*) or whipped cream (*tejszínhabbal*), should you request it. Ordering a cappuccino can be a very hit-or-miss affair as they vary dramatically in quality wherever you go, with the worst efforts consisting of little more than a regular coffee with a dollop of whipped cream unattractively slumped on top.

Tea-drinkers are in a minority here, perhaps because Hungarian **tea** with milk (*tejes tea*) is so insipid, although *tea citrommal* (with lemon) is pleasantly refreshing. However, there are a growing number of **teahouses** about, serving a terrific range of teas from around the world, as well as all manner of other beverages.

Most coffee houses have some pastries on offer, although you'll find much more choice in the **patisseries** (*cukrászda*), which pander to the Magyar fondness for sweet things. **Pancakes** (*palacsinta*) **with fillings** – *almás* (apple), *diós* (walnuts), *fahéjas* (cinnamon), *mákos* (poppy seeds), *mandulás* (almonds) or *Gundel*-style, with nuts, chocolate sauce, cream and raisins – are very popular, as are **strudels** (*rétes*) made with curds and dill (*kapros túrós rétes*), poppy seeds (*mákosrétes*) or plums (*szilvás rétes*). Even the humble dumpling is transformed into a *somlói galuska*, flavoured with vanilla, nuts and chocolate. But the frontrunners in the rich and sticky stakes have to be chestnut purée with whipped cream (*gesztenyepüré*); coffee soufflé (*kapucineres felfújt*); baked apple with vanilla, raisins and cream (*töltött alma*); and the staggering array of **cakes**. The average **cukrászda** displays a dozen or more types, including *dobostorta* (chocolate cream cake topped with caramel) and the pineapple-laden *ananásztorta*.

If you're still not satiated, there's **ice cream** (*fagylalt*), the opium of the masses, sold by the scoop (*gombóc*) and priced low enough so that anyone can afford a cone. The most common flavours are *vanília*, *csokoládé*, *puncs* (fruit punch), *citrom* and *kávé*, though mango, pistachio and various nutty flavours can be found too. And finally there's *metélt or tészta* – a rather unlikely-sounding but quite tasty dessert of chopped sweet noodles, served cold with poppy seeds or some other topping.

Drinking

Hungary's climate and diversity of soils are perfect for **wine** (*bor*), though cold winters mean that reds are usually on the light side. In the last few years the wine market has really begun to take off, and, though good vintages are still cheap by Western standards, prices are rising steadily. In bars and most restaurants you can either buy it by the bottle (*üveg*) or the glass (*pohár*). There are 22 wine-growing regions in the country, the best of which are Villány, Eger, Tokaj, Szekszárd and the Balaton. They even manage to grow grapes on the sandy soils around Kecskemét, at the edge of the Great Plain, but the wines from there are of poorer quality. Overall, though, standards are constantly rising as more vineyards try to win the right to label their bottles *minöségi bor* (quality wine), the equivalent of *appellation contrôlée*.

Wine bars (*borozó*) are ubiquitous and far less pretentious than in the West: the wine served is often pretty rough stuff, and there's usually a cluster of interesting characters round the bar. True devotees of the grape make pilgrimages to the extensive **wine cellars** (*borospince*) that honeycomb towns like Tokaj and Eger. By day, people often drink wine with water or soda water, specifying a *fröccs* or a yet more diluted *hosszú lépés* (literally, a "long step"). Wine can be sweet (*édes*), dry (*száraz*), semi-sweet (*félédes*) or semi-dry (*félszáraz*). Hungarians enjoy the ritual of **toasting**, so the first word to get your tongue around is *egészségedre* ("EGG-aish-shaig-edreh") – "cheers!". When toasting more than one other person, it's grammatically correct to change this to *egészségünkre* ("cheers to us!"). Hungarians only consider it appropriate to toast with wine or spirits. A simpler version that will get you by is *szia* (see-ya) for one person, and *sziasztok* (see-ya-stock) for more people.

As long as you stick to native brands, **spirits** are also cheap. The best-known type of *pálinka* – brandy – is distilled from apricots (*barack*), and is a speciality of the Kecskemét region, but spirits are also produced from peaches (*őszibarack*), pears (*körte*) and any other fruits available. This is particularly true of *szilva* – a lethal spirit produced on cottage stills in rural areas, allegedly based on plums. Hungarians with money to burn order whisky (*viszki*) to impress, but most people find its cost prohibitive.

Bottled **beer** (*sör*) of the lager type (*világos*) predominates, although you might come across brown ale (*barna sör*) and draught beer (*csapolt sör*). Hungarian beer production is almost totally in the hands of the big international breweries. Western brands like Tuborg, HB, Wernesgrünner and Gold Fassel are mostly brewed under licence in Hungary, while you can also find imported Czech brands like Urquell Pilsen and Staropramen. The old Austro-Hungarian beer Dreher has made a comeback in the hands of South African Breweries. Other brands to try are Arany Ászok, a very cheap light beer, and Pannonia Sör, a pleasant hoppy beer from Pécs. **Beer halls** (*söröző*) range from plush establishments sponsored by foreign breweries to humble stand-up joints where you order either a small glass (*pohár*) or a half-litre mug (*korsó*).

Communications

Both the Hungarian postal and telecommunications services are as efficient as anywhere else in Europe. Internet cafés are fairly ubiquitous, and you should be able to find some sort of access even in the smallest towns.

Mail

Post offices (*posta*) are usually open Monday to Friday 8am to 6pm and Saturday 8am to noon in most towns, and until around 4pm on weekdays (closed Saturdays) in smaller places. In Budapest you'll find several offices functioning around the clock. Mail from abroad should be addressed "poste restante, posta" followed by the name of the town; tell your friends to write your surname first, Hungarian-style, and underline it; even this may not prevent your mail being misfiled, so ask them to check under all your names. To collect mail, show your passport and ask "*Van posta a részemre?*". For express mail or packages, all the major **courier** companies, including DHL, Fedex and TNT, have offices in Budapest (see Budapest "Listings"). **Stamps** (*bélyeg*) can be bought at tobacconists or post offices, though the latter are usually pretty crowded and very few staff speak English. Note that letters and postcards have different rates, so don't buy a job lot of stamps – show your letter first. If you need to send a telegram (*távirat*), your best bet is the post office. In theory you can dictate them by dialling ☎192, but the line is often engaged and it's difficult to make yourself understood.

Telephones

In towns and cities, calls can be made from public phones with 10, 20, 50 and 100Ft coins (minimum call 20Ft), though **cardphones** are far more common and it's worth keeping a phonecard (*telefonkártya*) to hand; cards currently cost 800Ft and 1800Ft and are available from Matáv (the Hungarian telecommunications company) shops, post offices, tobacconists and some hotels. The best card for international calls is the Barangaló card (2000Ft and 5000Ft), available from post offices, which offers excellent per-minute rates to countries worldwide. To make a direct call outside the area you are in, dial ☎06 (which gives a burring tone), followed by the area code and the subscriber's number.

Calling home from Hungary

One of the most convenient ways of phoning home from abroad is via a **telephone charge card** from your phone company back home. Using a PIN number, you can make calls from most hotel, public and private phones that will be charged to your account. Since most major charge cards are free to obtain, it's certainly worth getting one at least for emergencies; enquire first though whether your destination is covered, and bear in mind that rates aren't necessarily cheaper than calling from a public phone.

In **the UK and Ireland**, British Telecom (Ⓣ0800 345 144, Ⓦwww.bt.com) will issue free to all BT customers the BT Charge Card, which can be used in 116 countries; AT&T (dial Ⓣ0800 890 011, then 888/641-6123 when you hear the AT&T prompt to be transferred to the Florida Call Centre; free, 24hr) offers the Global Calling Card.

In the **US and Canada**, AT&T, MCI, Sprint, Canada Direct and other North American long-distance companies all enable their customers to make credit-card calls while overseas, billed to your home number. Call your company's customer service line to find out if they provide service from Hungary, and if so, what the toll-free access code is.

To call **Australia and New Zealand** from Hungary, telephone charge cards such as Telstra Telecard or Optus Calling Card in Australia, and Telecom NZ's Calling Card can be used to make calls abroad, which are charged back to a domestic account or credit card. Apply to Telstra (Ⓣ1800 038 000), Optus (Ⓣ1300 300 937), or Telecom NZ (Ⓣ04/801 9000).

Telephone codes

When calling from abroad, dial the international access code +36 + area code + number. Note that the initial **zero** is omitted from the area code when dialing the UK, Ireland, Australia and New Zealand from abroad. When calling Hungary dial +36 + area code + number.

US and Canada +1 + area code.
Australia + 61 + city code.
New Zealand + 64 + city code.
UK + 44 + city code.
Republic of Ireland + 353 + city code.

Mobile phones

Hungarian **mobile phone** numbers have eleven digits, all prefixed with Ⓣ0620, Ⓣ0630, Ⓣ0660 or Ⓣ0670, followed by seven digits. Calling a mobile from a public or private phone, you have to dial all the numbers; calling from a phone on the same network, drop the first four digits; and calling from mobile phones on different networks, drop Ⓣ06 only.

Check with your phone provider if your mobile will work abroad, and what the call charges will be. For further information about using your UK phone abroad, check out Ⓦwww.telecomsadvice.org.uk/features/using_your_mobile_abroad.

Email

One of the best (and cheapest) ways to keep in touch while travelling is to sign up for a free **Internet email address** that can be accessed from anywhere, for example Yahoo! (Ⓦwww.yahoo.com) or Hotmail (Ⓦwww.hotmail.com). **Internet access** is now readily available in most places. If you can't locate an Internet café, seek out a Matáv shop, as they usually have at least a couple of terminals. Many of the more upmarket hotels have an ISDN line. Connections vary, but generally speaking are pretty slow, although prices are reasonable: expect to pay around 500Ft for an hour online.

For information regarding how to **plug in your laptop** whilst in Hungary, as well as a list of phone country codes around the world and information about electrical systems in different countries, see Ⓦwww.kropla.com.

The media

There are several main broadsheets available in Hungary, in addition to a handful of English-language papers. Television coverage, meanwhile, differs little from that in other European countries, with foreign cable and satellite television having made huge inroads in recent years.

Generally speaking, Hungarian **television** is pretty dismal, with state TV (MTV) screening a dreary diet of gameshows and low-budget soaps from morning to night. In addition, there are numerous commercial channels such as TV2, the German-Belgian owned RTK Klub and Duna TV, a state-supported channel geared to Hungarian minorities abroad, though these are little better. It is for this reason that many Hungarians subscribe to satellite channels, with whole apartment blocks sharing the cost of installation. Most half-decent hotels will now have access to foreign channels, though in some cases they will be German channels only, whilst the better-quality hotels will have the full satellite package.

Competing with the largest circulation broadsheet **newspaper**, *Népszabadság* (formerly Communist, but now avowedly Socialist), is the liberal-conservative leaning *Magyar Nemzet*. In addition, there are, of course, plenty of tabloids doing the daily rounds of sensationalism.

In Budapest you can find most of the **English** broadsheet papers in the classier hotels, some newsagents and in the street kiosks. There are several Budapest-based English-language weeklies including the *Budapest Sun* (Ⓦwww.budapestsun.com), a rather lightweight, newsy rag with entertainment and events listings, and the *Budapest Business Journal* (Ⓦwww.bbj.hu), which covers mainly business and politics. Of the many listings magazines, the irreverent *Budapest In Your Pocket* (Ⓦwww.inyourpocket.com) is by far the most informative and up to date. The *Budapest Week* (Ⓦwww.budapest-week.com) is a comprehensive online arts and entertainments weekly with excellent listings sections as well as a useful classifieds section. You could also drop into the British or American cultural centres in Budapest, which usually have a reasonable stock of recent newspapers and magazines. Whilst not in English, *Pesti Est* is a useful free weekly listings pamphlet available from tourist offices and hotels in most towns and cities throughout the country.

There are plenty of private **radio** stations, but for news, most listeners tune into foreign stations, especially the **BBC World Service** (Ⓦwww.bbc.co.uk/worldservice), **Radio Canada** (Ⓦwww.rcinet.ca), and **Voice of America** (Ⓦwww.voa.gov).

Opening hours, holidays and festivals

Shops are generally open Monday to Friday from 10am to 6pm, and on Saturdays from 9am to 1pm, with some (generally those in the capital, plus the larger shopping centres) open for a few hours on Sundays. Supermarkets and grocery stores open from 7 or 8am to 7 or 8pm, but again expect longer opening hours in the larger places, where there are also a growing number of 24-hour shops (Non-Stop, 0–24 or Ejjel-Nappali). Post offices in most places are open Monday to Friday 8am to 6pm and Saturdays 8am to noon, although in larger towns and cities these hours may be an hour or two longer. In Budapest you'll find several offices functioning around the clock. Those in smaller towns and villages typically close at 4pm on weekdays and do not open at all on Saturdays. Most banks open Monday to Thursday from 8am to 4pm, and on Fridays until 2 or 3pm. Pharmacy opening hours are normally Monday to Friday 9am to 6 or 7pm and Saturdays 9am to noon or 1pm; signs in the window give the location or telephone number of the nearest all-night (*éjjeli* or *ügyeleti szolgálat*) pharmacy.

Inevitably, **tourist office** opening times vary greatly, depending upon both their location and season. Summer opening times (typically June–Sept) are, generally speaking, weekdays 8 or 9am to 6 or 7pm and weekends 10am to 4 or 5pm, and during the winter Monday to Friday only from 9am to 4 or 5pm. Similarly, tourist agencies' opening hours vary enormously, with some even open until 8 or 9pm in the summer.

Museums are generally open Tuesday to Sunday 10am to 6pm (winter 9 or 10am to 4pm, or earlier), while some of the smaller museums may close down altogether over winter. Hungary's **thermal baths** are usually open daily from 8 or 9am to 6 or 7pm, although some open at 6am – as most of the baths in Budapest do. There are, of course, exceptions to the above – all specific opening times are detailed throughout the Guide.

Public holidays

On the following days, most things in Hungary shut down. When these **holidays** fall on a Tuesday or Thursday, the day between it and the weekend may also become a holiday, and the previous or next Saturday a working day to make up the lost day.

January 1 New Year's Day
March 15 Independence Day
Easter Monday
May 1 Labour Day
August 20 St Stephen's Day
October 23 National holiday
November 1 All Saint's Day
December 25 (Since Christmas celebrations start on the 24th, many shops will be closed the whole day, and by the afternoon everything closes down.)
December 26

Festivals

The Hungarian calendar is replete with some marvellous **festivals and events**, and whilst most of the bigger ones take place in Budapest, you'll find plenty happening throughout the rest of the country too. Naturally enough, most festivals take place over the summer, but if you're visiting any other time, you shouldn't have too much difficulty in tracking down some kind of event; Tourinform can fill you in on what's happening. The following festivals are covered in greater detail in their respective chapters.

Most Hungarian festivals typically feature a varied programme of classical and contemporary music mixed with art and theatrical performances, but there are many other uniquely "Hungarian" events taking place. **Wine festivals** are an integral and immensely enjoyable part of the Hungarian festival scene, with each wine-producing centre staging its own celebration at some time during the year (typically between May and October). The key ones occur in Balatonboglár, Eger, Kőszeg, Sopron, Szekszárd and Tokaj. **Historical pageants**, taking place at Veszprém, Tihany, Gyula, Esztergom and, most notably, Visegrád, are extremely popular, as are the **equestrian shows** with their "rodeo" atmosphere and amazing displays of horsemanship at Nagyvázsony, Apajpuszta, Tamási, Kisbér, Szántódpuszta and Hortobágy.

It is also worth knowing about the tradition of **name-day celebrations**, which are as important to Hungarians as birthdays are in other countries. Customarily, the celebrant invites relatives and friends to a party, and receives gifts and salutations. Lest you forget someone's name-day, tradition allows congratulations to be rendered up to a week afterwards.

Festivals

February

Busójárás Carnival Mohács, end of February. The biggest winter festival in Hungary sees displays of masked revellers re-enacting ancient spring rites and ritual abomination of the Turks.

March–April

Budapest Spring Festival Last two weeks in March. Hungary's largest, most prestigious arts festival; an intensive programme of classical music, theatre and film is run in conjunction with ten other towns and cities across the country.
Anniversary of the 1848 Revolution Countrywide, March 15. Wreaths are laid at monuments around the country to commemorate the revolution against the Habsburgs.
Hollókő Easter Festival Easter weekend. Authentic interpretations of old folk music, dancing and handicraft demonstrations.

May

Gizella Days Veszprém, beginning of May. Concerts, exhibitions and dance in the castle district in honour of the first Hungarian queen.
Balaton Festival Keszthely, May. Month-long festival of classical concerts, theatre programmes and art exhibitions.

June

Bartók + International Opera Festival Miskolc, June. Prestigious operatic festival featuring the work of Bartók alongside that of a different composer each year.
Danube Carnival Budapest, mid-June. Folk and contemporary dance troupes and classical musicians from Hungary and neighbouring countries. At several venues.
Pécs Weeks of Art and Gastronomy June. A fantastic array of mini-festivals related to music, art and food.
Győr Summer Days Mid-June to mid-July. Long-running festival of music, dance and theatre, some of which takes place on a water stage.
Sopron Festival Mid-June to mid-July. Month-long arts festival including musical programmes in the nearby Fertőrákos Caves.

July

Golden Shell Folklore Festival Siófok, first week of July. Folk and dance music featuring dance troupes from all over the world.
Beethoven Nights Martonvásár, July. Outdoor concerts performed by the National Philharmonic Orchestra in the beautiful park of the Brunszvik castle.
Baja Fish Soup Festival Mid-July. Over 2000 cauldrons of soups and casseroles to be devoured over two days.
Visegrád International Palace Games Mid-July. Jousting, archery and medieval arts festival.
Anna Ball Balatonfüred, end of July. Open-air events, cultural programmes and a grand ball to round things off.
Szeged Weeks July–August. Huge festival of music, drama and dance on numerous stages in Szeged's vast main square.

August

Eger Baroque Festival Beginning of August for three weeks. Terrific programme of dance and classical music, as well as jugglers, craftsmen and stall-keepers lining the streets.
Sziget Festival Budapest, August. Now firmly established amongst the premier pop and rock festivals in Europe, attracting some of the world's biggest artists.
Máriapócs August 15 and September 8. Religious pilgrimage in Eastern Hungary attracting thousands.
St Stephen's Day Countrywide, August 20. Honouring the death of Hungary's patron saint and "founding father", with day-long celebrations, the biggest of which is in Budapest with craft fairs, folk dancing, river parades and a spectacular fireworks display to round things off.
Flower Carnival Debrecen, August 20. Wonderfully colourful festival, the only one of its type in Central

and Eastern Europe.

Jewish Summer Festival Budapest, last week in August. Evenings of classical and Klezmer music, opera, dance and art exhibitions in the Budapest Jewish Museum.

September

Debrecen Jazz Days Debrecen, end of September. Oldest and best jazz festival in the country, with both local and international stars.

Wine-Song Festival Pécs and the Villány-Siklós wine region, end of September. One of Europe's premier festivals for male choir and vocal bands, run in conjunction with wine evenings.

Szolnok Goulash Festival Szolnok, first weekend of September. Hungary's most famous dish is celebrated in this convivial food-fest, which includes cooking competitions, lots of wine and a handicrafts market.

October

Kolbasz Sausage Festival Békéscaba, end of October. Another fabulous gastronomic festival, this time celebrating the spicy Csaba sausage.

Autumn Festival Budapest, last two weeks of October. Second only to the Spring Festival, this features programmes from the world of contemporary arts.

Sports and outdoor pursuits

Hungary has a stronger sporting pedigree than most people appreciate, and although the glory days of the national football team are long gone, there have been notable Olympic Games successes in recent years. The most prestigious and high-profile sporting event in the Hungarian calendar is the Formula One Grand Prix in Budapest each August.

Hungarian sport first came to international prominence thanks to its magnificent **football** (*labdarúgás*) team of the 1950s. In particular, it was a 6–3 demolition of England at Wembley in 1953 that alerted the wider footballing world to the marvellous Magyars. Whilst football might still be the nation's favourite sport, standards have declined alarmingly in recent years, with the international team struggling lamely, and unsuccessfully, to qualify for major tournaments and domestic football suffering from lack of finance and too few quality players to make it the thrilling spectacle it once was.

In the **Olympic** arena Hungary has achieved outstanding success, and is consistently in the top ten in the Olympic Games medals standings, an extraordinary feat given the size of the country and its hitherto limited resources. Its most successful Olympian is the little-known Aladár Grevich, who won seven gold medals in fencing between 1932 and 1960. More recently, sporting success has come in the pool, courtesy of the superb water-polo team which captured Olympic gold at the 2000 Sydney Olympics, and successfully retained the title in Athens in 2004 – the third time it has won successive Olympic golds in the sport.

Cycling

Hungary affords plentiful opportunities for cycling enthusiasts, from the easier, flatter routes on the Great Plain and around Lake Balaton, to the more challenging, hilly routes of the Northern Uplands, a more attractive proposition for mountain bikers.

The National Tourist Office produces a **cycling map**, available from Tourinform offices, which features twelve recommended routes, ranging from two to seven days' duration, as well as a list of hotels and guesthouses which offer a range of services to cyclists. There are also several other dedicated cycling maps available, the best of which is the 1:250,000-scale *Cycling Around*

Hungary (Frigoria; 1000Ft), which also includes sights of interest, accommodation and cycle maintenance and hire shops. If cycling in Budapest, then get hold of the free *On a Bike in Budapest* map from Tourinform. It is possible **to rent bikes** (by the hour, day or week) in most large towns and many of the Balaton resorts from private operators and certain campsites (details are given where appropriate in the Guide). Bike shops are fairly common, with repair shops in most larger towns, including several in Budapest.

For more **information** on cycling in Hungary contact the Hungarian Cyclists' Federation in Budapest, at Vadász utca 29 (⑦1/206-6223), or the Hungarian Mountain Bike Association at Visegrádi utca 50 (⑦1/339-9289).

Horse-riding

Hungarians profess a lingering attachment to the horse – their equestrian ally since the time of the great migration and the Magyar conquest – and the horse herds or *csikós* of the Plain are romantic figures of national folklore. Most native **horses** are mixed breeds descended from Arab and English thoroughbreds, crossed in recent years with Hanoverian and Holstein stock. The adjective most commonly used to describe their character is "spirited". In the competitive field, Hungary has produced some fine carriage drivers who have won a succession of individual and team gold medals at European and World Championships.

The current popularity and growth of equestrianism in Hungary is reflected in the number of schools (over 500) offering **riding programmes**. Schools, many of which have English-speaking guides, are graded according to a horseshoe classification system, with the highest, five, being a school of distinguished quality. Programmes available range from summer riding camps for children, to riding adventure tours for the more experienced lasting anywhere between one and ten days. There are also expeditions by **covered wagons** (*cigany kocsi*), which tourists drive and navigate across the *puszta* (Great Plain) and Northern Uplands. Although there are schools all over the country, the greatest concentration is on the Great Plain, around Lake Balaton and in the Northern Uplands.

A one-week adventure tour starts at around £450/€630/US$800, with tutorage, meals and lodgings included in the **price**. Many schools also offer additional recreational activities such as swimming and tennis as part of the package. Saddlery is provided, but you'll need your own riding clothes. Note that many schools will not accept you if you are not fully insured.

The Hungarian Equestrian Tourism Association in Budapest (Ⓦwww.equi.hu) has the most comprehensive file on riding schools in Hungary, and can advise on the range of programmes available. In addition, many Tourinform offices stock a glossy brochure in various languages detailing over 200 equestrian programmes throughout the country.

Hiking

The most beautiful areas for **walking** are the Börzsöny, the Bükk, the Bakony and the Pilis, though all the wooded hill regions in Hungary are crisscrossed with walking **trails**, which are signed with coloured stripes and symbols on trees, stones and buildings. At 1100km, the National Blue Trail is a roughly circular route which takes you through just about every region of the country, whilst, at 105km, the Red Trail is a considerably shorter route through the delightful western Őrség region.

Maps (*turistatérkép*) are available from most Tourinform offices and bookshops; walking paths are shown as red lines, with a letter above them to tell you what colour the stripes on the trees or boulders are: Z = green, K = blue, S = yellow and P = red. Most paths are marked with stripes or crosses, but some are marked with a coloured circle (circular routes), a square (leading to a building or village), a triangle (leading to a peak), or an L-shape (leading to a ruin).

Some of the more popular areas, such as the Börzsöny, to the east of the Danube, north of Budapest, have basic **accommodation** called *túristaház* or *kulcsosház* (see p.41), but it's wise to book in advance; tourist offices carry a list of phone numbers. If you plan to do some extensive walking in the country, then a useful companion is the **pocket guidebook**, *Walking in Hungary* (Cicerone, UK), which details some 32 routes through Uplands areas.

Other sports and activities

Swimming is hugely popular with Hungarians and most towns and cities have at least one indoor and one outdoor pool, whilst during the summer many retreat to the suitably clean and shallow waters of **Lake Balaton**. Here a host of other watersports can be enjoyed, including **windsurfing** (*szörf*) and **sailing**; equipment can be rented from the *kölcsönzo* at the main Balaton boat stations and at nearby Lake Velence.

Racquet sports are also gaining in popularity, with **tennis** (*tenisz*) leading the way; however, public courts are at a premium and so you'll probably have to go to the more upmarket hotels in Budapest and main resorts to find available ones. Few **squash** (*fallabda*) courts exist outside Budapest. Hungary's topography rules out any dramatic or lengthy slopes, but that doesn't stop enthusiasts from **skiing** in the Mátra Mountains and the Buda Hills. A final possibility is to pop along to the local **sports hall** (*sportcsarnok*), where facilities are usually of a fairly decent standard.

Crime and personal safety

Hungary is one of the safest European countries to travel in and you should have little reason to worry about your personal security. However, whilst violent crime is extremely rare, the incidence of theft is growing, with Budapest in particular a prime target for pickpockets, car thieves and other scams. Unfortunately, incidents of racist attacks are also steadily increasing, with Asians, Arabs and, most commonly, the Hungarian Roma bearing the brunt of physical assaults.

The police

The Hungarian **police** (*Rendőrség*), most of whom have at least a smattering of German but rarely any other foreign language, always had a milder reputation than their counterparts in other Eastern Bloc states, and are generally keen to present a favourable image, though in recent years there are signs that they have become increasingly intrusive, particularly where ethnic minorities are concerned. Having said that, unless you are suspected of black-marketeering, driving under the influence of alcohol, drug-smuggling or drug-taking, then there is little reason why you should have any dealings with the police. The most visible police presence is in Budapest, particularly during the summer, when **tourist police** patrol the streets and metro stations, there mainly to act as a deterrent against thieves, but also to assist in any problems tourists may encounter.

Specific offences and emergencies

Since police in towns and cities occasionally ask to inspect **passports and visas**, you should make sure that everything's in order. In border regions, solo travellers may be (politely and briefly) questioned by plain-clothes officers, but here too there shouldn't be any problem. **Drinking and driving** is totally prohibited and anyone caught doing so is liable for prosecution. The use of **drugs** is also illegal in Hungary, and should you be caught in possession the police have the power to detain you for up to 48 hours and administer a mandatory drugs test, which, if positive, can result in prosecution. To call the **police**, dial ⓣ107. Alternatively, you can call the English-speaking 24-hour Police Hotline (ⓣ438-8080). Should you be arrested or need legal advice, ask to contact your embassy or consulate (see Budapest "Listings" for contact details).

Prostitution and "consume girls"

Budapest could once lay claim to being the porn capital of Europe, but **streetwalking** is now illegal in Hungary except in "tolerated zones" – the catch being that there is only one such zone in the entire country, in Miskolc. Prostitution does of course still exist elsewhere, mainly in the capital, although these days it is largely confined to nightclubs, phoney hotels and escort agencies. A phenomenon of a different kind has hit the streets of Budapest in recent years, that of the "**consume girls**", who target solo male foreigners. A couple of attractive young women (they're not difficult to spot) will approach you, typically along Váci utca, get talking and, without wasting any time, "invite you" for a drink in a bar of their choice. A few drinks later you'll find yourself presented with a bill somewhat bigger than you bargained for and be strong-armed into paying up. The bars, and the waiters who work in them, are an integral part of the scam which makes any escape or complaint futile, although if you ever do find yourself caught up in such a situation (although the warning signs are pretty obvious) then report it to the police. To register a complaint for any scam contact the Bureau of Consumer Affairs, József krt 6 (☎1/459-4800), or the rip-off hotline (☎1/438-8080).

Religion

The majority of the Hungarian population affiliates itself to the Roman Catholic Church, with the remainder comprising Reformed Protestant (Calvinist), Evangelical Protestant (Lutheran) and other, smaller groups such as Serb and Greek Orthodox. As in many other former Communist countries there has been a steady rise in religious interest, with the church playing a more visible role in everyday life, although, Christmas and Easter aside, it's rare to see churches full.

Getting into **churches** (*templom*), however, may be more problematic. The really important ones charge a small fee to see their crypts and treasures, and may prohibit sightseeing during services (*mise* or *istentisztelet*, or Gottesdienst in German). In small towns and villages churches are usually kept locked except for worship in the early morning and/or the evening (between around 6pm and 9pm). A small tip is in order if you rouse the verger to unlock the building during the day; he normally lives nearby in a house marked *plébánia*. Visitors are expected to wear "decorous" dress – that is, no shorts or sleeveless tops. In Budapest, several churches offer religious services in English (see Budapest "Listings").

Hungary has a fabulously rich Jewish heritage with over forty **synagogues** (*zsinagóga*) across the country, the most outstanding of which are in Budapest – where the Dohány utca synagogue is the largest in Europe – Pécs and Szeged. However, most of Hungary's synagogues were ransacked during World War II and subsequently left derelict or given over to other functions, and whilst a number have since been reopened and restored, many lie in a desperate state of neglect. Budapest is the only place which retains a sizeable Jewish community, but in most places with a synagogue or Jewish cemetery, it is easy to get directions, although you may have to ask around for a key.

Hungary's few remaining **mosques** (*djami*) now qualify as museums rather than places of worship; Pécs, as well as housing a number of other reminders of the country's Ottoman past, is home to the only intact mosque in the country.

The Hungarian terms for the main **religious denominations** are: *Katolikus* (Catholic), *Református* (Calvinist), *Evangélikus* (Lutheran), *Görög* (Greek Orthodox), *Görög-Katolikus* (Uniate), *Szerb* (Serb Orthodox) and *Zsidó* (Jewish).

Work and study

Teaching English has traditionally been the main opportunity for work in Hungary, and now, more than ever, language teaching is big business. This is reflected in both the growing number of native speakers working in Budapest and in the number of schools which have opened up outside the capital in recent years. You might also find that some state primary and secondary schools are willing to take you on just by virtue of the fact that English is your mother tongue. There are also a growing number of opportunities in the voluntary sector, with several organizations arranging summer work camps.

Useful publications and websites

A pre-planning strategy for working abroad is to get hold of one of the **books** on summer jobs abroad and how to work your way around the world published by Vacation Work; call ⓣ01865/241 978 or visit ⓦwww.vacationwork.co.uk for their catalogue. Travel **magazines** such as the reliable *Wanderlust* (eight issues a year; ⓦwww.wanderlust.co.uk) have a Job Shop section which often advertises job opportunities with tour companies. ⓦwww.studyabroad.com is a useful website with listings and links to study and work programmes worldwide.

Teaching English

The most reputable **language school** in Hungary is International House, which has schools in Budapest, at Bimbó út 7 (ⓣ1/212-4010, ⓦwww.ih.hu), and Eger, at Mecset utca 3 (ⓣ36/413-770); their minimum requirement is a CELTA or TESOL qualification, and preferably one year's experience. There are also teaching opportunities at the British Council, Benczúr utca 26 (ⓣ1/478-4700, ⓦwww.britishcouncil.hu), whose minimum requirements are a CELTA and two years' experience. Salaries work out at about 120,000–130,000Ft for a 22-hour week, whilst some schools, such as International House, will provide accommodation and transport allowances, as well as one return flight. Although most language schools recruit year-round, the majority of teachers are in place by September. Assuming you can get enough clients, another option is to give **private lessons**, the going rate for which is anywhere between 2500Ft and 3000Ft for a 45-minute lesson.

For information on **TEFL courses** worldwide see ⓦwww.tefl.com/courses.

Although teaching in a **primary or secondary school** pays much less (around 70,000Ft per month), the deal usually includes subsidized or free accommodation. Expect to teach around twenty 45-minute periods a week, with a timetable that may also include exam preparation, marking, invigilation etc. Primary schools may take anyone who seems capable and enthusiastic, though you are likely to require at least a certificate in TEFL and/or a PGCE. For more information on teaching in a state school, your best bet is to contact the Centre for English Teacher Training (CETT) at Ajtosi Dürer sor 19 in Budapest (ⓣ1/460-4400, ⓦwww.btk.elte.hu/cett).

Study and work programmes

If you fancy taking up the challenge of **learning Hungarian**, or wish to brush up on your existing language skills, there are several schools in Budapest catering for foreigners, the best of which is the Hungarian Language School at Rippl Rónai utca 4 (Ⓣ1/351-1191, Ⓦwww.hls.hu). The school runs a comprehensive range of short- and long-term courses, from beginners to advanced, as well as organizing cultural programmes and workshops.

Eager to publicize their cultural achievements and earn foreign exchange, the Hungarians also organize **summer courses** in everything from folk art to environmental studies. Full details are contained in a booklet published in the spring, which can be obtained by writing to TIT (Society for the Dissemination of Scientific Knowledge), H-1088 Budapest, VIII, Bródy Sándor utca 16. The deadline for most applications is May 1, so it's advisable to write some months in advance. Students are of all ages and come from countries as diverse as Switzerland and Venezuela, so the chance to meet people can be as much an attraction as the subject to be studied. Hungary's major **summer school** is at Debrecen University (Ⓣ52/489-117, Ⓦwww.nyariegyetem.hu), whose main programme focuses on the Hungarian language and Hungarian history and culture. Other study subjects include photography (at Vác), fine arts (Zebegény), Esperanto (Gyula), Baroque recorder music (Sopron), jazz (Tatabánya), orchestral music (Pécs and Kecskemét), music-teaching by the Kodály method (Esztergom and Kecskemét), folk art (Zalaegerszeg) and nature studies (Keszthely). Fees include room and board and various excursions and entertainments. Courses typically run for two or four weeks; a two-week course, including full-board accommodation, costs around £320/€450/US$580.

Useful contacts

In the UK

British Council Ⓣ**020/7930 8466.** Produces a free leaflet which details study opportunities abroad. The Council's Central Management of Direct Teaching (Ⓣ020/7389 4931) recruits TEFL teachers for posts worldwide (check Ⓦwww.britishcouncil.org/work/jobs. for a current list of vacancies), and its Central Bureau for International Education and Training (Ⓣ020/7389 4004, Ⓦwww.centralbureau.org.uk) enables those who already work as educators to find out about teacher development programmes abroad. It also publishes a book, *Year Between*, aimed principally at gap-year students detailing volunteer programmes, and schemes abroad.

BTCV (British Trust for Conservation Volunteers) Ⓣ**01302/572 244,** Ⓦ**www.btcv.org.uk.** Large environmental charity organizing conservation projects in the farming village of Gőmőrszőlős in the northern part of the country during July and August.

Earthwatch Institute Ⓣ**01865/318 838,** Ⓦ**www.uk.earthwatch.org.** Long-established international charity offering the opportunity to work with eminent research scientists monitoring bird migration on the Ocsa wetland near Budapest (August/September, from around £700/US$1095).

Erasmus Ⓦ**europa.eu.int/comm/education/programmes/socrates/erasmus/erasmus_en.** EU-run student exchange programme enabling students at participating universities in Britain and Ireland to study in one of 26 European countries. Mobility grants available for three months to a full academic year. Anyone interested should contact their university's international relations office, or check the Erasmus website.

Field Studies Council Overseas Ⓣ**01743/852 150 or 0845 852 150,** Ⓦ**www.fscoverseas.org.uk.** Respected educational charity organizing one-week tours in September in the Northern Uplands, Lake Tisza and the Hortobagy puszta, which include the study of habitats or flora/fauna of these areas (£1080). Overseas Experiences brochure available.

GAP Activity Projects Ⓣ**0118/959 4914,** Ⓦ**www.gap.org.uk.** Volunteer teaching work for 17- to 20-year-olds in provincial schools throughout Hungary, as well as work in schools for partially sighted children, and in two orphanages. The six-month placements begin in September and February, with the fee (around £1250) covering training, living expenses and insurance.

International House Ⓣ**020/7518 6999,** Ⓦ**www.ihlondon.com.** Head office for reputable English-teaching organization which offers TEFL training leading to the award of a Certificate in English Language Teaching to Adults (CELTA), and recruits for teaching positions in Britain and abroad.

In the US and Canada

AFS Intercultural Programs US Ⓣ**1-800/727-2437 or 212/299 9000,** Ⓦ**www.afs.org.** Runs community service programmes aimed at fostering international understanding for teenagers and adults.

Bernan Associates US Ⓣ**1-800/274-4888,** Ⓦ**www.bernan.com.** Distributes UNESCO's encyclopedic Study Abroad.

Council on International Educational Exchange (CIEE) US Ⓣ**1-800/2COUNCIL,** Ⓦ**www.ciee.org.** The nonprofit parent organization of Council

Travel, CIEE runs summer, semester and academic-year programmes throughout Europe, and also publishes *Work, Study, Travel Abroad and Volunteer! The Comprehensive Guide to Voluntary Service in the US and Abroad.*

Earthwatch Institute US ⓣ1-800/776-0188 or 978/461-0081, ⓦ**www.earthwatch.org**. See p.55.

Harper Collins Perseus Division US ⓣ1-800/242-7737, ⓦ**www.harpercollins.com**. Publishes *International Jobs: Where They Are, How to Get Them.*

Vancouver English Centre Canada ⓣ604/687-1600, ⓦ**www.vec.ca**. Offers a four-week TEFL Certificate course which costs C$1440, with occasional 20 percent off deals in the winter.

Volunteers for Peace US ⓣ802/259-2759, ⓦ**www.vfp.org**. Nonprofit organization offering two-week summer workcamps (August/September), including community projects in an asylum centre in Békéscsaba, and work in a Roma community near Debrecen. Annual membership including directory costs $20.

In Australia and New Zealand

Australians Studying Abroad Australia ⓣ1800 645 755 or 03/9509 1955, ⓦ**www.asatravinfo.com.au**. High-end art and cultural tours; in Hungary, the offer is an eleven-day tour of Budapest (with visits to Esterházy and Sopron) and Vienna, with an option to extend the tour to Prague (August/September).

Communicative Language Training International New Zealand ⓣ03/377 8157, ⓦ**www.cltintl.com**. Offers a six-week TEFL course for NZ$3720.

Travellers with disabilities

Hungary has been painfully slow to acknowledge the needs of the disabled traveller, and, whilst progress is being made, don't expect much in the way of special facilities. Not surprisingly, Budapest is the one place where facilities are most advanced, with a number of hotels (albeit the more expensive ones) accommodating specially designed rooms, and an increasing number of museums providing ramps for wheelchairs. Aside from the M1 metro line and a handful of buses (including the airport minibus), public transport is largely inaccessible to wheelchair users. Outside Budapest, however, travellers with disabilities will have an even tougher time of it, although there have been some positive developments, such as at Lake Balaton, where several beaches have been fitted with lifts which can transport disabled people into the water. Furthermore, an increasing number of train stations are implementing ramps and lifts for disabled passengers so they can access platforms and carriages.

The **Hungarian Disabled Association** (MEOSZ), San Marco utca 76, 1032 Budapest (ⓣ1/388-5529, ⓦwww.meosz.hu), which is also the regional office for Eastern Europe, is currently doing a terrific job of trying to raise the profile of disabled persons' needs in Hungary. As well as advising on all aspects of coping with disabilities while in Hungary, they provide information on all tourist facilities in the country specifically equipped for the physically disabled, including hotels, museums, restaurants and transportation. MEOSZ also operates its own special transport service in Budapest whereby, for a fixed payment, a bus equipped with lift or ramp can take you to your chosen destination. Their website has an up-to-date list of all facilities in Budapest catering to disabled travellers.

Contacts for travellers with disabilities

In the UK and Ireland

Holiday Care ⓣ0845 124 9971 or ⓣ020/8760 0072, ⓦ**www.holidaycare.org.uk**. Provides free lists of accessible accommodation for European, American and long-haul destinations. Information on financial

help for holidays available.
Irish Wheelchair Association ⓣ01/818 6400, ⓦwww.iwa.ie. Useful information provided about travelling abroad with a wheelchair.
Tripscope ⓣ0845 758 5641, ⓦwww.tripscope.org.uk. This registered charity provides a national telephone information service offering free advice on UK and international transport for those with a mobility problem.

In the US

Access-Able ⓦwww.access-able.com. Online resource for travellers with disabilities.
Directions Unlimited ⓣ1-800/533-5343 or 914/241-1700. Travel agency specializing in bookings for people with disabilities.
Mobility International USA ⓣ541/343-1284, ⓦwww.miusa.org. Information and referral services, access guides, tours and exchange programmes.
Society for the Advancement of Travelers with Handicaps ⓣ212/447-7284, ⓦwww.sath.org. Nonprofit educational organization that has actively represented travellers with disabilities since 1976. Annual membership $45; $30 for students and seniors.
Wheels Up! ⓣ1-888/389-4335, ⓦwww.wheelsup.com. Provides discounted airfare, tour and cruise prices for disabled travellers, also publishes a free monthly newsletter and has a comprehensive website.

In Australia and New Zealand

ACROD (Australian Council for Rehabilitation of the Disabled) Australia ⓣ02/6282 4333 (also TTY), ⓦwww.acrod.org.au. Provides lists of travel agencies and tour operators for people with disabilities.
Disabled Persons Assembly NZ ⓣ04/801 9100 (also TTY), ⓦwww.dpa.org.nz. Resource centre with lists of travel agencies and tour operators for people with disabilities.

Gay and lesbian travellers

Attitudes towards gays and lesbians in Hungary have softened considerably over the last few years, particularly amongst the younger generation, and especially amongst those living in the larger towns and cities. Whilst Budapest is, unsurprisingly, still the centre of the gay and lesbian scene in Hungary, manifestations of gay life beyond the capital are becoming more visible, with gay bars to be found in several of the larger towns and cities and gay organizations working to support their local gay community.

In **Budapest** there are an increasing number of organizations dedicated to serving the gay and lesbian community; see p.140 for more information. The country's major gay celebration is the four-day **Gay and Lesbian Cultural Festival** (ⓦwww.gaypride.hu) in Budapest in late June to early July, which features art, film, music and dance amongst its many activities.

Contacts for gay and lesbian travellers

In the UK

Check out **adverts** in the weekly papers *Boyz* and *Pink Paper*, handed out free in gay venues.
ⓦ**www.gaytravel.co.uk** Online gay and lesbian travel agent, offering good deals on all types of holiday. Also lists gay- and lesbian-friendly hotels around the world.
Madison Travel ⓣ01273/202 532, ⓦwww.madisontravel.co.uk. Established travel agents specializing in packages to gay- and lesbian-friendly mainstream destinations, and also to gay/lesbian destinations.
Respect Holidays ⓣ0870 770 0169, ⓦwww.respect-holidays.co.uk. Offers exclusively gay packages to all popular European resorts.

In the US

ⓦ**www.gaytravel.com** US ⓣ1-800/GAY-TRAVEL. The premier site for trip-planning, bookings, and general information about international gay and lesbian travel.

International Gay & Lesbian Travel Association US ⓣ1-800/448-8550 or 954/776-2626, ⓦwww.iglta.org. Trade group that can provide a list of gay- and lesbian-owned or -friendly travel agents, accommodation and other travel businesses.

In Australia

Parkside Travel ⓣ08/8274 1222, ⓔparkside@herveyworld.com.au. Gay travel agent associated with local branch of Hervey World Travel; all aspects of gay and lesbian travel worldwide.
Silke's Travel ⓣ1800 807 860 or 02/8347 2000, ⓦwww.silkes.com.au. Long-established gay and lesbian specialist, with the emphasis on women's travel.
Tearaway Travel ⓣ1800 664 440 or 03/9510 6644, ⓦwww.tearaway.com. Gay-specific business dealing with international and domestic travel.

Travelling with children

From a practical point of view, travelling with children in Hungary will present few problems. Most of the better-quality hotels are well equipped to cope with children, whilst many restaurants (at least those of a decent standard) should be able to provide highchairs for younger children and babies. All supermarkets are well stocked with nappies, baby food and other essentials.

The real challenge will be keeping the youngsters entertained. Whilst Budapest has plenty of attractions for kids (see p.146), you'll have to use your imagination a little more once outside the capital. The most obvious attraction is Lake Balaton which, with its numerous **beaches** and clean, shallow waters, is ideal for young children. Some beaches also have water slides and various other play facilities. Hungary also has some wonderful **narrow-gauge trains** (detailed throughout the book), which are frequently full of screeching kids, while boat trips along the Danube are another possibility. A reliable fall-back option is the trusty **zoo**, and whilst Hungarian zoos might not be up to much compared to those in Western Europe – indeed some of them are rather tatty affairs – kids are sure not to mind.

Some larger towns and cities, such as Pécs and Kecskemét, have excellent **puppet theatres** which parents will probably enjoy as much as their offspring. Especially worth looking out for are those summer festivals which stage puppet shows, including the one in Pécs.

Children under the age of 6 get to travel free on all **public transport**, with further discounts offered to those between the ages of 6 and 14. Children under the age of 12 are forbidden to ride in the front seat of a **car**. Some **museums** offer discounted entry rates to children.

Directory

Addresses These usually begin with the postcode, which indicates the town or city and locality. The most common terms are *utca* (street, abbreviated to *u.*), *út* (or *útja*, avenue), *tér* (or *tere*, square) and *körút* (ring boulevard). You may also encounter *rakpart* (embankment), *sétány* (promenade), *híd* (bridge), *köz* (lane), *hegy* (hill) and *liget* (park). Town centres are signposted *Belváros*, *Városközpont* or *Centrum*. A *lakótelep* is a high-rise housing estate.

Electric power 220 volts. Round, two-pin plugs are used. A standard Continental adaptor allows the use of 13 amp, square-pin plugs.

Film All the major brands, such as Kodak, Fuji and Agfa, are readily available, and most towns offer colour-processing services, including one-hour processing.

Laundry Self-service launderettes (*mosoda*) are still pretty rare, even in Budapest, but there are a few companies offering service-washes such as Top Clean, which has many locations in the capital. Otherwise there is the competent but expensive Hungarian-American Ametiszt, which has quite a few outlets throughout the country. Staying in private lodgings, you may be allowed to use your host's washing machine for a small cost.

Left luggage Most train stations have a left-luggage office (*csomagmegőrző*), which has a daily charge of between 200Ft and 400Ft, depending on the size of your bag. Keep all of the scrappy little receipts, or you'll never get your gear back. A few main stations have automatic luggage lockers, which take specific coins and store your baggage for up to 24 hours.

Lost property Anything left on a train is kept for one month (three months at the three main stations in Budapest) at the final destination of the train, or where it was handed in. If, after this time, it remains unclaimed then it will be destroyed. Passports are first sent to the police and then forwarded to embassies. For property lost on Budapest city transport, see Budapest "Listings".

Museums Most of Hungary's museums have captions in Hungarian (and often German) only, although some of Budapest's more popular museums do have English labelling, whilst important museums in provincial centres might sell catalogues in various languages, including English. Village Museums, or Skanzens, are probably the most effective for surmounting the language barrier – fascinating ensembles of buildings and domestic objects culled from old settlements around the country, assembled on the outskirts of Szentendre, Nyíregyháza, Zalaegerszeg and Szombathely, or preserved in situ at Szalafő and Hollókő. In some of the grander palaces and mansions, it's likely that you'll be asked to don a pair of slippers, so as to prevent damage to the pristine clean flooring.

Names Surnames precede forenames in Hungary, to the confusion of foreigners. In this book, the names of historical personages are rendered in the Western fashion; for instance, Lajos Kossuth rather than Kossuth Lajos (Hungarian-style), except when referring to buildings, streets, etc.

Taxes Prices often include a sales tax (ÁFA), which ranges from 12 to 25 percent, so that any prices quoted are likely to jump sharply when it comes to paying. Check on whether ÁFA is included (*Árak nem tartalmaznak ÁFA*-t is Hungarian for "Prices do not include tax"). If you make a purchase over 50,000Ft, it's worth filling in the form that enables you to claim tax back when you leave the country (claims must be made within six months). For help in getting refunds, contact Global Refund, Bég utca 3–5 (Ⓣ1/212-4734, Ⓔtaxfree@hu.globalrefund.hu).

Time Hungary is one hour ahead of GMT, six hours ahead of Eastern Standard Time and nine ahead of Pacific Standard Time in North America. A word of caution: Hungarians express time in a way that might confuse the anglophone traveller. For example, 10.30am is expressed as "half eleven" (written 1/2 11 or f11), 10.45am is "three-quarter-eleven" (3/4 11 or h11), and 10.15am is "a quarter of the next hour" (1/4 11 or n11).

Tipping In restaurants it is usual to round up the bill or to tip around ten percent, although some may add a service charge – which should be indicated on the bill. Taxi drivers will expect a tip of between ten and fifteen percent.

Toilets Most public toilets (WC – *Férfiak* means "men", *Nők* means "women") are reasonably clean, and charge around 50Ft. This will include a sliver of rough paper, although you'd do well to carry your own.

Guide

Guide

Budapest

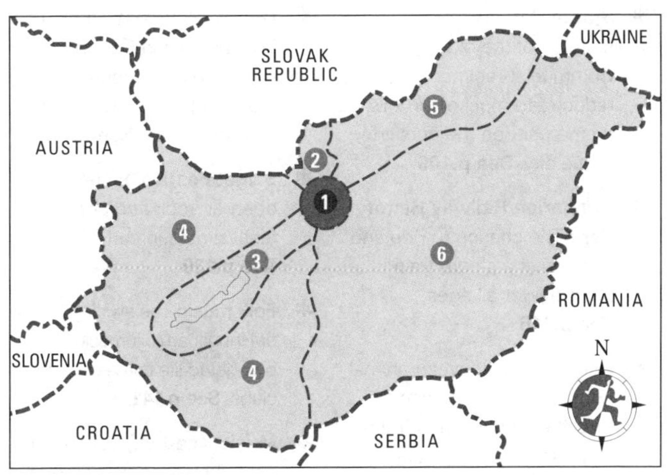
SLOVAK
REPUBLIC
UKRAINE
AUSTRIA
ROMANIA
SLOVENIA
CROATIA
SERBIA
N
1
2
3
4
4
5
6

CHAPTER 1

Highlights

* **The Vár** Laden with bastions, mansions and a huge palace, the Castle District preserves many medieval features. **See p.85**
* **Turkish baths** Experience unrivalled atmosphere and luxury in an original Ottoman bathhouse. **See p.98**
* **Statue Park** The epic statuary of the old Communist regime is reduced to mockery in this theme park on the outskirts of the city. **See p.100**
* **Hungarian Railway History Park** The chance to ride and even drive a steam train is a big draw for all ages. **See p.116**
* **Zoo** The Art Nouveau animal houses and the chance to feed the camels and giraffes make this a very special zoo. **See p.121**
* **Jewish quarter** Explore the atmospheric neighbourhood behind the Dohány utca Synagogue, the focal point of Budapest's Jewish community. **See p.123**
* **Coffee shops** This venerable Central European institution is alive and well in the streets of Pest. **See p.129**
* **Gundel Sunday brunch** The best bargain in Budapest, when the city's poshest restaurant opens its doors for a delicious feast. **See p.132**
* **Sziget Festival** Frenetic open-air rock and pop festival held in early August. **See p.139**
* **Folk music** The swirling tunes of Hungarian folk music are brought to life in the city's folk clubs. **See p.141**
* **Music Academy** A magnificent showcase for some of the best classical music in the country. **See p.142**

▲ Gellért Baths

1

Budapest

The importance of **BUDAPEST** to Hungary is difficult to overestimate. More than two million people live in the capital – one fifth of the population – and everything converges here: roads and rail lines; air travel (Ferihegy is the country's only civilian airport); industry, commerce and culture; opportunities, wealth and power. Like Paris, the city has a history

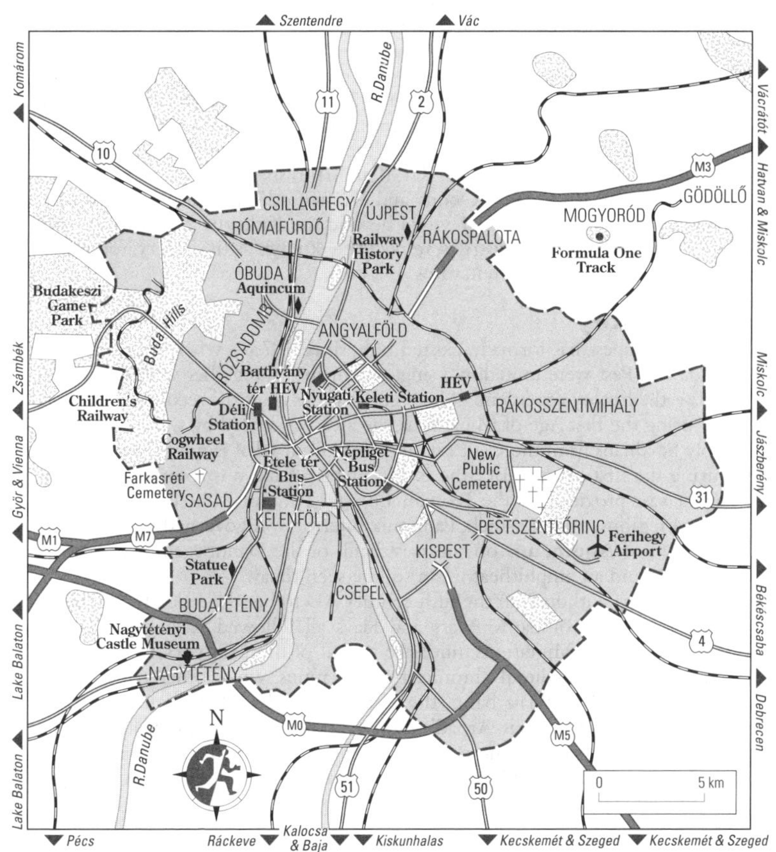

of revolutions – in 1849, 1918 and 1956 – buildings, parks and avenues on a monumental scale, and a reputation for hedonism, style and parochial pride. In short, Budapest is a city worthy of comparison with other great European capitals.

Surveying Budapest from the embankments or the bastions of the Vár (Castle Hill), it's easy to see why the city was dubbed the "Pearl of the Danube". Its grand buildings and sweeping bridges look magnificent, especially when floodlit or illuminated by the barrage of fireworks that explode above the Danube every August 20, St Stephen's Day. The eclectic inner-city and radial boulevards combine brash commercialism with a *fin-de-siècle* sophistication, while a distinctively Magyar character is highlighted by the sounds and appearance of the Hungarian language at every turn.

Since the Communist system expired, Budapest has experienced a new surge of dynamism. Luxury hotels and malls, restaurants, bars and clubs have all proliferated – as have crime and social inequalities. While the number of beggars and homeless people on the streets has risen inexorably, politicians and the media prefer moral posturing on other issues, such as toning down the sex industry that has earned Budapest the nickname of the "Bangkok of Europe", or cracking down on refugees and illegal immigrants among the new ethnic communities formed in the last decade. Though many Hungarians fear the erosion of their culture by foreign influences, others see a new golden age for Budapest, as the foremost world-city of Mitteleuropa.

The River Danube – which is never blue – determines basic **orientation**, with Buda on the hilly west bank and Pest covering the plain across the river. More precisely, Budapest is divided into 23 districts (*kerület*), designated on maps and street signs by Roman numerals; many quarters also have a historic name. In **Buda**, the focus of attention is the I district, comprising the Vár and the Víziváros (Watertown); the XI, XII, II and III districts are worth visiting for Gellért-hegy, the Buda Hills, Óbuda and Rómaifürdő. **Pest** is centred on the downtown Belváros (V district), while beyond the Kiskörút (Small Boulevard) lie the VI, VII, VIII and IX districts, respectively known as the Terézváros, Erzsébetváros, Józsefváros and Ferencváros.

Some history

Though Budapest has formally existed only since 1873 – when the twin cities of Buda and Pest were united in a single municipality, together with the smaller Óbuda – the history of settlement here goes back as far as the second millennium BC. During the first Age of Migrations, the area was settled by waves of peoples, notably Scythians from the Caucasus and Celts from what is now France.

During the first century BC, the Celtic Eravisci tribe was absorbed into Pannonia, a vast province of the Roman Empire. This was subsequently divided into two regions, one of which, Pannonia Inferior, was governed from the garrison town of **Aquincum** on the west bank of the Danube; ruins of a camp, villas, baths and an amphitheatre can still be seen today.

The Romans withdrew in the fifth century AD to be succeeded by the Huns. Germanic tribes, Lombards, Avars and Slavs all followed each other during the second Age of Migrations, until the arrival of the **Magyars** in about 896. According to the medieval chronicler, Anonymous, while other tribes spread out across the Carpathian basin, the clan of Árpád settled on Csepel sziget (Csepel Island), and it was Árpád's brother, Buda, who purportedly gave his name to the west bank of the new settlement. It was under the Árpád dynasty that Hungary became a Christian state, ruled first from Esztergom and later from Székesfehérvár.

The **development of Buda and Pest** did not begin in earnest until the twelfth century, and was largely thanks to French, Walloon and German settlers who worked and traded here under royal protection. Both towns were devastated by the Mongols in 1241 and subsequently rebuilt by colonists from Germany, who named Buda "Ofen", after its numerous limekilns. (The name Pest, which is of Slav origin, also means "oven".) During the fourteenth century, the Angevin kings from France established Buda as a **royal seat**, building a succession of palaces in the Vár. It reached its apogee in Renaissance times under the reign of "Good King" Mátyás (1458–90) and his Italian-born wife, Queen Beatrice, with a golden age of prosperity and a flourishing of the arts.

Hungary's catastrophic defeat at Mohács in 1526 paved the way for the **Turkish occupation** of Buda and Pest, which lasted 160 years until a pan-European army besieged Buda Castle for six weeks, finally recapturing it at the twelfth attempt. Under **Habsburg rule**, with control exerted from Vienna or Bratislava, recovery was followed by a period of intensive growth during the second half of the eighteenth century. In the first decades of the following century, Pest became the centre of the **Reform movement** led by Count Széchenyi, whose vision of progress was embodied in the construction of the **Chain Bridge** (Lánchíd), the first permanent link between Buda and Pest, which had hitherto relied on pontoon bridges or barges.

When the Habsburg Empire was shaken by revolutions which broke out across Europe in **March 1848**, local reformists and radicals seized the moment. While Lajos Kossuth (1802–94) dominated Parliament, Sándor Petőfi (1823–49) and his fellow revolutionaries plotted the downfall of the Habsburgs in the *Café Pilvax* (which exists today in a sanitized restaurant form in central Pest), from where they mobilized crowds on the streets of Pest. After the War of Independence ended in defeat for the Hungarians, Habsburg repression was epitomized by the hilltop Citadella on Gellért-hegy, built to cow the citizenry with its guns.

Following the Compromise of 1867, which established the Dual Monarchy familiarly known to its subjects as the K & K (from the German for "Emperor and King"), the twin cities underwent rapid **expansion** and formally merged. Pest was extensively remodelled, acquiring the Nagykörút (Great Boulevard) and Andrássy út, the grand thoroughfare that runs from the Belváros to the Városliget (City Park). Hungary's **millennial anniversary celebrations** in 1896 brought a fresh rush of construction, and Hősök tere (Heroes' Square) and Vajdahunyad Castle at the far end of Andrássy út are just two examples of the monumental style that encapsulated the age. New suburbs were created to house the burgeoning population, which was by now predominantly Magyar, although there were still large German and Jewish communities. At the beginning of the twentieth century the **cultural efflorescence** in Budapest rivalled that of Vienna and its café society that of Paris – a *belle époque* doomed by World War I.

In the aftermath of defeat, Budapest experienced the Soviet-ruled **Republic of Councils** under Béla Kun, and occupation by the Romanian army. The status quo ante was restored by **Admiral Horthy**, self-appointed regent for the exiled Karl IV – the "Admiral without a fleet, for the king without a kingdom" – whose regency was characterized by gala balls and hunger marches, bombastic nationalism and anti-Semitism. Yet Horthy was a moderate compared to the Arrow Cross Fascists, whose power grew as **World War II** raged.

Anticipating Horthy's defection from the Axis in 1944, Nazi Germany staged a coup, installing an Arrow Cross government, which enabled them to begin the massacre of the **Jews** of Budapest; they also blew up the Danube bridges as a way of hampering the advance of the Red Army. The six-month-long **siege of Budapest** reduced the Vár (Castle District) to rubble and severely damaged much of the rest of the city, making **reconstruction** the first priority for the postwar coalition government.

As the **Communists** gained ascendancy, the former Arrow Cross torture chambers filled up once again. A huge statue of the Soviet dictator (whose name was bestowed upon Budapest's premier boulevard) symbolized the reign of terror carried out by **Mátyás Rákosi**, Hungary's "Little Stalin". However, his liberally inclined successor, **Imre Nagy**, gave hope to the people, who refused to tolerate a comeback by the hardliners in 1956. In Budapest, peaceful protests turned into a city-wide **uprising** literally overnight: men, women and children defying Soviet tanks on the streets.

After Soviet power had been bloodily restored, **János Kádár** – initially reviled as a quisling – gradually normalized conditions, embarking on cautious reforms to create a "**goulash socialism**" that made Hungary the envy of its Warsaw Pact neighbours and the West's favourite Communist state during the late 1970s. A decade later, the regime saw the writing on the wall and anticipated Gorbachev by promising **free elections**, hoping to reap public gratitude. Instead – as Communism was toppled in Berlin and Prague – the party was simply voted out of power in Hungary. It was such an orderly transition from one system to another, yet so pregnant with consequences, that Hungarians simply refer to all that's happened since then as "**the Changes**".

While governments have come and gone since the historic 1990 elections, Budapest's administration has remained in the hands of the mayor, **Gábor Demszky**, who is now working with his fifth prime minister. People have voted for him partly because he is neither a Communist nor a nationalist, and his dour image invites a sense of reliability, perhaps fitting in well with the urban cynicism of the city dwellers. Under Demszky, Budapest has progressed gently without any major upsets, but his star is now waning; the city has precious little to show for his fifteen years in office, and he has recently been tainted by scandal, with talk of a villa built in dubious circumstances in Croatia, and various tax questions hanging over him. On present form he will be struggling for survival at the next elections in 2006.

Arrival and information

Other than the airport, all **points of arrival** are fairly central and most within walking distance or just a few stops by metro from downtown Pest. The city's three metro lines and three main roads meet at the major junction of Deák tér in Pest, making this the main transport hub of the city. Depending on when and where you arrive, it's definitely worth considering either arranging somewhere to stay before leaving the terminal or station (there are reservation services at all of them), or stashing your luggage before setting out to look for a room. For all **departure** information, see the relevant sections of "Listings", at the end of this chapter.

By air

Ferihegy Airport, 20km from the centre, has three passenger terminals: Ferihegy 2A, serving Malév and Malév's joint flights with other airlines; Ferihegy 1 for the no-frills airlines; and Ferihegy 2B, which is used by the rest. The easiest and most expensive option for heading into the centre is by taxi: the **airport**

Budapest addresses

Finding your way around Budapest is easier than the welter of names might suggest. Districts and streets are well signposted, and those in Pest conform to an overall plan based on radial avenues and semicircular boulevards.

Budapest addresses begin with the number of the district – for example, V, Petőfi tér 3 – a system used throughout this chapter. When addressing letters, however, a four-digit postal code is used instead, the middle digits indicating the district (so that 1054 refers to a place in the V district).

As a rule of thumb, **street numbers** ascend away from the north–south axis of the River Danube and the east–west axis of Rákóczi út/Kossuth utca/Hegyalja út. Even numbers are generally on the left-hand side, odd numbers on the right. One number may refer to several premises or an entire apartment building, while an additional combination of numerals denotes the floor and number of individual **apartments** (eg Kossuth utca 14/III/24). Confusingly, some old buildings in Pest are designated as having a half-floor (*félemelet*) or upper ground floor (*magas földszint*) between the ground (*földszint*) and first floor (*elsőemelet*) proper – so that what the British would call the second floor, and Americans the third, Hungarians might describe as the first. This stems from a nineteenth-century taxation fiddle, whereby landlords avoided the higher tax on buildings with more than three floors.

taxis that wait at the exits are mafia-controlled and known to physically threaten other cabs that enter their patch. They charge way above the odds, with fixed rates of 5000–7000Ft (€21–28) depending on your destination – almost twice the rate of other cabs – though they will charge unsuspecting foreigners many times that. Ask for help in ordering normal city cabs at Ferihegy's **Tourinform offices** (daily 8am–11pm), which can also give you information about Budapest. A cheaper option – especially if you are travelling alone – is the Airport Minibus, which will take you directly to your destination. Tickets (2100Ft) can be bought in the luggage claim hall while you are waiting for your bags, or in the main concourse; you give your address and then have to wait five to twenty minutes until the driver calls your destination. **Public transport** might be more inconvenient but it's not much slower, and it's certainly cheaper: take one of the Reptér-busz, which leave every 15 minutes from the stop between terminals 2A and 2B, and stay aboard until the final stop at the faded, red-and-yellow metro station at Kőbánya-Kispest; here you switch to the blue metro line, alighting ten stops later at Deák tér. It all takes about 45 minutes and costs 145Ft for each of the two tickets. Tickets are available at the newsagents in the terminals or from the machine by the bus stop – buying one from the driver on board will cost you 180Ft. Malév also runs a late-night bus service from the airport to the main **provincial cities**: Győr, Debrecen, Miskolc, Pécs and Szeged. It leaves the airport at 11pm, takes two to three hours and costs 6000–8000Ft. There are **ATMs** in all of the terminal buildings.

By train

The Hungarian word *pályaudvar* (abbreviated to *pu.* in writing only) is used to designate the seven Budapest **train stations**, only three of which are on the metro and of any use to tourists. Translated into English, their names refer to the direction of services handled rather than location, so that Western Station (Nyugati pu.) is north of downtown Pest, and Southern Station (Déli pu.) is in the west of the city; Eastern Station (Keleti pu.), however, is to the east of the city centre.

Most international trains terminate at Pest's **Keleti Station** on Baross tér in the VIII district. This station is something of a hangout for thieves and hustlers, and there are plenty of police about checking people's ID. In summer there are long queues at the 24-hour left-luggage office by platform 6 (260Ft or 520Ft for 24hr depending on size, half that amount for six hours) – the lockers (300Ft for 24hr) are a better bet if they are in operation. There are usually plenty of people offering accommodation as international trains arrive; the most reliable place for booking hostels is the Mellow Mood offices either side of the big glass doorways at the far end of the station. They will also organize transport to hostels, and should be able to offer other city information, too. Otherwise, head for the Tourinform office at Deák tér – three stops away on the red metro line towards Déli Station. Unmarked **taxis** lining the road outside the doors of the Keleti Station are worth avoiding, despite their drivers wearing badges saying "official taxi". Instead, look out for taxis from the companies listed on p.75, such as Főtaxi, which you can find by going out the main doors and turning right.

On the northern edge of Pest's Great Boulevard, **Nyugati Station** has a 24-hour left-luggage office (260Ft or 520Ft for 24hr) next to the ticket office beside platform 13. You can change money at the Budapest Tourist Information Office (Mon–Fri 9am–6pm, Sat–Sun 9am–3pm; ⓣ1/302-8580), by the police office (*rendőrség*) to the left of the main entrance of the station, which is also good for information on the city. To reach Deák tér, take the blue metro line two stops in the direction of Kőbánya-Kispest.

Déli Station, 500m behind the Vár in Buda, which has left-luggage facilities but no tourist office, is four stops from Deák tér on the red metro line.

By bus

International bus services wind up at the **Népliget Bus Station** in the IX district, southeast of the centre, which also handles buses from the Great Plain and Transdanubia. The bus station is six stops on the blue metro from Deák tér. The same warning applies here on **taxis** as to the airport above – it's best to ask the staff to help you order a regular taxi (see p.75), which will cost 1000–1500Ft to the centre. Within Hungary, buses from the Northern Uplands go to the **Stadion Bus Station** in the XIV district on the red metro line, those from the Danube Bend head for the **Árpád híd Bus Station** in the XIII district on the blue metro line, and ones from the Buda hinterland arrive at the **Etele tér Bus Station** in the XI district (take buses #173 or #7 to the centre). None of the four currently has any tourist facilities.

By hydrofoil

Hydrofoils from Vienna (April–Oct) dock at the **international landing stage**, on the Belgrád rakpart (embankment), near downtown Pest. Ibusz is five minutes' walk north, on Ferenciek tere, inland of the Erzsébet Bridge (Mon–Fri 8.15am–5pm).

Information, maps and tours

Leaving aside the business of finding accommodation, the best source of **information** is the **Tourinform** offices at several locations in the city. The one at V, Sütő utca 2, just around the corner from Deák tér metro (daily 8am–8pm; ⓣ1/438-8080, ⓦwww.tourinform.hu), is run by the National Tourist Office, and the polyglot staff can answer just about any question on Budapest or travel elsewhere in Hungary. (This is also the office of the tourist police, Policeinform,

The Budapest card

If you are doing a lot of sightseeing you might be tempted to buy a **Budapest Card**. For 4700Ft (48 hours) or 5900Ft (72 hours), you get free travel in most of the city, free entry to over sixty museums, and discounts of up to fifty percent in some shops and restaurants and on some sightseeing programmes and cultural and folklore events. The card is available from tourist offices, hotels, central metro stations and at the airport, and it comes with a booklet explaining where it can be used. However, the price means you'll have to work hard to save money on it, especially since the card is not valid for the funicular that goes up to the castle or for tours of Parliament, and because since May 2004, 21 national museums in Budapest, including the Hungarian National Museum and the National Gallery, do not charge admission fees for visiting their permanent displays. Note too that although the card allows entry into the Liszt Memorial Museum, it's not valid for the Sunday concerts held there – which are free if you pay to go into the museum. It does, however, give discounts on the Airport Minibus service, but only on one-way tickets.

where you can report any problems you might have and ask advice.) However, this office is often packed and the staff overstretched, so you might get more attention at the friendly **Yellow Zebra** at V, Sütő utca 2 – inside the courtyard behind Tourinform – which can help with all kinds of practical information. You can also access the Internet here and it's a good place to meet fellow travellers (daily 9.30am–6.30pm, till 8pm in summer; ⓣ1/266-8777 ⓦwww.discoverhungary.com). Alternatively, head for the Tourinform officess run by the Budapest Tourist Office (ⓦwww.budapestinfo.hu) at VI, Liszt Ferenc tér 11 (daily: May–Sept 10am–10pm; Oct–April 10am–6pm; ⓣ1/322-4098), and in the Vár on Szentháromság tér (daily 8am–8pm; ⓣ1/488-0453). There are also Tourinform offices at the airport in Terminal 2A and 2B.

It's a good idea to get hold of a proper **map** of the city at the earliest opportunity. The small freebies supplied by tourist offices give an idea of Budapest's layout and principal monuments, but lack detail. Larger, folding maps are sold all over the place, but their size makes them cumbersome. For total coverage you can't beat the wirebound *Budapest Atlasz*, available in bookshops for 1700Ft, which shows every street, bus and tram route, and the location of restaurants, museums and such like. It also contains enlarged maps of the Vár, central Pest, Margit sziget (Margit Island) and the Városliget (City Park), plus a comprehensive index.

Details of **what's on** can be found in the magazines *Where Budapest* (monthly; free in hotels), the weekly *Budapest Sun* (around 360Ft) and the free Hungarian-language listings weeklies, *Pesti Est* and *Exit* (widely available in cinemas and bars).

Although Budapest can easily be explored without a guide, if you're hard-pressed for time you might appreciate a two- to three-hour **city bus tour**. These range in price from €20–26 (or €40 if combined with a visit to the Parliament building) and can be booked through Ibusz (tickets from their office at V, Ferenciek tere 10 in the centre; ⓦwww.ibusz.hu) or Buda Tours (ⓣ1/374-7070, ⓦwww.budatours.hu; VI, Andrássy út 2). If you'd prefer to do a **walking tour**, the friendly Absolute Walking Tours offer a range of less conventional tours, such as around Communist Budapest or the city's bars, and the same office also handles **bike tours** of the capital (4000–5000Ft ⓦwww.absolute-tours.com or ⓦwww.yellowzebrabikes.com). For information on being guided round the old Jewish area behind the Dohány utca synagogue see p.122.

City transport

Most of Budapest's backstreets and historic quarters are eminently suited to **walking** – and this is much the best way to appreciate their character. Traffic is restricted in downtown Pest and around the Vár in Buda, and fairly light in the residential backstreets off the main boulevards, which are the nicest areas to wander around.

However, if you do need to make use of **public transport**, Budapest has an excellent system, which ensures that few parts of the city are more than thirty minutes' journey from the centre; many places can be reached in half that time. It doesn't take long to pick up the basics and it's also much better value than **taxis**, which sometimes overcharge tourists, and preferable to **driving** or **cycling** amidst the traffic jams and exhaust fumes that afflict the main thoroughfares. Budapest's outer suburbs are well served by the overground **HÉV train** network, while Danube **ferries** and the **Children's Railway** in the Buda Hills offer fun excursions. See the website of the Budapest Transport Company (BKV) for more information: Ⓦwww.bkv.hu.

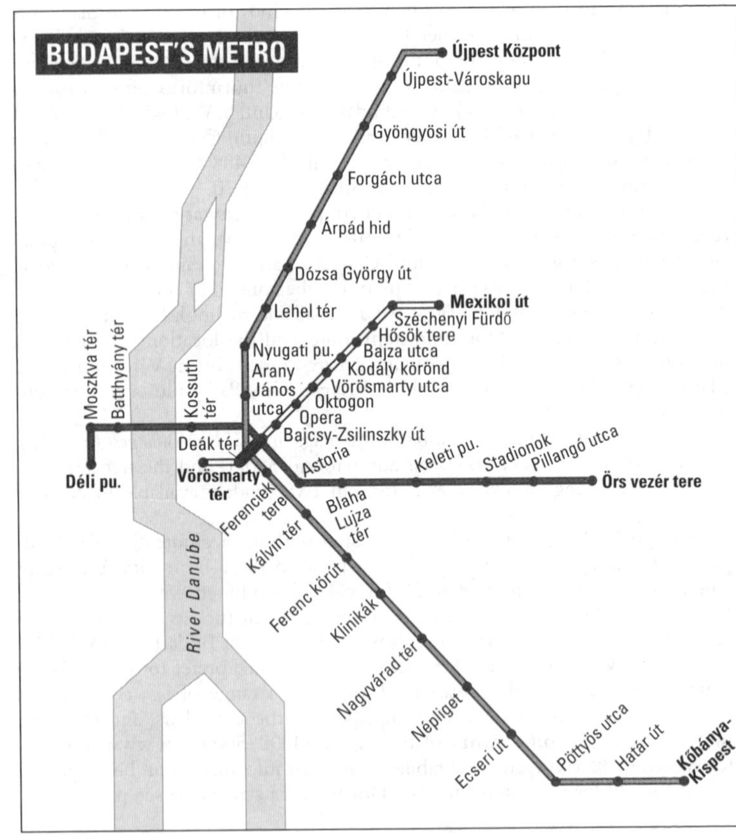

Useful bus and tram routes

Buses

#7 Bosnyák tér–Keleti Station–Móricz Zsigmond körtér (via Rákóczi út, Ferenciek tere, *Hotel Gellért*, Rác and Rudas Baths). Red #7-173 continues on to Kelenföld Station.
#16 Erzsébet tér–Dísz tér (Castle District).
#22 Moszkva tér–Budakeszi.
#26 Nyugati tér–Szent István körút–Margit sziget–Árpád híd metro station.
#27 Móricz Zsigmond körtér–near the top of Gellért-hegy.
#56 Moszkva tér–Szilágyi Erzsébet fasor–Hűvösvölgy, with the red #56E going almost without stopping.
#65 Kolosy tér–Pálvölgyi Caves–halfway up Hármashatár-hegy.
#86 Southern Buda–Gellért tér–the Víziváros–Flórián tér (Óbuda).
#105 Apor Vilmos tér–Chain Bridge–Deák tér.
Várbusz Moszkva tér– Dísz tér (Castle District) and back.

Night buses

#6É Moszkva tér–Margit sziget–Nyugati Station–Great Boulevard–Móricz Zsigmond körtér.
#78É Örs vezér tere–Bosnyák tér–Keleti Station–Buda side of Erzsébet Bridge.
#14É and **#50É** both run along Kispest (Határ út metro station)–Deák tér–Lehel tér along the route of the blue metro and on to the north and south.
#49É Moszkva tér–Erzsébet Bridge–*Hotel Gellért*–Móricz Zsigmond körtér.

Trams

#2 Margit Bridge–Petőfi Bridge along embankment–HÉV station at Közvágóhíd.
#4 Moszkva tér–Margit sziget–Nyugati Station–Great Boulevard–Petőfi Bridge –Október 23. utca.
#6 Moszkva tér–Margit sziget–Nyugati Station–Great Boulevard–Petőfi Bridge–Móricz Zsigmond körtér.
#19 Batthyány tér–Víziváros–Kelenföld Station.
#47 Deák tér–Szabadság Bridge–*Hotel Gellért*–Móricz Zsigmond körtér–Budafok.
#49 Deák tér–Szabadság Bridge–*Hotel Gellért*–Móricz Zsigmond körtér–Kelenföld Station.
#56 Moszkva tér–Szilágyi Erzsébet fasor–Hűvösvölgy.

Trolley buses

#72 Arany Janos utca metro station–Nyugati Station–Zoo–Széchenyi Baths-Petőfi Csarnok–Thököly út.
#74 Dohány utca (outside the Main Synagogue)–Városliget.

The metro, buses, trams and trolley buses

Running at two- to twelve-minute intervals between 4.30am and 11.10pm, Budapest's **metro** reaches most areas of interest to tourists, its three lines intersecting at Deák tér in downtown Pest (see map opposite). From nearby Vörösmarty tér, the **yellow line** (line 1) runs out beneath Andrássy út to Mexikoi út, beyond the Városliget. The **red line** (line 2) connects Déli Station in Buda with Keleti Station and Örs vezér tere in Pest; and the **blue line** (line 3) describes an arc from Kőbánya-Kispest to Újpest-Központ, via Ferenciek tere and Nyugati Station. There's little risk of going astray once you've learned to recognize the signs *bejárat* (entrance), *kijárat* (exit), *vonal* (line) and *felé* (towards). Drivers announce the next stop between stations and the train's direction is indicated by the name of the station at the end of the line.

A word of warning: there's an active **pickpocket** battalion on both the metro (especially the yellow line) and the city buses. Gangs distract their victims by pushing them or blocking their way, and empty their pockets or bags at the same time.

Buses (*autóbusz*) are useful for journeys that can't be made by metro – especially around Buda, where Moszkva tér (on the red line) and Móricz Zsigmond körtér (southwest of Gellért-hegy) are the main bus terminals. Bus stops are marked by a blue sign with the label "*autóbusz*" or with a picture of a bus in the centre, and have timetables underneath; most buses run every ten to twenty minutes from 5am to 11pm (*Utolsó kocsi indul* . . . means "the last one leaves . . ."). Regular services are numbered in black, buses with red numbers make fewer stops en route, and those with a red "E" suffix run nonstop between terminals. You should punch your own ticket on board; to get the bus to stop, push the button above the door or on the handrail beside the door. Busy routes are also served by **night buses** (up to four every hour), with black numbers and an "*É*" suffix.

Yellow **trams** (*villamos*) are chiefly good for travelling around the Great Boulevard or along the embankments. Services run from early in the morning to 11pm. **Trolley buses** (*trolibusz*) mostly operate northeast of the centre near the Városliget. The reason route numbers start at 70 is that the first trolley bus line was inaugurated on Stalin's seventieth birthday in 1949. Trolley bus #83 was started in 1961, when Stalin would have been 83.

Tickets and passes

There's a whole array of **tickets** available for travelling on public transport, but since validating your ticket can be complex and is easy to forget – and ticket inspections are much stricter than they were – the best advice if you are staying for more than half a day is to get a pass (see below).

Single **tickets** valid for the metro, buses, trams, trolley buses, the Cogwheel Railway and suburban HÉV lines (to the edge of the city) cost 170Ft and are sold at metro stations, newspaper kiosks and tobacconists. Tickets valid only on the **metro** come in a variety of types, depending on how many lines you want to use, and how many stops you want to go: a metro section ticket (120Ft) takes you three stops on the same line; a metro transfer ticket (270Ft) is valid for as many stops as you like with one line change; and a metro section transfer ticket (185Ft) takes you five stops with one line change. Tickets must be validated when you use them: on the metro and HÉV you punch them in the machines at the entrance (remember to validate a new ticket if you change lines); on trams, trolley buses and buses you punch the tickets on board in the small red or orange machines. You can get weekend family tickets (2040Ft) and books of ten and twenty tickets (1450Ft and 2800Ft) are also available – but note that if a ticket is separated from the book it will become invalid. Tickets bought on buses and trolley buses cost 200Ft.

Day passes (*napijegy*) cost 1350Ft and are valid for unlimited travel – on the metro, buses, trams, trolley buses, the Cogwheel Railway and suburban HÉV lines – until midnight; three-day passes cost 2700Ft and weekly passes 3100Ft. **Season tickets** cost 4050Ft for two weeks and 6250Ft for a month, and are available from metro stations, but you'll need a passport photo for the accompanying photocard, available from the BKV office, VII, Akácfa utca 22 (Mon–Fri 6am–8pm, Sat 8am–1.45pm), near Blaha Lujza tér metro, or from the ticket office at Kálvin tér.

There is a 2000Ft **fine** for travelling without a valid ticket and inspectors are very strict. If you have a season ticket but are not carrying it, the fine is higher, though most of it is refunded upon presentation of the season ticket within three days at the BKV office. **Children** up to the age of 6 travel free.

Taxis

Budapest's **taxis** have gained themselves a reputation for ripping off foreigners – the best advice is to use one of the following established companies: Főtaxi (☎1/222-2222) or Citytaxi (☎1/211-1111) are the most reliable; Tele-5-taxi (☎1/355-5555); and Volántaxi (☎1/466-6666). Avoid unmarked private cars and those hanging around the stations and airport – the latter often charge a far higher rate than the official taxi from the airport into town. There are also fake Fő- and Citytaxis, sporting copies of the red-and-white chequerboard or yellow shield logos, which will charge you a vastly inflated price.

Taxis can be flagged down on the street or, for a cheaper rate, ordered by phone – Főtaxi and Citytaxi are most likely to have English-speaking operators. There are ranks throughout the city and you can hop into whichever cab you choose – don't feel you have to opt for the one at the front of the line if it looks at all dodgy. Be sure your taxi has a meter that is visible, and that it is switched on when you get in; rates should also be clearly displayed. **Fares** begin at 300Ft, and the price per kilometre is around 200Ft. Főtaxi do a fixed-price fare to the airport of 3500–4000Ft.

Driving and cycling

All things considered, **driving** in Budapest can't be recommended. Road manners are nonexistent, parking space is scarce and traffic jams are frequent. The Pest side of the Chain Bridge (Lánchíd) and the roundabout before the tunnel under the Vár are notorious for collisions. Careering trams, bumpy cobbles and unexpected one-way systems make things worse. If you do have a car, you might be better off parking it somewhere outside the centre and using public transport to get in and out. It's best not to leave it unattended for too long, though. See "Listings", at the end of the chapter, for rental agency addresses.

Cyclists must contend with the same hazards as drivers, as well as sunken tramlines, and they are also banned from most major thoroughfares. However, cycle routes are now appearing, for example, up Andrássy út and along the Buda bank of the Danube to Szentendre and beyond, and the number of cyclists has shot up. Tourinform has free cycling maps of Budapest, or you can buy them in map shops. Budapest is the best place in Hungary for repairs or to buy a bike for use elsewhere; see "Listings" at the end of the chapter for details of bike shops and rental outlets. Bicycles can be carried on HÉV trains and the Cogwheel Railway for the price of a single ticket, but not on buses or trams.

HÉV trains

The green overground **HÉV trains** provide easy access to Budapest's suburbs, running at least four times an hour between 6.30am and 11pm. As far as tourists are concerned, the most useful line is the one from **Batthyány tér** (on the red metro line) out to **Szentendre** (see p.157), north of Budapest, which passes through Óbuda, Aquincum and Rómaifürdő. The other lines originate in Pest, with one running northeast from **Örs vezér tere** (also on the red metro line) to **Gödöllő** via the Formula One racing track at Mogyoród; another southwards from Boráros tér at the Pest end of Petőfi Bridge to Csepel; and the third from **Soroksári út** (bus #23 or #54 from Boráros tér) to **Ráckeve**. On all these routes, a normal city transport ticket will take you to the city limits, beyond which you must punch additional tickets according to the distance travelled. Alternatively, you can purchase a ticket that covers the whole journey at the ticket office in the station or from the conductor on board.

Ferries and other rides

Although **ferries** play little useful part in the transport system, they do offer an enjoyable ride. From May to September there are boats between Boráros tér (by Petőfi híd) and Batthyány tér up to Jászai Mari tér and Rómaifürdő – running every fifteen to thirty minutes between 7am and 7pm and costing 400–650Ft. From May to August there is also a boat from the Jászai Mari tér dock to Pünkösdfürdő in northern Buda (1hr; check times on the board at the main dock), though you might prefer to disembark at Margit sziget, before the boat reaches dismal Békásmegyer. Ferry tickets can be obtained from kiosks (where timetables are posted) or machines at the docks.

Other pleasure rides can be found in the Buda Hills, on the **Cogwheel Railway** (Fogaskerekű vasút), the **Children's Railway** (Gyermekvasút) – largely staffed by kids – and the **chairlift** (*libegő*) between Zugliget and János-hegy. Details for all of these are given in the "Buda Hills" section of this chapter.

Accommodation

The availability of **accommodation** in Budapest has improved markedly in recent years, but it has also become much more expensive. Predictably, the heaviest demand and highest prices occur over summer, when the city feels like it's bursting at the seams. Christmas, New Year, the Spring Festival in March–April and the Grand Prix in August are also busy periods, with rates marked up as much as twenty percent in some hotels. Even so, it should always be possible to find somewhere that's reasonably priced, if not well sited.

Budget travellers will find most **hotels** expensive even during low season (Nov–March, excluding New Year); only a few are viable options. Though cheaper, **pensions** are often much the same as small hotels, with en-suite bathrooms and other mod cons. For both hotels and pensions, it's essential to phone ahead and book. If you're on a tight budget, your safest bet is a **private room**, arranged through a tourist agency. Though its location might not be perfect, the price should be reasonable and you can be sure of finding one at any time of year, day or night.

Hostels vary in price: some offer the cheapest accommodation in the city, while others are more expensive than private rooms, although you have the bonus of the helpful young staff who are around 24 hours a day. Another cheap option is **campsites**, where tent space can usually be found, even if all the **bungalows** are taken.

Hotels

The rash of new hotels in Budapest has widened availability at the top end of the market, while **hotel** prices across the board have also rocketed in recent years. Hotels also fill up quickly so it's best to **book** before leaving home or, failing that, through an agency (see box opposite) or any airport tourist office on arrival.

Accommodation booking agencies

American Express V, Deák Ferenc utca 10 (Mon–Fri 9am–5.30pm, Sat 9am–2pm; ⓣ1/235-4330). Handles hotel bookings, with a $20 service fee for non-cardholders.
Express V, Semmelweis utca 4 (Mon–Thurs 8.30am–4.30pm, Fri 8.30am–3pm; ⓣ1/327-7092, ⓦwww.express-travel.hu). Books hotels.
Ibusz V, Ferenciek tere 10, on the corner of Petőfi Sándor utca (Mon–Fri 8.15am–5pm; ⓣ1/485-2716); V, Vörösmarty tér 6, facing the British Embassy (Mon–Fri 8.15am–5pm; ⓣ1/317-0532); VII, Dob utca 1 (Mon–Fri 8am–4pm; ⓣ1/322-7214; ⓦwww.ibusz.hu). Handles all forms of accommodation.
Vista Visitor Center VI, Paulay Ede utca 7 (Mon–Fri 9am–8pm, Sat 9am–6pm; ⓣ1/429-9950; ⓦwww.vista.hu). Books hotels and apartments.

Hotel star ratings give a fair idea of **standards**, though facilities at some of the older three-star places don't compare with their Western equivalents, even if prices are similar. Almost all hotels vary their prices according to **season** – the price codes given below are what you can expect to pay in high season (but not Grand Prix prices).

Buda

Buda has fewer hotels than Pest, with less choice in the mid-range in particular, though there are some cheaper places in the northern suburbs. Broadly speaking, Buda's hotels are in four main areas: the historic but expensive Vár and Víziváros; around Tabán and Gellért-hegy, another pricey area (and if you're behind the Vár and away from the river, not especially scenic); the Buda Hills, within easy reach of Moszkva tér; and out in Óbuda and Rómaifürdő, where you'll find some of the cheapest places in Buda, mostly near stops on the HÉV line from Batthyány tér. If the best locations are beyond your means, you should also check out the section on hostels (see p.83), a few of which enjoy superb settings.

The Vár and Víziváros

Art'otel I, Bem rakpart 16–19 ⓣ1/487-9487, ⓦwww.artotel.hu. The first boutique hotel in the city is an award-winning venture (part of a chain) that combines eighteenth-century buildings – comprising beautiful large rooms with original doors and high ceilings – with a modern wing overlooking the river with marvellous views. Well-equipped rooms come with all mod cons and bright-red dressing gowns. The furnishings, wall decorations and crockery were all designed by one American artist – they couldn't find a Hungarian artist who could mass-produce their art quickly enough. Wi-fi connection all round the hotel, and business centre Internet use for all. ❾
Astra I, Vám utca 6 ⓣ1/214-1906, ⓦwww.hotel-astra.hu. Small hotel in a converted 300-year-old building at the foot of the castle near Batthyány tér. Nine well-furnished rooms with minibar and a/c. ❽
Burg I, Szentháromság tér 7 ⓣ1/212-0269, ⓦwww.burghotelbudapest.hu. Small hotel right opposite the Mátyás Church. All rooms have en-suite bathrooms, a/c, minibar and TV. ❽
Carlton I, Apor Péter utca 3 ⓣ1/224-0999, ⓦwww.carltonhotel.hu. Four-star hotel well situated by the Chain Bridge, below Castle Hill. Modern, comfy interior, but slightly lacking in atmosphere. Rooms have minibar and TV and there's parking space. ❽
Hilton Budapest I, Hess András tér 1–3 ⓣ1/889-6600, ⓦwww.danubiusgroup.com/hilton. By the Mátyás Church in the Vár, with superb views across the river, this hotel incorporates the remains of a medieval monastery and hosts summertime concerts in the former church. Luxurious to a fault. ❾
Kulturinnov I, Szentháromság tér 6 ⓣ1/355-0122, ⓦwww.mka.hu. Well positioned for sightseeing, in a neo-Gothic building right by Mátyás Church. The hotel is badly signed in the main entrance on the first floor. Spacious quiet rooms with minibar, but no TV; breakfast included. Half the rooms have a/c – but the thick walls offer some protection. The hotel also hosts Hungarian cultural events, concerts and exhibitions. ❼
Victoria I, Bem rakpart 11 ⓣ1/457-8080, ⓦwww.victoria.hu. Very friendly small hotel on the

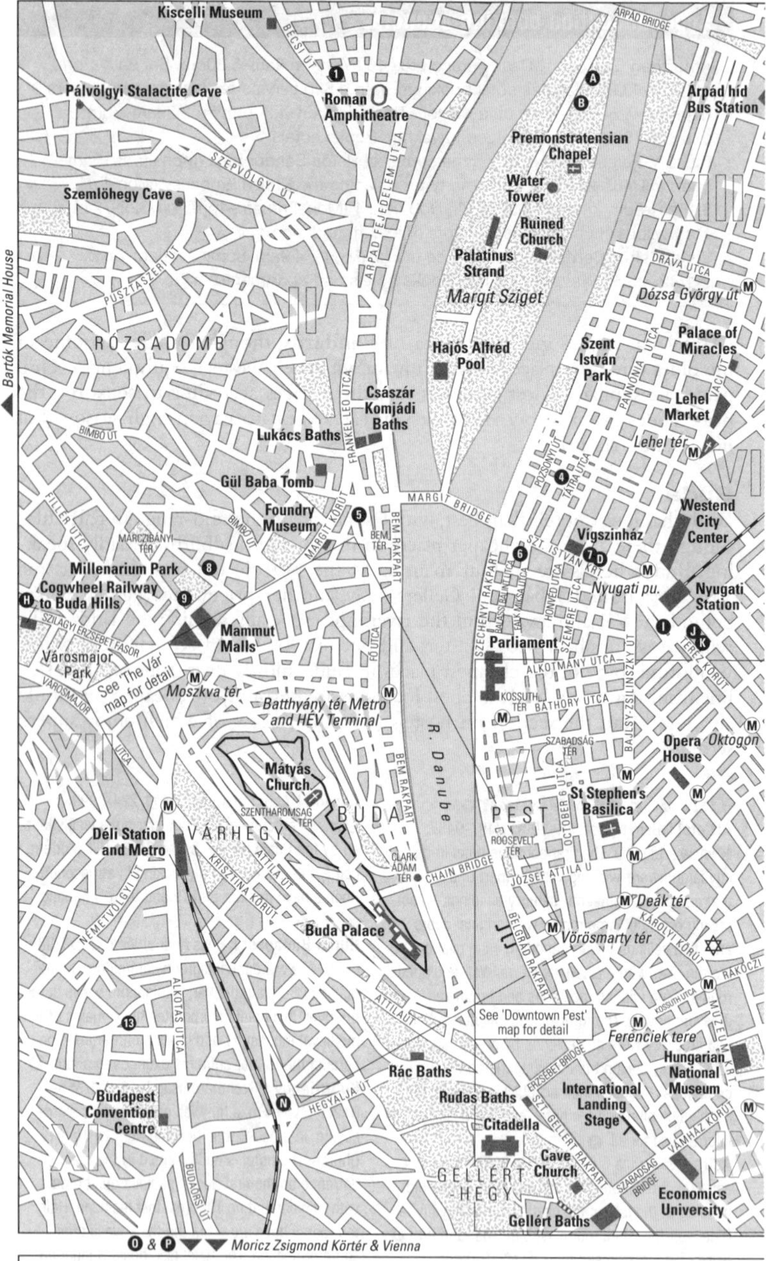

ACCOMMODATION

Ábel Panzió	O	Benczúr	F	Charles Hotel	N	Danubius Thermal	A	Nemzeti	M
Andrássy	E	Best Hostel	J	City Panzió Ring	D	Délibáb	C	Ráday Youth Hostel	Q
Béke Radisson	K	Budapest	H	Danubius Grand	B	Flamenco	P	Radio Inn	G

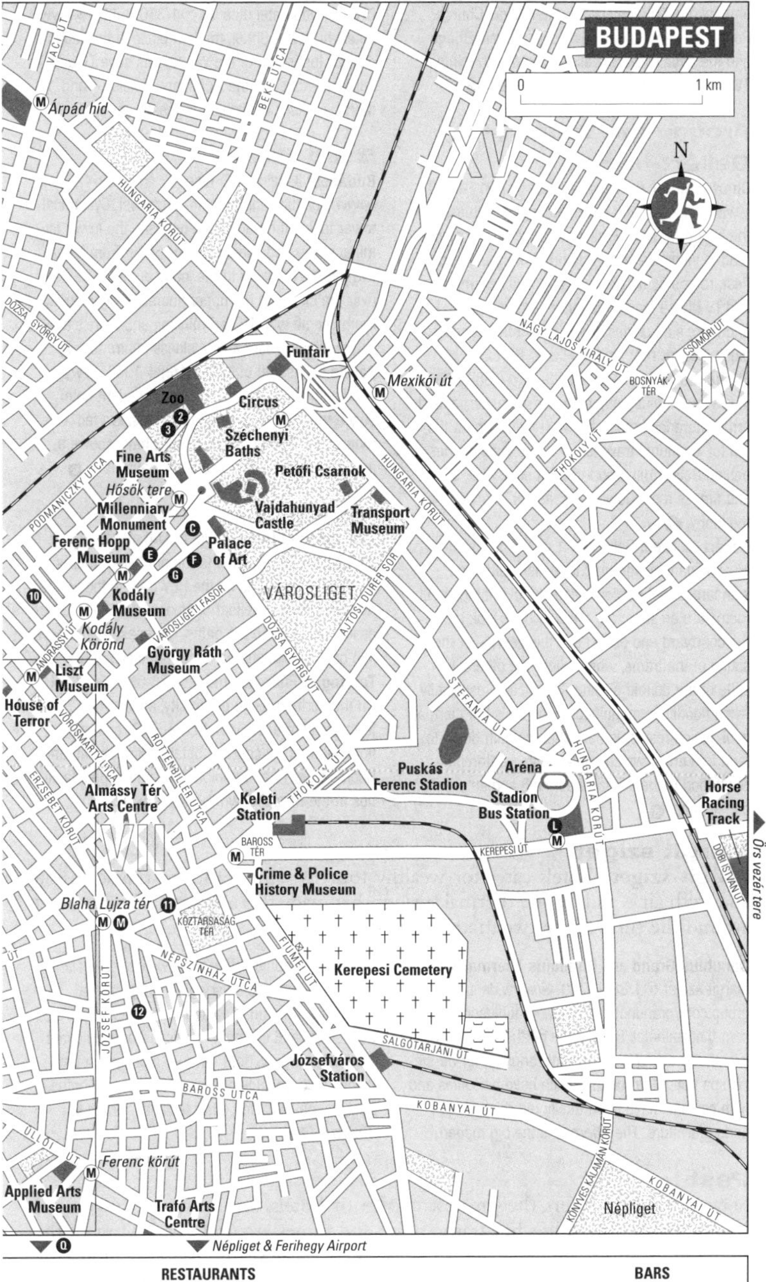

- Stadion L
- Yellow Submarine I

RESTAURANTS

- Arcade 13
- Bagolyvár 3
- Chez Daniel 10
- Firkász 4
- Gundel 2
- Gusto's 5
- Kerék 1
- Lanzhou 11
- Márkus Vendéglő 9
- Marxim 8
- Okay Italia 7

BARS

- Csiga 12
- Tokaji Borozó 6

embankment directly below the Mátyás Church. Rooms have excellent views of the Chain Bridge and the river, and are well equipped with minibar, TV and a/c. Sauna and garage facilities. ❽

Around the Tabán and Gellért-hegy

Charles Hotel XI, Hegyalja út 23 ⓣ1/212-9169, ⓦwww.charleshotel.hu. Friendly place situated on the hill up from the Erzsébet Bridge on the main road to Vienna, a short bus ride from the centre of Pest; rooms come with cooking facilities, minibar and TV (those facing the inner yard are quieter), and there's a business room with Internet access, plus bikes for rent. Parking costs €8 extra. ❻

Flamenco XI, Tas vezér utca 3–7 ⓣ1/889-5600, ⓦwww.danubiusgroup.com/flamenco. Large modern conference hotel – but with two floors at the top for individual travellers – in the leafy district behind Gellért Hill. Good-sized rooms. Pool, sauna and fitness room downstairs, and wi-fi access in the lobby. ❼

Gellért XI, Szent Gellért tér 1 ⓣ1/889-5500, ⓦwww.danubiusgroup.com/gellert. Old hotel with large, light corridors and lots of character. All rooms are en suite; the cheaper ones look on to the courtyard and don't have the views – or the sound of the trams, which blight the others, in spite of the double glazing. The facade, especially when floodlit, is magnificent, and so is the thermal pool, which residents have their own lift down to (and free entry, which comes with a bathrobe). Good food in the *söröző* (beer hall) and an excellent coffee shop. ❽

Orion I, Döbrentei utca 13 ⓣ1/356-8583, ⓦwww.hotels.hu/orion. Small, modern place in the Tabán district, just south of the Vár. Rooms have TV and minibar – those at the front can be noisy – and there's a sauna available for guests. ❽

Buda Hills

Budapest II, Szilágyi E. fasor 47 ⓣ1/889-4200, ⓦwww.danubiusgroup.com//budapest. Cylindrical tower facing the Buda Hills, opposite the lower terminal of the Cogwheel Railway, 500m from Moszkva tér. 1970s decor in the lobby but good views over the city from the upper floors. Air-conditioned rooms come with TV and minibar, and there's a sauna, fitness room and business centre too. ❼

Panda II, Pasaréti út 133 ⓣ1/394-1932, ⓦwww.budapesthotelpanda.hu. Pleasant, modern hotel only a ten-minute bus ride from Moszkva tér. All rooms have TV and minibar, most have showers, and three have baths. Sauna also available. ❻

Óbuda

Csillaghegy Strand III, Pusztakúti utca 3 ⓣ1/368-4012. Situated in the northern suburbs, but only ten minutes on the HÉV train to the centre. Attached to an excellent outdoor thermal pool. Prices include entry to the baths. Cheapest rooms have just basins, with shared bathroom facilities. ❸

Touring III, Pünkösdfürdő utca 38 ⓣ1/250-3184. On the northern edge of the city, about 11km from the centre. Basic but acceptable one-star hotel with tennis court, pool tables and restaurant. Rooms have TV and minibar. Swimming pool facilities at the *Strand* down the road. ❺

Margit sziget

Margit sziget's hotels cater for wealthy tourists who come for the seclusion and fresh air – and for the thermal springs that made this a fashionable spa resort around the turn of the twentieth century.

Danubius Grand and **Danubius Thermal** XIII, Margit sziget ⓣ1/889-4700, ⓦwww.danubiusgroup.com/grandhotel, ⓦwww.danubiusgroup.com/thermalhotel. Both at the northern end of the island, the *Grand* is the island's original, *fin-de-siècle* spa hotel; the rooms, which have balconies and high ceilings, have been totally refurbished with period furniture. The *Thermal* is the big modern one, with balconies offering views over the island. Both hotels provide a very wide range of spa facilities, with mud spas and massages, as well as medical and cosmetic services from pedicures to plastic surgery. Both have wi-fi access in the lobby. Prices include access to the thermal baths, pool, sauna, gym and other facilities. *Grand* ❽, *Thermal* ❾

Pest

Staying in **Pest** offers the greatest choice of hotels, and more in the way of restaurants and nightlife, but traffic noise and fumes are quite bad. Most of the outlying locations are easily accessible by metro. The prime spots are along the river bank with views across to the Royal Palace, although all the prewar grand hotels were destroyed during the war, and their replacements don't quite have the same elegance. The more expensive places tend to be in the downtown area, with prices falling as you go further out, though this is not always the case.

Moving out of the centre, more hotels are grouped around the Nagykörút, the larger ring road, and the City Park.

Downtown

Hotel Anna VIII, Gyulai Pál utca 14 ⓣ1/327-2000, ⓦwww.hotels.hu/annahotel. In a quiet street in central Pest, this hotel offers small, basic rooms – twin beds only – with TV and showers. Off-street parking. ❼

Astoria V, Kossuth utca 19 ⓣ1/889-6000, ⓦwww.danubiusgroup.com/astoria. Refurbished four-star hotel on a major junction in central Pest. Good-sized rooms have chairs and sofa, safe, minibar, phone and TV; half have baths, half showers. Very pleasant coffee house. ❽

ELTE Peregrinus Vendégház V, Szerb utca 3 ⓣ1/266-4911, ⓦwww.peregrinushotel.hu. Friendly elegant place in a quiet backstreet in central Pest with 25 rooms, complete with minibar and TV. Buffet breakfast included in the price. Rooms are spacious, unlike the bathrooms. It belongs to the university, and all rooms have writing tables to meet the needs of academic visitors. ❼

Four Seasons V, Roosevelt tér 5–6 ⓣ1/268-6000 ⓦwww.fourseasons.com/budapest. A magnificent restoration of this Budapest landmark (see p.111) has produced a new level of luxury in the city; the rooms all have Art Nouveau-style fittings (even down to the beautiful radiators) and are excellently equipped. Those overlooking the Danube naturally have the best aspect – several first-floor suites have views looking right through the tunnel across the river. Both the restaurants are excellent – the *kávéház* is the cheaper but still very good option – and the service throughout the hotel is superlative. Underground garage. ❾

K&K Opera VI, Révay utca 24 ⓣ1/269-0222, ⓦwww.kkhotels.com. Fully air-conditioned four-star hotel right by the Opera House, with its own parking space. The rooms are pleasantly furnished and have minibar, TV, safe and phone. Guests have free use of computers and Internet in the business centre. Buffet breakfast included. ❾

Kempinski Corvinus V, Erzsébet tér 7–8 ⓣ1/429-3777, ⓦwww.kempinski-budapest.com. Flashy five-star establishment in the centre of town, which seems to assume it is the best in town – Madonna, Michael Jackson and various Formula One Grand Prix stars have all stayed here. Facilities include wi-fi access in the lobby, swimming pool, sauna, solarium, fitness room and underground garage. ❾

Le Meridien V, Erzsébet tér 9–10 ⓣ1/429-5500, ⓦwww.lemeridien-budapest.com. Originally built for the Adria insurance company at the turn of the twentieth century, this building housed the police headquarters in the Communist years until it was totally gutted and reopened as a luxury hotel in 2000 – a welcome rival for the smug *Kempinski* next door. The hotel is magnificently furnished throughout, and its well-equipped rooms are perhaps the most tasteful in the city. The hotel's restaurant, *Le Bourbon*, topped by a domed glass ceiling, serves up top-class food. Parking and swimming pool. ❾

Marriott Budapest V, Apáczai Csere János utca 4 ⓣ1/266-7000, ⓦwww.marriott.com. All rooms in this older five-star a/c hotel overlook the Danube, and facilities include sauna, squash court, parking and baby-sitting service. ❾

Mercure Museum VIII, Trefort utca 2 ⓣ1/485-1080, ⓦwww.mercure-museum.hu. In a quiet street close to Astoria, this small hotel is housed in an imaginatively transformed Pest apartment block with the restaurant in the glass-roofed courtyard. Small but well-equipped a/c rooms come with en-suite bathrooms, hairdryers, satellite TV and minibar. Wi-fi acess in the lobby. Off-street parking available. ❽

Around the Nagykörút

Béke Radisson VI, Teréz körút 43 ⓣ1/301-1600, ⓦwww.radisson.com/beke. Refurbished vintage hotel on the Nagykörút, 200m south of Nyugati Station. Rooms have minibar, TV and safe. Facilities include sauna, pool, business centre, underground garage, restaurant and an excellent coffee house. ❽

Corinthia Royal Grand VII, Erzsébet körút 43–49 ⓣ1/479-4000, ⓦwww.corinthiahotels.com. Pleasant, new five-star hotel on the main boulevard. Once one of the grand prewar hotels, for forty years it was used as offices, while the ballroom acted as the very grand Red Star cinema. The rebuilding has been beautifully executed, using original drawings; only the facade is original, and even the gorgeous ballroom – except for the chandeliers – is totally reconstructed. The 414 rooms are very comfortable and the hotel will soon have its own pool when work is complete. The *Bock* wine bar serves excellent food and wine. ❾

Medosz VI, Jókai tér 9 ⓣ1/374-3000, ⓦwww.medoszhotel.hu. Pleasant hotel in an ugly modern block overlooking a square near Oktogon. Small, light, simply furnished rooms with bath and TV. Excellent value for the location. ❻

Nemzeti VIII, József körút 4 ⓣ1/477-2000, ⓦwww.mercure-nemzeti.hu. Small but elegant rooms with TV, a/c and minibar in this grand Art

Nouveau-style place on Blaha Lujza tér (red metro). Rooms overlooking the square have double glazing but the courtyard ones are quieter. The restaurant and staircases are magnificent. Breakfast included. ❼

Beyond the Nagykörút

Andrássy VI, Andrássy út 111 ⓣ1/462-2100, ⓦwww.andrassyhotel.com. Housed in a stunning, newly refurbished Bauhaus building, the Andrássy offers five-star accommodation without the corporate feel. It has a friendly atmosphere, and is well placed between the City Park and the Belváros. All double rooms have balconies and mod cons. (They also have cheaper, very small double rooms with massage showers, but without balcony.) Well-priced quality food in the *Zebrano* restaurant, wi-fi access in the lobby. ❾

Benczúr VI, Benczúr utca 35 ⓣ1/479-5650, ⓦwww.hotelbenczur.hu. Modern functional hotel on a leafy street off Andrássy út, with pleasant rooms – bath, TV, and minibar – and a nice garden at the back. Cheaper rooms have showers only. ❼

Délibáb VI, Délibáb utca 35 ⓣ1/342-9301, ⓦwww.hoteldelibab.hu. Simply furnished but pleasant. Standing right on Hősök tere, it is walking distance from the sights on Andrássy út and the City Park, and has excellent transport links too. No a/c. ❼

Radio Inn VI, Benczúr utca 19 ⓣ1/342-8347, ⓦwww.radioinn.hu. Spacious if slightly dark apartments complete with kitchen and TV. Situated in a nice leafy street, by the Chinese Embassy and opposite the Vietnamese Embassy. Pleasant garden. ❻

Pensions

There is little difference between the rates charged by hotels and **pensions** these days. The difference lies more in their characters, with pensions usually being smaller, family-run places. However, pensions still fill up fast during summer, so reservations are advisable. In most cases, you need to phone them direct.

Buda

Ábel Panzió XI, Ábel Jenő utca 9 ⓣ1/381-0553, ⓦwww.hotels.hu/abelpanzio. The most appealing pension in Budapest, a 1913 villa with beautiful Art Nouveau fittings in a quiet street twenty minutes' walk from the Belváros. Just ten rooms, so essential to book in advance. Discount available on cash payments. ❻

Beatrix Panzió II, Szehér út 3 ⓣ1/275-0550, ⓦwww.beatrixhotel.hu. Friendly eighteen-room pension with sauna in the Buda Hills; bar on ground floor. Price includes breakfast. ❻

Buda Villa Panzió XII, Kiss Áron utca 6 ⓣ1/275-0091, ⓦwww.budapansio.hu. Comfortable small pension in the hills just above Moszkva tér. Rooms have TV and there's a bar in the lounge on the first floor; breakfast is included. Small garden to relax in after a day's sightseeing. ❻

Pest

City Panzió Mátyás V, Március 15. tér 8 ⓣ1/338-4711, ⓦwww.taverna.hu/matyas. Centrally located place with 85 simply furnished rooms. Half have a/c, and all have en-suite bathrooms (mainly with showers), TV, minibar, and a buffet breakfast in the *Mátyás Pince* restaurant downstairs, which is painted inside like the Mátyás Church. The pension overlooks a big road, so ask for a courtyard room if you want some quiet, though the rooms on the corner have a great view of the river. ❼

City Panzió Ring XIII, Szt. István körút 22 ⓣ1/340-5450, ⓦwww.taverna.hu. Same chain as the *Mátyás*, near Nyugati Station. Rooms have shower, TV, radio, phone and minibar. ❼

Private rooms and apartments

There are **private rooms** throughout the city, many in the sort of locations where a hotel would be unaffordable. Depending on location and amenities, **prices** for a double room range from 5000–6000Ft a night. On the downside, solo travellers will almost certainly have to pay for a double, and rates are thirty percent higher if you stay fewer than four nights (making pensions or hostels more economical for short-staying visitors). **Apartments**, from 10,000Ft a night, are not as common as rooms, but you should be able to find an agency with one on its books.

It's easy enough to get a room from one of the **touts** at the train stations, but it's safer to go through a tourist agency, where you book and pay at the counter signposted *fizetővendég*. Ibusz (see box on p.77) handles private rooms, as does the To-Ma Travel Agency at V, Október 6 utca 22 (☎353-0819, Ⓦwww.tomatour.hu).

Since rooms are rented unseen, it pays to take some trouble over your choice. Your host and the premises should give no cause for complaint (both are checked out), but the **location** or ambience might. For atmosphere and comfort you can't beat the nineteenth-century blocks where spacious, high-ceilinged apartments surround a courtyard with wrought-iron balconies – most common in Pest's V, VI and VII districts, and the parts of Buda nearest the Vár. It's best to avoid the run-down VIII and IX districts unless you can get a place inside the *körút* (boulevard). Elsewhere – particularly in Újpest (IV district), Csepel (XXI) or Óbuda (III) – you're likely to end up in a box on the twelfth floor on a *lakótelep* (housing estate). The *Budapest Atlasz* is invaluable for checking the location of sites and access by public transport.

Because many proprietors go out to work, you might not be able to take possession of the room until 5pm. Some knowledge of Hungarian facilitates **settling in**; guests normally receive an explanation of the boiler system and multiple door keys (*kulcs*), and may have use of the washing machine (*mosógép*), which might require another demonstration.

Hostels

If you don't have a tent, a dormitory bed in a **hostel** is the cheapest alternative. Many also have rooms at much the same price as private accommodation, but with no surcharge for staying fewer than four nights. Prices are given per head, so that you can easily end up paying over 7000Ft for a double room. This does include 24-hour information from the English-speaking staff at the reception desk, but the rooms often have very basic student furniture. Unless stated otherwise, the hostels listed below are open year-round – student dormitories are open during July and August only, many of them located in the university area south of Gellért-hegy. You can't be sure of getting a bed in the hostel of your choice in summer without **booking** in advance (see box on p.77 for details).

If you arrive in the city on an international train, you will more than likely be given **information** about hostels even before the train pulls into the station. The competition between the private groups running the summer hostels is intense, but do not feel intimidated – you can afford to wait and choose. The larger organizations will also offer transport to the hostel, which can make arrival less daunting. The Mellow Mood group run some excellent all-year hostels in the city and also handle some of the university accommodation open during the summer. They have offices in Keleti Station, on either side of the doors at the far end as you arrive, and can give you information and make bookings (daily 7am–8pm; ☎1/413-2062, Ⓦwww.backpackers.hu).

Buda

Back Pack XI, Takács Menyhért utca 33 ☎1/385-8946, Ⓦwww.backpackbudapest.hu. Charming, clean fifty-bed hostel with a shaded garden, just twenty minutes from the centre. Lots of information on the city, sport and fitness, and they also organize cave trips. Tram #49 or bus #7 to Tétényi út stop. Dorm bed 2200Ft, doubles ❸

Citadella I, Citadella sétány, top of Gellért hegy ☎1/466-5794, Ⓦwww.citadella.hu. Breathtaking views of the city in this well-sited hostel, but note that the weekend disco in the neighbouring nightclub sets the whole place shaking. Get there early to get a bunk. Take bus #27 from Móricz Zsigmond körtér, and then it's a ten-minute walk from the last stop. Ten- and fourteen-bed dorms 4000Ft. ❺

Landler XI, Bartók Béla út 17 ☎1/463-3621. Near the Gellért Baths, housed in the Baross Gábor Kollégium. Two- and three-bed rooms, with high ceilings. Open July & Aug only. Dorm bed 5000Ft.

Pest

Best Hostel VI, Podmaniczky utca 27, 1st floor ☎1/332-4934, Ⓦwww.besthostel.hu. Rambling and friendly hostel in a typical tall Pest apartment, close to Nyugati Station. All rooms look on to the main streets, so it's noisy. Dorm bed 3000Ft, doubles ❹

Marco Polo VII, Nyár utca 6 ⓣ1/413-2555, ⓦwww.marcopolohostel.com. Clean and well positioned at the edge of the old Jewish quarter. Discount for IYHF cardholders. Dorm bed 4500–5000Ft, doubles ❻

Mellow Mood V, Bécsi utca 2 ⓣ1/411-1310, ⓦwww.mellowmoodhostel.com. Friendly, well-run and very centrally located hotel with 270 beds in doubles and rooms of four, six and eight beds, all overlooking the street, Internet access. If you book in Keleti Station you get a lift in the Mellow Mood van. Discount for IYHF cardholders. Dorm beds from 3200Ft.

Museum Guest House VIII, Mikszáth Kálmán tér 4, 1st floor ⓣ1/266-7770, ⓦwww.budapesthostel.com. In the streets behind the National Museum, handy for the bars and cafés of the centre. Three clean, spacious dorms, each sleeping seven or eight on mattresses on the floor. Cave trips organized. Free Internet access in the evening. Dorm bed 3000Ft.

Museum II V, Károly körút 10, upper 1st floor ⓣ1/266-7774. New, sister guest house to the one above, close to Astoria. The quieter rooms face the internal courtyard. Dorm bed 3000Ft.

Ráday Youth Hostel IX, Ráday utca 43–45 ⓣ1/218-4766. Near Kálvin tér, with basic student hostel furniture, tall rooms of two to six beds. Open July & Aug only. Dorm bed 3500Ft.

Yellow Submarine VI, Teréz körút 56. ⓣ & ⓕ1/331-9896, ⓦwww.yellowsubmarinehostel.com. Cheap hostel in a typical old Pest apartment near Nyugati Station, with 65 bunk beds in large rooms with high ceilings. Breakfast included in price, laundry facilities available. Rooms overlooking the main road are noisy. It's on the third floor (no lift). Also organizes canoeing, cycling and cave tours. Dorm bed 2800Ft, doubles ❹

Campsites

Budapest's **campsites**, by far the best of which are located in the Buda Hills, generally offer good facilities, and are pretty pleasant, with trees and grass and maybe even a pool, though they can become very crowded between June and September, and the smaller ones can run out of space. It is illegal to camp anywhere else, and the parks are patrolled to enforce this. The police usually tolerate people **sleeping rough** in train stations, but this is not to be recommended as there's a high risk of theft (or worse).

Budapest Tourist (see p.71 for details) can arrange detached **bungalows** of various sizes at several campsites and a number of other locations. Your best bet is to tell them more or less what you are looking for and let them handle the booking in the first instance, though if you decide to prolong your stay you can arrange this privately with the owners. Trying to sort it out for yourself over the phone can be a problem, as English is not always spoken, telephone numbers are liable to change, and opening times change from year to year depending on the weather. The campsites given below are all in Buda, since the Pest ones are far out and not very inviting. Tourinform can point you in their direction if you need them.

Csillebérc Camping XII, Konkoly Thege M. út 21 ⓣ1/395-6537, ⓦwww.datanet.hu/csill. Large, well-equipped site with space for 1000 campers. A range of bungalows also available. A short walk from the last stop of the #21 bus from Moszkva tér. Open year-round.

Római Camping III, Szentendrei út 189 ⓣ1/368-6260, ⓔromai@matavnet.hu. Huge site with space for 2500 campers beside the road to Szentendre in Rómaifürdő (25min by HÉV). Higher than average rates include use of the nearby swimming pool. Open year-round.

Zugligeti Niche Camping XII, Zugligeti út 101 ⓣ1/200-8346, ⓦwww.campingniche.hu. At the end of the #158 bus route, opposite the chairlift up to János-hegy. Small, terraced ravine site in the woods, with space for 260 campers and good facilities including a restaurant occupying the former tram station at the far end. Open April–Oct.

Buda

Viewed from the embankments of the Danube, **Buda** forms a collage of palatial buildings, archaic spires and outsize statues, crowning craggy massifs. This glamorous image conceals more mundane aspects, but at times, in the right place, Buda can really live up to it. To experience the **Vár** (Castle District) at its best, come early in the morning to visit the **museums** before the crowds arrive, then wander off for lunch or a soak in one of the Turkish baths, and return to catch street life in full swing in the afternoon. The outlying **Buda Hills** – accessible by chairlift and the **Children's Railway** – are obviously less visited during the week, while **Gellért-hegy**, with its superb views over the city, the **Rózsadomb** district and the **Roman ruins** of Óbuda and Rómaifürdő can be seen any time, but preferably when the weather's fine.

The Vár

The **Vár** (or Várhegy – Castle Hill) is Buda's most prominent feature, a long plateau laden with bastions, mansions and a huge palace, dominating the Víziváros (Watertown) below. The hill's grandiosity and strategic utility have long gone hand in hand: Hungarian kings built their palaces here because it was easy to defend, a fact appreciated by the Turks, Habsburgs and other occupiers. Its buildings, a legacy of bygone Magyar glories, have been almost wholly reconstructed from the rubble of 1945, when the Wehrmacht and the Red Army battled over the hill while Buda's inhabitants cowered underground – the eighty-sixth time that it was ravaged and rebuilt over seven centuries, rivalling the devastation caused by the recapture of Buda from the Turks in 1686.

Though the hill's appearance has changed much since building began in the thirteenth century, its main **streets** still follow their medieval courses, with Gothic arches and stone carvings in the courtyards and passages of eighteenth- and nineteenth-century Baroque **houses**, whose facades are embellished with fancy ironwork grilles. Practically every building displays a *műemlék* plaque giving details of its history (in Hungarian only), and a surprising number are still homes rather than embassies or boutiques – there are even a couple of schools and corner shops. At dusk, when most of the tourists have left, pensioners walk their dogs and toddlers play in the long shadows of Hungarian history.

There are several **approaches** to the Vár, mostly starting from the Víziváros (described on p.94). The simplest and most novel is to ride up to the palace by **Sikló** (see p.95; daily 7.30am–10pm, closed every other Monday; 600Ft uphill, 500Ft downhill), a renovated nineteenth-century funicular that runs from Clark Ádám tér by the Chain Bridge. Alternatively, you can start from Moszkva tér (on metro line 2) and either take the **Várbusz** – the small bus leaving from the raised side of Moszkva tér, that terminates by the palace – or walk uphill to the Vienna Gate at the northern end of the Vár. Walking from Batthyány tér via the steep flights of steps (*lépcső*) off Fő utca involves more effort, but the dramatic stairway up to the Fishermen's Bastion is worth the sweat. The most direct approach **from Pest** is to ride bus #16 from Erzsébet tér across the Chain Bridge to Clark Ádám tér – giving you the option of taking the Sikló or staying on the bus as far as Dísz tér, which is almost as close to the palace.

Restrictions on **traffic** in the Vár mean that private cars entering the district collect a ticket as they enter and pay as they leave – 450Ft per hour, or free if you leave within thirty minutes. Taxis, local residents, and guests of the *Hilton* do not have to pay, but hotel guests must get their card stamped by the reception desk.

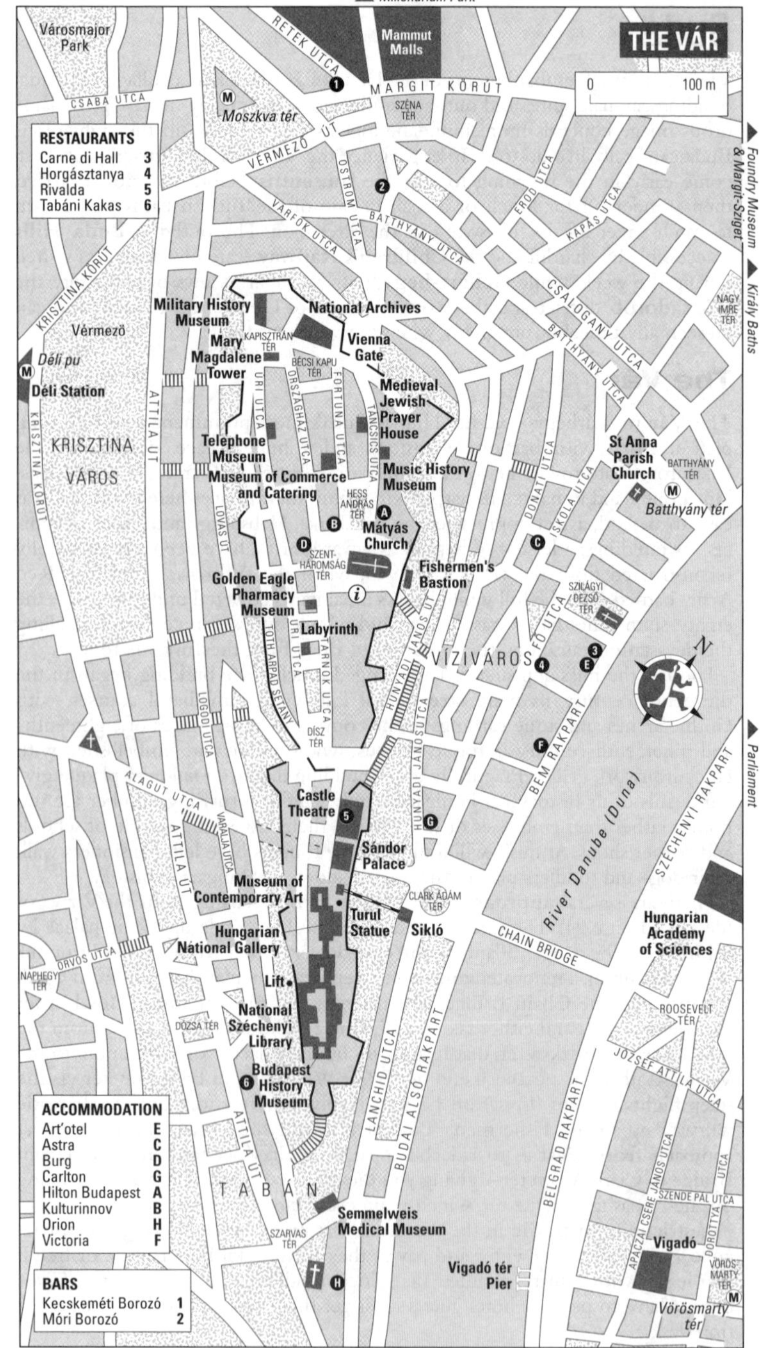
THE VÁR
0 100 m
Millenarium Park
Foundry Museum & Margit-Sziget
Király Baths
Parliament
Rác & Rudas Baths & Gellért-hegy
RESTAURANTS
Carne di Hall 3
Horgásztanya 4
Rivalda 5
Tabáni Kakas 6
ACCOMMODATION
Art'otel E
Astra C
Burg D
Carlton G
Hilton Budapest A
Kulturinnov B
Orion H
Victoria F
BARS
Kecskeméti Borozó 1
Móri Borozó 2
Városmajor Park
Mammut Malls
Moszkva tér
Széna tér
Margit körút
Retek utca
Csaba utca
Vérmező út
Ostrom utca
Varfok utca
Batthyány utca
Erőd utca
Kapás utca
Csalogány utca
Nagy Imre tér
Krisztina körút
Vérmező
Déli pu
Déli Station
Krisztina Város
Military History Museum
National Archives
Mary Magdalene Tower
Kapisztrán tér
Vienna Gate
Bécsi kapu tér
Medieval Jewish Prayer House
Úri utca
Országház utca
Fortuna utca
Táncsics utca
Telephone Museum
Museum of Commerce and Catering
Music History Museum
Hess András tér
Mátyás Church
Szentháromság tér
Fishermen's Bastion
Golden Eagle Pharmacy Museum
Labyrinth
Attila út
Lovas út
Donáti utca
Iskola utca
St Anna Parish Church
Batthyány tér
Szilágyi Dezső tér
Fő utca
Víziváros
Hunyadi János út
Tóth Árpád sétány
Tárnok utca
Dísz tér
Logodi utca
Alagút utca
Bem rakpart
Castle Theatre
Sándor Palace
Varalja utca
Museum of Contemporary Art
Clark Ádám tér
Turul Statue
Sikló
Hungarian National Gallery
Chain Bridge
River Danube (Duna)
Széchenyi rakpart
Hungarian Academy of Sciences
Orvos utca
Naphegy tér
Lift
National Széchenyi Library
Dózsa tér
Roosevelt tér
Budapest History Museum
Lánchíd utca
Budai alsó rakpart
József Attila utca
Belgrad rakpart
Tabán
Semmelweis Medical Museum
Szarvas tér
Szende Pál utca
Apáczai Csere János utca
Dorottya utca
Vigadó
Vigadó tér Pier
Vörösmarty tér

Szentháromság tér and around

To the north of the palace lies the area of the Vár where, for many centuries, residence was a privilege granted to religious or ethnic groups, each occupying a specific street. This pattern persisted through the 145-year-long Turkish occupation, when Armenians, Circassians and Sephardic Jews also established themselves under the relatively tolerant Ottomans. The liberation of Buda by a multinational Christian army under Habsburg command was followed by a pogrom and ordinances restricting the right of residence to Catholics and Germans, which remained in force for nearly a century. In 1944, the Swedish Red Cross established safe houses here for Jewish refugees, some of whom remained hidden in caves after the others were forced into the ghetto. By the time the Red Army finally took Buda on February 13, 1945, only four houses on the hill were habitable.

The obvious starting point is **Szentháromság tér** (Holy Trinity Square), the historic heart of the district, named after an ornate **Trinity Column** erected in 1713 in thanksgiving for the abatement of a plague. To the southwest on the corner of Szentháromság utca stands the former **Town Hall** of Buda, which functioned as a municipality until the unification of Buda, Pest and Óbuda in 1873. Down the road at Szentháromság utca 7, the tiny **Ruszwurm patisserie** has been a pastry shop and café since 1827, and was a gingerbread shop in the Middle Ages. Its Empire-style decor looks much the same as it did under Vilmos Ruszwurm, who ran the patisserie for nearly four decades from 1884.

The Mátyás Church

Szentháromság tér's most prominent feature is the neo-Gothic **Mátyás Church** (Mátyás templom; Mon–Sat 9am–5pm, Sun 1–5pm; 600Ft, crypt and treasury 400Ft, audioguide 300Ft), whose diamond-patterned roofs and toothy spires are wildly asymmetrical but nevertheless coherent in form. Officially dedicated to Our Lady, but popularly named after "Good King Mátyás", the building is a late nineteenth-century re-creation by architect Frigyes Schulek, grafted onto those portions of the original thirteenth-century church that survived the siege of 1686. The frescoes and altars had been whitewashed over or removed when the Turks turned it into a mosque. Ravaged yet again in World War II, the church was laboriously restored by a Communist regime keen to show its patriotic credentials, and the Changes saw the sanctity of this "ancient national shrine of the Hungarian people" reaffirmed – which means that visitors are expected to be properly dressed and respectfully behaved.

Entering the church through its twin-spired **Mary Portal**, the richness of the interior is overwhelming. Painted leaves and geometric motifs run up columns and under vaulting, while shafts of light fall through rose windows onto gilded altars and statues with stunning effect. Most of the **frescoes** were executed by Károly Lotz or Bertalan Székely, the foremost historical painters of the day. The **coat of arms of King Mátyás** can be seen on the wall to your left, just inside; his family name, Corvinus, comes from the raven (*corvus* in Latin) that appeared on his heraldry and on every volume in the famous Corvin Library.

Around the corner to the left, beneath the south tower, is the **Loreto Chapel**, containing a Baroque Madonna, while in the bay beneath the Béla Tower beyond the stairs you can see two medieval capitals, one carved with monsters fighting a dragon, the other with two bearded figures reading a book. The tower is named after Béla IV, who founded the church, rather than his predecessor in the second gated chapel along, who shares a double sarcophagus with Anne of Chatillon. Originally located in the old capital, Székesfehérvár, the **tomb of Béla III** and his queen, was moved here after its discovery in 1848. Although

Hungary's medieval kings were crowned at Székesfehérvár, it was customary to make a prior appearance in Buda – hence yet another sobriquet, the "Coronation Church".

By paying extra to visit the **crypt** you can see the red-marble tombstone of a nameless Árpád prince, and a small collection of **ecclesiastical treasures** and relics, including the right foot of St János. Otherwise, climb a spiral staircase to the **Royal Oratory** overlooking the stained-glass windows and embossed vaulting of the nave; here votive figures and vestments presage a **replica of the Coronation Regalia**, whose attached exhibition is more informative about the provenance of St Stephen's Crown than that accompanying the originals, on display in Parliament (see p.114).

To really do the church justice, attend a **Mass** (daily 7am, 8.30am & 6pm, plus 10am & noon on Sundays and public holidays). The 10am Sunday Mass is in Latin and has a choir and organ music. Otherwise, you can enjoy the acoustics at one of the many **concerts** performed during the festival seasons or **organ recitals** held throughout the year; details appear in listings magazines and on the church's own website Ⓦwww.matyas-templom.hu.

The Fishermen's Bastion

After the Mátyás Church, the most transfixing sight is the **Fishermen's Bastion** (Halászbástya) just beyond, which frames the view of Pest across the river. Although fishermen from the Víziváros reputedly defended this part of the hill during the Middle Ages, the existing bastion is purely decorative. An undulating white rampart of cloisters and stairways intersecting at seven tent-like turrets symbolizing the Magyar tribes that conquered the Carpathian Basin, it was designed by Schulek as a foil to the church. The view of Pest across the river is only surpassed by the vistas from the terrace of Buda Palace, and the Citadella on Gellért-hegy. (Occasionally, and at random, booths appear that charge 100–200Ft for the privilege of climbing up to the higher level.)

Between the bastion and the church, an equestrian **statue of King Stephen** honours the founder of the Hungarian nation, whose conversion to Christianity and coronation with a crown sent by the pope presaged the Magyars' integration into European civilization (see box opposite). The statue is reflected in the copper-glass facade of the **Hilton Budapest**, opposite, along with the church and the bastion. Incorporating chunks of a medieval Dominican church and monastery on the side facing the river, and an eighteenth-century Jesuit college on the other, the hotel bears a copy of the **Mátyás Relief** from Bautzen in Germany that's regarded as the only true likeness of Hungary's Renaissance monarch – who is shown being crowned by a pair of angels.

North towards Kapisztrán tér

If you're not in a hurry to reach the palace, it's worth exploring the quieter, **northern reaches of the Vár**, whose streets abound in period details. A common medieval feature that's survived are the sedilia, rows of niches with seats, in the passageway to the inner courtyard. For an example, look no further than the *Fortuna* restaurant on Hess András tér, which occupies the site of Hungary's first printing press, set up by András Hess in 1473. Also notice the hedgehog relief above the door of the former *Red Hedgehog Inn* at no. 3, where Janissaries were billeted in Turkish times.

Don't miss the fascinating **Museum of Commerce and Catering** (Kereskedelmi és Vendéglátóipari Múzeum; Wed–Fri 10am–5pm, Sat & Sun 10am–6pm; free, 500Ft for temporary exhibitions) at Fortuna utca 4, just off the square. In the Commerce section – through the door on the right in the

King Stephen

If you commit just one figure from Hungarian history to memory, make it **King Stephen**, for it was he who welded the tribal Magyar fiefdoms into a state and won recognition from Christendom. Born Vajk, son of Prince Géza, he emulated his father's policy of trying to convert the pagan Magyars and develop Hungary with the help of foreign preachers, craftsmen and merchants. By marrying Gizella of Bavaria in 996, he was able to use her father's knights to crush a pagan revolt after Géza's death, and subsequently received an apostolic cross and crown from Pope Sylvester II for his coronation on Christmas Day, 1000 AD, when he took the name Stephen (István in Hungarian).

Though noted for his enlightened views (such as the need for tolerance and the desirability of multiracial nations), he could act ruthlessly when necessary. After his only son Imre died in an accident and a pagan seemed likely to inherit, Stephen had the man blinded and poured molten lead into his ears. Naming his successor, he symbolically offered his crown to the Virgin Mary rather than the Holy Roman Emperor or the Pope; she has since been considered the Patroness of Hungary. Swiftly canonized after his death in 1038, **St Stephen** became a national talisman, his mummified right hand a holy relic, and his coronation regalia the symbol of statehood. Despite playing down his cult for decades, even the Communists eventually embraced it in a bid for some legitimacy, while nobody in post-Communist Hungary thinks it odd that the symbol of the republic should be the crown and cross of King Stephen.

entrance way – are antique shop fronts and interiors, and a model dog that raps on the glass with its paws, meant to attract passers-by into stores. The Catering – or Hospitality – section to the left pays homage to the restaurateur Károly Gundel and the confectioner Emil Gerbeaud and features furnishings from old coffee houses and a reconstructed bedroom from the *Hotel Gellért*.

The **Music History Museum** (Zenetörténeti Múzeum), at Táncsics Mihály utca 7, occupies the Baroque Erdödy Palace where Beethoven was a guest in 1800 and Bartók had his workshop before he emigrated. The museum is currently closed for refurbishment, and not due to reopen until 2007. The museum's collection includes scores of instruments representing three centuries of music, from a Holczman harp made for Marie Antoinette and a unique tongue-shaped violin to hurdy-gurdies, zithers, cowhorns and bagpipes, as well as the Bartók archives, amongst which are some of Bartók's scores and jottings.

Next door, **no. 9**, was once a barracks where the Habsburgs jailed Hungarian radicals such as Mihály Táncsics – after whom the street is named – but in an earlier age it was home to both Ashkenazi and Sephardic Jews, and called Zsidó utca (Jewish Street). The Ashkenazi community was established in the reign of Béla IV and encouraged by King Mátyás. Though you wouldn't think so from the outside, no. 26 contains a **Medieval Jewish Prayer House** (Középkori Zsidó Imaház; May–Oct Tues–Sun 10am–5pm; 400Ft) once used by the Sephardis. All that remains of its original decor are two Cabbalistic symbols painted on a wall, though the museum does its best to flesh out the history of the community with maps and prints – all the real treasures are in the Jewish Museum in Pest (see p.122).

Sparing a glance for the turbaned Turk's head above the doorway of no. 24, head on to **Bécsi kapu tér**, an inclined plaza named after the **Vienna Gate** that was erected on the 250th anniversary of the recapture of Buda. Beside it, the forbiddingly neo-Romanesque **National Archives** (no admission) guard the way to **Kapisztrán tér**, a larger square centred on the **Mary Magdalene Tower** (Magdolna-torony), whose accompanying church was wrecked in

World War II (though there are plans to rebuild it). In medieval times this was where Hungarian residents worshipped; Germans used the Mátyás Church. Today the tower boasts a peal of bells that jingles through a medley by the jazz pianist György Szabados, which includes Hungarian folk tunes, Chopin's *Études* and the theme from *The Bridge on the River Kwai*.

Beyond is a **statue of Friar John Capistranus**, who exhorted the Hungarians to victory at the siege of Belgrade in 1456, which the pope hailed by ordering church bells to be rung at noon throughout Europe. It shows Capistranus bestriding a dead Turk and is aptly located outside the **Military History Museum**, located in a former barracks on the north of the square (Hadtörténeti Múzeum; Tues–Sun: April–Sept 10am–6pm; Oct–March 10am–4pm; permanent displays free). This has gung-ho exhibitions on the history of hand-weapons from ancient times till the advent of firearms, and the birth and campaigns of the Honvéd (national army) during the 1848–49 War of Independence, but what sticks in the memory are the sections on the Hungarian Second Army that was decimated at Stalingrad – ask about seeing newsreel footage, as there are no regular shows. The entrance to the museum is on the Tóth Árpád sétány, a promenade lined with cannons and chestnut trees, overlooking the Buda Hills, which leads past a giant **flagpole** striped in Hungarian colours to the symbolic **grave of Abdurrahman**, the last Turkish Pasha of Buda, who died on the walls in 1686 – a "valient foe", according to the inscription.

Országház utca and Úri utca

Heading back towards Szentháromság tér, there's more to be seen on **Országház utca**, which was the district's main thoroughfare in the Middle Ages and known as the "street of baths" during Turkish times. Its present name, Parliament Street, recalls the sessions of the Diet held in the 1790s in a former Poor Clares' cloister at no. 28, where the Gestapo imprisoned 350 Hungarians and foreigners in 1945. No. 17, diagonally across the road, consists of two medieval houses joined together and has a relief of a croissant on its keystone from when it was a bakery. A few doors down from the former Parliament building, Renaissance sgraffiti survive on the underside of the bay window of no. 22 and a Gothic trefoil-arched cornice on the house next door, while the one beyond has been rebuilt according to its original fifteenth-century form.

The adjacent **Úri utca** (Gentleman Street) also boasts historic associations, for it was at the former Franciscan monastery at no. 51 that the five Hungarian Jacobins were held before being beheaded on the "Blood Meadow" below the hill in 1795. Next door is a wing of the Poor Clares' cloister that served as a postwar telephone exchange before being turned into a **Telephone Museum** (Telefónia Múzeum; Tues–Sun 10am–4pm; 200Ft; entrance from Országház utca 30 at weekends and holidays). The curator of the museum strives to explain the development of telephone exchanges since Tivadar Puskás introduced them to Budapest in the early 1900s – activating a noisy rotary one that's stood here since the 1930s – and you're invited to dial up commentaries in English or songs in Hungarian, check out the webcam and Internet facilities, and admire the personal phones of Emperor Franz Josef, Admiral Horthy and the Communist leader Kádár.

Further down the street on either side, notice the statues of the four seasons in the first-floor niches at nos. 54–56, Gothic sedilia in the gateway of nos. 48–50, and three arched windows and two diamond-shaped ones from the fourteenth and fifteenth centuries at no. 31.

South towards the palace

Heading south from Szentháromság tér towards the palace, you'll come to the intriguing **Golden Eagle Pharmacy Museum** (Arany Sas Patikamúzeum; Tues–Sun 10.30am–6.30pm; free) at Tárnok utca 18. The first pharmacy in Buda, established after the expulsion of the Turks, its original furnishings lend authenticity to dubious nostrums including the skull of a mummy used to make "Mumia" powder to treat epilepsy; there's also a reconstruction of an alchemist's laboratory, complete with dried bats and crocodiles, and other obscure exhibits such as the small, long-necked Roman glass vessel for collecting widows' tears. The museum has no handouts in English, but the staff can usually give a guide to the best bits. The *Tárnok* coffee house, next door but one, occupies one of the few buildings on the hill to have kept its Renaissance sgraffiti – a red and orange chequerboard pattern covering the facade.

A weirder attraction is the **Labyrinth of Buda Castle** (Budavári Labirintus), better known as the Várbarlang (Castle Caves). Cavities created by hot springs and cellars dug since medieval times form 10km of galleries, which were converted into an air-raid shelter in the 1930s and used as such in World War II. Having remained in military hands till the 1980s, it is now marketed as a New Age experience of shamanism and history. One section features copies of the cave paintings of Lascaux, while masked figures and a giant head sunken into the floor enliven other dank chambers. Guided tours leave from the main entrance at Úri utca 9 (daily 9.30am–7.30pm; 25min; 1200Ft; booking compulsory on ⓣ1/212-0207) and include a cup of tea at the end.

Both Tárnok utca and Úri utca end in **Dísz tér** (Parade Square), where the mournful Honvéd memorial presages the ramparts and gateways controlling access to the palace grounds. Ahead lies the scarred hulk of the old Ministry of Defence, while to your left is the **Castle Theatre** (Várszínház), where the first-ever play in Hungarian was staged in 1790 and Beethoven performed in 1808. The last building in the row is the **Sándor Palace** (Sándor Palota), formerly the prime minister's residence, where Premier Teleki shot himself in protest at Hungary joining the Nazi invasion of Yugoslavia. It is currently being restored.

Next door, the upper terminal of the **Sikló** funicular (see p.95) is separated from the terrace of Buda Palace by a stately gateway and the ferocious-looking **Turul statue**, a giant bronze eagle clasping a sword in its talons. In Magyar mythology the Turul sired the first dynasty of Hungarian kings by raping the grandmother of Prince Árpád, who led the tribes into Europe. During the nineteenth century it became a symbol of Hungarian identity in the face of Austrian culture, but wound up being co-opted by the Habsburgs, and has today been adopted as an emblem by Hungary's skinheads.

From here, you can descend a staircase to the **terrace** of the palace, commanding a sweeping **view** of Pest. Beyond the souvenir stalls prances an equestrian **statue of Prince Eugene of Savoy**, who liberated Buda in 1686. The bronze statues nearby represent **Csongor** and **Tünde**, the lovers in Vörösmarty's drama of the same name.

Buda Palace

As befits a former royal residence, the lineage of **Buda Palace** (Budavári palota) can be traced back to medieval times, with the rise and fall of various palaces on the hill reflecting the changing fortunes of the Hungarian state. The first fortifications and dwellings, hastily erected by Béla IV after the Mongol invasion of 1241–42, were replaced by the grander palaces of the Angevin kings, who ruled in more prosperous and stable times. This process reached its zenith in the reign of Mátyás Corvinus (1458–90), whose palace was a Renaissance extravaganza to which artists and scholars from all over Europe were drawn by the blandishments of Queen Beatrice and the prospect of lavish hospitality; the rooms had hot and cold running water, and during celebrations the fountains and gargoyles flowed with wine. After the Turkish occupation, and the long siege that ended it, only ruins were left – which the Habsburgs, Hungary's new rulers, levelled to build a palace of their own.

From Empress Maria Theresa's modest beginnings (a mere 203 rooms, which she never saw completed), the Royal Palace expanded inexorably throughout the nineteenth century, though no monarch ever lived here, only the Habsburg Palatine (viceroy). After the collapse of the empire following World War I, Admiral Horthy inhabited the building with all the pomp of monarchy until he was deposed by a German coup in October 1944. The palace was left unoccupied, and it wasn't long before the siege of Buda once again resulted in total devastation. Reconstruction work began in the 1950s in tandem with excavations of the medieval substrata beneath the rubble, which were incorporated in the new building, whose interior is far less elegant than the prewar version, being designed to accommodate cultural institutions.

Today, the complex houses the **Hungarian National Gallery** (Wings B, C and D), the **Budapest History Museum** (E) and the **National Széchenyi Library** (F). There are separate entrances for each.

The Hungarian National Gallery

Most people's first port of call is the **Hungarian National Gallery** (Magyar Nemzeti Galéria; Tues–Sun 10am–6pm; free for permanent displays, 800Ft for visiting shows), devoted to Hungarian art from the Middle Ages to the present. It contains much that's superb, but the vastness of the collection and the confusing layout can be fatiguing. Though all the paintings are labelled in English, other details are scanty, so it's worth investing in a guidebook or guided tour (3000Ft for up to five people; ⓣ60/20-439 7331). The main entrance is on the eastern side of Wing C, overlooking the river, behind the statue of Eugene of Savoy. Don't buy a special ticket (500Ft) to see the separate **Habsburg crypt** until you've checked that a tour is scheduled, as they require at least 25 people. The crypt contains the tombs of several Habsburgs who ruled as Palatine, or viceroy, of Hungary up until 1849.

On the **ground floor** of the museum, marble reliefs of Beatrice and Mátyás and a wooden ceiling from a sixteenth-century church are the highlights of a **Medieval and Renaissance Lapidarium**, which you need to pass through to reach the fantastic collection of fifteenth-century **Gothic altarpieces** at the rear of Wing D. Notice the varied reactions to the *Death of the Virgin* from Kassa and the gloating spectators in the Jánosrét *Passion*. From the same church comes a *St Nicholas* altar as long as a limo and lurid as a comic strip. The pointed finials on the high altar from Liptószentmária anticipate the winged altarpieces of the sixteenth century on the floor above. To get there without returning to the foyer, use the small staircase near the altarpieces and turn left, left and left again at the top.

The **first floor** picks up where downstairs left off by displaying **late Gothic altarpieces** with soaring pinnacles. Much of the **Baroque** art in the adjacent section once belonged to Prince Miklós Esterházy or was confiscated from private owners in the 1950s. Don't miss Ádám Mányoki's portrait of Ferenc Rákóczi II, a sober look at a national hero that foreshadowed a whole artistic genre in the nineteenth century. This and other **National Historical** art fills the central block, where you'll be confronted by two vast canvases as you come up the staircase: *Zrínyi's Sortie* by Peter Krafft depicting the suicidal sally of the defenders of Szigetvár, and the *Reoccupying of Buda Castle* by Gyula Benczúr. In Wing B, Benczúr's *The Baptism of Vajk* portrays St Stephen's conversion to Christianity, while Bertalan Székely's *Recovering the Corpse of Louis II* depicts the aftermath of the catastrophic defeat at Mohács. The rest of Wing B covers other trends in nineteenth-century art, with sections devoted to **Mihály Munkácsy** and **László Paál** – exhibited together since both painted landscapes, though Paál did little else whereas Munkácsy was internationally renowned for pictures with a social message – and **Pál Szinyei Merse**, the "father of Hungarian Impressionism", whose models and subjects were cheerfully bourgeois.

Walking upstairs to the **second floor**, you come face to face with three huge canvases by the visionary artist **Tivadar Kosztka Csontváry**, whose obsession with the Holy Land and the "path of the sun" inspired scenes like *Look Down on the Dead Sea* and *Ruins of the Greek Theatre at Taormina*. When Picasso saw an exhibition of his works years later, he remarked: "And I thought I was the only great painter of our century." There are six more, smaller, Csontvárys amongst the **twentieth-century art** in Wing D, which is largely attributable to members of the Gödöllő and Nagybánya artists' colonies. The chief exponent of Art Nouveau in Hungary was **József Rippl-Rónai**, whose portraits were little recognized in his lifetime but are now regarded as classics. Other trends such as Post-Impressionism are represented by works like Ödön Márffy's Cézanne-like *The Old Toll House at Vác*, but there's less abstract art than you'd expect from the 1930s and 1940s.

Since all the Socialist art was evicted in the 1990s, the **third floor** has been used for temporary exhibitions of graphics or photos by Hungarian artists.

The Mátyás Fountain and National Széchenyi Library

The courtyard outside is flanked on three sides by the palace, and overlooks Buda to the west. In the far corner stands the flamboyant **Mátyás Fountain**, whose bronze figures recall the legend of Szép Ilonka. This beautiful peasant girl met the king while he was hunting incognito, fell in love with him, and died of a broken heart after discovering his identity and realizing the futility of her hopes. The man with a falcon is the king's Italian chronicler, who recorded the story for posterity. It is also enshrined in a poem by Vörösmarty.

A lofty gateway guarded by lions – roaring on the inside, but peaceful on the outside – leads into the **Lion Courtyard**, flanked on the right by the **National Széchenyi Library** (Országos Széchenyi Könyvtár), whose full size is only apparent from the far side of the hill, where it looms over Dózsa tér like a mountain. Founded in 1802 on the initiative of Count Ferenc Széchenyi (the father of István who spearheaded the Reform era), it is a repository for publications in Hungarian and material relating to the country from around the world and receives a copy of every book and newspaper published in Hungary. Its reading room is open to the public (Mon 1–9pm, Tues–Sat 9am–9pm; free) and there are temporary exhibitions on diverse subjects. During library hours, a passenger **lift** (100Ft) at the rear of the adjacent building by the Lion gateway provides direct access to and from Dózsa tér, at the foot of the Vár.

The Budapest History Museum

On the far side of the courtyard, the **Budapest History Museum** (Budapest Történeti Múzeum; mid-May to mid-Sept daily 10am–6pm; mid-Sept to Oct daily except Tues 10am–6pm; Nov–Feb daily except Tues 10am–4pm; March to mid-May daily except Tues 10am–6pm; 800Ft) covers two millennia on three floors before descending into the vaulted, flagstoned halls of palaces of old. Due to the ravages inflicted by the Mongols and the Turks there's little to show from the time of the Conquest or Hungary's medieval civilization, so most of the second floor is occupied by **Budapest in Modern Times**, an exhibition that gives an insight into urban planning, fashions, trade and vices from 1686 onwards, with items ranging from an 1880s barrel organ to one of the Swedish Red Cross notices affixed to Jewish safe houses by Wallenberg (see p.115). The **remains of the medieval palace** are reached from the basement via an eighteenth-century cellar. A wing of the ground floor of King Sigismund's palace and the cellars beneath the Corvin Library form a stratum overlaying the **Royal Chapel** and a **Gothic Hall** displaying statues found in 1974. In another chamber are portions of red marble fireplaces and a massive portal carved with cherubs and flowers, from King Mátyás's palace. Emerging into daylight, bear left and up the stairs to reach another imposing hall, with a view over the castle ramparts.

If you feel like walking down the hillside into the Víziváros, the river-facing route switchbacks past a Rondella and the former **Palace Gardens** (whose crumbling statues and terraces are on the World Monument Fund's list of endangered sites) to end up at the lower terminal of the Sikló. Aiming for the Tabán (see p.97), it's better to leave the castle grounds by the **Ferdinánd Gate** near the Mace Tower, from which steps run directly down to Szarvas tér.

The Víziváros

Originally a poor quarter where fishermen, craftsmen and their families lived, the **Víziváros** (Watertown) between the Vár and the Danube was repopulated after the expulsion of the Turks by Croatian and Serbian mercenaries and their camp followers. Today it's a reclusive neighbourhood of mansions and old buildings meeting at odd angles on the hillside, reached by alleys which mostly consist of steps rising from the main street, **Fő utca**. Some of these are still lit by gas lamps and look quite Dickensian on misty evenings.

Batthyány tér and around

The Víziváros's main square, named **Batthyány tér** after the nineteenth-century prime minister, was originally called Bomba tér after the ammunition depot sited here for the defence of the Danube waterway. Now home to a long-established market and the underground interchange between the red metro line and the HÉV rail line to Szentendre, it's always busy with shoppers and commuters. To the right of the market is a sunken, two-storey building that used to be the *White Cross Inn*, where Casanova reputedly once stayed. Many of the older buildings in this area are sunken in this way: ground level was raised several feet in the nineteenth century to combat flooding. The twin-towered **St Anna Parish Church**, on the corner of the square, sports the Buda coat of arms on its tympanum.

Heading south along Fő utca, you'll see a spiky polychrome-tiled church on **Szilágyi Desző tér**, alongside the embankment. It was here that the Arrow Cross massacred hundreds of Jews, shooting them into the river in January of 1945, when Eichmann and the SS had already fled the city, which was by then encircled by the Red Army. An inconspicuous plaque commemorates the victims. Further on, you can see the old **Capuchin Church** featuring Turkish window arches, at no. 30 on the left-hand side, and the **Institut Français** at no. 17, a block or two before you emerge onto Clark Ádám tér, facing the Chain Bridge; the Institut celebrates Bastille Day with an outdoor concert beside the Danube.

The Chain Bridge, Sikló and Kilometre Zero

As the first permanent link between Buda and Pest, the majestic **Széchenyi Chain Bridge** (Széchenyi Lánchíd) has a special place in the hearts of locals, for whom it is a symbol of civic endurance. Austrian troops tried and failed to destroy it in 1849, but in 1945 the bridge fell victim to the Wehrmacht, who dynamited all of Budapest's bridges in a bid to check the Red Army. Their reconstruction was one of the first tasks of the postwar era; the Chain Bridge reopened on November 21, 1949, on the centenary of its inauguration. The bridge is now commemorated with its own **Bridge Festival** in June, and in summer it is often closed to traffic at weekends.

The bridge was the brainchild of **Count István Széchenyi**, a horse-fancying Anglophile with a passion for innovation, who founded the Academy of Sciences and brought steam engines to Hungary, amongst other achievements. Designed by **William Tierney Clark**, it was constructed under the supervision of a Scottish engineer, **Adam Clark** (no relation), who personally thwarted the Austrian attempts to destroy it by flooding the chain-lockers. Whereas Széchenyi later died in an asylum, having witnessed the triumph (and subsequent defeat) of Kossuth and the 1848 Revolution, Adam Clark settled happily in Budapest with his Hungarian wife.

During his time in Budapest, Clark also built the **tunnel** (*alagút*) under the Vár which, Budapesters joked, could be used to store the new bridge when it rained. Next to the tunnel entrance on the river end is the lower terminal of the **Sikló**, a nineteenth-century **funicular** running up to the palace (daily 7.30am–10pm, closed every other Monday; 600Ft uphill, 500Ft downhill). Constructed on the initiative of Ödön, Széchenyi's son, it was only the second funicular in the world when it was inaugurated in 1870, and functioned without a hitch until wrecked by a shell in 1945. The yellow carriages are exact replicas of the originals, but are now lifted by an electric winch rather than a steam engine. In the small park at its foot stands **Kilometre Zero**, a zero-shaped monument from which all distances from Budapest are measured.

Around the Király Baths and Bem tér

The area **north from Batthyány tér** to the Király Baths (strictly speaking part of the Víziváros) can be reached by heading up Fő utca, past the gloomy premises of the **Military Court of Justice** (nos. 70–72), where Imre Nagy and other leaders of the 1956 Uprising were tried and executed in 1958. The square outside has now been renamed after Nagy, whose body lay in an unmarked grave in the New Public Cemetery for over thirty years, and makes a suitably emollient site for the new Foreign Ministry building.

You can identify the **Király Baths** (women: Mon, Wed & Fri 7am–6pm; men Tues, Thurs & Sat 9am–8pm; 1100Ft; maximum stay 1hr 30min Mon–Fri, 1hr Sat; last tickets 1hr before closing), at Fő utca 82–86, by the four copper cupolas, shaped like tortoise shells, poking from its eighteenth-century facade. The octagonal pool – lit by star-shaped apertures in the dome – was built by the Turks in 1570 for the Buda garrison. The baths' name, meaning "king", comes from that of the König family who owned them in the eighteenth century. The baths have become a major meeting place for gay men.

A couple of blocks further north, **Bem tér** was named after the Polish general Joseph Bem, who fought for the Hungarians in the 1849 War of Independence. Traditionally a site for demonstrations, it was here that crowds assembled on October 23, 1956, prior to marching on Parliament, bearing Hungarian flags with the hammer and sickle cut out, hours before the Uprising. The square was also the focus for peace demonstrations and protests against the Nagymaros

▲ Chain bridge and Parliament

Dam (see box on p.185) during the 1980s.

At Bem utca 20, 200m west from the square, the **Foundry Museum** (Öntödei Múzeum; Tues–Sun 9am–4pm; free) is housed in the ironworks founded by Abrahám Ganz in 1844, which grew into a massive industrial complex. The huge ladles and jib-cranes are still in their original setting, while the museum's collection includes some fine cast-iron stoves.

The Tabán, Gellért-hegy and beyond

South of the Vár lies the **Tabán** district, once Buda's artisan quarter, inhabited by Serbs (known as *Rác* in Hungarian), and subsequently a seedy pleasure zone until the area was razed in the 1930s and replaced by an anodyne park that was later carved up by flyovers. Thankfully, the city planners spared Tabán's historic Turkish baths, and its traditions of lusty nightlife have been revived by the neighbouring outdoor bars.

The Tabán and its Turkish baths

In the more sedate reaches of the Tabán below the Vár, the **Semmelweis Medical Museum** at Apród utca 1–3 (March–Oct Tues–Sun 10.30am–6pm, Nov–Feb Tues–Sun 10.30am–4pm; Ⓦwww.semmelweis.museum.hu; free) honours the "saviour of mothers", Ignác Semmelweis (1815–65). He discovered the cause of puerperal fever (a form of blood poisoning contracted in childbirth) and a simple method for preventing the disease, which until then was usually fatal: the sterilization of instruments and the washing of hands with carbolic soap. Inside are displayed medical instruments through the ages, including such curios as a chastity belt. The small insignificant stones in the park behind the museum are in fact Turkish burial markers.

An even better reason to come to the Tabán, though, is to visit its Turkish baths, where you can immerse yourself in history. The relaxing and curative effects of Buda's **mineral springs** have been appreciated for two thousand years. The Romans built splendid bathhouses at Aquincum, to the north of Buda, and, while these declined with the empire, interest revived after the Knights of St John built a hospice on the site of the present Rudas Baths, near where St Elizabeth cured lepers in the springs below Gellért-hegy. However, it was the Turks who consolidated the habit of bathing – as Muslims, they were obliged to wash five times daily in preparation for prayer – and constructed proper bathhouses which function to this day.

Two lie at the southern end of the Tabán by the Buda bridgehead of the Erzsébet Bridge. Tucked under the main road that leads up the hill away from the bridge, Hegyalja út, the **Rác Baths** are closed as part of a major redevelopment due for completion in 2007 that includes building a hotel and an underground car park. The baths retain an octagonal stone pool from Turkish times. Heading on towards the Rudas Baths, you pass the **Ivócsarnok** (Water Hall) below the road to the Erzsébet Bridge – drinking water from three nearby springs is sold here (Mon, Wed & Fri 11am–6pm, Tues & Thurs 7am–2pm).

South of the Erzsébet Bridge, the men-only **Rudas Baths** (Mon–Fri 6am–7pm, Sat & Sun 6am–1pm; 1100Ft) are outwardly nondescript, but the interior has hardly changed since it was constructed in 1556 on the orders of Pasha Sokoli Mustapha. Tselebi called this place the "bath with green pillars", and these columns can still be seen today. Bathers wallow in an octagonal stone pool with steam billowing around the shadowy recesses and shafts of light pouring in from the star-shaped apertures in the domed ceiling.

Bathing matters

Most baths are divided into a **swimming** area and a separate section for **thermal baths** (*gyógyfürdő* or the *göz*, as they are popularly known). The bath experience can be daunting, as little is written in English once you are inside and attendants are unlikely to speak much more than Hungarian and a smattering of German. However, the basic system of attendants and cabins is the same in most baths, and once you get the hang of the rituals, it is most rewarding.

A basic ticket from the ticket office (*pénztár*) covers two hours in the sauna, steamrooms and pools; supplementary tickets will buy you a massage (*masszázs*), tub (*kádfürdő*) or mud bath (*iszapfürdő*). In some baths you pay for these treatments on the spot. Inside the changing room (*öltöző*) an attendant will direct you to a cabin, and in single-sex steam baths where swimsuits are still rare, they will give you a *kötény* – a small loincloth for men or an apron for women – which offers a vestige of cover. Once you've changed, find the attendant again, who will lock your door. You will get a key which you should tie to the strings of your *kötény* as you set off – taking with you any other tickets for massages etc and a towel if you want to use your own. A popular sequence in the thermal baths is: sauna, warm pool, steamroom, cold plunge, hot plunge (the last makes your skin tingle wonderfully), followed by a dip in warm water, and then start again. However, it's entirely up to you, and the main thing is not to stay longer in any one section if you feel uncomfortable. As you leave, take a sheet to dry yourself, relax in the rest room if you feel exhausted, and then find the attendant to unlock your cabin. It is usual to tip the attendant a couple of hundred forints. In many pools bathing caps (*uszósapka*) are compulsory; like swimsuits and towels, they can be rented at the *pénztár*.

Gellért-hegy

Gellért-hegy is as much a feature of the waterfront panorama as the Vár and the Parliament building: a craggy dolomite cliff rearing 130m above the embankment of the Danube, surmounted by the Liberation Monument and the Citadella. The hill is named after Bishop Ghirardus (Gellért in Hungarian), who converted pagan Magyars to Christianity at the behest of King Stephen. After his royal protector's demise, vengeful heathens strapped Gellért to a barrow and toppled him off the cliff, where a **statue of St Gellért** now stands astride a waterfall facing the Erzsébet Bridge.

Before ascending the hill, take a look at the **Gellért Hotel** facing the Szabadság Bridge, a famous Art Nouveau establishment opened in 1918, which Admiral Horthy commandeered following his triumphal entry into "sinful Budapest" in 1920. During the 1930s and 1940s, its balls were the highlight of Budapest's social calendar, when debutantes danced on a glass floor laid over its pool. The attached **Gellért Baths** are magnificently appointed with majolica tiles and mosaics, and a columned, Roman-style **thermal pool**, with lion-headed spouts. To enjoy its waters (May–Sept daily 6am–7pm, July & Aug Fri & Sat also 8pm–midnight; Oct–April Mon–Fri 6am–7pm, Sat & Sun 6am–5pm; 2400Ft for basic ticket with locker, 2900Ft with cubicle, and 900Ft back if you leave within 2hr, 500Ft in 3hr, 200Ft in 4hr), you must first reach the changing rooms by a labyrinth of passages; staff are usually helpful with directions. At the far end of the pool are steps leading down to the separate **thermal baths** (daily 6am–6pm), with segregated areas and ornate plunge pools for men and women. Tickets cover both sections, and towels, bathrobes, bathing caps and swimsuits can be rented. In the summer you can also use the **outdoor pools**, including one with a wave machine, on the terraces behind the main baths.

On the hillside opposite the entrance to the baths lies the sepulchral **Cave Church** (Sziklatemplom) where Mass is conducted by white-robed monks of the Pauline order – Hungary's only indigenous order (founded in 1256). The order once provided confessors to the monarchy, and had a monastery beside the church, until the whole order was arrested by the ÁVO at midnight Mass on Easter Monday, 1951, and the chapel was sealed up until 1989. Flickering candles and mournful organ music create an eerie atmosphere during services (daily 8.30–9.30am, 11am–noon, 4.30–6.30pm & 8–9pm), but tourists are only allowed to enter between times. Outside the entrance stands a **statue of St Stephen** with his horse.

The Liberation Monument and Citadella

By following one of the steep paths opposite the *Gellért Hotel* you can reach the **summit** of Gellért-hegy in about twenty minutes. Though it's quite a slog, it's not as laborious as the alternative: catching a #18 or #19 tram from Szt. Gellért tér to Móricz Zsigmond körtér and then bus #27 to the last stop, from where it's a ten-minute walk. Either way, the **panoramic view** from the top is stunning, drawing one's eye slowly along the curving river, past bridges and monumental landmarks, and on to the Buda Hills and Pest's suburbs, merging hazily with the distant plain.

On the summit stands the **Liberation Monument** – a female figure brandishing the palm of victory over 30m aloft. The monument's history is ironic, since it was originally commissioned by Admiral Horthy in memory of his son – killed in a plane crash on the Eastern Front – but was ultimately dedicated to the Soviet troops who died liberating Budapest from the Nazis. Its sculptor, Zsigmond Kisfaludi-Strobl, substituted a palm branch for the propeller it was meant to hold and added a statue of a Red Army soldier at the base of the monument, to gain approval as a "Proletarian Artist". Having previously specialized in busts of the aristocracy, he was henceforth known by his compatriots as "Kisfaludi-Strébel" (*strébel* meaning "to climb" or "step from side to side"). The monument survived calls for its removal following the end of Communism, but its inscription was rewritten to honour those who died for "Hungary's prosperity", and the Soviet soldier was banished to the Statue Park (see p.100).

The **Citadella** or fortress behind the monument was built by the Habsburgs to dominate the city in the aftermath of the 1848–49 Revolution. When the historic Compromise was reached in 1867, Budapest's citizens breached the walls to affirm that it no longer posed a threat to them – though in fact an SS regiment did later hole up in the citadel during World War II. Today, it contains a tourist hostel and an informative outdoor museum relating the hill's history, but it's the stunning view from the ramparts that justifies the 300Ft admission charge.

Farkasréti Cemetery

Two kilometres west of Gellért-hegy in the hilly XI district is the **Farkasréti Cemetery** (Farkasréti temető; Mon–Fri 7am–9pm, Sat & Sun 9am–5pm; free), easily reached by riding tram #59 from Moszkva tér to the end of the line. Of the many poets, writers and musicians buried in the "Wolf's Meadow Cemetery", the best known is **Béla Bartók**, whose remains were ceremonially reinterred in 1988 following their return from America, where the composer died in exile in 1945. His will forbade reburial in Hungary so long as there were streets named after Hitler or Mussolini, but the return of his body was delayed for decades to prevent the Communists from capitalizing on the event. In 1998 the Hungarian-born conductor **Sir Georg Solti** was buried alongside Bartók, having forged a career abroad since he left Hungary in 1939 to meet Toscanini and thus escape the fate of his Jewish parents. Farkasréti also contains the grave of **Mátyás Rákosi**, Hungary's Stalinist dictator, who died in exile in the USSR, as well as many wooden grave markers inscribed in the ancient runic Székely alphabet. However, the real attraction is the amazing **mortuary chapel** by Imre Makovecz – one of his finest designs – whose wood-ribbed vault resembles the throat and belly of a beast. Be discreet, however, for the chapel is in constant use by mourners. Visitors keen to see more of Makovecz's work could pay a visit to Visegrád (p.166), an hour's journey north of the capital.

Statue Park

Further out of the city is one of Budapest's most popular tourist attractions, the **Statue Park** (Szoborpark; daily 10am–dusk; 600Ft; ⓣ1/424 7500; ⓦwww.szoborpark.hu), which brings together 42 of the monuments that once glorified Communism. The park is situated way out beside Balatoni út in the XXII district, 15km from the city centre, and getting there involves taking a red-numbered bus #7-173 from Ferenciek tere to Etele tér, and then a yellow Volán bus from stand #7-8 towards Diósd, which takes twenty minutes to reach the park. More expensive but simpler is the special Statue Park bus that leaves from in front of *Le Meridien* hotel by Deák tér (see p.111) at 11am daily throughout the year, as well as at 3pm March to Oct, with additional services at 10am and 4pm in July and August (2450Ft including entry to the park).

Clearly visible from the highway, a bogus Classical facade frames giant statues of Lenin, Marx and Engels. Lenin's once stood beside the Városliget, while those of Marx and Engels are carved from granite quarried at Mauthausan, the Nazi concentration camp later used by the Soviets. Inside the grounds you'll encounter the Red Army soldier that guarded the Liberation Monument and dozens of other statues and memorials. Artistically, the best are the Republic of Councils Monument – a colossal charging sailor based on a 1919 revolutionary poster – and Imre Varga's Béla Kun Memorial, showing Kun making a speech from a platform amid a surging crowd of workers and soldiers (plus a bystander with an umbrella). Budapesters fondly remember the statue of Captain Ostapenko that once stood on the highway to the Balaton and Vienna, where hitchhikers would arrange to meet their friends.

Among the souvenirs on sale in the park are candles in the form of Stalin and Lenin, cans of air from "the last breath of socialism", and selections of old revolutionary songs, which can be heard playing from a 1950s radio set. There's also an informative English-language brochure available (600Ft).

The Nagytétényi Castle Museum

Even more distant than the Statue Park, the **Nagytétényi Castle Museum** (Nagytétényi Kastélymúzeum; Tues–Sun 10am–6pm; free, 400Ft for temporary displays; cameras 400Ft, videocameras 1000Ft; ⓦwww.nagytetenyi.hu) is strictly for furniture buffs – so think twice before undertaking the lengthy (30–45min) journey by bus #3 from Móricz Zsigmond körtér. Get off at the Petőfi utca stop in the XXII district, cross the road and follow Pohár utca into a park, to find the *kastély*. Though rendered as "castle" in English, "*kastély*" generally signifies a manor house or chateau without fortifications, which Hungarian nobles began building after the Turks had been expelled – in this case, by converting an older, ruined castle into a Baroque residence. Nowadays, its 29 rooms display furniture from the Gothic to the Biedermeier epochs, owned by the Museum of Applied Arts; the most outstanding is a walnut-veneered refectory from Trencsen Monastery. In July and August, **historical dances** and **concerts** are held in the grounds (ⓣ1/207 0005 for information).

Around Moszkva tér and the Rózsadomb

The area immediately north of the Vár is largely defined by the transport hub of **Moszkva tér** and the reclusive residential quarter covering the **Rózsadomb** (Rose Hill), but the **Millenarium Park** and Mammut malls have created a focus for the area, whose interest previously lay in the ambience of the Rózsadomb, Gül Baba's tomb in the backstreets, and easy access to the Buda Hills.

Moszkva tér and the Millenarium Park

Once a quarry, and subsequently an ice rink and tennis courts, the busy transport nexus of **Moszkva tér** (Moscow Square) has kept its name due to the sheer cost of renaming all the vehicles, maps and signs on which it appears. Among the useful services that run from here are the red metro; bus #22 to Budakeszi; bus or tram #56 to Hűvösvölgy; and trams #4 and #6 to Margit sziget and Pest's Nagykörút. Trams #4 and #6 run along Margit körút, past the **Mammut malls** (fronted by a statue of the woolly beast), and can get you within walking distance of Gül Baba's tomb (see below).

The main attraction of the area lies behind the mall, where the site of the former Ganz Machine Works has been transformed into the **Millenarium Park**, with water features, vineyards and plots of corn to represent different regions of Hungary. Kids can be let loose on the fantastic **playground**, while visitors of all ages can enjoy the performances at the outdoor theatre (1000Ft), concerts (800–1500Ft) and the diverse, ever-changing rota of events and exhibitions (mostly free) in the converted factory buildings (Ⓣ1/438 5335 Ⓦwww.millenaris.hu). A free Internet café – eMagyarország – operates in C Building (one-hour limit).

The Rózsadomb

Budapest's most exclusive neighbourhood lies beyond smog-ridden **Margit körút** and the backstreets off Moszkva tér. If you're coming from Bem tér, consider a preliminary detour to the rather over-restored **tomb of Gül Baba** on Mecset utca, just above Margit körút (May–Oct Tues–Sun 10am–6pm; 400Ft). This small octagonal building is a shrine to the "Father of the Roses", a Sufi Dervish who participated in the Turkish capture of Buda but died during the thanksgiving service afterwards. Restored in the late 1980s with funds from the Turkish government, the tomb now stands in a pristine little park with marble fountains and arabesque tiles. Carpets and examples of calligraphy adorn the shrine, which fittingly stands in a rose garden, surrounded by a colonnaded parapet with fine views.

The **Rózsadomb** (Rose Hill) itself is as much a social category as a neighbourhood, for a list of residents would read like a Hungarian *Who's Who*. During the Communist era this included the top Party *funcionárusok*, whose homes featured secret exits that enabled several ÁVO chiefs to escape lynching during the Uprising. Nowadays, wealthy film directors and entrepreneurs predominate, and the sloping streets are lined with spacious villas and flashy cars.

Heading downhill to the riverbank just north of Margit Bridge, you can find the Neoclassical **Lukács Baths**, harbouring a mixed thermal pool and a small swimming pool (Mon–Sat 6am–7pm, Sun 6am–5pm; 1400Ft, 500Ft back if you leave within 2hr, 300Ft in 3hr, 100Ft in 4hr). To reach the baths you pass through a ticket hall that wouldn't look amiss in a mansion, and a courtyard lined with plaques of gratitude in different languages from those who have benefited from the medicinal waters. The adjacent **Császár Komjádi Pool** has a Turkish bath-hall dating from the sixteenth century and still in use, plus an excellent modern outdoor swimming pool that gets covered over in winter (Mon–Sat 6am–9pm, Sun 6am–7pm; 800Ft; hats compulsory in the pool); the entrance to both is on the embankment side.

Óbuda and Aquincum

The district of **Óbuda**, up the river bank to the north, is the oldest part of Budapest, though that's hardly the impression given by the factories and high-rises that dominate the area today, hiding such ancient ruins as remain. Nonetheless it was here that the Romans built a legionary camp and a civilian town, later taken over by the Huns. This developed into an important town under the Hungarian Árpád dynasty, but after the fourteenth century it was eclipsed by the Vár. The original settlement became known as Óbuda (Old Buda) and was incorporated into the newly formed Budapest in 1873. The best-preserved ruins lie further north, in the **Rómaifürdő** district, accessible by HÉV train from Batthyány tér or Margit híd.

Óbuda

The section of Óbuda **around Fő tér** blends gaudy Baroque with modern art and overpriced gastronomy, within a minute's walk of the Árpád híd HÉV stop. At Szentlélek tér 1, the former Zichy mansion now contains the **Kassák Museum** (Tues–Sun 10am–6pm; 150Ft), dedicated to the Hungarian constructivist Lajos Kassák. Next door is the **Vasarely Museum** (Tues–Sun 10am–5.30pm; free), displaying eyeball-throbbing Op Art paintings by Viktor Vasarely, one of the founders of the genre. On cobbled Fő tér, just around the corner, you'll find the swanky *Sipos Halászkert* and *Postakocsi* restaurants. Whatever the weather, there are always several figures sheltering beneath umbrellas nearby: life-sized sculptures by Imre Varga, whose oeuvre is the subject of the **Varga Museum** at Laktanya utca 7 (Tues–Sun 10am–6pm; 400Ft). His sheet-metal, iron and bronze effigies of famous persons are full of pathos or humour.

Although the largest site lies further out in the Rómaifürdő district, Óbuda does have several excavated ruins to show for its past. The finest of them is the weed-choked, crumbling amphitheatre (*amfiteátrum*) at the junction of Nagyszombat and Pacsirtamező utca, which once seated up to 16,000 spectators. The amphitheatre can be reached by bus #86 (from Batthyány tér or anywhere along the embankment), or by walking 400m north from Kolosy tér (near the Szépvölgyi út HÉV stop). From here, you can continue on to Flórián tér and the Hercules Villa (see below) by bus #6 or #86. While you're in the area, sample two patisseries renowned for their ice creams: *Veress*, on the corner of Bokor utca leading south from the amphitheatre; and *Daubner*, up on Szépvölgyi út, which leads towards the hills and caves (see p.104).

Two kilometres north of the amphitheatre at Flórián tér, graceful Roman columns stand incongruously amid a shopping plaza and the legionary baths lurk beneath the Szentendrei út flyover. From here it's a ten-minute walk to the remains of the **Hercules Villa** (Tues–Sun: May–Sept 10am–6pm; late April & Oct 10am–5pm; 100Ft), sheltered by three canopies behind a block of flats at Meggyfa utca 19–21. The villa's name derives from the third-century mosaic floor beneath the largest canopy. Originally composed of 60,000 stones carefully selected and arranged in Alexandria, it depicts Hercules about to vomit at a wine festival. Another mosaic portrays the centaur Nessus abducting Deianeira, whom Hercules had to rescue as one of his twelve labours.

Aquincum and Rómaifürdő

The legionary garrison of six thousand spawned a settlement of camp-followers – Aquincum (meaning "Five waters") – which, over time, became a *municipium* and later a *colonia*, the provincial capital of Pannonia Inferior. The extensive **ruins of Aquincum** (Tues–Sun: May–Sept 9am–6pm; Oct & late April 9am–5pm; 700Ft) are visible from the Aquincum HÉV stop, while the remains of an **aqueduct** and another **amphitheatre** lie near the next HÉV stop, Rómaifürdő (Roman Bath).

Enough foundation walls and underground piping survive to give a fair idea of the layout of Aquincum, with its forum and law courts, its sanctuaries of the goddesses Epona and Fortuna Augusta, and the collegia and bathhouses where fraternal societies met. Its bare bones are given substance by an excellent **museum** (same hours; 300Ft) and smaller exhibitions around the site. You can discover how the Romans dressed (in clothes replicated by the Applied Arts Museum) and see a host of relics, some found only recently during the construction of shopping malls. A mummy preserved in natron, a cult-relief of the god Mithras and a reconstructed water-organ are the star attractions.

The Buda Hills

Thirty minutes or less by bus from Moszkva tér, the **Buda Hills** provide a welcome respite from Budapest's summertime heat. While some parts can be crowded at the weekend with walkers and mountain-bikers, it's possible to ramble through the woods for hours and see hardly a soul during the week. If your time is limited, the most rewarding options are the "**railway circuit**" or a visit to the **caves** – though the Bartók or Kiscelli **museums** will be irresistible to some.

The "railway circuit" and Budakeszi Game Park

An easy and enjoyable way to visit the hills that will especially appeal to kids is a return trip on the "railway circuit". This can can take anything from under two hours if connections click and you don't dawdle, to a full afternoon if the opposite applies. It begins with a short ride on tram #18 or #56 or bus #56 from Moszkva tér, out along Szilágyi Erzsébet fasor, to the lower terminal of the **Cogwheel Railway** (Fogaskerekű vasút; daily 5am–11pm; 145Ft, or ordinary public transport tickets also valid – see p.74). From here a small train clicks up through the **Svábhegy** suburb every ten minutes or so, past the world-famous **Pető Institute** for conductive therapy, to the summit of Széchenyi-hegy.

The terminal of the **Children's Railway** (Gyermekvasút), a narrow-gauge line that's almost entirely run by 10- to 14-year-olds, is a short walk across the park. Built by youth brigades in 1948, it enables kids who fancy a career with MÁV, the Hungarian State Railways, to get hands-on experience. Watching them wave flags, collect tickets and salute departures with solemnity, you can see why it appealed to the Communists. Until 1990 it was known as the Pioneers' Railway after the organization that replaced the disbanded Scouts and Guides movements (now re-formed). Trains depart regularly for the eleven-kilometre, 45-minute journey to Hűvösvölgy (every 45min–1hr; June–Aug daily 9am–5pm; Sept–May Tues–Sun same hours; 250Ft), stopping at various points en route.

The first stop, **Normafa**, is a popular excursion centre with a modest **ski-run**. Its name comes from a performance of the aria from Bellini's *Norma* given here by the actress Rozália Klein in 1840. Across the road, the humble *Rétes büfé* serves delicious strudel and coffee every day of the year including holidays. **János-hegy**, three stops on, is the highest point in Budapest. On the 527-metre-high summit, fifteen minutes' climb from the station, the **Erzsébet lookout tower** offers a panoramic view of the city and the Buda Hills. By the buffet below the summit is the upper terminal of the **chairlift** (daily: May–Sept 9.30am–5pm; Oct–April 9.30am–4pm; closed every other Mon; 400Ft) down to Zugliget, whence #158 buses return to Moszkva tér.

Nature-lovers can combine the circuit with a visit to the **Budakeszi Game Park** (daily 9am–dusk; 400Ft), bearing in mind that its ticket office closes at 4pm on weekdays and 6pm at weekends and on holidays. The park is accessible from the main road near the Szépjuhászné railway halt, one stop on from János-hegy (walk to the main road and catch bus #22), or from Moszkva tér, by express or regular bus #22 – get off at the MÁV Sanatorium stop and follow the Vadaspark signs for about 1km. Beyond the exhibition centre lie woods and fields inhabited by red, roe and shovel-antlered fallow deer, wild boar, mallards, pheasants and other birds. Shameless carnivores can savour these delicacies at the *Vadaspark* restaurant near the entrance.

Wild boars – which roam in the evening and sleep by day – are occasionally sighted in the forests above **Hárshegy**, one stop before Hűvösvölgy, the final stop of the Children's Railway. Also linked directly to Moszkva tér by #56 and #56E (nonstop) buses, **Hűvösvölgy** (Cool Valley) is the site of the popular *Náncsi Néni* restaurant (see p.133).

Stalactite caves and other sights

The more northerly Buda Hills harbour a second clutch of attractions, best reached in a separate excursion from Kolosy tér in Óbuda (near Szépvölgyi út HÉV stop). Ride bus #65 for five stops out to Szépvölgyi út 162 to find the **Pálvölgyi Stalactite Caves** (Pálvölgyi cseppkőbarlang; hourly tours Tues–Sun 10am–4pm; 40min; 700Ft, joint ticket with Szemlőhegyi Cave 900Ft). The tour of this spectacular labyrinth starts on the lowest level, which boasts rock formations such as the "Organ Pipes" and "Beehive". From "John's Lookout" in the largest chamber, you ascend a crevice onto the upper level, there to enter "Fairyland" and finally "Paradise", overlooking the hellish "Radium Hall" 50m below.

From the Pálvölgyi Caves, you can hurry through the sidestreets to catch the hourly tour of another labyrinth, the **Szemlőhegyi Cave** at Pusztaszeri út 35 (Szemlőhegyi barlang; Wed–Mon 10am–4pm; 600Ft, joint ticket with Pálvölgyi Stalactite Caves 900Ft), which abounds in pea-shaped formations and aragonite crystals resembling bunches of grapes. Coming from Kolosy tér by bus #29, alight at the fourth stop near the Pusztaszeri út turn-off. It's a twenty-minute walk from either cave to the **Kiscelli Museum** (Tues–Sun: April–Oct 10am–6pm; Nov–March 10am–4pm; 600Ft), which can also be reached by bus #165 from Óbuda's Kolosy tér and then an uphill stroll. Housed in a former Trinitarian monastery at Kiscelli utca 108, its collection includes antique printing presses and the 1830 Biedermeier furnishings of the Golden Lion pharmacy, which used to stand on Kálvin tér. Also on show are sculptures and graphics by twentieth-century Hungarian artists, and antique furniture exhibited in the blackened shell of the monastery's Gothic church, which makes a dramatic backdrop for operas, performances and fashion shows (Ⓣ1/388 8560 for details).

Music lovers can make a pilgrimage to the **Bartók Memorial House** at Csalán utca 29 (Bartók Béla Emlékház; Tues–Sun 10am–5pm; 500Ft), which can be reached by taking bus #29 from the Szemlőhegy Cave to the Nagybányai út stop, or bus #5 from Moszkva tér to the Pasaréti stop and then a short walk. Bartók and his family lived in the villa from 1932 until they emigrated to America in 1940. Besides an extensive collection of Bartók memorabilia, you can see some of his original furniture and possessions, including folk handicrafts collected during his ethno-musical research trips to Transylvania with Zoltán Kodály. Chamber music **concerts** are held here from September until May (ⓣ1/394 2100 for information; tickets 1200–2500Ft depending on the concert).

One final option for fresh-air fiends is to ride bus #65 from the Pálvölgyi Caves to the end of the line at the foot of **Hármashatár-hegy** and slog uphill to the summit. It provides a fabulous **view** of Budapest to the southeast, and is one of the best spots in the hills for **mushroom hunting**, a pastime that's almost as popular amongst locals as it is with city folk in Russia and Poland. People can take their fungi to special *gomba* stalls in the city's market halls, where experts distinguish the edible from the poisonous.

Margit sziget

A saying has it that "love begins and ends" on **Margit sziget** (Margaret Island), for this verdant expanse just upriver from the city centre has been a favourite spot for lovers since the nineteenth century, though until 1945 a stiff admission charge deterred the poor. Today it is one of Budapest's most popular recreation grounds, its thermal springs feeding outdoor pools and ritzy spa hotels. The easiest way of **getting here** is to catch bus #26 (which runs all the way along the island) from either Nyugati Station or Árpád híd metro in Pest. Alternatively, you can take tram #4 or #6 from Moszkva tér or the Nagykörút to the stop midway across Margit Bridge, and walk onto the island via the short linking bridge. Motorists can only approach from the north, via Árpád Bridge, at which point they must abandon their vehicles at a paying car park. You can **rent bikes**, **pedal cars** and **electric cars** on the island, but don't go for the first stall you come to: you'll find cheaper options by the Palatinus Strand in the middle of the island, ten minutes' walk away. The bikes and cars tend to be rather battered but are good enough to get around the five-kilometre circuit.

The southern part of the island is for chilling out and improving your tan. A huge circular fountain presages the 1930s **Hajós Alfréd Pool** (popularly known as the "Sport"; daily 6am–6pm; 500Ft), named after the winner of the 100m and 1200m swimming races at the 1896 Olympics, who was also the building's architect. The main attractions here are the all-season outdoor 50m pool and the fresh pastries at the buffet. Ten minutes' walk further on, a ruined thirteenth-century **Franciscan church** and a rose garden lie across the road from the **Palatinus Strand** (May to mid-Sept daily 8am–7pm; 1400Ft), which can hold as many as ten thousand people at a time in seven open-air thermal pools, complete with a water chute, wave machine and segregated terraces for nude sunbathing.

Further north, an **outdoor theatre**, by a conspicuous water tower, hosts plays, operas, concerts and fashion shows over summer, and is a handy spot for a beer or snack. To the east stands a **ruined Dominican church and convent**; Béla IV vowed to bring his daughter up as a nun here if Hungary survived the Mongol invasion, and duly confined 9-year-old Princess Margit when it did. She apparently made the best of it, acquiring a reputation for curing lepers and other saintly deeds, as well as for not washing above her ankles. Beatification followed her death in 1271, and a belated canonization in 1943. The convent fell into ruin during the Turkish occupation, when the island was turned into a harem.

A short way northeast of the water tower is a **Premonstratensian Chapel** whose Romanesque tower dates back to the twelfth century, when the order first established a monastery on the island; its fifteenth-century bell is one of the oldest in Hungary. Beyond lie two **spa hotels** catering to wealthy northern Europeans with a yen to be pampered: the *Danubius Grand*, a refurbished *fin-de-siècle* pile; and the equally well-equipped *Thermal Hotel*, built in the 1970s.

Pest

Pest is busier, more populous and vital than Buda: the place where things are decided, made and sold. While Buda grew up around the royal court, the east bank was settled by merchants and artisans, and commerce has always been its lifeblood. Much of its architecture and layout dates from the late nineteenth century, giving Pest a homogeneous appearance compared to other European capitals. Boulevards, public buildings and apartment houses were built on a scale appropriate to the Habsburg empire's second city, and the capital of a nation which celebrated its millennial anniversary in 1896. Now sooty with age or in the throes of restoration, these grand edifices form the backdrop to life in the **Belváros** (inner city) and the residential districts, hulking gloomily above the cafés, wine cellars and courtyards where people socialize. While there's plenty to see and do, it's the ambience that sticks in one's memory.

Away from the waterfront, you'll find that two semicircular boulevards are fundamental to **orientation**. The inner city lies within the **Kiskörút** (Small Boulevard), made up of Károly körút, Múzeum körút and Vámház körút. Further out, the **Nagykörút** (Great Boulevard) sweeps through the VI, VII, VIII and IX districts, where it is called Szent István körút, Teréz körút, Erzsébet körút, József körút and Ferenc körút respectively. Pest is also defined by **avenues** (*út*) radiating out beyond the Nagykörút – notably Bajcsy-Zsilinszky út (for Nyugati Station); Andrássy út, leading to the **Városliget** (City Park); Rákóczi út, for Keleti Station; and Üllői út, leading out towards the airport. As the meeting point of three metro lines and several main avenues, **Deák tér** makes a good jumping-off point for explorations.

The Belváros

The **Belváros** (Inner City) is the hub of Pest and, for tourists at least, the epicentre of what's happening – abuzz with pavement cafés, buskers, boutiques and nightclubs. Commerce and pleasure have been its lifeblood as long as Pest has existed, as a medieval market town or the kernel of a city whose *belle époque* rivalled Vienna's. After their fates diverged, the Belváros lagged far behind Vienna's Centrum in prosperity; in the last decade the gap has been superficially effaced by capitalism, but some of the old atmosphere lingers in the quieter backstreets south of Kossuth utca.

The **Kiskörút** (Small Boulevard) that surrounds the Belváros follows the course of the medieval walls of Pest, showing how compact it was before the phenomenal expansion of the nineteenth century swept the city far beyond its original boundaries. Within the Belváros there's little that's older than the eighteenth century, as the "liberation" of Pest by the Habsburgs left it in ruins. First-time visitors are struck by the statues, domes and mosaics on the skyline of Neoclassical and Art Nouveau piles, reflected in the mirrored banks and luxury hotels that symbolize the post-Communist era.

DOWNTOWN PEST

Nyugati Station

Hősök tere & the Városliget

Keleti Station

Rác Baths

BARS

Action	33
Capella	35
Captain Cook	17
Castro	38
Chaos	25
Darling	30
Darshan Udvar	34
Eklektika	26
Kuplung	12
Mystery	7
No. 1	20
Old Man's Music Pub	22
Paris-Texas	36
Picasso Point	3
Sark	18
Spoon	24
Vian	9

ACCOMMODATION

Hotel Anna	K
Astoria	M
Citadella	Q
City Panzió Mátyás	N
Corinthia Royal Grand	B
ELTE Peregrinus Vendégház	P
Four Seasons	D
Gellért	R
K&K Opera	C
Kempinski Corvinus	G
Le Meridien	F
Marco Polo	E
Marriott Budapest	I
Medosz	A
Mellow Mood	H
Mercure Museum	L
Museum Guest House	O
Museum II	J

RESTAURANTS

Al Amir	19
Baraka	29
Belcanto	11
Café Bouchon	4
Café Kör	13
Csarnok	5
Fausto's	27
Goa	16
Govinda	15
Il Terzo Cerchio	25
King's Hotel	23
Kiskacsa	21
Krizia	2
Lou Lou	14
Marquis de Salade	1
Menza	8
Múzeum Kávéház	31
Papageno	28
Rézkakas	32
Shiraz	37
Via Luna	6
Vörös és Fehér	10

Vörösmarty tér

The starting point for exploring the Belváros is **Vörösmarty tér**, the leafy centre of the district where crowds eddy around the portraitists, café tables and craft stalls that set up here over summer, Christmas and the wine festival. While children play in the fountains, teenagers lounge around the **statue of Mihály Vörösmarty** (1800–50), a poet and translator whose hymn to Magyar identity, *Szózat* (Appeal), is publicly declaimed at moments of national crisis. Its opening line – "Be faithful to your land forever, Oh Hungarians" – is carved on the pedestal. Made of Carrara marble, it has to be wrapped in plastic sheeting each winter to prevent it from cracking.

On the north side of the square is the **Gerbeaud patisserie**, Budapest's most famous confectioners. Founded in 1858 by Henrik Kugler, it was bought in 1884 by the Swiss confectioner Emile Gerbeaud, who invented the *konyakos meggy* (cognac-cherry bonbon) and sold top-class cakes at reasonable prices, making *Gerbeaud* a popular rendezvous for the middle classes. His portrait hangs in one of the rooms whose gilded ceilings and china recall the *belle époque*.

Beside *Gerbeaud*'s terrace is the entrance to the **Underground Railway** (Földalatti Vasút), whose vaguely Art Nouveau cast-iron fixtures and elegant tilework stamp it as decades older than the other metro lines. Indeed, it was the first on the European continent and the second in the world (after London's Metropolitan line) when it was inaugurated in 1896. Visit the Underground Railway Museum at Deák tér (see p.111) to learn more about its history.

At the lower end of the square, the **Bank Palace** was built (1913–15) in the heyday of Hungarian self-confidence by Ignác Alpár, and now houses the **Budapest Stock Exchange**, which was reborn in 1990.

Váci utca

Váci utca has been famous for its shops and **korzó** (promenade) since the eighteenth century. During the 1980s, its vivid **streetlife** became a symbol of the "consumer socialism" that distinguished Hungary from other Eastern Bloc states, but Budapesters today are rather less enamoured of Váci: dressed-to-kill babes and their sugar daddies would rather pose in malls, and teenagers can find *McDonald's* anywhere, leaving Váci utterly dependent on tourists for its livelihood and bustle.

The downside of this is visible in the overpriced souvenir shops and cafés, which compete with hustlers, buskers and bureaux de change for a share of the trade. Though people-watching is still a major diversion, **shopping** is less rewarding than it was when there were all kinds of small shops in the yards off the street, now driven out by soaring rents – and besides, Budapesters always did their serious shopping on the Nagykörút, anyway. A few landmarks along the way might catch your eye, such as the scantily clad **fisher-girl statue** on **Kristóf tér**, a small plaza running across to Szervita tér and Petőfi Sándor utca, or the **Pest Theatre** (no. 9) on the site of the *Inn of the Seven Electors*, where the 12-year-old Liszt performed in 1823.

Váci's looks improve slightly between Ferenciek tere and the Great Market Hall, since the southern stretch was only pedestrianized in 1997; unfortunately, this part is quickly catching up with its northern sibling as its more funky boutiques and specialist shops are overwhelmed by the numbers of tourists heading down to the market hall. The old buildings and cobbled sidestreets, however, have been tastefully facelifted; look out for the prewar **Officers' Casino** on the corner of Ferenciek tere (now a bank's headquarters) or the nineteenth-century hulk of the **Old Budapest City Hall** at nos. 62–64, where the city council still holds its meetings. Look out for the sculptural **plaque** on the wall of no. 47, commemorating the fact that the Swedish King Carl XII stayed here during his lightning fourteen-day horse-ride from Turkey to Sweden, in 1714.

Szervita tér and Petőfi utca

If the crowds on Váci utca deter you, head down Kristóf tér towards Szervita tér – named after the eighteenth-century **Servite Church**, but mainly distinguished by two buildings on the left-hand side of the street. No. 3 has a gable adorned with a superb **Secessionist mosaic** of *Patrona Hungaria* (Our Lady of Hungary) flanked by shepherds and angels, one of the finest works of Miksa Róth, while the **Rózsavölgyi Building**, next door, was built a few years later by the "father" of Hungarian Modernism, Béla Lajta; his earlier association with the National Romantic school is evident from the majolica decorations on its upper storeys. On the ground floor is the Rózsavölgyi music shop, one of the best in the city. Equally striking, but rather less attractive, is the **Telepont** phone, fax and email centre at the top of **Petőfi utca**, which runs down to Ferenciek tere parallel to Váci utca. Petőfi utca has none of the glamour and all the traffic, but you may be lured by the need to visit the **Central Post Office** (no. 13).

At the corner of Ferenciek tere and Petőfi utca, you'll find the **Párizsi Udvar**, a flamboyantly eclectic shopping arcade. Completed in 1915, its fifty naked figures above the third floor were deemed incompatible with its intended role as a savings bank. The old deposit hall now houses an Ibusz office, while the arcade is as dark as an Andalucian mosque and twice as ornate.

Ferenciek tere and further south

The Párizsi Udvar is just one of several impressive buildings round **Ferenciek tere**, although none can offset the fact that the square is dominated by a three-lane highway running from Erzsébet Bridge to Keleti Station. The bridge ramp runs down between twin *fin-de-siècle* office buildings called the **Klotild and Matilde Palaces** after two Habsburg princesses of that era. The square itself is named after the **Franciscan Church** on the corner of Kossuth utca, whose facade bears a relief recalling the Great Flood of 1838, which killed over 400 citizens. More would have died were it not for Baron Miklós Wesselényi, who rescued scores of people in his boat, as depicted on the plaque.

Walking southwards from the church you come to another thoroughfare, initially named after Count Mihály Károlyi, the liberal politician whose birthplace at no. 16 now houses the **Petőfi Literary Museum** (Petőfi Irodalmi Múzeum; Tues–Sun 10am–6pm, Ⓦwww.pim.hu; free, 280Ft for temporary shows), showcasing the personal effects of the national heroes Petőfi and Ady. Concerts are held in the courtyard here in the summer.

Heading on along Kecskeméti utca, past the **ELTE law faculty** that's the Hungarian equivalent of Oxbridge or Harvard for future high-fliers, a right turn into Szerb utca will bring you to the **Serbian Orthodox Church**, built by Serbian artisans and merchants who settled here after the Turks were driven out. Secluded in a garden, it is only open for High Mass (Sun 10.30–11.45am), when the singing of the liturgy, the clouds of incense and flickering candles create a powerful atmosphere. A block or so south, part of the **medieval wall of Pest** can be seen on the corner of Bástya utca and Veres Pálné utca.

Along the embankment

The **Belgrád rakpart** (Belgrade Embankment) bore the brunt of the fighting in 1944–45, when the Nazis and the Soviets exchanged salvos across the Danube. Like the Vár in Buda, postwar clearances exposed historic sites and provided an opportunity to integrate them into the environment – but the magnificent **view** of Buda Palace and Gellért-hegy is hardly matched by two colossal eyesores on the Pest side. While such historic architecture as remains can be seen in a fifteen-minute stroll between the Erzsébet and Chain bridges, **tram #2** enables you to see a longer stretch of the waterfront between Fővám tér and Kossuth tér, periodically interrupted by a tunnel.

Heading north from Fővám tér, the riverscape is dominated by the bold white pylons and cables of **Erzsébet Bridge**, the only one of the Danube bridges blown up by the Germans in 1945 that was not rebuilt in its original form. In the shadow of the approach road, the grimy facade of the **Belváros Parish Church** (Mon–Sat 7am–7pm, Sun 8am–7pm) masks its origins as the oldest church in Pest. Founded in 1046 as the burial place of St Gellért, it was rebuilt as a Gothic hall church, turned into a mosque by the Turks and reconstructed in the eighteenth century. By coming after Latin Mass at 10am on Sunday you can see Gothic sedilia and a Muslim *mihrab* (prayer niche) behind the high altar that are otherwise out of bounds; the nave and side chapels are Baroque.

On the square beside the church, a sunken enclosure exposes the remains of **Contra-Aquincum**, a Roman fort that was an outpost of their settlement in Óbuda. More pertinently to modern-day Hungary, the name of the square, **Március 15. tér**, refers to March 15, 1848, when the anti-Habsburg Revolution began, while the adjacent **Petőfi tér** is named after Sándor Petőfi, the poet whose *National Song* – the anthem of 1848 – and romantic death in battle made him a patriotic icon. The **Petőfi statue** has long been a focus for demonstrations as well as patriotic displays – especially on March 15, when it is bedecked with flags and flowers. Behind it looms the **Greek Orthodox Church**, built by the Greek community in the 1790s and currently the object of a tug-of-war between the Patriarchate of Moscow that gained control of it after 1945 and the Orthodox Church in Greece that previously owned it. Services (Sat 6pm & Sun 10am) are in Hungarian, but accompanied by singing in the Orthodox fashion.

The concrete esplanade on the Danube side of the gigantic **Marriott Hotel** is a sterile attempt to re-create the prewar **Duna-korzó** – the most informal of Budapest's promenades, where it was socially acceptable for strangers to approach celebrities. As you'd expect, its outdoor cafés are as expensive as the view is wonderful; in recent years, customers have also had a ringside view of the annual Gay and Lesbian parade.

The Vigadó

Like Váci utca, the Duna-korzó opens onto an elegant square full of stalls, named after the **Vigadó** concert hall, whose name translates as "having a ball" or "making merry". Inaugurated in 1865, this splendidly Romantic pile by Frigyes Feszl has hosted performances by Liszt, Mahler, Wagner and Von Karajan. Badly damaged in wartime, it didn't reopen until 1980, such was the care taken in re-creating its sumptuous decor. Its Large Hall and grand staircase can only be seen by concert-goers, though the foyer is accessible from 1pm, when the box office opens. The modern building on the right occupies the site of the *Angol királynő* (English Queen) hotel, where the likes of the Shah of Persia and Emperor Dom Pedro of Brazil used to stay during the city's *belle époque*. Don't overlook the statue of the **Little Princess** on the railings by the embankment. After dusk, you'll hardly notice that she isn't a person, if you notice her at all. By day, she looks like a cross-dressing boy in a Tinkerbell hat.

From Vigadó tér, the Duna-korzó continues past the *Inter-Continental Hotel* to end in a swirl of traffic at Roosevelt tér, on the edge of József Attila utca and the Lipótváros.

Deák tér and Erzsébet tér

Three metro lines, two segments of the Kiskörút and several important avenues meet at **Deák tér** and **Erzsébet tér** – two squares that merge into one another (making local addresses extremely confusing) to form a jumping-off point for the V, VI and VII districts. You'll recognize the area by two landmarks: the enormous mustard-coloured **Anker Palace** on the Kiskörút, and the **Lutheran Church** by the metro pavilion on the edge of the Belváros, which regularly hosts free concerts, including Bach's *St John Passion* over the fortnight before Easter. Next door, the **Lutheran Museum** (Evangélikus Múzeum; Tues–Sun 10am–6pm; 300Ft) displays a facsimile of Martin Luther's last will and testament, and a copy of the first book printed in Hungarian, a New Testament from 1541.

Accessible via the upper sub-level of Deák tér metro, the **Underground Railway Museum** (Földalattivasút Múzeum; Tues–Sun 10am–6pm; 145Ft or one BKV ticket) extols the history of Budapest's original metro. Its genesis was a treatise proposing a steam-driven tram network starting with a route along Andrássy út; an underground line was suggested as a fallback in case the overground option was rejected. Completed in under two years, in time for the Millennial Exhibition, it was inaugurated by Emperor Franz Josef and bore his name until 1918. The exhibits include two elegant wooden carriages (one used until 1973) and period fixtures and posters that enhance the museum's nostalgic appeal.

Lipótváros and beyond

The **Lipótváros** (Leopold Town) began to develop in the late eighteenth century, first as a financial centre and later as the seat of government. Though part of the V district, its ambience is quite different from that of the Belváros, with sombre streets of ponderously Neoclassical buildings interrupted by squares flanked by Art Nouveau or neo-Renaissance piles, busy with office workers by day but dead in the evenings and at weekends until *Café Kör* and *Lou Lou* brought some life to the area. Another source of vitality is the Central European University (CEU), funded by the Hungarian-born billionaire financier George Soros.

Depending on where you're coming from, it makes sense to start with Roosevelt tér, just inland of the Chain Bridge, or St Stephen's Basilica, two minutes' walk from Erzsébet tér. Most of the streets between them lead northwards to Szabadság tér, whence you can head on towards Kossuth tér – though the like-named metro station or tram #2 from the Belgrád rakpart will provide quicker access to Parliament.

Roosevelt tér

At the Pest end of the Chain Bridge, **Roosevelt tér** is blitzed by traffic, making it difficult to stand back and get a good view of the **Gresham Palace** on the eastern side of the square. This gorgeous Art Nouveau edifice was commissioned by a British insurance company in 1904, and is named after the financier Sir Thomas Gresham, the originator of Gresham's law, that bad money drives out good. His portrait high up on the facade, and the interior glass-roofed arcade and stained-glass windows, by the Art Nouveau master Miksa Róth, were rotting away gently until the building was given a new lease of life as the *Four Seasons* hotel. The restoration has been lovingly carried out, with period features restored – even the original companies were sought out, where they still existed, to recreate tiles and windows. It may be a luxury hotel, but the management is keen to show that it is handling a public treasure, so you can still walk in and ask to be shown around.

Statues of Count Széchenyi and Ferenc Deák stand at opposite ends of the square, the former not far from the **Hungarian Academy of Sciences** (Magyar Tudományos Akadémia), which was founded after Széchenyi pledged a year's income from his estates towards its establishment in 1825 – as depicted in a relief on the wall facing Akadémia utca. The Nobel Prize-winning scientist György Hevesy – discoverer of the element hafnium – was born at Akadémia utca 3, across the road.

While the Chain Bridge and the Academy are tangible reminders of Széchenyi's enterprise, Deák's achievement in forging an *Ausgleich* (Compromise) with the Habsburgs was symbolized by the crowning of Emperor Franz Josef as King of Hungary in 1867. Soil from every corner of the nation was piled into a Coronation Hill, atop which he flourished the sword of St Stephen and promised to defend Hungary against all its enemies – a pledge that proved almost as ephemeral as the hill itself. Eighty years later, the square was renamed Roosevelt tér in honour of the late US president – a rare example of Cold War courtesy that was never revoked.

St Stephen's Basilica and Bajcsy-Zsilinszky út

St Stephen's Basilica (Szent István-bazilika) took so long to build that Budapesters used to joke, "I'll pay you back when the basilica is finished". Work began in 1851 under the supervision of József Hild, continued after his death under Miklós Ybl, and was finally completed by Joseph Krauser in 1905. At the inaugural ceremony, Emperor Franz Josef was seen to glance anxiously at the dome, whose collapse during a storm in 1868 had naturally set progress back. At 96m it is exactly the same height as the dome of Parliament – both allude to the putative date of the Magyars' arrival in Hungary.

The basilica is best visited when its interior is open for sightseeing (Mon–Fri 9am–5pm, Sat 9am–1pm, Sun 1–4pm), as its beauty lies in the carvings, frescoes and chapels, the variegated marble, gilded stucco and bronze mouldings, and the splendid organ above the doorway. In a chapel to the left at the back is the gnarled **mummified hand of St Stephen**, Hungary's holiest relic, whose custodian solicits coins to illuminate the casket holding the *Szent Jobb* (literally, "holy right"), which is paraded around the church on August 20, the anniversary of Stephen's death. Although the **treasury** (same hours; 250Ft) is nothing special, don't miss the **Panorama Tower** (daily April–Oct 10am–6pm; 500Ft), offering a fabulous **view** of Pest from 65m; you can take a lift two-thirds of the way up if you don't fancy climbing the 302 steps.

While Stephen is revered as the founder and patron saint of Hungary, the pantheon of national heroes includes a niche for Endre Bajcsy-Zsilinszky (1866–1944). Originally a right-winger, he ended up an outspoken critic of Fascism, was arrested in Parliament (a statue on Deák tér captures the moment) and shot as the Russians neared Sopron. **Bajcsy-Zsilinszky út** runs northwards to **Nyugati tér**, dominated by **Nyugati Station**, an elegant, iron-beamed terminal built in 1874–77 by the Eiffel Company of Paris. During the summer, "nostalgia" steam trains run to Vác (p.181). The **Westend City Center**, a shopping mall with four hundred outlets and an artificial, but increasingly smelly, waterfall three storeys high, sits along the northern edge of the station. The mall boasts a new attraction, the **Budapest Eye** (Budapest Kilátó; weather permitting: May–Oct Mon–Thurs & Sun 11am–10pm, Fri & Sat 11am–midnight; Nov–April daily noon–8pm; 3300Ft; worth booking in summer on Ⓣ1/238 7623, Ⓦwww.budapestkilato.hu), a hot-air balloon on the first-floor roof above the railway tracks that takes visitors up 150m for excellent panoramic views over the city. It takes about twenty minutes, though you only spend five minutes at the top height.

Szabadság tér and around

For over a century the Lipótváros was dominated by a gigantic barracks where scores of Hungarians were imprisoned or executed, until this symbol of Habsburg tyranny was demolished in 1897 and the site redeveloped as **Szabadság tér** (Liberty Square). Invested with significance from the outset, it became a record of the vicissitudes of modern Hungarian history, where each regime added or removed monuments, according to their political complexion.

In the early years of the twentieth century, Hungary's burgeoning prosperity was expressed by two monumental temples to capitalism: the Stock Exchange, whose designer, Ignác Alpár, blended motifs from Greek and Assyrian architecture and crowned it with twin towers resembling Khmer temples; and the **National Bank** across the square, its facade encrusted with reliefs symbolizing honest toil and profit. While the former became the headquarters of Hungarian Television (Magyar Televizió, or MTV) after the Communists abolished the stock market, the latter still functions as intended and contains a small **Museum of Banknotes** (Thurs 9am–4pm; free), featuring such curiosities as the "Kossuth" banknotes that were issued in America during his exile and notes denominated in billions of forints from the period of hyperinflation in 1946. Today's capitalists have commissioned the mirrored-glass and granite International Bank Centre at the southern end of the square.

Turning from money to politics, notice the **statue of General Harry Bandholtz** of the US Army, who intervened with a dogwhip to stop Romanian troops from looting the Hungarian National Museum in 1919. The statue was erected in the 1930s, when Hungary was still smarting from the Treaty of Trianon that gave away two-thirds of its territory and a third of its Magyar population to Romania, Czechoslovakia and Yugoslavia. This deeply felt injustice inspired several other monuments on Szabadság tér, namely the Monument to Hungarian Grief – featuring a flag at half-mast and a quotation from Lord Rothermere (the proprietor of the *Daily Mail*, whose campaign against Trianon was so appreciated that he was offered the Hungarian crown) – and four statues called North, South, East and West, whose inauguration was attended by 50,000 people.

After 1945 all of these monuments were removed by the Communists, who converted the base of the Monument to Hungarian Grief into the **Soviet Army Memorial**, commemorating the liberation of Budapest from the Nazis. When the Socialists got the boot in 1990, there were calls to remove the Soviet memorial and restore all the old nationalist ones (Bandholtz had already been reinstated prior to President Bush's visit in 1989), but wiser counsels prevailed. There was once even a monument called "Gratitude", erected in 1949 in honour of Stalin's seventieth birthday – but of course nobody has proposed restoring that one.

To compound the irony, the Soviet memorial stands near the former headquarters of the Fascist Arrow Cross, and directly in front of the **US Embassy**, which for fifteen years gave shelter to Cardinal Mindszenty, the Primate of Hungary's Catholic Church. Though the US government was pleased to do so in the aftermath of the 1956 Uprising (when Mindszenty was freed from jail by insurgents), his presence later became an embarrassment to both the US government and the Vatican, which finally persuaded him to leave for Austria in 1971 (see box on p.175).

Behind the US embassy, the **former Post Office Savings Bank** on Hold utca is a classic example of Hungarian Art Nouveau – its facade patterned like a quilt, with swarms of bees (symbolizing savings) ascending to the polychromatic roof, which is the wildest part of the building and visible from the street. Its architect, Ödön Lechner, once asked why birds shouldn't enjoy his buildings, and amazing roofs are also a feature of his other masterpieces in Budapest, the Applied Arts Museum and the Geological Institute. The bank's interior is open to the public on only one day a year – European Heritage Day, in September (ask Tourinform for details). Across the street is a wrought-iron **market hall**, one of five opened on a single day in 1896, which continues to serve the centre of Budapest to this day.

At the junction of Hold utca and Báthory utca, a lantern on a plinth flickers with an **eternal flame** commemorating Count Lajos Batthyány, the prime minister of the short-lived republic declared after the 1848 War of Independence, whom the Habsburgs executed on this spot on October 6, 1849. As a staunch patriot – but not a revolutionary – Batthyány is a hero for conservative nationalists, and his monument the destination of annual marches on October 6 or other public holidays.

The refrains and paradoxes of Hungarian history are echoed on **Vértanuk tér** (Martyrs' Square), between Szabadság tér and Kossuth tér, where a **statue of Imre Nagy** – the reform Communist who became prime minister during the 1956 Uprising and was shot in secret afterwards – stands on a footbridge, gazing towards Parliament. With his raincoat, trilby and umbrella hooked over his arm, Nagy cuts an all too human, flawed figure, and is scorned by those who pay their respects to Batthyány.

Kossuth tér

The Lipótváros reaches its monumental climax at **Kossuth tér**, named after the leader of the 1848 Revolution, Lajos Kossuth, but also featuring a statue of an earlier hero of the struggle for Hungarian independence, Prince Ferenc Rákóczi II. The quote inscribed on the latter's plinth – "The wounds of the noble Hungarian nation burst open!" – refers to the anti-Habsburg war of 1703–11, but could just as well describe the evening of October 23, 1956, when crowds filled the square, chanting anti-Stalinist slogans at Parliament and calling for the appearance of Nagy – the prelude to the Uprising that night. An **eternal flame** burns in memory of those who died here on October 25, when ÁVO snipers opened fire on a peaceful crowd that was fraternizing with Soviet tank-crews. Thirty-three years later, the wheel turned full circle as the Republic of Hungary was proclaimed to an enthusiastic crowd from the same balcony that Nagy had spoken from, and the People's Republic of Hungary was officially consigned to the dustbin of history – symbolized by the removal of the red star from Parliament's dome, and the replacement of Communist emblems by the traditional coat of arms, featuring the double cross of King Stephen.

Parliament and the Museum of Ethnography

Budapest's stupendous **Parliament building** (Országház; Ⓦ www.parlament.hu) sprawls for 268m along the embankment, a grander version of the Houses of Parliament in London in an Eclectic or neo-Gothic style, scornfully described by the writer Gyula Illyés as "No more than a Turkish bath crossed with a Gothic chapel". Scores of flying buttresses and 88 statues of Hungarian rulers lift one's eyes towards the 96-metre-high cupola that straddles its symmetrical wings; the height of the dome is an allusion to the date of the Magyar conquest of Hungary. Although the nobility had maintained a Diet for centuries, which became a force for change during the Reform Era, it had no permanent home until work began on the building in 1885, and had grown sluggish by the time its grandiose seat was completed in 1902. Under Fascism, opposition MPs learned to fear for their lives, while after the Communists took over debates became a mere echo of decisions taken at Party headquarters on Akadémia utca, till Parliament began to recover its authority in the late 1980s.

Daily **guided tours** start at 10am, noon, 2pm & 6pm in English (free for EU citizens, passport needed for proof, 2070Ft for others; tickets from Gate X – you'll see a huddle of people to the right of the central span of the building, and guards will usually let you through to buy tickets 10min before tours start). Schedules can change at short notice according to parliamentary business or official visits. Besides the magnificent interior, visitors get to see **St Stephen's Crown**, the symbol of Hungarian statehood for over 1000 years. Its distinctive bent cross was caused by the crown being squashed as it was smuggled out of a palace in a baby's cradle; at other times it has been hidden in a hay-cart or buried in Transylvania, abducted to Germany by Hungarian Fascists and thence taken to the US, where it reposed in Fort Knox until its return home in 1978, together with the orb, sceptre and sword that comprise the **Coronation Regalia**. Since 2000 – when the regalia was moved from the National Museum to the Cupola Hall of Parliament – it has been flanked by guards in Ruritanian uniforms, holding drawn sabres.

Across the road at no. 12 stands a neo-Renaissance pile housing the **Museum of Ethnography** (Néprajzi Múzeum; Tues–Sun: March–Oct 10am–6pm; Nov–Feb 10am–5pm; free, visiting exhibitions 500Ft; Ⓦwww.neprajz.hu), one of the finest museums in Budapest. Its permanent exhibition on **Hungarian folk culture** is fully captioned in English and thematically arranged, and although such beautiful costumes and objects are no longer part of everyday life in Hungary, you can still see them in regions of Romania such as Maramureş and the Kalotaszeg, which belonged to Hungary before 1920. Upstairs, temporary exhibitions can cover anything from Bedouin life to Hindu rituals, while in the weeks leading up to Easter and Christmas the museum puts on **concerts** of Hungarian folk music and dancing, and **craft fairs**.

Further out

Szent István körút, running from Nyugati Station to the Danube, marks the end of the Lipótváros – but there are a few sights further out worth a mention. **Szent István Park**, opposite Margit sziget, is the social hub of the old wealthy Jewish neighbourhood, with the finest flowerbeds in the city – an apt site for a **monument to Raoul Wallenberg**, who gave up a playboy life in neutral Sweden to help the Jews of Budapest in 1944. Armed with diplomatic status and money for bribing officials, Wallenberg and his assistants plucked thousands from the cattle trucks and lodged them in "safe houses", manoeuvring to buy time until the Russians arrived. Shortly afterwards, he was arrested as a spy and vanished into the Gulag, never to return. The monument itself was constructed in the 1950s but "exiled" to Debrecen before being stashed away for decades, only taking its rightful place in Budapest in 1999.

The Danube bank below the park, the Ujpesti rakpart, is the site of a new summer development, the **Budapest Beach** (Budapest Plázs; Ⓦwww.budapestplazs.hu), which takes its cue from the Paris original. For the month of August the whole of the embankment facing Margit sziget is closed to traffic and covered in sand and palm trees, recreating a seaside feel, and there are stages, live music, children's programmes and numerous food stalls and restaurants to keep beach-goers happy.

Fifteen minutes' walk away from the river, visitors with kids or an interest in science should enjoy the **Palace of Miracles** (Csodák palotája; Jan to mid-April Tues–Fri 9am–5pm, Sat & Sun 10am–6pm; mid-April to Dec Mon–Fri 10am–5pm, Sat & Sun 10am–6pm; 650Ft; Ⓦwww.csodapalota.hu) at Váci út 19, three blocks north of Lehel tér metro. This interactive playhouse was the brainchild of two Hungarian physicists and aims to explain scientific principles to 6- to 12-year-olds, using optical illusions, a bed of nails, a simulated low-gravity "moonwalk" and a "miracle bicycle" on a tightrope – though the scarcity of explanations in English may leave you none the wiser.

The Hungarian Railway History Park

One of the best sights in the district is the **Hungarian Railway History Park**, sometimes called the Hungarian Railway Museum (Magyar Vasúttörténeti Park; Tues–Sun: April–Oct 10am–6pm; Nov–March 10am–3pm; 900Ft, family 1800Ft, cameras 200Ft, videocameras 800Ft; Ⓦwww.lokopark.hu), in the freight yards of the XVI district. Its sheds and sidings house over seventy kinds of locomotives and carriages from 1900 onwards, and between April and October (10am–4pm) you can even **drive** a steam train (1000Ft) or a luggage cart (300Ft) – wear old clothes. Many of the staff are ex-employees of MÁV (Hungarian State Railways), proud of a tradition inherited from the Royal Hungarian Railways. The museum above the information centre displays information in Hungarian only, but books, videos and MÁV souvenirs are sold downstairs. From April to October, the ticket price includes travel to the museum **by special train** (*különvonat*) from Nyugati Station (9.45am, 10.45am, 1.45pm & 3.45pm); this might sound attractive, but since this special train is an old diesel van, it will appeal more to enthusiasts who don't mind being choked by the fumes for half an hour or more. Tickets are available from the MÁV Nosztalgia office next to platform 10 in the station. Otherwise, the park gates at Tatai út 95 are a short walk from the Rokolya utca stop, a longish ride by bus #20 or #30 from Keleti Station or Dózsa György út.

The Terézváros

The **Terézváros** (Theresa Town), or VI district, bordered by Bajcsy-Zsilinszky út and Király utca, was laid out in the late nineteenth century and heavily influenced by Haussmann's redevelopment of Paris. At that time it was one of the smartest districts in the city – especially at the Városliget (City Park) end – but later much of the area became run-down and deprived. Although the villas near the park have recovered their value, the much touted "Hungarian Broadway" on Nagymező utca – which cuts across the main avenue, Andrássy út – sees café society rubbing shoulders with winos and outcasts.

Andrássy út

Running in a perfect straight line for 2.5km up to Hősök tere on the edge of the Városliget, Budapest's longest, grandest avenue was inaugurated in 1884 as the Sugár (Radial) út but soon renamed **Andrássy út** after the statesman Count Gyula Andrássy. The name stayed in popular use throughout the years when this was officially Stalin Avenue (1949–56) or the Avenue of the People's Republic (1957–89), until it was formally restored. With its greystone edifices laden with dryads, its Opera House and coffee houses, the avenue retains something of the style that made it so fashionable in the 1890s, when "Bertie", the Prince of Wales, drove its length in a landau, offering flowers to women as he passed. The initial stretch up to the Oktogon is within walking distance of

Erzsébet tér, but if you're going any further it's best to travel from sight to sight by the yellow metro beneath the avenue, or bus #4.

At Andrássy út 3 the **Post Office Museum** (Posta Múzeum; Tues–Sun 10am–6pm; 100Ft) occupies a fabulous old apartment, complete with parquet floors, marble fireplaces, Venetian mirrors and frescoes by Károly Lotz; its owners fled to the US in 1938. Exhibits include a compressed-air mail tube, vintage delivery vehicles, and a display on the inventor Tivadar Puskás, a colleague of Thomas Edison, who set up the world's first switchboard and telephonic news service in Budapest in the early 1900s.

The **State Opera** (Állami Operaház) was founded by Ferenc Erkel, the composer of Hungary's national anthem, and occupies a magnificent neo-Renaissance pile built in 1875–84 by Miklós Ybl. It can boast of being directed by Mahler (who complained about the anti-Semitism in Hungary), hosting performances conducted by Otto Klemperer and Antal Doráti, and sheltering two hundred local residents (including Kodály) in its cellars during the siege of Budapest. Tours of the grand interior run daily (3 & 4pm; 2200Ft, tickets from the shop to the right of the main entrance). In a similar vein, don't miss the **New Theatre** (Új Színház) on Paulay Ede utca, off the other side of Andrássy, whose blue and gold Art Nouveau facade and foyer (by Béla Lajta) are superb.

One block north of the Opera, Andrássy út is crossed by **Nagymező utca** – dubbed "**Broadway**" after the clubs and theatres on either side. The magnificence of the recently restored Operett Szinház (Operetta Theatre) at no. 19 reflects the high standing of this genre in Hungary, which has spawned such operetta composers as Ferenc Lehár and Imre Kálmán. During the interwar years the most famous club was the *Arizona*, run by Sándor Rozsnyai and his wife Miss Arizona, which inspired Pal Sándor's film of the same name, starring Hanna Schygulla and Marcello Mastroianni; the Rozsnyais were murdered by the Arrow Cross in 1944. Their club was at Nagymező utca 20, in the former home of the Habsburg court photographer who lends his name to the **Mai Manó Photography Museum** (Mon–Fri 2–7pm, Sat, Sun & holidays 11am–7pm; 400Ft; Ⓦwww.maimano.hu) – worth a visit for both the fine exhibitions and the well-stocked photographic bookshop. Across Andrássy at Nagymező utca 8 the **Ernst Múzeum** has excellent temporary fine arts exhibitions on the first floor (Tues–Sun 11am–7pm; 500Ft) – but it's worth visiting for the building alone. Dating from 1911, the museum – which takes its name from Lajos Ernst, a Hungarian art collector – has Art Nouveau designs by József Rippl-Rónai and Ödön Lechner, and, if it is open, pop into the Tivoli theatre in the same building to see its Art Deco lobby.

Further up Andrássy, two elongated squares with pavement **cafés** provide an interlude. On the left is **Jókai tér**, with a large statue of Jókai himself, while across the road on **Liszt Ferenc tér**, the composer hammers an imaginary keyboard with his vast hands, blind to the strolling, flirting crowds or the Music Academy that bears his name, further along.

Continuing up Andrássy brings you shortly to the intersection with the Nagykörút (Great Boulevard) at the **Oktogon**, an eight-sided square flanked by eclectic buildings. With 24-hour fast-food chains ensconced in two of them, and buses and taxis running along the Nagykörút through the small hours, the Oktogon never sleeps. During the Horthy period it rejoiced in the name of Mussolini tér, while under the Communists it was called November 7 tér after the date of the Bolshevik revolution.

Beyond the Oktogon

A minute's walk past the Oktogon on the left-hand side, you can't miss the **House of Terror** (Terror Háza; Tues–Fri 10am–6pm, Sat & Sun 10am–7.30pm; 1200Ft; ⓦwww.terrorhaza.hu) at Andrássy út 60, an otherwise ordinary corner house surrounded by an ominous black frame. In the mid-twentieth century this was the most terrifying address in Budapest – the headquarters of the secret police. Jews and other victims of the Arrow Cross were tortured here during World War II, and the ÁVO (see box opposite) later used the building for the same purpose. When it was captured by insurgents in 1956, no trace was found of the giant meat-grinder rumoured to have been used to dispose of corpses.

It's not so much a museum, more a macabre theme park, with a series of powerful images – such as the Soviet tank that fills the courtyard – linked together by loud music; the moment you step in through the spooky automatic door you are bombarded with funereal sounds. The exhibitions start on the second floor with a couple of rooms quickly dealing with the Nazi terror and the Holocaust, and continues down to the basement with rooms covering the Soviet "liberation", the deportations, rigged elections, collectivization, and the crushing of the 1956 Uprising. The most harrowing part is the lift that leads down to the basement: when the doors shut you cannot escape the video of an executioner quietly explaining his job. When the doors open at the bottom, you emerge in the re-created old torture section, which gives you a strong feel for how the cells must have been when prisoners were brought down to be softened up before being taken for interrogation. Here, the music mercifully stops as the exhibits are allowed to speak for themselves. Set up by the right-of-centre Fidesz government, the House was accused of bias in its emphasis on the Stalinist terror; for example, the video in the ticket hall repeatedly plays the image of a man weeping at the many deaths at the hands of the Communists, and saying "this was their socialism". However, balance is impossible here in such a sensitive area, and the public treatment of the Stalinist years is at least a much-needed beginning. The English-language audio-guides only repeat the same text as you'll find on the sheets in each room, and you could choose to save the 1000Ft for a coffee and cake afterwards to cheer yourself up. A little further on the opposite side, the Old Music Academy at no. 67 harbours the **Liszt Memorial Museum** (Liszt Ferenc Emlékmúzeum; Mon–Fri 10am–6pm, Sat 9am–5pm; closed in Aug; 380Ft), entered from around the corner at Vörösmarty utca 35, where the composer lived from 1881 until his death in 1886. His glass piano and travelling keyboard are the highlights of an extensive collection of memorabilia and scores. Concerts are performed here by young pianists every Sunday at 11am (250Ft). Another great Hungarian composer lends his name to the **Kodály körönd** (named Hitler tér during World War II), one of Budapest's most elegant squares, flanked by four neo-Renaissance mansions (one with gilt sgraffiti). At no. 1 on the northeast corner, the flat where Kodály lived until his death in 1967 is now the **Kodály Memorial Museum** (Wed 10am–4pm, Thurs–Sat 10am–6pm, Sun 10am–2pm; 200Ft), preserving his library, salon, dining room and folk-art collection.

Two fine collections of Asian art lurk just beyond the *körönd*. The **György Ráth Museum** (Tues–Sun: April–Oct 10am–6pm; Nov–March 10am–4pm; free) displays lovely artefacts from all the great civilizations, in an Art Nouveau villa at Városligeti fasor 12 – reached via Bajza utca – whose garden contains a statue of the Hungarian Orientalist Sándor Körösi-Csoma, as a Buddhist monk. The **Ferenc Hopp Museum** (Wed & Thurs 1–5pm, Fri 1–4pm; 400Ft) at Andrássy út 103 hosts temporary shows of Asian art. From here, the final stretch of Andrássy út up to Hősök tere is lined by spacious villas set back from the avenue, mostly housing embassies.

The ÁVO

The **Communist secret police** began as the party's private security section during the Horthy era, when it betrayed Trotskyites to the police to take the heat off their Stalinist comrades. After World War II it became the Államvédelmi Osztály or **ÁVO** (State Security Department), its growing power implicit in a change of name in 1948 – to the State Security Authority or **ÁVH** (though the old acronym stuck). Ex-Nazi torturers were easily persuaded to apply their skills on its behalf, and its network of spies permeated society. So hated was the ÁVO that any members caught during the Uprising were summarily killed, and their mouths stuffed with banknotes (secret policemen earned more than anyone else).

Hősök tere and around

Laid out in 1896 to mark the thousandth anniversary of the Magyar conquest, **Hősök tere** (Heroes' Square) is appropriately grandiose. The **Millenniary Monument** at its centre consists of a 36-metre-high column topped by the figure of Archangel Gabriel who, according to legend, appeared to Stephen in a dream and offered him the crown of Hungary. Around the base are Prince Árpád and his chieftains, who led the Magyar tribes into the Carpathian Basin. As a backdrop to this, a semicircular colonnade displays statues of Hungary's most illustrious leaders, from King Stephen to Kossuth. During the brief Republic of Councils in 1919, when Hungary was ruled by revolutionary soviets, the square was decked out in red banners and the column enclosed in a red obelisk. More recently, it was the setting for the ceremonial reburial of Imre Nagy and other murdered leaders of the Uprising (including an empty coffin to represent the "unknown insurgent") on June 16, 1989 – an event which symbolized the dawning of a new era in Hungary. Today it's more likely to be filled with rollerbladers and skateboarders who make use of this huge space on summer evenings.

Museum of Fine Arts

To the left of the square stands the **Museum of Fine Arts** (Szépmsvészeti Múzeum; Tues–Sun 10am–5.30pm; free, temporary exhibitions 800Ft), the international equivalent of the Hungarian National Gallery, housed in an imposing Neoclassical building completed in 1906. Although the majority of exhibits are now labelled in English, explanatory captions are few, so art lovers should invest in a catalogue, or join one of the tours in English at 11am (Tues–Fri). On the lower ground floor there's an excellent art bookshop and some of the snazziest toilets in Budapest.

Also on the lower ground floor is a small **Egyptian Collection**, chiefly from the Late Period and Greco-Roman eras, whose highlights are four huge painted coffins and a child-sized one, a mummified crocodile, cat and falcon, and a tautly poised bronze of the cat-goddess Bastet. The **Twentieth-Century Art Collection** across the way features few artists you're likely to have heard of but is nonetheless stimulating – look out for Chagall's *Village in Blue* in the Majovszky Hall, and Victor Vasarely's Op Art view of the Giza pyramids. While the Ionic Pyramid room features a changing selection of contemporary artists, the Doric Pyramid room hosts a superb collection of **Gothic sculptures**.

On the ground floor, most visitors make a beeline for the **Nineteenth-Century Art Collection**, where the drama of Courbet's *Wrestlers* and the delight of Monet's *Plum Trees in Blossom* or Corot's *Remembrance of Coubrou* aren't sustained by weaker efforts by Manet, Cézanne and Toulouse-Lautrec. The hall at the end displays **historical** paintings like *Nero on the Ruins of Rome*, while **Symbolist**

and Decadent pictures such as Franz von Stuck's *The Kiss of the Sphinx* adorn the last room. Don't spend long on the Mediterranean antiquities across the foyer, but check what's showing in the **Prints and Drawings Room**, where works by Raphael, Leonardo, Rembrandt, Rubens, Dürer, Picasso and Chagall alternate with solo retrospective exhibitions.

Upstairs are the **Old Masters**, many once owned by Count Miklós Esterházy. The **Spanish Collection** of seventy works is perhaps the best in the world outside Spain, with seven El Grecos (most notably *Christ Stripped of His Garments* and *The Agony in the Garden*) in Room XV, and five Goyas, several Murillos (including *Ecce Homo*) and a Velásquez in Room XVI. The **Italian Collection** is almost as impressive, with Raphael's "Esterházy Madonna" and portraits by Giorgione and Titian in Room XVIII, Veroneses and Tintorettos in Room XXIII. The **German Collection** contains Holbein's *Dormition of the Virgin*, Dürer's *Young Man* and works by Altdorfer and Cranach the Elder, while Room XXI exhibits such artists as Canaletto, Tiepolo and Kauffmann. Whereas the **Dutch Collection** has such gems as Van Dyck's *St John the Evangelist* (Room B) and a whole room of fantastic Brueghels, the single room of **English art** can only muster a dull portrait apiece by Hogarth, Reynolds and Gainsborough.

The Palace of Art and Dózsa György út

On the other side of the square is the **Palace of Art** (Műcsarnok; Tues–Sun 10am–6pm, Thurs noon–8pm; 600–900Ft), a Grecian edifice with gilded columns and a mosaic of St Stephen as patron of the arts. Its magnificent facade and foyer are in contrast to the four austere rooms used for **contemporary art exhibitions**, which are often first-rate. Since the palace was inaugurated in 1896, its steps have been a stage for the state funeral of the painter Munkácsy, the reburial of Nagy, and other public ceremonies.

Before heading into the Városliget, take a glance down **Dózsa György út**, the wide avenue running off alongside the park, where domes or tents serve as **circus** or **concert** venues. In Communist times it was here that Party leaders reviewed parades from a grandstand, beneath a 25-metre-high statue of Stalin that was torn down during the Uprising, dragged to the Nagykörút and hammered into bits for souvenirs. A statue of Lenin was erected in its place, which remained until it was taken away "for structural repairs" in 1989 and finally ended up at the Statue Park (see p.100).

The Városliget

The leafy **Városliget** (City Park) starts just behind Hősök tere, where the fairytale towers of **Vajdahunyad Castle** rear above an island girdled by an artificial lake that's used for boating in the summer and is transformed into the most splendid ice rink in Europe in winter. Like the park, the castle was created for the Millenniary Anniversary celebrations of 1896, so dramatic effects were the order of the day. This "stone catalogue" features replicas of the Chapel at Ják in western Hungary (see p.284) and two Transylvanian castles, enclosing a Renaissance courtyard that makes a romantic setting for evening **concerts** from July to mid-August (details of concerts from Tourinform or from ticket offices).

In the main wing is an **Agricultural Museum** (Mezőgazasági Múzeum; March to mid-Nov Tues–Fri & Sun 10am–5pm, Sat 10am–6pm; mid-Nov to Feb Tues–Fri & Sun 10am–4pm, Sat 10am–5pm; free) tracing the history of hunting and farming in Hungary, though its English captions peter out long before you reach the gift shop. However, few can resist the hooded **statue of Anonymous** outside. This nameless chronicler to King Béla is the prime source of information about early medieval Hungary, though the existence of several monarchs of that name during the twelfth and thirteenth centuries makes it hard to date him or his chronicles with any exactitude.

Leaving the island by the causeway at the rear, you're on course for the **Petőfi Csarnok**, a shabby 1970s "Metropolitan Youth Centre" that regularly hosts good concerts (outdoors in summer), films, parties, and a fine flea market at weekends (Ⓣ1/363-3720 or Ⓦwww.petoficsarnok.hu for information in English). Accessible by a staircase around the back, the **Aviation and Space Flight Exhibition** (Repüléstörténeti és arhajózási kiállítás; April–Nov Tues–Fri 10am–5pm, Sat & Sun 10am–6pm; free) features some vintage planes and a space capsule. The museum is an offshoot of the **Transport Museum** (Közlekedési Múzeum; Tues–Fri 10am–5pm, Sat & Sun 10am–6pm; free), 250m away on the edge of the park, which contains antique cars, mothballed steam trains and models galore – don't miss the model railway that runs every hour on the hour, nor the outdoor wagon-bar (a quiet nightspot).

The Széchenyi Baths, Zoo, Circus and Vidám Park

On the far side of the park's main axis, Kós Károly sétány, the **Széchenyi Baths** could be mistaken for a palace, so grand is its facade. Outside is a statue of the geologist Zsigmondy Vilmos, who discovered the thermal spring that feeds its outdoor pool and Turkish baths (daily 6am–7pm; 1900Ft, 2200Ft with cabin, 900Ft back if you leave within 2hr, 500Ft in 3hr, 200Ft in 4hr). In the huge mixed-sex outdoor pool you can enjoy the surreal spectacle of people playing **chess** while immersed up to their chests in steaming water – so hot that you shouldn't stay in for more than twenty minutes. The best players sit at tables round the pool's edge – the former world champion **Bobby Fischer** has been known to visit when in Budapest. Bring your own set if you wish to participate.

Beyond the baths on the other side of Állatkerti körút, the **Municipal Circus** (Fővárosi Nagycirkusz) traces its origins back to 1783, when the Hetz Theatre played to spectators on what is now Deák tér (performances mid-April to Aug Wed, Fri & Sun 3pm & 7pm, Thurs 3pm, Sat 10am, 3pm & 7pm; 1200–1900Ft). To the right is **Vidám Park**, an old-fashioned fairground known as the "English Park" before the war (daily 11am–6pm, open till 8pm July–Aug; 300Ft, free for children under 120cm in height); the funfair was the setting for Ferenc Molnár's play *Liliom*, which inspired the musical *Carousel*.

Further down towards Hősök tere you'll find the delightful Elephant Gates of Budapest's **Zoo** (Állatkert; Ⓦwww.zoobudapest.com; daily: May–Aug 9am–6pm; March, April, Sept & Oct 9am–5pm; Nov–Feb 9am–4pm; 1300Ft), which opened in 1866. Its Art Nouveau pavilions by Károly Kós seemed the last word in zoological architecture when they were constructed in the early 1900s, but the zoo slowly stagnated until the 1990s, when a new director aided by private sponsors began long-overdue improvements to give the animals better habitats and make the zoo more visitor-friendly. Don't miss the exotic Elephant House resembling a Central Asian mosque or the Palm House with its magnificent aquarium below (300Ft). The children's corner is signposted "Állatóvoda". Besides the zoo stands *Gundel's*, one of the grandest restaurants in Budapest (see p.135).

The VII district: Erzsébetváros

The **Erzsébetváros** (Elizabeth Town) or VII district, between Andrássy and Rákóczi út, is mainly residential, composed of nineteenth-century buildings whose bullet-scarred facades, adorned with wrought-ironwork, conceal a warren of dwellings and leafy courtyards. It is also traditionally the **Jewish quarter** of the city, which was transformed into a ghetto and nearly wiped out during the Nazi occupation of 1944–45, but has miraculously retained its cultural identity. This identity has recently come under threat, however, as the local council pursues its campaign to "revive" the district, knocking down the old blocks and replacing them with bright, modern office buildings. The streets around Király utca have been the most affected, and if too much of the quarter is redeveloped it will be a great loss, since there is no better part of Pest to wander around, savouring the atmosphere and discovering things for yourself. But the area still retains enough of its original architecture to make a visit worthwhile, and the impending development has meant that vacant lots are being turned into lively summertime beer gardens. Approaching the area from Deák tér, as most people do, the first landmark is the Dohány utca (Tobacco Street) Synagogue, just off Károly körút. **Walking tours** of the quarter (daily except Sat noon & 3pm; 4900Ft; ⓣ1/317 2754 for tickets and information) reveal local colour and historical details you might otherwise miss; you can sign up at the Dohány utca Synagogue.

The Dohány utca Synagogue and Jewish Museum

The splendid **Dohány utca Synagogue** (Dohány utcai Zsinagóga; Mon–Thurs 10am–5pm, closing at 3pm Oct–March, Fri 10am–3pm, Sun 10am–2pm; 1000Ft for synagogue and museum), designed by Ludwig Förster and built between 1854 and 1859, is one of the landmarks of Pest. Europe's largest synagogue and the second biggest in the world after the Temple Emmanuel in New York, it can hold 3000 worshippers of the Neolog community – a Hungarian denomination combining elements of Reform and Orthodox Judaism. Its design epitomizes the Byzantine-Moorish style that was popular in the 1850s, and the colours of its brickwork (yellow, red and blue) are those of Budapest's coat of arms. In the 1990s the synagogue was restored at a cost of over $40 million, funded by the Hungarian government and the Hungarian-Jewish diaspora, notably the Emmanuel Foundation, fronted by the actor Tony Curtis, born of 1920s emigrants.

You have time to admire the gilded onion-domed towers while waiting to pass through a security check, and can opt for a guided tour (1900Ft), though this doesn't add much to the experience. The magnificent **interior** of the synagogue is by Frigyes Feszl, the architect of the Vigadó, and its layout reflects its Neolog identity, with the *bemah*, or Ark of the Torah, at one end in the Reform fashion, but men and women seated apart, according to Orthodox tradition. The ceiling is decorated with arabesques and Stars of David, the balconies surmounted by gilded arches and the floor inset with eight-pointed stars. On Jewish festivals it is filled to the rafters and is a great meeting place for the local community. At other times, the hall is used for **concerts** of classical or klezmer music, as advertised outside.

Alongside is a courtyard full of simple headstones, marking the **mass grave** of 2281 Jews who died here during the winter of 1944, and a remnant of the brick **wall** that enclosed the ghetto, with a plaque commemorating its liberation by the Red Army. Behind looms the cuboid, domed **Heroes' Temple**, erected in honour of the 10,000 Jewish soldiers who died fighting for Hungary during World War I, which serves as an everyday synagogue and is not open to tourists.

To the left of the main entrance and up the stairs is the **Jewish Museum** (Zsidó Múzeum). Notice a relief of Tivadar (Theodor) Herzl, the founder of modern Zionism, who was born and taught on this spot. In the foyer is a gravestone from the third century AD – proof that there were Jews in Hungary six hundred years before the Magyars arrived. The first three rooms are devoted to Jewish festivals, with beautifully crafted objects such as Sabbath lamps and Seder bowls, while the final one covers the Holocaust, with chilling photos and examples of anti-Semitic propaganda. Oddly, the museum says nothing about the huge contribution that Jews have made to Hungarian society, in every field from medicine to poetry. Upon leaving, turn the corner onto Wesselényi utca and enter the **Raoul Wallenberg Memorial Garden**, named after the Swedish diplomat who saved 20,000 Budapest Jews by lodging them in safe houses or plucking them from trains bound for Auschwitz (see p.115). The park's centrepiece is a **Holocaust Memorial** shaped like a weeping willow, each leaf engraved with the names of a family killed by the Nazis. Behind it are glass panels by the artist Klára Szilárd, commemorating the sixtieth anniversary of the Holocaust. Also within the grounds is the **Goldmark Hall**, named after Károly Goldmark, the composer of the opera *The Queen of Sheba*.

Around the backstreets

Fanning out behind the synagogue is what was once the **Jewish ghetto**, created by the Nazis in April 1944. As their menfolk had already been forced into labour battalions intended to kill them from overwork, the 70,000 inhabitants of the ghetto were mainly women, children and old folk, crammed into 162 blocks of flats – over 50,000 of them around Klauzál tér alone.

Directly across the road from the Wallenberg Garden, Rumbach Sebestyén utca leads westwards to the **Synagogue** of the so-called Status Quo or middling-conservative Jews, which is outwardly akin to the Dohány utca synagogue but inwardly conforms to Orthodox prescriptions, and isn't open to the public.

Returning in the same direction as far as Dob utca, you'll see a **monument to Carl Lutz**, the Swiss Consul who began issuing *schutzpässes* to Jews, attesting that they were Swiss or Swedish citizens, as Wallenberg did later. Lutz was a more ambiguous figure, who ceased issuing passes and tried to prevent others from doing so after being threatened by the Gestapo. His monument – a gilded angel swooping down to help a prostrate victim – is known locally as "the figure jumping out of a window".

Just beyond, a portal at no. 16 leads into the **Gozsdu udvar**, an eerie 200-metre-long passageway connecting seven courtyards that runs through to Király utca. A hive of life and activity before the Holocaust, it is now just gently rotting and is scheduled for redevelopment in the district's grand scheme.

Király utca was the major thoroughfare of the district in the nineteenth century until Andrássy út was built, and for many years has been an atmospheric backwater. But the recent pedestrianization and influx of new boutiques is transforming the area, and it boasts an excellent café, bar and Syrian restaurant. The fifty-year-old kosher *Fröhlich* patisserie on parallel Dob utca at no. 22 is one of several Jewish businesses on and around the **Kazinczy utca Orthodox Synagogue**, the centre of the 3000-strong Orthodox community. There's a butcher's in the yard of Dob utca 35, with wigmakers at nos. 31 and 46, while down to the right at Kazinczy utca 28 is a kosher baker and the non-kosher Jewish *Carmel* restaurant at no. 31. Near the latter stands an Art Nouveau edifice that melds into the curve of the street. Though its interior is off limits to the public, the gate to the right leads into an L-shaped courtyard containing a Jewish school and the *Hanna* kosher restaurant – also accessible via an arcade on Dob utca.

For something quite different, visit the **Museum of Electrotechnology**

(Magyar Elektrotechnikai Múzeum; phone to book visits on ⓣ1/342 5750 or ⓔinfo@emuzeum.hu; free) in a former electricity sub-station at Kazinczy utca 21. Its curators demonstrate the world's first dynamo (invented in 1859 by Ányos Jedlik) and other devices in rooms devoted to such topics as the history of light bulbs, or the Hungarian section of the Iron Curtain. Though the current was too weak to kill and the minefields were removed in 1965, patrols kept it inviolate until 1989, when the Hungarians ceased shooting escapees, thereby spelling the end of the Iron Curtain as a whole.

Further east along Dohány utca, at the junction with the Nagykörút, stands the **New York coffeehouse**, another of the old Budapest landmarks. The coffeehouse is on the ground floor of a magnificent building which, like the Gresham Palace, is being turned into a luxury hotel, in this case by the Italian Boscolo chain. The exterior is spectacular, and when the hotel opens in late 2005 the coffeehouse's Art Nouveau interior should be worth making time for. This was one of the few great literary cafés in prewar Budapest to have survived, though whether this tradition is revived by its new owners remains to be seen. Going on along Dohány utca beyond the Nagykörút you leave the Jewish quarter, to enter an area that becomes more working class and populated by Arab and Chinese immigrants the nearer you get to the "Garment District" around **Garay tér** and Keleti Station.

The VIII district: Józsefváros

The VIII district – otherwise known as **Józsefváros** (Joseph Town) – is separated from the VII district by Rákóczi út, which runs out to Keleti Station, and from the Belváros by Múzeum körút, part of the Kiskörút. Nicknamed "Chicago" during the 1920s and 1930s, this area has a mixed reputation, being the site of prestigious institutions but also traditionally a red-light and thieves' quarter.

Múzeum körút resembles Andrássy út in miniature, lined with trees, shops and imposing facades as it curves around to meet Kálvin tér. Immediately beyond the East-West business centre by the Astoria junction stands the **natural sciences faculty of ELTE university** (Eötvös Loránd Tudományos-egyetem), whence a group of scientists who worked on the US atomic bombs graduated before World War II, including Edward Teller, the "Father of the Hydrogen Bomb". Further on and across the street, a substantial crenellated section of the **medieval wall of Pest** can be seen in the courtyard of no. 21. The walls gradually disappeared as the city was built up on either side, but fragments remain here and there.

The National Museum, the Radio Building and Kálvin tér

Like the National Library in the Vár, the **Hungarian National Museum** (Magyar Nemzeti Múzeum; Tues–Sun 10am–6pm; free; ⓦwww.hnm.hu) was the brainchild of Count Ferenc Széchenyi, who donated thousands of prints and manuscripts to form the basis of its collection in 1802. Shortly after it opened, this Neoclassical edifice, by Mihály Pollack, became the stage for a famous event in the 1848 Revolution, when Sándor Petőfi first declaimed the *National Song* with its rousing refrain – "Choose! Now is the time! Shall we be slaves or shall we be free?" – from its steps. Ever since, March 15 has been commemorated here with flags and speeches.

By way of amends for losing the Coronation Regalia in 2000 (now on display in the Parliament building – see p.114), the National Museum has undergone a major refit. The basement is devoted to medieval and Roman sculptures (including a mosaic floor from the Roman villa at Balácapuszta – see p.236). Also accessible from the foyer is a darkened room displaying King Stephen's silk coronation robe. The upper floor covers Hungarian history from prehistoric times until the present day, with treasures and curios ranging from Renaissance pews to Freemasons' regalia, and Stalin kitsch to multiparty election posters, while in room 20 is a typical sitting room from the 1960s, complete with a television showing the Communist leader János Kádár speaking.

Bródy Sándor utca, beside the museum grounds, seems an unlikely place for a revolution to start – yet this is where the Uprising began, outside the **Radio Building** at no. 7, when ÁVO guards fired upon students demanding access to the airwaves, an act which turned the hitherto peaceful protests of October 23, 1956, into a revolt against the secret police and other manifestations of Stalinism.

Street fighting was especially fierce around **Kálvin tér**, on the far side of the museum at the junction of Üllői út and the Kiskörút, where insurgents battled tanks rumbling in from the Soviet base on Csepel island. It seems almost miraculous that the ornate reading rooms of the **Szabó Ervin Library** (Mon–Fri 10am–8pm, Sat 10am–4pm; free), on the corner of Baross utca, survived unscathed. The library, which was built in 1887 by the Wenckheim family who controlled most of Hungary's onion production, has just come through a thorough modernization in sparkling form and is very busy in term time. Entering via the main entrance on Reviczky utca, you can ask at the information desk about visiting the reading rooms up on the fourth level. They may ask you to register (which you will also have to do to use the Internet), but will probably just wave you through.

In front of the library stands the "**Fountain of Hungarian Truth**" (Magyar Igazság kútja), and its very name sets alarm bells ringing. Below the figure of Justice comforting poor Hungary, the text speaks of the gratitude of the Hungarian people to Lord Rothermere. Set up in 1928 in honour of the peer, whose profile is featured on the fountain, this is one of the few surviving public monuments marking the Trianon treaty. On June 4, the anniversary of the treaty's signing, right-wing and Fascist groups gather to pay their respects. Further up Reviczky utca you come to Mikszáth Kálmán tér, the centre of a web of busy backstreets.

Beyond the Nagykörút

The József körút is one of the sleazier arcs of the Nagykörút, with *lezbiánus* shows that have survived the crackdown on **Rákóczi tér**, following a law in 1999 that restricted **prostitution** to "tolerated zones" – a move which merely drove the trade into brothels more easily controlled by the mafia. While theatregoers bestow bourgeois respectability upon **Köztársaság tér** – the home of Budapest's "second" opera house, the **Erkel Theatre** – the grittier side of life prevails at **Keleti Station** on Baross tér. As Budapest's "gateway to the east", it's not surprising that Chinese takeaways and Arab shops are a feature of the area – nor the incessant ID checks by the **police**, who patrol here in threes ("One can read, one can write, and the third one keeps an eye on the two intellectuals", as the old joke has it).

The Crime and Police History Museum

Handily for the police, their precinct HQ is only two blocks from the station, at Mosonyi utca 5. Tourists who'd never go there otherwise can visit its bizarre **Crime and Police History Museum** (Bűnügyi és Rendőrség-Történeti

Múzeum; Tues–Sun 10am–5pm; free) at no. 7, guarded by a dummy sentry. Since the museum is captioned in Hungarian only, you can easily miss the ideological cast of the display of uniforms and memorabilia going back to Habsburg times, which harbours a tribute to the Communist border guards and militia, and CIA leaflets inciting the Uprising. Be thankful you're not an exhibit in the other hall, where many displays depict murders and mutilations in horrific detail, unlike the staged – and very Sixties – crime scene with a sign listing key points for trainee investigators. Stuff on forgery and art theft in the 1980s begs the question why there's nothing about crime in Hungary nowadays. The show ends with a fraternal display of police uniforms from the fellow forces in the EU.

Kerepesi Cemetery

Five minutes' walk from the museum, along Fiumei út, you'll find **Kerepesi Cemetery**, the Père Lachaise of Budapest, where the famous, great and not-so-good are buried (daily: April & Aug 7am–7pm, May–July 7am–8pm, Sept 7am–6pm, Oct 7am–5.30pm, Nov–March 7.30am–5pm; free). Vintage hearses and mourning regalia in the **Funerary Museum** near the main entrance illuminate the Hungarian way of death and set the stage for the necropolis. On the far side of the museum, a starkly ugly **Pantheon of the Working Class Movement** enshrines personages who "Lived for Communism and the People" (some have been removed by relatives since 1989), while Party leader János Kádár – who ruled Hungary from 1956 to 1988 – rates a separate tomb, heaped with wreaths from admirers (his reputation has risen in recent years, and there's even talk of a public monument).

Further in lie the florid **nineteenth-century mausoleums** of Kossuth, leader of the 1848 Revolution against the Habsburgs; Count Batthyány, executed for rebellion; and Ferenc Deák, who engineered the Compromise between Hungary and the empire. The great diva Lujza Blaha, the "Nation's Nightingale", is also buried in Kerepesi, as is the confectioner, Gerbeaud. A more recent addition to the roll of honour is József Antall, the first prime minister of post-Communist Hungary, whose grave was originally marked by a simple cross but now features a large allegorical monument with horses struggling to burst free of a sheet.

The stadiums

The **stadion** district, north across Kerepesi út, is chiefly notable for the 76,000-seat **Puskás Ferenc Stadium**, where league championship and international **football** matches, **concerts** by foreign rock stars and events such as the national dog show are held. Originally known as the **People's Stadium** (Népstadion), it was built in the 1950s as a showcase for Communist sport, but was renamed after the great Hungarian footballer (also of the 1950s). Stalinist statues of healthy proletarian youth line the court that separates it from the smaller **Kisstadion**, while the latest member of the family is the **Aréna** or Sportaréna, a mushroom-shaped building that hosts concerts and sporting events. The **Stadion Bus Station** completes this concrete ensemble. All are best reached by red metro (from Keleti Station or downtown) or by trolley bus #75 along Dózsa György út from the edge of the Városliget.

Further out

Pressing on out into the X district and Kőbánya, 15km from central Pest, the **New Public Cemetery** (Új köztemető; daily dawn–dusk; free) is the final resting place of Imre Nagy and 260 others executed for their part in the Uprising, who were buried in unmarked graves in 1958. Any flowers left at **Plot 301** were removed by the police until 1989, when the deceased received a state funeral on Hősök tere. The plot is 2km from the main gates, with minibuses running there every twenty minutes. Near the graves, an ornate wooden gateway and headposts mark a mass grave now designated as a **National Pantheon** – as opposed to the Communist pantheon in Kerepesi (see opposite).

In the adjacent **Jewish cemetery**, where famous rabbis and Ernő Szép, author of *The Smell of Humans*, are buried, look for the lovely blue Art Nouveau tomb of Sándor Schmidl, designed by Lechner and Lajta. Getting to the cemeteries entails a 35-minute ride by tram #37 or #28 from Népszínház utca (near Blaha Lujza tér metro), out past the breweries of Kőbánya, to the main gates on Kozma utca. Tram #37 runs on past the entrance to the Jewish cemetery, 700m up the road.

Ferencváros and beyond

The **Ferencváros** (Francis Town), or IX district, was built to house workers in the 1880s and remains the most working-class of Budapest's inner suburbs, with tenements that are swelteringly hot in the summer. During the 1930s and 1940s its population confounded Marxist orthodoxy by voting for extreme right parties that returned the favour by supporting the local football team **FTC** – popularly known as "**Fradi**" – which became the unofficial team of the opposition under Communism and is nowadays known for its racist "ultras", hard-core hooligan supporters. The club's green and white colours can be seen throughout the district. See p.145 for more on Budapest's football teams.

Initially, Ferencváros takes its tone from two institutions on **Vámház körút**, the section of the Kiskörút that separates it from the Belváros. The wrought-iron **Great Market Hall** (Nagycsarnok; Mon 6am–5pm, Tues–Fri 6am–6pm, Sat 6am–2pm) is as famous for its ambience as for its produce, with tanks of live fish downstairs and stalls festooned with strings of paprika at the back, where former British prime minister Mrs Thatcher once endeared herself by haggling during a visit. Nearer the Danube, the **Economics University** (named after Karl Marx during Communist times) makes a fine sight at night, reflected in the river, and adds to the liveliness of the area by day. The building was originally Budapest's main Customs House (Vámház) – hence the name of the körút. On the Belváros side of the boulevard, a freestanding section of the **medieval walls** of Pest can be found in the courtyard of no. 16. Everything else of interest in the district is too far away to walk, but readily accessible by public transport.

Along Üllői út

Don't bother with **Üllői út** unless you have a particular destination in mind, since this grimy thoroughfare of ponderous Neoclassical blocks runs for miles out to the airport. Fortunately, its principal attraction is only one block back from the Ferenc körút metro stop, at the junction with the Nagykörút.

The **Applied Arts Museum** (Iparművészeti Múzeum; Tues–Sun: mid-March to Oct 10am–6pm; Nov to mid-March 10am–4pm; free) is worth a visit purely to see the building by Ödön Lechner, who strove to create a uniquely Hungarian form of architecture emphasizing the Magyars' Ugric roots. Topped by a huge green and yellow dome, its portico adorned with Turkish motifs on a yolk-coloured background, the museum's pure white interior is reminiscent of Moghul architecture (it was once thought that the Magyars came from India). A fine show of **Arts and Crafts** since medieval times is surpassed by **Style 1900**, devoted to the movement known as Art Nouveau, Jugendstil or Secessionist, with a superb collection ranging from William Morris wallpaper to stained-glass panels by Hungarian masters like József Rippl-Rónai and Miksa Róth. The museum's hoard of furniture from other epochs is on show in the Nagytétény Castle Museum (see p.100).

Beyond the Nagykörút, on the right-hand side of Üllői út, stands the former **Kilián Barracks**, whose garrison was the first to join the 1956 insurgents. As the Uprising spread, it became the headquarters of Colonel Pál Maleter and teams of teenage guerrillas, who sallied forth from the alleys surrounding the **Corvin Cinema** on the other side of the road to lob Molotov cocktails at Soviet tanks. Since the fall of Communism they have been honoured by a **statue of a young insurgent** outside the cinema. A couple of streets further down on the left are two very different buildings. On Liliom utca an old transformer plant has been turned into the **Trafó**, an outstanding contemporary arts centre (see p.140), while on the parallel Páva utca you'll find the newly established **Budapest Holocaust Memorial Centre** (Holocaust Emlékközpont; Tues–Sun 10am–6pm; free; Ⓦwww.hdke.hu). Designed by Leopold Baumhorn (responsible for some of Hungary's finest synagogues), the core of the centre is a beautiful 1920s synagogue. A new wing was added to the old building to house the first government-funded documentation centre in the region, which has been set up to collect information about the Holocaust in Hungary, promote educational activities in schools and hold exhibitions. The centre doesn't just cover the Jewish extermination, but also that of the Roma and others, hence the importance of its location outside the main Jewish quarter. A permanent exhibition should have opened by mid-2005, which may give this fine setting greater ballast.

Further out: Népliget FTC

Two and a half kilometres further out along Üllői út lies the **Népliget** or People's Park, which lacks the allure of the Városliget but does have a **Planetarium**, 100m from Népliget metro, hosting astronomical programmes by day, and nightly **laser shows** with music by Pink Floyd, Mike Oldfield, Madonna, Bizet and Carl Orff (mid-Jan to May & early July to mid-Dec Mon–Sat at 7.30pm; 1990Ft; Ⓦwww.lasertheatre.hu). At the same crossroads you will also find the **Népliget Bus Station**, but for **football** fans, the biggest draw will be the **FTC Stadium** on the other side of Üllői út, where Fradi does its stuff (see p.127).

South to the National Theatre

Further south on the banks of the Danube lies what looks like a Ceausescu folly, stranded by the decline of Communism. This is the latest stage in the pilgrimage of the **National Theatre** (Nemzeti Szinház), a forlorn creation with a tortured history (see box on p.143). This national institution is to be at the centre of a major new development, but all that has been built so far is a couple of peculiar constructions miles from the centre and surrounded by wasteland. The theatre's exterior and surroundings is strewn with random architectural references – the Classical facade lying under water is the front of the old National Theatre torn down in 1964 by the Communists – and assorted statuary and theatrical symbolism, such as the prow at the front which makes the building appear like a prop from *Carry on Cruising*.

Next door is the **Palace of the Arts** (Művészetek Palotája Ⓦwww.mupa.hu), the new home of the Ludwig Museum, the Philharmonic Orchestra and the National Dance Theatre, all of which began moving in 2005. The **Ludwig Museum** or **Museum of Contemporary Art** (Kortárs Művészti Múzeum; Tues–Sun 10am–6pm; 600Ft; Ⓦwww.ludwigmuseum.hu) was established in

1996 to build upon an earlier bequest by the late German industrialist Peter Ludwig. The **Ludwig Collection** includes US Pop Art such as Warhol's *Single Elvis* and Lichtenstein's *Vicky*, Picasso's *Musketeer with a Sword* and a felt-and-fat *Sealed Letter* by Beuys, but most of the recent acquisitions are works by lesser-known Europeans, in such styles as Hyperrealism and neo-Primitivism.

Eating and drinking

Hungarians relish **eating and drinking**, and Budapest is great for both. Though Magyar cuisine naturally predominates, you can find everything from Middle Eastern to Japanese food, bagels to Big Macs. The diversity of cuisine is matched by the range of outlets and prices – from de luxe restaurants where a meal costs an average citizen's monthly wage, to backstreet diners that anyone can afford. Many restaurants and bars have live music in the evenings; places where the emphasis is on music and dancing are covered under "Entertainment".

Coffee houses, cafés and patisseries

Daily life in Budapest is still punctuated by the consumption of black coffee drunk from little glasses, though cappuccinos and white coffee are becoming ever more popular. These quintessentially Central European coffee breaks are less prolonged these days than before the war, when Budapest's **coffee houses** (*kávéház*) were social club, home and haven for their respective clientele. Free newspapers were available to the regulars – writers, journalists and lawyers (for whom the cafés were effectively "offices") or posing revolutionaries – with sympathy drinks or credit to those down on their luck. Today's coffee houses and **patisseries** (*cukrászda*) are less romantic but still full of character, whether fabulously opulent, with silver service, or homely and idiosyncratic.

Buda

Ági Rétes II, Retek utca 19. Best *rétes* (strudel) in town just near Moszkva tér, all baked on the premises. Mon–Fri 10am–6pm, Sat 10am–2pm.
Angelika I, Batthyány tér 7. Quiet but smoky atmosphere in a former convent, with a lively terrace. Daily 10am–midnight.
Ruszwurm I, Szentháromság tér 7. Diminutive Baroque coffee house near the Mátyás Church; so packed that it's almost impossible to get a seat in summer. Delicious cakes and ices. Daily 10am–8pm.

Pest

Astoria Kávéház V, Kossuth utca 19. Early twentieth-century coffee house-cum-bar in the *Astoria* hotel; the comfy armchairs have sadly disappeared, but it's still popular with the locals. Daily 7am–11pm.
Café Picard V, Falk Miksa utca 10. Elegant small French café near Parliament, serving good breakfasts – fresh croissants and excellent coffee – and lunches. Mon–Fri 7am–10pm, Sat 9am–10pm.
Central Kávéház V, Károlyi Mihály utca 9. Large old coffee house recently restored to its former grandeur. Also serves a wide range of food throughout the day, from cheap favourites like creamed spinach to more expensive dishes. Daily 8am–midnight/1am.
Eckermann VI, Andrássy út 24. Attached to the Goethe Institute right by the Opera House, this is popular with young artists and writers – and also with bag thieves, take note. Mon–Sat 8am–10pm.
Fröhlich VII, Dob utca 22. Excellent kosher patisserie five minutes' walk from the Dohány utca synagogue, and a great people-watching place. Specialities such as *flodni* (apple, walnut and poppy-seed cake) are worth tasting. Mon–Thurs 9am–6pm, Fri 7.30am–3pm, Sun 10am–4pm; closed Sat & Jewish holidays.
Gerbeaud V, Vörösmarty tér 7. A Budapest institution with a gilded salon and terrace. Always packed with tourists but the service is good; head round the corner to the *Kis Gerbeaud* ("Little Gerbeaud")

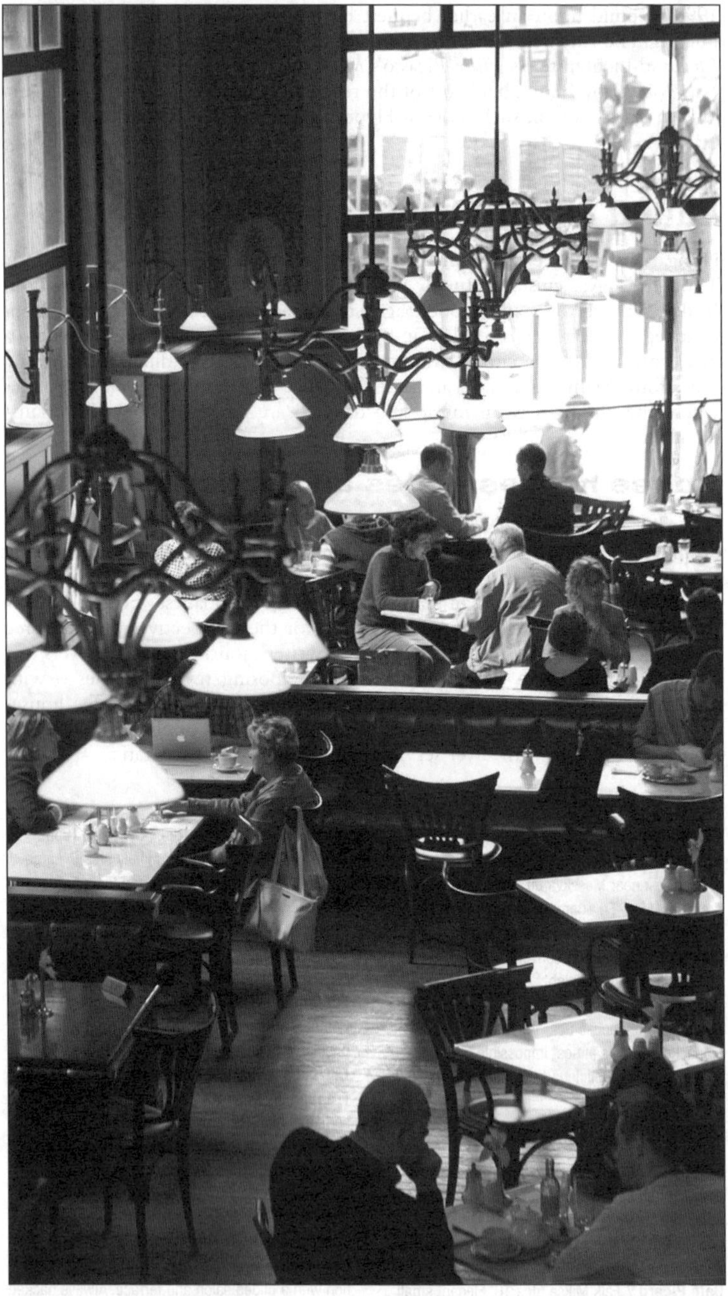

▲ Central Kávéház

where you can get the same cakes far cheaper and without the scrum. Daily 9am–9pm.

Ibolya V, Ferenciek tere. Iced coffee outside in the summer, sticky cakes, Szalon beer from the southern Hungarian town of Pécs, and a smoky atmosphere indoors all year round in this popular meeting place. Mon–Sat 8am–midnight, Sun noon–11pm.

Király V, Király utca 19. Patisserie serving excellent cakes and ice cream, with a very cosy café upstairs. Daily 10am–midnight.

Lukács VI, Andrássy út 70. One of the old coffee houses, restored to its full grandeur by a bank, so you get cakes called "the banker", and have to walk in through the bank's main entrance. Mon–Fri 8am–8pm, Sat 10am–8pm.

Művész VI, Andrássy út 29. There's an air of faded grandeur in this old coffee house that's more noted for its decor – chandeliers and gilt – than for its rather standard cakes. But it still retains some of its old clientele, such as old ladies in fur hats. Daily 8am–midnight.

Múzeum Cukrászda VIII, Múzeum körút 10. Friendly hangout near the National Museum. Fresh pastries arrive early in the morning. Open 24hr.

Sport V, Bank utca 5. 1970s furniture and service and good cakes in this fine example of an *ancien-régime* café.

Szalai V, Balassi Bálint utca 4. Old-style cake shop, one of the few remaining in Budapest, serving very good cakes in a fine location near Parliament. Daily except Tues 9am–7pm.

Zsolnay VI, Teréz körút 43. Elegant café on the first floor of the *Béke Radisson* hotel that is surprisingly popular with intellectuals, and also serves good cakes. Daily 10am–10pm.

Snack and sandwich bars and fast food

Budapest took to **fast food** in a big way and has over forty branches of *McDonald's* and plenty of *Pizza Huts* and *Burger Kings* too. On a more positive note, you'll find excellent Chinese stand-up joints – *gyors büfé* – all over town, many of them serving very good and cheap fare. A Hungarian peculiarity is the *étkezde* – small, lunchtime diners where customers sit at shared tables to eat hearty home-cooked food.

Buda

Lánchíd I, Fő utca 4. Atmospheric small bar serving hot and cold sandwiches, handily placed at the Buda end of the Chain Bridge. Daily 9am–11pm.

Pest

Duran Sandwich Bar V, Október 6 utca 15, & XII, Retek utca 18. A sandwich and coffee bar chain – filling a surprising gap in Budapest. Mon–Fri 8am–6pm, Sat 9am–1pm.

Falafel V, Paulay Ede utca 53. Budapest's most popular falafel joint, where you stuff your own pitta breads. Seating upstairs. Mon–Fri 10am–8pm, Sat 10am–6pm.

Három Testvér ("Three Brothers"), VI, Teréz körút 62, & XIII, Szent István körút 22. Chain of Turkish kebab bars offering quick, cheap and good food. Good range of salady bits too. Many other branches all over Pest. Daily 9am–3am.

Kádár Étkezde VII, Klauzál utca 10. Cheap diner in Pest with delicious home cooking; traditional non-kosher Budapest Jewish food on Friday. Mon–Sat 11.30am–3.30pm; closed mid-July to mid-Aug.

Marie Kristensen Sandwich Bar IX, Ráday utca 7. The Danish flavour is hard to spot; this is just a decent regular sandwich bar behind Kálvin tér. Mon–Fri 8am–9pm, Sat 11am–8pm.

Mirákulum V, Hercegprímás utca 19. Handy breakfast joint near Arany János utca station (blue metro), with smoking and non-smoking sections. Open daily 9am–1am.

Szahara VIII, József körút 82 ☎1/313-0257, close to the Corvin cinema at Ferenc körút metro station. Clean, bright joint with a wide range of tasty Middle Eastern food, eaten at shared tables. No smoking inside, though there are some tables outside in summer. It's easy to order: just point to the pictures of the food on the menu. Sun–Thurs 10am–midnight, Fri & Sat 10am–3am.

Tower Restaurant 10th floor of the Central European University, V, Nádor utca 9. Excellent inexpensive university café open to all, run by the same people as the café in the Museum of Contemporary Art. Mon–Fri 10am–8pm (from noon to 2pm university members get priority).

Restaurant prices

As forint prices rise continuously, we have classified restaurants in comparative terms. Expect to pay under 4000Ft per head for a full meal with drinks in a **cheap** place; 4000–10,000Ft in a **moderate** restaurant; and 10,000Ft upwards in an **expensive** one.

Restaurants

The biggest change in the city's **culinary scene** has been the appearance of a number of very good restaurants offering high-quality food and the best in Hungarian wine. Places such as *Arcade*, *Krizia*, *Chez Daniel* and *Lou Lou* are hardly cheap even by Western standards, but are extremely popular regardless and always packed. There has also been a welcome diversification in recent years, with many new places offering Chinese and Japanese food, mainly to wealthy tourists and nouveau-riche natives. Restaurants with Hungarian Gypsy bands tend to be touristy, but do have a certain distinctive charm. It is wise to **reserve** a table if you're determined to eat somewhere in particular, though you can usually find an alternative within a couple of blocks. We've included phone numbers where booking is advisable.

Some of the places listed below are rough-and-ready, others glittering citadels of *haute cuisine* – it's worth checking out both ends of the spectrum. You can generally reckon that the places further from the Belváros or the Vár are likely to be cheaper. It is worth noting that **hotels** such as the *Kempinski* (*Kempi Brauhaus*), *Le Meridien* (*Le Bourbon*), *Corinthia Royal* and *Four Seasons* (*Páva*) have outstanding French, German or Italian chefs who produce exceptionally good food. A popular development with foreign residents in the city is **Sunday brunch**, giving you as much as you can eat for a fixed price: *Gundel* by the Városliget is the best location, but many of the top hotels, including the *Marriott*, *Le Meridien* and the *Hilton*, also offer an excellent spread. If a restaurant doesn't have a menu (*étlap*) in German (which most waiters understand) or English, the food and drink vocabulary on pp.482–485 should help when **ordering meals**. Simply pointing to dishes on the menu or neighbouring tables is a bit risky.

Waiters in Budapest do very easily make "mistakes" with the bill, and foreign visitors are especially easy targets for overcharging. The worst **rip-offs** have been when single male visitors are lured into restaurants by women they have befriended and are then landed with an astronomical bill – which the unfortunate diner is forced to pay by beefy bouncers. Other more common tactics include issuing menus without prices, offering expensive "specials of the day", hiking up the bill or charging exorbitant amounts for the wine. Insist on a proper menu (including prices for drinks), don't be shy about querying the total, and avoid the seedier tourist joints in the centre of town.

Buda

Despite the plethora of tourist traps in the Vár, **Buda** offers some excellent possibilities if you don't mind a bit of a journey. There is no typical style of Buda restaurant: they range from grand villas in the hills to small friendly locals. The "**historic**" **restaurants** in the Vár tend to charge exorbitant prices for mediocre food – the *Rivalda* is the exception, and is the only one included in the list below.

The Vár and the Víziváros

Carne di Hall II, Bem rakpart 20 ⓣ1/210-8137, ⓦwww.carnedihall.com. Under the same management as *Lou Lou* in Pest, the food here is just as good, even if the pun in the name – Carnegie Hall – doesn't quite work. Service is leisurely. Delicious steaks and chocolate torte. Open noon–midnight. Expensive.

Gusto's II, Frankel Leo utca ⓣ1/316-3970. Near the Buda side of Margit Bridge, a charming little bar serving light meals – as well as very good tiramisu. Booking essential. Mon–Sat 10am–10pm. Moderate.

Horgásztanya I, Fő utca 27 ⓣ1/489-0236. Enjoyable fish restaurant near the Danube that has resisted the forces of modernization, remaining unchanged for many years. Serves up some of the best fish soups in the city. Daily noon–11pm. Cheap.

Rivalda I, Szinhaz utca 5–9 ⓣ1/489-0236. Smart new restaurant close to the Royal Palace that attracts a loyal local clientele, not just tourists – unlike so many other places on Castle Hill. High-standard cooking (the chicken with mustard maple syrup and the chocolate gateau are especially recommended) and wacky, theatrically inspired decor. Daily 11.30am–11.30pm. Expensive.

Tabáni Kakas I, Attila út 27 ⓣ1/375-7165. Popular old place specializing in poultry – it does an excellent goose leg with mashed potatoes and cabbage (*sült libacomb*) – but also serving good fish dishes, such as catfish paprika (*paprikás harcsa*). Daily noon–midnight. Cheap.

Moszkva tér and further out

Arcade XII, Kiss János alt. utca 38 ⓣ1/225-1969. Upmarket place serving excellent international cuisine, including delicious duck steak in maple syrup. Good range of top Hungarian wines includes Gere Kopár. Tues–Sun 11am–11pm. Expensive.

Márkus Vendéglő II, Lövőház utca 17 ⓣ1/212-3153. Friendly Hungarian restaurant near Moszkva tér, right by the Millenarium Park. Large portions of traditional Hungarian dishes, such as *Jokai bableves* and variously stuffed turkey dishes, all recommended. Menus in English available. Daily 9am–1am. Cheap.

Marxim II, Kisrókus utca 23. Popular pizza restaurant, whose decor makes humorous digs at Stalin. Daily 11am–1am. Cheap.

Náncsi Néni II, Ördögárok út 80 ⓣ1/397-2742. Popular family restaurant with a large terrace in the leafy suburb of Hűvösvölgy, ten minutes' walk from the terminus of bus #56. Excellent, well-cooked Hungarian food – very tasty starters and the best *turos gomboc* (sweet curd dumpling) in the city – and live music too. Booking essential. Mon–Sat noon–9pm, Sun noon–5pm. Moderate to expensive.

Óbuda

Kerék III, Bécsi út 103 ⓣ1/250-4261. A small place serving traditional Hungarian food at very reasonable prices with *srámli* (accordion) music provided by a couple of old musicians (daily except on Sundays). Outside seating in summer. Daily noon–11.30pm. Cheap.

Kisbuda Gyöngye III, Kenyeres utca 34 ⓣ1/368-6402. Good food in finely decorated *fin-de-siècle* surroundings. Booking essential. Daily noon–midnight. Expensive.

Pest

There's a much wider range of places in **Pest**, particularly within the Nagykörút, where rip-offs await the unwary. It's also possible to find some excellent restaurants, especially if you're prepared to do a bit of exploring. Most of the following are easily accessible from downtown Pest, though you should reserve a table to avoid a wasted journey.

Within the Nagykörút

Al Amir VII, Király utca 17 ⓣ1/352-1422. Syrian restaurant offering one of the cheapest and best vegetarian options in the city, with delicious starters and salads – but also a wide range of Middle Eastern meat dishes. No alcohol served. Daily 11am–11pm. Cheap.

Baraka V, Magyar utca 12–14 ⓣ1/483-1355, ⓦwww.barakarestaurant.hu. Stylish and pricey restaurant on two floors with contemporary decor, an intimate feel and a modern European menu. Attentive service. Mon–Sat 6–11pm. Moderate to expensive.

Belcanto VI, Dalszínház utca 8 ⓣ1/269-2786.

Good international fare in a smart establishment right by the Opera House – though you'll hardly want to go after the opera as the *Belcanto*'s speciality is that the waiters burst into song. Makes for a lively atmosphere. Daily noon–3pm & 5.30pm–midnight. Expensive.

Café Bouchon VI, Zichy Jenő utca 33 ⓣ1/353-4094. Set up by breakaway staff from *Café Kör*, the *Bouchon* has a similar friendly style, good Continental cuisine – and specials written up on the wall. Mon–Sat 9am–11pm. Moderate.

Café Kör V, Sas utca 17 ⓣ1/311-0053. Buzzy, friendly place near the basilica with a very relaxed feel. Good grilled meats, salads and wines. The specials of the day, displayed on a board, are recommended – the staff speak English and can advise on your choice. Booking essential. Mon–Sat 10am–10pm. Moderate.

Csarnok V, Hold utca 11, one block east of Szabadság tér ⓣ1/269-4906. Good, down-to-earth Hungarian restaurant specializing in mutton, lamb and bone-marrow dishes. Mon–Fri 9am–11pm. Cheap.

Fausto's VII, Dohány utca 5 ⓣ1/269-6806. Run by masterchef Fausto DiVora, this is one of the best Italian restaurants in town, serving up exquisite food in elegant surroundings. Mon–Sat noon–3pm & 6–11pm. Expensive.

Goa VI, Andrássy út 8. New, fashionable and fairly expensive restaurant near Deák tér. Slightly overdoing the trendy Eastern feel, but the food is very good: a range of cuisines covered, including Thai and Japanese. Daily noon–midnight. Expensive.

Govinda V, Vigyázó Ferenc utca 4 ⓣ1/473-1310. Hare Krishna vegetarian restaurant which does good cheap set meals, accompanied by the whiff of soporific incense. Mon–Sat noon–9pm. Cheap.

Il Terzo Cerchio VII, Nagydiófa utca 3. A cellar restaurant in a central location, this place is full of elderly Italian blokes watching football, and if that doesn't make it authentic enough, the food is excellent and inexpensive. Daily noon–midnight. Cheap.

King's Hotel VII, Nagydiófa utca 25–27 ⓣ1/352-7675. Mehadrin kosher food, which is rare in this town, and it's reasonably good too. You have to pay in advance for Sabbath meals. Daily noon–9.30pm. Cheap.

Kiskacsa VII, Dob utca 26. Small, friendly joint ten minutes up from the Dohány utca synagogue, serving traditional Hungarian fare. You get three dice with your bill and if you roll three sixes your meal is on the house. Mon–Sat noon–midnight. Cheap.

Krizia V, Mozsár utca 12 ⓣ1/331-8711. Top-class Italian restaurant, one of the best in town, conveniently located near the Opera. Mon–Sat noon–3pm & 6.30pm–midnight. Expensive.

Lou Lou V, Vigyázo Ferenc utca 4 ⓣ1/312-4505, ⓦwww.lou-lou.hu. One of the top restaurants in town. The menu has French influences but goes far wider than that, with interesting dishes such as a delicious lamb steak in an orange and coffee-bean sauce. Top Hungarian wines too. No-smoking section. Mon–Fri noon–3pm & 7–11pm, Sat 7–11pm. Expensive.

Marquis de Salade VI, Hajós utca 43 ⓣ1/302-4086. Big portions of food from all round the world. Its large basement is decorated with beautiful Persian carpets. Daily 11am–midnight. Moderate.

Menza VI, Liszt Ferenc tér ⓣ1/413-1482 Excellent and moderately priced establishment on Liszt Ferenc tér with stylish retro decor and retro Hungarian dishes, too, that evoke nostalgic memories among the locals. Daily 10am–midnight. Moderate.

Múzeum Kávéház VIII, Múzeum körút 12 ⓣ1/267-0375 ⓦwww.muzeumkavehaz.hu. Excellent food in a grand nineteenth-century restaurant – note the Zsolnay tiles and the frescoes on the ceiling. Rather old-school, with a kitsch singing pianist in the background. Near Astoria metro. Booking essential. Mon–Sat 10am–midnight. Moderate.

Okay Italia XIII, Szent István körút 20. A lively restaurant, popular with expats and locals alike, serving up very good pasta and pizza at reasonable prices. A second branch is located on Nyugati tér, diagonally across from the station. Daily noon–midnight. Cheap.

Papageno V, Semmelweis utca 19 ⓣ1/485-0161. Small bistro with an experienced chef specializing in pasta dishes in a small street near the Astoria. A very good lunchtime place, though you'll need to book. Mon–Fri 11.30am–midnight, Sat 12.30pm–midnight. Moderate.

Rézkakas V, Veres Pálné utca 3 ⓣ1/318-0038, ⓦwww.extra.hu/rezkakas. If you want to eat in traditional Hungarian style, with an excellent Gypsy band playing away in the corner, one of the best places to try is the smart "Golden Cockerel", close to Ferenciek tere. Daily noon–midnight. Expensive.

Shiraz IX, Ráday utca 21. Friendly Persian establishment serving tasty regional dishes – good salads make it attractive to vegetarians. Daily noon–midnight. Cheap.

Via Luna V, Nagysándor József utca 1 ⓣ1/312-8058. Popular Italian-style restaurant in the heart of central Pest. Good filling salads. Daily noon–11.30pm. Moderate.

Vörös és Fehér ("Red and White") VI, Andrássy út 41 ☏1/413 1545. This wine bar is one of the best restaurants in town. Very good tapas-style food, salads and snacks accompanied by top Hungarian vintages – you can drink most wines by the glass and the friendly staff can advise what goes well with what. Worth booking. Daily 11am–midnight. Moderate.

Beyond the Nagykörút

Bagolyvár XIV, Állatkerti körút 2 ☏1/468-3110. Sister to the *Gundel* (see below), but offering traditional Hungarian family-style cooking at far lower prices. George Habsburg comes here especially for the creamed spinach (*spenot főzelék*). Three-course menu 3010Ft. Daily noon–11pm. Moderate.

Chez Daniel VI, Szív utca 32 ☏1/302-4039. Excellent French restaurant, one of the best in town, run by idiosyncratic master chef Daniel Labrosse. In summer it spreads into its very atmospheric courtyard. Fresh ingredients, including fish. Booking recommended. Daily noon–10.30pm. Expensive.

Firkász XIII, Tátra utca 18 ☏1/450-1118. Done up like a turn-of-the-twentieth-century journalists' haunt, this establishment serves good trad Hungarian food, with creamed veg stews and the like at an excellent price. Daily noon–midnight. Cheap.

Gundel XIV, Állatkerti körút 2, near the zoo in the Városliget ☏1/468-4040. Budapest's most famous restaurant offers plush surroundings and a fantastically expensive menu. Bookings and smart dress required. *Gundel*'s Sunday brunch – all you can eat for just 4900Ft – is one of the city's biggest bargains (booking essential, and dress can be relaxed, though not too scruffy). Daily noon–4pm & 7pm–midnight, Sunday brunch 11.30am–3pm. Expensive.

Lanzhou VIII, Luther utca 1b ☏1/314-1080. One of the best Chinese restaurants in Budapest, with a large menu of specialities, such as spicy tripe. Popular with the local Chinese community. Daily noon–11pm. Cheap.

Bars, wine bars and beer halls

It's hard to draw a firm line between places to eat and places to **drink** in Budapest, since some patisseries double as cocktail bars, and restaurants as beer halls (or vice versa), while the provision of live music or pool tables blurs the distinction between drinking spots and clubs. Budapest's **bar** scene has burgeoned in recent years, and is centred on three main areas: Liszt Ferenc tér – the place to see and be seen – running between Andrássy út and the Music Academy; semi-pedestrianized Ráday utca, which with its innumerable cafés and terraces styles itself as the Budapest Soho; and Krudy Gyula utca, behind the National Museum. Another big growth area has been **outdoor bars**, but these come and go with frightening regularity – some have dance floors and are covered under "Clubs" below. There is another new trend for **beer gardens** to be set up in the empty lots in the VII District in the streets behind the synagogue, such as Holló utca and Kisdiofa utca, but as they may move from year to year, it's best to look in the listings magazines (see p.71) for bars such as *Szodakert* and *Mummus*. The majority of *borozó* or **wine bars** are nothing like their counterparts in the West, being mainly working men's watering holes, offering such humble snacks as *zsíros kenyér* (bread and pork dripping with onion and paprika). Conversely, **beer halls** (*söröző*) are often quite upmarket, striving to resemble an English pub or a German *bierkeller*, and serving full meals. The addition of *pince* to the name of an outlet signifies that it is in a cellar; many of the newer places stink of mould until the crowds arrive.

Most places open around lunchtime and stay open until after midnight, unless otherwise stated. The following list is not exhaustive, since it excludes various **club-type places** (covered under "Clubs" below). See p.132 for warnings about rip-offs in restaurants, which apply equally to bars.

Buda

Bambi I, Frankel Leó utca 2–4. One of the few surviving socialist-realist bars, with red plastic covered seats and stern waitresses, serving breakfast, omelettes, snack lunches, cakes and alcohol all day long. Mon–Fri 7am–9pm, Sat & Sun 9am–8pm.
Kecskeméti Borozó II, Széna tér. By Moszkva tér on the corner of Retek utca. Smoky, sweaty, crowded stand-up wine bar. A notice on the wall says: "We do not serve drunks", but that would rule out most of the people inside. However, they do serve that staple Hungarian bar fare, *zsíros kenyér*. Mon–Sat 9am–11pm.
Móri Borozó I, Fiáth János utca 16, just up from Moszkva tér. Cheap and cheerful neighbourhood wine bar attracting a young crowd. Darts and bar billiards in the room at the far end. June–Aug daily 4–11pm; Sept–May Mon–Sat 2–11pm, Sun 2–9pm.
Ponyvaregény XI, Bercsényi utca 5. The books around the walls (the name means "pulp fiction") and the sofas give this spacious cellar bar a very friendly feel. Daily 10am–2am.

Pest

Captain Cook VI, Bajcsy-Zsilinszky út 19/A. Popular café/pub with seats outside in summer. Daily till 2am.
Castro IX, Ráday utca 35. A popular new place on Ráday utca attracting a good mix of locals and expats. The Serb chef rustles up excellent food, such as spinach pies. Internet access too. Daily 10am–midnight/1am.
Csiga VIII, Vásár utca 2. Friendly smoky bar, popular with locals and expats. Good food and occasional live music. Mon–Sat 11am–1am.
Darshan Udvar VIII, Krudy Gyula utca 7. The largest bar in a growing complex of bars, cafés and shops. Set at the back of the courtyard, with exuberant Gaudíesque decorations, generous and tasty servings, outdoor terrace in the summer and live music, but leisurely service. Mon–Wed 11am–1am, Thurs–Sat 11am–2am, Sun 6pm–midnight.
Kuplung VII, Király utca 46. A new and surprisingly large bar down a narrow alleyway in what was once a police stable and later a moped repair shop (the name means "clutch"). Daily till late.
No. 1 V, Sas utca 9. Popular old-style hangout with a friendly crowd, near the basilica. Mon–Fri 9am–midnight, Sat 6pm–midnight.
Old Man's Music Pub VII, Akácfa utca 13, Ⓦwww.oldmans.hu. Large, popular joint near Blaha Lujza tér. Live local acts, and good food. Daily 3pm–dawn.
Paris-Texas IX, Ráday utca 22. Stylish café with good atmosphere near Kalvin tér. Pool tables. Mon–Fri 10am–3am, Sat & Sun 1pm–3am.
Picasso Point VI, Hajos utca 31. Popular, relaxed venue in the streets behind the Opera House with a spacious bar with comfortable chairs upstairs and a disco downstairs. Also serves food. Mon–Wed & Sun 11am–midnight, Thurs–Sat 4pm–3am.
Sark VII, Klauzál tér 14. Heaving bar, decorated with massive murals; DJs and good live music downstairs. Daily 10am–2am.
Spoon V, on the river by the *Inter-Continental* hotel, Ⓦwww.spooncafe.hu. If you don't want to splash out in the good, but expensive, restaurant with cocky waiters, the bar here offers the same grand setting, looking across to the Chain Bridge and the Buda Palace, as well as access to the toilets with the best views in Budapest. Open daily noon–2am.
Tokaji Borozó V, Falk Miksa utca 32. Crowded smoky old-style wine bar serving wines from the Tokaj region as well as snacks such as *lapsánka* (potato pancakes) and *zsíros kenyér*. Mon–Fri noon–9pm.
Vian VI, Liszt Ferenc tér 11. Less pretentious than others on this posiest of squares, with pleasant staff and a relaxed atmosphere. Daily 9am–midnight.

Entertainment

The range of **entertainment** available in Budapest includes everything from clubbing and folk dancing to opera-going and jazz. To find out **what's on**, check out *Where Budapest*, a free magazine distributed in hotels; the listings in *Budapest in your Pocket* and *Budapest Sun*; or the Hungarian-language weekly *Pesti Est* (available free in cinemas and bars; published on Wednesdays) for its English-language film section. A number of festivals and events which occur annually are described in the box on pp.138–139.

Clubs

Budapest is catching up fast in both the quantity and quality of its **clubs**, and its growing popularity as a destination for young Westerners will speed up the process. The city has a varied scene, especially in the summer when it expands into several large outdoor venues, and there are also one-off events held in such places as the old Turkish baths or sites further out of town; look out for posters which are put up at bus stops. **DJs** to look out for include Yonderboi, Keyser and Shuriken (easy listening), Palotai, Titus and Mango (drum'n'bass) and Superbeat (nujazz); anything run by Tilos Rádió, the old pirate radio, is usually good. You can expect to pay 1000–4000Ft to get into a club – be warned that bouncers are a common feature of Budapest nightlife and it's worth keeping on the right side of them. You'll also find dancing in some of the bars listed above, including the *Old Man's Music Pub* and *Picasso Point*, as well as in the three big arts centres, the Petőfi Csarnok (see below), Almássy téri Szabadidő Központ (see p.141), and the Trafó (see p.140). The gay and lesbian scene is covered separately below.

Cha Cha Cha IX, Kálvin tér subway. Glam 1970s bar with fake zebra furnishings and a louche feel. Despite its strange location, it attracts a big crowd spilling out into the concourse, and there are DJs Thursday to Saturday nights. Mon–Fri 7am–2am, Sat 10am–2am.

E-Klub X, Népliget (at the Planetarium) ⓦwww.e-klub.hu. Formerly in block E of the Technical University, this once-wild cattle market for engineering students has been exiled to outer Pest. Today a more mixed crowd packs in for the two discos on different floors and beer galore. Live rock music on Fridays. Fri & Sat 8pm–5am.

Franklin Trocadero Café V, Szent István körút 15. Excellent Latin music and dancing just up from Nyugati Station. Daily 9pm–5am.

Petőfi Csarnok XIV, Zichy M. út 14 ⓣ1/363-3730, ⓦwww.petoficsarnok.hu. Huge purpose-built youth centre near the back of the Városliget, hosting the Madonna Club, the Pet Shop Boys Club and other band-specific DJ nights, concerts by local and big-name foreign bands, contemporary dance performances and Greek folk dancing (Sun in summer). Exhibitions are also held here, and there's a very good flea market on Saturday and Sunday mornings. Ring the above number for more details in English.

Piaf VI, Nagymező utca 20. This old favourite on "Broadway" charges 500Ft to enter – unless you come with a regular. Basically a room and a cellar graced by the odd film star and lots of wannabes, with occasional jazz or rock sets. Daily from 10pm until well after dawn.

SOTE Club IX, Nagyvárad tér 4 (in the Semmelweis Medical University – Orvosi Egyetem – near Nagyvárad tér metro stop) ⓦwww.soteklub.hu. A heaving disco plus sideshows including jazz gigs, rock concerts and movies. Closed July & Aug.

West Balkan IX, Kisfaludy utca 16. Lively dance spot which can migrate; if it has moved, check listings magazines under the same name. Indoor and outdoor dance areas. May–Sept daily 5pm–dawn.

Zöld Pardon XI, Goldmann György tér ⓦwww.zp.hu. Large, heaving outdoor bar near the Petőfi bridgehead, where you can dance to drum'n'bass, deep house and jungle. Great venue, marred by punch-ups and knifings despite heavy security. Daily 9am–6am (kitchen noon–6am).

Gay bars and clubs

Most of the places listed below levy an **entry fee** or set a minimum consumption level – being gay in Budapest is an expensive privilege. Some, like the *Capella*, give you a card when you enter, which all your drinks are written down on; you then pay for your drinks and the entry fee as you leave – though be warned that if you lose the card you'll have to pay a lot of money.

In this very male-dominated town, there is one explicitly **lesbian-friendly** bar, the *Eklektika* (see p.138), but the *Angyál* and *Capella* are also good for women.

Festivals and events: the Budapest year

The two highlights of Budapest's cultural calendar are the **Spring Festival** (Ⓦwww.festivalcity.hu/btf) in late March and the **Autumn Festival** (Ⓦwww.festivalcity.hu/bof) from late September to late October. Both offer music, ballet and drama, including star acts from abroad.

The ten-day **Budapest Film Festival** is usually in February, while the first major national holiday of the year is on **March 15**, when Budapest decks itself out in flags and cockades in honour of the 1848 Revolution, and there are patriotic gatherings at the Petőfi statue and the National Museum. **Easter** is marked by church services and outbreaks of *locsolkodás* (splashing) – when men and boys visit their female friends to spray them with cologne and receive a painted egg or pocket money in return. The fall of Communism has put paid to grandiose parades on April 4 and May 1, but **May Day** remains a national holiday, with a big party in the Városliget organized by the trade unions. In early June Vörösmarty tér is packed with bookstalls for the very popular **Book Week** (Könyvhét), and there are long queues for the book signings by top authors. Politicians have now joined the book circus, competing for who can attract the largest numbers of followers coming to get their book autographed.

While many theatres close down for the season, there are plenty of outside concerts and events over the summer, as well as the **Hungarian Grand Prix**, usually held in mid-August. **World Music Day** (a French invention that celebrates music across the world, not to be confused with "world music") is held on June 21, while the **Budapest Bucsú** or Farewell (Ⓦwww.festivalcity.hu/bucsu), first held in 1991 to celebrate the departure of the last Russian troops from Hungary, takes place on the last weekend of June, with open-air music, dance and events across the city. **Gay Pride Budapest**, a four-day festival taking place in late June or early July, is the largest event in the gay calendar, culminating in a march down Andrássy út to the Danube (see p.140). The **Bridge Festival** (Hid Fesztval; Ⓦwww.festivalcity.hu/hidunnep) at the end of June commemorates the building of the Chain Bridge in the 1840s. The bridge itself is closed to traffic, and there is a river cavalcade and general festivities. A new development in 2004 saw the bridge closed to traffic and returned to the people at weekends in July and August, which the authorities say they will continue to do. Another new summer feature is the **Budapest Beach** (Budapest Plazs; Ⓦwww.

Action V, Magyar utca 42 Ⓦwww.action.gay.hu. The hardest of the gay bars, full of young men looking for one-night stands. Dark room and video room. Entry 1300Ft. Daily 9pm–4am.

Angyál Bár VII, Szövetség utca 33. Budapest's premier gay club looks like an airport lounge, but has an interesting crowd. Men-only on Saturdays, but popular with women on Fridays and Sundays. Entry 800–1000Ft. Thurs–Sun 10pm–dawn.

Capella V, Belgrád rakpart 23 Ⓦwww.extra.hu/capellacafe. Drag queens, jungle music and lots of kitsch, with decor as outrageous as the acts. Shows start at 11.30pm and 2am. A very mixed joint, attracting as many straights if not more. Entry 1000Ft. Wed–Sun 10pm–4am or later.

Chaos V, Dohány utca 38 Ⓦwww.chaospub.hu. The most cultured of the gay bars, this is a friendly place to meet. The ground floor is a gallery and Internet café and downstairs is the *Coxx Club* with a small dance floor. Entry 700Ft. Daily 9pm–5am.

Darling V, Szép utca 1. A beer-house and gallery that gets "warmer" after 9pm and stays open till late. Attracts a lot of Romanian prostitutes. Free entry. Daily 7pm–3am.

Eklektika V, Semmelweis utca 21. Lesbian-friendly bar – a pleasant space with 1960s furniture – that has a women-only evening on the second Saturday of every month. No entry fee, but entry 500Ft on women's night. Mon–Fri noon–1am, Sat & Sun 5pm–1am.

Mystery Bar V, Nagysándor József utca 3 Ⓣ1/312-1436, Ⓦwww.mysterybar.hu. Very small bar near the Arany József utca metro, for talking rather than dancing – there's no disco. If the door's locked you might have to wait to be let in. Internet café too. Free entry. Mon–Fri 10pm–4am, Sat & Sun 4pm–4am.

budapestplazs.hu); for most of August a kilometre and a half of the Pest riverside opposite Margit sziget, from Margit Bridge northwards, is closed to traffic and turned, like its Paris forebear, into a beach (see p.115). The biggest music event of the summer is the **Sziget Festival**, one of the largest open-air rock and pop gatherings in Europe, held on an island north of the city in early August (Ⓦwww.sziget.hu). The **BudaFest opera festival** takes place in the opera house during the summer recess, and at the end of August the **Jewish Festival** (Ⓦwww.jewishfestival.hu) attracts an international range of artists presenting classical, jazz and klezmer music and exhibitions. **St Stephen's Day** (August 20), honouring the founder of the Hungarian state, occasions day-long celebrations at the basilica (see p.112), a craft fair and folk dancing at different venues in the Vár, another river parade and finally a spectacular display of fireworks at 9pm from barges in the river between the Erzsébet and Margit bridges – check at Tourinform for the precise location so that you can get the best vantage point. Up to one million people gather on the river bank, and the traffic jam that follows the display is equally mind-blowing. If you want to eat out that night, you should book a place well in advance, as all the restaurants are packed. Soon after is the **Budapest Parade** on August 25, a mini version of London's Notting Hill Carnival, when a procession of floats set up by radio stations and clubs parades through the city, ending up on Dózsa György út by City Park for a rave into the early hours.

September heralds the start of the grape harvest, marked in Budapest by the annual **Wine Festival**, which fills Vörösmarty tér with stalls – and merriment, as the wine flows. As the Autumn Festival winds down and trees in the parks turn russet and gold, it is nowadays permitted to honour the **anniversary of the 1956 Uprising**. October 23 was a taboo anniversary for decades, then suddenly accorded cathartic, televised recognition; however, interest now seems to be waning among the majority of Hungarians who are too young to have experienced the Uprising, while others find their memories too painful to want to reawaken them. On **December 6**, children hang up Christmas boots for "little Jesus" to fill, and people prepare for the Christmas Eve feast of jellied carp or turkey. Festivities build up towards **New Year's Eve**, when revellers gather on the Nagykörút, engaging in noisy battles with toy trumpets at the junction with Rákóczi út.

Live music: rock and pop

Budapest attracts every Hungarian band worth its amplifiers and a growing roll call of international stars, making it the best place for **rock concerts** in Hungary. Major foreign acts appear at the vast Puskás Ferenc Stadion, the smaller Kisstadion or the Aréna, all in the same complex, and their appearances are well publicized in the media. Don't get too excited by flyposters advertising Michael Jackson or the Cure, however, as these usually refer to light shows or DJs at clubs and discos. Posters around town – particularly around Deák tér, Ferenciek tere and the Astoria underpass – also publicize concerts by Hungarian bands. Prices range from 1000Ft up to as much as 10,000Ft for international superstars. For an authentically grim Magyar rock-opera, you can't beat *István a király* (Stephen the King) or the new *Attila Sword of God*, both of which are about the early heroes of the Hungarian nation.

Local bands often perform at the **Petőfi Csarnok**, a big youth centre near the Városliget (see p.137), and world music groups regularly perform at the *Darshan Udvar* (see p.136). The following cultural centres are also popular venues, as are many of the clubs on p.137.

A 38 XI, Pázmány Péter sétány Ⓣ1/464-3940, Ⓦwww.a38.hu. Tram #4 or #6. Excellent concerts on this boat moored on the bank just below Petőfi Bridge on the Buda side.

Gay Budapest

Budapest's **gay scene** has taken wing in recent years, with new, overtly gay clubs replacing the old, covert meeting places, and the appearance of a trilingual monthly listings magazine, *Mások* ("Outsiders"). However, gays must still tread warily and lesbians even more so. The Hungarian word for gay is *meleg* – "warm" – while the pejorative term is "buzi" (from the word "buzeráns", which has the same roots as "bugger"). The **websites** ⓦwww.gayguide.net/Europe/Hungary/Budapest and ⓦwww.gay.hu have the latest on gay accommodation, bars, clubs, restaurants, baths and any events that might be happening in the city, and the Hattér **helpline** (daily 6–11pm; ⓣ1/329-3380, ⓦwww.hatter.hu), run by the largest gay and lesbian organization in the country, is another good source of information.

Aside from the bars and clubs listed on p,138, the **Turkish baths** are a popular meeting place – Király Baths for the younger crowd, where you'll find a lot of Romanian prostitutes, and the thermal baths at the Gellért. The first private gay bath is at Magnum Sauna & Gym at VIII, Csepreghy utca 2 (Mon–Thurs & Sun 1pm–1am, Fri & Sat 1pm–6am; from 1300Ft; ⓣ1/267 2532, ⓦgayguide.net/Budapest/Magnum; Ferenc körut metro). A **restaurant** with a particularly gay clientele is *Club 93* (V, Vas utca 2; 11am–midnight), a cheap pizzeria near Astoria that is popular after 8pm, while *Clifton* (I, Batthyány utca 63, ⓦwww.clifton.hu; Mon–Sat noon–midnight) is gay and lesbian friendly.

The major event in the gay calendar is **Gay Pride Budapest**, a four-day festival taking place in late June or early July. Organized by Hattér, this is fast becoming a well-established event in the capital, incorporating a varied programme of film festivals, public discussion forums and gay parties. The event culminates with the very colourful Pride March on the Saturday which wends its way from Dózsa György út to the Chain Bridge via Andrássy út.

Fonó Budai Zeneház XI, Sztregova utca 3 ⓣ1/206-5300, ⓦwww.fono.hu. Tram #18 or #47. Lively international folk, world music and jazz venue out past Móricz Zsigmond körtér.

Millenáris II, Millenarium Park ⓦwww.millenaris.hu. The concert hall in the park below Moszkva tér regularly hosts good concerts, including international acts and festivals, including the Hungarian folk stars Muzsikás and the top local ethno-jazz group, the Dresch Quartet.

Trafó IX, Liliom utca 41 ⓣ1/456-2040, ⓦwww.trafo.hu. Major contemporary arts centre attracting top foreign acts, with an excellent bar downstairs.

Live music: jazz

Don't be fooled by the small number of jazz venues in Budapest – the country boasts some brilliant jazz players, some of them well known abroad. For the top names, keep an eye out for pianists Béla Szakcsi Lakatos, György Szabados and György Vukán, double bassist Aladár Pege and saxophonist Mihaly Dresch. Some bands appear at local cultural centres (see above), others in some of the places listed on pp.137 under "Clubs", such as the *Petőfi Csarnok*.

Hades Jazztaurant VI, Vörösmarty utca 31 ⓣ1/352-1503. Pleasant bar/restaurant with a jazz trio (Mon & Fri) and piano music (Tues–Thurs). No live music June–August. Open till 2am (midnight on Sun).

Jazz Garden V, Veres Pálné utca 44A ⓣ1/266-7364, ⓦwww.jazzgarden.hu. Cellar jazz bar and restaurant. Guests include Hungarian stars Béla Szakcsi Lakatos and Aladár Pege, as well as local resident American blues guitarist Bruce Lewis. Daily noon–1am.

New Orleans Jazz Club VI, Lovas utca 5 ⓣ1/354-1130. New modern bar attracting big international names – but tickets can be astronomical even by Western standards. Daily noon–2am.

Tickets

Tickets for most big events are available from numerous outlets in the city: TicketExpress (no credit cards), VI, Andrássy út 18 (Mon–Fri 9.30am–6.30pm, Sat 9am–1pm; ⓣ1/312-0000, ⓦwww.ticketexpress.hu); Filharmónia, V, Madách utca 3 (Mon–Fri 10am–5pm; ⓣ1/321-4199); Rózsavölgyi ticket office in the record shop of the same name at V, Szervita tér 5 near Deák tér (Mon–Fri 10am–6pm, Sat 10am–3pm); and Publika (no credit cards) at VII, Károly körút 9 (ⓣ1/322-2010). The opera has its own ticket office. Ticket prices for major international acts will often have a small handling fee slapped on them, too.

Folk music and táncház

Hungarian **folk music and dancing** underwent a revival in the 1970s, drawing inspiration from Hungarian communities in Transylvania, regarded as pure wellsprings of Magyar culture. Enthusiasts formed "dance houses" or **táncház** to revive traditional instruments and dances, and get people involved. Visitors are welcome to attend the weekly gatherings (350–800Ft admission) and learn the steps. Groups such as Muzsikás, Téka, Ökrös and Kalamajka play Hungarian folk music, while other groups are inspired by South Slav music from Serbia, Croatia and Bulgaria, or, in the case of Di Naye Kapelye, klezmer music from around the region (far better than the easy-listening mainstream Budapest Klezmer Band).

Details of events are available in events magazines or on the website ⓦwww.tanchaz.hu. Bear in mind that many cultural centres close for summer, so check before you go.

Almássy téri Szabadidő Központ (see p.137). Greek and African dance houses; there are often big Hungarian or Gypsy (Roma) gatherings too. Closed July & Aug.

Aranytíz V, Arany János utca 10 ⓣ1/311-2248, ⓦwww.aranytiz.hu. The Kalamajka ensemble plays to a packed dance floor on Saturday nights at this downtown Pest cultural centre. Instruction from 7pm. There is also music in the bar upstairs, and as the evening rolls on a jamming session often develops. Closed early June–late Sept.

Fonó Budai Zeneház (see opposite). Folk musicians from around the Carpathian Basin play every Wednesday evening, followed by a local band.

Marcibányi tér Művelődési Ház II, Marcibányi tér 5A ⓣ1/212 0803. The best place in the city to catch the pulsating sounds of Csángó music from eastern Romania – it's a meeting point for Csángó people living in Budapest. Members of Muzsikás sometimes play on Thursday night from 8pm – check in *Pesti Est*. Not a dance house as such – the group just plays and people sit around in a very informal atmosphere.

Opera, ballet and classical music

Opera is highly esteemed in Hungary, a country whose composers and writers have created such works as *Bánk Bán*, *László Hunyadi*, *The Queen of Sheba* and *Blood Wedding*. Most productions are in Hungarian, a custom introduced by Mahler when he was director of the State Opera House in Budapest; fans prefer their opera "old style", with lavish sets and costumes, and they interrupt with ovations after particularly bravura passages. Operas by Mozart, Verdi, Puccini, Wagner and national composers are staged throughout the year, while several new productions are premiered during the Spring and Autumn festivals, when you can also catch performances by the State Opera **ballet** and visiting foreign companies.

The city excels in its variety of **classical music** performances, although pre-Baroque stuff is poorly represented. There are several concerts every night of the year, especially during the two main festivals. Look out for performances by the **Budapest Festival Orchestra** (the city's only privately financed orchestra), conducted by the charismatic Iván Fischer, and the **Radio and Television Symphony Orchestra**, conducted by Tamás Vásáry – both orchestras are below par when their inspirational directors are not at the helm – as well as two excellent **chamber ensembles**: the Liszt Ferenc Chamber Orchestra and the Weiner Száz Orchestra. Pianists Zoltán Kócsis, András Schiff and Dezső Ránki, violinist Vilmos Szabadi and cellist Miklós Perényi are other names to catch, while young stars to watch out for include two violinists, Barnabás Kelemen and Kristóf Baráti. The **Lutheran Church** on Deák tér in central Pest has regular concerts including Bach Passions before Easter; information for these is posted by the church's entrance. **St Stephen's Basilica** and the **Kálvín tér church** in central Pest also host occasional concerts; consult Tourinform for details.

Over the **summer**, smaller concerts take place outdoors on Margit sziget, and in many historic buildings, including the **Mátyás Church**, the **Dominican Yard** of the *Hilton* hotel in the Castle District, and the **Vajdahunyad Castle** in the Városliget. Choral or organ recitals are also held at the Mátyás Church on Fridays and Saturdays between June and September (from 8pm), and less frequently the rest of the year. Bear in mind that many city venues – the opera, theatre and concert halls – **close for the summer** at the end of May, reopening in mid-September. There is a summer season of concerts at Martonvásár (see p.196) and Vácrátót, within commuting distance of Budapest. A comprehensive **listing** of classical music events in Hungarian can be found at ⓦwww.koncertkalendarium.hu, or in the free monthly *Koncert Kalendárium* found in ticket offices, but you can also check out the other listings magazines (see p.71). The Opera House has its own box office (Mon–Sat 11am–5pm, Sun 4–7pm) for events there and in the Erkel Theatre, and also sells tickets for outdoor performances in and around Budapest (Martonvásár, Vácrátót, etc). These ticket offices also sell tickets to most classical concerts, as well as other events such as fashion shows and pop concerts.

Budapest Kongresszusi Központ (Budapest Convention Centre) XII, Jagelló út 1–3 ⓣ1/209-1990. This modern and uninspiring concert hall behind the *Novotel* is the venue for big orchestral concerts.

Erkel Színház VIII, Köztársaság tér 30 ⓣ1/333-0540. A modern venue for operas, ballet and musicals, on the edge of the red-light district near Keleti Station.

Liszt Ferenc Zeneakadémia (Music Academy) VI, Liszt Ferenc tér 8 ⓣ1/342-0179, ⓦwww.liszt.hu. Nightly concerts and recitals in the magnificent Nagyterem (Great Hall) or the smaller Kisterem. The former is usually shut during summer, as it gets too hot.

Magyar Állami Operaház (Hungarian State Opera) VI, Andrássy út 22 ⓣ1/353-0170, ⓦwww.opera.hu. Budapest's grandest venue, with gilded frescoes and three-tonne chandeliers – a place to dress up for.

Operetta Színház VI, Nagymező utca 17 ⓣ1/332-0535. Located on "Broadway", a few blocks from the opera house, this magnificent theatre stages classical Hungarian operettas and modern musicals – Hungarians' favourite musical genres.

Vigadó V, Vigadó tér 1 ⓣ1/327-4322. Another fabulously decorated hall, though the acoustics are not so hot. Closed for restoration at the time of writing.

Theatre

Mainstream Hungarian **theatre** is in the doldrums at present, and there is little to tempt the visitor in its melodramatic and unsubtle productions in an

A national farce

The sorry saga of Budapest's **National Theatre** (Nemzeti Színház) is a source of much shame and amusement in the city. The theatre used to be housed in a grand building on Blaha Lujza tér until the construction of the metro in the 1960s – which many saw as an evil plot by the Communist regime to undermine the nation's identity. For many years the theatre was temporarily housed in a hideous building in the backstreets of Pest, while the debate continued as to where the great national institution should stand. In 1997 the centre-left city authorities finally started the construction of a huge development on Erzsébet tér, which incorporated specially constructed and very costly foundations so that the underground car park would not disturb the performances. Hardly had the foundations been laid, however, when the new centre-right national government halted the construction in 1998 and started a new debate about where to put the theatre. In the end it chose a site on the Pest riverbank, but the controversy has gone on: the government minister in charge of the project gave the job of designing the building to the architect who designed his own holiday house; the site of the new theatre is some way south of the centre, with poor transport links; and even the end product has been widely mocked (see below).

incomprehensible language. The newly constructed **National Theatre**, IX, Bajor Gizi park 1 (Ⓣ1/476-6800, Ⓦwww.nemzetiszinhaz.hu), is aimed at reviving Hungary's proud traditions, but it has had a troubled birth and less dramatic impact than first hoped (see box, above). Of the established theatres, both the **Új Színház**,VI, Paulay Ede utca 35 (Ⓣ1/351-1406, Ⓦwww.szinhaz.hu/ujszinhaz), and **Radnoti Színház**,VI, Nagymező utca 11 (Ⓣ1/321-0600), however, offer reliably solid performances, while locals dress up in their finest for the beautiful **Vígszínház**, XIII, Szent István krt 14 (Ⓣ1/329 2340). It is also worth looking out for performances by the provincial theatre company from the town of **Kaposvár** in Transdanubia, which has attracted some good actors out from the city. The best Hungarian mainstream theatre is to be found outside the borders, in places like Cluj in Transylvania, where for the Hungarian minority the theatre still plays a vital role in communication.

Alternative theatre is where the quality is to be found. One Hungarian group that has received considerable critical acclaim abroad is the **Mozgó haz** (Moving House) theatre company, whose inventive combination of music and movement under the direction of László Hudi won the top award at the International Theatre Festival in Sarajevo in 1998 and was well received at the London International Festival of Theatre in 2001. Look out for them – they also perform as HUDI – at the Trafó (see p.140), the best venue for alternative dance and theatre. Other names to keep in mind are the **Krétakör** group, under the young director Árpád Schilling, which has won wide recognition abroad, and performances by **Péter Halász**, a big bald actor-director who spent many years in New York before returning to Hungary.

Alternative theatre **venues** include the **MU Színház**, XI, Körössy József utca 17 (Ⓣ1/209 4014, Ⓦwww.mu.hu); **Szkéné Színház**, XI, Műegyetem rakpart 3 (Ⓣ1/463-3741, Ⓦwww.szkene.hu); **Studio K**, IX, Mátyás utca 9 (Ⓣ1/216-7170, Ⓦwww.szinhaz.hu/studiok); and the **Merlin Theatre** in the centre of town at V, Gerlóczy utca 4 (Ⓣ1/317-9338, Ⓦwww.szinhaz.hu/merlin), which often hosts visiting British companies. Look out for flyers and check out the theatre listings publication *Súgó* (published in English in July and Aug). During summer there are easy-to-understand performances at the outdoor theatre on Margit sziget. The puppet theatre is covered under "Children's Budapest" on p.146.

Hungarian cinema

What the Hungarian film industry lacks in funds it makes up for in ideas. In recent years some really good films have been released, which unfortunately probably never make it beyond the art film festivals in the West, making a visit to the cinema a must for film buffs while they are here. Older **directors** include István Szabó (*Mephisto*, *Colonel Redl*, *Being Julia*), Márta Mészáros (*Diary for My Children*, *Nine Months*) and Károly Makk (*Another Way*, *The Gambler*). They were followed by Peter Gothár, with his absurd humour and love of the fantastic (*Time Stands Still*, *Let Me Hang Vaska*), Ildikó Enyedi (*My Twentieth Century*, *The Magic Hunter* and *Simon the Magician*), János Szász, whose latest film *The Witman Boys* won the best international film at Cannes, and Béla Tarr (*Werckmeister Harmonies* and the epic eight-hour *Satan Tango*), who has won considerable praise abroad. With the film industry getting a considerable boost from the present Socialist coalition government, there are a couple of young names to watch: Ferenc Török, whose film *Moszkva ter* – about apolitical youths in 1989 – won many fans, and Nimrod Antal, whose first film, the black comedy *Kontroll*, was a big hit abroad.

Cinema

Hollywood blockbusters and Euro soft-porn films currently dominate Budapest's mainstream **cinemas**, though the city has a chain of "arts cinemas" which specialize in the latest releases and obscure films from Eastern and Western Europe. Their provenance is indicated thus: *angol* (British), *lengyel* (Polish), *német* (German), *olasz* (Italian) and *orosz* (Russian). *Budapest Sun* runs listings of all movies playing in English. If you understand Hungarian, the fullest **listings** appear in *Pesti Est* and *Pesti Műsor* (*PM*) under the heading *Budapesti mozik műsora*. Here, the times of shows are cryptically abbreviated to *n8* or *1/4 8* for 7.15pm; *f8* or *1/2 8* for 7.30pm; and *h8* or *3/4 8* for 7.45pm. "*Mb.*" indicates the film is dubbed, and "*fel.*" or "*feliratos*" means that it has Hungarian subtitles.

Budapest has some of the most beautiful movie houses around. It is worth checking out the Moorish interior of the **Uránia National Film Theatre**, at VIII, Rákóczi út 21 (Ⓦwww.urania-nf.hu) – as a showcase for Hungarian film – and the coffered ceiling of the turn-of-the-twentieth-century **Pushkin**, at V, Kossuth Lajos utca 18, while the **Cirkógejzir**, at V, Balassi Bálint utca 15–17 (Ⓣ1/260-0904), is an alternative joint complete with Chinese tea before showings. A host of **multiplex** cinemas has now also appeared in the city, including the Corvin Film Palace at VIII, Corvin köz 1 (Corvin Filmpalota; Ⓣ1/459-5050, Ⓦwww.corvin.hu), and the Palace Westend in the Westend City Center by Nyugati Station (Ⓣ1/336-5555). Cinema-going is still cheap, with tickets from 600Ft in the smaller cinemas to more than 1100Ft in the multiplexes. In the summer there are also outdoor and drive-in cinemas on the edge of town. For more details about these, contact Tourinform.

The three main **film festivals** during the year are the Hungarian Film Festival (Magyar Filmszemle; Ⓦwww.magyar.film.hu), a parade of the year's new films in February, and two festivals of alternative Hungarian and foreign films, the Titanic Film Festival (Ⓦwww.datanet.hu/titanic) in October and the Europa Film Festival in December.

Sports

Apart from popular spectator sports such as soccer, horse-racing, and the Grand Prix, the city offers a range of **sports facilities** for participators. **Swimming** is very popular in Hungary, and Budapest has plenty of pools, such as the Hajós Alfréd Pool in the southern part of Margit sziget (see p.105) and the Császár Komjádi Pool (see p.101) – both have an indoor and an all-season outdoor pool. In summer you can find big outdoor pools (*strand*) surrounded by grass and fried-food stalls on the Margit sziget (see p.105), at Csillaghegy, III, Pusztakúti utca 3 (Szentendre HÉV to Csillaghegy), and at Rómaifürdő, a water park with three big slides, a family slide and sauna, III, Rozgonyi Piroska utca 2 (Szentendre HÉV to Rómaifürdő) – all three are open daily in the summer (May–Sept) from 9am to 7pm. The thermal baths – including the Rudas, the Lukács and the Gellért – also have swimming pools.

Tennis courts can be booked all year round at the Városmajor Tennis Academy in Városmajor Park near Moszkva tér (ⓣ1/202–5337) – you can also hire racquets – while **squash** enthusiasts should head for the City Squash Club at II, Marcibányi tér 13 (ⓣ1/325-0082). To organize **horse-riding** contact the Hungarian Equestrian Tourism Association at Ráday utca 8 (ⓣ1/456-0444, ⓦwww.equi.hu); alternatively, head out for the Great Plain (see Chapter 6), where there are many small riding schools. In winter, it's possible to **ski** at Normafa and Jánoshegy in the Buda Hills – equipment can be rented from Suli Sí in the Komjádi swimming complex at II, Árpád fejedelem utca 8 (ⓣ1/212-0330). Skates can be rented at the **ice rink** in the Városliget between November and March. Finally, most of the larger hotels have **fitness centres** open to non-residents.

Soccer

Hungary's great footballing days are long past – the golden team of the 1950s that beat England 6–3 with stars such as Ferenc Puskás and József Bozsik is a world away from today's national team that struggles to qualify for any big tournaments. The club scene is also in deep crisis, with teams floundering in a financial desert amid poor infrastructure and bad management. While **international matches** are held at the Puskás Ferenc Stadion – generally filling just a third of its 76,000 seats – club football revolves around the turf of three **premier league teams**. Ferencvárosi Torna Club (aka FTC or Fradi) is the biggest club in the country, based at IX, Üllői út 129, near the Népliget metro (ⓦwww.ftc.hu). Fradi is almost a national institution, and its supporters, dressed in the club's colours of green and white, are the loudest presence at international matches too. The club has long had right-wing ties – this was the fascists' team before the war, and in recent years it has attracted a strong skinhead – and anti-Semitic – element. When a businessman of Jewish origin bought the club in 2001, it resulted in an outpouring of violently anti-Semitic comments from the nationalist right wing. Fradi fans try to pick fights with supporters of Újpesti Torna Egylet, whose ground is at IV, Megyeri út 13 (four stops on bus #30 from Újpest Központ metro station). Their main rivals are MTK, whose club is at VIII, Salgótarján utca 12–14 (tram #37 from Blaha Lujza tér).

See the daily paper *Nemzeti Sport* for details of fixtures. The **season** runs from late July to late November and then from late February to mid-June. Matches are played on Saturday afternoons. Tickets cost around 1800Ft.

Horse-racing

Horse-racing has flourished for many years in Hungary, but is currently in a state of turmoil. It was introduced from England by Count Széchenyi in 1827 and flourished until 1949, when flat racing (*galopp*) was banned by the Communists. For many years punters could only enjoy **trotting races**, but in the mid-1980s flat racing resumed at the horse-racing track, Kincsem Park, further east of the centre. The sport since then has been dogged by financial problems and mismanagement, and the trotting track was sold off for redevelopment in 2000, causing uproar in racing circles.

You can watch both flat racing and trotting at Kincsem Park, X, Albertirsai út 2–6 (Pillangó utca on the red metro, and then either walk or catch #100 bus). **Flat racing** takes place on Sundays from spring to autumn; **trotting** is all year round, on Wednesdays and Saturdays (and on Sundays in winter when the flat racing stops). The atmosphere at the tracks is informal, but photographing the racegoers is frowned upon, since many attend unbeknownst to their spouses or employers. Races are advertised in *Fortuna* magazine. **Betting** operates on a tote system, where your returns are affected by how the odds stood at the close of betting. The different types of bet you can make are *tét* (placing money on the winner); *hely* (on a horse coming in the first three); and the popular *befutó* (a bet on two horses to come in either first and second or first and third). Winnings are paid out about fifteen minutes after the end of the race.

The Hungarian Grand Prix

First held in 1986, the **Hungarian Grand Prix** takes place every summer at the purpose-built Formula One Racing track at **Mogyoród**, 20km northeast of Budapest. It is usually scheduled for mid-August, and financial uncertainties surrounding the event spark off rumours every year that that is the last year it will be held. Details are available from Tourinform, any listings magazine or the website Ⓦ www.hungaroring.hu. You can reach the track by special buses from the Árpád híd Bus Station; trains from Keleti Station to Fót, and then a bus from there; or by HÉV train from Örs vezér tere to the Szilasliget stop, which is 1800m northeast of Gate C. **Tickets**, available from Ostermann Forma 1 Kft., Apáczai Csere János utca 11, 3rd floor (Ⓣ 1/266-2040), online at the address above or from booths in Ferenciek tér, range from €35–90 for the first day, to €100–290 the final day, and €110–400 for a three-day pass – the price being partly determined by the location, and whether you book in advance or risk disappointment on the day.

Children's Budapest

Facilities for **children** in Budapest do leave something to be desired, though that is not a reflection of Hungarian attitudes to kids: Hungarians love children and will often talk to them on the bus, give up their seats for them, and roundly criticize you if they think your child is not sufficiently wrapped up in winter.

From Klauzál tér's scaled-down assault course to the folksy wooden seesaws and swings erected on Széchenyi-hegy, there are children's **playgrounds** all over Budapest – the best are in the **Millenarium Park** (see p.101) and the **Zoo** (p.121). Improvements to the Zoo have made it a great place to visit; kids can feed the camels and giraffes, tickle the rhinos, stroke the goats, sheep and farm animals and explore the restored aquarium and Palm House. Nearby is

Városliget (p.120) with its mock castle and lake – allowing skating or rowing according to the season – as well as the **Transport Museum** with its old trains (p.121), the **fairground** (p.121) and the **circus** (p.121). The "**railway circuit**" of the Buda Hills (p.103) should also appeal to all ages, but the best place for young train buffs is the **Hungarian Railway History Park**, where kids can clamber over all kinds of locomotives and even get to drive a steam train (p.116). Finally, the **Labyrinth of Buda Castle** under the Vár (p.91) offers an exciting exploration for 6–12-year-olds, and there's fun hands-on science at the **Palace of Miracles** (see p.116).

Budapest has a strong tradition in puppetry but at present has only one **puppet theatre** (*bábszínház*); this occasionally puts on English-language performances. Morning and matinée performances are for kids, while the evening's occasional masked grotesqueries or renditions of Bartók's *The Wooden Prince* and *The Miraculous Mandarin* are intended for adults. Tickets are available from the puppet theatre itself at VI, Andrássy út 69 (Ⓣ1/341-2166), or the ticket offices detailed on p.141.

Another popular destination for kids is the **Görzenál Skatepark** at III, Árpád fejedelem útja (March–Oct Mon–Fri 9am–7pm, Sat & Sun 9am–9pm; Nov–Feb Sat & Sun 9am–6pm; Ⓣ1/250-4800; Szentendre HÉV to Timár utca), where you can rollerblade, skateboard and cycle on ramps and jumps to your heart's content.

Shopping

Budapest's range of **shops** has expanded massively in recent years, as big international names such as Mango and Benetton have appeared in its streets, and more especially in its malls. Most shops are **open** Monday to Friday 10am–6pm, and Saturday until 1pm, with most foodstores opening from 8am to 6 or 7pm. Recently some shops in the centre of the city have been staying open later on Saturdays. The new shopping malls on the edge of the city also tend to have longer opening hours, and are open on Sundays as well. You can usually find a 24-hour – *non-stop* – shop serving alcohol, cigarettes and some food in the centre of town, though in the residential parts of Buda they may be harder to find.

Main **shopping areas** are located to the south of Vörösmarty tér in central Pest, in particular in and around pedestrianized Váci utca and Petőfi Sándor utca, which have the biggest concentration of glamorous and expensive shops. The main streets radiating out from the centre – Bajcsy-Zsilinszky, Andrássy and Rákóczi út – are other major shopping focuses, as are the two ring boulevards, the Great Boulevard (especially from Margit Bridge to Blaha Lujza tér) and the Kiskörút, while the small streets inside the Nagykörút are also worth exploring.

Modern **shopping malls**, combining major shopping centres with entertainment facilities under one roof, have now spread right across the city, and most stay open all weekend. Two of the closest to the centre are Mammut and Mammut II (Ⓦwww.mammut.hu) by Moszkva tér, Mom Park (Ⓦwww.mompark.hu), XII, Alkotás utca 53, above Déli Station, and Westend (Ⓦwww.westend.hu), by Nyugati Station.

Budapest has three **flea markets**: Petőfi Csarnok (Sat & Sun 7am–2pm; see p.137) in the Városliget, which has expanded fast and is probably the best in town; the expensive Ecseri piac at XIX, Nagykőrösi utca 156 (Mon–Fri

7am–4pm, Sat 7am–noon; take bus #54 from Boráros tér at the Pest end of Petőfi Bridge), where Saturday is the biggest day and sellers are aware of the money to be made from rich foreign tourists, but where there are also bargains to be found, either early on a Saturday or at closing time; and Nowák piac at Dózsa Gy. utca 1–3, behind Keleti Station (head up Verseny utca), which has excellent bargains and shady characters, although it is weak in the snack department.

The most popular **souvenirs** to bring home are wine, porcelain, foodstuffs (such as paprika, salami and goose liver) and CDs. Budapest's **Antiques Row** is Falk Miksa utca, at the Pest end of Margit Bridge. Shops in the Vár are almost exclusively given over to providing foreign tourists with folksy **souvenirs**, embroidered tablecloths, hussar pots, fancy bottles of Tokaji wine and so forth. Another good source of presents is the **market halls** in Pest: the spectacular Great Market Hall (Nagycsarnok), or smaller ones on Hold utca (behind the American Embassy) and on Rákóczi tér. Other interesting shops include Hephaistos, at V, Molnár utca 27, which sells beautiful wrought-iron items, from candle holders to bookshelves; Lekvárium, VII, Dohány utca 39 (Mon–Fri 10am–6pm), which has a range of locally made and unusual jams and preserves, as well as delicious elderflower syrup; the puppet shop in the courtyard at V, Párizsi utca 3, which has marvellous glove puppets; and the Diófa toy shop, with wooden old wind-up toys at Wesselényi utca 23.

The emergence of a thriving **wine industry** is reflected in the number of new wine shops in the city. The Budapest Wine Society at I, Batthyány utca 59, near Moszkva tér, has a good selection and the English-speaking staff know their wines (Mon–Fri 10am–8pm, Sat 10am–6pm, free wine tastings on Sat afternoons; ⓣ1/202-2569, ⓦwww.bortarsasag.hu) – other outlets can be found at IX, Ráday utca 7 and in the Mom Park centre. Another good store is La Boutique des Vins at V, József Attila utca 12, near Deák tér (Mon–Fri 10am–8pm, Sat 10am–3pm; ⓣ1/317-5919, ⓦwww.malatinszky.hu). Outlets for the main **porcelain** makers are Haas & Czjzek, at VI, Bajcsy-Zsilinszky út 23, opposite the Arany János metro station, which stocks all the main brands, or the shops of the producers, such as Herend at V, József nádor tér 11, or Zsolnay at V, Váci utca 19–21.

For rock, pop and jazz **records** and **CDs** (including bootlegs), try DOB Records, VII, Dob utca 71, Indiego in the courtyard at VIII, Krudy Gyula utca 7 (Mon–Fri 11am–8pm), or Lemezkucko, VI, Király utca 67. The best place for folk CDs is the shop in the Fonó concert hall (Tues–Sat 10am–11pm; see p.140). For classical music, try the Zeneszalon at V, Deák Ferenc utca 19 or the CD Bar at Krudy Gyula utca 6 (Mon–Fri 10am–8pm, Sat 10am–4pm, ⓦwww.cd-bar.hu), across the way from Indiego. The friendly Rózsavölgyi at V, Szervita tér 5, has an excellent selection of classical music, with pop and folk downstairs, plus sheet music. The best selection of secondhand classical records and CDs is at Concerto Records, VII, Dob utca 31 (Mon–Fri noon–7pm, Sun noon–4pm), and for secondhand rock and blues records and CDs try Lemez Dokk, VIII, Horánszky utca 27 and Rockin' Box at VI, Paulay Ede utca 8 (both Mon–Fri noon–6pm).

Listings

Airlines Air France, V, Váci utca 19 ⓣ1/483-8800; British Airways/Qantas, V, East-West Business Centre, VIII, Rákóczi út 1–3 ⓣ1/777-4747; KLM, VIII, Rákóczi út 1–3 ⓣ1/373-7737; Lufthansa, V, Váci utca 19 ⓣ1/266-4511; Malév, V, Dorottya utca 2 ⓣ1/235-3565.

Airport information Flight information: ⓣ1/296-7000, ⓦwww.bud.hu.

Banks and exchange You can transfer money from abroad through the Magyar Külkereskedelmí Bank, V, Szent István tér 11, by the basilica; through Interchange, the regional agents for Western Union, which have branches at the main stations and in the city centre; and through the American Express Moneygram service (minimum $100), V, Deák utca 10 ⓣ1/235-4330. Money transfers allegedly take only a few minutes. The Magyar Külkereskedelmi Bank also has safe-deposit boxes for storing valuables.

Bike rental Try Charles Rent-a-Bike at the *Charles Hotel* (see p.80); Yellow Zebra (see p.71); and Nella Bikes off Bajcsy-Zsilinszky út at V, Kálmán Imre utca 23 ⓣ1/331-3184.

Bookstores English-language bookstores include Bestsellers at V, Október 6 utca 11; Libri at V, Váci utca 22; the foreign-language bookshop in the Párizsi Udvar at V, Petőfi Sándor utca 2; Fókusz at VII, Rákóczi út 14–16; Litea at I, Hess András tér 4. The Red Bus bookstore, V, Semmelweis utca 14, deals exclusively in secondhand English books, or there are small English sections in Hungarian secondhand bookstores (*antikvárium*) at V, Váci utca 28 & 75; V, Múzeum körút 15; and Bibliotéka on the corner of Andrássy út and Bajcsy-Zsilinszky út.

British Council VI, Benczúr utca 26 ⓣ1/478-4700, ⓦwww.britishcouncil.hu. Library, newspapers and a noticeboard. Mon–Thurs 11am–6pm, Fri 11am–5pm; closed Aug.

Car breakdown The Magyar Autóklub runs a 24-hour breakdown assistance ⓣ188.

Car rental Avis, V, Szervita tér 8 (by the Jet petrol station under the multistorey car park) ⓣ1/318-4240, ⓦwww.avis.hu; Budget at the *Hotel Mercure Buda*, I, Krisztina körút 41–43 ⓣ & ⓕ1/214-0420, ⓦwww.budget.hu; Europcar V, Deák Ferenc tér 3 ⓣ1/328-6464, ⓦwww.europcar.hu; Hertz, V, Apáczai Csere János utca 4 (beside the *Marriott Hotel*) ⓣ1/296-0999, ⓦwww.hertz.hu; Recent Car, III, Hajógyári sziget 131, ⓣ1/453-0004, ⓦwww.recentcar.hu. All except Recent Car also have offices at the airport.

Driving information For motoring information contact Magyar Autóklub, II, Rómer Floris utca 4A ⓣ1/345-1800, ⓦwww.autoklub.hu; for traffic conditions in Budapest contact Fővinform ⓣ1/317-1173.

Embassies Australia, XII, Királyhágó tér 8–9 ⓣ1/457-9777; Canada, XII, Budakeszi út 32 ⓣ1/392-3360; Germany, I, Úri utca 64 ⓣ1/488-3500; Ireland, V, Szabadság tér 7, Bank Center, 7th floor ⓣ1/302-9600; UK, V, Harmincad utca 6 ⓣ1/266-2888; US, V, Szabadság tér 12 ⓣ1/475-4400.

Emergencies Ambulance ⓣ104; police ⓣ107; fire service ⓣ105.

Hospitals and dentistry There are 24-hour casualty departments at V, Hold utca 19, behind the US embassy (ⓣ1/311-6816), and at II, Ganz utca 13–15 (ⓣ1/202-1370). The Országos Baleseti Intézet VIII, Fiumei út 17 (ⓣ1/333-7599), specializes in broken limbs and accidents; Profident, VII, Károly körut 1, is a round-the-clock dentist where they speak English. A private clinic with English-speaking personnel is the IMS (International Medical Services) at XIII, Váci út 202 (ⓣ1/329-8423; Mon–Fri 7.30am–7pm), and at III, Vihar utca 29 ⓣ1/388-8257 (24-hour). Embassies can also recommend private, foreign-language-speaking doctors and dentists.

International buses and trains International train tickets should be purchased 24–36 hours in advance, at the stations or the MÁV booking office, VI, Andrássy út 35 (Mon–Fri 9am–5pm, until 6pm April–Sept; ⓣ1/461-5500, ⓦwww.mav.hu, booking service and timetables on ⓦwww.elvira.hu). Bookings are required on all international train routes but it may not be possible to obtain them on trains leaving from Kőbánya-Kispest. This also applies to services from Zugló Station, which sometimes handles international traffic. The Vienna-bound *Wiener Waltzer* often runs late, so reserve sleepers on from Austria in Budapest. Also bring drinks, as the buffet staff overcharge shamelessly. International bus services depart from Népliget Bus Station, where you can buy tickets (Mon–Fri 6am–6pm, till 9pm mid-June to mid-Sept, Sat–Sun 6am–4pm; English information on ⓣ1/219-8021).

Internet access Smaller places tend to be cheaper but do not have such fast machines, or as many printers or games as the larger places. Only those specified have English keyboards. CEU Net, V, Október 6 utca 14 (daily 11am–10pm; all English keyboards); Electric Café, VII, Dohány utca 37 (daily 9am–midnight, some English keyboards); Millenarium Park C Building (free for one hour); Internet Ráday, IX, Mátyás utca 17 (daily 10am–11pm; some English keyboards); Ami, V, Váci utca 40 (daily 9am–2am; some English keyboards; 50 terminals, plus games available); Budapest Internet Café, V, Kecskeméti utca 5 (daily 10am–10pm; some English keyboards); Castro, IX, Ráday utca 35 (Mon–Fri 10am–midnight, Sat & Sun 2pm–midnight; five terminals); Szabó Ervin Library, VIII, Reviczky utca (Mon–Fri 10am–8pm, Sat 10am–4pm – register at the desk in reception); and Matávpont, V, Petőfi utca 17–19 and all large shopping malls (daily 9am–8pm).

Laundry Házimosoda, V, Galamb utca 9 ⓣ1/200-5305 (Mon–Fri 8am–7.30pm, Sat 9am–1pm), offers laundry and dry cleaning; Irisz Szalon V, Városház utca 3–5 (Mon–Fri 7am–7pm) is one of the few self-service launderettes left in the city.
Lost property For items left on public transport go to the office at VII, Akácfa utca 18 (ⓣ1/267-5299; Mon, Tues & Thurs 7.30am–3pm, Wed 7.30am–7pm, Fri 7.30am–2pm). Lost or stolen passports should be reported to the police station in the district where they were lost. Any found are handed to the relevant embassy.
Pharmacies Details of each district's 24-hour pharmacy are posted in every pharmacy's window. Central 24-hour pharmacies include those at Alkotás utca 2, opposite Déli Station, and at Teréz körút 41, near Oktogon. For herbal remedies try Herbária, VIII, Rákóczi út 49, and V, Bajcsy-Zsilinszky út 58.
Post offices Main office/poste restante at V, Petőfi Sándor utca 13 (Mon–Fri 8am–8pm & Sat 8am–2pm), and a late-night post office by Keleti Station at VII, Baross tér 11c (daily 7am–9pm).
Religious services in English Anglican: Sun 11am at VI, Vörösmarty utca 51; Baptist: Sun 10.30am, International Baptist Church, II, Törökvész út 48–54 (Móricz Zsigmond Gimnázium); Roman Catholic: Sat 5pm, Pesti Jézus Szíve Templom, VIII, Mária utca 25 ⓣ1/318-3479.
Taxis Citytaxi has an English-speaking service ⓣ1/211-1111, but other reliable companies include: Fő taxi ⓣ1/222-2222; Buda-taxi ⓣ1/233-3333; and Tele-5-taxi ⓣ1/355-5555.
Telephones International calls can be made from any phone booth on the street or from Telepont, V, Petőfi Sándor utca 17–19 (Mon–Fri 9am–8pm, Sat 10am–3pm); the international operator can be reached on ⓣ199.

Travel details

Trains

Where only InterCity are given, there are also slightly slower express services to the same destination.
Batthyány tér (HÉV) to: Pomáz (every 10–15min; 30min); Szentendre (every 10–20min; 40min).
Déli Station to: Balatonfüred (every 1–2hr; 2hr–2hr 15min); Balatonszentgyörgy (every 1–2hr; 3hr–3hr 30min); Dombóvár (7 InterCity daily; 1hr 30min–2hr); Kaposvár (2 daily; 2hr); Pécs (6 InterCity daily; 2hr 30min); Siófok (hourly June–Sept, otherwise 8 daily; 1hr 45min); Székesfehérvár (every 20–30min; 1hr); Szekszárd (5 daily; 2hr 45min); Szombathely (5 InterCity daily; 2hr 45min); Tapolca (every 1–2hr; 4–5hr); Veszprém (7 daily; 1hr–1hr 30min); Zalaegerszeg (5 daily; 3hr 20min).
Keleti Station to: Békéscsaba (hourly; 3hr); Eger (4 daily; 2hr); Győr (hourly; 1hr 30min–2hr); Komárom (13 daily – also from Déli Station; 1hr 15min–1hr 50min); Miskolc (hourly; 2hr–2hr 30min); Sárospatak and Sátoraljaújhely (2 daily; 3hr 45min–4hr); Sopron (7 daily; 2hr 50min); Szolnok (hourly; 1hr 30min); Tata (every 2hr; 1hr).
Nyugati Station to: Debrecen (hourly; 2hr 30min–3hr 30min); Esztergom (every 40min–1hr; 1hr 30min–1hr 40min); Kecskemét (12 daily; 1hr 30min); Nyíregyháza (hourly; 3hr–3hr 30min); Szeged (11 daily; 2hr 30min); Szob (hourly; 1hr 20min); Szolnok (hourly; 1hr 30min); Vác (every 30min; 45min); Vácrátót (hourly; 1hr 10min).

Buses

Árpád híd to: the Danube Bend: Dobogókő (2 daily; 1hr 20min); Esztergom via the Bend (every 30–40min; 1hr 15min) or Dorog (every 30min; 55min); Pilisszántó (every 20–30min; 1–2hr); Pilisvörösvár (every 20min; 40min); Szentendre (every 30min–1hr; 30min); Vác (hourly; 30min); Visegrád (every 30min–1hr; 1hr).
Népliget to: Lake Balaton and Transdanubia: Balatonfüred (5 daily; 2hr–2hr 40min); Dunaújváros (hourly; 1hr 20min); Győr (every 30min–1hr; 1hr 50min); Herend (10 daily; 2hr 45min); Harkány (2 daily; 4hr 30min); Hévíz (3 daily; 4hr); Kaposvár (3 daily; 3hr 30min); Keszthely (3 daily; 3hr 45min); Mohács (3 daily; 4hr); Nagyvázsony (2 daily except Sun; 3hr); Pécs (5 daily; 4hr); Siklós (1 daily; 4hr 50min); Siófok (7 daily; 1hr 35min–2hr 10min); Sopron (5 daily; 3hr 50min); Sümeg (3 daily; 3hr 40min); Székesfehérvár (every 15–45min; 1hr 15min); Szekszárd (hourly; 3hr); Szombathely (2 daily; 4hr 25min); Velence (8 daily; 1hr); Veszprém (every 10–15min; 2hr 10min); Zalaegerszeg (6 daily; 4hr 45min); Zirc (3 daily; 2hr 30min).
Stadion to: northern Hungary and the Great Plain: Aggtelek (2 daily; 5hr); Baja (every 1–2hr; 3hr 15min); Balassagyarmat (every 1–2hr; 2hr 10min); Békéscsaba (3 daily; 4hr); Eger (hourly; 2hr); Gödöllő (every 1hr–1hr 30min; 45min); Gyöngyös (hourly; 1hr 35min); Kalocsa (every 1–2hr; 2hr); Kecskemét (every 10min–1hr; 1hr 45min); Kiskunfélegyháza (8–10 daily; 2hr); Mátraháza (every

2–3hr; 1hr 50min); Miskolc (1 daily; 4hr 30min); Salgótarján (every 1hr–1hr 30min; 2hr 30min); Szeged (6 daily; 3hr 25min).

Hydrofoils and ferries

Ferries operate from April to October or November, as weather permits, with more running June to August.

Belgrád rakpart international landing stage to: Vienna (April–Oct 1–2 hydrofoils daily; 6hr).

Vigadó tér pier to: Esztergom (1 daily; 4hr 30min); Szentendre (2 daily; 1hr 25min); Vác (1 daily; 1hr 45min); Visegrád (2–3 daily; 3hr 30min); Zebegény (1–2 daily; 4hr 20min).

The Danube Bend

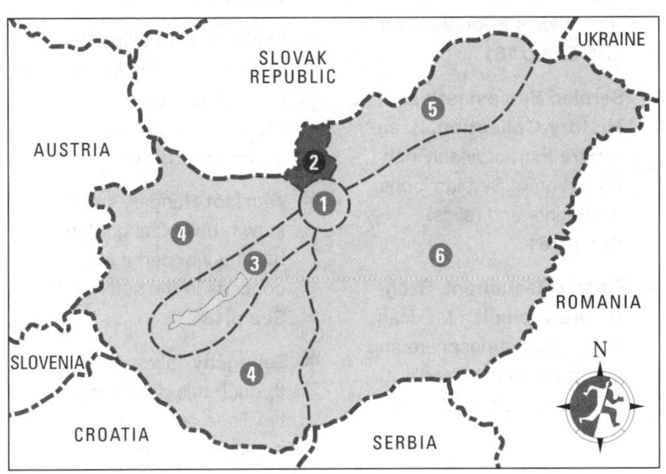

CHAPTER 2 Highlights

* **Ferry ride along the Danube** A leisurely cruise along the river is the nicest way to reach the historic Danube towns. See p.156

* **Margit Kovàcs Museum, Szentendre** Unique and entertaining collection of sculptures and reliefs from the nation's favourite ceramicist. See p.161

* **Serbian Ecclesiastical History Collection, Szentendre** Extraordinarily rich collection of Serbian icons, vestments and relics. See p.161

* **Palapa Restaurant, Szentendre** Top-notch Mexican food, great atmosphere and live music in the Bend's grooviest restaurant. See p.163

* **Hungarian Open-Air Museum** The best of Hungary's open-air museums, with a fantastic cross-section of dwellings from around the country. See p.163

* **Visegrád Hills** Good hiking and superb panoramas of the sweeping Danube Bend. See p.171

* **Esztergom Basilica** Hungary's largest cathedral, with an atmospheric crypt holding the tomb of Cardinal Mindszenty. See p.175

* **Vácrátót** Hungary's best-known botanical garden, hosting wonderful evening concerts in the summer. See p.184

* **Zebegény** Take a stroll through this delightfully pretty village on the quieter east bank. See p.186

▲ Esztergom Basilica

2

The Danube Bend

To escape Budapest's humid summers, many people flock north of the city to the **Danube Bend** (Dunakanyar), one of the grandest stretches of the river, outdone only by the Kazan Gorge in Romania. Entering the Carpathian Basin, the Danube widens dramatically, only to be forced by hills and mountains through a narrow, twisting valley, almost a U-turn – the "Bend" – before dividing for the length of Szentendre Sziget (Szentendre Island) and flowing into Budapest. The **historic towns and ruins** of Szentendre, Esztergom and Visegrád on the west bank can be seen on a long day-trip from Budapest, but it would be a shame not to linger here and visit the quieter east side too, boasting the sedate town of Vác, the gardens of Vácrátót and the charms of Nagymaros and Zebegény, as well as the neighbouring Pilis and Börzsöny highlands, with opportunities for **hiking** or **horse-riding**.

The west bank

The natural defence presented by the broad river and the hilly western bank has long attracted the inhabitants of this region to build their castles here. The Romans built a camp to keep the barbarians at bay, unwittingly staking out the sites of the future castles of the Magyar kings, who, a thousand years later, had to repel the Mongols arriving from the east. **Esztergom**, the scene for the Hungarians' official conversion to Christianity in the tenth century, served as the royal seat for three hundred years, after which the kings moved their base downriver to the citadel of **Visegrád**. With the expulsion of the Turks in the seventeenth century, the fertility and beauty of the landscape became the main attractions. Baroque **Szentendre** was established in the eighteenth century when Serbs fleeing up the Danube from the Turks settled here. Later, in the 1920s, it became an artists' colony. The **Pilis range** of mountains, filling the countryside between the three towns, makes for excellent hiking.

Its proximity to Budapest makes Szentendre the logical place to start your trip. With frequent onward **bus** services, it's easy to travel to Visegrád and then continue westward to Esztergom. Both these towns are also accessible direct from

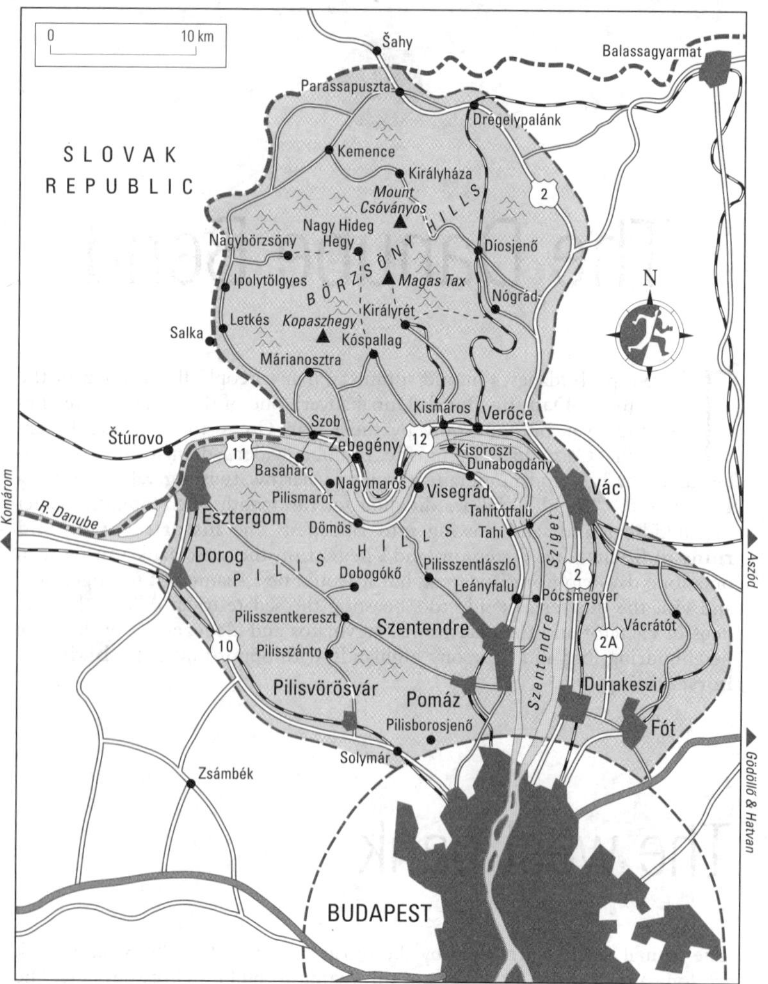

Budapest: hourly buses from the Árpád híd terminus follow an anticlockwise route around the Bend – although Esztergom can be reached more directly by the less scenic clockwise route that goes via Dorog; this is also the route taken by **trains** to Esztergom from the capital's Nyugati Station. Train access is otherwise limited in the Bend: you can catch a train to Visegrád only by going up the east bank to Nagymaros via Vác and taking the ferry across the river, but there is no onward train to Esztergom.

In summer you can take the more leisurely option of travelling by **ferry** from Budapest's Vigadó tér pier to Visegrád and Esztergom via Vác, as well as Szentendre. For further information, contact any Tourinform office or the Mahart shipping company (Ⓦwww.mahartpassnave.hu) by Vigadó tér pier. To

The Danube

The Danube is the second longest river in Europe after the Volga, flowing 2857km from the Black Forest to the Black Sea. Between the confluence of the Bereg and Briach streams at Donaueschingen and its shifting delta on the Black Sea, the Danube is fed by over three hundred tributaries from a catchment area of 816,000 square kilometres, and has nine nations along its banks. Known as the Donau in Germany and Austria, it becomes the Dunaj in Slovakia and then the Duna in Hungary before taking a course through Croatia, Serbia and Bulgaria as the Dunav, Romania as the Dunarea and the Ukraine as the Dunay, forming the frontier for much of the way. Used by armies and tribes since antiquity, this "dustless highway" deeply impressed the German poet Hölderlin who saw it as an allegory for the mythical voyage of the ancient German forefathers to the Black Sea, and for Hercules' journey from Greece to the land of the Hyperboreans. Attila József described it as "cloudy, wise and great", its waters from many lands as intermingled as the peoples of the Carpathian Basin. While the Danube's strategic value ended after World War II, economic and environmental concerns came to the fore in the 1980s, when the governments of Hungary, Austria and Czechoslovakia began to realize a plan to dam the river between Gabčikovo and Nagymaros (see box, p.185). The project, however, was finally and controversially shelved.

make a **day-trip** from Budapest, you might want to combine transport, taking a boat up to Esztergom and then catching the bus round to Visegrád and back to Budapest.

Szentendre and around

With its fabulous Baroque heart, **SZENTENDRE** (St Andrew), 19km north of Budapest, is unlikely to disappoint. Called "the Montmartre of the Danube" by Claudio Magris (see p.462), it remains a delightful maze of houses painted in autumnal colours, with secretive gardens and lanes winding up to hilltop churches. The town's location on the lower slopes of the Pilis range is not only beautiful, but ensures that Szentendre enjoys more hours of sunlight than anywhere else in Hungary, making it a perfect spot for an artists' colony.

Before the artists moved in, Szentendre's character had been formed by waves of refugees from **Serbia**. The first influx followed the catastrophic Serb defeat at Kosovo in 1389, which foreshadowed the Turkish occupation of Hungary in the sixteenth century, when Szentendre fell into ruin. After Hungary had been liberated, the Turkish recapture of Belgrade in 1690 precipitated the flight of 30,000 Serbs and Bosnians led by Patriarch Arsenije Carnojević, 6000 of whom settled in Szentendre, which became the seat of the Serbian Orthodox Church in exile. Prospering through trade, they replaced their wooden churches with stone ones and built handsome town houses. However, as Habsburg toleration waned and phylloxera (vine-blight) and floods ruined the local economy, they began to trickle back to Serbia, so that by 1890 less than a quarter of the population was Serb. Today, only a few dozen families of Serbian descent remain.

In 1928, thanks to its close proximity to Budapest and the excellent light conditions, Szentendre became a working artists' colony, and today its links with art are as strong as ever, with some two hundred artists working here and the town's countless museums and galleries vying for the attention of the peak-season tourist crowds. The town is extremely popular and can get swamped in

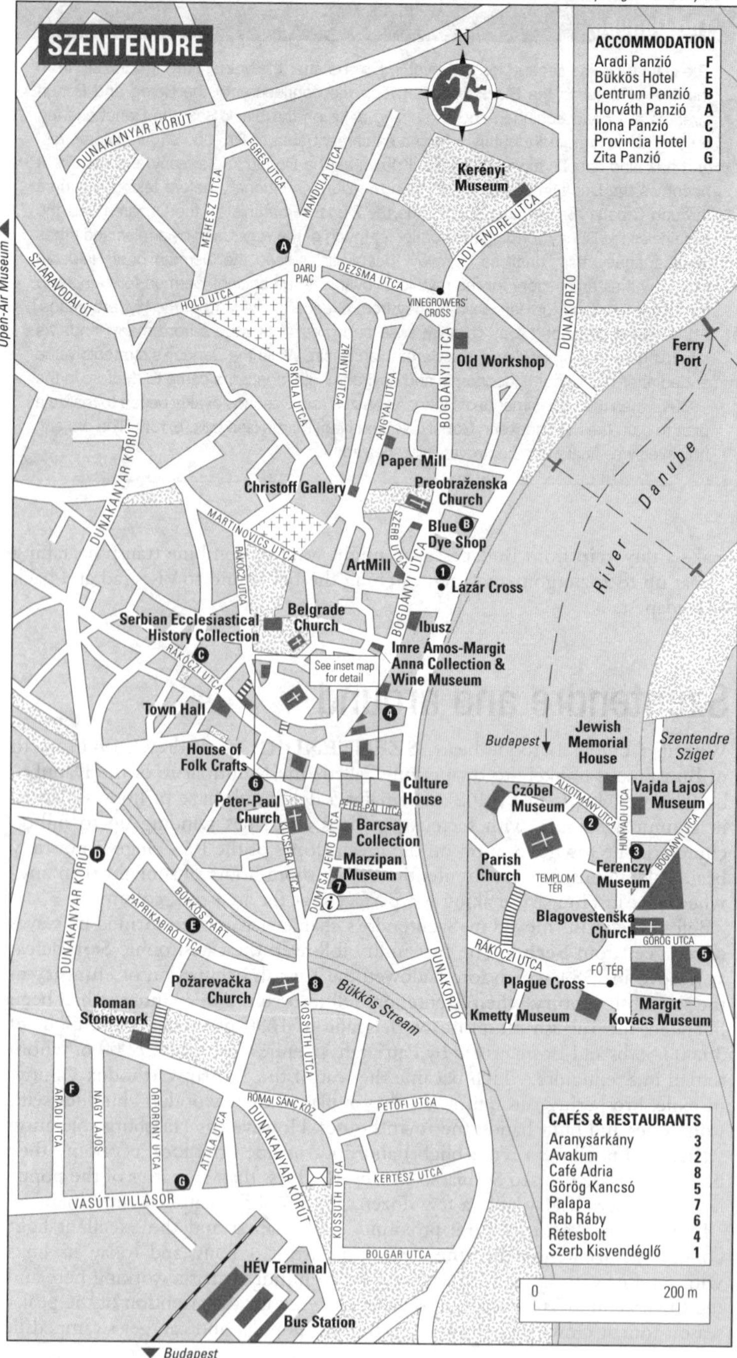
SZENTENDRE
ACCOMMODATION
Aradi Panzió F
Bükkös Hotel E
Centrum Panzió B
Horváth Panzió A
Ilona Panzió C
Provincia Hotel D
Zita Panzió G
CAFÉS & RESTAURANTS
Aranysárkány 3
Avakum 2
Café Adria 8
Görög Kancsó 5
Palapa 7
Rab Ráby 6
Rétesbolt 4
Szerb Kisvendéglő 1
Pap Sziget and Leányfalu
Open-Air Museum
Visegrád and Esztergom
Budapest
Kerényi Museum
Old Workshop
Ferry Port
Paper Mill
Christoff Gallery
Preobraženska Church
Blue Dye Shop
ArtMill
Lázár Cross
Serbian Ecclesiastical History Collection
Belgrade Church
Ibusz
Imre Ámos-Margit Anna Collection & Wine Museum
See inset map for detail
Town Hall
House of Folk Crafts
Jewish Memorial House
Szentendre Sziget
Culture House
Peter-Paul Church
Barcsay Collection
Marzipan Museum
Požarevačka Church
Roman Stonework
Bükkös Stream
River Danube
HÉV Terminal
Bus Station
Czóbel Museum
Vajda Lajos Museum
Parish Church
Ferenczy Museum
Blagovestenška Church
Plague Cross
Kmetty Museum
Margit Kovács Museum
TEMPLOM TÉR
FŐ TÉR
DARU PIAC
VINEGROWERS' CROSS
DUNAKANYAR KÖRÚT
EGRES UTCA
MÉHÉSZ UTCA
MANDULA UTCA
ADY ENDRE UTCA
DEZSMA UTCA
HOLD UTCA
SZTÁRAVODAI ÚT
DUNAKORZÓ
BOGDÁNYI UTCA
ZRÍNYI UTCA
ISKOLA UTCA
ANGYAL UTCA
MARTINOVICS UTCA
RÁKÓCZI UTCA
SZERB UTCA
PÉTER-PÁL UTCA
KUCSERA UTCA
DUMTSA JENŐ UTCA
BÜKKÖS PART
PAPRIKABÍRÓ UTCA
KOSSUTH UTCA
ALKOTMÁNY UTCA
HUNYADI UTCA
GÖRÖG UTCA
ARADI UTCA
NAGY LAJOS
ŐRTORONY UTCA
ATTILA UTCA
RÓMAI SÁNC KÖZ
PETŐFI UTCA
KERTÉSZ UTCA
VASÚTI VILLASOR
BOLGÁR UTCA
0 200 m

the summer months, but it's still possible to escape the tourists and enjoy the quieter side of the place.

A good time to visit is for Szentendre's **summer festival** (Szentendrei Nyár), which runs from late June to late August and encompasses jazz and folk music evenings, organ concerts, dancing and theatrical performances; it culminates with a pop concert and fireworks on August 20. On the preceding day, a **Serbian festival** with *kolo* (circle) dancing takes place at the Preobrazenska Church. Tourinform can furnish you with more specific information on the festival's events.

Arrival and information

Szentendre's **bus and train (HÉV) stations** are next door to one another, ten minutes' walk south of the town centre. Local buses run to the centre via Dunakanyar körút. There are two docks for **Danube ferries**: one for the boat to Szentendre Sziget (Szentendre Island), located 100m north of the *Centrum Panzió* pension on Dunakorzó (hourly; 140Ft); the other, 500m further north, for services between Budapest and Esztergom.

For **information** on the town and the Danube Bend, the busy but very helpful Tourinform office is at Dumsta Jenő utca 22 (June–Aug Mon–Fri 9am–7pm, Sat & Sun 9am–6pm; Sept–May Mon–Sat 9.30am–4.30pm, Sun 10am–2pm; ⓣ26/317-965, ⓔszentendre@tourinform.hu). They have a comprehensive list of accommodation but do not book rooms. Szentendre's main **post office** is at Kossuth ucta 23–25 (Mon–Fri 8am–7pm, Sat 8am–noon). There is a currency exchange machine on Fő tér. **Internet access** is available at Game Planet, Petőfi utca 1 (daily 10am–10pm).

Accommodation

There is no agency to help you find private rooms in Szentendre, but plenty of *Zimmer frei* signs advertising vacancies. Another budget option is to **camp** on Pap Sziget (Priest's Island), 1.5km north of the centre. The *Pap Sziget* site (ⓣ26/310-697; May–Sept) also has two- to four-person chalets by the river (❹), a pension (❷), a hostel (❶) and a restaurant. The camping fee includes use of the swimming pool on the island. To get there take any bus heading towards Visegrád or Esztergom and get off at the Pap Sziget stop, by the *Danubius Hotel*.

Aradi Panzió Aradi utca 4 ⓣ26/314-274. Friendly, if somewhat plain, but some rooms have little balconies which make up for the uninspiring decor. Located in a quiet street 200m beyond the *Zita Panzió*. ❸

Bükkös Hotel Bükkös part 16 ⓣ26/312-021, ⓕ310-782. Idyllic location by a stream lined with weeping willows, 100m west of the Požarevačka Church. Comfy rooms with TV, phone and minibar. Restaurant, laundry service, secure parking and car rental. ❹

Centrum Panzió Dunakorzó ⓣ & ⓕ26/302-500, ⓦwww.hotels.hu/centrum_panzio. Delightful, air-conditioned pension with warm, peach-coloured rooms, three of which overlook the Danube. ❺

Horváth Panzió Daru piac 2 ⓣ & ⓕ26/313-950, ⓦwww.option.hu/horvath. Small pension in the quieter, northern part of the old town, with its own small bar; en-suite double rooms furnished with traditional folk crafts. ❸

Ilona Panzió Rákóczi utca 11 ⓣ & ⓕ26/313-599. Ideally located pension, tucked away a couple of minutes' walk from the centre of town. Rooms are on the small side, but are lovely and peaceful and there's a breakfast terrace. ❸

Beta Provincia Hotel Paprikabíró utca 21–23 ⓣ26/301-083, ⓦwww.reise.info.hu/hotel-provincia. Despite its horrible location on the busy ring road, this is the classiest place in town, with sauna, pool, spacious airy rooms and two restaurants. ❻

Zita Panzió Őrtorony utca 16 ⓣ & ⓕ26/313-886. Modest six-room pension 200m from the bus and train stations. The quiet rooms come with and without shower, but all have TVs. Breakfast not included. ❷

The Town

Most of Szentendre's main tourist attractions are centred on the main square, Fő tér. On your way in from the station, along Kossuth utca, you can make a detour to examine a hoard of **Roman stonework** at Dunakanyar körút 1 (March–Oct Mon–Fri 10am–4pm); turn left up Római sánc köz and carry straight on up for five minutes. Its opening times are unreliable, however, and you may have to look at the stones from behind the wire fence. The eroded lintels and sarcophagi belonged to Ulcisia Castra, a military town named after the Eravisci, an Illyrian-Celtic tribe subdued by the Romans during the first century AD.

Back on Kossuth utca, another five minutes' walk up the street, just before the Bükkos stream, you'll encounter the first evidence of a Serbian presence – the **Požarevačka Church** (Sat & Sun 11am–5pm; 200Ft). Typical of the churches in Szentendre, this was built in the late eighteenth century to replace an older wooden church, although its Byzantine-style iconostasis was inherited rather than specially commissioned. Beyond the stream, Dumtsa Jenő utca continues past the Tourinform office, on the corner, and the **Marzipan Museum and Pastry Shop** at no. 12 (daily 9am–7pm; 350Ft), where the marzipan creations include a model of the Hungarian parliament; a plaque on the wall opposite marks the birthplace of nineteenth-century Serbian novelist Jakov Ignjatovic, who created the Serb realist novel. Further up the street on the right is the **Barcsay Collection** (Tues–Sun: March–Nov 10am–6pm; Dec–Feb 1–5pm; 400Ft), a museum housing drawings and paintings by Jenő Barcsay (1900–88), who was born in Transylvania but lived and worked in Szentendre from 1928. His dark prewar canvases give way to more abstract works after the war, avoiding the strictures of the regime. His anatomical drawings at the end of the display confirm his skill as a draughtsman. During the summer festival, concerts are held in the courtyard of the museum.

A little further on, the road is crossed by Péter-Pál utca where a left turn brings you to the **Peter-Paul Church**, a yellow and white Baroque church built in 1708. Its original furnishings were taken back to Serbia after World War I, and the church is now Roman Catholic. Organ recitals take place at the church regularly; ask at Tourinform for details. From here, or from the last uphill stretch of Dumtsa Jenő utca, it's just a block to the main square.

Around Fő tér

Swarming with buskers and tourists during summertime, Szentendre's main square, **Fő tér**, is a place either to savour or avoid. At the centre of the square stands the Plague Cross, its triangular marble base decorated by icons, which was erected by the merchants' guild after Szentendre escaped infection in 1763. From here, diverging streets and alleys lead to an assortment of galleries and museums around the square, as well as to the many tourist shops, especially down Bogdányi utca.

The **Kmetty Museum**, immediately on your left if entering the square from Dumsta Jenő utca (Tues–Sun: March–Nov 10am–6pm; Dec–Feb 1–5pm; 400Ft), contains some delightful watercolours by János Kmetty (1889–1975), and, downstairs, his blue, Cubist paintings from a later period.

On the north side of the square is the Church of the Annunciation, or **Blagovestenška Church** (Tues–Sun 10am–5pm; 200Ft), the most accessible of the Orthodox churches in the town. Painted by Mihailo Zivković (1776–1824) of Buda in the early eighteenth century, the church's icons evoke all the richness and tragedy of Serbian history. The building itself is thought to have been designed by András Mayerhoffer in the 1750s, on the site of an earlier wooden church dating from the time of the Serbian migration in 1690. Look out for the tomb of a Greek merchant of Macedonian origin to the left of the entrance, and the Rococo windows and gate facing Görög utca (Greek Street).

Just behind the church, at Vastagh György utca 1, is by far the most popular of the town's galleries, the **Margit Kovács museum** (daily: March–Nov 10am–6pm; Dec–Feb 9am–5pm; 600Ft). This is a wonderful collection that never fails to delight, the themes of legends, dreams, religion, love and motherhood giving Kovács' graceful sculptures and reliefs universal appeal. Her expressive statues with their big eyes aren't particularly well known abroad, but in Hungary, Kovács, who died in 1977, is duly honoured as the nation's greatest ceramicist and sculptor.

Back on the main square, next door to the church, a portal carved with emblems of science and learning provides the entrance to a former Serbian school, now the **Ferenczy Museum** (Tues–Sun: March–Nov 10am–6pm; Dec–Feb 9am–5pm; 400Ft). Károly Ferenczy (1862–1917) pioneered Impressionism and *plein air* painting in Hungary, while his eldest son Valér (1885–1954) swung towards Expressionism. His younger sons, twins Nóemi (1890–1957) and Béni (1890–1967), branched out into textiles and bronzeware, with diminishing returns. The museum holds plenty of examples from each of the artists.

Several of the square's buildings (nos. 8, 17, 19 and 22) are old Baroque **trading houses** with their dates and trades engraved above the gates. The former Pálffy House (no. 17) bears the sign of the merchants' guild, combining the patriarchal cross of Orthodoxy with an anchor and a number four to symbolize Danube trade and the percentage of profit deemed appropriate by the guild.

A short walk out of the top western end of the square brings you into Rákóczi utca with the Baroque **Town Hall** on your left, which hosts summer concerts in its courtyard, while opposite at Rákóczi utca 1 is the **House of Folk Crafts** (Tues–Sun: March–Nov 10am–6pm; Dec–Feb 1–5pm; 400Ft), in an old bellhouse, with small temporary displays on blacksmithing and wine-making. The covered wooden steps leading up the hill behind are presently closed – the nearest stairs are just back along Rákóczi utca towards the main square.

Templom tér and Bogdányi utca

From Fő tér or Rákóczi utca, you can ascend an alley of steps to gain a lovely view of Szentendre's rooftops and gardens from **Templom tér**, where **craft stalls** plying their wares are regularly set up under the acacia trees to help finance the restoration of the Catholic **parish church**. Of medieval origin, with Romanesque and Gothic features, it was rebuilt in the Baroque style after falling derelict in Turkish times; the frescoes in its sanctuary were collectively painted by the artists' colony. Across the square, the **Czóbel Museum** (Tues–Sun: March–Nov 10am–6pm; Dec–Feb 1–5pm; 400Ft) exhibits paintings of brooding nudes by Béla Czóbel (1883–1976) and his wife Mária Modok (1896–1971), whose fierce brush strokes challenged the Neoclassical trend of the Horthy era.

A minute's walk north of Templom tér, the burgundy spire of the Orthodox episcopal cathedral, **Belgrade Church** (April–Oct daily 10am–5pm; 400Ft), rises above a walled garden off Alkotmány utca. The entrance to the grounds is from the corner of Alkotmány utca and Pátriárka utca. Built during the late eighteenth century, it has a lavishly ornamented interior with icons, painted by Vasilije Ostoic, depicting scenes from the New Testament and saints of the Orthodox Church. There are many old tombstones in the churchyard with Cyrillic inscriptions. This tale of demographic decline is echoed by the **Serbian Ecclesiastical History Collection** in the episcopal palace (April–Oct Wed–Sun 10am–5pm; 400Ft), whose outstanding hoard of icons, vestments and crosses comes from churches in Hungary that fell empty after the Serbs returned to the Balkans and the last remaining parishioners died out. The museum also houses various relics from Serbia including a pair of wedding crowns donated by the Karadjordjević dynasty in 1867. If you fancy attending a service you can do so at 6pm on Saturdays and 10am on Sundays during the summer and at 5pm on Saturdays and 4pm on Sundays during the winter.

From the Belgrade Church you can follow Alkotmány utca back down towards the main square. Just before you get there, you pass two more museums hiding in Hunyadi utca on your left. The **Vajda Lajos Museum** at no. 1 (Tues–Sun: March–Nov 10am–6pm; Dec–Feb 1–5pm; 400Ft) commemorates the work of a Szentendre painter who died in the Holocaust. Vajda's early work reveals Cubist and constructivist influences, while his later charcoal works seem to foretell the approaching torment. Although the museum is housed in a wealthy bourgeois villa, the artist himself was poor – as you can see from the materials he worked with. Downstairs is an excellent display of works by artists of the "European School", including Bálint Endre and Jenő Barcsay. This group formed after the war but was quickly stopped by the Communists. On the other side of Hunyadi utca, a few steps further along, is the **Szántó Jewish Memorial House and Synagogue** (April–Oct Tues–Sun 11am–5pm; donations accepted), set up by the grandson of a Holocaust victim, Lajos Szántó, who lived in the town. Most of Szentendre's Jewish community, which never numbered more than 250, were deported and killed during the Holocaust. The documents and relics are few, but they make a moving display.

Heading northeast from Fő tér, Bogdányi utca is packed with stalls, attended by shop assistants dressed up in folk gear. The **Wine Museum** at no. 10 (daily 10am–10pm; 100Ft, plus 1600Ft for wine tasting) is really there to lure people into the *Labirintus* restaurant, but otherwise does a fair job of describing Hungary's wine-making regions using maps, wine-bottle labels and other artefacts. Next door at no. 10b a painterly couple is commemorated by the **Imre Ámos-Margit Anna Collection** (Tues–Sun: March–Nov 10am–4pm; Dec–Feb 1–5pm; 400Ft). Imre Ámos was sent to a Jewish labour camp in 1940, where he died in 1944. The museum contains works from the last years of his life, including *Self Portrait with Angel* from 1938 and the disturbing Apocalypse series of 1944. Downstairs, his wife Margit Anna's works are split into two periods: the warm, mellow pictures from before the Holocaust to the right of the entrance, and to the left the uncomfortably bright, sometimes grotesque images that she produced after the war.

A little further along, Bogdányi utca opens onto a square at the far corner of which stands the **Lázár Cross**, a small iron cross that's easy to miss behind the parked cars that fill the square. It honours King Lázár of Serbia, whom the Turks beheaded after the battle of Kosovo in revenge for the death of Sultan Murad. His body was brought here by the Serbs and buried in a wooden church. When the relic was taken back to Serbia in 1774, the place was marked by a cross in his memory. Horse-drawn carriages can be rented here (and along Dunakorzó) between March and October for trips round the town; prices start at 1500Ft per person for half an hour, though it's possible to bargain them down.

Beyond the square, and the welter of tourist shops and stalls, is the **ArtMill** (daily 10am–6pm; 500Ft, free Mon), a contemporary art centre constructed out of the remnants of an old sawmill. Realized with considerable local government support, this impressive exhibition hall holds a varied collection of paintings by local artists, plus a smattering of international ones, and also serves as the focus for community-based art projects and events. Ongoing development means that a café and library will eventually materialize. A few steps on at no. 36, the

Kovács Blue Dye Shop (daily 10am–6pm) showcases a traditional style of folk dyeing: everything – pillow cases, skirts, oven cloths, you name it – is blue, and there's a small display to show how it is done.

The **Preobraženska Church**, a few steps further along Bogdányi utca, was erected by the tanners' guild in 1741–76, and its *embonpoint* enhanced by a Louis XVI gate the following century. Though its lavish iconostasis merits a look, the church is chiefly notable for its role in the Serbian festival on August 19, when it hosts the Blessing of the Grapes ceremony (recalling Szentendre's former role as a wine-producing centre). This is followed by a traditional procession round the church and further celebrations in the town square and elsewhere.

At the far end of Bogdányi utca, five minutes' walk further on, is another cross, the **Vinegrowers' Cross**, raised by a local guild and fittingly wreathed in grapevines. Having come this far, you might as well check out the hulking outdoor creations of Jenő Kerényi in the **Kerényi Museum**, a few minutes' walk away at Ady Endre utca 5, just past the *Vadászkert* restaurant (April–Oct Wed–Sun noon–6pm; 400Ft).

Eating and drinking

Like most things in Szentendre, **restaurants** tend to be pricey by Hungarian standards, and crowded during the summer. Tour groups tend to make for the ones on Fő tér, but there are more agreeable alternatives away from the main square.

Likewise, there are some choice **drinking** options on the fringes of the centre. *Café Adria* at Kossuth utca 4 (daily 10am–10pm) is a lovely Balkan themed café by the Bükkös stream, while *Avakum*, a cool cellar café near the Belgrade Church at Alkotmány utca 14 (daily 8am–10pm), is a good place to escape the heat and enjoy a refreshing cup of tea or glass of wine.

Restaurants

Aranysárkány Alkotmány utca 1a ⓣ26/311-670. The "Golden Dragon", a minute's walk up from Fő tér, is a smart Hungarian restaurant with air conditioning – useful as it's got an open kitchen. One of the pricier options in town. Booking is advisable. Daily noon–10pm.

Görög Kancsó Görög utca 1. One of several restaurants down by the river, this is a stylish establishment serving both Greek and Hungarian dishes (and wines). Daily 11am–2am.

Palapa Dumsta Jenő utca 14a. Brilliant Mexican restaurant/bar with quality food and unusually attentive service. Add to this regular live music in the courtyard and some fine cocktails and you've got the most enjoyable place to eat in town. Arrive early to bag a table. Daily 11am–midnight.

Rab Ráby Kucsera utca 1a. Just across from the Peter-Paul Church, this old restaurant is similar to the *Aranysárkány* but more traditionally Hungarian in style and a touch cheaper. Daily noon–11pm.

Rétesbolt Bercsényi utca. Snack-type place with pizzas, hot dogs and delicious strudels. Daily 9am–6pm.

Szerb Kisvendéglő Dunakorzó 4. Serbian restaurant with typically meaty and filling dishes such as *Pljeskavica* and *Čevapi*, lamb and beef burgers and meatballs served in thick soft pittas. Enjoyable place to eat, if you don't mind the 15 percent service charge. Daily 10am–midnight.

Hungarian Open-Air Museum

The **Hungarian Open-Air Museum** (Szabadtéri Néprajzi Múzeum; March–Oct Tues–Sun 9am–5pm; 600Ft, free Tues & Wed; ⓦwww.skanzen.hu) on Sztaravodai út, 4km to the west of town, is easily the most enjoyable local attraction. Hungary's largest open-air museum of rural architecture (termed a *skanzen*, after the first such museum, founded in a Stockholm suburb in 1891), it will eventually include "samples" from nine different regions of the country – five have been finished so far – and the remains of a Roman villa. The

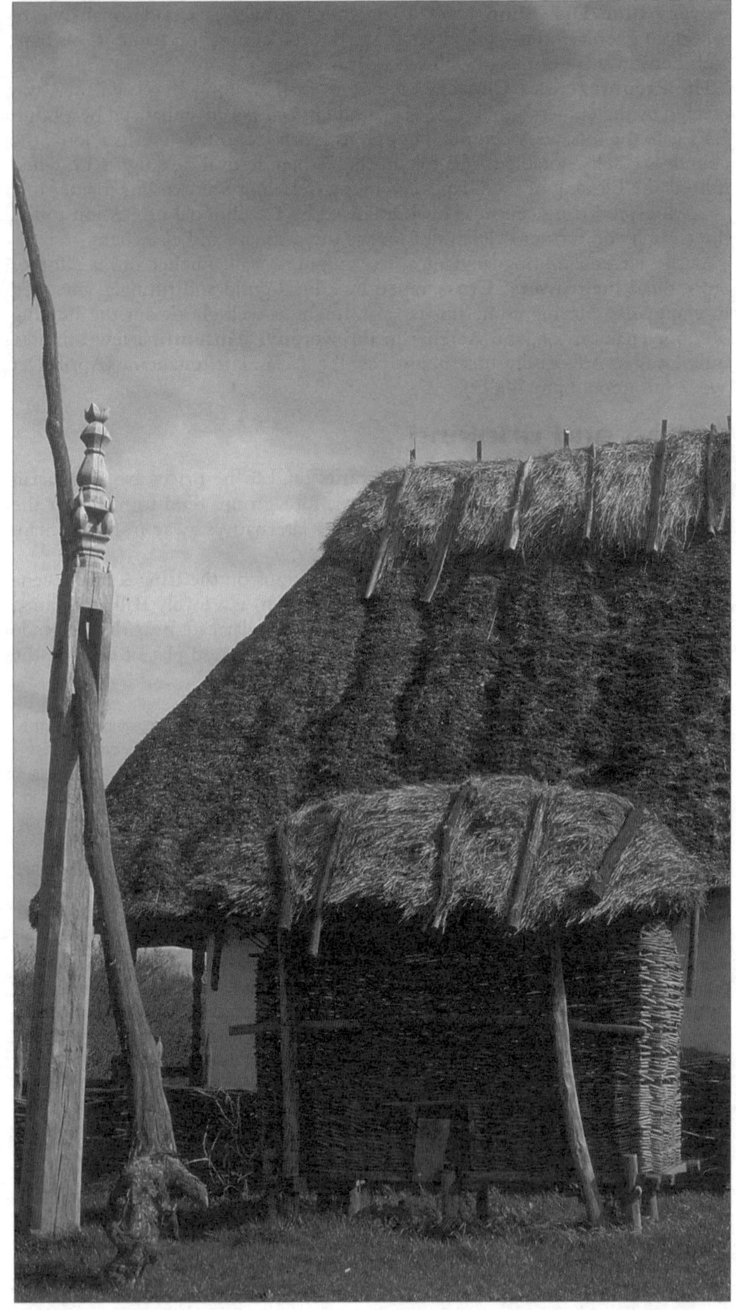

▲ Hungary Open-Air Museum

museum is accessible by **buses** running roughly every hour from stand 7 of the bus terminal; get off when you see the spires in a field to the right; the entrance is 100m off the road. You can get an excellent **book** on the contents of the museum, which guides you round building by building, and has maps both of the layout of the museum and of the villages. Each building also has its warden, who can explain everything in great detail, though usually only in Hungarian.

Downhill to the right from the entrance is a composite village from the **Upper Tisza** region in northeast Hungary, culled from isolated settlements in the Erdőhát. The guide points out the finer distinctions between the various humble peasant dwellings scattered among the barns and woven pigsties. As you walk towards the church, the houses move up the social scale, as even the fences show, going from rough wickerwork to a smart plank fence. The first house, a poor cottage from Kispalad, has mud floors, which the warden sprinkles in the traditional way to stop the dust rising, and a rough thatch. Further down is a house with wooden roof tiles and wooden floors. Rural carpenters produced highly skilled work, examples of which are the circular "dry mill" from Vámosoroszi, the wooden bell-tower from Nemesborzova, and the carving inside the Greek Catholic church from Mándok (on a hilltop beyond).

As you walk up past the Calvinist graveyard, where the grave markers from four villages include the striking boat-shaped markers from Szatmárcseke in eastern Hungary, signs point you to the remains of the third-century Roman village, and on to the **Western Transdanubia** section. The thatched houses from the Orség region are often constructed of wood and covered in adobe. The school from the village of Kondorfa has its old benches with slates for writing on, a towel and basin for washing, and behind the door the children's little home-spun bags. The teacher's living quarters are at the other end of the building, separated by a kitchen with an apron chimney, where the smoke goes out of a hole in the roof. At one end of the L-shaped house from Szentegyörgyvölgy dating from the nineteenth century, a small hen ladder runs up to the roof for the poultry, and in the open end of the attic you can see large woven straw baskets for storing grain. By contrast, the next section, originating from the ethnic German communities of the Kisalföld (Little Plain) in **Northwest Transdanubia**, seems far more regimented. Neatly aligned and whitewashed, the houses are filled with knick-knacks and embroidered samplers bearing homilies like "When the Hausfrau is capable, the clocks keep good time". The next region is **The Great Hungarian Plain**, which is still under construction. The house from Süsköd has a beautiful facade on the street, with the visitors' room or "clean room" laid out for Christmas celebrations with a nativity crib and a church-shaped box. In the fields of the Great Plain region stands a windmill from Dusnok, built in 1888 and with its sails still operating. The newest region is the **Bakony and Balaton-Uplands**, located near the hilly part of the museum to the north. The constructions here are perhaps the most interesting in the museum, with several communal buildings on display including a fire station, a working watermill and a Catholic church. The four neatly aligned stone dwelling houses reflect the varying financial standings of those living in the region during the early twentieth century. Walking through the sections brings you back to the entrance of the museum.

Demonstrations of folk dancing and traditional crafts such as weaving, pottery and basket-making take place at the museum most Sundays as well as on public holidays, but check at the museum (☎26/502-500) or at the Tourinform office in town for precise dates of events. Local **festivals** are also celebrated here, such as the wine festival in September, when folkloric programmes and grape-pressing take place. The huge *Jászárokszállás* **restaurant** (daily 10am–10pm) inside the museum serves up dishes and wines from the various regions. Shops outside the museum entrance sell snacks and ice creams as well as local crafts, including beautiful handmade paper from the Vincze paper mill.

Szentendre Sziget

Across the water from Szentendre is the sparsely populated **Szentendre Sziget** (Szentendre Island), stretching from below Szentendre up almost to Visegrád. Its open expanses have escaped the holiday-home development seen on the road north of Szentendre, and the villages here give you the feeling that time has passed them by. Access to the island is poor, with only one bridge connecting it to the mainland at **Tahitótfalu**, 10km north of Szentendre. Buses run from the Budapest Árpád híd bus terminal to Tahitótfalu, and ferries from each main settlement on the bank go across to the island. There's also one car ferry connecting Vác on the east bank with the road to Tahitótfalu.

KISOROSZI, the small village near the northern tip of the island, is so quiet that it has no official accommodation, though if you ask around, you might be able to find a room. Ferries connect the village to the west bank hourly, linking with the bus from Budapest (Árpád híd terminal). Along the main road, at 43 Széchenyi utca, is the superb *Diófa* restaurant which serves up delicious and surprisingly light Hungarian food. Up to the left at the crossroads, a half-hour walk brings you to the peaceful, sandy north tip of the island, with stunning views across to Visegrád, and a very basic campsite amidst the trees (Ⓣ26/398-178; May to mid-Sept). A couple of kilometres back along the road to Tahitótfalu is an eighteen-hole **golf course**, one of the first in Hungary, created in 1984 (9,000Ft for one round; March to mid-Nov; Ⓣ26/392-463). The island also makes excellent terrain for horse-riding, and one of the island's several **riding** schools is the Hubert Lovarda, 2km south of Tahitótfalu, on the road to Pócsmegyer (1800Ft for one hour; Ⓣ30/952-6384), which is well served by buses.

One of the more curious local events, and one which befits an island covered in strawberry fields, is the **Eperfesztival** (Strawberry Festival), which takes place during the first weekend of June. Staged on the mainland by the bridge, the festival involves various shows and concerts, the highlights being a monumental tug-of-war across the bridge between the two communities and a competition to see who has, amongst other things, the biggest, smallest and fattest strawberries.

Visegrád and around

When the hillsides start to plunge and the river twists, keep your eyes fixed on the mountains to the west for a first glimpse of the citadel and ramparts of **VISEGRÁD**, 23km north of Szentendre. The citadel is almost as it appeared to János Thuroczy in 1488, who described its "upper walls stretching to the clouds floating in the sky, and the lower bastions reaching down as far as the river". At that time, courtly life in Visegrád, the royal seat, was nearing its apogee, and the palace of King Mátyás and Queen Beatrice was famed throughout Europe. The papal legate Cardinal Castelli described it as a "paradiso terrestri", seemingly unperturbed by the presence of Vlad the Impaler, who resided here under duress between 1462 and 1475.

Tucked in between the hills and the river as the Danube flows north, Visegrád is a compact town, with most local activity centred around the ferry and the church. The three main **historical sites** all lie north of the centre: the Royal

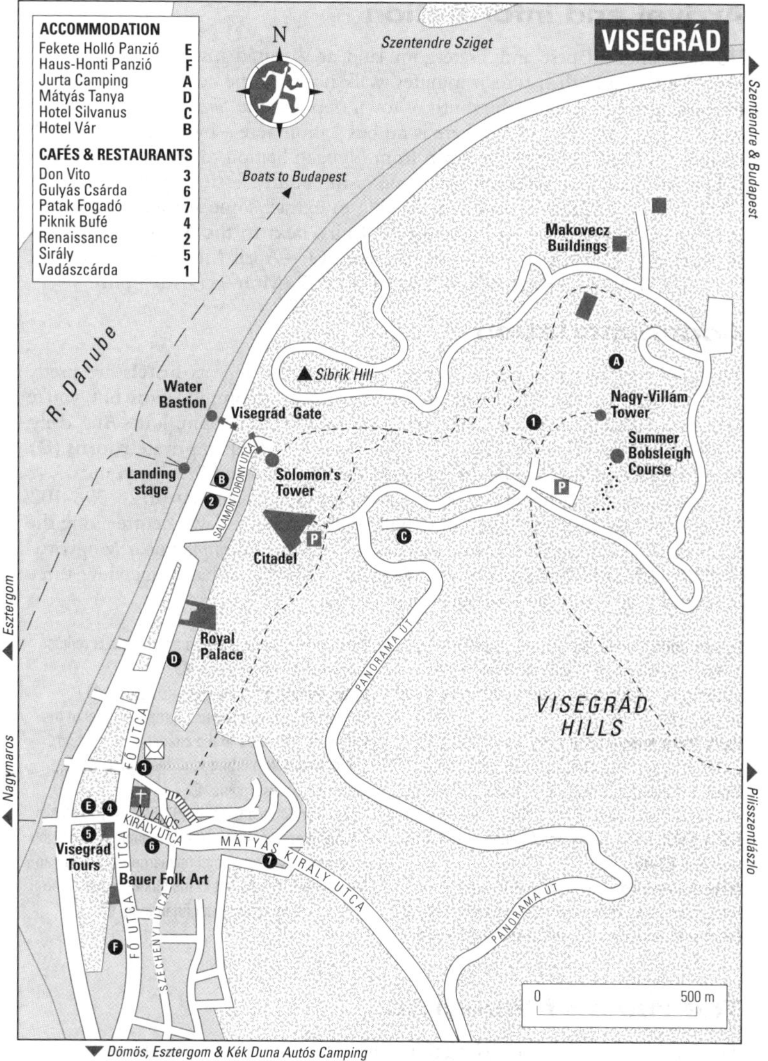

Palace and Solomon's Tower down near the river, and the citadel perching on top of the hill above. All the river sites are within easy walking distance, but you might prefer taking a bus up to the citadel if the climb is too forbidding. While here, you can also visit the surrounding **Visegrád Hills**, boasting gorgeous views, and providing an unexpected but appropriate setting for several works by the visionary architect Imre Makovecz (see box, p.172). Though the ruins can be visited on a flying visit, the hills require a full day and a fair amount of walking, with the option of longer hikes or pony-trekking.

Arrival and information

Boats from Budapest and Esztergom land at Visegrád just below Solomon's Tower, little more than fifteen minutes' walk north of the centre. Ferries to and from Nagymaros dock to the south of town opposite the *Sirály* restaurant. **Buses** make two stops in Visegrád – there is no bus station here – by the ferry and boat stations. You can also travel by **train** from Nyugati Station to Nagymaros-Visegrád on the Szob line, and then catch one of the hourly ferries across to Visegrád.

Try hard enough and you might be able to extract some **information** from the distinctly unhelpful staff at Visegrád Tours, next to the *Sirály* restaurant at Rév utca 15 (May–Sept daily 8am–5.30pm; Oct–April Mon–Fri 10am–4pm; ⓣ26/390-160). The **post office** is at Fő utca 77 (Mon–Fri 8am–4pm).

Accommodation

Though Visegrád has a limited range of accommodation, its **hotels** are pretty good value. Visegrád Tours (see above) can book accommodation but you're better off heading to Bauer Folk Art, Fő utca 46 (10am–6pm: June–Aug daily; Sept–May Mon–Fri; ⓣ26/397-127), who can help in finding private **rooms** (❷). You'll also see plenty of *Zimmer frei* signs along Fő utca and Széchenyi utca.

The nearest place to **camp** is at *Kék Duna Autós Camping* (ⓣ26/398-102; May–Sept), which is well placed by the Danube, near the town centre along the main road to Esztergom. Not so easy to reach is *Jurta Camping* near Mogyoró-hegy (Hazelnut Hill; ⓣ26/398-217; May–Sept), though it has a nice view; three buses a day go from the Visegrád ferry station.

Fekete Holló Panzió Rév utca 12 ⓣ26/397-290, ⓕ398-158. Sited next to the restaurant of the same name, this five-room pension is the cheapest in town. ❷

Haus-Honti Panzió Fő utca 66 ⓣ26/398-120, ⓕ397-274, ⓦwww.hotels.hu/honti. Good-value family-run pension comprising renovated rooms in an older building overlooking a stream and a newer building with rooms facing the Danube. Bike rental available. ❸–❹

Mátyás Tanya Fő utca 47 ⓣ26/398-309, ⓦwww.hotels.hu/matyas_tanya. Mid-range option situated near the Royal Palace. An elegant setting down by the river with large gardens and spacious rooms furnished with dark wood. ❹

Hotel Silvanus Fekete-hegy ⓣ26/398-311, ⓦwww.hotels.hu/silvanus. Upmarket hotel at the top of the hill, close to the citadel and boasting comprehensive sporting facilities and splendid views from most rooms. ❻

Hotel Vár Fő utca 9 ⓣ26/397-522, ⓔvarhotelvisegrad@matavnet.hu. Formerly a hunting lodge, this handsome riverfront hotel has large rooms and an atmospheric restaurant in the stone-arched wine cellars, serving great Hungarian food. ❺

The ruins of Visegrád

The layout of the **ruins of Visegrád** (whose Slavic name means "High Castle") dates back to the thirteenth century, when Béla IV began fortifying the north against a recurrence of the Mongol invasion. Its most prominent features are the citadel on the hill and Solomon's Tower near the riverside below, part of the fortification that forms a gate over the road that you pass through arriving from Budapest. The Royal Palace itself is inconspicuously sited, further inland and 500m south of Solomon's Tower. As Visegrád fell into dereliction after the Turkish occupation, mud washing down from the hillsides gradually buried the palace entirely, and later generations doubted its very existence. In 1934, however, the archeologist János Schulek made a breakthrough. While at a New Year's Eve party, after he had been in Visegrád for some time hunting for the lost palace without success, the wine ran out and Schulek was sent to get some more from the neighbours. An old woman told him to go down to the wine cellar, and there he found clues in the stones that convinced him the palace was here, later unearthing one of the palace vaults.

In July each year the ruins provide the setting for **medieval pageants** intended to re-create the splendour of Visegrád's Renaissance heyday (see p.172).

The Royal Palace

Now largely excavated and partially reconstructed, the **Royal Palace**, ten minutes' walk from the centre at Fő utca 27–29 (Tues–Sun 9am–5pm; free), spreads over four levels or terraces. Originally founded in 1323 by the Angevin king Charles Robert, the palace was expanded by subsequent kings, the largest development occurring in the reign of Mátyás Corvinus.

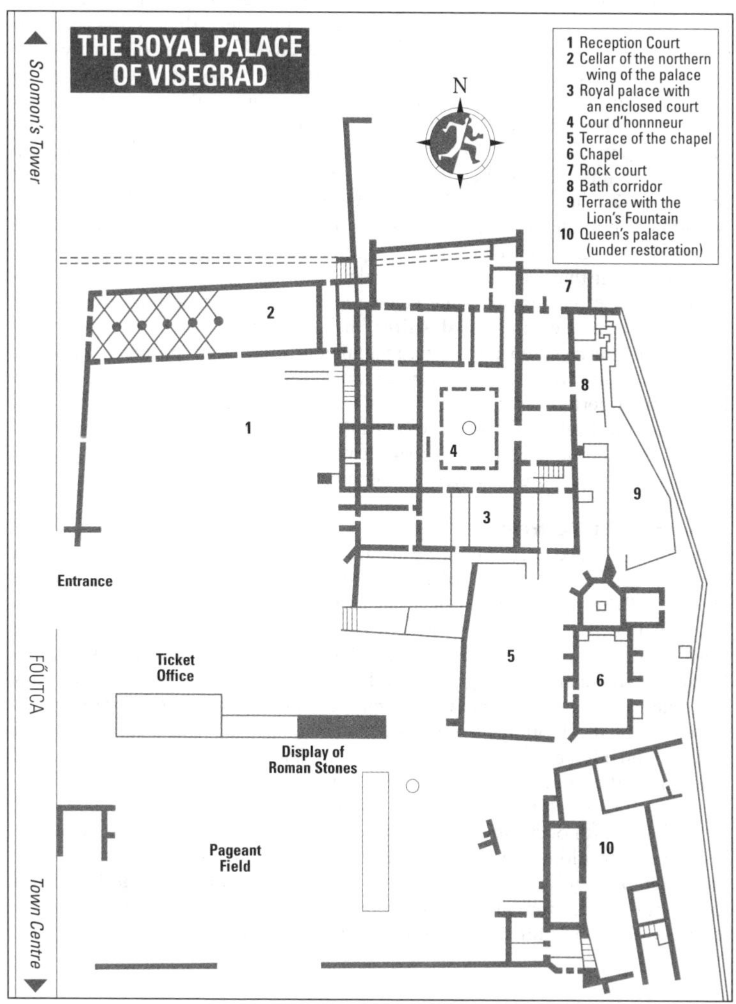

Walking up from the entrance, you pass the *kőtár*, a collection of excavated stones from Roman to medieval times, before arriving at the palace proper. Here you enter at the second level, the **cour d'honneur**, which was constructed for Charles's successor, Louis, and provided the basis for subsequent building by Sigismund and, later, Mátyás Corvinus. Much work on this inner courtyard has been completed in recent years, with pristine reconstructions of the pilastered **Renaissance loggia** and the cloistered walks, plus a replica of the **Hercules Fountain** which would spout wine during important events; the original is displayed, like an impossible jigsaw, in an adjoining room. Work is continuing on the vaulting of the large hall and other rooms surrounding the courtyard.

Down the steps in the exhibition room, you enter the **wine cellar**, where the Hungarian, Czech and Polish kings signed the closing document at the Visegrád Congress of 1335. Called to discuss the growing Habsburg threat, they failed to agree on any concrete steps, but nevertheless managed to consume 10,000 litres of wine and vast amounts of food in the process. In February 1991, Visegrád played host to another less extravagant summit, when the prime ministers of Hungary, Poland and Czechoslovakia met here to put together a joint strategy for trade and EC membership in the post-Communist era. Again the setting for signing the final document was the cellar, and again the results were limited – although it did mean that the present display of stonework from the age of King Mátyás was put together so that the cellar would not be totally empty. Work has begun on creating an entrance at ground level into the cellar, but this is taking some time to realize.

Legend has it that Mátyás was eventually poisoned by his wife Beatrice, who wanted to rule on her own. The chalice containing the fatal potion may well have passed between the **royal suites** that once stood beneath an overhang on the third terrace, separated by a magnificent **chapel**. Reportedly, the finest sight at this time was the garden on the fourth terrace, embellished by the **Lion Fountain**. A perfect copy of the original (carved by Ernő Szakál) bears Mátyás's raven crest and piles of sleepy-looking lions, although, unlike the original, it's not fed by the gutters and pipes that channelled water down from the citadel. The original pieces are displayed in Solomon's Tower.

Solomon's Tower

Five minutes' walk north along Fő utca, just after it rejoins the main highway, you can take a right onto Salamon torony utca, which climbs up through the gate of the old castle fortifications to reach **Solomon's Tower**, a mighty hexagonal keep, buttressed on two sides by unsightly concrete slabs (Tues–Sun 9am–4.30pm; free), and named after an eleventh-century Hungarian king. The **Mátyás Museum** on the ground and first floor of the tower exhibits finds from the palace, including the white Anjou Fountain of the Angevins; the original pieces of the Lion and Hercules fountains, together with a reconstruction of the child Hercules struggling with the hydra; and the red marble *Visegrád Madonna*, a Renaissance masterpiece that shows many similarities to the works of Tomaso Fiamberti nearby. The next two floors present the history of Visegrád up to the Turkish occupation. It's worth climbing to the top for the view of the lines of fortification running down from the citadel on both sides, meeting at the Water Bastion by the river. However, neither this, nor the **ruined Roman fort** to the north, atop Sibrik Hill, is worth a special detour, so you might want to save your energy for the climb to Visegrád's citadel.

The citadel

Dramatically sited on a crag directly above Solomon's Tower and commanding a superb view of Nagymaros and the Börzsöny mountains on the east bank, Visegrád's triangular **citadel** (March 15–Nov 15 daily 9.30am–6pm; rest of the year Sat & Sun 10am–3pm; closed when it snows, as the battlements are too slippery; 550Ft including all displays) served as a repository for the Hungarian crown jewels until they were stolen by a treacherous maid of honour in the sixteenth century. Restoration of the castle began in the late nineteenth century, after an eager local priest brought the government's attention to the dire state of the place, and work still continues slowly. Its state before the work began in 1870 is shown inside in a photograph in the **exhibition** on the history of the castle, which includes a hologram of the crown and drawings of how the castle looked at different periods; you can see the same drawings in the Royal Palace and Solomon's Tower. The waxworks display on instruments of torture and execution in the Middle Ages is fairly tame, with careful descriptions of how the different instruments were used. In the innermost courtyard is a display on hunting, fishing and quarrying, with mock-ups of medieval scenes showing hunters and their tools, a stuffed deer lying dead in a cart and an animal caught in a trap. All information is in Hungarian and German only, but you get the general idea from the displays.

You can reach the citadel from the centre of town via the "Calvary" **footpath** (signposted *Fellegvár* and marked by a red cross on the way), heading up to the left off Nagy Lajos Király utca, 50m behind the church. It takes its name from the calvary of reliefs that you follow on your way up. Alternatively, you can start from Solomon's Tower and walk through the top gate and uphill, looking out for signs up to the right after ten to fifteen minutes. Both routes involve around forty minutes of steep walking; the latter track is slightly tougher. There are also three buses a day (April–Sept 9.30am, 12.30am & 3.30pm), which stop at both the boat and the ferry stations on the river side of the road, and follow the scenic Panorama Route into the hills. Alternatively, you can tackle the same four-kilometre trip in a car, heading into the hills up Mátyás Király utca.

The Visegrád Hills

Thickly wooded and crisscrossed with paths, the **Visegrád Hills** are a popular rambling spot. From the car park near the citadel, it's a 400-metre walk up the main road to another car park; from here you can follow a signposted path off to the left, which leads to the **Nagy-Villám observation tower** (kilátó; 10am–5pm: April–Oct daily; Nov–March Sat & Sun; 100Ft). Sited at the highest point on the Danube Bend, it offers wonderful panoramas of Szentendre Sziget and the Bend and, on a clear day, views as far as Slovakia. You can also hike from here over into the Pilis range (see p.178). The *Vadászcárda* (closed Dec–Feb) on the way up is a good spot to stop for a moderately priced meal with fine views. You can also visit the collection of wooden buildings designed by **Imre Makovecz** at Mogyoró-hegy (Hazelnut Hill), 1km north of the observation tower (see box, p.172). Back down by the car park is the **Summer Bobsleigh Course** (Nyári Bob), where for 280Ft you can race down a one-kilometre run (April–Oct daily 9am–7pm; Nov–March Sat & Sun 10am–4pm; ☎26/397-397), except on rainy days when the brakes are rendered ineffective.

If you feel like **hiking**, you could try the twelve-kilometre trail marked with blue stripes running from the tower, via Paprét (Priest's Meadow), to Pilisszentlászló, which takes two to three hours. Although Visegrád itself has nowhere to swim, there is a salubrious terraced strand and natural warm-water **pool** 4km away at Lepence, at the Pilisszentlászló turn-off towards Dömös

Imre Makovecz at Visegrád

Imre Makovecz was a promising architect in the Kádár years, but was branded a troublemaker for his outspoken nationalism, banned from teaching, and "exiled" to the Visegrád forestry department in 1977. During this time he made many of the wooden buildings which can be seen at Mogyoró-hegy in Visegrád. Over the next decade he refined his ideas, acquiring a group of student followers for whom he held summer schools. Employing cheap, low-technology methods in a way he branded as specifically Magyar, he taught his students how to construct temporary buildings using raw materials such as branches and twigs. The Cultural House near Jurta Camping in Visegrád is an excellent example, with a turfed roof and a light homely interior that has worn well.

Now one of the most influential architects in Hungary, Makovecz's buildings can be found all over the country. They include the community centres in Sárospatak, Zalaszentlászló and Szigetvár, churches at Paks and Siófok, and the oesophagus-like crypt of the Farkasréti cemetery in Budapest. Makovecz also designed the much admired Hungarian Pavilion at the 1992 Expo in Seville, with its seven towers representing the seven Magyar tribes. He has won a considerable amount of praise abroad, with strong support from Prince Charles, for whom his anti-modernist, back-to-nature style has a strong appeal. However, his generous use of wood does not appeal to all environmentalists, and his dabbling in right-wing politics turns his whole idea of a return to the "real" Hungarian style of building, once a righteous tool against the old regime, into something less appealing.

(May–Aug daily 6am–6.30pm; 1100Ft; ⓣ26/398-208). A series of pools has been cut into the hillside overlooking the Danube, making it one of the most spectacular open-air pool complexes in Hungary.

Eating, drinking and entertainment

Two of the best **restaurants** in Visegrád are up on the road towards the citadel: the *Gulyás Csárda* at Nagy Lajos király utca 4 is a well-established Hungarian restaurant serving good food at reasonable prices; while the *Patak Fogadó*, a few hundred metres further on at Mátyás király utca 92, is a more stylish alternative with better-quality food. Other options include the medieval-themed *Renaissance*, next to *Hotel Vár*, where you can feast on suckling pig while wearing a cardboard crown, and be serenaded by a pantalooned man with a lute. *Don Vito*, next to the church at Fő utca 83, is always understandably heaving, due to their impressive stone-baked pizzas. For a simple quick fill, the self-service *Piknik Büfé* just across the road on Rév utca does the job. In summer there are **discos** at the *Sirály* restaurant, and sporadic disco **cruises** between Visegrád and Esztergom, which leave from the main landing stage as advertised. The main event in town each year (usually during the second weekend in July) is the **International Palace Games**, a series of rousing medieval pageants with jousting and archery tournaments, crafts workshops and considerable amounts of eating and drinking, most of which takes place within the grounds of the Royal Palace. For more information contact Tourinform in Szentendre (see p.159).

Esztergom

Beautifully situated in a crook of the Danube facing Slovakia, **ESZTERGOM**, 25km on from Visegrád, is dominated by its basilica, whose dome is visible for miles around. The sight is richly symbolic, since it was here that Prince Géza

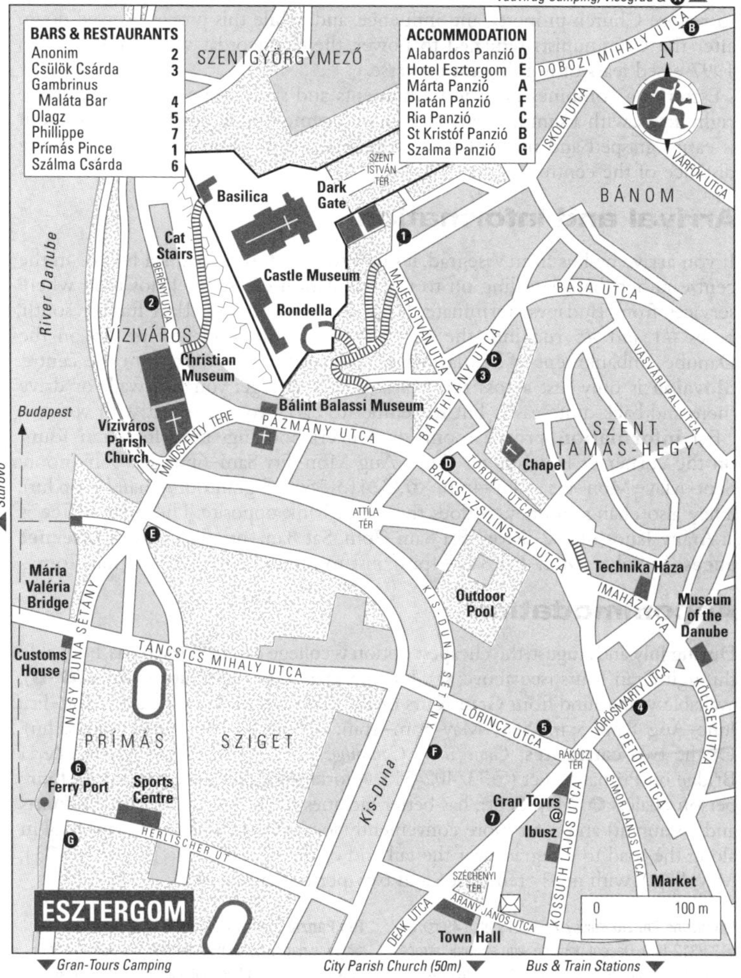

and his son Vajk (the future king and saint Stephen) brought Hungary into the fold of Roman Catholic (not Orthodox) Christendom, in the nation's first cathedral. Even after the court moved to Buda following the Mongol invasion, Esztergom remained the **centre of Catholicism** until the Turkish conquest, when the clergy dispersed to safer towns and it became an Ottoman stronghold, besieged by Christian armies. While the town recovered in the eighteenth century, it wasn't until the 1820s that it became the Primal See again, following a nationwide campaign. As part of the *ancien régime*, the Church was ruthlessly persecuted during the Rákosi era (though the basilica was well maintained, allegedly because the wife of the Soviet leader Khrushchev liked it). From the 1960s onwards, however, the Communists settled for a *modus vivendi*, hoping to enlist the Church's help with social problems and to harness the patriotic spirit of the faithful. The avowedly Christian government elected in 1990 did its best to restore Church property and influence, and, while this process slowed down after the Communists returned to power, their concordat with the Vatican in 1997 eased fears of it going into reverse.

Esztergom combines historic monuments and small-town charm in just the right doses, with a summer festival as an inducement to linger. The town's layout is easily grasped and most of the restaurants and pensions are within walking distance of the centre.

Arrival and information

If you arrive by bus from Visegrád, it's best to get off near Basilica Hill or in the centre rather than travelling on to the bus station on Simor János utca, where services from Budapest terminate. From the train station, 1km further south, buses #1 and #5 run into the centre. Ferries from Budapest tie up on the Danube embankment of Prímás Sziget, fifteen minutes' walk from the centre. **Slovakia** is only just across the Mária Valéria Bridge; you can walk or drive there and back quite easily, but remember to carry your passport with you.

For **information**, private rooms or concert bookings head for Gran Tours, on the corner of Rákóczi tér (June–Aug Mon–Fri 8am–6pm, Sat 9am–noon; Sept–May Mon–Fri 8am–4pm; ⓣ33/413-756, ⓔgrantour@mail.holop.hu). They also change money, as does the K&H bank opposite. The **post office** is at Arany János utca 2 (Mon–Fri 8am–7pm, Sat 8am–noon). There is **Internet access** at Solva (Mon–Fri 8am–4pm), just round the corner from Gran Tours.

Accommodation

During July and August, the cheapest option is college **dormitory beds**, bookable through Gran Tours (see above; ❶). The next best deal is **private rooms** (❶–❷), available year-round from Gran Tours or Ibusz at Kossuth Lajos utca 5 (Mon–Fri: June–Aug 8am–5pm; Sept–May 8am–4pm; ⓣ33/520-920, ⓔi048@ibusz.hu). Of the two **campsites**, *Gran-Tours Camping*, 500m south of the Mária Valéria Bridge on Prímás Sziget (ⓣ33/402-513, ⓔfortanex@axelro.hu; pension ❸, four-person chalets ❹; May–Sept), has better facilities (including a pool, tennis courts and restaurant) and is far more conveniently located than *Vadvirág Camping*, 3km along the road to Visegrád near the tail end of the #6 bus route (ⓣ33/312-234; May–Sept), with grassy tent space and two-person chalets (❶).

Alabardos Panzió Bajcsy-Zsilinszky utca 49 ⓣ & ⓕ33/312-640. Decent pension with a small terrace and a Mediterranean feel, on an alley off the main road, midway between the upper and lower town. ❹

Hotel Esztergom Nagy Duna sétány, Prímás Sziget ⓣ33/412-555, ⓦwww.hotel-esztergom.hu. Rather tired 1970s three-star hotel in a pleasant setting on the island, with a restaurant and roof terrace. ❻

Márta Panzió Bocskoroskuti út 1 ⓣ & ⓕ33/311-983. Quiet, modern pension twenty minutes' walk from town near the Visegrád road. It has its own little bar and offers thoughtfully furnished rooms with TV and bathroom. Secure parking. ❷

Platán Panzió Kis-Duna sétány 11 ⓣ & ⓕ33/411-355. The cheapest pension in Esztergom; a basic place pleasantly located opposite Prímás Sziget, close to the centre of the lower town. ❷

Ria Panzió Batthány utca 11–13 ⓣ33/313-115, ⓦwww.riapanzio.com A comfortable pension with spotless rooms in two buildings in a good location below Basilica Hill. Secure parking, a pocket-sized garden and beer terrace. Bicycle rental available. ❺

St Kristóf Panzió Dobozi Mihály utca 11 ⓣ & ⓕ33/414-153, ⓔkristoph@elender.hu. Outstanding pension on the Visegrád road, ten minutes from the basilica, with spacious, air-conditioned rooms and apartments, a lovely garden and a splendid restaurant. If it's full, there are also rooms for rent opposite. ❺

Szalma Panzió Nagy Duna sétány 2 ⓣ & ⓕ33/315-336, ⓦwww.col.hu/szalmacsarda. Run by the owners of the *Szalma* restaurant 50m away, this is a clean, bright place with basic pine-furnished rooms, all with small bathrooms. Good discounts for children. ❸

The Town

The main focal point of the town is **Basilica Hill**, whose landscaped slope appears on maps as Szent István tér. After seeing the basilica and the castle remains here, you'll probably want some refreshment before heading downhill to the **Víziváros**, where art buffs can get stuck into the **Christian Museum** and others will be drawn to the shady *korzó*, a weeping-willow-lined promenade beside the Kis-Duna, separating **Prímás Sziget** from the lower town. In the **lower town**, the emphasis is on enjoyment, with cafés, bars and discos and an outdoor thermal pool.

The basilica

Built on the site of the first cathedral in Hungary, where Vajk was crowned as King Stephen by a papal envoy on Christmas Day, 1000 AD, Esztergom's Neoclassical **basilica** (daily 7am–6pm; free) is the largest in the country, measuring 118m in length and 40m in width, and capped by a dome 100m high. Representing a thousand years of faith and statehood, it was begun by Pál Kühneland and János Packh in 1822, and finally completed by József Hild in 1869, thirteen years after its consecration, once the dome was in place. Liszt's *Gran Mass* was composed for the occasion (*Gran* being the German name for Esztergom). In 1991, the church hosted two events symbolizing its triumph over Communism: the reburial of the exiled Cardinal Mindszenty and the first papal visit to Hungary.

The exterior of the basilica is unadorned except for the primates' coats of arms flanking the great bronze doors that are only used on special occasions. Its nave is on a massive scale, clad in marble, gilding and mosaics. To the left of the entrance is the lavish red and white marble **Bakócz Chapel**, whose Florentine altar was salvaged by Archbishop Tamás Bakócz from the original church. The basilica's main altarpiece was painted by the Venetian Michelangelo Grigoletti, based on Titian's *Assumption* in the Frari Church in Venice. To the right lies the **treasury** (kincstár; daily: March–Oct 9am–4.30pm; Nov & Dec 10am–3.30pm; 400Ft), an overpowering collection of bejewelled croziers and chalices and kitsch papal souvenirs.

Towards the nave are two stairways, the first leading to a **crypt** (krypta; daily 9am–5pm; 100Ft), which is like a set from a Dracula film, with seventeen-

The return of Cardinal Mindszenty

When the much travelled body of Cardinal József Mindszenty was finally laid to rest with state honours in May 1991, it was a vindication of his uncompromising heroism – and the Vatican realpolitik that Mindszenty despised. As a conservative and monarchist, he had stubbornly opposed the postwar Communist takeover, warning that "cruel hands are reaching out to seize hold of our children, claws belonging to people who have nothing but evil to teach them". Arrested in 1948, tortured for 39 days and nights, and sentenced to life imprisonment for treason, Mindszenty was freed during the Uprising and took refuge in the US Embassy, where he remained for the next fifteen years, an exile in the heart of Budapest.

When the Vatican struck a deal with the Kádár regime in 1971, Mindszenty had to be pushed into resigning his position and going to Austria, where he died in 1975. Although his will stated that his body should not return home until "the red star of Moscow had fallen from Hungarian skies", his reburial occurred some weeks before the last Soviet soldier left, in preparation for the pope's visit in August of that year. Nowadays the Vatican proclaims his greatness, without any hint of apology for its past actions.

metre-thick walls to support the enormous weight of the basilica, and giant stone women flanking the stairway down to gloomy vaults full of entombed prelates. Though several other mausolea look more arresting, it is the **tomb of Cardinal Mindszenty** (see box on p.175) that transfixes Hungarians. The other stairway ascends for over three hundred steps to the stiflingly hot interior of the **cupola** (kupola; May–Oct daily 9am–5pm; 200Ft), though any discomfort is forgotten the moment you step outside and see the magnificent **view** of Esztergom, with the Slovak town of Štúrovo across the water.

The Castle Museum and around

On higher ground, thirty metres south of the basilica, are the red-roofed, reconstructed remains of the palace founded by Prince Géza, now presented as the **Castle Museum** (Tues–Sun 10am–6pm; 400Ft). A royal seat for almost three hundred years, it was here that Béla III entertained Philip of France and Frederick Barbarossa on their way to the Third Crusade. After Buda became the capital, Hungary's primates lived here, and the Renaissance prelate János Vitéz made it a centre of humanist culture, where Queen Beatrice spent her widowhood. Although the palace was sacked by the Turks in 1543 and twice besieged before they were evicted in 1683, enough survived to be excavated by Leopold Antal in the 1930s – indeed, it is more impressive than the remains of Buda's royal palace.

Though foreigners are expected to join a tour in Hungarian, you can slip away to the rooms displaying visualizations of the palace in various epochs to reach the royal suite ahead of the crowd. Traces of the frescoes that once covered every wall in the palace can be seen in the vaulted living-hall from Béla III's reign, whence a narrow stairway ascends to the study of Archbishop Vitéz – known as the **Hall of Virtues** after its allegorical murals of *Intelligence*, *Moderation*, *Strength* and *Justice*. Beyond lies the **royal chapel**, whose Gothic rose window and Romanesque arches were executed by craftsmen brought over by Béla's two French wives; its frescoes of saints and the Tree of Life reflect his Byzantine upbringing. A spiral staircase leads to the palace rooftop, offering a panoramic view of Esztergom and the river, and a fresh perspective on the basilica.

During June and July, **plays** and **dances** are staged in the **Rondella** bastion, whose exit is guarded by a giant statue of a warrior. As you descend the hillside, notice the monumental **Dark Gate**: a tunnel built in the 1820s as a short cut between church buildings on either side of the hill and later exploited by the Soviet army, which maintained a base there until 1989. The former primate's wine cellars, next door, have been converted into a restaurant, the *Prímás Pince* (see opposite).

The Víziváros and Prímás Sziget

Leading down from the ramparts of the basilica, the **Cat Stairs** are cut into the side of the hill and it's an unrelenting, but breathtaking, climb down to the **Víziváros** (Watertown), a small district of Baroque churches and seminaries where practising choirs are audible along the streets. Turning into Pázmány utca, you come to the **Bálint Balassi Museum** at no. 13 (Tues–Sun 9am–5pm; 100Ft), which mounts temporary historical exhibitions rather than dwelling on the romantic poet Bálint Balassi (1554–94), who died trying to recapture Esztergom from the Turks. This half-crazed philanderer was famous for sexually assaulting women and then dedicating verses to them – behaviour that resulted in him being beaten unconscious on several occasions.

A couple of minutes further on you'll come to the Italianate Baroque **Víziváros Parish Church** and the old Primate's Palace at Berényi utca 2.

The latter now houses the **Christian Museum** (Tues–Sun 10am–6pm; 250Ft), Hungary's richest hoard of religious art, which includes the largest collection of Italian prints outside Italy, Renaissance paintings and wood carvings by German and Austrian masters, and the unique "Lord's Coffin of Garamszentbenedek" – a wheeled, gilded structure used in Easter Week processions, from around 1480. From the parish church you can cross a bridge onto **Prímás Sziget** (Primate's Island), a popular tourist spot with a couple of hotels, a restaurant, campsite and sporting facilities. A little way south of the landing stage for ferries to Štúrovo is the reconstructed **Mária Valéria bridge** that connects the two towns. Blown up by retreating Germans at the end of World War II, the bridge was left neglected until, after years of wrangling and protracted negotiations between Hungarian and Slovakian ministers, an intergovernmental agreement to rebuild the bridge was finally signed in 1999. The renovated **Customs House** houses a free exhibition on the history of the bridge.

The lower town and Szent Tamás-hegy

While Rákóczi tér, with its supermarkets and banks, is the de facto centre of the **lower town**, its most attractive feature is the **Kis-Duna sétány**, a riverside walk lined with weeping willows and villas, popular with promenaders. Inland, civic pride is manifest in the brightly painted public buildings on **Széchenyi tér**, including a town hall with Rococo windows that once belonged to Prince Rákóczi's general, János Bottyán, whose statue stands nearby. The old part of town extends as far south as the **City Parish Church**, built on the site of a medieval monastery where Béla IV and Queen Mária Lascaris were buried. To the right of its gateway is a plaque showing the level of the flood of 1832.

The taming of the river is one of the themes of the **Museum of the Danube** at Kölcsey utca 2 (March–Oct Mon & Wed–Sun 10am–6pm; free). Count Széchenyi was the prime mover of the plan to curb flooding and improve navigation on the Danube, using the labour of thousands of Hungarian navvies and technology imported from England – including the steam-dredger *Vidra*, a model of which can be seen. There is also an exhibition on the controversial Danube barrages at Nagymaros and Gabcikovo – until recently a bone of contention between Hungary and Slovakia (see box on p.185).

To end with an overview of the lower town, walk up Imaház utca past a flamboyant, Moorish-style edifice that was once Esztergom's synagogue and is now a science club, or **Technika Háza**. Shortly afterwards you'll find a flight of steps leading to **Szent Tamás-hegy** (St Thomas's Hill), a rocky outcrop named after the English martyr Thomas à Becket. A **chapel** was built here in his honour by Margaret Capet, whose English father-in-law, Henry II, prompted Thomas's assassination by raging "Who will rid me of this turbulent priest?" Even after her husband died and Margaret married Béla III of Hungary, her conscience would not let her forget the saint. The existing chapel (postdating the Turkish occupation) is fronted by a trio of lifesize statues representing Golgotha.

Eating, drinking and entertainment

Hungarian food rules the menus in Esztergom, and **restaurants** near the tourist sites are geared to coach parties and a fast turnover, though none of them is so bad or expensive that you feel compelled to look elsewhere. Indeed, it's hard to resist a meal in the cavernous cellars of the *Prímás Pince* (daily 10am–10pm), beneath Basilica Hill. On Prímás Sziget, the terraced rustic-style *Szálma Csárda* (daily noon–9pm) near the Budapest ferry-dock serves fish, poultry and game in large portions. In the Víziváros, *Anonim* at Berényi utca 4 (Tues–Sun noon–10pm) specializes in exotically sauced game dishes, while the *Csülök*

Csárda (daily noon–midnight), next to the *Ria Panzió*, serves up large portions of moderately priced Hungarian food, and is popular with locals and tourists alike. There's Belgian cooking at *Phillippe*, Széchenyi tér 16 (Wed–Sun noon–11pm), a stylish place serving wild boar sausages, or for something a little less complicated try the good-value pizzas at *Olagz*, Lőrincz utca (daily 11am–11pm). Finally, the restaurant in the *St Kristóf Panzió* (daily 10am–10pm) is worth the walk for its tremendous home cooking, the best and most reasonably priced in town. If you're catering for yourself, there's a daily outdoor **market** on Simor János utca. Almost any of these restaurants are feasible **drinking** spots, as are the **pavement cafés** between Rákóczi tér and Széchenyi tér, which are also good for sandwiches, cakes and ices – though only the *Gambrinus Maláta Bar* at Vörösmarty utca 3 (Mon–Thurs & Sun 11am–2am, Fri & Sat till 3am) could be described as trendy, an intimate tangle of varnished branches with dance music on the jukebox.

Summer is the time for **concerts** in Esztergom, with an annual programme of choral and organ music in the basilica and the Víziváros parish church, plus a **Guitar Festival** during the first half of August in odd-numbered years (Ⓦwww.esztergom.hu/guitar); further details of both can be obtained from Gran Tours. By day, you can work up a sweat in the sports centre (daily 8am–10pm) or the tennis courts near *Gran-Tours Camping*, or pass the time soaking in the large outdoor **swimming pool** with saunas and steam rooms (daily: June–Aug 6am–7pm; May & Oct 6am–6pm; 450Ft), behind the defunct *Hotel Fürdő* on Bajcsy-Zsilinszky utca.

The Pilis range and around

Whether you describe them as mountains or hills, the **Pilis range** (Pilis hegység), behind the west bank, offers lots of scope for **hiking** amidst lovely scenery. The beech and oak woods on these limestone slopes are most beautiful in the autumn, but there's a possibility of sighting red deer or wild boar at any time of year. Ruined monasteries and lodges attest to the hermits of the Order of St Paul and the royal hunting parties who frequented the hills in medieval times.

Pilisvörösvár and Pillisszánto are directly accessible by bus from Árpád híd terminal in Budapest, as is Pomáz, from where buses go on to Pilisszentkereszt and on up to Dobogókő. Buses to Pomáz frequently make the short trip from Szentendre. There are no direct buses from Esztergom. You can also catch the **HÉV train** to Pomáz (near Szentendre) from Budapest's Batthány tér, or you can hike up from the Nagy-Villám Tower at Visegrád. If you're planning any walking, buy a **map** of the Pilis in Budapest or the Danube Bend towns, which shows the paths (*turistaút/földút*), caves (*barlang*), and rain shelters (*esőház*) throughout the highlands.

Pomáz

POMÁZ, on the HÉV line between Budapest and Szentendre, is an excellent place from which to step off into the Pilis, with regular buses leaving from the HÉV station, on the eastern edge of town, to Dobogókő, 18km northwest of Pomáz. Before doing so, though, it's worth exploring the town, most of which is fairly recent, though the Roman sarcophagus outside the town hall on the main street indicates that people have been living and dying here for quite some time. Serbian immigrants fleeing from the Turks arrived in the late seventeenth century, and by the nineteenth century there was a flourishing German community here too.

The first point of interest you come to as you walk up to the town from the HÉV station is the **ethnographical collection** of folk costumes and embroidery (Magyar Néprajzi Gyűjtemény; Tues 2–6pm, Sat & Sun 10am–noon & 1–6pm; 400Ft), behind the colourful Transylvanian gate at József Attila utca 28b. It was put together by private collector János Hamar and covers four regions of Hungarian-speaking communities; every spare inch of furniture here is covered with decoration. The **Community History Collection** at Kossuth Lajos utca 48 (Község Történeti Gyűjtemény; daily 10am–6pm; closed Dec & Jan; 150Ft), a ten-minute walk up the road just past Hősök tere, on the left of the main road, offers something more local. It re-creates homes in Pomáz belonging to the Serbian and German communities, and includes a very nice enamel stove which also served as a boiler, with a tap on one side to let out the hot water. Archeological finds from the area are housed to the left of the entrance. The Swabian community, originally from Germany, was mostly deported back there after World War II, and links with the deported families have only been officially re-established over the last decade or so.

Pomáz's Serb community has been shrinking steadily during the last century, although you can still hear old ladies chatting to each other in Serbian on street corners, and the town is proud of its traditional Serbian dance group which has won prizes in Belgrade. Ten minutes further up Kossuth Lajos utca, at Szabadság tér, is a **Plague Cross** erected in 1792. Five minutes' walk up to the right along the suitably named Szerb utca stands the **church of St George**, which holds masses for the small community at 10am on the second and fourth Sundays of the month. Your best chance to look around the church is to go in just before the service starts. The church's main **annual celebration** is the feast of its patron saint on May 6. The square behind the church, Vujicsics tér, takes its name from the Serbian composer Tihamer Vujicsics (1929–75), who was born in the street beyond; a plaque on Plébánia utca marks the spot. The **Vujicsics Ensemble**, which preserves his memory, started in Pomáz and performs frequently in the town in the summer, although it's now based in Szentendre. Ask at Tourinform in Szentendre about concert dates.

Pomáz has a couple of **places to stay**: the *Kara Hotel* at Beniczky utca 63 (Ⓣ26/322-114, Ⓕ325-355; ❸), ten minutes' walk up the main road past the Plague Cross, has both pension and hotel rooms and its cellar restaurant is the best place to **eat** in town. All buses from the HÉV terminal pass by here. The *Tutti Panzió*, ten minutes' walk from the station along the main road at Budakalász út 14 (Ⓣ26/325 888, Ⓔtuttipanzio@freemail.hu; ❸), is the alternative – a bland place with worn rooms.

Dobogókő and Dömös

Standing in the shadow of 756-metre-high Pilis-tető, **DOBOGÓKŐ** has been a hiking centre since the late nineteenth century, when one of Hungary's first hostels was established here, and is still the best base for walking in the Pilis. The most popular way to see the area is to take the bus up to the resort, and then to walk down the Rám precipice – a four- to five-hour hike that's not advisable in wet weather – to Dömös, which offers fabulous views down to the river.

The hostel building at Dobogókő, just up through the trees from where the buses turn round, is now home to the small **Museum of Rambling and Nature Tourism** (Thurs, Sat & Sun 9am–2pm; free). Exhibits include old photos of the area, showing that there was hardly a tree around the village a hundred years ago, and some old equipment, including skis with a strip of seal fur on the bottom to prevent the ski from slipping downhill. Behind the museum is an observation point which affords lovely views of Szob and Zebegény.

The *Eötvös Loránd Tourist House* (Ⓣ26/347-534; dorm beds 1500–3000Ft), next to the museum, offers the cheapest **accommodation** around, whilst, with permission, tents can be pitched on the grassy area in front of the house. Campers can use the *Tourist House*'s bathroom and restaurant, which serves strudels and other snacks during the week, and lunch at weekends from noon to around 6pm. Just down from here is the *Hotel Nimród* (Ⓣ26/547-003, Ⓦwww.hotels.hu/nimrod_hotel; ❹), an unappealing place swamped in heavy brown decor, although boasting a pool. There are two further possibilities on the main road leading up to Dobogókő, about 1km from the top of the hill: the *Platán Panzió* (Ⓣ & Ⓕ26/347-680, Ⓦwww.hotels.hu/platan_dobogoko; ❷) has bright, wood-furnished rooms and an attractive restaurant, while the *Pilis Hotel* (Ⓣ26/347-522, Ⓕ347-557, Ⓦwww.hotels.hu/pilis_hotel; ❺) is only marginally more dour than the *Nimrod*.

Aside from the hotels, for **food** there is the *Ízek Háza*, opposite the *Hotel Nimród* (Fri–Sun noon–8pm), or the *Bohém Tanya* by the car park at the bus terminus (Mon–Sat noon–10pm, Sun noon–6pm), both serving solid Hungarian fare; or for a filling bean goulash or toasted sandwiches head 300m down past the *Hotel Nimród* to the *Zsindelyes Csárda*, a wooden construction by Imre Makovecz, which also houses the engine house of the ski lift. At busy times of year you may also find some steaming stew cooking over a fire, or an impromptu grill set up on the ends of the trails, at the edges of the bus terminus.

Walking up to Dobogókő from the river, the best starting point is **DÖMÖS**, 7km west of Visegrád, where buses between Visegrád and Esztergom stop off. Inconspicuous wooden signposts near the stream in the centre of the village indicate the start of trails into the hills, where raspberries abound in early summer. Follow the Malom tributary for 2.5km and you'll reach a path that forks right for the Rám precipice (3hr) and Dobogókő (4–5hr), and left for the Vadálló Rocks (3hr) beneath the towering "Pulpit Seat" – a 641-metre crag that only the experienced should attempt to climb.

The east bank

Compared to its western counterpart, the Danube Bend's **east bank** has fewer monuments and, consequently, fewer visitors. **Vác**, the only sizeable town, has a monopoly on historic architecture, styling itself the "city of churches". Not far from the town is the beautiful botanical garden at **Vácrátót**, while further north you can view some of the finest scenery in the Danube Bend at **Zebegény** and **Nagymaros**, which, like other settlements beneath the **Börzsöny range**, mark the start of trails into the highlands.

Starting **from Budapest**, you can reach anywhere along the east bank within an hour or two by train from Nyugati Station, or by bus from the Árpád híd terminal. The slower alternative is to catch a boat from Budapest's Vigadó tér pier to Vác (2hr 30min), or on to Nagymaros and Zebegény. There are also regular ferries from the west bank.

Vác and around

The town of **VÁC**, 40km north of Budapest, has a worldlier past than its sleepy atmosphere suggests, allowing you to enjoy its architectural heritage in relative peace. Its bishops traditionally showed a flair for self-promotion, like the cardinals of Esztergom, endowing monuments and colleges. Under Turkish occupation (1544–1686), Vác assumed an oriental character, with seven mosques and a public *hammam*, while during the Reform Era it was linked to Budapest by Hungary's first rail line (the second continued to Bratislava). In 1849 two battles were fought at Vác, the first a victory for the town over the Austrian army, followed a few months later by a defeat in July 1849 when the town was captured; the battles are commemorated by a bright green **obelisk** by the main road from Budapest, shortly before you enter the town. More recently Vác became notorious for its prison, which has one of the toughest regimes in the country and was used to incarcerate leftists under Admiral Horthy and "counter-revolutionaries" under Communism. Though Vác's legacy of sights justifies a visit, it's not worth staying unless you're planning to visit Vácrátót (see p.184) or Zebegény (see p.186), or are coming especially for the annual festival at the end of July (see p.184).

Arrival and information

Arriving by bus, train or ferry, you can walk into the centre of town in around ten minutes. From the **train station**, head 400m along Széchenyi utca to reach Március 15 tér. Coming from the **bus station**, cross over Dr Csányi László körút to get onto Széchenyi utca. Disembarking at the landing stage for **ferries**

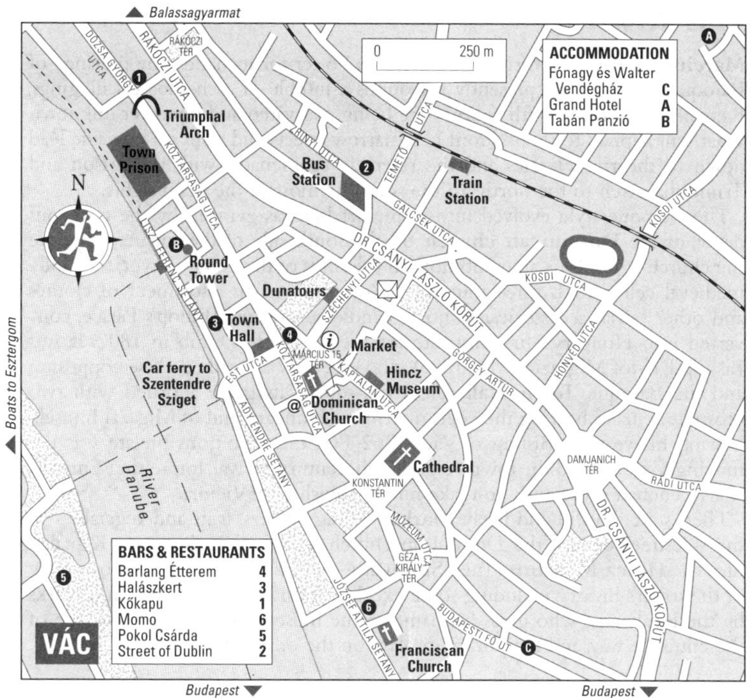

from Budapest, you can see the prison and triumphal arch to the north; head south along the promenade and the town centre is on the left, up Est utca as you reach the wharf for **ferries to Szentendre Sziget** (hourly; 270Ft for passengers, 1000Ft for a car; last ferry leaves around 9pm). From the ferry you can walk across the island to Tahitótfalu (4km), or take the waiting bus.

Tourinform, at Március 15 tér 16–18 (May–Sept Mon–Fri 9am–5pm, Sat 9am–2pm; Oct–April Mon–Fri 9am–4pm; ⓣ27/316-160, ⓔvac@tourinform.hu), has all the **information** you need, both on the town and other attractions along the east bank. There's **Internet** access at Matrix, Rev Koz 2 (Mon–Sat 9am–10pm, Sun 12am–10pm).

Accommodation

For a reasonably large town, Vác has surprisingly little **accommodation**, so you might have to opt for private rooms (❷), bookable through Dunatours at Széchenyi utca 14 (Mon–Fri 8am–4pm, Sat 8am–noon; ⓣ27/310-950). The only hotel in town is the *Grand Hotel*, Végh Dezső utca 34 (ⓣ & ⓕ27/305-297; ❹), an apt name for this highly conspicuous, pale-blue building perched on a hill fifteen minutes' walk north of town; with its well-equipped, elegantly furnished rooms, it is remarkably good value. Otherwise there's the cheerful four-room *Tabán Panzió*, on Korvin Lepsco, which has river views from its terrace down the narrow alleyway next to the Round Tower (ⓣ27/315-607; ❸), or there are cool and comfortable rooms at the friendly *Fónagy és Walter Vendégház* at Budapest fő út 36, ten minutes south of the main square (ⓣ & ⓕ27/310-682, ⓔfonwal@irvitel.hu; ❹), with its own wine cellar and leafy courtyard restaurant where you can taste and buy Hungarian wines.

The Town

Március 15 tér, which rivals Szentendre's Fő tér for its handsome melange of Baroque and Rococo, presently surrounds a jumble of archeological diggings. Remains from the twelfth century are being excavated and it's as yet unknown what will happen to them. From here narrow streets and steps on one side lead down to the river, ferries and the riverside promenade, with the prison and Triumphal Arch to the north. To the south lie most of the main sights.

The Baroque style evolved into a fine art here, as evinced by the gorgeous decor of the **Dominican church** on the south side of the square. Opposite the church at no. 19 is an exhibition on the finds of the church crypt; the chilly medieval cellar holds three mummified corpses and an assortment of clothes and other burial accessories. At no. 6 stands the original Bishop's Palace, converted into Hungary's first Institute for the Deaf and Dumb in 1802. It was Bishop Kristóf Migazzi (1714–1803) who erected Vác's cathedral (see opposite) and the Baroque **Town Hall** across the square, its gable adorned with two prostrate females bearing the coats of arms of Hungary and of Migazzi himself. During his years as Bishop of Vác (1762–86), this ambitious prelate was the moving force behind the town's eighteenth-century revival, impressing Empress Maria Theresa sufficiently to make him Archbishop of Vienna.

There's a colourful and lively **market** selling flowers, fruit and vegetables in the sidestreet behind the Dominican church, and further down on Káptalan utca the **Hincz Museum** (Tues–Sun 10am–6pm; 400Ft) gives a brief overview of the town's history, including some excellent photos. You will also find works by the local artist who gives his name to the museum upstairs on one side of the entrance way, and temporary displays on the other side.

The cathedral

A few minutes on down Káptalan utca brings you to the back of Vác's **cathedral** on Konstantin tér. Chiefly impressive for its gigantic Corinthian columns, Migazzi's church is a temple to self-esteem more than anything else. Its Neoclassical design by Isidore Canevale was considered revolutionary in the 1770s, the style not becoming generally accepted in Hungary until the following century. Migazzi himself took umbrage at one of the frescoes by Franz Anton Maulbertsch, and ordered *The Meeting of Mary and Elizabeth*, above the altar, to be bricked over. His motives for this are unknown, but one theory is that it was because Mary was depicted as being pregnant. The fresco was only discovered during restoration work in 1944. From the cathedral you can head along Múzeum utca to Géza király tér, the centre of Vác in medieval times, where there's a Baroque **Franciscan church** with a magnificent organ, pulpits and altars.

Along the waterfront to the prison

From the Franciscan church you can follow the road down to the **riverside promenade**, József Attila sétány, where the townsfolk of Vác walk on summer weekends and evenings. The northern stretch of the promenade, named after Liszt, runs past the **Round Tower**, the only remnant of Vác's medieval fortifications. Beyond the dock for ferries to Budapest and Esztergom rises the forbidding hulk of the town's **prison**. Ironically, the building was originally an academy for noble youths, founded by Maria Theresa. Turned into a barracks in 1784 – you can still see part of the older building peering awkwardly above the blank white walls of the prison – it began its penal career a century later, achieving infamy during the Horthy era, when two Communists died here after being beaten for going on hunger strike to protest against maltreatment. Later, victims of the Stalinist period were imprisoned here, but in October 1956 a mass escape occurred. Thrown into panic by reports from Budapest where their colleagues were being "hunted down like animals, hung on trees, or just beaten to death by passers-by", the ÁVO guards donned civilian clothing and mounted guns on the rooftop, fomenting rumours of the Uprising among prisoners whose hopes had been raised by snatches of patriotic songs overheard from the streets. A glimpse of national flags with the Soviet emblem cut from the centre provided the spark: a guard was overpowered, locks were shot off, and the prisoners burst free. Edith Bone was an inmate at the time, an English journalist who had been accused of spying and imprisoned for fifteen years in 1949. Robert Maxwell was also imprisoned here during World War II, accused of spying, then using his original name of Ludvik Hoch.

The **Triumphal Arch** flanking the prison was another venture by Migazzi and his architect Canevale, occasioned by Maria Theresa's visit in 1764. Migazzi initially planned theatrical facades to hide the town's dismal housing (perhaps inspired by Potemkin's fake villages in Russia, created around the same time), but settled for the Neoclassical arch, from which Habsburg heads grimace a stony welcome.

Eating, drinking and entertainment

Whereas the medieval traveller Nicolaus Kleeman found Vác's innkeepers "the quintessence of innkeeperish incivility", modern visitors should find things have improved. The best **restaurant** in town is *Momo*, near the river at Tímár utca 9 (Mon–Thurs & Sun 11.30am–midnight, Fri & Sat till 2am), which has three levels of terracing and an outdoor bar – the international menu is pricey but hugely enticing, as is the wine list. Five hundred metres further along the riverfront, at Liszt sétány 9, the *Halászkert* is a touch dated but good for fish; while the *Kőkapu*, just past the Triumphal Arch at Dózsa György utca 5, serves up standard Hungarian fare in a rather old-fashioned setting – the courtyard is a nicer place to eat. The most central eating option – and a good spot for a beer – is the *Barlang Étterem* (Mon–Thurs & Sun noon–11pm, Fri & Sat till 1am), whose main staple is pizzas; you'll find it in an old cellar under Március 15 tér, reached by some steps in the middle of the square. Finally, the *Pokol Csárda* by the ferry station on Szentendre Sziget (daily noon–10pm; last ferry to Szentendre Sziget leaves at 9pm and around 9.30pm back to Vác) caters for tourist groups with huge plates of grilled meats and gets quite boisterous.

Aside from the *Momo* and *Barlang* restaurants, the town's major **drinking** venue is the *Street of Dublin*, across from the bus station at Zrinyi utca 3; you'll also catch live music here (daily until 1am). Vác's major annual **festival** is the three-day Váci Világi Vigalom (literally, the Vác Secular Entertainment, though why secular no one seems able to say) at the end of July, which includes music and exhibitions and takes place on Március 15 tér and down by the river.

Vácrátót

VÁCRÁTÓT, 35km from the centre of Budapest in the hinterland of Vác, has one of Hungary's best-known **botanical gardens** (daily: April–Sept 8am–6pm; Oct–March 8am–4pm; 500Ft). Founded in the 1870s by Count Vigyázó, it was subsequently bequeathed by him to the Hungarian Academy of Sciences. Complete with waterfalls and mock ruins, the garden contains thousands of different trees and shrubs from around the world, covering 2.3 square kilometres and taking a good two hours to walk round. On some Saturday evenings in the summer, concerts are held on the lawns in front of the former manor house, with a backdrop of tall copper beeches on one side and a lake on the other. Tickets are available from the Filharmónia ticket office in Budapest (see p.141).

Motorists can reach Vácrátót from Budapest by turning east off Route 2, north of Sződliget (about 5km before Vác). Although the village is accessible by **train** from Nyugati Station in Budapest, the station is 3km away from the gardens and connecting coaches can be unreliable. Hourly **buses** from the northern end of the blue metro (Újpest) in Budapest and from Vác stop directly outside the gardens.

Nagymaros and Zebegény

The north bank of the Danube gradually becomes steeper as you head towards two settlements, **Nagymaros** and **Zebegény**, both of which merit attention for their atmosphere and as starting points for reaching the Börzsöny hills.

Nagymaros

Twenty kilometres west from Vác along the bank of the Danube, **NAGYMAROS**, the home of nobles in the age of royal Visegrád, is a quietly prosperous village with an air of faded grandeur – an unlikely focus for years of environmental protest. The cause is not Nagymaros itself, where a drunk's ejection from an *italbolt* (local bar) counts as a major disturbance, but a short way upriver, where extensive environmental landscaping has been employed over the remains of the aborted **dam** (see box opposite).

The Gabčikovo-Nagymaros dam

Controversy concerning the building of a **dam** at Nagymaros became a focus of opposition to the Communist regime in the 1980s and was even an element in hastening its demise. The dam was part of the Gabčikovo-Nagymaros Hydroelectric Barrage, a grandiose project dreamt up by Hungarian and Czechoslovak planners in 1978, and supported and partly financed by the Austrians, who hoped to gain access to a cheap source of electricity. The barrage was intended to make use of 200km of the River Danube, diverting it for 25km and tapping its energy with two dams. While work on the dam at Nagymaros was abandoned in 1989 after five years of opposition by Duna Kör (the Danube Circle), the dam at Gabčikovo was almost completed at the time of the Velvet Revolution. Having invested heavily in the project, the newly constituted Slovak government pressed ahead and diverted the Danube away from Hungary onto the Gabčikovo turbines, but, as an operating dam at Nagymaros had been an essential part of the original project, environmental havoc was wreaked on the stretch of the Danube above Győr for comparatively little energy gain.

In 1994 the Hungarian government began demolishing the unused dam at Nagymaros, and both sides turned to the International Court at The Hague for a ruling in the vain hope that this would end the dispute. When the judges finally spoke in early 1998, the Hungarian government promptly declared that the ruling compelled them to go ahead with a dam somewhere on the river. It seemed like Gyula Horn's sweet revenge: the man who had always advocated the dam and watched it destroy the old one-party system could now push the same line as leader of a democratically elected government. Horn was too cocky, however, and the elections later in 1998 swept him and the Socialists from power. The new government declared in one of their first statements that the dam would not be built, and the issue now finally seems closed.

The village lies across the river from Visegrád, with a superb view of the latter's citadel: "Visegrád has the castle, but Nagymaros has the view", as the locals have always boasted. The railway line cuts the village firmly in two; above the line, whitewashed houses straggle up the hillside, while below is the main road, and beyond that the river and ferry to Visegrád. From the Nagymaros-Visegrád Station, duck under the bridge and walk past the *Mátyás Király Restaurant* to the main road, Váci utca; 100m to the right is the leafy main square, Fő tér. At the bottom of the square, across the main road, is the ferry, while at the top, on the other side of the rail line, is a **Gothic church**, parts of which date back to 1509. After 1500m, the path divides at a car park – one fork heads south to Hegyes-tető, where you can enjoy a **panoramic view of the Bend**, while the other heads up into **the Börzsöny**, towards Törökmez, a five-kilometre walk away along a footpath marked with red signs.

Private **accommodation** in Nagymaros is best found on the spot by wandering the streets in search of *Zimmer frei* signs. Alternatively, you can stay at the *Fehér Hattyú* (Ⓣ & Ⓕ27/350-057, Ⓦwww.hotels.hu/feherhattyu-hotel; ❺), a magnificently kitsch hotel and restaurant complex just north of the ferry station, complete with garden gnomes, tinkling waterfalls and a view of the Visegrád Castle opposite; or you can head up through the beech woods to the unassuming but picturesquely located *Törökmező Hostel* (Ⓣ27/350-63; dorm bed 1800Ft). For **food**, try *Fehér Hattyú*, whose garden restaurant backs onto the river bank, or the *Mátyás Király Restaurant* on Magyar utca, near the train station, which serves goulash soups and poultry dishes. Both are open daily until 10pm.

Zebegény

At **ZEBEGÉNY**, 5km further along the bank of the river, where the Danube turns south, the excellent light and the magnificent view of the Bend have lured painters for years. Most of this exceptionally pretty village lies to the east of the rail tracks. From Route 12 you pass under the train station and immediately come to the distinctive **Catholic Church** (1908–14), the only one in Hungary to be built in the National Romantic style, an amalgam of Art Nouveau and folk art, designed by Károly Kós. Inside, frescoes by Aladár Körösfői Kriesch depict Emperor Constantine's vision of finding the Holy Cross in Jerusalem with his mother, St Helena. Five minutes' walk behind the church over the stream and down to the right brings you to one of Zebegény's curiosities, the so-called **Museum of Navigation and Seafaring People** at Szőnyi utca 9 (April–Oct daily 9am–6pm; 500Ft), housing the bizarre private collection of Captain Vince Farkas, who has sailed the world and amassed some nifty carved figureheads in the process (though how tigers and totem poles fit in is a puzzle). Following Szőnyi utca for another ten minutes brings you to Bartóky József utca, where at no. 7 you'll find the **memorial house and studio** of one of Zebegény's best-known artists, István Szőnyi, who died in 1960 (March–Oct Tues–Sun 10am–6pm; Nov–Feb Fri–Sun 10am–4pm; 300Ft). Szőnyi first began to paint here, and the house hosts an international **art school** every summer.

If you're looking to **stay**, there are several places signed *Zimmer frei* ten minutes' walk past the church along Kossuth utca. Five minutes further on, over the stream to the left, is the welcoming *Malomkerék Vendégfogadó* at Malom utca 21 (ⓣ27/373-010, ⓦwww.malomkerek.de.tf; ❷), which also acts as the **information office** for the village; there are well-kept rooms in the house, and the guesthouse has a couple of equally pleasant apartments, as well as a pool, open-air fire for cooking goulash, and bicycles and canoes available for rent. Twenty minutes' walk further on, turn right at the end of the village to get to the *Almáskert Pension* at Almáskert utca 13 (ⓣ27/373-037; ❷), which has timber-balconied rooms overlooking a neat lawn. If the prospect of a room directly overlooking the river appeals, five minutes' walk from the church (under the railway, left on the main road, left and then first right) brings you to cheap rooms at Táncsics Mihály utca 2 (ⓣ27/373-255; ❷). There is a more luxurious option 1km to the south at the modern *Kenderes Hotel* on Dózsa György út 26 (ⓣ & ⓕ27/373-444, ⓔkenderes@dunaweb.hu; ❸–❹), where rooms have a bathroom, television and safe; you can also rent watersport equipment and use the sauna and swimming pool.

The restaurants in the *Almáskert* and *Kenderes* are the best places to **eat**, the latter serving some Balkan and Transylvanian dishes.

Into Slovakia

The main claim to fame of Szob, the last town on the Hungarian north bank of the river, is as the border crossing for trains to Slovakia. Crossing into Slovakia by road is either unnecessarily long or overcomplicated depending on how you choose to do it: you can either take the ferry from Szob across the Danube to Basaharc, travel 12km up the road to Esztergom, and there catch another ferry back across to Slovakia; or you drive 30km north to Parassapuszta on the Ipoly River, which demarcates the frontier. The neighbouring village of Drégelypalánk, 7km away, is on the Vác–Diósjen–Balassagyarmat train line (trains roughly every 2hr). The crossing at Letkés/Salka can be used only by Hungarians and Slovakians.

The Börzsöny range

The **Börzsöny range**, squeezed between the Danube and Slovakia, sees few visitors despite its scattering of hostels and forest footpaths, and its abundance of rabbits, pheasants and deer is watched only by circling eagles. It's feasible to camp rough here, though most of the places covered below offer some form of accommodation. Would-be walkers should buy Cartographia's *Börzsöny-hegység* map of the hills (available at the Tourinform office in Vác or from map shops), which shows paths and the location of hostels (*túristaház*).

Mount Csóványos (939m) is the highest peak in the Börzsöny, and also the most challenging. Hikers usually approach it from the direction of **DIÓSJENŐ**, a sleepy mountain village that's accessible by bus or train from Vác. Diósjenő's **campsite** (Ⓣ35/364-134; May–Sept), at Petőfi Sándor utca 55, lies just over 1km from the village and 2km from the train halt. Six kilometres further up the road towards Kemence, there is a **pension** (Ⓣ27/365-139; ❷) and riding school (same Ⓣ; 1500Ft for 1hr) at **KIRÁLYHÁZA**; the road runs along a delightful wooded valley, but there is no bus from Diósjenő.

An alternative route into the mountains begins at Kismaros, 12km up the Danube from Vác. From here narrow-gauge trains trundle to **KIRÁLYRÉT** (April–Oct 5 daily; Nov–March 4 daily Sat & Sun only; 55min), with connecting trains to and from Budapest from the main-line station across the road. Close to the station is the *Fővárosi Önkormányzat Üdülője*, a hostel with cheap beds (Ⓣ27/375-033; dorm bed 2300Ft), and you can eat cheaply at the local restaurant. Supposedly once the hunting ground of Beatrice and Mátyás, this "Royal Meadow" has paths going in several directions. One trail, marked in green, goes across to the village of Nógrád with its ruined castle, 5km from Diósjenő on the Diósjenő–Vác railway line. Another, marked in red, leads to the Magas-Tax peak about ninety minutes' walk away, with another cheap hostel, the *Magas Tax Turistaház* (Ⓣ60/346-150; dorm bed 2600Ft). The path goes on to the "Big Cold" peak, **Nagy Hideg Hegy**, which has excellent views, and branches out to Mount Csóványos and the villages of Nagybörzsöny and Kóspallag; use the *Börzsöny-hegység* map to guide you.

Nagybörzsöny, Kóspallag and Márianosztra

From Nagy Hideg Hegy, a trail marked by blue squares leads westwards to **NAGYBÖRZSÖNY**. You can also get here by bus from Szob and make this your starting point for walking east. A wealthy town during the Middle Ages, Nagybörzsöny declined with the depletion of its copper, gold and iron mines in the eighteenth century, and is now a mere logging village with an overdose of churches – four in all. The walled thirteenth-century Romanesque **Church of St Stephen**, on the left as you enter the village, was left stranded as the cemetery chapel when the village moved closer to the mines in the fifteenth century. If you are walking from the centre of the village, stop in at Petőfi utca 17 en route to ask for the gigantic church key, as the church is normally closed. Just across the road from the house is the Gothic **Miners' Church**, some of whose features have survived later alterations; again, if the church is closed, ask at Petőfi utca 17. Just below the church, an exhibition of folk costumes, home furnishings and mining accessories can be found at the **Mining Museum** at Petőfi utca 19 (Tues–Sun 10am–4pm; 100Ft), with explanations in Hungarian and German only, but you get the general feel anyway. Just up from the main square, where the bus terminus is located, you will find the village's still-working watermill along to the left by the stream (Tues–Sun 10am–4pm; 60Ft). For **accommodation**, there are basic doubles (shared bathrooms) above the *Butella Borozó* (☎27/378-035; ❷), just above the main road near the Romanesque church; or a ten-minute walk along the track past the wine bar leads down to the *Nagybörzsöny Község Vendégháza*, by a fishing lake – a rather out-of-the-way site where you can get a room (☎27/377-450; ❷). Otherwise it is worth asking in the village about private rooms.

The other trail from Nagy Hideg Hegy (marked with a blue horizontal line) runs south down to **KÓSPALLAG**, another prosaic village, notable only as a place to catch **buses** to Vác (six daily; last bus at 3pm). However, pursuing the path onwards, things improve beyond the Vác–Szob road junction below the village, where the path wanders through beech woods to a lovely open meadow graced with a solitary tree and the first view of the Danube. Cutting southwest across the meadow puts you back on the path to the *Törökmező Hostel* (see p.185). The path divides by the exercise camp in the woods, and heading west along the path marked with green signs you come down to Zebegény (5km). Alternatively, you can head on another 4km along the blue path, past the hostel, to a car park at the junction of paths to Hegyes-tető (Hilly Peak) and Nagybörzsöny.

If you take the road from Kóspallag to Szob, you come to **MÁRIANOSZTRA**, a place of pilgrimage 9km from Szob and served by hourly buses. These **pilgrimages** take place on the second Sunday in May, and on the Sundays preceding August 15 and September 14. The Baroque church in the centre of the village (now in the courtyard at the entrance of a men's prison) dates from 1360, and retains some original fragments. One curiosity is the copy of the *Black Czestochowa Madonna*, the original of which was taken to Poland in 1382 by Hungarian monks sent to found the monastery there. An hour's walk north from the village takes you to **Kopasz hegy** (Bald Hill) which affords some of the best views in the region.

Travel details

Trains

Esztergom to: Budapest (every 40min–1hr; 1hr 30min); Komárom (3 daily; 1hr 20min).
Kismaros to: Királyrét (April–Oct 5 daily; 35min).
Vác to: Balassagyarmat (10 daily; 2hr 20min); Budapest (every 30min; 45min); Diósjenő (11 daily; 45min); Nagymaros (hourly; 20min).
Vácrátót to: Aszód (4 daily; 1hr 30min); Budapest (hourly; 1hr 10min); Vác (hourly; 15min).
Pomáz to: Budapest (every 30min; 25min).

Buses

Esztergom to: Budapest via the Bend (every 30–40min; 1hr 15min) or via Dorog (every 30min; 55min); Győr (2 daily; 2hr); Komárom (5 daily; 90min); Sopron (2 daily; 4hr); Szentendre (hourly; 1hr 30min); Veszprém (2 daily; 2hr); Visegrád (hourly; 40min).
Pomáz to: Dobogókő (Mon–Fri every 30min–1hr, Sat & Sun hourly; 40min).
Szentendre to: Budapest (every 30min–1hr; 30min); Esztergom (hourly; 1hr 30min); Pomáz (every 20–30min; 10min); Visegrád (hourly; 40min).
Szob to: Nagybörzsöny (hourly; 35min).
Vác to: Budapest (hourly; 30min); Diósjenő (6–8 daily; 1hr); Kóspallag (7 daily; 90min); Vácrátót (hourly; 45min); Nagymaros (hourly; 20min).
Visegrád to: Budapest (every 30min–1hr; 1hr); Dömös (hourly; 15min); Esztergom (hourly; 40min).

Ferries

The following ferries operate April to September.
Basaharc to: Szob (hourly; 10min).
Esztergom to: Budapest (1 daily; 4hr 30min); Štúrovo, Slovakia (hourly; 10min); Szentendre (2

daily; 1hr 25min); Vác (1 daily; 2hr 30min); Visegrád (1–2 daily; 1hr 25min).
Kismaros to: Kisoroszi (every 30min–1hr 30 min; 10min).
Leányfalu to: Pócsmegyer (every 30–60min; 10min).
Nagymaros to: Visegrád (hourly; 10min).
Pilismarót to: Zebegény (hourly; 10min).
Szob to: Basaharc (hourly; 10min).
Tahitótfalu to: Vác (hourly; 10min).
Vác to: Budapest (1 daily; 1hr 20min); Esztergom (1 daily; 2hr 30min); Tahitótfalu (hourly; 10min).
Visegrád to: Budapest (1 daily; 3hr 30min); Esztergom (1–2 daily; 1hr 45min); Kisoroszi (2 daily; 20 min); Nagymaros (hourly; 10min); Vác (1 daily; 45min); Zebegény (1–2 daily; 50min).

Lake Balaton and the Bakony

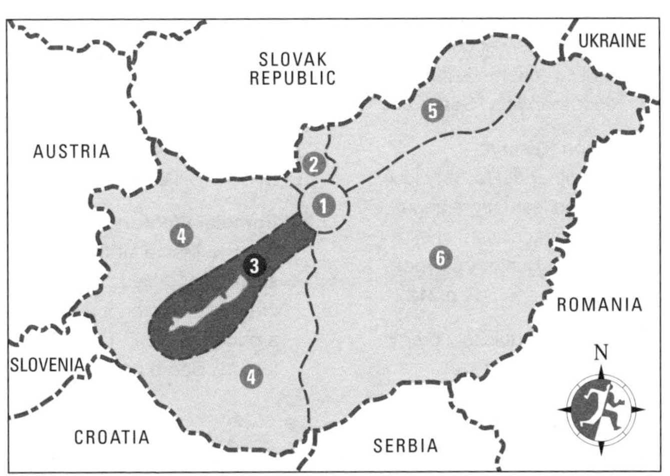

CHAPTER 3

Highlights

* **Watersports on Lake Balaton** The clean, shallow waters of Lake Balaton are ideal for sailing or windsurfing – head for Siófok, Balatonfüred or Keszthely. **See p.205, p.216 and p.226**

* **Bory's Castle, Székesfehérvár** Take a wander around this marvellously eccentric mid-twentieth-century suburban folly. **See p.202**

* **Bison Reserve, Kápolnapuszta** Get close to, and learn more about, these magnificent animals, in Hungary's largest buffalo park. **See p.212**

* **Tihany** Exquisitely pretty village located in Hungary's first national park. **See p.221**

* **Festetics Palace, Keszthely** Imposing palace with a wonderful library set in a charming lakeside town. **See p.229**

* **Thermal lake, Hévíz** Wallow in temperatures of 30°C in Europe's largest thermal lake. **See p.231**

* **Várhegy, Veszprém** The elevated position of this beautifully preserved castle district affords terrific views of the Bakony Hills. **See p.238**

* **Porcelain factory, Herend** Marvel at the supremely skilled craftsmanship on a tour around the world-famous factory. **See p.240**

▲ Festetics Palace, Keszthely

3

Lake Balaton and the Bakony

Lake Balaton, affectionately known to Hungarians as "Balcsi", is the nation's substitute for a coastline. Millions of people come here every summer to enjoy the lake's remarkably clean, milky green waters, which, with an average depth of only 3m, are warm enough to swim in from May to October. Though few would subscribe to the old romantic view of Balaton as the "Hungarian sea", it is still the largest freshwater lake in Europe – nearly 80km long and varying in width from 14km to a mere 1.5km at the point where the lake is almost cut in two by the Tihany peninsula – and all that remains of the ancient Pannonian Sea that once covered the region.

Though its **history** is hardly writ large, the region was first settled in the Iron Age, and has been a wine-growing centre since Roman times. During the sixteenth century, it formed the front line between Turkish and Habsburg-ruled Hungary, with an Ottoman fleet based at Siófok and an Austrian one at Balatonfüred. Spas and villas began to appear from 1765 onwards, but catered largely to the wealthy until the Communists began promoting holidays for the masses after World War II. During the 1960s, footloose youths started flocking here, and in the 1970s and 1980s there was a boom in private holiday homes and room-letting, fuelled by an influx of tourists from Germany and Austria. Today, visitors from these two countries still provide the bulk of tourists, although an increasing number of other foreigners are beginning to discover some of the undoubted charms of the lake. If visiting, it's best to do so outside July and August as this is the time when the natives descend upon the lake in their masses.

Balaton's low-lying **southern shore** is almost entirely built up with a continuous chain of fairly indistinguishable resorts, with brash and bustling **Siófok** the model for others, such as **Fonyód** further along. By contrast, waterfront development on the **northern shore** has been limited by reed beds and cooler, deeper water, and the attractions, such as the beautiful **Tihany peninsula** and the wine-producing **Badacsony Hills**, are of a less hedonistic bent, instead offering splendid scenery and sightseeing. The compact western end is perhaps the most appealing part of the lake, providing the setting for the delightful university town of **Keszthely**, the world's second-largest thermal lake at nearby **Hévíz** and the reedy **Kis-Balaton** nature reserve, home to a bison reserve and a superb venue for bird-watching.

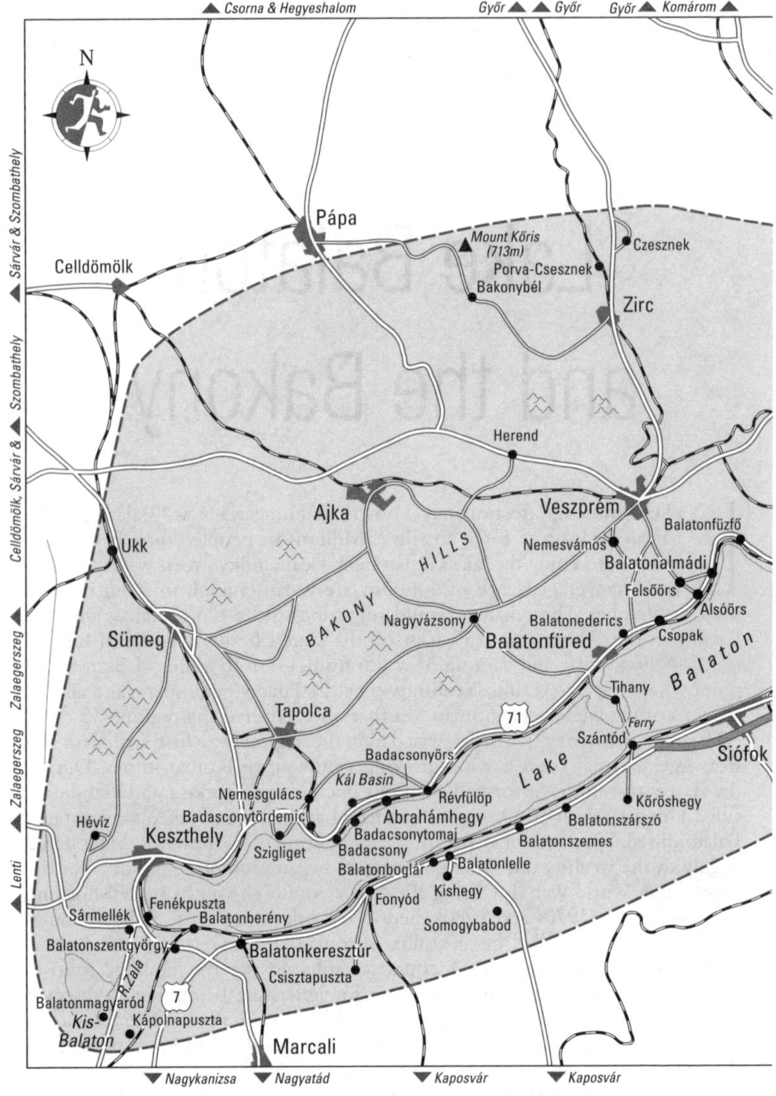

Midway between Budapest and Balaton, **Lake Velence**, a miniature version of Balaton, lies close to **Martonvásár**, where summer Beethoven concerts in the grounds of the Brunswick Mansion draw many visitors from the capital. Beyond Lake Velence is **Székesfehérvár**, well worth a visit for its romantic Belváros (Inner Town) and "Bory's Castle", whilst the wooded **Bakony** region north of Balaton, dotted with picturesque villages and ruined castles, is the setting for the historic towns of **Veszprém**, **Sümeg** and **Tapolca**, plus the world-famous porcelain factory at **Herend**.

Lake Balaton is easily accessible from Budapest and Transdanubia. **Trains** from

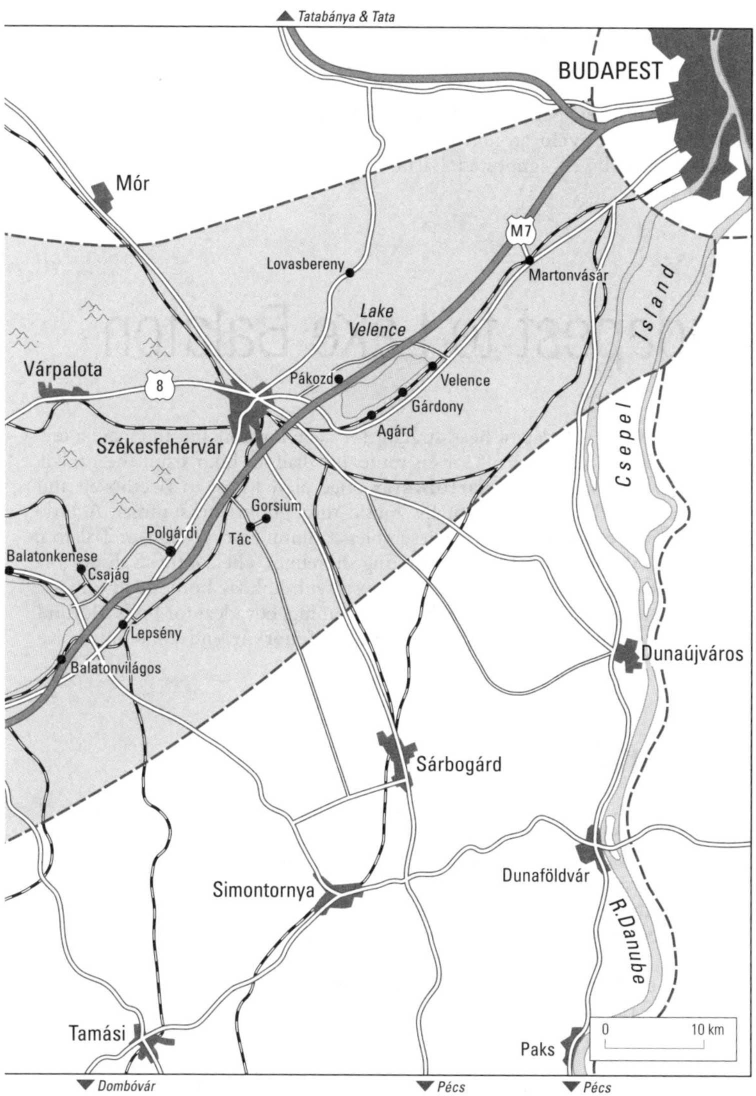

Budapest's Déli Station run to all the main resorts, with daily InterCity services providing the fastest access to Keszthely (2hr 30min) via the southern shore. **Buses** to Székesfehérvár, Veszprém and Balaton leave from the Népliget depot. If you're driving to Balaton, the M7 to Siófok is the quickest road; to get to the northern shore, turn off the M7 onto Route 71 for Balatonfüred. Over summer, however, you can expect long tailbacks on the M7 on Friday evenings and Saturday mornings, and also on the way back to Budapest on Sunday evenings.

A great way to see – and get around – the lake is by ferry. From mid-April to October, **passenger ferries** run from Siófok to Balatonfüred and Tihany on the opposite bank, and between Fonyód and Badascony and Keszthely. During July and August, a number of other services shuttle back and forth across the lake connecting the smaller resorts. Between March and November, there is also a **car ferry** between Tihany-rév and Szántód-rév. Another attractive proposition is to **cycle** around the lake, now possible thanks to the recently inaugurated, and well signposted, Balaton cycleway (Balaton Kőrűt).

Budapest to Lake Balaton

Most visitors from Budapest head straight for Lake Balaton, but there are a few attractions worth stopping off for en route. Just half an hour from the capital, the Brunswick Mansion at **Martonvásár** once played host to Beethoven and today holds outdoor concerts of his music throughout the summer. A little further southwest, **Lake Velence** resembles a diminutive version of Balaton, with hills to the north and two contrasting shorelines. The southern shore, followed by Route 70 and the rail line, is awash with holiday homes and tourists, while the opposite bank is too reedy for swimming, but ideal for birds. Beyond Lake Velence is the atmospheric town of **Székesfehérvár**, and some impressive Roman ruins at nearby **Tác**.

Martonvásár

Situated about halfway between Budapest and Velence, the small town of **MARTONVÁSÁR** is renowned for the neo-Gothic **Brunswick Mansion** (Brunszvik Kastély), set in a lovely park where **Teréz Brunswick** founded Hungary's first nursery school in 1828; sadly, the mansion isn't open to the public but the park is a wonderful place to stroll around (daily 8am–5.30pm; 170Ft). Beethoven came to the mansion several times in the early years of the nineteenth century, teaching music to Teréz and her sister, Josephine, who may have been the "immortal beloved" of **Beethoven**'s love letters, and the inspiration for his *Moonlight* and *Appassionata* sonatas. Some reckon, though, that his muse was Giulietta Guiccardi, the "beautiful devil" whom he also met here between 1800 and 1806.

A handful of Beethoven's letters, as well as a medallion containing a lock of his hair, and a *hammerklavier* that Beethoven himself might have played, are displayed in the **Beethoven Memorial Museum** (Tues–Fri 10am–noon & 2–4pm, Sat & Sun 10am–noon & 2–6pm; 200Ft) adjoining the mansion. In addition there are numerous items belonging to the Brunswick family, including portraits, books and musical instruments, though the only guidance you can get on the exhibits in English is a small leaflet sold at the ticket desk (50Ft). Housed in a small hut to the left of the mansion, the **Nursery Museum** (Óvodamúzeum; mid-March to mid-Oct Tues–Fri 10am–2pm, Sat & Sun 11am–6pm; 200Ft) offers a cramped display of artefacts, including a row of enamel potties set in a wooden bench, and photos from the past 150 years illustrating Hungary's pioneering role in nursery education.

A more compelling reason to come to the mansion is for the **summer evening concerts**, held on an island in the middle of the park beneath a great bower of beech and sycamore. Armed with mosquito repellent and a couple of bottles from the bar-buffet, you can listen to the music as the sun sets through the trees. Tickets (1500–2800Ft) are available from the booth at the park entrance, or from the Central Box Office or Filharmónia in Budapest (see p.141).

Arriving by **train**, it's a ten-minute walk down Brunszvik utca to the park entrance, while **buses** drop you off at the post office by the traffic lights, from where it's a two-minute walk. Should you miss the last train back to Budapest (11.32pm), or to Lake Velence and Székesfehérvár (11.15pm), there are a couple of places to **stay** on Budai űt, the main road towards Budapest (turn left at the traffic lights up from the park); try the friendly but simple *Macska Pension* at no. 21 (Ⓣ22/460-127; ❸), or the very smart *Hotel Marton*, 450m further up at no. 83 (Ⓣ22/460-342, Ⓦwww.hotelmarton.com; ❸). The only **restaurant** here is *Postakocsi* at Fehérvári utca 1, on the corner of Dósza György út, leading up to the park.

Lake Velence

It's hard not to smile when told that Velence, 50km from Budapest and just 15km from Székesfehérvár, is the Hungarian name for Venice, though the town probably came by the name because Italian craftsmen working in Székesfehérvár lived here in the Middle Ages, rather than from any more romantic similarities. Today, the 26 square kilometres of **Lake Velence** (Velencei-tó) serves as a lesser Balaton, though its resort aspect is balanced by a strong wildlife presence. Reeds cover up to a half of the lake's surface, helping to maintain the quality of the water, and the western end is a nesting ground for some 30,000 **birds**, which migrate here in spring. According to legend, three sisters, who turned themselves into herons to escape the Turks, return home here every year.

The **southern and eastern shores** of the lake are one continuous strip of holiday homes and campsites, along an enclosed, mainly grassy, *strand*. If it weren't for the individually named train stations, **Velence**, **Gárdony** and **Agárd**, you'd never realize that there were three separate settlements along the shore. The **beaches** alternate between ones where you have to pay for a swim and the dubious privilege of using the changing rooms, and *szabad strand*, free ones with fewer facilities, such as the *strand* a few minutes' walk north of Velence train station in front of the *Hotel Helios*. **Watersport** facilities are widely available along this stretch of the lake, and it's an ideal spot to learn windsurfing as the water is only 1–2m deep, warming up to an acceptable 22–26°C over summer. In winter, the lake often freezes solid and ice-skating becomes the favoured sport. For something less energetic, you can always head for the **thermal baths** in Agárd, 1km or so south of the lake at the end of Határ utca (daily 8am–7pm; 600Ft).

The most interesting of the lake's sights are located on the less built-up **northern shore**, close to the peninsula where ferries dock. A ten-minute walk uphill brings you to **Mészeg Hill**, where an obelisk commemorates the Battle of Pákozd on September 29, 1848, the first Hungarian victory of the 1848–49 Revolution. The small **museum** (Tues–Sun 10am–5pm; 260Ft), close by, exhibits various paraphernalia from the battlefield, as well as some photos of the unveiling of the obelisk in 1951 – there's also a decent café here, serving light snacks. A further ten minutes uphill brings you to a **memorial** to the Hungarian soldiers who died in Russia during World War II, fighting on the side of the Nazis. This canopy-chapel is designed to ease an old wound for Hungarians, who lost over 100,000 men in Russia, mainly at the River Don, but were unable to mourn them during the Communist era.

One kilometre east from Mészeg Hill is the **Pákozdi Arborétum** (mid-March to Oct Tues–Sun 10am–6pm; 250Ft), a rather dreary collection of local trees, plants and rocks. A better reason for heading this way is to climb the wooden lookout tower (*kilató*), which affords some splendid views of the lake and the Velence hills, some of the oldest in Hungary, formed from magma and granite. There is more geology above the village of **PÁKOZD**, thirty minutes' walk under the motorway and left along the main road. Turning off the main road just past another 1848 monument, it's a stiff walk up the 241-metre-high **Pogány-kő** (Pagan Rock), where several colossal "rocking stones" (*ingókővek*) – blocks of granite polished in the shapes of various animals – sway perceptibly in the wind.

Practicalities

Arriving at the southern shore, orientation couldn't be easier: wherever you get off the **train**, simply head for the lake. The Tourinform office is located in Gárdony, at Szabadság utca 16 (mid-June to mid-Sept Mon–Fri 9am–6pm, Sat & Sun 10am–5pm; mid-Sept to mid-June Mon–Fri 8am–4pm; ⓣ22/570-078, ⓔgardony@tourinform.hu), while another good source of **information** is Sol Tours at Szabadság utca 12 (July & Aug daily 9am–8pm; March–June & Sept–Oct Mon–Sat 9am–5pm; ⓣ22/570-158, ⓦwww.soltours.inf.hu); both are located across the road from the *Ponty* restaurant by the group of small apartment blocks. Sol Tours also has an office at the northeastern end of the lake in Velence, at Ország utca 25 (same hours; ⓣ22/470-497).

The **northern shore** is accessible by hourly buses from Székesfehérvár or by ferry from Agárd (May to mid-June & Sept to mid-Oct Sat & Sun only every 1hr 30min; mid-June to Aug hourly; 360Ft one way), which docks at the small peninsula, Szúnyog Sziget (Mosquito Island).

Accommodation

Like Balaton, Lake Velence closes down from October to April and is very busy the rest of the year, so it's worth booking accommodation in advance rather than just turning up. Velence and Agárd have the greatest variety of places to stay, including **private rooms**, **flats** and **cottages** (❷–❹), bookable through Sol Tours (see above) or rented direct from householders (look for *Zimmer frei* signs), although they may not be any cheaper than the rest of the accommodation on offer. There are numerous **campsites**, all open mid-April to mid-October, spread between the three resorts, the largest of which is *Panoráma Camping* on Kemping utca (ⓣ22/472-043; chalets ❷) on the eastern shore of the lake, roughly 2km from Velence station; facilities include tennis courts, a minigolf course, water-bikes, restaurants, and masseurs for post-beach relaxation. In Agárd, try *Park Strand Camping* (ⓣ22/579-220), some 500m west of the train station at Chernel István út 56, or *Termál Camping* (ⓣ22/579-008), which also has a pension (❸) and is down by the resort's thermal baths on Határ utca; guests qualify for reduced admission prices to the baths. Four buses run daily from the centre to the baths.

Családi Panzió Templom köz 12 ⓣ & ⓕ22/472-710. Clean and modern pension at the northern end of Velence near the church and 600m from the water. Rooms have TV and bathroom. ❸
Hotel Helios Tópart utca 34 ⓣ22/589-330, ⓦwww.hoteljuventus.hu. Just ten minutes' walk from Velence station and very near the lake, this pleasant small hotel has comfortable en-suite rooms plus its own pool. There's a free beach opposite, but you can use the *strand* and facilities of the nearby *Hotel Juventus*, run by the same people. ❺
István Panzió Templom köz 10 ⓣ22/472-702, ⓕ474-424. Next door to the *Családi Panzió* and identically priced, but with much better furnished rooms and a delightful garden restaurant. ❸
Hotel Juventus Kisköz 6 ⓣ22/589-330, ⓦwww.hoteljuventus.hu. Peaceful, unprepossessing lakeside hotel five minutes on from the *Hotel Helios*, with reasonably smart rooms, a sauna and tennis courts, and watersports on its own bit of beach. ❼
Touring Hotel Tópart utca 1 ⓣ22/370-113, ⓦwww.hotels.hu/touring. Small and friendly lakeside hotel, ten minutes' walk west of Agárd station, beside the pier, with somewhat dated rooms. Bikes and water-bikes can be rented here. May–Sept. ❹

Eating

Of the **restaurants**, the *Ponty*, 100m left along the main road as you exit the station in Gárdony, is one of the most popular around the lake, serving up fresh fish dishes and salads (daily 11am–10pm). In Agárd, two places worth trying are the *Nádas Csarda*, just up from the train station on the main road, Balatoni utca, and the *Csutora*, a fifteen-minute walk west along the same road at no. 131; both knock up better than average Hungarian cuisine accompanied by live music and are open daily from 11am to 11pm. In Velence itself you could opt for *Velence Pizzeria* at Tópart utca 2 (daily noon–10pm), which also has a limited Hungarian menu, or the very good restaurant in the *Juventus Hotel*, which offers a comprehensive buffet menu (see above).

Székesfehérvár and around

Reputedly the site where Árpád pitched camp and founded his dynasty, **SZÉKESFEHÉRVÁR**, 60km southwest of Budapest, was probably the first Hungarian town. Its name (pronounced "**saik**-esh-fehair-var") comes from the white castle (*fehérvár*) founded by Prince Géza, whose son Stephen made it his royal seat (*szék*). As the centre of his efforts to civilize the Magyars, it was named in Latin "Alba Civitas" or "Alba Regia". Since this medieval town was utterly destroyed by the Turks, Székesfehérvár today owes its Belváros to the Habsburgs, and its high-rise suburbs to the final German counterattack in 1945, which levelled almost everywhere else. The town's principal attractions are its narrow winding streets and diverse galleries in the **Belváros**, and the wonderful suburban folly known as **Bory's Castle**.

Arrival and information

Székesfehérvár's **train station** is 1km south of the centre; catch any bus heading up Prohászka Ottakár út, which subsequently becomes Várkörút, and get off near the *Hotel Alba Regia*. The **bus station** is more conveniently located on Piac tér, just a few minutes' walk from the Belváros. **Information** is available from Tourinform at Városház tér 1 (July to mid-Sept Mon–Fri 9am–7pm, Sat & Sun 9am–6pm; mid-Sept to June Mon–Fri 9am–4pm; ⓣ22/312-818, ⓔfejer-m@tourinform.hu) or Sol Tours, in the courtyard at Kossuth utca 14 (June–Aug Mon–Fri 9am–6pm, Sat & Sun 9am–5pm; Sept–May Mon–Fri 9am–5pm; ⓣ22/385-321, ⓦwww.soltours.inf.hu). The main **post office** is on Szent István tér (Mon–Fri 8am–7pm).

Accommodation

Székesfehérvár has a reasonable, if largely uninspiring, stock of **hotels**. Alternatively, **private rooms** (❷) can be booked through Ibusz at Táncsics Mihaly utca 5 (Mon–Fri 8am–5pm, Sat 9am–1pm; Ⓣ22/329-393, Ⓔi088@ibusz.hu) and Sol Tours (see p.199), while Tourinform can advise on **hostel** accommodation (❶–❸) over the summer and at weekends throughout the year – though be warned that some hostels are on the outskirts of town. For **camping**, *Ifjúsági Camping* is at Bregyó köz 1 (Ⓣ22/313-433; May–Sept), about fifteen minutes' walk north of the centre (or buses #12 and #14).

Hotel Alba Regia Rákóczi utca 1 Ⓣ22/313-484, Ⓔreserve.hotelalbaregia@mail.datanet.hu. Functional three-star 1970s establishment overlooking the Romkert with dull rooms and small, rather shabby, bathrooms. ❺

Két Góbé Gugásvölgyi út 4 Ⓣ & Ⓕ22/327-578. Unattractively sited on the main ring road 2km northeast of the centre, this eight-room thatched pension has fairly glum-looking rooms, but it's cheap. Buses #26 and #32. ❸

Magyar Király Hotel Fő utca 10 Ⓣ22/311-262, Ⓕ327-786. A grand hotel built in the 1870s, but which now has disappointingly ordinary rooms. ❹

Novotel Ady Endre utca 19–21 Ⓣ22/534-300, Ⓦwww.novotel-szekesfehervar.hu. Efficient chain hotel featuring all the requisite four-star comforts, including pristine rooms with Internet access and safe. ❼

Rév Hotel József Attila utca 42 Ⓣ22/327-015, Ⓕ327-061. 500m east of the centre, this *üdülőház* (workers' hotel) has ten rooms, each with washbasin only, available throughout the year. ❷

Szent Gellért Hotel Mátyás király körút 1

☎22/510-810, ©szentgellert@axelero.hu. Bright hotel in a cracking location near the bus station and Belváros, containing a good mix of doubles and triple rooms, as well as dorms sleeping up to six people. Terrific value. Dorm beds ❶, doubles ❷–❹

The Town

Székesfehérvár's **Belváros** occupies approximately the same area as the great castle once did, as evinced by a section of the medieval walls alongside the **Romkert** (April–Oct Tues–Sun 9am–5pm; 260Ft, free on Sun). Among the stonework in this "Garden of Ruins" is a richly carved Roman sarcophagus found in 1803 and believed to hold the remains of King Stephen, minus his right hand which resides in St Stephen's Basilica in Budapest. Alongside the garden are the excavated **foundations of the cathedral** where Stephen was buried. Designed for him by Italian architects in an attempt to rival St Mark's in Venice, it hosted the coronations of 38 Hungarian kings. After the town fell to the Turks in 1543, the cathedral was plundered of its gold and jewels, and then blown up.

Városház tér, the gorgeous, elongated main square beside the ruins, recalls Székesfehérvár's revival under Maria Theresa, with its Baroque town hall, Franciscan church and Zopf-style **Bishop's Palace**, built with stones from the ruined cathedral by Bishop Milassin, whose coat of arms appears on the gable. Running off to the north, **Fő utca** is so perfectly preserved that you expect to see crinoline-clad ladies emerging from the **Black Eagle Pharmaceutical Museum** at no. 5 (Fekete Sas Patika Műzeum; Tues–Sun 10am–6pm; 250Ft, free on Sun). This eighteenth-century pharmacy operated right up until 1971, and visitors can see the original Baroque fittings and fixtures dating from 1758, along with displays on traditional remedies. Like the Baroque church of St John across the street, it was founded by the Jesuits.

The City Gallery and Szent István Király Museum

Around the back of St John's Church, at Oskola utca 10, is the **City Gallery** (Városi Képtár; Tues–Sun: April–Oct 10am–6pm; Nov–March 9am–5pm; 150Ft), which has a brilliant display of nineteenth- and twentieth-century Hungarian art. The Deák Collection, which was bequeathed to the city by a local collector, is housed in three medieval houses that have been joined together, with a labyrinth of small rooms exhibiting works by top Hungarian artists, such as Victor Vasarely, Lajos Kassák, Endre Bálint and Rippl-Rónai. In the same block is a collection of sculptures by Erzsébet Schaár (same hours as the gallery; 100Ft); ask the people at the main desk to guide you through the labyrinth to get to the sculptures.

Back on Fő utca, at no. 6, next to the church, is the permanent collection of the **Szent István Király Museum** (Tues–Sun: May–Sept 10am–4pm; Oct–April 10am–2pm; 260Ft, free on Sun), a lively exhibition on local history featuring a superb collection of archeological finds and domestic treasures from the Neolithic period through to the time of Turkish rule. Especially notable is the hoard of Celtic goods, including pottery, urns and jewellery, and a stone dedication block featuring a relief of Mithras, the sun god, ritually slaying the bull. The museum also puts on temporary shows of contemporary Hungarian art at Országzászló tér 3, at the top of Fő utca (Tues–Sun 2–4pm; 260Ft, free on Sun).

South of Városház tér

More of the historic architecture is clustered south of Városház tér. Walking south down Arany János utca, you'll pass the Baroque **St Stephen's Cathedral**, a much rebuilt edifice that dates back to the thirteenth century. The **Chapel of St Anna** alongside is the only remnant of medieval Székesfehérvár spared by the Turks, who put it to use as a mosque – notice the Koranic inscriptions and arabesque murals. Continuing south along Arany János utca, you'll come to the fanciful Zopf-style **Budenz House** at no. 12 (Tues–Sun: March–April & Oct 10am–2pm; May–Sept 10am–4pm; 260Ft), which has a collection of beautiful old furniture and Hungarian art belonging to the Ybl family. Architect Miklós Ybl (1814–91) was born in this house, and in one of the rooms downstairs you can see his drawing cabinet and photos of buildings he designed, including the Budapest Opera House. The house itself is over two hundred years old and named after its former owner Budenz József, a researcher of Finno-Ugrian languages and founder of Hungarian comparative linguistics. Further down the street, a left turn takes you into **Petőfi utca**; a **plaque** on the wall of the cinema marks the house where the ubiquitous Sándor Petőfi lived for a couple of months at the end of 1842 as a travelling actor. Close by, at Megyeház utca 17, the **Dolls' House Museum** (Fehérvári Babaház; March–Oct Tues–Sun 9am–5pm; 280Ft) features an exquisite collection of eighteenth-century dolls' houses and porcelain dolls, while, for the boys, there's a small assemblage of model toys. In the same building there is a small gallery for temporary art exhibitions (same times and included in same ticket).

Bory's Castle

The town's most popular, and curious, sight is **Bory's Castle** (Bory Vár; March–Nov daily 9am–5pm; 400Ft), situated out in the eastern suburbs at Máriavölgy utca 54, beyond the microchip and TV factories. An extraordinary and wildly eclectic structure combining features of Scottish, Romanesque and Gothic architecture, it was built between 1923 and 1959 in an ordinary suburban street by a group of students directed by the architect and sculptor **Jenő Bory** (1879–1959). Originally just a small cottage with a vineyard, Bory gradually enlarged the premises so as to include a gallery, loggia and a large courtyard spotted with numerous columns and towers. The castle's rooms (only open Sat & Sun 10am–noon & 3–5pm) are stuffed with paintings of Ilona Komocsin, Bory's wife, while the colourful gardens are filled with statues of Hungarian kings and other eminent characters. Although the overall effect of Ilona's multiple images is slightly morbid, the castle is a marvellous place to wander around and explore. **Buses** #26 and #26A from the bus station, and #32 from the train station, run regularly to the castle.

Eating and drinking

Though the town is not blessed with an abundance of places to eat, there are several **restaurants** worth investigating: the refined *Kiskulacs Vendéglő* at Budai út 26 (daily 11am–11pm), with its elegantly designed interior and rather more prosaic outdoor dining area, offers moderate to expensively priced Hungarian food plus an accomplished wine list; while the *Isolabella*, in a small courtyard at Kossuth utca 14 (daily 10am–11pm, Fri & Sat till midnight), is an imaginative place with separate rooms for different cuisines (Mexican, Greek, Hungarian and Italian) and decor to match – with good options for vegetarians. On the slightly more expensive side is the *Belgian Beer Café* at Szent István tér 14 (daily 10am–midnight), serving all manner of inventively titled and extremely filling Belgian dishes, accompanied by some of the best beer in town. Other **drinking** possibilities include the *Szin Kávéház* and the *Eden Kávéház*, two funky little places located a few paces apart from each other on Vasvári Pál utca (both open Mon–Sat till 1am, Sun till 10pm); the former has a terrific terrace overlooking the Romkert, while the latter has live jazz at weekends as well as a basement **Internet** room. During the day, the masses congregate at the sprawling *Pátria Kávéház* on Városház tér.

Tác

TÁC, 10km south of Székesfehérvár and 3km off the M7 motorway, is the site of Hungary's largest archeological park; by **train** (6 daily) you'll need to get off at Szabadbattyán station and catch a local bus, or take a **bus** from Székesfehérvár's bus terminal (every 2hr) and get off in the centre of the village at the Soviet war memorial (a rare sight in Hungary now), where signs point towards the **Roman ruins of Gorsium**, twenty minutes' walk away (daily: April–Oct 8am–6pm; Nov–March 8am–4pm; 360Ft including entry to the museum). Gorsium began life as a military camp, but by the beginning of the second century had become the religious centre of Pannonia. Following heavy damage during the third century, Emperor Diocletian founded the city of Herculia over the ruins; it then remained a settlement of sorts until the late sixteenth century when it was finally destroyed by the Turks. Covering two square kilometres, the site has been under excavation since 1958, though to date barely a third has been uncovered. The foundations so far revealed include a palace, a temple, the forum, a theatre and a cemetery, with some well-preserved grave markers lining the paths of the site. It is worth getting a map at the entrance as it is hard to make sense of it otherwise. Carved stonework and other finds are displayed in a **museum** to the right of the entrance (same hours). The ruins host an annual **festival** called the "Floralia" at the end of April, which celebrates the arrival of spring; its highlights are a flower show, craft stalls, Greek plays and gladiatorial combat. Tickets are available from Tourinform in Székesfehérvár (see p.199).

Lake Balaton: the southern shore

The **southern shore** of Lake Balaton is almost entirely built up, with an endless procession of *strand* – the generic term for any kind of bathing place. Hungarians call these **beaches**, though they are in fact grassy sunbathing areas with concrete embankments along the shoreline. While the discerning head for **Balatonvilágos**, the masses plump for **Siófok**, which has no peers when it comes to partying, although other resorts, such as **Fonyód**, try hard to imitate. In **Balatonszárszó** and **Balatonszemes**, you can even find a touch of history, while the South Balaton wine route covers the region around the villages of **Balatonlelle**, **Balatonboglár** and **Kishegy**, which are also notable for their festivals. Nature only reasserts itself at the western end of the lake, where the River Zala flows through the reeds into the **Kis-Balaton** (Little Balaton) – the location for a bird and bison reserve. All the resorts along the southern shore are accessible by **train** from Budapest or Székesfehérvár.

Storm warnings

From May to September Balaton is prone to occasional **storms**. Twenty-four storm signalling stations dotted around the lake indicate when storms are approaching, or when the wind is getting up, via a series of yellow flashing lights: thirty flashes per minute indicates winds of 40–60km per hour; sixty flashes per minute means winds of over 60km per hour. In the case of sixty flashes per minute it is forbidden to enter the water and windsurfers or sailors should head for land at once.

Balatonvilágos

Approaching the southern shore by train, you'll catch your first glimpse of Balaton at **BALATONVILÁGOS**, a five-kilometre-long village that came into being following the amalgamation of two resorts, Aliga and Világos. Built on wooded cliffs along the shore, the village was once a favoured haunt of Party officials and boats were forbidden to dock in its harbour – even those seeking refuge from a storm. Today it is one of the lushest, least commercialized resorts around the lake. Moreover, unlike many other resorts, it has what can properly be called a **beach**.

The Tourinform office at Dózsa György utca 1, next to the post office in the upper part of the village, can give **information** on accommodation (June–Aug Mon–Fri 9am–7pm, Sat & Sun 9am–5pm; Sept–May Mon–Fri 8am–4pm;

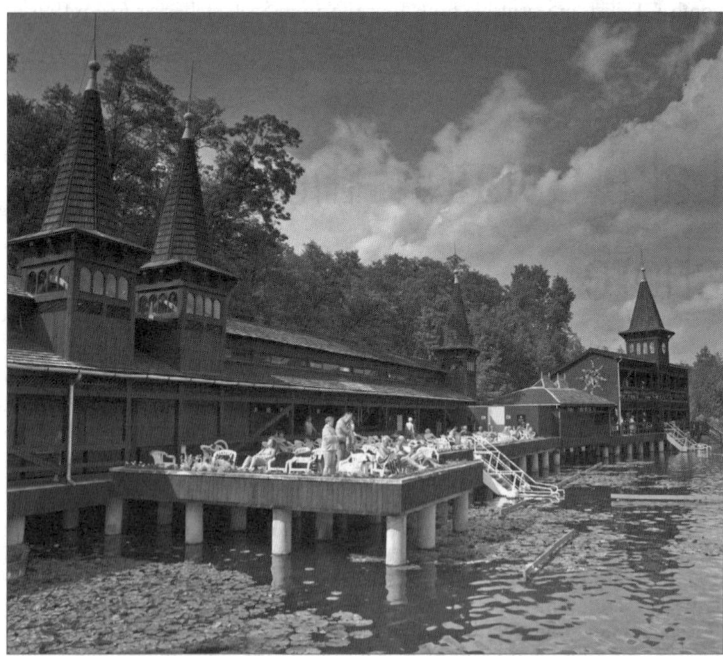

▲ Gyógy-tó, Hévíz

Ⓣ88/446-034, Ⓔbalatonvilagos@tourinform.hu). Heading down the steep road that runs past the train station at the western end of the village, you'll find plenty of lakeside **accommodation**, all of which is available between April or May and September. The extremely pleasant *Napfény Hotel,* at Rákóczi út 12 (Ⓣ30/901-8316, Ⓦwww.hotels.hu/napfeny; ❸), is by far the best place to stay, with nine intimate, air-conditioned rooms and a terrific restaurant and lakeside beer garden. Five hundred metres further on, at no. 33, is the much larger but less agreeable *Dalma Panzió* (Ⓣ88/480-883; ❹). The *Aranyhid üdülő* (Ⓣ480-616; dorm bed 2500Ft), next door to the *Napfény Hotel*, is one of several hostels along Rákóczi út and Zrínyi út; others worth trying include the *Tópart Ifjúsági üdülő* at Rákóczi út 19 (Ⓣ88/480-741; dorm bed 2500Ft), and the *Kék-Balaton üdülő* at Zrinyi út 3 (Ⓣ88/480-827; dorm bed 2500Ft). About 500m along from the *Kék-Balaton üdülő* is a paying beach (200Ft), while the free beach (*szabad strand*) is another 1km further on.

Siófok

SIÓFOK, 6km down the shore from Balatonvilágos, is the largest, busiest and most vibrant resort on Balaton: crammed with bars and restaurants, it has long been the choice venue for young party-goers and was the first to introduce strip bars and sex clubs to augment the traditional pleasures of boozing, guzzling, sunbathing and dancing. Though its vitality might appeal for a while, you'll probably find that a day or two here will suffice – and finding accommodation can be tough.

Arrival and information

The **bus** and **train stations** are next to each other on Fő utca, the town's main axis, just across the road from the **post office** (Mon–Fri 8am–7pm, Sat 8am–noon). **Ferries** to and from Balatonfüred on the northern shore dock to the west of Jókai Park, at the mouth of the Sió Canal. **Information** can be obtained from the incredibly busy Tourinform office, housed in the water tower (Víztorony) on Szabadság tér (mid-June to mid-Sept Mon–Fri 8am–8pm, Sat & Sun 9am–6pm; mid-Sept to mid-June Mon–Fri 9am–4pm; Ⓣ84/315-355, Ⓦwww.siofok.com). There's **Internet access** at Net-Game-Pont at Fő utca 45 (daily 10am–10pm).

Accommodation

There's plenty of accommodation to go around in Siófok, though the town gets completely swamped during July and August, and booking ahead is strongly advised. **Private rooms** (❸–❹) are bookable through Tourinform (see above), Siótour at Szabadság tér 6 (June–Aug Mon–Fri 8.30am–7pm, Sat 9am–2pm; Sept–May Mon–Fri 9am–4pm; Ⓣ84/310-900, Ⓦwww.siotour.hu) and Ibusz, inside the atrium at Fő utca 176 (June–Aug Mon–Fri 8am–6pm, Sat 9am–6pm, Sun 9am–1pm; Sept–May Mon–Fri 8am–4pm; Ⓣ84/510-720, Ⓔi081@ibusz.hu). If the accommodation situation looks bleak then head for Balatonvilágos, just three stops and fifteen minutes away on the train, where there are further options (see above).

There are several **campsites** around, the largest and most accessible of which are *Aranypart Camping*, 5km east of the centre (bus #2) at Szent László utca 183–185 (Ⓣ84/352-801; chalets ❹; mid-April to mid-Sept), and *Ezüstpart*

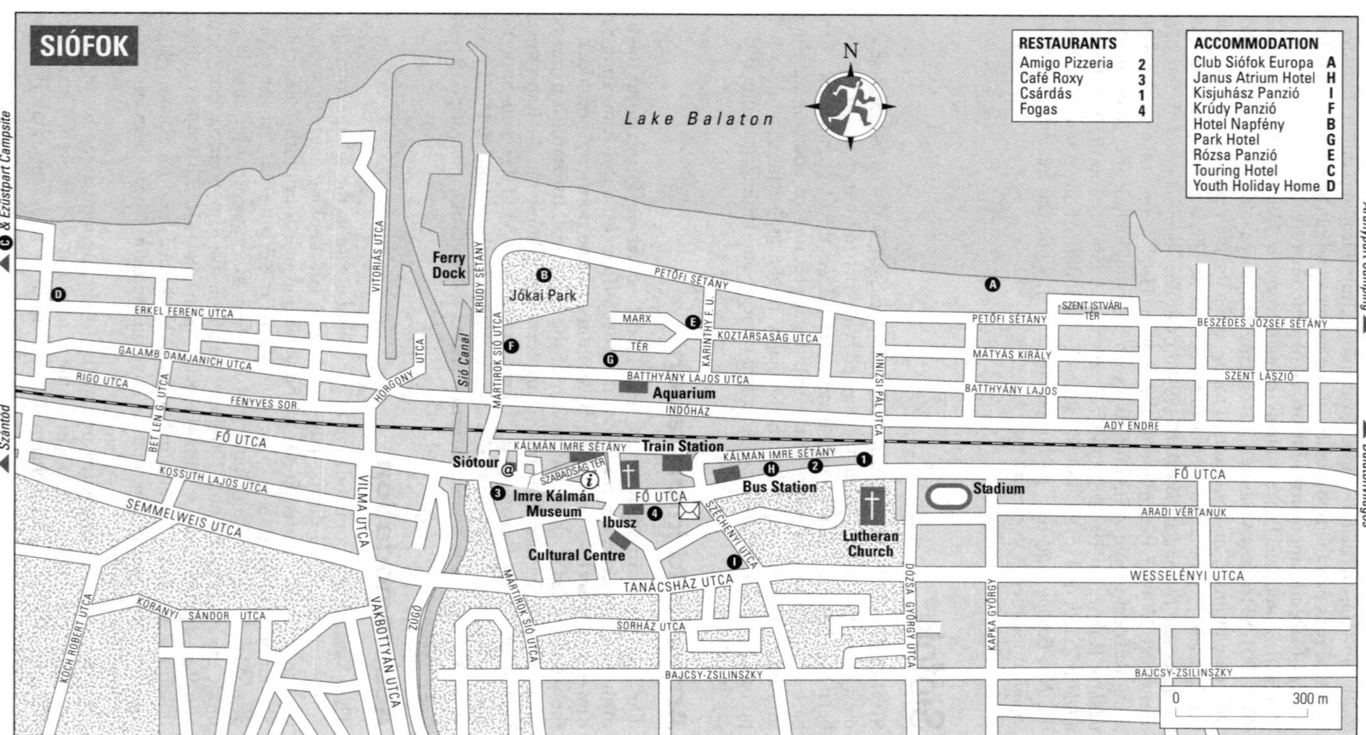
SIÓFOK
RESTAURANTS
Amigo Pizzeria 2
Café Roxy 3
Csárdás 1
Fogas 4
ACCOMMODATION
Club Siófok Europa A
Janus Atrium Hotel H
Kisjuhász Panzió I
Krúdy Panzió F
Hotel Napfény B
Park Hotel G
Rózsa Panzió E
Touring Hotel C
Youth Holiday Home D
N
Lake Balaton
Aranypart Camping
Balatonvilágos
C & Ezüstpart Campsite
Szántód
Ferry Dock
Jókai Park
Sió Canal
Aquarium
Train Station
Siótour
Imre Kálmán Museum
Ibusz
Cultural Centre
Bus Station
Stadium
Lutheran Church
0
300 m
PETŐFI SÉTÁNY
SZENT ISTVÁRI TÉR
BESZÉDES JÓZSEF SÉTÁNY
MÁTYÁS KIRÁLY
SZENT LÁSZIÓ
BATTHYÁNY LAJOS
BATTHYÁNY LAJOS UTCA
ADY ENDRE
INDÓHÁZ
KINIZSI PÁL UTCA
MARX
TÉR
KARINTHY F. U.
KOZTÁRSASÁG UTCA
KRÚDY SÉTÁNY
VITORIÁS UTCA
ERKEL FERENC UTCA
GALAMB
DAMJANICH UTCA
RIGO UTCA
HORGONY UTCA
MÁRTIROK SIÓ UTCA
FENYVES SOR.
BET LEN G. UTCA
FŐ UTCA
KÁLMÁN IMRE SÉTÁNY
SZABADSÁG TÉR
KOSSUTH LAJOS UTCA
SEMMELWEIS UTCA
VILMA UTCA
SZÉCHENYI UTCA
TANÁCSHÁZ UTCA
ARADI VÉRTANUK
WESSELÉNYI UTCA
DÓZSA GYÖRGY UTCA
KAPKA GYÖRGY
SORHÁZ UTCA
BAJCSY-ZSILINSZKY
KORÁNYI SÁNDOR UTCA
KOCH ROBERT UTCA
VAKBOTTYÁN UTCA
ZUGÓ

Camping, 4km west of the centre (bus #1 from the Baross Bridge) at Liszt Ferenc sétány 5 (☎84/350-374; chalets ❸; May–Sept). There are also two **hostels** west of the centre: the *Youth Holiday Home*, at Erkel Ferenc utca 46 (☎84/310-131; ❷; June–Aug), has doubles with shared bathrooms, as does the *Touring Hotel* (☎84/350-185; ❶; May–Sept) at Cseresznye utca 1/0.

Club Siófok Europa Petőfi sétány 17 ☎84/313-411, Ⓦwww.pannoniahotels.hu. Unattractive high-rise down on the waterfront with average-looking rooms, swimming pool, sauna and massage facilities. The identical *Lido* and *Hungária* hotels next door are run by the same team. May–Sept. All ❼
Janus Atrium Hotel Fő utca 93–95 ☎84/312-546, Ⓦwww.janushotel.hu. Classy and quiet hotel on the busy main road, with modestly sized and darkly furnished rooms; also boasts a gorgeous little basement pool and Jacuzzi. ❽
Kisjuhász Panzió Széchenyi utca 14 ☎84/311-289, Ⓔkisjuhas@axelero.hu. Five minutes south of the rail and bus stations, this cordial pension has spotless, air-conditioned rooms with fridge. Triples and quads available too. ❹
Krúdy Panzió Batthyány Lajos utca 1a ☎84/310-416, Ⓕ458-001. Set back from the street on the edge of leafy Jókai Park, this pleasantly secluded pension has large, spartan rooms. May–Sept. ❺
Hotel Napfény Mártirok Sió utca 8 ☎84/311-408, Ⓔnapfeny@mail.datanet.hu. Fairly run-of-the-mill place, and a touch overpriced, but it does occupy a great location in Jókai Park near the lakeside. April–Sept. ❺
Park Hotel Batthyány Lajos utca 7 ☎84/310-539, Ⓦwww.parkhotel.hu. Big, high-ceilinged rooms in this welcoming, ideally located hotel by Jókai Park. ❹–❺
Rózsa Panzió Karinthy Frigyes utca 5 ☎ & Ⓕ84/310-722. Located between the station and the beach, this is a peaceful place with basic, modernish rooms. Triples, quads and apartments available. May to mid-Sept. ❺

The Town and beaches

With its high-rise hotels and packed beaches, there's little trace of Siófok's prewar reputation as a quietly elegant resort, nor much evidence of the town's long history. The canal that the Romans began in 292 AD was later made use of by the Turks, who stationed a fleet of 10,000 men here to confront the Austro-Hungarian fleet across the water at Balatonfüred. A small **gallery** at the top of the 45-metre-high water tower on central Szabadság tér displays photos of Siófok a century ago and offers a view of the town today, though you have to climb over 120 steps to get there (above Tourinform, same hours, see p.205; 200Ft). The streets between the train station and the shore are an enjoyable place to wander around, with avenues of plane trees screening some magnificent turn-of-the-twentieth-century **villas**, many of them turned into garishly decorated restaurants or pensions, or, in the case of the one at Batthyány Lajos utca 22, an **aquarium** (daily: June–Aug 10am–9pm; Sept–May 10am–6pm; 500Ft), which houses some colourful marine life, although most people come for the daily shark shows (between 10am & 5pm).

Siófok's most famous son is the composer of operettas **Imre Kálmán** (1882–1953), who was born in a house near the train station at what is now Kálmán Imre sétány 5, where there's a **museum** (Tues–Sun 9am–5pm; 250Ft) featuring his piano, desk and dressing gown, as well as photos and programmes from operettas such as the *Countess Maritza* and the *Csárdás Princess*, unfortunately without any explanations in English.

From the museum, head down to Fő utca, and walk east for ten minutes to reach the striking modern **Lutheran Church** (May–Sept daily 9am–noon & 3–7pm; Oct–April Sun only 11am–noon), designed by the visionary architect Imre Makovecz (see box on p.172). It not only embodies his ideas about organic architecture and nationhood, but constitutes a rebuke to the immorality and materialism of Siófok – or at least that's assumed to be the significance of the hollow-eyed face of an old man carved into the wooden facade. The points of the roof are meant to be the shoulders of his sheepskin coat.

Back at the lakeside there are two main waterfront resort areas: **Aranypart** (Gold Shore) to the east of the Sió Canal, and **Ezüstpart** (Silver Shore) to the west. Though the central stretch of shoreline consists of paying **beaches** (daily mid-May to mid-Sept 7am–7pm; 700Ft), there are free *strand* 1km further along at both resort areas. Having larger hotels and more nightlife in the vicinity, Aranypart is the livelier and noisier of the two. You can rent **windsurfing** boards and small **sailing** boats at most beaches, while **horse-riding** and **pleasure cruises** can be arranged through Siótour (see p.205).

Eating

Restaurants abound in Siófok but, predictably enough, the majority are geared towards tourists and the bulk of these are concentrated along Aranypart, and in particular on Petőfi sétány. Away from the waterfront, however, there is an impressive line-up of restaurants scattered along Fő utca.

Amigo Pizzeria Fő utca 99. The pick of the restaurants along this street, this thoroughly modern, very large and very enjoyable place has an outstandingly varied menu including fish, poultry and beef, as well as a "sharpfood" menu (ie very hot) – the pizzas, meanwhile, are fantastic. Daily noon–midnight.

Asia Fő utca 93–95. Inside the *Janus Atrium Hotel* (see p.207), this is as authentic a Chinese restaurant as you'll find outside Budapest; there's also a Thai menu and some very appealing vegetarian options. Tues–Fri 6–10pm, Sat & Sun noon–2pm & 6–10pm.

Café Roxy Szabadság tér 1. Informal and very popular restaurant-cum-bar offering a choice selection of dishes including pickled salads, stews and grills, and wild boar. It's also a good spot for a daytime coffee or evening glass of wine. Daily 11am–10pm.

Csárdás Fő utca 105. Old-fashioned joint with a reliably solid Hungarian menu as well as some surprisingly attractive vegetarian choices; there's live Gypsy music to boot. Daily 11.30am–10pm.

Fogas Fő utca 184. Slightly more colourful than the *Csárdás*, this seasoned eatery opposite the train station offers decent Hungarian food, and is also the best place in town to sample fish. Daily noon–10pm.

Nightlife and entertainment

As befits Balaton's number-one party town, Siófok has more than its fair share of **nightlife**, with dozens of bars and clubs stretching along Petőfi sétány – three of the most popular bars being *Renegade*, *Baccardi* and *La Siesta*. The two big-hitters, and the place for serious clubbers, are the *Palace Dance Club*, to the west of town at Deák Ferenc utca 2 (mid-May to mid-Sept; Ⓦwww.palace.hu), which regularly attracts big-name DJs; and *Flört* (mid-May to mid-Sept; Ⓦwww.flort.hu), a high-energy techno club just off Fő utca on the east bank of the canal – both are open till the very early hours. There are also regular **pop and rock concerts** on one of the *strand* by the hotels in the centre of town – look out for flyers around town or check with Tourinform (see p.205).

Siófok being the birthplace of Imre Kálmán, **operetta** dominates summer entertainment, with performances of his works (usually in German) in the Cultural Centre (Kulturális Központ; 4000Ft) behind the water tower. Another key component of the summer programme is **organ concerts** and **piano recitals**, most of which also take place in the Cultural Centre. In early July Siófok hosts the **Golden Shell International Folklore Festival**, a five-day event with parades and dancing by troupes from around the world. Details of all concerts and festivals are available from Tourinform.

The southern shore to Kis-Balaton

Beyond Siófok the southern shore abounds with smaller resorts, such as **Balatonszárszó** and **Balatonszemes**, both of which boast interesting museums, and the villages of **Balatonlelle** and **Balatonboglár**, which lie at the heart of the region's main wine road. The shore winds up at **Kis-Balaton**, site of a peaceful nature and bison reserve, the latter in particular worth visiting.

Szántód and around

The small village of **SZÁNTÓD**, 11km down from Siófok, is the point of departure for **car ferries** to Tihany-rév (see p.219) on the northern shore (daily: March–May & early Sept–Nov every hour, last ferry at 6pm; June to early Sept every 40min, last ferry at 10pm; 10min; 1060Ft per car, 340Ft per person & 260Ft per bike). If for some reason you need to **stay** here, try the friendly, hostel-like *Rév Hotel*, five minutes' walk from the ferry at Szent István út 162 (Ⓣ84/348-245, Ⓔrevhotel@elender.hu; May–Sept; ❹), or *Rév Camping*, next door (Ⓣ84/348-859; mid-May to Aug). One kilometre back towards Siófok along Route 7 is a cluster of eighteenth- and nineteenth-century farm buildings converted into a "tourist and cultural centre" at **Szántódpuszta** (daily: mid-April to June & Sept to mid-Oct 9am–5pm; July & Aug 8.30am–7pm; 400Ft). *Puszta* has two meanings: one is the flat plains of eastern Hungary, and the other, of which Szántódpuszta is a good example, is a large farmstead common in western Hungary. The restored thatched buildings house a local history exhibition with beautiful old photos, a poor craft display, a blacksmith's workshop that's sometimes in operation, and a Balaton aquarium, plus two restaurants, and a stables offering horse-and-carriage rides. You can stay here at the simple and old-fashioned *Patkó Fogadó* (Ⓣ84/348-714; ❹; May to mid-Sept), run by the Siótour office at the entrance to the complex.

Balatonszárszó and Balatonszemes

The boundary of the small town of **BALATONSZÁRSZÓ**, 5km further on from Szántód, is marked by a cemetery containing the **grave of Attila József**, the tragic proletarian poet. Dismissed by his literary peers and rejected by both his lover and the Communist Party, he threw himself under a local freight train on December 3, 1937. Attila spent his last days in a pension that's now a **memorial museum** at József Attila utca 7 (Tues–Sun: April–Oct 10am–6pm; Nov–March noon–4pm; 300Ft), a couple of streets south of the train station. The museum contains some of his manuscripts, photographs and personal effects, as well as the crumpled, blood-stained shirt he was wearing when struck by the train; unfortunately all captions are in Hungarian only. If you're looking to **stay** here then your best bets are the comfortable *Cseri Panzió*, 400m south of the train station at Fő utca 30 (Ⓣ84/363-221, Ⓔcseripanzio@matavnet.hu; ❹), or the less attractive but perfectly acceptable *Főnix Hotel* (Ⓣ84/362-961; ❹), 100m west of the station down by the lake. The clean and pleasant *Tura Camping* is 100m along the tracks from the station in József Attila Park (Ⓣ84/362-754; mid-June to Aug). As for **eating**, the two pizzerias by the station might not occupy the best location in the world but are agreeable all the same.

BALATONSZEMES, 5km further west, has a relaxed feel, with pleasant plane-tree-lined avenues curling down to the lakeside, and an old coaching inn converted into a **Postal Museum** at Bajcsy-Zsilinszky utca 46 (May–Sept Tues–Sun 10am–6pm; 200Ft), which is primarily concerned with documenting the history of postal transportation, as illustrated by the antique stage coaches standing in the courtyard. Although they do not have an information office here, Siótour runs the *Lídó* **campsite** (Ⓣ84/360-112; mid-May to mid-Sept) and **hostel** (❷; same months) at Ady Endre utca 8, and the *Vadvirág* campsite, just off the main road at Arany János utca 101 (Ⓣ84/360-114; June to mid-Sept), which also has chalets (❹).

Balatonlelle, Balatonboglár and around

During the Kádár era, the settlements of Balatonlelle and Balatonboglár were merged into a single entity called Boglárlelle, but since 1991 they have re-established their own identities and also made the most of the revival of the wine industry since then, becoming the main centre of **wine tourism** on the southern shore of the lake. The fifty-kilometre-long strip of land that makes up this, the fifth largest wine region in the country, yields an equal number of quality red and white wines. For more information contact the South-Balaton Wine Route Association in Balatonboglár (Ⓣ85/351-311, Ⓔbalatonboglar@somogy.hu).

Balatonlelle and around

The tidy little resort of **BALATONLELLE** does its bit to attract tourists by staging the lively **Wine Week Festival** during the first week of August, featuring wine and music, and an arts and crafts fair. There's some good **accommodation** here, too, the best of which is the lovely *Viktória Panzió*, some 400m west of the station at Szent István utca 13 (Ⓣ85/554-233, Ⓦwww.viktoriapanzio.hu; ❺), which has polished, well-furnished rooms; the *Lelle Park*, 200m east of the station at Köztársaság út 11 (Ⓣ85/450-317; Ⓦwww.lellepark.com; ❹–❻), which has immaculate air-conditioned apartments sleeping two to six people; and, just along from here at no. 31, the bright *Hotel Francoise* (Ⓣ85/352-429, Ⓦwww.francoise.hu; ❹). The large and well-equipped *Aranyhíd* campsite is at Köztársaság út 53 (Ⓣ85/350-449; mid-May to mid-Sept). Both the *Viktória* and the *Lelle Park* have very good **restaurants** offering above-average Hungarian fare, while the latter also has a smart pub.

Wine lovers should also venture 3km inland to **KISHEGY** (you'll have to walk or take a taxi if you don't have your own transport), where you can taste and buy wine in the **Szent Donatus winery** at Kishegyi utca 42 (Mon–Fri 7.30am–noon & 12.30–3.30pm; Ⓣ85/454-701, Ⓔstdonatus@mail.datanet.hu); expect to pay around 50–60Ft per glass. It's another 2km to the *Szent Donatus Csárda* at the top of the hill (the staff at the winery can direct you), where you can get stuck into solid Hungarian fare and sample more wines while gazing over the lake (May to mid-Sept daily noon–10pm).

Balatonboglár and around

BALATONBOGLÁR, 3km west of Balatonlelle, plays host to several more good festivals, most notably the five-day **Jazz and Wine Festival** at the end of July, and the massive **Grape Gathering Festival** (Boglári Szüreti) from August 18 to 20, which takes place on two stages down by the Platán *strand*, with a big fair and a procession, a competition for the title of Wine Queen, nightly firework displays, and, of course, lots of wine. In neighbouring Várhegy, a spherical **lookout tower** commands a sweeping view from Keszthely to Tihany, while atop Temetődomb (Cemetery Hill), behind the two chapels, there are regular exhibitions by artists from June to August. Another fun time to be here is the last Saturday in July when the **swim across Balaton** takes place; each year several thousand greased-up swimmers set off from **Révfülöp**, 5.2km away on the northern shore, to Balatonboglár in this popular amateur swim-fest.

Balatonboglár's **Tourinform** office is at Erzsébet utca 12–14, a couple of minutes' walk up off the main road (mid-June to mid-Sept Mon–Sat 9am–8pm, Sun 9am–6pm; mid-Sept to mid-June Mon–Fri 9am–noon & 1–4pm; Ⓣ85/550-168, Ⓔbalatonboglar@tourinform.hu). You can book private **rooms** through Fredo Tourist, located across the tracks at Tinódi utca 16 (June–Aug daily 8am–8pm; Ⓣ85/350-288, Ⓦwww.fredotourist.hu). The *Vasutas Üdülő* at Kodály Zoltán utca 9–15, by the tracks to the east of the station (Ⓣ85/350-634; ❶), has cheap beds, or for something more comfortable, head along to the *Família Hotel* at no. 64 (Ⓣ84/350-604, Ⓦwww.hotels.hu/bb_familia; ❸; May–Sept). The *Sellő Campsite* (Ⓣ85/550-367; April–Sept) is on the west of the landing stage at Kikötő sétány 3. Balatonboglár is as good a place as any along the southern shore to **buy wine** and there's a well-established cellar and discount wine shop at Szabadság utca 28 (Mon–Fri 8am–4pm, Sat 8am–noon), 300m up from central Vörösmarty tér; the entrance is on the right-hand side of the road, directly opposite no. 29, through the rusty gate. If driving, carry on another 200m and you'll see the signs.

During the first weekend of June the small village of **SOMOGYBABOD**, 12km south of Balatonboglár, stages the **Somogybabod Off-Road Festival**, an established event for off-road enthusiasts with lively concerts and huge beer tents complementing the series of races on the reconditioned track; more information can be obtained from Tourinform in Balatonboglár.

Fonyód

FONYÓD, 10km further on from Balatonboglár, grew up between the Sipos and Sándor hills and subsequently spread itself along the lakeside. Its built-up shoreline, with bleak modern architecture, is not particularly appealing, and most people come here only for the **ferries to Badacsony** on the northern shore, from where the symmetry of Fonyód's setting is best appreciated. However, there are a couple of places of interest away from the water. Heading uphill from the station along Szent István utca and turning right into winding József utca, you come to some fantastic **villas** high above the lakefront. About fifteen minutes' walk along, the salmon-coloured "**Crypt Villa**" was built above a red marble crypt with room for two by a grieving widower who lived here in seclusion for many years, waiting to join his wife below. A further ten minutes' walk brings you to some more fine villas, on the tree-lined Bartók Béla utca promenade, which offer marvellous views across the lake to the Badacsony Hills, and can be reached by local buses running from the bus station to the suburb of Bélatelep.

Sticking to Szent István utca and heading up past the Balaton Travel office for twenty minutes, you'll find **Fácán Park** on your right, where the earthworks of a medieval castle are still visible. Its Hungarian defenders escaped their Turkish besiegers by using wooden columns sunk below the surface of the water to cross the surrounding marshes, while the Turks were left stranded on the other side.

Practicalities

Fonyód's **bus** and **train stations** and **ferry terminal** are all conveniently close to the centre of town on Ady Endre utca, from where it's a hop across the road to the **Tourinform** office on the corner of Ady Endre utca and Szent István utca (June–Aug daily 9am–noon & 4–8pm; Sept–May 8am–noon & 12.30–

4.30pm; ⓣ85/560-313, ⓔfonyod@tourinform.hu). You'll find everything else of a practical nature, including a bank, supermarket and **post office** (Mon–Fri 8am–4pm), opposite the train station on Ady Endre utca.

There's very little in the way of **accommodation** here, so you'll need to book ahead if you want to stay, especially in July and August. P&P Tours, at Szent István utca 5 (June–Aug daily 8am–8pm; Sept–May Mon–Fri 8am–4pm; ⓣ85/362-125, ⓔpptours@axelero.hu), can arrange private rooms (❷), while there are a couple of identically (over-) priced, and not particularly exciting, hotels close at hand: the *Hotel Balaton*, just up from Tourinform at Szent István utca 1 (ⓣ85/560-335, ⓔhbalaton@ax.hu; ❺), and *Fonyód Hotel* (ⓣ85/561-900; ⓦwww.hotelfonyod.hu; ❺) just below the Crypt Villa by the sports stadium at József utca 21. The *Napsugár* **campsite** at Wekerle utca 5, 2km east of the centre in Fonyód-Bélatelep (ⓣ85/361-211; mid-May to mid-Sept), also has chalets (❷–❹). The Balaton Surf Club, based at the site, has **windsurfers** for rent.

From May to August, you can enjoy tasty, inexpensive homestyle Hungarian **food** and wine at the *Présház* restaurant behind Fácán Park, which is named after the winepress that operated here in the eighteenth and nineteenth centuries.

Kis-Balaton

At the far end of the lake, reeds obscure the mouth of the River Zala and stretch for miles upstream to **Kis-Balaton** (Little Balaton). This lake once covered forty square kilometres, but was half-drained in the 1950s to provide irrigation for new crop land, and was nearly destroyed by the dumping of pollutants into the Zala during the 1980s. Its rehabilitation was begun in the 1980s, as attempts were made to improve the quality of water in Lake Balaton. The first stage of the process, diverting water back through the reed beds that act as a filter for the lake, has been completed, but there is much debate about how successful this has been, and whether further steps should be taken. It has certainly restored the area as a paradise for birds and bird lovers, with over eighty species of birds found here. The Research Centre in Fenékpuszta, north of the lake, and just 4km south of Keszthely, arranges **bird-watching tours** for groups only, although individuals can phone the reserve (ⓣ83/315-341) on the off chance of being able to tag along.

The settlement of **Kápolnapuszta**, about 20km south of Keszthely, is home to Hungary's largest **Bison Reserve** (Bivalyrezervátum; daily 9am–7pm; 500Ft). Established in 1992 with just sixteen buffalo, the reserve now keeps some 200 of the animals, which account for about a third of Hungary's total stock; prior to World War II there were over 200,000 buffalo in the territory of Hungary. A well marked-out trail – which takes approximately 45 minutes to walk – allows you to get close (but not too close – there's an electric fence) to the animals, while regular information boards do an excellent job of explaining their various habits and activities. The buffalo are herded out to pasture from spring to late autumn, though they can still be visited indoors during the winter. Without your own transport, however, getting here is both tricky and time-consuming: the best way is to take a **bus** from Keszthely to either Balatonmagyaród or Sármellék, from where there are more frequent buses to Balatonmagyaród – from here, though, it's still a good thirty-minute walk to the reserve.

Lake Balaton: the northern shore

The resorts of **Balatonalmádi** and **Balatonfüred** on the **northern shore** of the lake are more genteel than their southern counterparts, with a certain faded elegance, but the crowds of tourists are just as big, while the Tihany peninsula, and in particular the pretty village of **Tihany**, attracts even greater numbers. The shoreline beyond Tihany is dominated by holiday homes and nondescript resorts, although the local vineyards make a few visits to wine cellars a temptation. The biggest wine centre, however, is on the slopes of the **Badacsony Hills**, whose picturesque village, **Badacsony**, draws big crowds throughout the summer. For walkers, there is plenty to explore in the hinterland, including the volcanic shapes around Badacsony Hills. Buses run alongside the shore to the enjoyable university town of **Keszthely**, whilst trains follow the lake for most of its length before turning inland to Tapolca, where you should change for Keszthely.

Balatonalmádi

The first major settlement along the northern shore is **BALATONALMÁDI**, a resort since 1877, which now has a pleasantly faded air, although most visitors to this part of the shore pass straight through, favouring instead the more buoyant resort of Balatonfüred. However, its decent beaches, pleasant lakeside walks and varied cultural programme make it worth stopping off for. The best time to visit is during the **Balatonalmádi Days** at the end of July, a nine-day cultural festival featuring folk dancing, operetta and a big craft fair around the lakeside area. The **grape harvest** celebration in mid-September is a smaller event – a day of wine and music, with a grand procession through the town.

All the sights in the town are church-related. A few minutes' walk west of the centre, the small **Chapel of the Holy Right Hand** (Szent Jobb Kápolna), tacked on to the left side of the Church of Szent Imre, at Óváry Ferenc utca 47, was originally located in the Royal Palace in Buda and housed the holy right hand of St Stephen, which is now in St Stephen's Basilica in Budapest. During the reconstruction of Buda Palace after World War II, the chapel was spared from destruction by Stalinists, and rebuilt at Balatonalmádi in 1957. Peering through the bars of the gate you can see the impressive gold mosaic executed by Károly Lotz in 1896.

Two other unusual churches lie in the older suburb of **Vörösberény**, a thirty-minute slog uphill along Petőfi utca and Veszprémi út (or take one of the regular buses from the bus station). The Baroque **parish church**, built in 1779 for the Jesuits, contains interesting frescoes depicting the order's founder, St Ignatius, as well as some contemporary figures; you can get the key from the *plébánia*, two houses behind the church. Just uphill stands a fortified thirteenth-century **Calvinist church**, whose shape has undergone many changes over the years; only fragments of frescoes and a couple of windows remain from the original. The key is available from the priest's house (Református Lelkész Hivatal), directly below the church at Veszprémi út 105. On Friday evenings in July and August the church hosts **concerts** of Renaissance and Baroque music – check with Tourinform for details (see below). If you've got time, and some energy, you could walk the **Red Sandstone Path**, a six-kilometre-long, circular trail which takes in the **Óvári lookout tower** in the forest to the north of town – you can pick up a guiding leaflet from Tourinform.

Balatonalmádi has a paying **beach** (May–Sept daily 8.30am–7pm; 300Ft) by Városház tér in the centre of town, and a free beach (*szabad strand*) half an hour's walk west at Káptalanfüred.

Practicalities

The **bus** and **train** stations are situated at the top and bottom of the main square, Városház tér, respectively, while in July and August **boats** from Balatonfüred and Tihany arrive at the pier, ten minutes' walk east of the main square through the lakeside park. Tourinform, between the stations at Városház tér 4 (mid-June to mid-Sept Mon–Fri 9am–7pm, Sat & Sun 9am–5pm; mid-Sept to mid-June Mon–Fri 8.30am–4.30pm; ⓣ88/594-081, ⓔbalatonalmadi@tourinform.hu), can supply **information** on events and accommodation, but doesn't handle bookings. Although they can't arrange private rooms, Balatontourist, at Petőfi utca 6 (May to mid-June & Aug 20 to Sept Mon–Fri 8.30am–4.30pm, Sat 8.30am–noon; mid-June to Aug 19 Mon–Sat 8.30am–7pm, Sun 9am–noon; Oct–April Mon–Fri 8.30am–3.30pm; ⓣ88/584-106, ⓔbalmadi@balatontourist.hu), do have a good selection of **flats** (❸–❺), sleeping between two and ten people. The **post office** is at Petőfi utca 19 (Mon–Fri 8am–4pm, Sat 8am–noon).

Unlike many resorts on the northern shore, Balatonalmádi has few appealing options when it comes to **accommodation**. The best of a limited bunch is the *Wellness Hotel*, nicely positioned in the park near the pier at Véghely utca 1 (ⓣ88/438-514, ⓔwellnesshotel@vnet.hu; ❻), which has very modern, though not particularly large, rooms; and the friendly and mellow *Hotel Viktória*, a fifteen-minute walk north at Bajcsy-Zsilinszky utca 42 (ⓣ88/438-940, ⓦwww.hotels.hu/viktoria_panzio; ❸). The latter's facilities include a sauna, solarium and terraced restaurant. The cheapest option around is the *Pedagógus Üdülő* (Teachers' Holiday Home) at Dózsa György utca 13, just behind the Church of St Imre (ⓣ88/438-518; ❶; May–Sept), offering basic rooms with basins and shared bathrooms. The best of the town's several **campsites** are the very welcoming and neat *Kristóf Motel and Camping*, 400m to the right of the train station and across the tracks at Véghely utca 8 (ⓣ88/584-201, ⓔckristof@balatontourist.hu; chalets ❹; mid-April to Sept), and, a little further along, the much larger *Yacht Camping* (ⓣ88/584-101, ⓔcyacht@balatontourist.hu; mid-May to mid-Sept), which also has apartments for four people (❺). Both sites have excellent facilities, including tourist information, minimarkets, sports facilities and exchange offices. Campers at the *Yacht* have direct access to the lake, while those at the *Kristóf* can get to the town beach, next door, free of charge.

The town's two outstanding **restaurants** are located down by the ferry pier on Véghely Dezső út. The stylish *Kikötő*, at no. 5 (daily 8am–midnight), is part of the Almadi Yacht Club but isn't as haughty as you might expect, with a tempting, and moderately priced, international menu, as well as live jazz and flamenco music on Sundays evenings during the summer. A few paces across the park, at no. 1, is the *Liget Kávéház*, a slightly more reserved place housed in a Baroque building with period furnishings, which serves high-quality, but respectably priced, Hungarian meals and coffees (daily 11am–11pm).

Csopak

The dispersed village of **CSOPAK**, 9km down Route 71 towards Balatonfüred, has made a name for itself in recent years for its **wine**, and this is the main reason for visiting. There are numerous **cellars** around the old village, and many houses advertise dens where you can pop in to taste – and buy – the local hock. Csopak wines are mainly white, of which the best-known is Olaszrizling; most locals sell it straight from the barrel. One of the best in the village is the Varga Borház (daily 8am–7pm), located in the large factory-like building at Simoga kőz 4, a fifteen-minute walk north of the village just off Route 71. Smaller cellars, where you can also eat as you taste the wines, include the Linczy Pince at Berekháti utca 34, a few minutes' walk up from the train station (May–Oct daily 5–11pm), and the Söptei Pince at Istenfia utca 5, 200m down from the Varga Borház and then twenty minutes' walk west along Füredi utca (May–Oct daily 11am–11pm). Csopak's **Wine Days Festival** (*Borhét*) takes place in the third week of August, with wine, singing and dancing down by the waterfront at the entrance to the *strand*.

Practicalities

Arriving by train, walk up the main street, Kossuth utca, to the old village, or, to get to the *strand* and the resort area, walk across Route 71 and then along Fürdő utca; the ferry is a couple of minutes' walk beyond. **Information** on wine tasting in the village is provided by Csopaktourist, down by the lake at Őrkény Sétány 1 (June–Aug daily 8am–8pm; Ⓣ87/455-025, Ⓦwww.csopak-tourist.hu).

Accommodation is available down near the waterfront at the *Rozmaring Panzió*, a series of low buildings containing fairly nondescript rooms spread over large pleasant grounds by the *strand* at Ifjúság sétány 4 (Ⓣ & Ⓕ87/446-583; ❸; May–Sept) – there is also a small camping area here. The *Ifjúsági Üdülő*, a large, hostel-like complex a few minutes' walk east of the *strand* at Sport utca 9 (Ⓣ87/446-505; dorm bed 2000Ft, doubles ❷–❸; May–Sept; no IHYF discounts in July & Aug), has the most basic rooms with showers; while the *Hotel Piroska* next door at Sport utca 5–7 (Ⓣ87/446-461; ❹; mid-May to mid-Sept) is outwardly unappealing but has perfectly fine rooms with balconies overlooking the gardens.

Two pleasant places to **eat**, both with outside seating and serving traditional Hungarian cuisine, are the *Dobó Restaurant* at the top of Kossuth utca near Csopaktourist, and the *Malom Csárda* in an old watermill ten minutes' walk up at Veszprémi út 3, on the northern edge of the village (daily 11am–10pm).

Balatonfüred

Seventeenth-century chronicles tell of pilgrims descending on **BALATONFÜRED** to "camp in scattered tents" and benefit from the mineral springs. Some 30,000 people come here every year for treatment at the springs, mingling with hordes of tourists, giving this popular Balaton resort a distinctive, sedate air. Füred, as it is often called, is split into two, with the older centre a couple of kilometres away from the lake; here you'll find shops, churches and a market along its Baroque main street, Kossuth utca. Most visitors head for the resort area beside Balaton, whose centrepiece is the leafy Gyógy tér, with its

sanatorium, springs and run-down nineteenth-century facades, leading down to a tree-lined lakeside promenade. On either side are beaches and a mix of modern hotels and antebellum villas.

Arrival and information

The **bus** and **train stations** are conveniently located next door to each other on Castricum tér – midway between the old town and the lakeside resort, both of which are within comfortable walking distance. Alternatively, bus #1 takes a roundabout route to the embankment before heading west along Széchenyi út. **Ferries** from Siófok and Tihany dock at the pier at the western end of the promenade.

The **Tourinform** office is at Petőfi Sándor utca 68, tucked away amongst a cluster of red, kiosk-type buildings next to the Balatonederics train station, the station before Balatonfüred (mid-June to mid-Sept Mon–Fri 9am–7pm, Sat 9am–6pm, Sun 9am–1pm; mid-Sept to Oct Mon–Fri 9am–5pm, Sat 9am–1pm; Nov to mid-June Mon–Fri 9am–4pm; ⓣ87/580-480, ⓦwww.balatonfured.hu); they also have a summer-only office (same times), 2km west of the centre (buses #1 and #1B or any Tihany bus) at Széchenyi utca 47, by the *Füred* campsite. The **post office** is just up from the *Hotel Blaha Lujza* at Zsigmond utca 14 (Mon–Fri 8am–noon & 12.30–4pm), and there's **Internet access** at

Net Espresso, Horváth Mihály utca 3 (Mon–Fri 8am–10pm, Sat & Sun 10am–10pm), and CyberClub, Kőztársaság utca 6 (daily 11am–8pm).

Accommodation

The town has a reasonable stock of good-value **accommodation** but it's advisable to book ahead, and essential in the period from the last weekend in July to August 20. Budget accommodation can be found at the *Széchenyi Ferenc Kollégium* on Hősök tér, up in the main town (Ⓣ87/342-641; ❶; July & Aug only). Twenty minutes' walk west of the promenade (bus #1 or #1B), at Széchenyi utca 24, lies the huge *Füred* **campsite** (Ⓣ87/580-241, Ⓔcfured@balatontourist.hu; mid-April to mid-Oct), offering a swimming pool, tennis, watersports and bungalows (❷–❹) on the lakefront.

Hotel Annabella Deák Ferenc utca 25 Ⓣ87/889-431, Ⓦwww.danubiushotels.com/annabella. The town's major package-tourist hotel, complete with tidy, modern rooms all with balcony and some with views over to the lake. They also have indoor and outdoor pools and an enormous beer garden. April–Oct. ❺–❻

Hotel Árkád Gyógy tér 1 Ⓣ87/581-246. Located on the northwestern side of the square, this crumbling, ghost-like building has definitely seen better days; bare rooms and shared bathrooms, but it's the cheapest option around. June–Sept. ❸

Hotel Blaha Lujza Blaha Lujza utca 4 Ⓣ87/581-210, Ⓦwww.hotelblaha.hu. Formerly the summer home of the nineteenth-century actress and singer Lujza Blaha, this magnificently sumptuous Neoclassical hotel has snug rooms with all mod cons, and also sports a sauna, solarium, fitness centre and a very accomplished restaurant (see p.218). ❻

Korona Panzió Vörösmarty utca 4 Ⓣ87/343-278, Ⓦwww.koronapanzio.hu. Decent, family-run pension with neatly furnished rooms, some with balcony, just five minutes from the train and bus stations and ten minutes' walk from the waterfront. ❺

Hotel Marina Széchenyi utca 26 Ⓣ87/889-500, Ⓦwww.danubiusgroup.com/marina. Lakeside high-rise with comfortable rooms, although those in the adjoining *Marina Lido* building are much better. Also has its own bit of *strand* and play area. May to mid-Oct. ❹–❺

Hotel Vasutas Erkel Ferenc utca 1 Ⓣ87/342-492, Ⓔhotelvasutas@axelero.hu. One of the more agreeable workers' hotels, with very spartan, but very clean, rooms in a peaceful spot 150m north of the lake. ❹

The lakeside

Walking around Balatonfüred's resort area makes you feel like an extra in Resnais' film, *Last Summer in Marienbad*, and you almost expect to come across tubercular countesses and impoverished artists. Despite the crowds and a few high-rise hotels, this once elegant spa has managed to retain most of its old Central European charm. The tone is set by the elegant tree-lined promenade that runs east from the pier, where you can admire the view across to the Tihany promontory and the far side of the lake. The promenade is named Tagore sétány after the Bengali poet Rabindranath Tagore who came here in 1926 and planted a tree near the pier in gratitude for his cure. Indira and Rajiv Gandhi and a host of other Indian figures have followed suit, as have various Nobel prize-winners and the odd Soviet cosmonaut.

A few minutes up from the middle of the promenade, you come to the aptly named **Gyógy tér** (Health Square). Its columned, pagoda-like **Kossuth Well** gushes carbonated water, while other springs feed the sanatorium and cardiac hospital on the northern and eastern sides of the square. Excavations suggest that the Romans were the first to exploit the springs, using the waters to treat stomach ailments and, when mixed with goats' milk whey, as a cure for lung diseases. The hospital's **mineral baths** are reserved for patients only. On the western side of the square stand two former trade union holiday homes, the

boxh1/The Anna Ball and other events

The big event in Füred's calendar is the **Anna Ball** on the last Saturday of July. Magnate Zsigmond Horváth held the first ball on Anna's Day, July 26, 1825, in honour of his granddaughter Anna, and since the collapse of Communism this traditional social occasion has gained in stature. Crowds gather around Gyógy tér to watch the ball-goers, before they retire to the Hotel Árkád for the main ball. The following day the beauty queen elected at the ball is paraded around town in a horse-drawn carriage. Besides the sailing competitions on the lake, Füred has two other regular events in August. On the second weekend of the month, keen **swimmers** set off on the 3.6km to Tihany – a challenge that usually attracts in excess of four thousand participants. The same weekend sees the start of the two-week Wine Festival (Borhetek), with stalls set up along the promenade, where you can taste local vintages. There are also concerts during summer in the Calvinist church on Kossuth utca in the main town (the whitewashed church rather than the red sandstone one at the top of Ady utca).

dilapidated *Hotel Árkád* and the eighteenth-century **Horváth House**, one of the first inns in a land where innkeeping developed late, patronized by writers and politicians during the Reform era. A sanatorium for uranium miners in the Communist era, the inn has been closed for years, though is now in the formative stages of being slicked up as a luxury hotel.

Running westwards between the two is Blaha Lujza utca, named after the "Nation's Nightingale", who spent her summers here in a **villa** at no. 4 (now the *Hotel Blaha Lujza*) and had her tea at the *Kedves Cukrászda* across the road. Just past the hotel at the junction with Jókai utca stands the mid-nineteenth-century **Round Church**, modelled on the Pantheon in Rome. Across the road, the **Jókai Memorial House** (May–Sept Tues–Sun 10am–6pm; 260Ft) was built by the nineteenth-century novelist Mór Jókai, whose novels are often compared to those of Dickens; Queen Victoria is said to have been among his fans. He came to Balatonfüred at the age of 37, half expecting to die from a lung infection, and built the villa as a refuge; he didn't die, however, until the ripe old age of 84. The museum preserves Jókai's furniture, a selection of his paintings, sketches and books, and a handful of personal effects.

Eating and drinking

Decent eating possibilities are woefully thin on the ground in Balatonfüred; most of the lakeside **restaurants** are fairly samey – big, open-terraced places knocking up grilled meat and fish dishes for the masses, such as the *Borcsa* (daily 10am–11pm) and *Stefánia Vitorlás Étterem* (daily 10am–midnight) at either end of Tagore sétány. Away from the lakeside, the restaurant in the *Hotel Blaha Lujza* is the most sophisticated place in town, with moderately priced steaks the choice dish on offer (daily 7am–10pm). Otherwise, there's the *Arany Csillag*, a refined little pizzeria with cosy indoor seating at Zsigmond utca 1 (daily 11am–11pm), or, in the main town at Kossuth utca 11, the old-fashioned *Arany Korona Vendéglő*, which just about qualifies as the most "Hungarian" restaurant in Balatonfüred. For **coffee and cakes**, you can't beat Lujza Blaha's favourite coffeeshop, the cool *Kedves Cukrászda* at Blaha Lujza utca 7 (daily 8am–9pm), while, for a more vigorous bout of **drinking**, pop into the *Macho Pub*, a Mexican-themed haunt behind the train station at Vasút utca 4 (daily 8pm till late), or the rather predictably named, and not very Irish, *Irish Pub*, next to the *Kedves*.

Balatonfüred activities

With wooded hills on one side and water on the other, Füred offers plentiful opportunities for recreation. Balatonfüred's two main **beaches** are located at the eastern end, of Tagore sétány: the Eszterházy (mid-June to mid-Sept daily 9am–6pm; 330Ft), and, fifteen minutes' walk further east, the Kisfaludy (same dates and times; 300Ft). The Városi strand on Széchenyi utca west of the centre by the Hotel Marina is best for **swimming** (though not for kids, as it drops away quickly). **Pedaloes** and **windsurfing** boards are available at every strand and yachts can be rented from Opticonsor at Köztársaság utca 1 (Ⓣ87/341-188), Lisa Hajó at Füred Camping (Ⓣ06-30/9373-044) and the Fekete Péter School at Zákonyi utca 8 (Ⓣ06-30/9378-519), which also offers **sailing** lessons. You can rent **bicycles** (350Ft per hr, 2500Ft per day) from Papp Kristóf at Petőfi Sándor utca 62/b or Tempo 21 at Ady Endre utca 54, as well as some of the big hotels. **Tennis courts** (1500Ft per hr) can be found at various locations, including the tennis centre next to the Margareta Hotel at Széchenyi utca 27 (daily 6am–11pm) and at the Kiserdő Park in the centre of town. Tourinform can help arrange **horse-riding** at the riding school in the Koloska Valley, a few kilometres outside town (Ⓣ87/20-4213-634).

Tihany peninsula

A rocky finger of land that was declared Hungary's first national park in 1952, the **Tihany peninsula**, 7km west of Balatonfüred, is historically associated with the Benedictine order and a castle (no longer in existence) that withstood 150 years of Turkish hostility. As one of the most beautiful regions of Balaton, Tihany gets swamped with visitors over summer, though it's easy to escape the crowds by hiking into the interior.

The lakeshore road from Balatonfüred passes along the eastern side of the peninsula, through Diós (where Avar graves have been discovered) and Gödrös, entering **Tihany village** above the inner harbour (Belső Kikötő), where ferries from Balatonfüred and Siófok arrive. At the tip of the peninsula, 2km on, lies **Tihany-rév**, where car ferries cross to Szántód. Next to the ferry is the expensive *Club Tihany* resort complex. Besides the paying **beaches** by *Club Tihany* and the Tihany docks, there are free *strand* along the reedier shores between Gödrös and Diós, and south of Sajkod on the other side of the peninsula.

Arrival and information

Tihany is connected to Balatonfüred by hourly **buses**, which stop in the village by András tér below the abbey church, and at Balatontourist on Kossuth utca. The peninsula is also connected by bus with Badacsony to the west. **Ferries** from Balatonfüred and Siófok (mid-April to Oct) arrive at the inner harbour, while from March to November the car ferry from Tihany-rév goes across to Szántód on the southern shore (daily: March–May & early Sept–Nov hourly, last ferry at 6.30pm; June to early Sept every 40min, last ferry at 10.20pm; 1060Ft per car, 340Ft per person, 260Ft per bike). Regular buses link the ferries with the upper village, or, alternatively, you could jump on the naff **tourist train** that stops below the abbey (June–Sept 9.30am–8.30pm, every 30min; 300Ft).

Information is available from Tourinform, located down from the abbey at Kossuth utca 20 (mid-April to mid-June Mon–Fri 9am–4pm, Sat 9am–1pm; mid-June to mid-Sept Mon–Fri 9am–8pm, Sat & Sun 10am–6pm; mid-Sept to mid-April Mon–Fri 9am–3pm; Ⓣ87/438-016, Ⓦwww.tihany.hu), or the much

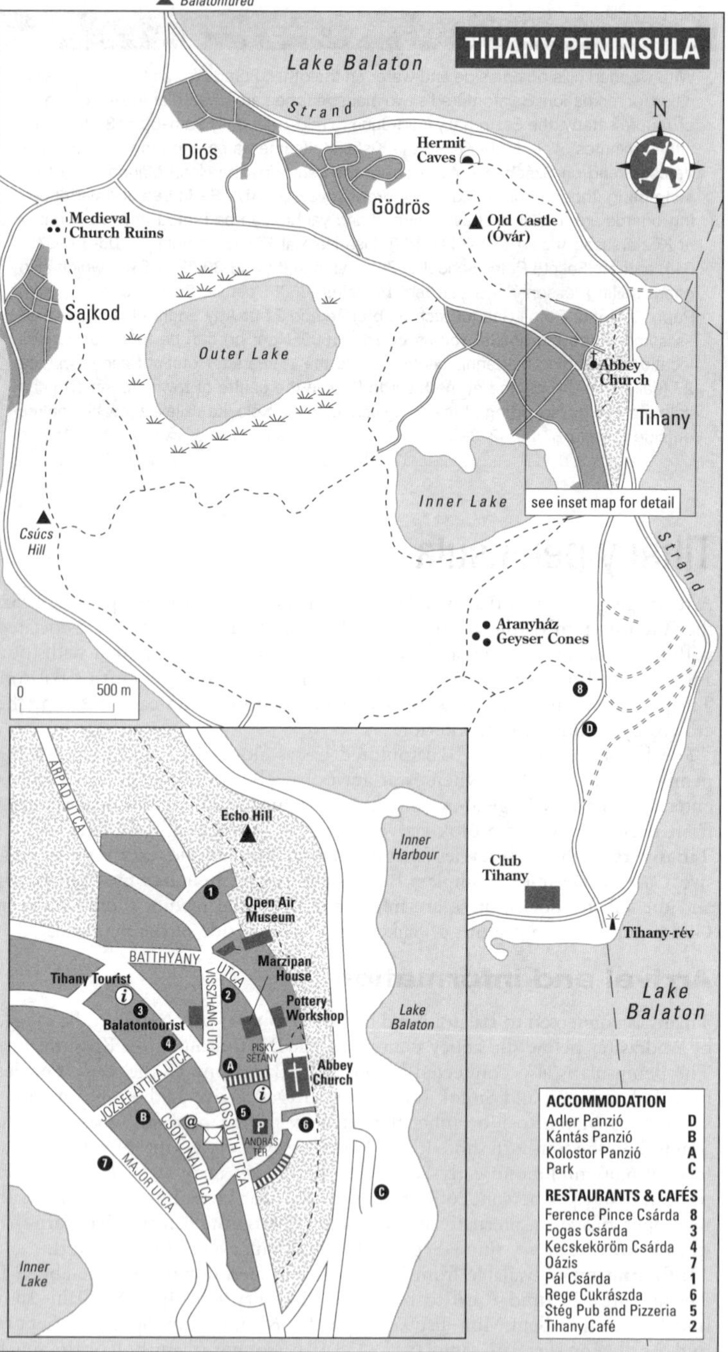

TIHANY PENINSULA
Balatonfüred
Badacsony
Balatonfüred
Siófok
Szántód
Lake Balaton
Strand
Diós
Hermit Caves
Gödrös
Old Castle (Óvár)
Medieval Church Ruins
Sajkod
Outer Lake
Abbey Church
Tihany
Inner Lake
see inset map for detail
Strand
Csúcs Hill
Aranyház Geyser Cones
0
500 m
Club Tihany
Tihany-rév
Lake Balaton
ÁRPÁD UTCA
Echo Hill
Inner Harbour
Open Air Museum
BATTHYÁNY UTCA
Marzipan House
Tihany Tourist
VISSZHANG UTCA
Pottery Workshop
Balatontourist
Lake Balaton
PISKY SÉTÁNY
Abbey Church
JÓZSEF ATTILA UTCA
KOSSUTH UTCA
CSOKONAI UTCA
ANDRÁS TÉR
MAJOR UTCA
Inner Lake
ACCOMMODATION
Adler Panzió D
Kántás Panzió B
Kolostor Panzió A
Park C
RESTAURANTS & CAFÉS
Ference Pince Csárda 8
Fogas Csárda 3
Kecskeköröm Csárda 4
Oázis 7
Pál Csárda 1
Rege Cukrászda 6
Stég Pub and Pizzeria 5
Tihany Café 2

more helpful Tihany Tourist at Kossuth utca 11 (daily: April–June & Sept–Oct 9am–5pm; July & Aug 9am–8pm; Ⓣ87/448-481, Ⓦwww.tihanytourist.hu), where you can also change money. **Internet access** is available at Postakőz 1 (daily 10am–8pm), just behind the **post office** (Mon–Fri 8am–4pm). If you'd like to explore some of the inland areas but don't fancy walking, **bicycle rental** is available at Kossuth utca 32 (May–Sept 10am–6pm; 3000Ft per day, 2000Ft half-day).

Accommodation

There is a reasonable, if largely dull, choice of **accommodation** in the village, although prices are rather inflated, which might tempt you to opt for a private room (❷–❸), or apartment (❹), bookable through Tihany Tourist (see above), or Balatontourist at Kossuth utca 12 (June–Aug Mon–Sat 8.30am–7pm, Sun 8.30am–1pm; Sept to mid-Oct Mon–Fri 8.30am–4.30pm, Sat 8.30am–1pm; Ⓣ87/538-071, Ⓔtihany@balatontourist.hu). Alternatively, if you simply wander the streets you'll see plenty of *Zimmer frei* signs dotted around.

Adler Panzió Felsőkopaszhegyi 1 Ⓣ87/448-755, Ⓦwww.adler-tihany.hu. 1km south of the upper village, this homely place has large rooms with showers and TV and some with small balcony, as well as a swimming pool, sauna and restaurant. April–Oct. ❺

Kántás Panzió Csokonai utca 49 Ⓣ87/448-072, Ⓦwww.hotels.hu/kantas. Ordinary but restful and friendly six-room pension just down behind the post office. ❹

Kolostor Panzió Kossuth Lajos utca 14 Ⓣ87/448-408. A somewhat gloomy place with sombre rooms above a restaurant along the main road. Mid-May to Sept. ❹

Park Fürdőtelepi utca 1 Ⓣ87/448-611, Ⓦwww.hotelfured.hu. Tihany's principal hotel is the *Park*, on the east side of the peninsula. The hotel's two wings comprise the *Kastély* (Castle), a grand mansion confiscated by the Communist Party as their summer house, which has moderately impressive rooms, and the *Park* itself, a marginally cheaper, more modern building next door. Mid-April to mid-Oct. ❻–❼

Tihany village and around

In contrast with Tihany-rév, **TIHANY** village, on the top of the hill halfway along the eastern side of the pensinsula, is a traditional-looking place, full of old houses built of grey basalt tufa, with thatched roofs and porticoed terraces, their windows and doors outlined in white. However, it rivals Szentendre as the most touristy place in Hungary, with folksy stalls lining the streets, parking as expensive as in Budapest, and coach-loads of tourists descending in almost unmanageable levels.

In days gone by, the village was dominated by a Benedictine abbey overlooking Balaton, established in 1055 at the request of Andrew I and founded, true to the biblical injunction, upon a rocky promontory; it was later transformed into a fortress, and eventually demolished in the seventeenth century. Andrew's body lies in the crypt of the **abbey church** – the only one of the Árpád line to remain in the place where he was buried. The building itself is Baroque, the original having succumbed to the ravages of wars and time. Inside are virtuoso **woodcarvings** by Sebestyén Stulhoff, who lived and worked in the abbey for 25 years after his fiancée died (her features are preserved in the face of an angel to the right of the altar), and grandiose **frescoes** by Károly Lotz, Székely and Deák-Ebner. Recently restored, the church (daily: May–Sept 9am–6pm; Oct–April 10am–3pm; 400Ft) provides a magnificent setting for **organ concerts** over summer – contact Tourinform for programme details (see p.219). The abbey's foundation deed, held at Pannonhalma Monastery in Transdanubia (see p.260), is the earliest document to include Hungarian words among the Latin.

From the church, it's a few minutes' walk down Pisky sétány, a parapet overlooking the waterfront, to a small **Open-Air Museum** (Szabadtéri Múzeum; May–Oct Tues–Sun 10am–6pm; 180Ft) exhibiting two well-preserved houses. The first, with a beautiful entrance way, was built in the early nineteenth century and inhabited up until 1960; note the cross on the chimney, a common feature in this region. Behind this is an old Fishermen's Guild House, its mud-brick walls clad in thin stone to give an impression of wealth. Inside are the old boats the fishermen used, and a "wooden dog" sledge for fishing on ice. In the traditional way, the mud floor of the veranda is washed with mud daily to deal with the dirt and cracks. Folk dancing performances are held on the open-air stage most Sunday evenings throughout July and August at 6pm.

Behind the museum at Batthyány utca 26 is a **pottery workshop** (daily: May–Sept 8am–7pm, Oct–April till 4pm), where earthenware made from the red clay of the area and glazed in bright greens and blues is made and sold. Opposite, at no. 17, the seductively titled **Marzipan House** (Marcipán Ház; daily 10am–6pm; 250Ft) contains one room of marzipan-moulded Disney characters (and, somewhat bizarrely, models of Naomi Campbell and Karl Lagerfeld), while the other is brimming with a tempting assortment of marzipan, chocolates and confectionery. Continuing along the lakeside walk for another five minutes, you come to the scenic vantage point of **Echo Hill**. An echo can theoretically be produced by standing on a short concrete pedestal and projecting your voice onto the wall of the abbey church. Legend goes that the echo is the voice of a princess, drowned in the lake by the King of the Water following her refusal to fall in love with his son. By taking a well-marked path onwards, you can circumambulate the **Óvár** (Old Castle), a volcanic outcrop riddled with cells carved by Russian Orthodox monks in the eleventh to fourteenth centuries, whence hot springs gush forth.

Inland walks

A trek inland will allow you to escape the crowds and enjoy the beauty of the peninsula, whose geology and microclimate have produced an unusual flora and fauna. The **Inner Lake** (Belső-tó), whose sunlit surface is visible from the abbey church, fills a volcanic crater 25m above the level of Balaton. From its southern bank, you can follow a path for a couple of kilometres through vineyards, orchards and lavender fields to the **Aranyház geyser cones** – rock funnels forced open by hot springs.

The northerly **Outer Lake** (Külső-tó) was drained for pasture in 1809, but started to be refilled in 1975. Its reed beds are harvested by hand over winter in the traditional manner, and provide a sanctuary for mallards, gadwalls and other **birds**. On the western side of the peninsula, a lookout tower atop **Csúcs Hill** (232m) offers a **panoramic view** of Balaton. The trail, marked in red, is a ninety-minute round-trip from Tihany village.

Eating

While **bars** and snack stalls cluster round the dock at Tihany-rév, **restaurants** are concentrated in the village, with some less expensive, less frequented wine cellars and restaurants in the streets around the Inner Lake. Homestyle Hungarian cuisine with frills is the rule in Tihany, and you'll be paying over the odds in most restaurants. For **coffee and cakes** head for the *Rege Cukrászda*, in the little courtyard just up from Tourinform – there are glorious views of the lake from the outdoor terrace; or *Tihany Café*, a frantic little place at the junction of Batthyány utca and Visszhang utca.

Ference Pince Csárda Cserhegy 9. This secluded, sprightly restaurant and wine cellar 1km south of the village is well worth the trek – you'll see the sign pinpointing its location 200m up a dusty track. April–Oct daily noon–11pm.
Fogas Csárda Kossuth utca 9. Great fish is the order of the day in this perky little place on the main street. March–Nov daily 11am–11pm.
Kecskeköröm Csárda Kossuth utca 19. This restaurant has a solid reputation, with game an established favourite, while its sloping terrace with wooden tables and benches gives it a relaxed, casual feel. Daily 11am–10pm.
Oázis Major utca 49. Down towards the inner lake away from the crowded centre, this place offers wholesome Hungarian meals in a relaxed atmosphere, with obliging staff. Noon–11pm.
Pál Csárda Visszhang utca 19. Very popular place with a pretty, vine-shaded courtyard and a highly creditable regular menu, in addition to a different set menu each day. March to mid-Nov daily 9am–10pm.
Stég Pub and Pizzeria Kossuth utca 18. Informal gaff offering oven-baked pizzas, salads and good beer. Daily 10am–1am.

The Badacsony

A hulk of volcanic rock with four villages at its feet, backed by dead volcanoes ranged across the Tapolca basin, **the Badacsony** is one of Balaton's most striking features. When the land that was to become Hungary first surfaced, molten magma erupted from the sea bed and cooled into a great semicircle of **basalt columns**, 210m high, which form Badacsony's southeastern face. The rich volcanic soil of the lower slopes has supported **vineyards** since the Age of Migrations, when the Avars buried grape seeds with their dead to ensure that the afterlife wouldn't be lacking in wine. Nowadays, the harvest consists of Zöldszilváni, Szürkebarát (Pinot Gris), Olaszrizling and Kéknyelő (Blue Stem); the last variety is exclusive to the region. The **wine harvest festival** in the village of Badacsony during the second week in September is a time of street processions, folk dancing and music – and of course lots of wine to be drunk.

Arrival and information

Although trains and buses also call at the other villages – Badacsonytomaj, Badacsonylábdihegy and Badacsonytördemic – Badacsony proper is where everyone gets off, with ferries arriving from Balatonboglár, Fonyód and Szigliget. Badacsony's **train station** is right in the centre of the village, just up from the **ferry** pier, while **buses** stop on the main street, Park utca. Beyond Badacsony the train line veers northwards up to Tapolca in the Bakony, so it's easier to continue along the shore by **bus**, changing at Balatonederics if necessary.

Maps and **information** are available from Tourinform, 100m north of the train station at Park utca 6 (mid-June to mid-Sept Mon–Fri 9am–7pm, Sat & Sun 9am–6pm; mid-Sept to Oct & May to mid-June Mon–Fri 9am–5pm, Sat 9am–1pm; Nov–April Mon–Fri 9am–3.30pm; Ⓣ87/431-046, Ⓔbadacsonytomaj@tourinform.hu), and the **post office** is close by at no. 3 (Mon–Fri 8am–5pm, Sat 8am–noon).

Accommodation

Given the popularity of the place, **accommodation** in Badacsony is scarce, though nearby Badacsonytomaj (2km east on the road to Balatonfüred) has further options. Moreover, there is a reasonable stock of **private rooms** (❷–❸) bookable through Balatontourist, next door to Tourinform at Park utca 4 (May–June & Sept Mon–Fri 8am–3.30pm, Sat 8am–noon; July & Aug Mon–

Sat 8am–9pm, Sun 8am–noon; ⓣ87/531-021, ⓔbadacsony@balatontourist.hu), and Miditourist, at Egry sétány 3 (daily: July & Aug 8am–9pm; May, June & Sept to mid-Oct 9am–6pm; ⓣ87/431-117, ⓦwww.miditourist.hu) and Park utca 53 (June–Sept daily 8am–8pm; Oct–May Mon–Sat 9am–4pm; ⓣ87/431-028). Badacsony's **campsite** is on the shore, fifteen minutes' walk west of the ferry pier (ⓣ87/531-041; mid-May to Sept), while, a kilometre or so beyond Badacsonytomaj, in Badacsonyörs, is the larger *Balaton Camping* (ⓣ87/571-031; May to mid-Sept).

Badacsony

Hotel Neptun Római út 158 ⓣ87/431-293, ⓕ471-597. Just up the road from Tourinform, this is by far the best place to stay in the village. An old building, modestly but stylishly renovated to incorporate both a neat and colourful pension and a clean, bright hostel with shared bathrooms and a large communal area. April–Oct. Hostel doubles ❶, pension ❸

Orbán Panzió Egry sétány 2 ⓣ87/431-188, ⓕ431-001. Rather dour, but very cheap, pension next to Miditourist. ❷

Hotel Volán Római út 168 ⓣ87/431-013, ⓦwww.vhotel.hu. Neo-Baroque heap with a 1980s annexe possessing rather lacklustre rooms (note that the actual hotel entrance is on Egry sétány, just along from Miditourist). April–Oct. ❹

Badacsonytomaj

Egry József Fogadó Római út 1 ⓣ & ⓕ87/471-057. Five minutes up from the station, this friendly hostel offers accommodation in two- to five-bedded rooms with shared bathrooms. April to mid-Oct. Dorm bed ❶

Borbarátok ("Wine Friends") Római út 78 ⓣ87/471-597, ⓦwww.borbaratok.hu. Lovely six-room pension some 15mins' walk along from *Egry József Fogadó*, with tidy rooms, and which also makes its own wine (see opposite). April–Oct. ❸

Badacsony village and around

In high summer **BADACSONY** village is absolutely packed, and however you get here, you'll arrive in the midst of a mass of stalls selling folksy crafts, wine and fried fish. Just over the level crossing at Egry sétány 12, the **Egry József Museum** (May–Sept Tues–Sun 10am–6pm, till 8pm July & Aug; 350Ft) exhibits the works of local lad József Egry (1883–1951), one of Hungary's foremost painters. Born into a poor family, Egry worked as a locksmith and roofer before winning a scholarship to the Academy of Fine Arts. He moved to Balaton after World War I, thus beginning a thirty-year love affair with the lake, as evinced by an exquisite series of paintings, which capture the changing light and moods of the lake beautifully. This enjoyable collection also features some interesting family and self-portraits, as well as some of his sketches and photographs.

From May till October you can take one of the **jeep-taxis** (600Ft per person), which leave from in front of the Tourinform office on Park utca and whizz you, at alarmingly high speeds, 3km uphill through the vineyards to the charming **Róza Szegedy House** (Szegedy Róza Ház; May–Sept Tues–Sun 10am–6pm; 260Ft). Róza Szegedy met her future husband, poet Sándor Kisfaludy, on the slopes of the Badacsony in 1795, and when they married five years later they used her Badacsony house as a summer home; its views proved to be an inspiration to his poetry. As well as a selection of his literature, the museum contains some of her old furniture, including an ornate card table and her bed. The former wine-press room now houses a cool little wine bar (same times as museum), where you can sample and buy a selection of local wines.

From the museum you can follow a path up to the **Rose Rock** (Rózsakő), where it's said that if a man and woman sit upon it with their backs to Balaton and think about each other, they'll be married by the end of the year. The trail continues through the beechwoods to the **Kisfaludy lookout tower** (437m), about an hour's walk from the museum, and on another twenty minutes to the

Stone Gate (Kőkapu), two massive basalt towers flanking a precipitous drop. For **longer hikes** into the hills further north, offering an escape from the crowds, it's a good idea to buy a 1:80,000-scale map of the region from one of the tourist offices. A four-kilometre walk northwest from the Stone Gate will bring you to **Gulács-hegy**, a perfectly conical hill (393m) near the Nemesgulács halt for trains en route to Tapolca. The **Szent György-hegy** (415m), on the far side of the tracks, boasts some impressive basalt **organ pipes** and the region's finest vineyards, where Szürkebarát is produced. A few kilometres to the east, the 375-metre-high **Csobánc-hegy** is crowned by a **ruined castle**; this hike will probably take the best part of a day and leave you closer to Tapolca than Balaton. Don't be alarmed if you hear bangs in the fields around you: it's just the local way of scaring birds off the grape crop.

Three kilometres northeast of Badacsony, near the settlement of **BADACSONYÖRS**, signposts point up the hill to the **Folly Aborétum** (April–Nov Tues–Sun 9am–6pm; 250Ft), a stiff twenty-minute climb that rewards visitors with excellent views and a small park offering a peaceful contrast to Balaton. This private collection of cedars and pines from all over the world was started in 1905, and takes about an hour to walk around.

Eating and drinking

There are several **restaurants** to choose from in Badacsony, the best of which is the *Bacchus*, a ten-minute walk north of the centre towards Badacsonytomaj at Kossuth Lajos utca 1. Planted amongst lush vineyards, its elevated position affords magnificent views of the lake, whilst the food is exceptional and the service swift. Another remote spot, also with tremendous views, is the *Kisfaludy Ház* by the Róza Szegedy museum, which offers excellent food and Hungarian gypsy music. Back in the centre, the *Hárksert Vendéglő* (daily noon–9pm), in the *Hotel Neptun*, offers a more standard Hungarian menu, but is a pleasant antidote to the *Halászkert* at Park utca 5 – the definitive tourist restaurant, with pricey food, waiters touting at the entrance and musicians eagerly plucking away in the background (April–Nov daily 11am–midnight). Aside from the restaurants there are stacks of **snack** and **wine stalls** in between the train station and Park utca. In Badacsonytomaj, the restaurant at the *Borbarátok* (daily noon–10pm) has a fine wine selection, with tastings also possible (around 800Ft for five wines).

Szigliget

After the crowded Badacsony, the lush **Szigliget peninsula** is a marked contrast. Both the main road and the train line go inland of the picturesque village of **SZIGLIGET**, 5km west of Badacsony, giving it a pleasant secluded feel. Though the peninsula has been built up with holiday homes, these are mainly privately owned, and accommodation is almost entirely in private houses. Earlier inhabitants of the region included a people known as the Lads, who occupied this area when the Magyars entered the region in the tenth century.

The centre of the village, which lies on the west of the peninsula at the top of Kossuth utca, is dominated by a former Esterházy mansion (closed to the public), now a holiday resort for the Writers' Union, and the ruins of **Szigliget Castle** (daily 9am–6pm; 250Ft), a twenty-minute signposted walk uphill. Originally commissioned in 1260 by Pannonhalma Monastery in the wake of the Mongol invasion, the present remains date from the sixteenth century. During the Turkish occupation, the Hungarian fleet moored at Szigliget under the protection of the castle, but in the seventeenth century lightning struck the castle and burnt it down. Although there remains a fair bit to see – including several of the towers, a section of the living quarters and part of the former stables – the main reason for visiting is to take in the superlative views of the lake and the Bakony Hills. Just below the castle is the *Vár Vendéglő* (daily 11am–10pm), a touristy, but decent enough, restaurant, while, a little further down at Kossuth utca 3, is the **Esterházy Wine Cellar** (June–Oct daily noon–10pm; ⓣ87/461-044), which offers tours of its enormous eighteenth-century cellars. During the summer they also stage folklore programmes, comprising music, dance and food (July & Aug Mon, Wed & Fri 6pm; 4000Ft), and though these are generally the preserve of big tour groups, you could always try and see if there are places available. Heading down Kossuth utca for 2km you come to the **strand**, which is slightly quieter than your average Balaton beach (May–Sept daily 9am–6pm; 250Ft); boats from Keszthely and Badacsony arrive at the port 500m further on. Just before the turning for Badacsonytördemic, another couple of kilometres on, are the remains of a twelfth-century **church** with a restored octagonal tower.

Access to the village is by **bus** running between Tapolca and the train station at Badacsonytördemic (10 daily), serving all points around the peninsula. Here you'll find the tourist office, Familia Turist, at no. 51 (June to mid-Sept daily 9am–6pm; ⓣ87/461-011). They can help with **accommodation**, as can Tourinform in Badacsony, or you can try one of the many places advertising *Zimmer frei*.

Keszthely and around

A tradition of freethinking that dates back to the eighteenth century gives **KESZTHELY** a sense of superiority over other resorts, and its university ensures that life isn't wholly taken over by tourism. Perched at the far western tip of the lake, and the hub of several ferry, bus and train routes, the town gracefully absorbs thousands of visitors during peak season and yet manages not to look bleak and abandoned the rest of the year. With the Belváros and Festetics Palace to admire, and a thermal lake awaiting bathers at nearby **Hévíz**, Keszthely is one of the most appealing and enjoyable towns on Balaton. It's also the best place from which to approach the attractions at Kis-Balaton (see p.212).

Arrival and information

Arriving by ferry near the main *strand*, you can walk up Erzsébet királyné útja to the centre in less than fifteen minutes. The **train** and **bus stations**, with services to Budapest, the Bakony and major towns in Transdanubia, are further south, at the bottom end of Mártírok útja, but most buses entering town drop passengers on downtown Fő tér, sparing them a 600-metre trudge along Kossuth utca, Keszthely's main axis.

Information can be obtained from Tourinform at Kossuth utca 28 (mid-June to mid-Sept Mon–Fri 9am–8pm, Sat & Sun 9am–6pm; mid-Sept to mid-June Mon–Fri 9am–5pm, Sat 9am–1pm; ⓣ83/314-144, ⓦwww.keszthely.hu). The main **post office** is at no. 44 (Mon–Fri 8am–6pm, Sat 8am–noon).

Accommodation

There is no shortage of **accommodation** in Keszthely and even during July and August you should be able to find something. Dormitory beds are available

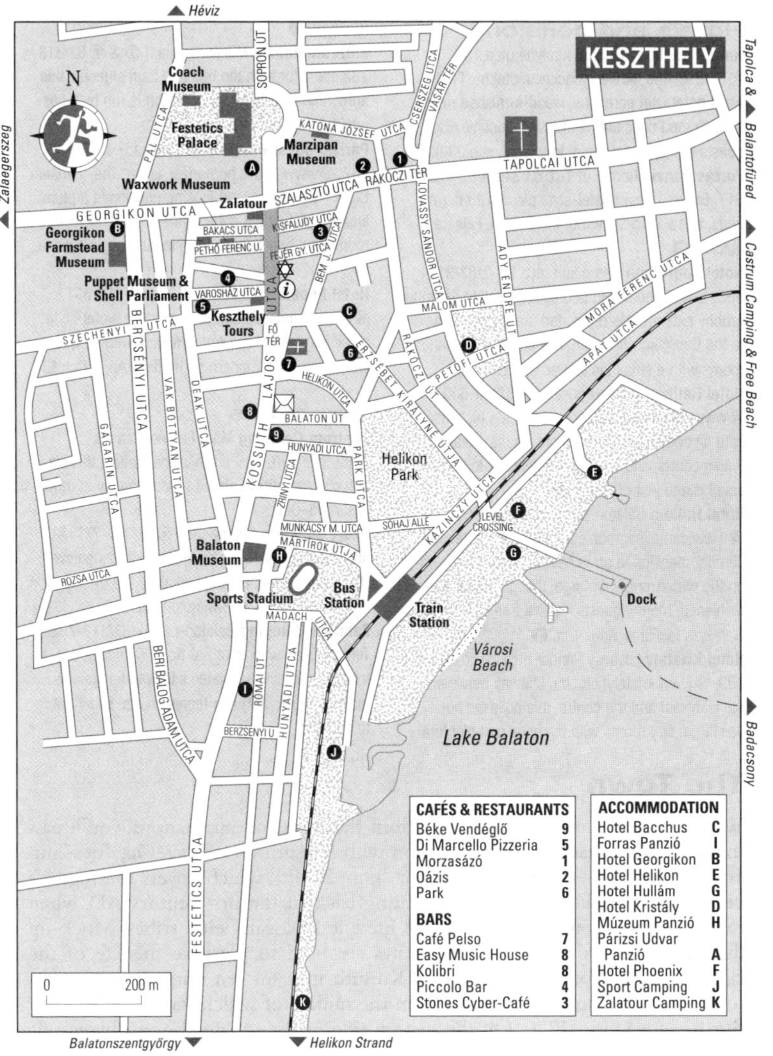

at the *Vajda Hostel*, Gagarin utca 2 (Ⓣ83/311-361; dorm beds 2000Ft; mid-June to Aug), and the *Pethe Ferenc Kollégium*, Festetics utca 5 (Ⓣ83/311-290; dorm beds 2000Ft; July & Aug). **Private rooms** (❷–❸) are bookable through Zalatour at Kossuth utca 1, near the palace (May–Sept Mon–Fri 9am–6pm, Sat 9am–1pm; Oct–April Mon–Fri 9am–5pm, Sat 9am–1pm; Ⓣ83/312-560, Ⓕ314-301), while Keszthely Tours at Kossuth utca 25 (June–Aug Mon–Fri 8am–6pm, Sat 9am–1pm; Sept–May Mon–Fri 8am–4pm; Ⓣ83/314-287, Ⓔkhtours@axelero.hu) have a good selection of affordable apartments (❺) in town; alternatively, searching the backstreets south of the station should turn up something, or, as a last resort, you could always head to nearby Hévíz.

Hotels and pensions

Hotel Bacchus Erzsébet királyné utca 18 ⓣ83/510-450, ⓦwww.bacchushotel.hu. First-class hotel with gorgeous, wood-furnished rooms, all with mod cons and some with balcony. Also boasts the best restaurant in town (see p.230). ❺

Forras Panzió Római út 1 ⓣ83/311-418, ⓕ314-617. Big and busy hostel-style place with dorm beds, a few blocks west of the station. Fills up quickly. ❸

Hotel Georgikon Georgikon utca 20 ⓣ83/312-363, ⓦwww.hotels.hu/georgikon. Despite its rather grubby exterior, this renovated manor house, next to the Georgikon Museum, has clean, utilitarian rooms with a small kitchen area in each. ❹

Hotel Helikon Balaton-part 5 ⓣ83/889-600, ⓦwww.danubiusgroup.com. Lakeside high-rise with smoothly furnished rooms, sauna, pool and tennis courts, and a causeway leading to its own small island just offshore. ❻

Hotel Hullám Balaton-part 1 ⓣ83/312-644, ⓦwww.danubiusgroup.com. Palatial nineteenth-century mansion in an unbeatable location down on the waterfront, with large, though a little old-fashioned, rooms; guests receive free use of the *Helikon*'s facilities. April–Oct. ❻

Hotel Kristály Lovassy Sándor utca 20 ⓣ83/318-999, ⓦwww.kristalyhotel.hu. Midway between the lakefront and the centre, this polished hotel has large, airy rooms with big beds and plentiful furniture. ❻

Műzeum Panzió Műzeum utca 3 ⓣ & ⓕ83/313-182, Ideal for both the bus and train stations, this agreeable little five-room pension is run by a hospitable proprietor. ❸

Párizsi Udvar Panzió Kastély utca 5 ⓣ83/311-202, ⓦwww.hotels.hu/parizsi_udvar. The "Parisian Court" is a fresh, good-looking pension in a plum location just by the palace gates; the three-bed rooms and apartments are particularly good value. ❹

Hotel Phoenix Balaton-part 3 ⓣ83/312-631, ⓦwww.danubiusgroup.com. Austere motel-style place just behind the *Hotel Hullám*, with boxy, care-worn rooms but modern bathrooms. April–Oct. ❸

Campsites

Castrum Camping Móra Ferenc utca 48 ⓣ83/312-120. 1km north of the station, this clean and pleasant site is aimed predominantly at motorists. April–Oct.

Sport Camping Csárda utca ⓣ83/313-777. A noisy and unappealing campsite with bungalows (❷), situated five minutes south of the train station beside the tracks. Mid-May to Sept.

Zalatour Camping Balaton-part ⓣ83/312-782. Ten minutes' walk south of *Sport Camping*, this is a large, attractively located site with bungalows for four people (❷) and tennis courts. Mid-April to mid-Oct.

The Town

Walking uphill along Mártírok útja from the train and bus stations, you'll pass the **Balaton Museum** at the junction with Kossuth utca (May–Oct Tues–Sun 10am–6pm; Nov–April Tues–Sat 9am–5pm; 200Ft), which covers the region's history and wildlife, with artefacts dating back to the first century AD, when road-building Romans disrupted the lifestyle of local Celtic tribes. Mock-up displays of fishing and thatching scenes are used to illustrate the life of the lakeside population. Heading on up Kossuth utca for ten minutes brings you to **Fő tér**, a strangely shaped square in the middle of which stands the **Trinity Statue**, erected in 1770. On the eastern side of the square, the much-remodelled **Church of Our Lady of the Hungarians** was originally constructed in the fourteenth century, and was at one point rebuilt as a fortress to repel the Turks, before becoming the property of György Festetics (see opposite) in 1799. Further reconstruction in the late nineteenth century included the addition of the neo-Gothic tower, and the church still retains a Gothic rose window above its portal. North of Fő tér is Kossuth utca, a bustling pedestrianized thoroughfare given over to cafés, buskers and strollers, with a **flea market** on Wednesday and Saturday mornings.

Heading towards the Festetics Palace, you'll pass a plaque on the right at Kossuth utca 22 marking the **birthplace of Karl Goldmark**. Born in 1830, the son of a poor Jewish cantor who enrolled him in Sopron's school of music, Goldmark went on to study at the Vienna Conservatory. Almost shot as a rebel for giving concerts in Győr during the 1848 Revolution, he survived to compose *Merlin*, *Zrínyi* and *The Queen of Sheba*. In the courtyard behind is the newly restored **synagogue**, dating from 1852; if it's closed you can arrange to get keys from István Goldschmidt (Ⓣ83/312-188). A black **obelisk** nearby commemorates the 829 Jews who were deported from here in 1944.

A little further down Kossuth utca you come to a triple-header of attractions on the left-hand side at no. 11 (all daily: June–Sept 9am–6pm; Oct–May 10am–5pm). The first one you come to is the **Waxwork Museum** (Panoptikum; 300Ft), featuring life-size models of legendary and eminent Hungarians such as King Stephen, Árpád and Petőfi; it is made all the more enjoyable thanks to the English captions explaining each person's role in Hungarian society. Just around the corner is the **Shell Parliament** (200Ft), an extraordinary seven-metre-long, 2.5-metre-high reconstruction of the Budapest Parliament building – extraordinary in the sense that it took one indefatigable woman, Ilona Miskei, fourteen years of her life to piece together 4.5 million Pannon sea-snail shells to get the finished result. The building next door houses the delightful **Folk Costume Puppet Museum** (Népi Babamúzeum; 300Ft), a vast collection of exquisite porcelain dolls dressed up in folk costumes representing the multifarious regions of Hungary. Ten minutes' walk north, beyond the end of Kossuth utca and 200m down from the palace gates at Katona József utca 19, the **Marzipan Museum and Pastry Shop** (March–Dec Tues–Sun 10am–6pm; 120Ft) is well worth a stop, not only to view the exquisitely made marzipan works, but also to sample one of the many tempting marzipan desserts.

Keszthely has three **beaches**. There's a free *strand* at the end of Lóczy Lajos utca east of the centre and two more paying beaches: the Városi *strand*, near the ferry dock, with its own quay, is the nicer of the two, while the Helikon *strand* is between the two campsites further south (both mid-May to mid-Sept daily 8am–8pm; 300Ft, free after 5.30pm). You can rent **windsurfing** gear at both of the paying beaches (500Ft per hour, 2000Ft per day).

The Festetics Palace and Georgikon

The imposing neo-Baroque **Festetics Palace** assumed its present form in 1887, and with one hundred halls and rooms, some eighteen of which can be visited, it is one of the largest, and most expensive to visit, in Hungary (May & June Tues–Sun 9am–6pm; July & Aug daily 9am–6pm; Sept–April Tues–Sun 10am–5pm; 1200Ft or 1500Ft if combined with the Coach Museum). The Festetics family are chiefly remembered for Count György, founder of Keszthely's agricultural university, the Georgikon, in 1797. During the early nineteenth century, the palace's salons attracted the leading lights of Magyar literature and became Hungary's first public forum for criticism. More recently, there was a national scandal in 1989 when it was discovered that a porn version of the life of spy Mata Hari had been filmed here while school parties were touring other parts of the palace.

The highlights of the palace are a gilt, mirrored **ballroom** and the **Helikon Library**, a masterpiece of joinery by János Kerbl, built in 1801 and containing over 90,000 books in diverse languages, the oldest of which – *Chronica Hungarorum* – dates back to 1488. Chinese vases and tiled stoves jostle for space with portraits of the family racehorses and dachshunds (whose pedigrees are proudly noted), and the pelts and heads of tigers, bears and other animals shot by Count Windishgrätz. Housed in the immaculately renovated former stables at the rear of the palace is the quite splendid **Coach Museum** (Hintőmuzeum; same times; 500Ft), which proudly displays an assortment of eighteenth- and nineteenth-century carriages – principally parade and hunting coaches, though the oldest one here is a Hungarian bride coach from 1770.

Ten minutes' walk southwest of the palace, at Bercsényi utca 67, is the **Georgikon**, the first college of its kind in Europe. Students attending the three-year course lived and worked together in a cluster of whitewashed buildings, some of which have been converted into the **Farmstead Museum** (May–Oct Tues–Sun 10am–5pm; 150Ft). Sheltered here is an impressive and voluminous gathering of dairy and viticultural equipment, cartwrights' and blacksmiths' tools, as well as old Ford tractors and two enormous steam ploughs manufactured by the British company John Fowler in 1912. The Georgikon was the forerunner of today's **Agricultural University**, a green and daffodil-yellow pile halfway along Széchenyi utca.

Eating, drinking and entertainment

Given Keszthely's size and popularity, its **restaurant** scene is hugely disappointing. The restaurant in the *Hotel Bacchus* (daily 11am–10pm) is by far and away the best, offering an upscale take on familiar Hungarian dishes, and great wine to boot, whilst the *Park*, down at Vörösmarty utca 1a, is a distinctly more modest affair, where you can get stuck in to generous portions whilst the accordionist squeezes away in the background (daily noon–10pm). The *Béke Vendéglő* (daily 10am–11pm), at Kossuth utca 50, also has reasonable homestyle Hungarian food, while the *Di Marcello Pizzeria*, at Városház utca 4, serves up tasty thin-crust pizzas in rustic surrounds (daily 11am–10pm). Two appealing self-service places are *Oázis*, down from the palace at Rákóczi tér 3 (Mon–Sat 11am–4pm), which has a decent salad and vegetarian menu, and the more wide-ranging *Morzasázó*, 200m further down the road at no. 12 (Mon–Fri 11am–7pm, Sat & Sun 11am–4pm).

Rather dispiritingly, Keszthely's nightlife largely revolves around a string of tacky, neon-lit clubs and strip bars scattered around town. Otherwise, most **drinking** venues are, predictably enough, student focused and include the *Easy Music House* across from the post office at Kossuth Lajos utca 79, which has live dance and Latin music, the *Kolibri* next door, and the *Piccolo Bar* at Városház utca 9 – all are similarly rowdy and stay open till midnight or later. More refined is *Café Pelso*, occupying a wonderful spot on Fő tér, and the place to go for coffee – during the summer the top terrace opens up and it becomes a really vibrant place (daily: May–Sept 8am–midnight; Oct–April 9am–9pm). There's **Internet access** at *Stones Cyber-Café*, a posey little bar, with pool tables, at Kisfaludy utca 17 (Mon–Sat 10am–midnight, Sun 5pm–midnight). The *Hotel Bacchus* (see p.228) offers several terrific **wine-tasting** programmes in its beautiful eighteenth-century cellar (daily noon–11pm; 2200Ft for six wines with snacks).

Festivals

Keszthely has a rich festival tradition, the highlight being the month-long **Balaton Festival** each May. One of the largest festivals on Balaton, it brings pop and classical concerts, theatre programmes and art exhibitions to venues across town, including the lakeside, the palace, the Balaton Museum and the pedestrian stretch of Kossuth utca. In May of even-numbered years, the **Helikon Festival of Chamber and Orchestral Music**, a celebration featuring young musicians, takes place in the palace. Another regular event is the five-day **Wine Festival**, starting at the end of July or beginning of August, with folk music, dance performances and a plethora of stalls selling wine and offering tastings along the avenue between the *Helikon* and *Hullám* hotels near the lake. The **Theatre Festival**, featuring plays by Shakespeare, is performed on an open-air stage in the palace grounds at the end of July/beginning of August. The palace is also the setting for frequent **philharmonic concerts** throughout July and August, while there are **organ recitals** at the Lutheran church. The summer months are further enlivened by rock, folk and jazz **concerts** on Fő tér, and buskers and jugglers along Kossuth utca. Tourinform can provide further details on all of the above.

Hévíz

HÉVÍZ, 8km northeast of Keszthely, boasts the second-largest **thermal lake** (Gyógy-tó) in the world after Lake Tarawera in New Zealand. The temperature rarely drops below 30°C even during winter, when steam billows from the lake and its thermal stream, and Indian waterlilies flourish on its surface. The lake is replenished by up to eighty million litres of warm water a day gushing up from springs 1km underground, and is completely flushed out every couple of days.

Exploited since medieval times for curative purposes as well as for tanning leather, the lake was salubriously channelled into a bathhouse by Count György Festetics in 1795. By the end of the nineteenth century, Hévíz had become a grand **resort**, briefly favoured by crown princes and magnates like those other great spas of the Habsburg empire, Karlsbad and the Baths of Hercules. They'd be hard-pressed to recognize it today, with high-rise hotels, tacky bars and a raft of souvenir stalls setting the tone.

Although the wooden terraces and catwalks surrounding the **baths** (*tófürdő*; daily: summer 8.30am–5pm; winter 9am–4pm; 1600Ft per day, 900Ft for 3hr) have a vaguely *fin-de-siècle* appearance, the general ambience is modern, with people sipping beer or reading newspapers while bobbing on the lake in rented inner tubes. Prolonged immersion isn't recommended on account of the slightly radioactive water, though mud from the lake is used to treat locomotive disorders. The busiest months are May and September, when the water is at its optimum temperature for bathing. You can rent all the necessary equipment here – rubber rings, swimsuits and towels.

Practicalities

With half-hourly buses from Fő tér in Keszthely, there's no need to linger in Hévíz, but, should you decide to stay, there's plenty of accommodation, with fewer vacancies in May and September, when the town is at its fullest. **Private rooms** (❷) can be booked through Hévíz Tourist at Rákóczi utca 2 (May–Sept Mon–Fri 8.30am–5.30pm, Sat 9am–1pm; Oct–April Mon–Fri 8.30am–4.30pm; Ⓣ83/341-348, Ⓔheviztur@axelero.hu) and Zalatour at no. 8 (June–Sept Mon–Fri 9am–6pm, Sat 9am–3pm, Sun 9am–1pm; Oct–May Mon–Fri 9am–5pm, Sat 9am–1pm; Ⓣ83/341-048). Otherwise, Kossuth and Zrínyi utcas are both teeming with *Zimmer frei* signs. At the southern end of the lake, the four-star *Castrum Gyógycamping* rents plots for tents and trailers at high rates (Ⓣ83/343-198).

The cheapest **hotel**, in a resort not exactly bursting with them, is *Hotel Alba*, a modest, homely place at Petőfi utca 18 (Ⓣ83/343-123, Ⓕ343-402; ❹). Two superb-value hotels lie just next door to each other on Széchenyi utca: at no. 23 is *Pannon* (Ⓣ83/340-482, Ⓦwww.hotels.hu/pannon_heviz; ❹), a colourful, characterful place with inviting rooms; and the only marginally less attractive *Napfény*, at no. 21 (Ⓣ83/340-642, Ⓦwww.napfenyhotelheviz.hu; ❺), which also rents out bikes. The *Danubius Thermal Hotel*, up at Kossuth utca 9–11 (Ⓣ83/889-400, Ⓦwww.danubiusgroup.com; ❽), is by far the swishest, and most expensive, hotel in town, with luxury rooms and several thermal pools (for use by the general public as well as hotel guests); while the *Park Hotel* at Petőfi utca

26 (Ⓣ83/341-190; Ⓦwww.danubiusgroup.com; ❼) is an elegant thirty-room hotel housed in two villas linked by a walkway; its facilities include sauna, Jacuzzi and fitness centre.

Hévíz's **restaurants** are very tourist-orientated. The two best places, both combining standard Hungarian and fish dishes, are somewhat inconveniently located fifteen minutes' walk southwest of the centre on Tavirózsa utca, the street north of Kossuth utca; although there's little to choose between the *Tavirózsa* at no. 4 and the *Magyar Csárda* at no. 1, the former is a touch more polished and has vegetarian dishes – both are open daily till 11pm. Of those down by the baths, the *Rózsakert* on Rákóczi utca, offering lots of grilled meats, is about the best there is (daily 10am–11pm).

The Bakony

The Bakony range cuts a swathe across central Transdanubia, as if scooped from the ground to provide space for the lake and piled as a natural embankment behind the lowlier Balaton highlands. Abundant vineyards testify to the richness of the volcanic soil, and mineheads to the mineral wealth beneath it. With dense woods and narrow ravines, the Bakony was the Hungarian equivalent of Sherwood Forest during the centuries of warfare and turmoil, and the setting for a dozen castles, the finest of which stand at **Sümeg** and **Nagyvázsony**. The regional capital, **Veszprém**, boasts a wealth of historic architecture and serves as a base for trips to **Herend**, location of the world-famous porcelain factory, while **Tapolca** is currently enjoying a revival, belying its old reputation as a dour mining centre. During autumn, pink crocuses spangle the meadows between Sümeg and Balaton, and, if you want to do some walking, the hills around **Zirc** and **Bakonybél** are ideal.

Access to the western end of the Bakony is from Tapolca, where **buses** and **trains** go to Sümeg. Buses also run from Tapolca here via Nagyvázsony and Nemesvámos towards Veszprém, the main transport hub, from where buses serve all the Bakony villages and towns, as well as the major Route 8 to Herend.

Tapolca

Ten kilometres inland from Balaton, the charming small town of **TAPOLCA** was a relatively unimportant village until the 1960s, when it became the capital of Hungary's mining industry. Today, it offers several interesting tourist attractions, as well as serving as something of a transport hub, with regular buses and trains from Keszthely, including *nosztálgia* **steam trains** in July and August, and services to and from Balatonfüred.

The town's biggest draw is the **Cave Lake** (Tavasbarlang; June–Aug daily 10am–6pm; Sept–May Tues–Sun 10am–5pm; 400Ft entry, plus 400Ft boat rental), a ten-minute walk east of the main square, Fő ter, on Kisfaludy utca. Discovered in 1902 during a well-digging, the cave was robbed of its water by mining until 1990, when the mine was closed and the water returned. You can now explore about 100m of the cave on foot, although to really make the visit worthwhile, pay the extra for the boat, from which you can discover a further 300m.

Just behind Fő tér to the south is the wonderfully serene and picturesque **Mill Lake** (Malom-tó), fed by thermal springs and bisected by a low footbridge and the *Hotel Gabriella*, housed in an eighteenth-century watermill – the mill wheel, with its slowly turning blades, still hangs precariously outside. A delightful strolling spot, the smaller, narrower lake (Kis-tó) is fringed by weeping willows whilst the larger lake (Nagy-tó) is encircled by softly-coloured buildings and a couple of cafés. During the summer, the pontoon on the larger lake stages **classical concerts** – details are available from Tourinform. In the group of buildings behind the hotel, signs point you to an old school housing the **School Museum** (Iskola or Városi Múzeum; June–Aug Tues–Sun 9am–4pm; Sept–May Tues–Fri 9am–4pm; 500Ft), where you can see a rather unexciting assemblage of books, desks and school uniforms among other accessories from a hundred years ago; there's also a teacher's bedroom next door. Across the lake from the hotel, the **Szent Antal Wine Museum** (Bormúzeum; Sat & Sun 9am–9pm; 350Ft) houses an exhibition on the history of Balaton wines; tastings are included in the entry price and you can buy a selection of wines from the region.

Practicalities

While the **train station** is 1.5km southwest of the town centre, served by regular buses or a fifteen-minute walk along Dózsa György utca, the **bus station** is on Deák Ferenc utca, a minute's walk from Fő tér. **Information** can be obtained from Tourinform at Fő tér 17 (mid-June to mid-Sept Mon–Fri 9am–6pm, Sat & Sun 9am–5pm; mid-Sept to mid-June Mon–Fri 9am–4pm; ⓣ87/510-777, ⓔtapolca@tourinform.hu). The **post office** is at Deák utca 19 (Mon–Fri 8am–6pm, Sat 8am–noon).

You can book **private rooms** (❷) through Balatontourist at Deák utca 7 (June to mid-July Mon–Fri 8am–4pm, Sat 9–11.30am; mid-July to Aug 20 Mon–Fri 8am–5pm; Aug 21–May Mon–Fri 8am–3.30pm; ⓣ87/510-131, ⓔtapolca@balatontourist.hu). Otherwise, there's a healthy stock of good-quality **accommodation** in town: 400m north of the Cave Lake at Kőztársaság 10 is the plush four-star *Hotel Pelion* (ⓣ87/513-100, ⓦwww.hunguesthotels.hu; ❽), whose facilities include indoor and outdoor thermal pools, tennis and squash courts, and, somewhat uniquely, a medicinal cave. Right next to the Cave Lake, at Kisfaludy utca 1, sits the well-run *Szent György Panzió* (ⓣ & ⓕ87/413-809; ❹), which has alluringly bright, open rooms. For the best views, though, you can't beat the lovely *Hotel Gabriella*, overlooking the Mill Lake at Batsányi tér 7 (ⓣ87/511-070, ⓦwww.hotelgabriella.hu; ❹–❺), while some 100m east of here at Arany János utca 14, there is the top-notch value *Varjú Fogadó* (ⓣ87/510-522, ⓕ510-713; 4), with simply furnished but colourful rooms.

Both the *Szent György Panzió* and *Hotel Gabriella* have the best **restaurants** in town; the former, a gorgeously decorated place with enticing chef's specials, is marginally more superior. Less formal is the cracking pizzeria inside the *Varjú Fogadó*. For coffee, cakes and ice cream head to *Café One* on the corner of Fő tér and Kossuth utca.

Sümeg

SÜMEG, 14km north of Tapolca, has always drawn crowds of tourists, thanks to its dramatic-looking castle dating from the eighteenth century, when Sümeg was the seat of the bishops of Veszprém. All of Sümeg's sights are located less than a couple of minutes' walk from Kossuth Lajos utca, the town's main thoroughfare. Baroque mansions line Deák utca, which leads down from Kossuth Lajos utca to the **Church of the Ascension** (March–Sept Mon–Sat 9am–noon & 1–6pm, Sun 1–6pm; Oct–Feb Mon–Sat 9am–noon & 1–3pm, Sun 1–6pm); if it's shut, ask for the key at the *plébánia*, across the road at Biró Marton utca 3. Outwardly unprepossessing, the church contains magnificent **frescoes** by Maulbertsch, who, with a team of assistants, managed to cover the whole interior within eighteen months, mostly in biblical scenes. Exceptions are the rear wall, which depicts his patron, Bishop Biró (1696–1762), and the wall facing the choir, which shows the churches Biró sponsored in Sümeg and Zalaegerszeg. In the former, the man kneeling before the bishop has Maulbertsch's features, as does the shepherd in the Adoration scene.

Retracing your steps to cross Kossuth utca you come to Kisfaludy tér. To the left is the **Town Museum** (Városi Múzeum; May–Sept Tues–Sun 10am–6pm; Oct–April Mon–Fri 8am–4pm; 400Ft), which houses archeological finds from the area, furniture and other objects belonging to Sándor Kisfaludy, the romantic poet of Balaton; best of all, however, are a dozen or so typically demonstrative sculptures by Margit Kovács, Hungary's best-known ceramicist and sculptor (see p.161). Up from the square behind the trees, the crumbling, overgrown **Bishop's Palace** (Püspöki Palota), commissioned by Bishop Biró in the mid-eighteenth century, is currently being renovated; it's still possible to visit the wine cellar, part of which is now an excellent wine bar and shop (*Palota Pince*; Mon–Sat noon–7pm, Sun 1–7pm), although proper tasting sessions are reserved for groups only. On the right side of the square is the second-oldest building in town after the castle, the **Franciscan Church and monastery**, originally dating from the seventeenth century, though the present church owes more to alterations the following century. The church hosts special celebrations on September 13, when the miraculous statue of the Virgin draws crowds of believers. Heading up Vak Bottyán utca to the right of the church, a five-minute walk brings you to the former **Bishop's Stables** (Váristálló), where some forty horses are still kept today; the riding school (Capári Lovasiskola) here offers an excellent programme, including lessons for beginners, trots around the yard and cross-country rides (1500–2500Ft). You can also just wander around the stables to view the horses or take a look at the small Hussar exhibition tucked away in a corner of the stable office (daily 9am–6pm; free). Just beyond the stables is a cluster of souvenir stalls that leads up from Route 84 to the entrance of the castle.

Sümeg Castle

The most impressive sight in town is **Sümeg Castle** (daily: May–Oct 9am–7pm; Nov–April 9am–5pm weather permitting; 500Ft; Ⓦwww.sumegvar.hu), one of the best-preserved fortifications in Hungary and worth visiting for its tremendous views alone. Dominating Sümeg from a conical limestone massif, a unique Cretaceous outcropping among the basalt of the Bakony, the castle was built during the thirteenth century as a defence against marauding Mongols. It was reinforced several times over the next few hundred years, proving impregnable to the Turks, but eventually falling to the Habsburgs in 1713. If the long climb up to the castle is beyond you, take one of the **jeep taxis** which leave from the top of Városdal utca, where the path to the castle begins (April–Oct; 350Ft).

From June to August each year the so-called "Castle Captain", who is currently renting the castle, organizes evenings of folk dancing, gypsy music, jousting and the like, which cost 1000Ft for entry only and around 6000Ft for an evening including a medieval feast. In the daytime, medieval knights wander around inviting tourists to join in spear- and axe-throwing.

Practicalities

Arriving in Sümeg by **train**, head along Darnay Kálmán utca for ten minutes before turning left at the church and on to Kossuth Lajos utca; the **bus** station is on Florián tér, at the southern end of Kossuth Lajos utca. **Information** can be obtained from Tourinform at Kossuth utca 15 (mid-June to mid-Sept Mon–Fri 9am–6pm, Sat & Sun 9am–5pm; mid-Sept to mid-June Mon–Fri 8am–4pm; ⓣ87/550-276, ⓔsumeg@tourinform.hu), whilst Balatontourist in the adjoining office (Mon–Fri 8.30am–4pm, Sat 8.30am–noon; ⓣ87/550-259, ⓔsumeg@balatontourist.hu) can arrange private **accommodation** (❷). Alternatively, *Hotel Kapitány* at Tóth Tivadar utca 19, round the far side of the Várhegy (ⓣ87/550-166, ⓦwww.hotelkapitany.hu; ❹), has comfortable rooms with great views up to the castle. In the centre, up past the Franciscan church at Vak Bottyán utca 2, is the *Hotel Vár* (ⓣ87/352-352, ⓦwww.hotelvar.hu; ❹; mid-March to mid-Nov), an outwardly unappealing, chunky stone-walled building, which conceals big, colourful and modern wood-furnished rooms, including some triples and quads. Cheapest of all is the basic student accommodation at Városdal utca 5, above the Bishop's Stables near the castle (ⓣ87/550-087; dorm bed 2000Ft, doubles ❷), although only the most fanatical equine-lover is likely to be enticed by the horsey smells.

Eating choices in town are poor: the only half-decent **restaurants** are the *Kisfaludy Étterem* at Kossuth Lajos utca 13 (daily 9am–11pm), which knocks up cheap Hungarian food, and *Scotti*, opposite the Kisfaludy Museum, providing the full gamut from pizzas and spaghetti to steak and fish (daily 10am–9pm). Otherwise, there's the *Vár Csárda* up by the castle, though it's a rather hollow place aimed squarely at tourists, or the medieval-styled restaurant in the *Hotel Kapitány* (daily noon–10pm), where beef and game constitute the bulk of the menu.

Nagyvázsony and Nemesvámos

NAGYVÁZSONY, a sleepy market town 20km from Tapolca (and also accessible by bus from Balatonfüred), harbours **Kinizsi Castle** (April–Oct Tues–Sun 9am–5pm; 400Ft), given by King Mátyás to Pál Kinizsi, a local miller who made good as a commander. Formidably strong, he is said to have wielded a dead Turk as a bludgeon and danced a triumphal jig while holding three Turks, one of them between his teeth. During the sixteenth century, this was one of the border fortresses between Turkish and Habsburg-ruled Hungary. It is now a ruin, except for the pale stone keep housing an exhibition of weapons and fetters, and the chapel across the way containing Kinizsi's red marble sarcophagus.

The town livens up in the first weekend of August, when there are three or four days of **show-jumping and jousting** in the former Zichy mansion at Kossuth utca 12, north of the castle. The mansion is now the luxurious and expensive *Kastély Hotel* (ⓣ80/264-109; ❸), and during this period it is essential to reserve a place here, or above the mansion's stables in the cheaper *Lótel* – a play on the Hungarian word for horse, *ló* (same phone; ❷). Closer to the castle, you'll find the *Vázsonykő Pension* at Sörház utca 2 (ⓣ80/264-344, ⓕ264-707; ❸; mid-April to Nov), where you can also get good Hungarian home cooking and wine.

Approaching Veszprém, you can't miss the roadside *Betyár Csárda* (mid-April to mid-Oct daily noon–midnight), an eighteenth-century **inn**, 600m before the village of **NEMESVÁMOS**. If you ignore the odd modern fixture and today's clientele, it's possible to imagine it as it once must have been: servants hurrying from the tap-room with its huge casks to the cellar, where swineherds, wayfarers and outlaws caroused, seated upon sections of tree trunk. Poor though most were, Bakony folk were proud of their masterless lives among the oak forests, esteeming the *kondás*, with his herd of pigs, and the highwaymen who robbed rich merchants. These highwaymen called themselves *szegénylegények* ("poor lads"), and the most audacious, Jóska Savanyú, claimed the tavern as his home. Although the food and atmosphere are undeniably enjoyable, it's all rather hammed up for the tourists, with kitsch folklore programmes at 6pm each day throughout July and August.

Another 300m past the inn, a right turn brings you to the village of Nemesvámos itself, 2km beyond which are the **ruins of a Roman villa** (Római Kovi Villagazdaság; May–Sept Tues–Sun 10am–6pm; 250Ft). Its reconstructed frescoes and mosaics convey an impression of the lifestyle of wealthy Roman colonists in the early centuries of the Christian era.

Veszprém

VESZPRÉM, 15km northwest of Lake Balaton, spreads over five hills cobbled together by a maze of streets that twist up towards its old quarter on a precipitous crag overlooking the Bakony Hills. Like Székesfehérvár, it became an episcopal see in the reign of Prince Géza, who was converted to Christianity in 975. It was here in 997 that King Stephen crushed a pagan rebellion with the help of knights sent by Henry of Bavaria, father of his queen, Gizella. During medieval times, Veszprém was the seat of the queen's household and the site of her coronation – hence its title the "Queen's Town". Utterly devastated during the sixteenth century and rebuilt after 1711, its castle district (Vár) and downtown parks are now juxtaposed with apartment buildings, a technical university and chemical factories. Considering its proximity to the lake, Veszprém makes a good base for visiting the Balaton resorts without having to stay there, and is also good for excursions to Nagyvázsony, Nemesvámos and Herend.

Arrival and information

Arriving at the **train station** 2km out to the north, catch bus #2 or #4 to the tall tower block near downtown Szabadság tér (built by the Communists so that the view of the town would not be dominated by the castle and cathedral); the intercity **bus station** is more conveniently situated five minutes' walk northeast of the town centre on Piac tér. From Szabadság tér, you can head north towards the Vár or strike out into the lower town. **Drivers** coming in from the west cross the 150-metre-long Valley Bridge over the River Séd, glimpsing the Vár en route to the centre.

Information is available from Tourinform, by the Heroes' Gate at Vár utca 4 (mid-June to Aug Mon–Fri 9am–6pm, Sat & Sun 10am–4pm; Sept to mid-June Mon–Fri 9am–5pm; ⓣ88/404-548, ⓦwww.veszpreminfo.hu); between June and August they also organize a free two-hour city walking tour – check with the office for days and times. The **post office** is on Kossuth utca (Mon–Fri 8am–6pm, Sat 8am–noon).

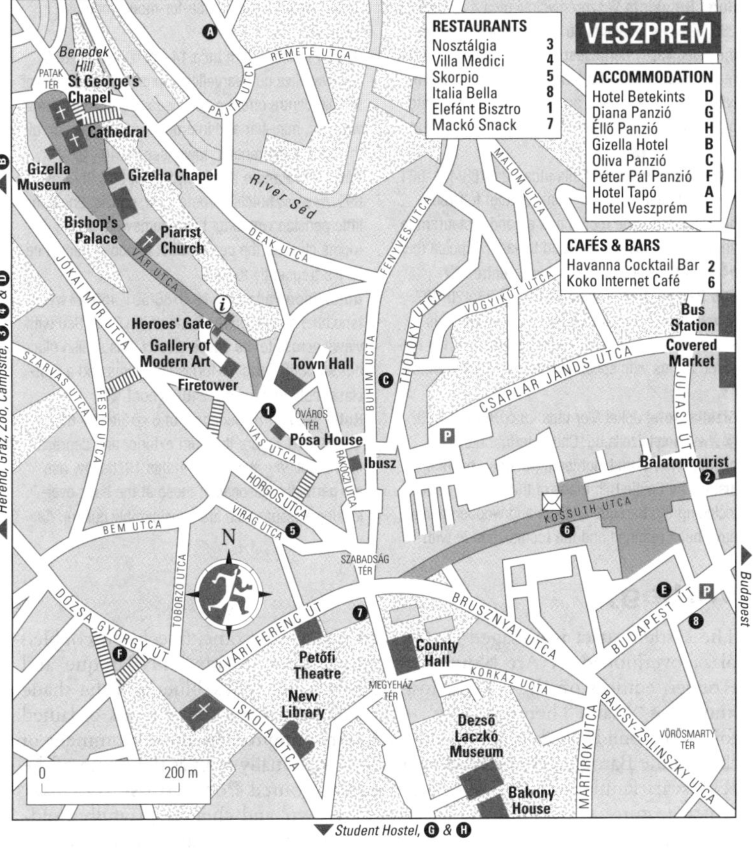

Accommodation

The town is blessed with numerous very fine **hotels** and **pensions**, but if you're looking for something a little cheaper, both Balatontourist, Kossuth utca 21 (June–Aug Mon–Fri 8.30am–5pm, Sat 9am–noon; Sept–May Mon–Fri 8.30am–5pm; ⓣ88/591-142, ⓔveszprem@balatontourist.hu), and Ibusz, Rákóczi utca 6 (Mon–Fri 8am–5pm, Sat 8am–noon; ⓣ88/565-540, ⓔi093@ibusz.hu), have plenty of private **rooms** (❷). In July and August there is cheap accommodation in the student hostel at Egyetem utca 12, beyond Veszprém University, 1km south of the centre (ⓣ88/429-811; bus #2Y, #4, #8 or #14Y; dorm bed 2500ft), and at the Theological Academy (Hittudomány Akadémia; ⓣ88/426-116; dorm bed 2500Ft) at Jutási út 11, which is easier to reach, being twenty minutes' walk up the main road from the bus station – buses into town pass it. The tiny *Erdei* **campsite**, out by the zoo at Kittenberger Kálmán utca 14 (ⓣ88/326-751; mid-April to mid-Oct), also has a motel attached (❷).

Hotel Betekints Veszprémvölgyi utca 4 ⓣ88/579-280, ⓦwww.betekints.hu. Classy hotel down in the Fejes Valley northwest of town, featuring all the requisite comforts of a four-star: big, plush rooms with large beds, chairs and sofa, and immaculate bathrooms. Price includes use of pool, sauna and fitness suite. ❼
Diana Panzió József Attila utca 22 ⓣ88/421-061, ⓦwww.hotels.hu/diana_panzio. Quiet ten-room pension with large rooms and a good restaurant in an attractive villa on the road towards Tapolca (bus #4 from the train station or town centre). ❹
Éllő Panzió József Attila utca 25 ⓣ88/420-097, ⓦwww.hotels.hu/ello. Opposite the *Diana*, this smart, secure villa has fancily furnished, richly-coloured rooms with spectacularly clean bathrooms. ❺
Gizella Hotel Jókai Mór utca 48 ⓣ88/579-490, ⓦwww.hotelgizella.hu. Characterful hotel in a beautifully restored eighteenth-century building just below Castle Hill; many of the original details, including the Baroque ceilings and wooden beams, have been retained and the rooms sparkle with character – the best value-for-money hotel in town. ❻
Oliva Panzió Buhim utca 14–16 ⓣ88/403-875, ⓦwww.oliva.hu. Marvellous pension in the heart of the old centre offering cool, wood-furnished rooms with a/c, mini-bar and Internet access, plus one of the best restaurants in town (see p.240). ❻
Péter Pál Panzió Dózsa György út 3 ⓣ88/328-091, ⓦwww.hotels.hu/peter_pal_panzio. Engaging little pension with bright, but somewhat small, rooms close to the centre. Best to book in advance as it's frequently full. ❹
Hotel Tapó Pajta utca 19 ⓣ88/591-450, ⓦwww.tapo.hu. Located on the bank of the River Séd with views across to the castle district, this stylish place has smooth, designer-furnished rooms and a first-class restaurant (see p.240) to boot. ❺
Hotel Veszprém Budapest út 6 ⓣ88/424-677, ⓕ424-076. Ignore the grim exterior and depressing reception – the rooms in this 1970s low rise are perfectly reasonable; those at the back overlooking Kossuth utca are considerably quieter. ❹

Várhegy

The castle district is presaged by **Óváros tér**, a handsome, tree-laden cobbled plaza overlooked by Art Nouveau buildings on one side and Baroque and Rococo edifices on the other. Most are painted in pinks, blues and the shade known as "Maria Theresa yellow" – the colour scheme the empress ordained for public buildings throughout the Habsburg Empire. The most prominent of these is the Baroque **Town Hall** (Városháza), originally built as the home of the Kaposvári family, and, opposite, the custard-coloured **Pósa House** (Pósaház), which features a striking pediment with a crown, and cherubs playfully holding a garland. From Óváros tér, the path leads up to the **Vár** (Castle District), accessed via the **Heroes' Gate**, a neo-Romanesque portal erected in 1936 to commemorate the dead of World War I. In the courtyard to the left of the gate the 48-metre-high Baroque **Firetower** (Tűztorony; April–Oct daily 10am–6pm; 300Ft) offers exceptional views of Veszprém's rooftops and the Bakony hills, while a traditional recruiting tune is played every hour on the hour by a carillon in the dome. Housed in a renovated building in the same courtyard is the **Gallery of Modern Art** (Vass Gyűjtemény; daily 10am–6pm; 500Ft), an enjoyable and smartly presented little exhibition of mostly abstract works.

Continue for five minutes along Vár utca, past well-preserved eighteenth-century buildings, and you'll come to a **Piarist Church and Monastery** (Piarista templom; Tues–Sun May–Aug 10am–6pm, Sept to mid–Oct till 5pm), now used for temporary exhibitions, whose facade bears three Greek letters encapsulating the Piarist credo "Mary, Mother, God". Soon after, the street broadens out into the main square, **Szentháromság tér** (Trinity Square), in the centre of which is the **Trinity Statue**, erected in 1750 on the orders of Bishop Márton Padányi Biró. The square's single most impressive, and dominant, building is the **Bishop's Palace** (Püspöki Palota; May–Aug Tues–Sun 10am–6pm; Sept to mid–Oct till 5pm; 500Ft), a typically massive Baroque pile by Jakab Fellner, with the distinction of having had the first flush toilets in Hungary, installed in the late eighteenth century. It's possible to view some half a dozen of the palace's rooms, the most impressive of which is the Dining Hall, by virtue of its ceiling frescoes depicting the four seasons, and the wall paintings of Veszprém and Sümeg castles as they probably once were. During the palace's construction, workmen unearthed a vaulted chamber believed to be part of Queen Gizella's palace, which stood on the site until the fourteenth century. Dubbed the **Gizella Chapel** (Gizella-kápolna; Tues–Sun May–Aug 10am–6pm; Sept to mid–Oct till 5pm; 150Ft), this tiny space contains Byzantine-style frescoes of the apostles from the thirteenth century. Across the square, at no. 35, you can view the **Gizella Museum** (Gizella királyné Múzeum; Tues–Sun May–Aug 10am–6pm; Sept to mid–Oct till 5pm; 300Ft), which keeps a small but rich collection of eighteenth- and nineteenth-century ecclesiastical objects, such as votive statues, chasubles, vestments and paintings.

Behind the Trinity Statue looms the **St Michael Cathedral**, whose interior is every bit as austere as its exterior. Having been razed and resurrected half a dozen times since the eleventh century, its current neo-Romanesque incarnation, dating from 1907–10, has only a Gothic crypt to show for its origins. However, a glass dome behind the cathedral shelters the excavated remains of **St George's Chapel** (Szent György kápolna; Tues–Sun May–Aug 10am–6pm; Sept to mid–Oct till 5pm; 150Ft; access from Vár utca), where Stephen's son Imre is said to have taken an oath of celibacy. His canonization, like that of Stephen and the latter-day King László, cemented the Árpáds' adherence to Catholicism and gave the Hungarians their own saints with whom to identify. Statues of Stephen and Gizella duly watch over the parapet at the far end of Vár utca, while a flight of steps round the far side of the cathedral leads down to **Benedek Hill**, the spur which commands a fine panoramic view of the Séd Valley and the Bakony Hills.

The lower town

Returning to Óváros tér, head down Rákóczi utca, and at the lights in Szabadság tér turn right onto Óvári Ferenc út to find the Art Nouveau **Petőfi Theatre**, built in 1908. The first large building in Hungary to be constructed from reinforced concrete, it boasts a circular stained-glass window entitled *The Magic of Folk Art*, whose symbolic figures represent the attachment of Hungarians to their land. Its designer, Sándor Nagy, was one of the Gödöllő Pre-Raphaelites; another of his designs, *The Hunting of the Magic Deer*, a depiction of a Magyar myth, decorates the rear of the building.

A five-minute walk past the Eclectic-style **County Hall** brings you to the **Dezső Laczkó Museum**, behind the trees at Erzsébet sétány 1 (Tues–Sun: April–Sept 10am–6pm; Oct–March noon–4pm; 250Ft), which features an array of local history exhibits from all periods, including Bronze Age pottery and Roman mosaics unearthed in the villa at Balácapuszta (see p.236), regional folk costumes, and material on the Bakony's highwaymen. Standing somewhat incongruously next door is the **Bakony House** (same hours; entry on the same ticket), a 1930s clone of a traditional homestead, filled with peasant artefacts.

West of town

Two more sights lurk to the west of the castle district, either side of the impressive, fifty-metre-high **St Stephen's viaduct**. About ten minutes' walk along Jókai Mór utca, below the castle, is an antique **watermill** – one of many that once lined the banks of the Séd – and, passing under the viaduct, on Kittenburger Kálmán utca, is the **Kittenberger Zoo** (daily: May–Sept 9am–6pm;

April & Oct 9am–5pm; Nov–March 9am–3pm; 720Ft), named after the nineteenth-century zoologist Kálmán, where the lions and tigers have hardly enough room to pace their cages.

Eating, drinking and entertainment

The best **restaurants** in town are those in the hotels and pensions, but that is certainly no bad thing here – indeed you'll find few better ones anywhere in the region. The covered **market**, next to the bus station (Mon–Fri 6am–6pm, Sat 6am–2pm), is a good place to pick up bread, fruit and dairy products.

There are few obvious **drinking** venues in town, but for starters you could try the *Patrióta Lokál Bar* in the *Skorpio* restaurant (Mon–Thurs 10am–2am, Fri & Sat till 4am, Sun 5pm–1am), featuring regular live music, or the *Havanna Cocktail Bar* at Kossuth utca 25, which, in addition to its repertoire of fancy cocktails, has a tastefully designed gaming room out back (daily 10am–2am). *Koko Internet Café*, opposite the post office on Kossuth utca, is a swish café providing coffees, beers, cakes and ices and three terminals for **Internet access** (Mon–Thurs 9am–10pm, Fri & Sat 9am–midnight, Sun 2–10pm). **Theatre** tickets can be purchased at the Petőfi ticket office at Szabadság tér 7 (Mon–Fri 9am–1pm & 2–5pm; ⓣ88/424-235; 1600–2500Ft).

One of the largest events in the Veszprém calendar is the **Gizella Days** (Gizella Napok), held every year in the second week of May in honour of István's wife. To mark the occasion, a series of concerts, exhibitions and dance events is held in the castle district and in the cultural centre at Dózsa György utca 2.

Restaurants

Elefánt Bisztro Óváros tér 6. The pleasant people-watching terrace in this relaxed bistro is an enjoyable venue from which to enjoy the mix of pizza, pasta and salad dishes. Daily 9am–10pm.

Italia Bella Budapest út 7. Just across from the *Hotel Veszprém*, this vaguely Italian-styled place is perfect for steaming plates of pasta and risottos. Mon–Thurs & Sun noon–10pm, Fri & Sat 11am–11pm.

Mackó Snack Megyeház tér 2. Just the job for a quick sit-down or take-away bite, including salads and burgers; coffee and cakes also available. Mon–Sat 7am–7pm, Sun 10am–7pm.

Oliva Buhim utca 14–16. The restaurant in the *Oliva* pension, with its eclectic menu and wine list, mellow decor and Mediterranean-style grill garden, is the most enjoyable place to eat in town. Daily 11.30am–11pm.

Skorpio Virág utca 1. Easy-going, cosy, wood- and brick-designed establishment offering a nice twist on standard meat and grill dishes. Daily 10am–11pm.

Tapó Pajta utca 19. Stylish place in the hotel of the same name, which leans heavily towards game dishes, a theme continued by the animal heads on the walls and the wooden/fur seating. Pop into the adjoining *Safari Bar* afterwards for a drink. Daily noon–10pm.

Villa Medici Kittenburger Kálmán utca 1. Located 1km northwest of town out in the Fejes Valley, this very posh and fantastically pricey restaurant offers superb international fare. No less impressive, or expensive, is the *Nosztálgia* restaurant immediately next door, which sticks to Hungarian cuisine. Both daily noon–11pm.

Herend and around

Twelve kilometres west of Veszprém, **HEREND**'s famous **porcelain factory** makes for an enjoyable side-trip or an interesting stopover en route to Pápa or Szombathely, in Transdanubia. A pottery was founded in the village by Vince Stingl in 1826, and in 1851 Herend porcelain gained international renown when Queen Victoria ordered a chinoiserie dinner service at the Great Exhibition. Other famous buyers have included Tsar Alexander II, Kaiser Wilhelm I, the

Shah of Iran and the British royal family. The factory remains one of the largest porcelain manufacturers in the world, exporting over 75 percent of its products – mainly to Japan and America – and employing some 1600 people, all of whom must attend a three-year training school before beginning in the factory.

A new visitors' complex lies a five-minute walk from the **bus** station at Kossuth Lajos utca 140. The highlight of the complex is the **mini-factory** (April–Oct daily 9.30am–5.30pm; Nov–March Tues–Sat 9.30am–4.30pm; 1500Ft, includes entrance to museum; Ⓦwww.porcelanium.com), where you can see how porcelain is made; the fascinating forty-minute tour starts with a short film on the history of Herend porcelain before you are whisked around the various stages of production, observing plaster mould-makers, clay basket-weavers, glazers and painters all demonstrating their supreme, and highly individual, skills. Your guide will be keen to point out that, for all the technological advances, every single piece made here is still done by hand.

The visitor centre's well-presented **museum** (April–Oct daily 9am–4.30pm; Nov–March Tues–Sat 9am–3.30pm), just across the courtyard, displays a vast number of hand-painted dinner services, vases and statuettes; although many pieces are rather over the top and just a little too fanciful, it is nevertheless an impressive collection – in particular, look out for the ornamental wine canteen with pierced walls from 1867 and a Chinese Imari Plate from the 1850s.

Adjacent to the factory is the hugely elegant, and very expensive, *Apicus* **restaurant** (Tues–Sat noon–8pm, Sun noon–5pm) and **coffee house** (daily 9am–6pm); coffee is served, naturally enough, from the finest Herend porcelain cups. Each summer the centre puts on a number of open-air programmes with brass-band music, folk dancing and the like.

After Herend the scenery deteriorates around Ajka, but 6km beyond Devecser (where the rail line turns northwards towards Celldömölk) there's a great view of the Bakony from a lookout tower near **Sómlóvásárhely**. In clear weather Mount Kőris (see p.242) and even the Austrian Alps may be visible.

Zirc, Csesznek and Bakonybél

Heading north from Veszprém, the train tracks and Route 82 follow the River Cuha through the Bakony Hills up to Pannonhalma, with its famous monastery, and Győr, in northern Transdanubia. The first stop en route is the small town of **Zirc**, dominated by its eighteenth-century Cistercian Abbey. From here roads head off into the Bakony Hills in two directions: Route 82 continues northwards past the village of **Csesznek**, with its ruined castle; while to the west lies **Bakonybél**, with excellent hiking opportunities.

Zirc

Twenty kilometres north of Veszprém, the small, conservative town of **ZIRC** is best known for its large **Cistercian Abbey** (Barokk apátsági templom), whose muddy yellow towers loom large over the area. Outstanding features of the church, built between 1732 and 1752, are the altar paintings and frescoes by Maulbertsch and the gorgeous wood-carved furnishings; although the church is currently undergoing painstakingly slow restoration work, it remains open to visitors. The adjacent abbey houses a **natural history museum** (Természettudományi Múzeum; daily 9am–5pm; 350Ft) on the first floor, displaying a very ordinary collection of botanical, geographical and zoological exhibits from the Bakony, and a **library** (Műemlék Könyvtár; Tues–Sun 10am–noon & 2–4pm; 200Ft) with

Empire-style furnishings, named after Zirc-born Antal Reguly (1819–58), the pioneer of Finno-Urgic linguistic research. Established by the Cistercians in the eighteenth century, the library holds over 60,000 books and periodicals, including the complete issues of *Pesti Hírlap* ("Pesti News"), edited by Lajos Kossuth. Reguly's birthplace, on the south side of the central, park-like Rákóczi tér at no. 10, is now the **Antal Reguly Museum** (Mon–Sat 9am–5pm, Sun 10am–noon & 2–4pm; 180Ft), containing artefacts picked up from his travels in Northern Europe, as well as a small ethnographic collection displaying folk art and ancient crafts from the Bakony region. A short walk south of Rákóczi tér along Széchenyi utca, a left turn brings you to the **Arborétum** (Tues–Sun: May–Sept 9am–5pm; March 15 to April & Oct–Nov 9am–4pm; 300Ft), which used to belong to the abbey. Its tall trees provide an oasis of coolness on a hot day.

Practicalities

From the **train station** on Állomás utca it's a ten-minute walk along Köztársaság utca into town, while **buses** stop in the centre of Rákóczi tér, from where it's a short walk across to Tourinform on the same square at no. 1 (mid-June to mid-Sept Mon–Fri 9am–6pm, Sat & Sun 9am–5pm; mid-Sept to mid-June Mon–Fri 8am–4pm; ⓣ88/416-816, ⓔzirc@tourinform.hu); they can provide **information** on both the town and hiking in the area. Should you wish to **stay**, there are a couple of pensions a short walk south of Rákóczi tér along Kossuth utca: at no. 28, the rather bland *Jeskó Panzió* (ⓣ88/414-390, ⓔjeskopanzio@mail.uti.hu; ❸), which has quieter rooms at the back away from the road, and, 500m further along, behind the petrol station at no. 68, the *Király Fogadó*, (ⓣ & f88/585-275; ❸), with neat, compact rooms. A twenty-minute walk north of Rákóczi tér, along Deák Ferenc utca and up to the right on Pintér-hegyi Erdősor, is the *Erdőalja Panzió* (ⓣ88/414-148; ❶–❸; May–Sept), a former hunting lodge that has small dark rooms with shared bathrooms, and a bungalow that sleeps five. There's a basic **campsite** (ⓣ88/416-788) just beyond the train station at Győru űt 16.

Czesznek

Eleven kilometres north of Zirc, along Route 82, a road breaks off towards the village of **CSESZNEK**, where a **ruined castle** (Cseszneki vár; daily 8am–sunset; 200Ft) on a steep hill affords a fine view of the region. Founded in the thirteenth century, steady decay, followed by an earthquake in 1810, has reduced the castle to its present, paltry state, and with only a shell of the original castle remaining there is little to see once you climb up here except the view, though it looks very striking from a distance. The castle plays host to a good summer programme of concerts and medieval events, most of which take place on Saturdays during July and August (1000–2000Ft); the information centre at Vár útca 51 (ⓣ88/436-110, ⓦwww.cseszprog.hu), or Tourinform in Zirc (see above), can supply further information. **Buses** offer the best access, with ten a day from Zirc going right to the village. **Trains** stop some distance away at Porva-Csesznek, but the journey is a scenic one, winding between cliffs, over bridges and through tunnels, along a line built in 1896. The *Lovag Vár*, just below the castle, offers refreshments.

Bakonybél

The scattered village of **BAKONYBÉL**, 17km to the west and served by ten daily buses from Zirc, is situated at the foot of **Mount Kőris**, the highest peak in the Bakony at 713m. The village, long known for its wood-carving trade, has several popular **hiking trails** emanating from it, details of which can be obtained from Tourinform in Zirc (see opposite). There's a smattering of **accommodation** in the village, including the tremendous-value *Bakony Hotel* (Ⓣ88/461-125, Ⓦwww.bakonyhotel.hu; ❹), hidden away on the edge of the forest at Fürdő út 57, which also rents out bikes; the *Tamás Panzió*, about 400m further north, on the road towards Pápa at Jókai út 62 (Ⓣ & Ⓕ88/461-121; ❷), which has excellent views from its simple rooms; and the *Gerence Fogadó* at Fürdő út 59 (Ⓣ & Ⓕ88/461-042; dorm bed 3000Ft), an old hiking hostel with basic facilities near the *Bakony Hotel*. The only place worth **eating** is the reasonably decent restaurant in the *Bakony Hotel*.

Travel details

Trains

Balatonfüred to: Budapest (every 1–2hr; 2hr 15min–3hr); Székesfehérvár (hourly; 1hr–1hr 30min); Tapolca (every 1–2hr; 50min–1hr 30min).
Balatonszentgyörgy to: Keszthely (hourly; 15min); Nagykanizsa (every 1–2hr; 30–45min).
Fonyód to: Kaposvár (8 daily; 1hr).
Keszthely to: Balatonszentgyörgy (hourly; 15min); Budapest (3 daily; 2hr 30min); Tapolca (hourly; 30min).
Siófok to: Budapest (hourly June–Sept, otherwise 8 daily; 1hr 45min); Székesfehérvár (hourly; 30–50min).
Székesfehérvár to: Balatonfüred (hourly; 1hr–1hr 30min); Budapest (every 1hr–1hr 30min; 1hr–1hr 15min); Fonyód (hourly; 1hr 30min–2hr 30min); Komárom (7 daily; 1hr 15min–1hr 45min); Siófok (hourly; 30–50min); Szombathely (4 daily; 2hr 30min); Veszprém (hourly; 45min–1hr).
Tapolca to: Balatonfüred (every 1–2hr; 50min–1hr 20min); Celldömölk (every 1–2hr; 50min–1hr 15min); Keszthely (hourly; 30min); Sümeg (every 1–2hr; 30min); Szombathely (2 daily; 1hr 30min).
Veszprém to: Budapest (6 daily; 1hr 45min–2hr 15min); Györ (7 daily; 2hr 30min); Székesfehérvár (hourly; 45min–1hr); Szombathely (4 daily; 1hr 30min–3hr).

Buses

Badacsony to: Keszthely (8 daily; 1hr).
Balatonalmádi to: Budapest (4 daily; 2hr); Csopak (6 daily; 15min); Veszprém (10 daily; 25min).
Balatonfüred to: Budapest (5 daily; 2hr 15min); Győr (6 daily; 2hr); Nagyvázsony (3 daily; 45min); Sopron (2 daily; 4hr); Székesfehérvár (7 daily; 1hr 15min); Tapolca (4 daily except Sun; 1hr 30min); Tihany (hourly; 30min); Veszprém (every 30min–1hr 30min; 30min).
Hévíz to: Keszthely (every 30min; 15min); Zalaegerszeg (every 45min; 45min).
Keszthely to: Badacsony (8 daily; 1hr); Balatonmagyaród (Mon–Fri 2 daily; 40min); Budapest (6 daily; 3hr 45min); Hévíz (every 30min; 15min); Pécs (4 daily; 3hr 45min); Sármellék (8 daily; 30min); Sopron (2 daily; 3hr); Sümeg (every 40–60min; 1hr); Tapolca (hourly; 40min); Zalaegerszeg (every 45min; 1hr).
Siófok to: Budapest (3 daily; 1hr 45min–2hr 15min); Pécs (4 daily; 2hr 30min); Szekszárd (5 daily; 1hr 45min); Veszprém (6 daily; 1hr 30min).
Sümeg to: Györ (6 daily; 2hr 15min); Keszthely (9 daily; 45min); Pápa (6 daily; 1hr 20min); Sárvár (4 daily; 1hr 15min); Sopron (3 daily; 2hr 15min); Tapolca (hourly; 35min).
Székesfehérvár to: Balatonfüred (7 daily; 1hr 15min); Budapest (every 30–40min; 1hr); Győr (6 daily; 1hr 40min); Kalocsa (2 daily; 3hr); Martonvásár (7 daily; 40min); Pécs (2 daily; 4hr); Siófok (7 daily; 1hr); Szekszárd (6 daily; 2hr); Tác (7 daily; 30min); Velence (10 daily; 40min); Veszprém (every 30–60min; 1hr).
Tapolca to: Balatonfüred (2 daily except Sun; 1hr 30min); Keszthely (hourly; 40min); Nagyvázsony (12 daily; 45min); Sümeg (hourly; 30min); Szigliget (6 daily; 25min); Veszprém (every 2hr; 1hr).
Tihany to: Balatonfüred (hourly; 30min).
Veszprém to: Balatonfüred (every 1hr–1hr 30min; 30min); Budapest (every 1hr–1hr 30min; 2hr 15min); Györ (10 daily; 2hr); Herend (every 30–40min; 30min); Nagyvázsony (7 daily; 25min); Nemesvámos (hourly; 25min); Siófok (8 daily; 1hr 30min); Székesfehérvár (every 1hr–1hr 30min; 1hr); Tapolca (hourly; 1hr); Zirc (every 30–40 min; 45min).
Zirc to: Bakonybél (10 daily; 25min); Budapest (3 daily; 2hr 30min); Györ (10 daily; 1hr 15min); Székesfehérvár (4 daily; 1hr 15min); Veszprém (hourly; 40min).

Ferries

Badacsony to: Balatonboglár (July–Aug 4 daily; 1hr); Balatonföldvár (July–Aug 1 daily; 2hr 45min); Fonyód (mid-April to May & Sept–Oct 6 daily; June 8 daily; July–Aug 9 daily; 25min); Keszthely (July–Aug 4 daily; 2hr); Siófok (June–Aug 1 daily; 4hr 30min); Szigliget (July–Aug 4 daily; 30min); Tihany (June–Aug 2 daily; 3hr).
Balatonboglár to: Badacsony (July–Aug 4 daily; 45min); Révfülöp (June 4 daily; July–Aug 6 daily; 25min).
Balatonföldvár to: Balatonfüred (July–Aug 1 daily; 1hr); Tihany (June 4 daily; July–Aug 5 daily; 30min).
Balatonfüred to: Balatonalmádi (July–Aug 2 daily; 1hr 30min); Balatonföldvár (July–Aug 1 daily; 1hr); Siófok (mid-April to May & Sept–Oct 4 daily; June 8 daily; July–Aug 9 daily; 1hr); Tihany (mid-April to May & Sept–Oct 3 daily; June 7 daily; July–Aug 9 daily; 20min).
Fonyód to: Badacsony (mid-April to May & Sept–Oct 5 daily; June 8 daily; July–Aug 9 daily; 25min); Keszthely (1 daily; 3hr).
Keszthely to: Badacsony (July–Aug 4 daily; 2hr); Szigliget (July–Aug 4 daily; 1hr 30min).
Révfülöp to: Balatonboglár (June 4 daily; July–Aug 6 daily; 25min).
Siófok to: Badacsony (July–Aug 2 daily; 4hr 30min); Balatonfüred (mid-April to May & Sept–Oct 4 daily; June 7 daily; July–Aug 8 daily; 50min); Tihany (mid-April to May & Sept–Oct 3 daily; June 7 daily; July–Aug 8 daily; 1hr 20min).
Szántódrév to: Tihany-rév (March–Nov every 40–60min; 10min).
Szigliget to: Badacsony (July–Aug 5 daily; 25min); Keszthely (July–Aug 4 daily; 1hr 30min).
Tihany to: Badacsony (July–Aug 2 daily; 3hr); Balatonalmádi (July–Aug 2 daily; 2hr); Balatonföldvár (July–Aug 5 daily; 35min); Balatonfüred (mid-April to May & Sept–Oct 3 daily; June 8 daily; July–Aug 10 daily; 30min); Siófok (mid-April to May & Sept–Oct 3 daily; June 7 daily; July–Aug 7 daily; 1hr 15min).
Tihany-rév to: Szántódrév (March–Nov every 40–60min; 10min).

Transdanubia

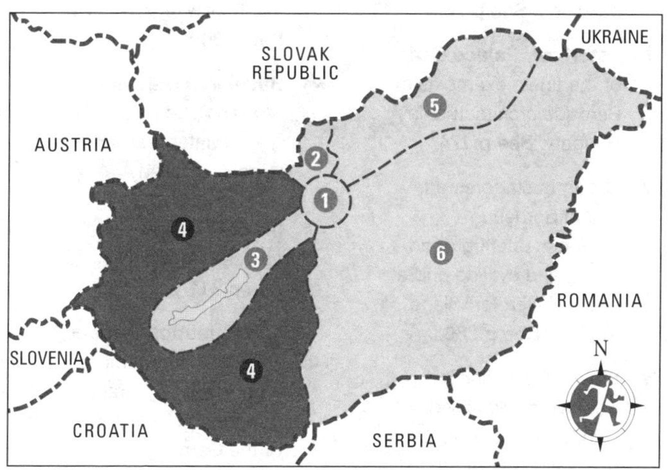

CHAPTER 4

Highlights

* **Pannonhalma Monastery** Hungary's most impressive monastery is also a UNESCO World Heritage site. See p.260
* **Sopron** Atmospheric town featuring a gorgeous Belváros stuffed with Baroque buildings. See p.265
* **Esterházy Palace** One of the finest examples of Baroque architecture in Hungary. See p.274
* **Őrség** Lush, forested region bordering Slovenia, offering good hiking and cycling and a popular area for village tourism. See p.286
* **Steiner Collection in Kaposvár** Unique and wonderful private collection of cast-iron objects and ornaments. See p.295
* **Pécs** One of Hungary's most vibrant cities, with sights galore and the eclectic Pécs Weeks festival of arts and food. See p.297
* **Villány-Siklós wine road** Hungary's most established wine route is a must for wine lovers. See p.309
* **Busójárás Carnival, Mohács** The country's major winter festival sees spooky masked revellers parading through the town and across the Danube. See p.311
* **The Forest of Gemenc** Take a hike (or jump on a narrow-gauge train) through the thick forests of the Gemenc. See p.313

▲ St Peter and St Paul Basilica, Pécs

4

Transdanubia

A vast area encompassing the western half of the country, **Transdanubia** – the Dunántúl – is a region of considerable charm and variety, and one which, perhaps more than any other region in Hungary, is a patchwork land, an ethnic and social hybrid. Enclosed to the north and the east by the River Danube, its valleys, hills, forests and mud flats have been a melting pot since Roman times, when the region was known as Pannonia. Settled since then by Magyars, Serbs, Croats, Germans and Slovaks, it has been torn asunder and occupied by the Turks and the Habsburgs, and only within the last 150 years has it emerged from a state of near-feudalism.

Stark testament to these centuries of warfare are the fortified castles which stand at the core of every main town in the region. Around each weathered *vár* (castle) sprawls a Belváros, with rambling streets and squares overlooked by florid Baroque and the odd Gothic or Renaissance building. In the predominantly flat region of northern Transdanubia – which borders Slovakia to the north – the small lakeside town of **Tata** and the larger, more ebullient city of **Győr** both provide fine examples of this genre, whilst close by is the superb **Pannonhalma Monastery**.

By way of contrast, western Transdanubia, which neighbours Austria and Slovenia, has a far more varied topography, with the hilly, idyllic **Őrség region** presenting great opportunities for rambling, cycling and other leisurely pursuits. Though **Szombathely** has the most to show for its Roman origins, with its Temple of Isis and other ruins, the must-see towns in this region are **Sopron**, with its cobbled streets and beautifully distinct Belváros, and delightfully sleepy **Kőszeg**.

Cossetted by the rolling **Mecsek Hills**, the dashing city of **Pécs**, boasting a Turkish mosque and minaret, is the outstanding highlight of southern Transdanubia – a relatively flat tract of land sandwiched between Lake Balaton in the north and Croatia to the south. In the southernmost reaches, almost scraping the Croatian border, the **Villány-Siklós** wine road has some of the lushest vineyards in the country, and there are more excellent wine-tasting opportunities at **Szekszárd**, close to the **Forest of Gemenc** on the way back to Budapest.

While many towns host spring or summer **festivals** of classical music, drama, folk music and dancing, the most interesting events take place in southern Transdanubia, such as the masked Busójárás Carnival at **Mohács**, seven weeks before Easter, and the Pécs Weeks of Art and Gastronomy in June and July. During summer, **concerts** are also held in two unique settings – the **Esterházy Palace** at **Fertőd** and the rock chambers of **Fertőrákos**,

both close to Sopron. At the monthly **market** in Pécs, you'll sense the peasant roots underlying many Transdanubian towns, whose sprawling *lakótelep* (apartment buildings) house recent immigrants from the countryside.

Transport links between the towns and cities in the region are excellent. Express trains from Budapest run regularly to the major centres, and there are also plenty of buses and trains to and from Lake Balaton.

Northern Transdanubia

Most of **Northern Transdanubia** consists of the **Kisalföld** (Little Plain), a fertile but rather monotonous landscape that focuses your attention on the region's towns. The first of these on the approach from Budapest is **Tata**, a delightful small town nestled around a large lake, with a medieval castle cocooned amid Baroque and Neoclassical buildings. By far the largest and liveliest city in the region is **Győr**, which also makes a good base for excursions to **Pannonhalma**, Hungary's most impressive monastery, and the wetlands of the **Szigetköz** with their abundant birdlife. If heading south towards Balaton, the appealing small town of **Pápa** is worth a brief stopoff.

The main transport routes interconnect at **Komárom**, the chief border crossing between Hungary and Slovakia, and site of one of Europe's largest fortresses, and **Mosonmagyaróvár**, the last town before Vienna and Bratislava. All the towns en route are served by frequent trains from Budapest's Déli or Keleti stations, and can also be reached by bus from Népliget Station.

Tata

TATA, 74km northwest of Budapest, is a small lakeside town interlaced with canals and streams, at its most charming on misty mornings, when its castle, mills and riding school appear as wraiths from olden days on the shores of the central lake. There's enough to see in a leisurely day, plus horse-riding, fishing and swimming for the more actively inclined.

Historically, Tata had the misfortune to be right on the war-torn border between Turkish and Habsburg Hungary for 150 years. It was almost wholly rebuilt in the eighteenth century under the direction of the Moravian-born architect Jakab Fellner, resulting in an extremely harmonious Baroque town centre up on the hill, which has been left untouched by later developments in the Tóváros (Lake Town) to the east, where most of the tourist facilities are located.

Arrival and information

Tata has two **train stations**: the main (Vasútállomás) station, 1.5km north of the centre just off Bacsó Béla utca (bus #1); and the Tóvároskert Station, 1km east of the centre (bus #5), where mostly local trains stop. The intercity **bus station** is a few blocks north of the castle on Május 1 út. Motorists coming off the M7 drive through the old town round to the top of Ady Endre utca.

Information is available from Tourinform at Ady Endre utca 9 (mid-June to mid-Sept Mon–Fri 9am–6pm, Sat & Sun 9am–5pm; mid-Sept to mid-June Mon–Fri 8am–4pm; Ⓣ34/586-045, Ⓔtata@tourinform.hu). The main **post office** is in the old town on Kossuth tér (Mon–Fri 8am–6pm, Sat 8am–11am), and there's a smaller one in the modern district on the corner of Ady Endre utca and Somogyi Béla utca (Mon–Fri 8am–4pm).

Accommodation

Tata has a decent array of accommodation, including **private rooms** (❷), bookable through Gerecse Travel at Ady Endre utca 13 (Mon–Fri 8am–5pm;

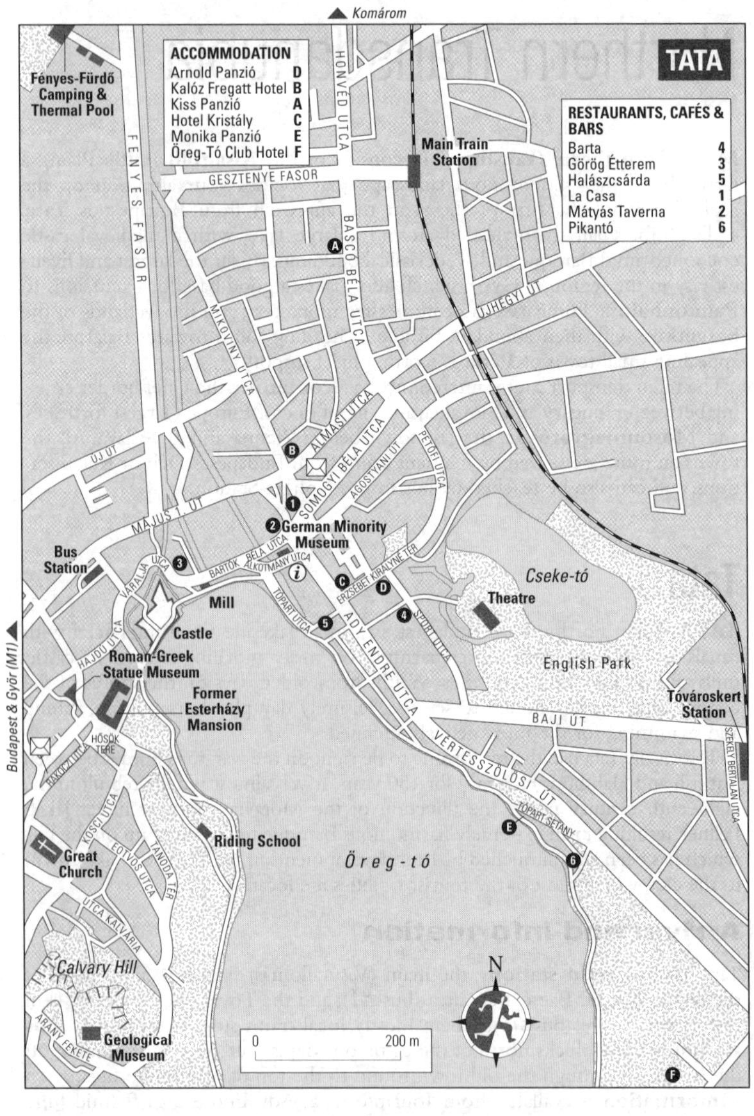

Ⓣ & Ⓕ34/483-384). The *Fényes-Fürdő* **campsite**, which also has chalets and a motel (both ❶), is by the thermal baths, where bus #3 terminates (Ⓣ34/481-208; May–Sept), and there's extremely basic, hostel-type accommodation at the optimistically named *Öreg-Tó Club Hotel*, down by the lake at Fáklya utca 4 (Ⓣ34/487-960, Ⓦwww.hotels.hu/oreg_to_tata; dorm bed 1200Ft).

Arnold Panzió Erzsébet királyné tér 8 Ⓣ34/588-028, Ⓦwww.hotels.hu/arnold. Located in a peaceful spot behind the *Hotel Kristály*, this is a pretty classy place, with ultramodern rooms, and a stylish restaurant. ❺

Kalóz Fregatt Hotel Almási út 2 Ⓣ34/382-382,

Ⓦ www.hotels.hu/kaloz. Smack-bang in the centre of town, this colourful building houses five cramped and dreary rooms, though its pub is worth a visit (see p.252). ❹

Kiss Panzió Bacsó Béla utca 54 Ⓣ 34/586-888, Ⓦ www.hotels.hu/kispanzi. This unmistakeable pink building, 500m from the train station en route to the centre, contains nine magnificently furnished, air-conditioned rooms, all with Internet access. Stunning indoor pool, sauna, solarium and whirlpool. ❻

Hotel Kristály Ady Endre utca 22 Ⓣ 34/383-577, Ⓦ www.hotels.hu/kristaly_tata. This late eighteenth-century building on the noisy main road now accommodates two wings; the older one has huge, but rather staid, doubles and singles with showers or baths, while the newer building has infinitely smarter rooms. ❺–❻

Monika Panzió Tópart sétány Ⓣ 34/383-208. Large and very dull rooms, though the pleasant lakeside setting compensates somewhat. ❹

The Town

All Tata's attractions are located within close proximity to the **Old Lake** (Öreg-tó), with the best place to start being the **German Minority Museum**, just north of Tourinform at Alkotmány utca 1 (Német Nemzetiségi Múzeum; mid-April to mid-Oct Tues–Sun 10am–6pm; mid-Oct to mid-April Wed–Fri 10am–2pm, Sat & Sun 10am–4pm; 200Ft). Swabians, Bavarians and other German settlers have long inhabited Transdanubia, and Tata (like Székesfehérvár and Pécs) was almost entirely German-speaking for many centuries. In keeping with their ethic, the folk costumes are less flamboyant than Magyar attire. The museum is housed in the former Nepomucenus Mill, built in 1758 and straddling a weir. A hundred metres further east, at Bartók Béla utca 3, is the **Cifra Mill** (Cifra-malom), dating back to the sixteenth century.

Just beyond here lies Tata's moated fourteenth-century **castle** (mid-April to mid-Oct Tues–Sun 10am–6pm; mid-Oct to mid-April Wed–Fri 10am–2pm, Sat & Sun 10am–4pm; 400Ft). Once the hunting lodge of King Sigismund, it was badly damaged by both the Turks and the Habsburgs, and only one of the original corner towers remains. Its residential "keep" was reconstructed in 1897 for a visit by Franz Josef II, and now contains a museum of Roman miniatures and faïence by the eighteenth-century local craftsman Domokos Kuny.

From the castle a path heads up through the park to an impressive, decrepit pile that was formerly an **Esterházy Mansion** (May to mid-Sept Wed-Sun 10am–6pm; 300Ft), where the Habsburg King Francis took refuge from Napoleon in 1809 and later signed the Schönbrunn peace treaty. After years of being used as a psychiatric hospital, it's now possible to nose around a handful of the mansion's rooms. From here you can wander up to Hősök tere and the Baroque old town, laid out by Fellner. Down to the right, Tata's former synagogue now houses the **Roman-Greek Statue Museum** (Görög Római Szobormásolatok Múzeum; April–Oct Tues–Sun 10am–6pm; Nov–March by appointment; 200Ft; Ⓣ 34/381-251), containing life-sized plaster casts of the Elgin Marbles, Hercules and Laocoön.

The climax to Fellner's endeavours occurs further along on Kossuth tér, where his statue stands in front of the twin-spired **Great Church** designed by himself and József Grossman, but which wasn't completed until seven years after Fellner's death in 1780. A crag behind the church is named **Calvary Hill** (Kálvária-domb) and has a crucifixion monument, to which a more secular age has added an outdoor **Geological Museum** (Szabadtéri Geológiai Múzeum; April–Oct Tues–Fri 10am–4pm, Sat & Sun 10am–5pm; 80Ft), a **nature reserve** and a **lookout tower** offering fine views of the town and into Slovakia (May–Sept Tues–Sun 9am–5pm; 140Ft).

East of busy Ady Endre utca, which is also the main road up to Komárom, peace returns as you turn off by the *Hotel Kristály* into Erzsébet királyné tér, leading to the 200-hectare **English Park** (Angol Kert) surrounding the **Small**

Lake (Cseke-tó). Laid out in 1780 in the naturalistic English style, the park contains an outdoor **theatre** and **swimming pool**, and a fake ruined church cobbled together from Roman and Benedictine stonework. Hungary's Olympic team has its main training facility along the southern edge of the park.

Activity seekers will also find plenty to occupy them in Tata. On the western shore of the Old Lake, at Fekete utca 2, is a grandiose **Riding School** (Lovasiskola; daily 9am–noon & 2–6pm; ⓣ30/2422-233), modelled on the Spanish Riding School in Vienna, which has been going for over a century; it offers lessons (700-1200Ft for 1hr), cross-country riding through the woods (1000Ft), and carriage rides (3000Ft). Tourinform can supply details on **angling** in the lakes out towards the **thermal pool** (May–Sept 9am–7pm; 700Ft) on Fényes Fasor, reached by bus #3. Rowing **boats** (*csónak*) and pedal boats (*vízibicikli*) can be rented on the eastern side of the Old Lake, from a spot 500m beyond the *Monika Panzió*.

Eating, drinking and entertainment

The classiest **restaurants** in town are *La Casa* at Országgyűlés tér 3 (daily noon–10pm), which excels with its richly diverse menu of fish, including barbecued crabs and grilled swordfish, and the *Pikantó*, down by the lake at Tópart sétány 13 (daily 11.30am–11pm), which has a similarly Mediterranean flavour in addition to some sophisticated Hungarian specials such as paprika-filled spiced pancakes. Aside from these, the *Mátyás Taverna* at Bartók Béla 1 might not look like much from the outside, but it's the most intimate place around and the Hungarian food is reassuringly solid (Sun–Thurs 11am–10pm, Fri & Sat till midnight), whilst further along towards the castle, the *Görög Étterem* at Váralja utca 20 (March–Oct daily noon–10pm) does a fair job of preparing authentic Mediterranean dishes using the freshest vegetables, fruits and spices. The lakeside *Halászcsárda*, at Tópart sétány 10 (daily noon–midnight), should satisfy even the most demanding of seafood connoisseurs with its array of freshly caught fish.

For **drinking**, just about the liveliest place is the *Kalóz Fregatt Pub*, attached to the hotel of the same name (see p.251), a breezy, pirate-themed place knocking up jugs of beer, cocktails and a varied live music programme at weekends (daily noon–midnight, Sat till 2am). A gem of a coffee house is the very ornate *Barta*, by the entrance to the English Park at Sport utca 1 (daily 10am–8pm), which serves fine coffees in its best china.

Tata's main annual happening is the **Water-Music-Flower Festival** on the last weekend of June, featuring concerts and dancing, a flower show, and a craft fair in the castle grounds.

Komárom and around

KOMÁROM, 18km northwest of Tata, is the main crossing between Hungary and Slovakia, linked by a 500-metre-long road and rail bridge to Komárno, across the Danube. The two towns formed a single municipality until 1920 and ethnic Magyars still predominate on the Slovak side, where streets and shops are signposted in both languages. Though neither town has much to offer in the way of sights, the easy crossing and good **connections** between Komárno and Bratislava make this a useful stepping stone en route to the Slovak capital.

The confluence of the Danube and the Váh has been a fortified crossing point since Roman times, reaching its apotheosis in the nineteenth century with the building of three Habsburg fortresses. The most accessible of these is the **Mon-**

ostori Fortress (Monostori Erőd; mid-March to Oct Tues–Sun 9am–5pm; 900Ft; ⓦwww.fort-monostor.hu), 1km west of the train station, which can lay fair claim to being one of the largest fort complexes in Central Europe. Covering over a hundred square kilometres and containing 4km of underground passages, Monostori was built following the 1848–49 Hungarian Revolution, and was also one of the most technologically advanced fortresses of its day, with a highly complex system of bastions, trenches and gun shelters. Thereafter it served as a training base for the Hungarian army, and, during World War II, as a transportation camp and prison, before Soviet troops moved in. Following their departure in 1990 the fort underwent a major restoration programme, reopening as a public monument in 1998. The decently presented **museum** inside the fortress relates its history.

Built between 1871 and 1877, the **Igmándi Fortress** (Igmándi Erőd; mid-April to Oct Tues–Fri 9am–4pm, Sat & Sun 9am–5pm; 200Ft), 2km down Igmándi út from the centre, is far less impressive and contains little more than a museum displaying Roman stoneworks; to get to the entrance take a left down Térffy Gyula and follow the path to the right. The star-shaped **Csillag Fortress**, east of the centre, was originally built in 1586 as a means of keeping the mouth of the Váh-Danube river under control; nowadays it serves as a storage depot and isn't open to the public. For a more relaxing time, head to the **thermal baths** on Táncsics utca, fifteen minutes' walk from the station, which is open all year (daily 9am–7pm; 540Ft).

Practicalities

The **Tourinform** office is located ten minutes east of the bus and train stations, just before the bridge across to Slovakia, at Igmándi út 2 (mid-June to mid-Sept Mon–Fri 9am–6pm, Sat & Sun 9am–1pm; mid-Sept to mid-June Mon–Fri 8am–4pm; ⓣ34/540-590, ⓔkomarom@tourinform.hu). There's plenty of **accommodation** in town, much of it located in the vicinity of the baths along Táncsics utca; best of the bunch is the colourful and welcoming *Forrás Hotel* at no. 34 (ⓣ34/540-177, ⓦwww.hotelforras.hu; ❺), while, less excitingly, there's the *Thermal Hotel* at no. 38 (ⓣ34/342-447, ⓦwww.hotels.hu/thermal_komarom; ❹–❺), which has a mix of dingy older rooms and perfectly acceptable newer ones. The marginally better *Hotel Juno* is across the road at Bem utca 21 (ⓣ34/340-568, ⓦwww.hotels.hu/juno_komarom; ❺). There are **campsites** attached to both hotels, and a third site, *Solaris*, at Táncsics utca 34–36 (ⓣ34/344-777), which is open all year and has apartments with shared showers (❸). Rates at all the above hotels and campsites include admission to the baths. The cheapest place to sleep is the thoroughly downtrodden and depressing *Béke Hotel*, just around the corner from Tourinform at Bajcsy-Zsilinszky utca 8 (ⓣ34/340-333; ❷). The best **restaurants** are in the *Hotel Juno* and the *Bogáncs Étterem*, beside the *Thermal* hotel, although there's little to choose between their Hungarian menus. *Riviera Snack and Drink* at Táncsics utca 34 (daily 11am–midnight) is a breezy place serving both hot sandwiches and fuller meals, and it also has a bar.

Into Slovakia: Komárno

It takes five minutes to walk from Komárom train station to the bridge, which is usually thronged with people **crossing the border**. Both countries' passport controls are at the Slovak end of the bridge, where formalities are straightforward. If you don't fancy walking, there are four buses a day running from Komárom train station to Komárno, and three in the opposite direction. From

Komárno, there are regular local trains to **Bratislava**, 95km away, eliminating the need to use international services. If you're **entering Hungary**, there are fairly frequent trains and buses from Komárom to Budapest, Győr or Esztergom (for the Danube Bend).

At Palatinova ulica 32, the small **Podunajské Museum** (Tues–Sun 10am–noon & 2–4pm; free) pays tribute to two local sons, **Franz Lehár** and **Mór Jókai**. The former, the composer of *The Merry Widow*, was born here in 1870 and initially followed in his father's footsteps as bandmaster with the local garrison, while Jókai was a prolific writer of sentimental novels. You'll need Slovak or Hungarian to appreciate the displays. The museum stands next to a small **Orthodox Church** (Pravoslávny kostol) built in the early eighteenth century by Serbian refugees who had fled from the Turks. Komárno's **bus and train stations** are 2km northwest of the main street, Záhradnícka Slovanská, where the **tourist office** at Župná 5 (Mon–Fri 9am–5pm; ⓣ00421/35/7730-063, ⓔtik@komarno.sk) can arrange **accommodation** in one of the town's hotels or pensions.

Győr and around

The industrial city of **GYŐR** (pronounced "dyur"), 40km east of Komárom, harbours a waterfront Belváros stuffed with Baroque mansions and churches, where streets bustle and restaurants vie for custom. With so much to enjoy around the centre, you can easily forget the high-rise apartments and factories that form the rest of Győr, whose Rába Engineering Works, producing trucks and rolling stock, is one of the country's most successful industries. The city also makes an excellent base for excursions to Pannonhalma Monastery (see p.260) and the Szigetköz wetlands (see p.263).

Győr's **history** owes much to its location at the confluence of three rivers – the Rába, Rábca and Mosoni-Duna – in the centre of the Kisalföld. The place was named Arrabona by the Romans, after a local Celtic tribe whom they subjugated, while its current name derives from *gyürü*, the Avar word for a circular fortress. During the Turkish occupation of Hungary, Győr's castle was a Habsburg stronghold and the town was known as Raab (after the Rába River). After its military role diminished, Győr gained industrial muscle and a different kind of clout. In the 1956 Uprising, its town hall was occupied by a radical Provisional National Council that pressed the Nagy government to get Soviet troops out and to quit the Warsaw Pact immediately.

Arrival and information

Győr's **bus and train stations** are on the southern edge of the centre, behind the very grand wedding-cake-like town hall, only ten minutes' walk from the Belváros along Baross Gábor utca and across Szent István út – a veritable wind tunnel of an avenue that separates the new and old towns.

Tourinform, housed in a glass pavilion on the corner of Baross utca and Árpád utca (June to mid-Sept Mon–Fri 8am–8pm, Sat & Sun 9am–6pm; mid-Sept to May Mon–Fri 9am–5pm, Sat 9am–3pm; ⓣ96/311-771, ⓔgyor@tourinform.hu), can supply all the **information** required, as well as book accommodation and change money. The main **post office** is opposite the theatre at Bajcsy-Zsilinszky út 46 (Mon–Fri 8am–6pm), although the one by the train station has longer opening hours (Mon–Fri 8am–8pm, Sat 8am–noon). **Internet access** is available at the loungey Different Club, at Liszt Ferenc utca 20 (Mon–Fri 9am–9pm, Sat 3–9pm; 500Ft for 1hr), though the entrance is actually on Pálffy utca.

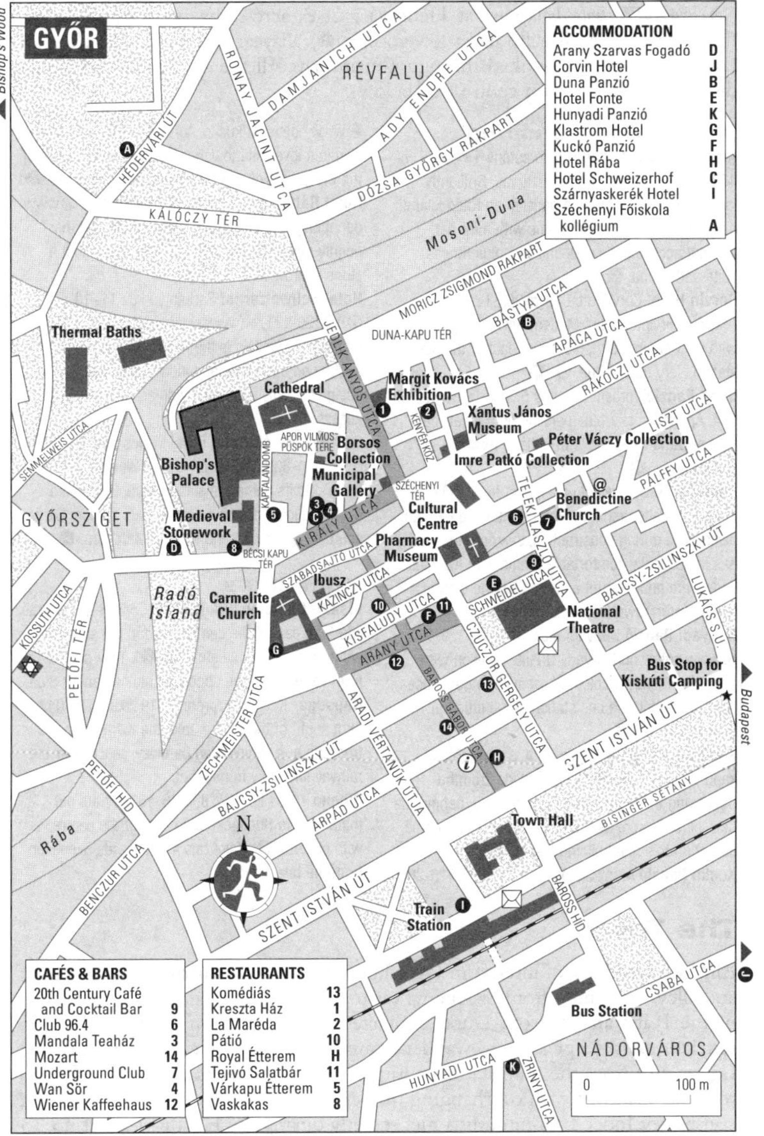

Accommodation

Győr is bursting with good-value **hotels** and pensions, many of which are tucked away amongst the narrow streets and squares of the old town. For **private rooms** (❷–❸), head to Ibusz at Kazinczy utca 3 (Mon–Fri 8am–5pm, Sat 9am–1pm; ⓣ96/311-700, ⓔi051@ibusz.hu). The cheapest option is the

Széchenyi Főiskola kollégium at Hédervári út 3, across the bridge in Révfalu (bus #11), which usually has a few rooms (❶) all year round, though they go fast – these can be booked through Tourinform. All the **campsites** are some distance from the town centre (see below).

Hotels and pensions

Arany Szarvas Fogadó Radó sétány 1 ⓣ96/517-452, ⓦwww.hotels.hu/aranyszarvas. Brilliantly located, nautically themed pension on Radó Island; delightful pine-furnished rooms with mini-bar, Internet access and small balcony, plus fitness suite and sauna. ❹

Corvin Hotel Corvin utca 19 ⓣ96/312-171, ⓦwww.corvinhotel.hu. Modern hotel and pension with well-equipped rooms 400m east of the bus station. Very good value. ❸–❹

Duna Panzió Vörösmarty utca 5 ⓣ & ⓕ96/329-084. Appealing sky-blue pension on a quiet road east of Duna-kapu tér, with antique furniture in some rooms. ❹

Hotel Fonte Schweidel utca 17 ⓣ96/513-810, ⓦwww.hotelfonte.hu. So named after the fountain discovered during construction, this gorgeous hotel has fantastically comfortable rooms with luscious beds, safe and Internet access, plus the classiest restaurant in town (see p.259). ❻

Hunyadi Panzió Hunyadi utca 10 ⓣ96/329-162, ⓦwww.hotels.hu/hunyadi. Quality pension with bright, exuberantly coloured rooms in a good location just behind the bus station. Good little bar downstairs too. ❹

Klastrom Hotel Zechmeister utca 1, off Bécsi kapu tér ⓣ96/516-910, ⓦwww.klastrom.hu. Occupying the eighteenth-century priory behind the Carmelite Church, the hugely disappointing rooms do not do this fine building justice. ❻

Kuckó Panzió Arany János utca 33 ⓣ96/316-260, ⓦwww.hotels.hu/kucko. Agreeable nine-room pension in a lovely old townhouse, right in the centre of the Belváros. Note that the stairs are very steep. ❹

Hotel Rába Árpád utca 34 ⓣ96/889 400, ⓦwww.danubiusgroup.com/raba. Comfortable and thoroughly modern hotel with big, airy rooms just a stone's throw from the Belváros.

Hotel Schweizerhof Sarkantyú köz 11–13 ⓣ96/329-171, ⓦwww.schweizerhof.hu. Along with the *Fonte*, this is the finest hotel in town: a lobby on each floor and individually styled, designer-furnished rooms with a/c and Internet access. ❻–❼

Szárnyaskerék Hotel Révai Miklós utca 5 ⓣ96/314-629, ⓕ317-844. The "Winged Wheel Hotel", as its name translates, occupies the old hostel building across from the train station. Large, spartan rooms with and without bathroom. ❷–❸

Campsites

Kiskúti Camping Kiskútliget ⓣ96/318-986. Large site 3km east of the centre, beyond the stadium, with a motel and chalets (both ❷). Take bus #8 from Szent István út, opposite Lukács Sándor utca.

Napsugár Külső Veszprémi út 19 ⓣ96/411-042. 5km south of the centre; take the Kismegyer bus from the bus station. Can be noisy, as it's near the railway line. May to mid-Oct.

Pihenő 10-es Fő út ⓣ96/316-461. By the old main road to Budapest, 5km east of the centre, with chalets (❷). Take bus #11 towards Szentiván from the bus station.

The Town

Almost everything of interest in Győr lies within the **Belváros**, a web of streets and alleys stretching from Széchenyi tér to Káptalandomb, near the confluence of the Rába and Mosoni-Duna. Protected by preservation orders and traffic restrictions, it is a pleasure to wander around. Heading up pedestrianized Baross Gábor utca from the train station, antique side streets beckon on your left, narrow and shadowy with overhanging timbered houses – the perfect setting for a conspiracy. Indeed, Communists met secretly during the Horthy years at no. 15 on Sarló köz, a cobbled alley forking off Kazinczy utca.

Turning off Baross Gábor utca down Kazinczy utca, you come out into **Bécsi kapu tér**, overlooking the River Rába, which reputedly escaped flooding in the eighteenth century thanks to a miracle-working statue of Mary of the Foam occupying a chapel beside the former **Carmelite Church**. Entering the church through a portal whose inscription proclaims "I worked zealously for the Lord of Hosts", you'll find a richly decorated high altar and other furnishings carved by Franz Richter, a lay brother in the order. Behind the church stands the erstwhile monastery, subsequently used as a refugee centre and military prison and now converted into the *Klastrom Hotel*.

On the eastern side of the square are two **mansions** with finely wrought ironwork. The Zichy Palace at no. 13, built in 1778–82, has a balconied Zopf-style facade bearing the coat of arms of the Ott family, who owned it at a later date. Next door, at no. 12, stands the Altabek House, with two corner oriel windows dating back to the sixteenth century, and a Baroque portico. Just around the corner, at Király utca 4, is the so-called Napoleon House, where the emperor stayed during a visit in 1809.

From Bécsi kapu tér you can carry on uphill to the surviving bastions of Győr's sixteenth-century **castle**, where visitors can see a courtyard full of Roman and medieval stonework and underground casements (April–Oct Tues–Sun 10am–6pm; 300Ft). The castle successfully resisted the Turks for decades – unlike the town, which was frequently devastated.

Káptalandomb and the waterfront

Káptalandomb (Chapter Hill) has been crowned by a **cathedral** (daily 9.15am–noon & 2–6pm; free) ever since King Stephen made Győr an episcopal see in the eleventh century, so the existing building incorporates Romanesque, Gothic and Baroque features. Just inside the entrance, the Gothic Hederváry Chapel contains a **reliquary bust of St László**, the canonized monarch who ruled from 1077 to 1095. Sensitively moulded and richly enamelled, it is a superb example of the goldsmith's art from the workshop of the Kolozsvári brothers. The frescoes inside the cathedral were painted by Maulbertsch, who decorated numerous Hungarian churches in the eighteenth century, while the Bishop's throne was a gift from Empress Maria Theresa.

The building behind the cathedral, at Apor Vilmos püspök tere 2, houses the **Miklós Borsos Collection** (Tues–Sun 10am–6pm; 500Ft), a marvellous assemblage of sculptural art by the self-taught artist who designed the Kilometre Zero monument in Budapest. Using a range of mediums, Borsos (1906–1990) composed a prolific number of sculptures – mostly female nudes, torsos and mythological figures – in addition to statuettes and copper discs with reliefs of eminent Hungarian and European composers, artists and writers. On the other side of the cathedral lies the **Bishop's Palace** (Püspökvár), a much remodelled edifice whose oldest section dates from the thirteenth century. Although the palace is not open to the public, a section of the old cellars has been cleverly converted into a small **museum** (Apor Kiállitás; April–Oct Tues–Sun 10am–6pm; Nov–March Sat 10am–4pm; 600Ft), with exhibitions on Győr during World War II and the city's wartime bishop, **Vilmos Apor**. Apor was shot by Russian soldiers on March 29, 1945 whilst trying to protect women and girls seeking refuge in the palace (you can see the bullet holes in the ceiling of the first room), only to die a few days later. Guided tours are in Hungarian, though it's possible to arrange an English guide if you call a day or two in advance (Ⓣ96/525-090).

From here you can walk down Káptalandomb, past the Zopf-style Provost House at no. 15, to reach **Duna-kapu tér**, a waterfront square alongside which Danube grain ships once moored, and where food **markets** are still held on Wednesdays and Saturdays. Notice the iron weathercock on top of the well – an allusion to the one that the Turks fixed above the town's gate, boasting that they would not leave Győr until it crowed.

Around Széchenyi tér

Heading up Jedlik Ányos utca from Duna-kapu tér, you'll find the **Ark of the Covenant** (Frigyláda emlékmű), a splendid Baroque monument erected by Emperor Karl III by way of an apology for the Habsburg soldiers who knocked the monstrance from a priest's hands during a Corpus Christi procession in 1727. At the same junction, on the corner of Káposztás köz (Cabbage alley), the upstairs rooms of the medieval style Kreszta House holds the **Margit Kovács Collection** (Tues–Sun 10am–6pm; 300Ft), featuring ceramic pieces by the Győr-born artist. Whilst the work on display is not as enlightening as the museum of her work in Szentendre (see p.161), it is still a delight and worth viewing for its highly distinctive vases, figurines and reliefs.

On the other side of the road, Kenyér köz (Bread Alley) and Szappanos köz (Soap Alley) lead to **Széchenyi tér**, traditionally the main square, overlooked by eye-like attic windows from the steep roofs of surrounding buildings. Notice the **Iron Stump House** at no. 4, so-called after a wooden beam into which travelling journeymen hammered nails to mark their sojourn. It now contains the stimulating **Imre Patkó Collection** (Tues–Sun: May–Sept 10am–6pm, Oct–April noon–4pm; 300Ft), which, in addition to housing a number of African and Asian objects rounded up by the art historian Imre Patkó, has an impressive display of Hungarian and Western European twentieth-century fine art. Next door is the **Xantus János Museum** (Tues–Sun: May–Sept 10am–6pm; Oct–April noon–4pm; 300Ft), named after a locally educated nineteenth-century archeologist who emigrated to America and subsequently travelled in China. The free English-language leaflet describes the varied and fascinating artefacts relating to local history, while the collection of tiled stoves needs no explanation.

On the south side of the square, beyond an ornate **Marian Column** commemorating the recapture of Buda from the Turks, stands the Benedictine **Church of St Ignatius**, designed by the Italian Baccio del Bianco in the 1630s. A painting in the sanctuary by the Viennese artist Troger depicts the saint's apotheosis. Beside the adjacent monastery is the **Pharmacy Museum** (Mon–Fri 7.30am–4pm; free), a beautifully furnished seventeenth-century apothecary's that still functions as a pharmacy. North of the square, at Nefelejcs köz 3, an ex-hospice with two minuscule Renaissance-style yards contains the fabulous **Péter Váczy Collection** (Tues–Sun 10am–6pm; 300Ft) of seventeenth- and eighteenth-century Hungarian and European furniture – look out for the English chair that magically converts into a mini stepladder–sculpture and paintings. In the fine old pink-peach building at Király utca 17 is the **Municipal Gallery of Art** (Tues–Sun 10am–6pm; 300Ft), which houses the Radnai Collection, a permanent exhibition of paintings and drawings by eminent Hungarian artists such as Egry, Kmetty and Barcsay, and further temporary exhibitions by Hungarian and international contemporary artists.

Across the river

Should you want a change of scenery, walk across the bridge over the Mosoni-Duna to the **Révfalu** district, where a fifteen-minute walk will bring you to the **Bishop's Wood** (Püspök-erdő), a large park with deer and other fauna. Alternatively, you can cross the Rába via a small island linked by bridge to Bécsi kapu tér and the **Győrsziget** district. On the far side, on Fűrdő tér, is the newly renovated **thermal baths complex** (daily 9am–9pm; 1600Ft per day, 1300Ft for 3hr), which features both indoor and outdoor baths, as well as an indoor **swimming pool** that's only open during the summer (700Ft). Down Kossuth utca, at no. 5, stands the partially restored former **synagogue**, a domed construction built in 1869 according to the designs of Károly Benkő. It's now most often used for concerts, particularly during the Mediawave festival (see p.260), though you can ask at the music academy next door whether you can get inside at other times.

Eating, drinking and entertainment

Tracking down somewhere to eat here will be easy, as Győr has no shortage of good **restaurants** to choose from. Whilst not quite so prevalent, there are enough **drinking** spots for a good evening out.

Restaurants

Fonte Schweidel utca 17. The restaurant in the *Hotel Fonte* is a wonderfully lit and supremely sumptuous affair, with first-class international food and a marvellous wine list. Expensive. Daily noon–midnight.

Komédiás Czuczor Gergely utca 30. Understatedly cool place with an attractive menu of moderately priced fish, game, grilled meats and stews, plus good vegetarian options. Mon–Sat 11am–midnight.

Kreszta Ház Jedlik Ányos utca 3. Tasty, wholesome and extremely generous portions of stock Hungarian dishes, in convivial surrounds. Daily 10am–11pm.

La Maréda Apáca utca 4. The restaurant here is a pretty posh affair, featuring some impressive dishes such as hot smoked salmon, roast lamb and guinea fowl, while the bistro is good for salads, sandwiches and hot breakfasts. Daily 11am–midnight (bistro from 8am).

Pátió Sarló köz 7. Overly glitzy place above the *cukrászda* of the same name, offering a fairly exotic menu including cream soups, stuffed pheasant, deer steak and catfish in paprika and sour cream. Daily 11am–10pm.

Royal Étterem Árpád utca 34. Despite its somewhat sterile location inside the *Hotel Rába*, the food here is excellent, as are the (expensive) Belgian beers. Daily 11am–11pm.

Tejivó Salatbár Kisfaludy utca 30. Hectic, canteen-style place with salads and pastas priced by weight – perfect for a breezy snack stop. Mon–Fri 8am–5pm, Sat 8am–1pm.

Várkapu Étterem Bécsi kapu tér 7. Located on a lovely square, this little restaurant has a wide choice of dishes, including a particularly impressive number of steaks – a good place to dine in summer. Daily 10am–11pm.

Vaskakas Bécsi kapu tér 2. Cavernous cellar restaurant which, when full, has a terrific atmosphere. Live music several nights a week. Mon–Thurs & Sun 11am–9pm, Fri & Sat till 1am.

Bars and cafés

The coolest hangout in town is the terrific *Underground Club* at Teleki László utca 21, which, in addition to its film shows and world music events, has lots of alternative happenings (daily 4pm–midnight). More straightforward **drinking** venues include the saloony *Captain Drake's Pub* (Mon–Fri & Sun 11.30am–midnight, Sat 1pm–1am), inside the *Arany Szarvas Fogadó* (see p.256), the *20th Century Café and Cocktail Bar* at Schweidel utca 25 (daily 11am–midnight, Fri & Sat till 2am), and *Club 96.4*, an enjoyable cellar bar at Liszt Ferenc 8 (daily 11am–midnight, Fri & Sat till 2am). The *Wan Sör*, down a tiny alley at Király utca 9, is a smoky little boozer with head-thumpingly loud music that draws a youngish crowd (daily till 2am). The shiny *Pátió Cukrászda* (see above) has good **coffee** as well as an eye-popping selection of cakes, or there's the *Wiener Kaffeehaus*, in the courtyard at Arany János utca 18–20 (daily 9am–7pm), and the *Mozart* at Baross Gábor utca 30 (Mon–Sat 8am–10pm, Sun till 9pm). Best of all is the beautifully scented *Mandala Teaház*, behind the *Hotel Schweizerhof* at Sarkantyú köz 7 (Mon–Fri 9am–10pm, Sun 2–8pm), a great place to kick back and partake in a pot of tea.

Entertainment and festivals

Culture-wise, Győr has plenty to offer visitors. In particular it's worth looking out for performances by the **Győr Ballet Company**, which achieved international renown under its founder Iván Márko, formerly the lead dancer of Maurice Béjart's Twentieth Century Ballet Company. Although Márko has moved on, the locals still cherish it, and performances frequently sell out at the brashly tiled **National Theatre**, on the corner of Bajcsy-Zsilinszky út and Czuczor Gergely utca; tickets (800–1800Ft) can be obtained from the designated ballet box office in the theatre (Tues–Fri 10am–noon & 3–5pm, Sat & Sun 1hr before performances). Tickets for the **Philharmonic Orchestra**, who mostly perform at the Richter Hall at Aradi vértanúk utca 16, can be obtained at Kisfaludy utca 25 (Mon–Thurs 8am–4pm, Fri 8am–2pm).

The **Cultural Centre** at Czuczor Gergely utca 17 is a regular venue for foreign **films**, exhibitions and concerts, especially during the **Mediawave festival** in late April/early May – one to two weeks of avant-garde film, theatre and music (Ⓦwww.mediawavefestival.com). The **Summer Events** (Gyori Nyár) from mid-June to mid-July is a larger festival of music, theatre and dance at various venues throughout town, including Széchenyi tér, the Synagogue and Radó Island. Finally, the **Baroque Nostalgia Art Festival**, featuring guitar music, theatrical performances and a Bach concert, takes place during the first two weeks of October at several venues including the Zichy Palace. Tourinform can supply you with further details on all the city's festivals and events.

Pannonhalma Monastery

Twenty kilometres southeast of Győr, the low-lying Kisalföld meets a spur of the Bakony, a glorious setting for the fortress-like **Pannonhalma Monastery** atop St Martin's Hill (282m). According to Anonymous, the medieval chronicler, it was here that Árpád was "uplifted by the beauty of Pannonia" after the Magyar conquest, and Prince Géza invited the **Benedictine Order** to found an abbey in 969. The Order helped Géza's son Stephen weld the pagan Magyar tribes into a Christian state, and remained influential until its suppression in 1787 by Emperor Josef II. Re-established by his successor, the Benedictines thereafter confined themselves to prayer and pedagogy. Today there are around fifty monks resident at the monastery, with some 350 boys living and studying in the school here.

The monastery manifests a variety of styles, its chiefly Romanesque wings contrasting with the Baroque exterior of the **basilica** and a Neoclassical **tower**. The late-Romanesque/early-Gothic church is the third on this site since the monastery's foundation, and although it was subsequently enlarged and tinkered with, the Gothic elements have been faithfully retained, most notably in the superb, high-vaulted ceiling. The interior design, however, is mostly nineteenth century, remodelled by Ferenc Storno after the Turks plundered the original furnishings. Notice, too, the marble sepulchres containing the bones of two abbots and a princess. From the church you pass through an exquisitely carved Gothic portal (though the door is nineteenth century) and into the splendid **cloisters** dating from the first quarter of the thirteenth century, when Pannonhalma was remodelled under Abbot Oros, who later gave King Béla IV 220 kilos of silver to help him rebuild the country after the Mongol invasion. Near the doorway is a fourteenth-century fresco, discovered by accident just ten years ago, whilst on the wall by the doorway are some sixteenth-century graffiti – "Hic fuit", which translates as nothing more spectacular than "I Was Here".

Although Pannonhalma's most sacred treasures are displayed on only a couple of days around August 20, its medieval codices and ancient books are permanently on show in the magnificent Empire-style **library**. The 400,000-volume collection (around 120,000 of which are on display) includes the foundation deed of Tihany Abbey, dating from 1055 and the earliest known document to include Hungarian words (55 of them) amongst the customary Latin. The monastery's **art gallery** displays a portrait of King Stephen and paintings by Italian, Dutch and German artists of the sixteenth and seventeenth centuries, plus more recent works marking the monastery's millennium, which was celebrated in 1996 – an apt time for UNESCO to add it to their World Heritage List. A ten-minute walk away is the monastery's modern **wine cellar**, where you can taste a selection of wine harvested on the surrounding slopes (900Ft).

Visitors are only admitted on **guided tours**, which begin at the new, and very ugly, visitor centre 200m down the road from the monastery. Following a fifteen-minute film, visitors are escorted along a specially constructed walkway to the monastery where the tour proper begins. Tours in English run from March 21 to November 11 (Tues–Sun at 11.20am, 1.20pm & 3.20pm; 2000Ft), or there are more frequent tours in Hungarian – with English text – running year-round (June–Sept daily 9am–5pm, hourly; March 21 to May & Oct to Nov 11 Tues–Sun 9am–4pm, hourly; Nov 12 to March 20 Tues–Sun 10am–3pm, hourly except midday; 1400Ft). Churchgoers have a choice of three **masses** on Sunday: Hungarian ones at 9am and 11.30am, and a service at 10am with Gregorian singing. Fully fledged **organ recitals** (1500Ft) usually occur on Easter Monday, Whit Monday, August 20, September 11, October 23 and December 26 (all at 3.30pm), drawing crowds of music lovers; book at least a week in advance through the Tricollis office (see below). Another profitable sideline is the selling of **lavender** *(levendula)* from the fields surrounding the monastery. The oil's efficacy is advertised as a remedy for depression, insect bites, and moths in clothes, and you can buy it from shops in the village or from the visitor centre.

Practicalities

Pannonhalma can be reached from Győr by any bus or train heading for Veszprém (or vice versa). The train station is 2km west of the village, whilst buses pass through the village centre – a steep, fifteen-minute walk away from the monastery up Váralja – with several a day continuing right up to the monastery (check in Győr before leaving). **Information** is available from Tourinform in the cultural centre at Petőfi utca 25 (mid-June to mid-Sept Mon–Fri 9am–6pm, Sat & Sun 9am–5pm; May to mid-June & mid-Sept to Oct daily 10am–4pm; ⓣ96/471-733, ⓔpannonhalma@tourinform.hu), or Tricollis in the visitor centre (open same times as monastery; ⓣ96/570-191, ⓔtricollis@osb.hu).

While neither can arrange private **accommodation**, both offices can give a few addresses. Otherwise, there are three places to stay in town: the most comfortable is the *Pannon Panzió* at Hunyadi utca 7b (ⓣ96/470-041, ⓦwww.hotels.hu/pannon; ❹), with the alternatives being the smaller *Familia Panzió* at Béke utca 61, 600m off Petőfi utca (ⓣ96/470-192; ❸), and the extraordinarily bland *Pax Hotel* at Dózsa György utca 2, just off Petőfi utca (ⓣ96/470-006, ⓦwww.hotels.hu/paxhotel_pannonhalma; ❹). The *Panorama* campsite (ⓣ96/471-240; May–Sept) is beautifully sited on the hillside at Fenyvesalja utca 4a, 300m south of the village centre.

Of the several **restaurants** in the village, the best is the one in the *Pannon Panzió*, which is surprisingly accomplished. The *Szent Márton*, across the car park from the visitor centre, is fine enough, although frequented in the main by coach parties (Tues–Sun 10am–9pm). Finally, the *Borpince* on Szabadság tér has wine tasting and also serves up hot and cold plates (daily 11am–7pm).

Pápa

Forty-five kilometres south of Győr, down towards the Bakony Hills, the small town of **PÁPA** grew up in the Middle Ages as a milling village, with 26 mills along the Tapolca stream. It missed out on the nineteenth-century industrialization drive, thus preserving its elegant Baroque centre, though during the Communist era the Tapolca suffered the same fate as many other streams and springs in the region, being destroyed by pollution and mining. Today, the town is best known for its Calvinist school, one of the few religious schools to remain in church hands during Communist times, whose illustrious alumni include the national poet Sándor Petőfi and the novelist Mór Jókai.

Dominating the main square is the Catholic **Church of St Stephen**, built by Jakab Fellner and József Grossman in 1774–86, with frescoes by the Austrian painter Maulbertsch from the life of the saint (not the Hungarian king but the original martyr). The church was commissioned by Bishop Károly Esterházy, who had the same team build the U-shaped mansion behind the church on the ruins of the old castle. The finest Baroque parts of the **Esterházy Mansion** have been closed for some time now and there are few signs that the profoundly slow restoration work is nearing completion. Instead, you could take a walk through **Kastély-park**, an extensive area of parkland behind the mansion and a favourite spot with the locals.

Walking down Fő utca, the street leading south from the main square, there are delightful Baroque buildings on either side. At no. 6, the **Calvinist History and Art Museum** (Református Egyházművészeti Múzeum; May–Oct Tues–Sun 9am–5pm; 250Ft), housed in the former chapel, has temporary exhibitions downstairs and a few pieces of peasant-style painted church furniture from the eighteenth and nineteenth centuries upstairs. When the chapel was built in 1783, Catholic restrictions required that it should not face onto the street, and should have no tower. Later the congregation was allowed to build a larger church just down the road on Március 15 tér.

Across the road from the church, at no. 12, is the delightful **Blue Dyers' Museum** (Kékfestő Múzeum; Tues–Sun: April–Oct 9am–5pm; Nov–March 9am–4pm; 300Ft), one of the largest of its kind in Central Europe. Blue dyeing was a method of colouring cotton that was popular among the German communities of western Hungary, and which went into a decline after the postwar deportation of Germans and was an endangered craft by the 1960s (when the museum opened), but is now back in fashion with Hungarians. The museum fronts a workshop that was run by the Kluge family from 1783 until 1957, and where the original vats and drying attic can still be inspected and demonstrations are held; you can also buy blue-dyed items here.

Retrace your steps to Fő tér and walk through the archway down pedestrianized **Kossuth utca**, full of turn-of-the-twentieth-century shops and buildings. By turning right down Petőfi Sándor utca, you can find the house, no. 11, where Petőfi lived while attending school in Pápa, which is right next to the school itself. Further down on the left is an empty **synagogue**, a beautiful but battered relic of a community that barely survived the Holocaust. The family living at Eötvös utca 24 holds the key.

Practicalities

Arriving by bus, you'll be dropped five minutes' walk east of the centre on Szabadság utca, while the train station is fifteen minutes' walk from the centre, to the north on Béke tér. All the sights in town are concentrated on Fő utca and Kossuth utca, leading off Fő tér. **Information** can be obtained from the small Tourinform office at Fő utca 5 (June–Aug daily 9am–5pm; Sept–May Mon–Fri 8.30am–3.30pm; ⓣ89/311-535, ⓔpapa@tourinform.hu) and **private rooms** (❷) can be booked through Balatontourist at Kossuth utca 18 (Mon–Fri 8.30am–4pm, Sat 8.30am–noon; ⓣ89/510-014, ⓔpapa@balatontourist.hu). Two excellent places to **stay** are the *Caesar Panzió* at Kossuth utca 32 (ⓣ89/320-320, ⓦwww.caesarpanzio.hu; ❸), a cracking little pension whose cool, air-conditioned rooms incorporate some neat touches; and the *Arany Griff Hotel*, in the Baroque row on Fő tér (Ⓣ89/312-000, Ⓦwww.hotelaranygriff.hu; ❹–❺), with pastel-furnished rooms and more than ample space, including a little entrance hall and gleaming bathrooms. If you can't get in to either of these, there's the small and grubby *Főnix Panzió* at Jókai utca 4, just past the Blue Dyers' Museum (Ⓣ89/324-361; ❷). The *Arany Griff* also has the best **restaurant** in town, serving Hungarian specialities (daily 7am–10pm), as well as a funky café (open daily till midnight) which spills out onto the pavement at the front. The *Vadásztanya*, at Rákóczi út 21, leading off Kossuth utca, also has Hungarian food in more modest surrounds (daily 11am–10pm).

The **post office** is at Kossuth utca 27 (Mon–Fri 8am–6pm, Sat 8am–noon). In mid-June, the town hosts the **United Games Festival**, a series of classical and rock concerts, exhibitions and children's activities, most of which take place in Kastély-park. There's also a four-day **wine festival** at the end of August.

The Szigetköz

Twenty kilometres from Győr, you can turn off the highway to **LÉBÉNY**, but it's only recommended if you're a fan of ecclesiastical architecture, since the village's sole attraction is a thirteenth-century **Benedictine Church** that once came under the jurisdiction of Pannonhalma. Alongside the church in Ják (see p.284), this is touted as one of the oldest and finest examples of Romanesque architecture in Hungary, though it was actually restored to its original style after receiving a Baroque face-lift from the Jesuits in the mid-seventeeth century.

On the other side of the highway, however, lies the **Szigetköz** or "island region", bounded by the meandering Mosoni-Duna and the "old" or main branch of the Danube. This picturesque wetland abounds in rare flora, **birdlife** and fish, making it something of a paradise for hikers and naturalists alike. Unfortunately, the **Gabčikovo hydroelectric barrage** has reduced water levels sharply, thus badly affecting the ecology and wildlife of the region. If you want to explore the area on horseback, there are lots of local **riding** stables; one of the best, awarded the five horseshoe grade, is the Szelle Lovasudvar at Sérfenyő utca 99, in **DUNASZIGET**, 10km northeast of Mosonmagyaróvár (Ⓣ96/233-515, Ⓦwww.go.to/szelle); the stables organize a number of riding tours around the region. The minor road that traverses Szigetköz, running between Győr and Mosonmagyaróvár, is ideal for **cyclists**, and there's plenty of **accommodation** along the way. In **MECSÉR**, 3km off the road, there's the *Dunaparti Panzió* at Ady Endre út 45 (Ⓣ96/213-386, Ⓦwww.hotels.hu/dunaparti_panzio; ❸), which also rents out **kayaks**, while a good place to eat is *Pusztacsárda 1804* (Thurs & Fri 6–11pm, Sat & Sun noon–11pm), an enormous thatched barn of a place 2km south of the village near route 1. In **HÉDERVÁR**, about 5km north of Mecsér, you can try the *Kék Apartman* at Kossuth utca 13 (Ⓣ & Ⓕ96/215-430; ❸), which rents out **bikes**, or, if you've got the money, the 300-year-old *Kastely Hotel* at Fő út 47 (Ⓣ96/213-433, Ⓦwww.hedervar.hu; ❼), which also has a very posh restaurant. Close by, in **LIPÓT**, there's the *Hort-Duna Panzió* at Fő út 65 (Ⓣ & Ⓕ96/216-196; ❷), and the basic *Termál* campsite (Ⓣ96/215-734; May–Sept), also on Fő út. Fishing enthusiasts can obtain **angling licences** from Tourinform in Mosonmagyaróvár (see p.264).

Mosonmagyaróvár and around

MOSONMAGYARÓVÁR, 39km northwest of Győr, is a fusion of two settlements near the confluence of the Mosoni-Duna and Lajta rivers. While **Moson** is utterly prosaic, dominated by the main road that runs through the middle of it, **Magyaróvár** – where you'll find all the restaurants and hotels – is a pleasant, fairly touristy, old town with a picturesque castle and bridges. Both are visibly prosperous, thanks in the main to all the Austrians who come here to shop or to receive inexpensive medical attention – there are well over one hundred dentists in town. If you have the choice, the best time to visit is late autumn, when the crowds have thinned and the first pressing of grapes takes place at **vineyards** in the locality.

The chief attraction is **Magyaróvár Castle**, at the north end of the town (follow the signposts for Bratislava). Founded in the thirteenth century to guard the western gateway to Hungary, it gave the town its medieval name, Porta Hungarica. Much remodelled since then, it now houses a section of Keszthely's Agricultural University and a small exhibition on the fauna of the Hanság region (Mon–Fri 9am–noon & 1–2pm; free).

The cobbled streets running down through the town are worth exploring, even if they have been strongly kitschified for the big tourist crowds that come across the border from Austria. On Fő utca, the main road running round the west side of the old centre, the **Cselley Ház** at no. 19 (Tues–Sun: May–Sept 10am–6pm; Oct–April noon–4pm; 250Ft) is one of the oldest buildings in the town, with some features dating back to the fourteenth century. It's notable for its stone-framed windows, wrought-iron window grilles, and its panelled ceilings on the first floor. It houses an **Exhibition of Fine and Applied Arts** from the seventeenth century onwards, as well as the collection of an art-loving doctor, including paintings by some of the big names in Hungarian art such as Munkácsy Mihály. In the basement are Roman stoneworks. Following Fő útca on down for ten minutes to the junction with Kossuth utca, you come to the **Hanság Museum** at Szent István Király út 1 (Tues–Sun: May–Sept 10am–6pm; Oct–April noon–4pm; 250Ft), with its classical front, which has one of the oldest provincial collections in Hungary. There are some worthy exhibits on show, such as Roman and Celtic grave goods, Hussars' uniforms, furniture from a peasant household, and documents pertaining to the events of October 26, 1956, when one hundred demonstrators were shot dead by secret police in front of the town's barracks. The town's **thermal baths** are in Magyaróvár at Kolbai utca 10 (daily 8am–7pm; 1100Ft).

Practicalities

The **bus** and **train stations** are located in the south of Moson on Hild tér; buses #1, #2, #5 and #6 run along Szent István Király út, past Tourinform at Kápolna tér 16 (mid-June to mid-Sept Mon–Fri 9am–6pm, Sat & Sun 9am–5pm; mid-Sept to mid-June Mon–Fri 9am–4pm; Ⓣ96/206-304, Ⓔmosonmagyarovar@tourinform.hu), and then into Magyaróvár, 1.5km further on.

Most of the town's **hotels** are located in Magyaróvár, the best of which are the *Hotel Thermal*, part of the thermal baths complex at Kolbai utca 10 (Ⓣ96/206-871, Ⓦwww.thermal-movar.hu; ❻) and where there are bikes for rent; and the *Solaris Hotel*, in a quiet, leafy road at Lucsony utca 19 (Ⓣ96/215-300, Ⓦwww.hotels.hu/solaris; ❹). In Moson the only decent place is the hospitable *Hotel Corvina*, 500m on from Tourinform at Mosonyi Mihály utca 2 (Ⓣ96/218-131, Ⓦwww.corvinahotel.hu; ❺), which has bright, airy rooms. For those with transport, *Vizpart Camping* in Dunakiliti (Ⓣ96/224-579), 12km north of the town near the Danube, is a better option than the crowded *Kis-Duna* site by the river at Gabona rakpart 6 (Ⓣ96/216-443; May–Oct), which also has a motel (❸).

Of the several brazenly tourist-orientated **restaurants** spilling out onto Magyar utca, the *Magyaros Vendéglő* at no. 3 is the best option (daily 9am–10pm). Beyond the tourist zone, the pleasantly informal *Muskétás* at Lakatos utca 10,

Into Slovakia and Austria

Mosonmagyaróvár is the last stop before two major border crossings. **Rajka**, 19km north, handles traffic bound for the Slovak capital of Bratislava, 15km away, while **Hegyeshalom** is the main road and rail crossing into Austria, from where it's 45km to Vienna. While the latter used to be famous for its queues of Ladas and Trabants carrying families of Hungarians to the hypermarkets on the Austrian side, traffic now moves quickly in both directions.

split into two contrasting rooms, has a good salad bar and a canopied terrace (Mon–Sat 9am–11pm), and the *Főrum*, opposite, is of a similar bent but has better vegetarian dishes (daily 8am–10.30pm). For **coffee** head to the *Anna Café*, near *Muskétás* at Kapu ut 7.

Western Transdanubia

Western Transdanubia, part of the region bordering Austria and Slovenia, has a sub-Alpine topography and climate, ideal for wine growing and outdoor pursuits. Its Baroque towns and historic castles evince centuries of Habsburg influence and doughty resistance against the Turks, and the region's proximity to Austria has given it a wealthier and more developed status than any other part of Hungary. The beautiful town of **Sopron**, with its magnificent Belváros, makes an ideal place to start, with several enjoyable attractions nearby: the Esterházy Palace at **Fertőd**, the Széchenyi Mansion at **Nagycenk** and the **Fertő-Hanság National Park** – excellent cycling country. Heading south, **Kőszeg** is one of the prettiest towns in Hungary, whilst larger **Szombathely** has plenty to show for its Roman past. It is also a good base from which to explore the castle at **Sárvár** or the picturesque **Őrség region**, where village tourism is thriving.

The following north–south itinerary is possible by public transport, since Sopron is easily accessible by express trains and buses from Budapest or Győr, whereas other places are easier to reach using local services. Starting from Balaton, however, it's easier to work your way north via Szombathely or **Zalaegerszeg** (in which case, you should backtrack through the following sections).

Sopron

With its 115 monuments and 240 listed buildings, **SOPRON**, tucked away in the far northwestern corner of the country, 79km west of Győr, can justly claim to be "the most historic town in Hungary", as well as one of the most attractive. Never having been ravaged by Mongols or Turks, the inner town retains its medieval layout, with a melange of Gothic and Baroque that rivals the Várhegy in Budapest – and here there are even fewer cars on the streets. Sopron is also

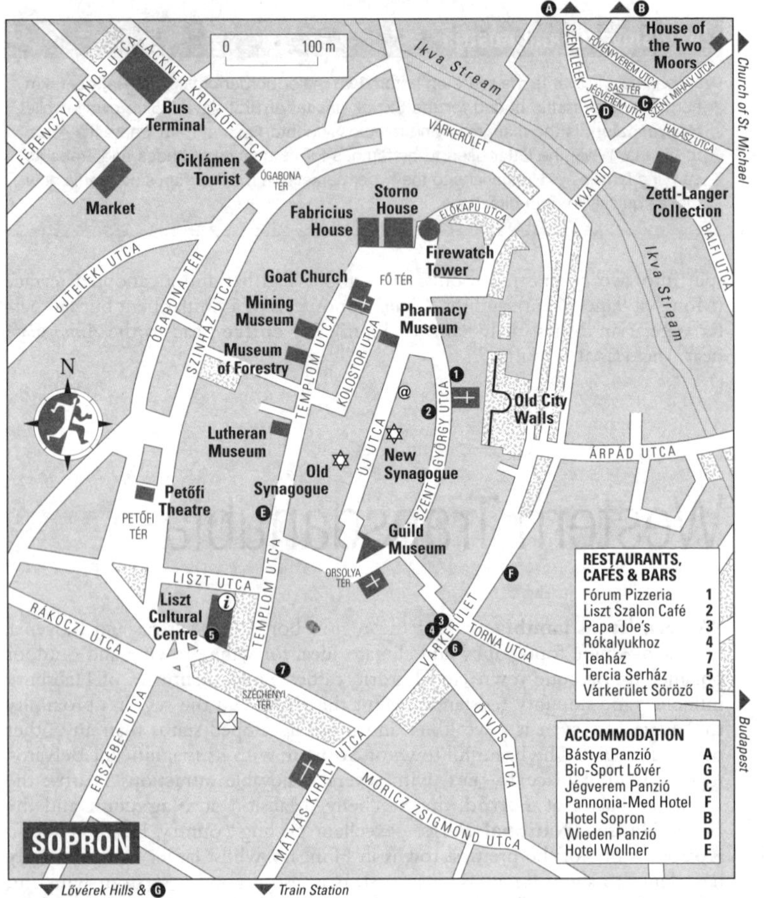

a major wine-producing centre and the base for excursions to the Esterházy Palace and the vintage steam train at Nagycenk amongst others. Its proximity to Vienna means that Austrians have long come here to shop, eat out and get their teeth fixed (there are dentists everywhere in Sopron). While the local economy benefits, visitors will find that prices are almost at Budapest levels and accommodation can be in short supply in the high season. If you're visiting in the winter, be warned that some museums are closed from October until March.

Arrival and information

From Sopron's **train station**, it's just 500m up Mátyás király utca to Széchenyi tér, on the southern edge of the Belváros. Arriving by **bus**, it's five minutes' walk along Lackner Kristóf utca to Ógabona tér, on the northwest side of the Várkerület that surrounds the Belváros.

Information is provided by Tourinform, inside the Liszt Cultural Centre at Liszt utca 1 (mid-June to mid-Sept Mon–Fri 9am–7pm, Sat & Sun 9am–6pm;

mid-Sept to mid-June Mon–Fri 9am–5pm, Sat 9am–3pm; ☎99/517-560, Ⓦwww.tourinform.sopron.hu). If you're in the mood to visit several museums in one day then purchase a **museum pass** (*felonőtteknek*; 2000Ft), available from the Firewatch Tower, which allows entry into all museums. The **post office** is at Széchenyi tér 7–10 (Mon–Fri 8am–7pm, Sat 8am–noon) and there's **Internet access** at Új utca 3 (Mon–Wed 1–7pm, Thurs & Fri 11am–7pm).

Accommodation

There's a decent choice of **accommodation** in town, though it's at a premium over summer, so it's wise to book ahead. During July and August **dormitory beds** are available at the *Középiskolai Fiu kollégium* at Erzsébet utca 9 (☎99/311-260) and the *Hetvényi Leány kollégium* at Mátyás király utca 21 (☎99/320-211), both just down from Széchenyi tér, or at the *Nyugat-Dunántúli Egyetem* at Ady Endre utca 5 (☎99/518-194), ten minutes' walk southwest of the centre. Though **private rooms** (❷–❸) are scarce over summer, it's worth enquiring at Ciklámen Tourist, Ógabona tér 8 (Mon–Fri 8am–4.30pm, Sat 8am–1pm; ☎99/312-040).

Hotels and pensions

Bástya Panzió Patak utca 40 ☎99/325-325, Ⓦwww.hotels.hu/bastya_panzio. Large pension just west of Sas tér, with neat, compact rooms and shiny clean bathrooms. ❹

Bio-Sport Hotel Lővér Várisi utca 4 ☎99/888-400, Ⓦwww.danubiusgroup.com/lover. Peaceful, secluded hotel on the fringes of the Lővérek Hills, twenty minutes' walk from the city centre (bus #1 or #2). Well-appointed rooms and good facilities, including a pool and tennis courts. ❻

Jégverem Panzió Jégverem utca 1 ☎99/510-113, Ⓦwww.jegverem.hu. Just uphill from the Belváros, this converted eighteenth-century inn is named after the old ice pit in the middle of its restaurant (see p.271). Very popular, with just five rooms, so essential to reserve. ❹

Pannonia-Med Hotel Várkerület 75 ☎99/312-180, Ⓦwww.pannoniahotel.hu. A lovely old building with wrought-iron balconies and comfortable rooms with fluffed-up pillows, fancy towels and so on. Underground car park, pool and gymnasium are just some of the facilities. ❼–❽

Hotel Sopron Fövényverem utca 7 ☎99/512-261, Ⓦwww.hotelsopron.hu. Up on Koronázó-domb (Coronation Hill) just north of the Belváros, with a mix of very ordinary older rooms and newer, more modern ones, some of which have terrific views of the old town. Facilities include sauna, solarium, tennis courts and parking. ❻–❼

Wieden Panzió Sas tér 13 ☎99/523-222, Ⓦwww.wieden.hu. Across from the *Jégverem*, this pension has various sized, but rather staid, doubles. ❹

Hotel Wollner Templom utca 20 ☎99/524-400, Ⓦwww.wollner.hu. Housed in a 300-year-old building in the heart of the Belváros, this outstanding hotel oozes class. Gorgeous rooms come with minibar, oak bureaus and large, handsome beds, and the hotel also boasts a beautiful inner courtyard and hanging garden, and a superb restaurant and wine cellar (see p.271). ❼

Campsites and hostels

Brennbergi Youth Hostel Brennbergi utca 82, 4km west of the city centre ☎99/313-116. Take bus #3 or #10 from the bus station. Open July & August. Dorm beds 1500Ft.

Lővér Camping Pócsi-domb ☎99/311-715. Huge site with chalets (❷–❸), located 4km south of the centre and accessible by hourly bus #12 from Deák tér and the bus station. Open mid-April to mid-Oct.

Ózon Camping Erdei Malom köz 3 ☎99/331-144. A four-star site with a few rooms (❷), in the garden district 5km outside town, off the #10 bus route. Open mid-April to mid-Oct.

Around the Belváros

Compact and easily explored on foot, the **Belváros** is where most of the sights are located. Templom utca provides a direct route from Széchenyi tér to the heart of the Belváros, but you should take a detour along the first turning to the right, to admire **Orsolya tér**, in the centre of which is the now defunct Maria Fountain (Mária Kút), dating from 1780. This romantic-looking cobbled square gets its name from an Ursuline convent that once occupied the site of the **Church of the Virgin**, sandwiched between two neo-Gothic edifices dripping with loggias, one of which contains the **Catholic Collection of Ecclesiastical Art** (Katolikus Gyűjtemény; May–Oct Mon, Thurs & Sun 10am–4pm; 300Ft). The square was the site of the Salt Market in olden days, and animals were butchered under the arcades of the building at no. 5. Today, this houses a museum, with temporary displays only.

From Orsolya tér you can head north up **Új utca** (New Street), which is actually one of Sopron's oldest thoroughfares. Its chunky cobblestoned pavements follow a gentle curve of arched dwellings painted in red, yellow and pink, with a view of the Firewatch Tower above them. During the Middle Ages it was called Zsidó (Jewish) utca and housed a flourishing mercantile community, until they were accused of conspiring with the Turks and expelled in 1526, only returning to Sopron in the nineteenth century. At no. 22, a tiny medieval **synagogue** (Ó-Zsinagóga; May–Oct Tues–Sun 10am–6pm; 400Ft) stands diagonally opposite another one, at no. 11, that now contains an office. At the end of the street you emerge onto Fő tér.

Fő tér

The focal point of **Fő tér** is the cherubim-covered **Holy Trinity Statue**, which local Protestants took as an affront when it was erected in 1700 by Cardinal Kollonich, who threatened: "First I will make the Hungarians slaves, then I will make them beggars, and then I will make them Catholics." Behind it stands the triple-aisled **Goat Church** (Kecsketemplom) built for the Franciscans in 1300, where three kings were later crowned and Parliament convened on seven occasions. Its curious name stems from the legend that the church's construction was financed by a goatherd whose flock unearthed a cache of loot – in gratitude for which an angel embraces a goat on one of the pillars of its interesting Gothic and Baroque interior.

Before crossing the square to visit the mansions on its northern side, check out the **Pharmacy Museum** at no. 2 (Patikamúzeum; Tues–Sun April–Sept 10am–6pm; Oct–March 10am–2pm; 300Ft), which preserves the Angel apothecary's founded by Tóbiás Marb in 1601. Though remodelled since then, its Biedermeier-style walnut furnishings and artefacts from the Dark Ages of pharmacology certainly deserve a look.

Directly opposite the church stands the **Fabricius House** at no. 6 (Régészet Kőtár; Tues–Sun: April–Sept 10am–6pm; Oct–March 10am–2pm; 500Ft), which unites a Baroque mansion built upon Roman foundations with a patrician's house from the fifteenth century. A Renaissance stairway leads up to a small museum of archeological finds, also noted for its "whispering gallery", while the Gothic cellar contains three large Roman statues unearthed during the construction of the town hall. Next door at no. 7 is the **Lackner House**, named after the seventeenth-century mayor who bequeathed it to Sopron; his motto "Fiat Voluntas Tua" ("Thy will be done") appears on the facade.

The Renaissance **Storno House** (Storno-gyűjtemény) at no. 8 has the finest pedigree, however. King Mátyás stayed here in 1482–83, as did Franz Liszt in 1840 and 1881. It is still owned by descendants of Ferenc Storno, painter, architect and master chimney-sweep, who restored Pannonhalma and other medieval churches during the nineteenth century. The family's private collection of Liszt memorabilia and Roman, Celtic and Avar relics is displayed in an enjoyably eccentric **museum** on the second floor (Tues–Sun: April–Sept 10am–6pm; Oct–March 10am–2pm; 600Ft).

The Firewatch Tower

North of Fő tér rises Sopron's symbol, the **Firewatch Tower** (Tűztorony; April–Oct Tues–Sun 10am–6pm, May–Aug till 8pm; 500Ft), founded upon the stones of a fortress built by the Romans, who established the town of Scarbantia here during the first century AD. As its name suggests, the tower was intended to give warning of a fire anywhere in town. Its sentries, while standing watch, blew trumpets to signal the hours. Ascending from its square tenth-century base, up through a cylindrical seventeenth-century mid-section, you emerge onto a Baroque balcony offering a stunning **view** of Fő tér and the Belváros.

At the base of the tower stands the **Gate of Loyalty**, erected in honour of the townfolks' decision to reject the offer of Austrian citizenship in 1921. The motif shows Hungaria surrounded by kneeling citizens, and Sopron's coat of arms, which henceforth included the title "Civitas Fidelissima" ("the most loyal citizenry"). Walking through the gate, you'll emerge onto **Előkapu** (Outer Gate) utca, where the houses are staggered for defensive purposes, and "errant burghers" and "gossiping, nagging" wives were once pinioned in stocks for the righteous to pelt with rotten food.

At the junction with the Várkerület, you can cross the road to examine the colourfully tiled facade of the **Golden Lion Pharmacy** at no. 29, or head to the right along the boulevard to espy a section of the **medieval town walls**.

Templom utca

Templom utca, a picturesque street of Baroque facades, heads south from Fő tér. Standing just around the corner from the Goat Church on Fő tér is the square's finest sight, a fourteenth-century **chapterhouse** (Káptalanterem; May–Oct daily 10am–noon & 2–5pm; free) behind the Baroque facade of no. 1, whose Gothic pillars and vaults are decorated with images of the seven deadly sins and the symbols of the Evangelists.

On the opposite side of the road, at no. 2, the **Mining Museum** (Központi Bányászati Múzeum; Tues–Sun: April–Oct 10am–6pm; Nov–March 10am–4pm; 300Ft) occupies a former Esterházy mansion where Haydn often stayed, and has some curious artefacts from the Brennberg pits near Sopron, the oldest coal mines in Hungary. Next door at no. 4 is the **Museum of Forestry** (Erdészeti Gyűjtemény; daily except Wed; May–Oct 1–5pm; Nov–April 10am–1pm; 200Ft), although you'd have to be a real die-hard to appreciate the vast collection of instruments, tools and appliances.

At no. 12 a medieval building given an extra floor in the 1770s contains the **Lutheran History Museum** (Országos Evangélikus Múzeum; May–Sept Wed–Fri 10.30am–2pm, Sat & Sun 2–5pm; 100Ft), which explains how all the Evangelical churches were confiscated in 1674, obliging Lutherans to worship at home until the authorities relented. The adjacent **Lutheran Church** dates from 1782, but only acquired its Romanesque bell-tower eighty years later, due to restrictions on the faith decreed by Emperor Josef II. On the other side, the profusely ornamented Töpler House at no. 22 is named after a physician who devoted his life to fighting epidemics, while the courtyard of no. 15 contains a neo-Renaissance loggia.

Beyond the Belváros

While the Belváros is spectacular, there is more to see as you move out of the centre, with art and architecture to the north, a folly to the west, and beautiful countryside to the south.

Ikva híd, crossing a narrow stream which used to flood noxiously in the nineteenth century, points towards some more sights. Off to the right at Balfi utca 11 is the private **Zettl-Langer Collection** (Tues–Sun 10am–noon; 300Ft) of porcelain, earthenware and weaponry, assembled by nineteenth-century businessman and sometime painter Gusztáv Zettl. His descendants still live here and will give you a guided tour through the collection.

A five-minute walk up Dorfmeister and Szent Mihály utca from Ikva híd takes you past the **House of the Two Moors** (so-called after the turbaned statues flanking its gate) on your left, to the partially Gothic **Church of St Michael** further uphill, whose gargoyles leer over a decaying thirteenth-century Chapel of St Jacob. Nearby stand the tombstones of Soviet soldiers killed liberating Sopron from the Arrow Cross puppet government, which massacred hundreds of hostages before fleeing with the Coronation Regalia in April 1945.

The Fool's Castle

In the southwestern garden suburbs, 3km from the centre, at Csalogány köz 28, lurks a bizarre "**Fool's Castle**" (Taródi-vár; 300Ft), built by local eccentric Istvan Taród in the 1950s. The castle's cold, dark rooms are crammed with a ramshackle assortment of paintings, furniture and other curios, including a couple of rusting motorbikes, while up on the roof you can view the crumbling stone turrets and pillars, and the not-so-distant Lővérek Hills. Whilst it can't compare to the extravagant Bory Castle in Székesfehérvár (see p.202), it's still an oddly enjoyable place to wander around. It's still inhabited by Taród's descendants, and though there are no set opening hours, you can usually gain admission whenever someone's at home. To get here, take bus #1 from Széchenyi tér, which drops you near the covered pool (Fedett Uzsoda) outside town, walk 50m back, turn left up Fegyves Sor, another left up Harsfa Sor, and then follow the road round.

The Lővérek Hills and the Burgenland

A kilometre or so further south of the castle are the sub-Alpine **Lővérek Hills**, a standing invitation to hikers. Bus #1 or #2 will drop you at the *Bio-Sport Hotel Lővér* near the start of the path up to the **Károly lookout tower** (Károlymagaslati Kilátő; daily: May–Aug 9am–8pm, April, Sept & Oct till 7pm, Nov–March till 4pm; 250Ft), which offers marvellous views of the surrounding countryside. Although several **hiking trails** continue into Austria, only locals are allowed to pass through the low-key checkpoints. Both sides of the border are inhabited by bilingual folk engaged in viticulture, following the division of the **Burgenland** region between Hungary and Austria (which got the lion's share) after the collapse of the Habsburg empire – an amicable partition, it seems, since nobody complains about it today.

Eating, drinking and entertainment

Given the town's popularity, the range of places to **eat** and **drink** is somewhat disappointing, though wine buffs can choose from several good cellars.

Restaurants

Fórum Pizzeria Szent György utca 3. Enjoyable pizzeria also offering spaghetti, lasagne and a salad bar. Despite the waiters being overworked, the service is excellent. Daily 11am–11pm.

Jégverem Fogadó Jégverem utca 1. Mammoth portions of fine homestyle cooking in this popular, frenetic restaurant inside the pension of the same name. The menu is adventurous, but the service is slow and with an open kitchen it can get a bit stuffy. Daily 11am–11pm.

Rókalyukhoz Várkerület 112. A fairly prodigious pizza menu awaits at this informal restaurant/pub. Head downstairs for a more intimate dining experience. Daily 10am–midnight.

Tercia Serház Liszt Ferenc utca 1. Large, modern and pleasantly informal basement restaurant under the Cultural Centre, offering a very reasonably priced and colourful menu, including stews, dumplings, lamb, fish, and, for the more adventurous, baked brain. Daily 11am–11pm, Fri & Sat till midnight.

Várkerület Söröző Várkerület 83. Fairly basic place opposite the *Rókalyukhoz*, serving Hungarian cuisine and grilled meats, with a buzzing beer garden and drinking bar. Mon–Sat 9am–1am, Sun 11am–1am.

Wollner Templom utca 20. You're guaranteed an exquisite dining experience in the *Hotel Wollner*'s distinguished restaurant. Expensive – but first-class – helpings of Hungarian and international cuisine. Daily 11.30am–10pm.

Cafés, bars and cellars

The two best **cafés** in town are the *Liszt Szalon Café* (and chocolate shop), a classy, relaxing place in the heart of the Belváros at Szent György utca 12 (daily 10am–10pm), and the cosy *Teaház* at Széchenyi tér 16 (daily 10am–10pm), offering a complete range of teas alongside some delicious strudels and roulades. The sociable *Hungariá Kaveház* in the Liszt Cultural Centre has the best summer terrace (daily 9am–10pm).

Beer drinkers should head for *Rókalyukhoz* (see above) or *Papa Joe's*, a few paces along at Várkerület 108 (daily 11am–midnight, Fri & Sat till 2am). Hearty red Kékfrankos and white, apple-flavoured Tramini can be sampled in **wine cellars** such as the Cezár Borozó on the corner of Oroslya tér and Hátsókapu utca (Mon–Sat 11am–midnight, Sun 1–11pm), which boasts vintage oak butts and leather-aproned waiters and also serves meat platters; or the less refined Gyógygödör Borozó at Fő tér 4 (Tues–Sun 9am–10pm). There's also good wine tasting to be had in the more formal surrounds of the *Hotel Wollner*'s cellar (see p.267).

Festivals

Sopron is at its liveliest during the **Spring Days** (late March) and **Festival Weeks** (mid-June to mid-July), when all manner of concerts and plays are staged at the Petőfi Theatre on Petőfi tér, the Liszt Cultural Centre on Széchenyi tér, and many other venues in the region. You can get details from Tourinform and tickets from the festival office, in the same building (Tues–Fri 9am–5pm, Sat 9am–noon; ⓣ99/511-730, ⓦwww.prokultura.hu). In mid-October the town hosts a festival to celebrate the **Grape Harvest**, when there is wine tasting, folk dancing and music.

Around Sopron

There are several attractions around Sopron worth visiting. East of town is the lovely **Fertő-Hanság National Park**, to the north of which is **Fertőrákos**, whose old quarry is a splendid venue for summertime concerts. Travelling eastwards will bring you to the village of **Nagycenk**, with its own stately home and a popular steam railway, and continuing on you'll find the magnificent, but slowly decaying, **Esterházy Palace** in Fertőd. There are buses every thirty to sixty minutes (every 1hr 30min–2hr to Lake Fertő) to the following places from the bus station in Sopron.

The Fertő-Hanság National Park

Fifteen kilometres to the east of Sopron lies the **Fertő-Hanság National Park**, a once extensive swampland that has gradually been drained and brought under cultivation since the eighteenth century. Prone to thick fogs, the area is traditionally associated with tales of elves and water sprites, and with the dynastic seats of the Esterházy and Széchenyi families at Fertőd and Nagycenk. The most obvious feature on the map is the shallow, reedy expanse known to Hungarians as **Lake Fertő** and to Austrians as the Neusiedler See, which was out of bounds under Communism to prevent escapes, but is now being developed as a nature reserve and resort, noted for its wild beauty and varied **birdlife**. The lake makes especially good **cycling** country, having a 110-kilometre-long cycle track all the way around it (35km of which is in Hungary), with campsites en route and *Zimmer frei* signs in most of the villages. This track forms part of a longer track from Sopron to Fertőd via Fertőrákos, which is highly recommended.

Fertőrákos Quarry

Eight kilometres north of Sopron, on the fringes of the park, the village of **FERTŐRÁKOS** presumably gets its name "cancerous slough" from the local **quarry** (Kőfejtő; daily: March–April 8am–5pm; May–Sept 8am–7pm; Oct 8am–5pm; Nov, Dec & Feb 8am–4pm; 300Ft), where limestone has been hewn since Roman times. Vienna's St Stephen's Cathedral and Ringstrasse were built with stone from Fertőrákos, where quarrying only ceased in 1945. The result is a Cyclopean labyrinth of gigantic chambers and oddly skewed pillars, resembling the mythical cities imagined by H.P. Lovecraft; animal and plant fossils attest that the land was once submerged beneath a prehistoric sea. A better reason for visiting the quarry is to attend one of the **concerts** staged in the Cave Theatre, carved out in 1970 and holding some 800 people. The majority of concerts take place during the Sopron Festival Weeks (tickets available from the Sopron festival office – see p.271).

Everything in the village is situated on Fő utca, the very long main street running downhill from the quarry – the bus makes several stops along this street. A five-minute walk downhill from the quarry brings you to the **Mineral Museum** at no. 99 (Ásványműzeum; April–Oct Tues–Sun 9am–5pm; 250Ft), exhibiting all manner of rocks and stones hewn from the quarry, followed by the former **Bishop's Palace** at no. 153, which dates back in parts to the Middle Ages; there are tentative plans to reopen it as a local history museum.

Should you feel like staying, there's stacks of **accommodation** in the village, including dozens of households advertising private rooms – look out for the *Zimmer frei* signs. The best of the guesthouses are the cosy *Horváth Ház Panzió* (Ⓣ99/355-368, Ⓦwww.hotels.hu/horvathhaz; ❸), in an old peasant dwelling at Fő utca 194, and the four-room *Várfal Panzió*, a further 200m down the road at no. 222 (Ⓣ99/355-115, Ⓦwww.hotels.hu/varfal_fertorakos; ❸), with neat little rooms complemented by charming hospitality. Cheapest of all is the basic and grubby *Vízmalom Hostel*, set back from the road at no. 141 (Ⓣ99/355-034; ❷). The *Ráspi* **restaurant** at Fő utca 78 (daily 11am–11pm) is renowned for the quality of its Hungarian dishes and wine, whilst the interior, with its thick wooden beams and benches, and candle-topped tables, is a delight – the patrons also rent out **bikes** (150Ft for 1hr, 800Ft for a day).

The Széchenyi Mansion and Railway

One of the region's major feudal seats lies on the southern fringe of Fertő-Hanság National Park in the village of **NAGYCENK**. Buses from Sopron can drop you at the **Széchenyi Mansion** (Széchenyi Emlékmúzeum) on Route 84 (the Budapest road), 800m outside the village, which is on the Balaton road. Arriving at the train station, turn right and walk along the path for ten minutes until you enter the village – the mansion is signposted from the village. As the family home of Count Széchenyi, "the greatest Hungarian" (see box below), it has never been allowed to fall into ruin, and was declared a museum in 1973. The first part of the museum (Tues–Sun: April–Oct 10am–6pm; Nov–March 10am–2pm; 500Ft) includes portraits, personal effects and furniture from his household – the first in Hungary to be lit by gas lamps and to have flush toilets – whilst also detailing his many achievements. There's useful guidance in this section, in the form of a button on the wall of each room which, when pressed, gives a short spiel about the contents – though it can get rather chaotic when several people are all vying at once to hear one of the six different languages available. The museum then proceeds to document the development of Hungarian industry since Széchenyi's day, with particular emphasis on transportation and communications.

Adjoining the mansion is a 200-year-old **Stud Farm** (Tues–Sun 10am–5pm; 200Ft), which houses an exhibition of carriages, saddles and other equipment – or you can just wander around the yard and admire the magnificent horses. If you'd rather go for a walk, cross the road running past the mansion's front garden to find a lovely **avenue of limes** that's now a nature conservation area. At the far end of the three-kilometre-long avenue there used to be a cell inhabited by the "Nagycenk Hermit", whom the Széchenyis employed to pump the church organ on Sundays.

Just up the road to the left of the avenue is a shining example of Hungary's heritage industry – the **Széchenyi Railway**. This outdoor museum of **vintage steam trains** comes alive every weekend from April to October, when hundred-year-old engines run along a special line, past fields full of stooks of drying reeds, to terminate at Fertőboz, 4km away, though some turn back earlier. Tickets (400Ft) can only be bought on site, so you'll just have to turn up and hope for the best. Bicycles may be taken on the trains for an additional 160Ft each way.

Count Széchenyi

Count István Széchenyi (1791–1860) was the outstanding figure of Hungary's Reform Era. As a young aide-de-camp he cut a dash at the Congress of Vienna and did the rounds of stately homes across Europe. The "odious Zoltán Karpathy" of Bernard Shaw's *Pygmalion* (and the musical *My Fair Lady*) was based on his exploits in England, where he steeplechased hell for leather, but still found time to examine factories and steam trains. Back in Hungary, he pondered solutions to his homeland's backwardness and offered a year's income from his estates towards the establishment of a Hungarian Academy. In 1830 he published *Hitel* (Credit), a hard-headed critique of the nation's feudal society.

Though politically conservative, Széchenyi was obsessed with **modernization**. A passionate convert to steam power after riding on the Manchester–Liverpool railway, he invited Britons to Hungary to build rail lines and the Chain Bridge. He also imported steamships and dredgers, promoted horsebreeding and silk-making, and initiated the taming of the River Tisza and the blasting of a road through the Iron Gates of the Danube. Alas, his achievements were rewarded by a melancholy end. The 1848 Revolution and the triumph of Kossuth triggered a nervous breakdown, and, although Széchenyi resumed writing after his health improved, he committed suicide during a relapse.

Down in the **village** stands the neo-Romanesque **Church of St Stephen**, designed by Ybl in 1864. Its portal bears the Széchenyi motto "If God is with us, who can be against us?" In the cemetery behind the church stands the **Széchenyi Mausoleum** (May–Oct 10am–6pm; 200Ft), with a chapel decorated by István Dorfmeister, and a crypt including the graves of István and his wife Crescentia Seilern.

The seemingly permanent closure of the once grand *Kastély Hotel* (and its restaurant), located in the west wing of the mansion, means that the only options if you want to stay here are **private rooms** (❷), advertised widely around the village.

Fertőd and the Esterházy Palace

The village of **FERTŐD**, some 15km further east of Nagycenk, began life as an appendage to the palace and was known as "Esterháza" until the family decamped in 1945. As you enter the village, postwar housing gives way to stately public buildings endowed by the Esterházys, presaging the palace at the eastern end – which is impossible to miss so long as you stay on the main street.

The Esterházy Palace

Built on malarial swampland drained by hundreds of serfs, the **Esterházy Palace** was intended to rival Versailles and remove any arriviste stigma from the dynasty (see box below). Gala balls and concerts, hunting parties and masquerades were held here even before it was completed in 1776, continuing without a let-up until the death of Prince Miklós "the Ostentatious" in 1790. Neglected by his successor, who dissolved the orchestra and moved his court back to Eisenstadt, the palace rapidly decayed. Its picture gallery, puppet theatre and Chinese pavilions disappeared, while its salons became storerooms and stables. Though basic repairs were made after World War II, restoration only began in earnest in the 1950s, and is still unfinished due to the prodigious cost.

Ornate Rococo wrought-iron gates lead into a vast horseshoe courtyard where hussars once pranced to the music of Haydn, Esterházy's resident maestro. The U-shaped wings and ceremonial stairway sweep up to a three-storey Baroque facade, whose distinctive rich ochre colour has recently been repainted a rather more sombre grey. **Guided tours** (every 40min; April–Oct Tues–Sun 10am–6pm; Nov–March Fri–Sun 10am–4pm; 1000Ft) cover 23 of the 126

The Esterházy family

Originally of the minor nobility, the **Esterházy family** began its rise thanks to **Miklós I** (1583–1645), who married two rich widows and sided with the Habsburgs against Transylvania during the Counter-Reformation, for which he was rewarded with the title of count. His son Paul was content to make his mark by publishing a songbook, *Harmonia Celestis*; but **Miklós II** "the Ostentatious" (1714–90) celebrated his inheritance of 600,000 acres and a dukedom by commissioning the palace in 1762. Boasting "anything the Kaiser can do, I can do better!", he spent 40,000 gulden a year on pomp and entertainment. Thereafter the family gradually declined, until under the Communists they were expropriated and "un-personed". Today, one descendant drives trams in Vienna, while two others (from a separate branch of the family) are respected figures back home: the writer **Péter Esterházy** and his cousin, **Marton Esterházy**, formerly centre forward on the national football team. Internationally, however, the best-known bearer of the family name is **Joe Esterhasz**, the Hollywood scriptwriter of *Basic Instinct* and *Showgirls*.

rooms in the palace, whose decaying splendour speaks of its one-time magnificence. The highlights of the ground floor are the panelled and gilded **Sala Terrena** and several blue-and-white **chinoiserie salons**, their walls painted by fairly mediocre artists – unlike the superb fresco on the ceiling of the **Banqueting Hall** upstairs, by J.B. Grundemann, which is so contrived that Apollo's chariot seems to be careering towards you across the sky whatever angle you view it from.

An adjacent room displays **Haydn memorabilia** from the period following his appointment as the Esterházy *Kapellmeister* in 1761, though the exhibition mainly consists of photocopied texts and old Hungaroton record sleeves. Haydn subsequently took over the direction of palace orchestra, opera house and marionette theatre, and wrote six great masses for performance here between 1796 and 1802. The palace also witnessed the premiere of Beethoven's Mass in C, personally conducted by the maestro in 1807. **Concerts** (5000Ft) are held here during July and August, usually on Friday, Saturday and Sunday evenings; tickets can be purchased from the palace. The tour over, you can wander around the **French Gardens** at the back, although these can be visited free of charge anyway.

Practicalities

Arriving at the Fertőszéplak-Fertőd **train station**, it's a long thirty-minute walk (turn right as you exit the station) along Fő utca to the centre of Fertőd. Far more convenient are **buses**, which stop outside the palace gates. Tourinform is located opposite the gates at Haydn utca 3 (April–Oct Mon–Sat 9am–5pm; Nov–March Tues–Sat 10am–4pm; Ⓣ99/370-544, Ⓔfertod@tourinform.hu). There are several **accommodation** possibilities in the village, including two very pleasant pensions: the *Újvári Panzió*, about 500m from the palace at Kossuth utca 57a (Ⓣ99/537-097, Ⓦwww.hotels.hu/ujvari_fertod; ❸), whose genial host will ensure that you have a most accommodating stay; and the *Kata Vendégház*, 1km down Vasút utca at Mikes Kelemen utca 2 (Ⓣ99/370-857, Ⓦwww.hotels.hu/kata_fertod; ❸), which has large rooms and shared bathrooms plus use of the kitchen and living room. A third option is the *Dori Hotel*, a bizarre-looking wooden structure near the palace at Pomogyi utca 1 (Ⓣ99/370-838; Ⓦwww.hotels.hu/dori; ❹); it also has a campsite (mid-April to mid-Oct) and chalets (❸-❺) sleeping up to seven people.

The *Kastélykert* and *Gránátos* **restaurants** (both daily 10am–10pm), both serving stock Hungarian meals, are sited just outside the palace. You can grab a simple snack at the *Joco Ételbár*, Fő utca 24 (daily 9am–midnight), and coffee and pastries at *Elit*, Fő utca 1 (daily 8am–10pm). For really good local food, however, it's worth travelling 2km down the road towards Sopron, to the village of **Fertőszéplak**, where you'll find the *Polgármester Vendéglő* up behind the church at Széchenyi utca 39 (daily 10am–10pm).

Kőszeg and around

Nestled amidst the sub-Alpine hills along the Austrian border, the small town of **KŐSZEG**, 50km south of Sopron, cherishes its status as the "Hungarian Thermopylae", and a town centre which can justifiably claim to be one of the prettiest in Hungary. While its castle recalls the medieval Magyar heroism that saved Vienna from the Turks, its Baroque houses and *bürgerlich* ambience reflect centuries of Austrian and German influence, when Kőszeg was known

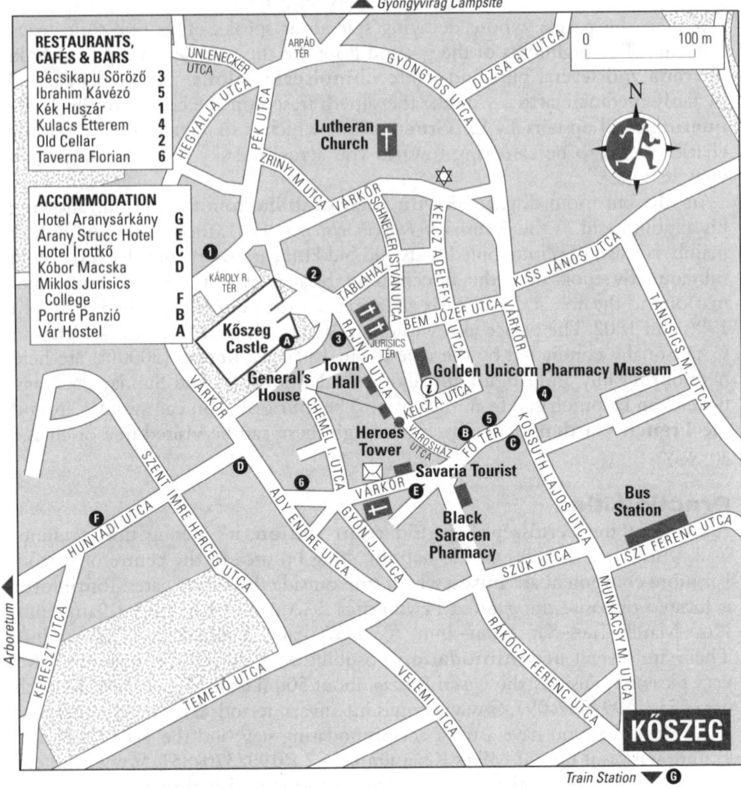

as Güns. Despite a summer blitzkrieg of tourists that briefly arouses excitement and avarice, this is basically a sleepy, old-fashioned town where people still leave cartons of raspberries and blackberries outside their houses and trust you to leave money for it.

Arrival and information

On **arrival** at Kőszeg's bus station on Liszt Ferenc utca, walk 150m up Kossuth utca to the Várkör, a horseshoe-shaped road that follows the course of the long-demolished medieval town walls; most things of interest lie within this area. Arriving at the train station 1.5km to the south of town, take a bus as far as the junction of Fő tér and the Várkör.

The Tourinform office at Jurisics tér 7 (mid-June to mid-Sept Mon–Fri 8am–6pm, Sat 9am–1pm; mid-Sept to mid-June Mon–Fri 8am–4pm; Ⓣ94/563-120, Ⓦwww.koszeg.hu) also doubles up as the Írottkő Natúrpark Information Centre (Ⓦwww.naturpark.hu), and so can advise on information on both the town and the outlying regions, including suggested walks – they also have **bikes** for hire (1500Ft per day). If you're planning to visit all four of Kőszeg's museums, it makes sense to buy a **day ticket** (*napibérlet*; 500Ft) which covers them all, available from the General's House by the entrance to the Heroes' Tower. The **post office** is opposite the church at Várkör 65 (Mon–Fri 8am–4pm, Sat 8am–noon).

Accommodation

There's ample **accommodation** to go around in Kőszeg, all of it very affordable. The *Vár Hostel* (☎94/360-227; dorm bed 2000Ft, doubles ❶), inside the yard through the first gate of the castle, is cheap but a bit of a shambles and has shared showers. There are also beds available during July and August at the *Miklos Jurisics College* at Hunyadi János utca 10 (☎94/361-404; 1400Ft per person). Although they don't offer private rooms, Savaria Tourist at Várkör 69 (Mon–Fri 8am–4pm, Sat 8am–noon; ☎94/563-048, ⓔtompasav@matavnet.hu) do have three-bed apartments (❸) in town. The small but neat and idyllic *Gyöngyvirág* **campsite**, at Bajcsy-Zsilinszky utca 6, also has rooms in its adjoining pension (☎94/360-454, ⓦwww.gyongyviragpanzio.hu; ❷).

Hotel Aranysárkány Rákóczi Ferenc utca 120 ☎94/362-296, ⓦwww.clubhotel-aranysarkany.hu. Agreeable, and cheap, pension-type place near the train station with neat, pine-furnished rooms. ❸
Arany Strucc Hotel Várkör 124 ☎94/360-323, ⓦwww.hotels.hu/aranystrucc. One of the oldest hotels in Hungary, "The Golden Ostrich" is a characterful place with fairly simple double rooms with showers; the bigger rooms have minibar. ❹
Hotel Írottkő Fő tér 4 ☎94/360-373, ⓦwww.hotelirottko.hu. Characterless hotel on the main square, with tatty, musty-smelling rooms with either bath or shower. Triples are good value. ❹
Kóbor Macska Várkör 100 ☎94/362-273, ⓦwww.hotels.hu/kobor. Eighteenth-century inn occupying a splendid spot just to the west of the inner town; large rooms with showers literally *in* the bedroom and shared toilets. Breakfast not included. ❸
Portré Panzió Fő tér 7 ☎94/363-170, ⓦwww.portre.com. Stylish pension on the main square, with sunny yellow-and-blue rooms, subtly furnished with wooden desks and chairs, and smart rugs. ❹

The Town

The focal point of the town, and hub of most of the activity, is **Fő tér**, whose main landmark is the **Church of the Sacred Heart**, built in 1894 and worth a peek to see the fancifully patterned interior. Off to the west of Fő tér, Városház utca leads up to the 27-metre-high **Heroes' Tower** (Hősök kapuja; Tues–Sun 10am–5pm; 200Ft). Erected to mark the four-hundredth anniversary of the siege of Kőszeg, this fake medieval portal was one of several commemorative gates raised in the 1920s and 1930s, when Hungary was gripped by nostalgia for bygone glories and resentment towards the Successor States. The entrance to the tower is via the former Baroque **General's House** (Tábornok Ház; Tues–Fri 10am–5pm, Sat 10am–1pm; 460Ft), containing several rooms of exhibits on bookbinding, carpentry and other historic guilds and crafts.

Beyond the archway lies **Jurisics tér**, an engaging cobbled square whose antique buildings are watched over by two churches and a limestone-carved Trinity statue. The most eye-catching facades are those of the seventeenth-century **Town Hall** (embellished with oval portraits of the Hungarian coat of arms, the Virgin and Child and St Stephen) and the so-called **Lada House** at no. 12, whose interesting features include heraldic figures, angels' heads, and a niche with a statue of St Imre. Across the square, at no. 7, is a beautifully sgraffitoed building (now a pizzeria), where the pillory stood in medieval times, and, further along at no. 11, is the **Golden Unicorn Pharmacy Museum** (Patikamúzeum; March–Nov daily 10am–5pm; 360Ft), which preserves an eighteenth-century apothecary. The superb oak and chestnut furnishings were removed from the Jesuit Cloister in 1773 following the dissolution of the order, and brought to the pharmacy a few years later when it was opened – you can have a look, too, at the upstairs drying area, where the raw materials were cleaned, chopped and stored. There's another, much smaller, such establishment, the **Black Saracen Pharmacy**, at Rákóczi utca 3 (April–Nov Tues–Fri 1–5pm; 360Ft), just south of Fő tér.

Past Jurisics tér's fountain, the Baroque **Church of St Imre** precedes the older **Church of St James**, a handsome Gothic edifice containing the tomb of Miklós Jurisics (see below) and some barely discernible frescoes dating back to 1403, the year the church was built. From here you can head north to Várkör, where you'll find a former **synagogue** at no. 38, which can only be viewed from the street. Built in 1859, the redbrick complex resembles an outlying bastion, having two crenellated towers with slit windows, and originally included a *yeshiva* and a ritual bath. Its dereliction is a sad reminder of the provincial Jewish communities that never recovered from the Holocaust, for – unlike the Budapest ghetto – their extermination was scheduled for the summer of 1944, when Eichmann's death-machine still ran at full throttle. Indeed, many of the buildings in this part of the inner town are in a similarly terrible state, with some completely gutted. Oddly, a **Lutheran bell-tower** stands next to the synagogue. When the Lutheran church behind it was built in 1783, József II had decreed that non-Catholic churches could not have bell-towers or steeples; this bell-tower was only built in 1930.

From Várkör you can head up Hunyadi utca to the west for ten minutes, passing a number of fortress-like villas, to the **Chernel Arboretum** of sub-Alpine trees (Chernel-Kert; Mon–Thurs 9am–3pm, Fri till 1pm); towards the rear of the gardens is a one-roomed museum dedicated to the works of local ornithologist István Chernel (same times; 200Ft). Heading the same distance in the opposite direction you'll come to the outdoor **swimming pool**, across the river: follow Kiss János utca eastwards from Várkör – a signpost in Fő tér points towards the *strand*. Otherwise, head back the other way to the castle.

The Castle

The Turks swore that **Kőszeg Castle** was "built at the foot of a mountain difficult to climb; its walls wider than the whole world, its bastions higher than the fish of the Zodiac in heaven, and so strong that it defies description". Since the castle is actually quite small, with not a mountain in sight, the hyperbole is probably explained by its heroic defence during the month-long **siege of 1532**, when Sultan Süleyman and a hundred thousand Turks were resisted by four hundred soldiers under Captain Miklós Jurisics. After nineteen assaults the Sultan abandoned campaigning until the following year, by which time Vienna was properly defended. Today's visitors to the castle won't find anything dramatic when they cross the grassy moat into an ugly yard that postwar additions have done nothing to enhance, although its **museum** (Tues–Sun 10am–5pm; 460Ft) has a reasonable display of military relics and various properties of town officers, as well as the "Grape Book" – a log book which has documented, largely in the form of sketches, European viticulture since 1740 and is still updated every year on St George's Day. In summer the castle really comes to life with the staging of **medieval games** in the moat and concerts in the yard (see opposite).

Eating, drinking and entertainment

The best **restaurants** in town are the *Taverna Florian* at Várkör 59, a smart place serving Mediterranean cuisine (Tues–Sat 5–10pm, Fri, Sat & Sun also 11.30am–2.30pm), and the one in the *Portré Panzió* (see p.277), which sports a garden terrace and pavement café (daily 8am–10pm). Two humbler places are the *Kulacs Étterem* at Várkör 12 (daily 10am–9pm), which is also good for a lighter snack, and the *Kék Huszár* on Károly Róbert tér behind the castle, which has an agreeable straw-covered beer garden (daily 11am–9pm).

The pace of life here dictates that **drinking** options are few and far between. Aside from the bar at the *Portré*, you could try the *Bécsikapu Söröző*, opposite St James' Church at Rajnis utca 5 (daily 11am–10pm), or the beer garden at the back of the *Kék Huszár*. If you enjoy quaffing wine in medieval surroundings, the vaulted ceiling and high Gothic windows of the *Old Cellar* at Rajnis utca 10 (daily 9am–9pm) provide an ideal setting. The best coffee and strudel is to be had at the *Ibrahim Kávézó*, a few paces along from the *Portré Panzió* on Fő tér, whose long, narrow and dark wood-panelled interior leads to a lovely terrace area (daily 8am–10pm). There's coffee, hot chocolate, cakes and pastries at Soproni Zoltán's lovely old-fashioned shop at Rákóczi utca 4 (Mon–Fri 5am–noon & 12.30–4pm, Sat 5am–noon).

Wine lovers are well catered for in Kőszeg, with the **Grape Festival** on April 24 celebrated with events such as wine contests, concerts and folklore programmes, and a **Wine Festival** on the last weekend of September featuring a carnival, brass band and horse shows. The **Summer Festival** takes place in July and August, with theatre and opera in the castle yard.

Around Kőszeg: Cak, Velem and Bozsok

There are plenty of opportunities for **hiking** in the delightful countryside, with a well-signposted trail through the hills to the **Óház lookout tower**, 5km away. Set out along Temetö utca and then head back into town past the Fountain of the Seven Leaders, a spring with seven waterspouts named after the Magyar tribal chieftains, and a church with shrines of the stages of the cross. At the bottom of the hill you can turn left to reach a boating lake, or bear right for town, passing a chamber in the hillside where **St Stephen's Crown** was hidden for ten days in 1945, as it was being smuggled out of Hungary.

If you want to explore further afield, there are three attractive villages grouped south of Kőszeg. Local buses bound for Velem can drop you off in the pretty village of **CÁK**, 6km south of Kőszeg, with a protected row of old thatched cottages at Petőfi utca 19 (Szabadtéri Muzeűm; April–Oct Tues–Sun 10am–6pm; 200Ft), actually little more than wattle-and-daub hovels with straw hats on, used at one time for wine-making and storage. The *Csikő Csárda* (daily 11am–10pm), near the bus stop at the entrance to the village, is a good place for lunch, and if you want to continue you can pick up the walking trails, marked with a yellow stripe, to the neighbouring villages of Bozsok and Velem.

VELEM, 4km further down the road, is famous for its handicrafts and on August 20 each year holds the **Craftsmen's Feast** at the Creative House, where the traditional crafts and trades of the village are celebrated, along with wine drinking and other folklore programmes. At the entrance to the village is the sprawling **Millennium Memorial Park and Holiday Village** (Milleniumi Emlékpark és Űdűlőfalu), a somewhat kitsch assemblage of mini attractions – including a Dolls Museum and waxworks exhibition – built to commemorate the Hungarian millennium in 2001. The bulk of the site, however, is consumed by the holiday village (Ⓣ94/360-035; ❺), which comprises over fifty small, wood-furnished, two-bed houses, each with a small kitchen and dining area – there are also five larger houses for families. You'll also find a large, rustically-styled restaurant here. If you don't fancy this, there is the *Borőka Villa* at Kossuth utca 8 (Ⓣ94/360-036; ❸), while village tourism is flourishing here and you'll find many houses advertising rooms for the night.

Five kilometres further to the southwest is **BOZSOK**, basically a one-street village with a seventeenth-century manor house set in a lovely park at Rákóczi utca 1. It now serves as the very bland *Sibrik Castle Hotel* (Ⓣ &

Ⓕ94/360-960; ❹), while, in the same grounds, the Dobrádi Riding School offers **riding lessons** and trips in the region (daily: April–Oct 9am–noon & 2–6pm; Nov–March 10am–noon & 2–5pm; Ⓣ94/363-342). A cheaper option is the *Szilvia Panzió* at Rákóczi utca 120 (Ⓣ94/361-009; ❷), which also has **camping** facilities (April–Oct), or you could opt for a bed in one of the many houses along this street offering rooms. For **refreshments** head to the *Aranypatak* at Rákóczi utca 29, or the *Imperial Pub*, 500m further along the road at no. 101.

Szombathely and around

Commerce has been the lifeblood of **SZOMBATHELY** ("Saturday market") ever since the town was founded by Emperor Claudius in 43 AD to capitalize on the Amber Road from the Baltic to the Mediterranean. Savaria, as it was then called, soon became the capital of Pannonia, and a significant city in the Roman Empire. It was here that Septimus Severus was proclaimed emperor in 193 AD and Saint Martin of Tours was born in 317. Under Frankish rule in the eighth century, the town, known as Steinamanger, prospered through trade with Germany. Nowadays, it is Austrians who boost the economy, flooding across to shop, get their hair done or seek medical treatment in the town which they have nicknamed "the discount store".

From a tourist's standpoint, the chief attractions are the outdoor **Village Museum** (Skanzen) and **Roman ruins**, and a **Belváros** stuffed with Baroque and Neoclassical architecture. Szombathely is also the base for a side-trip to the beautiful Romanesque church at **Ják** and, further out, the spa and castle at **Sárvár**, home of the infamous "Blood Countess" Báthori. If you're here at **Easter** time, there are colourful religious processions in Szombathely and other towns in the region.

Arrival and information

Arriving at the **train station**, walk west along Széll Kálmán utca – 100m to the left of the station as you exit – to get to the centre (just under 1km), or catch a #2, #3, #5, #7, #7Y or #11 bus to Mártírok tere, close to Fő tér. The intercity **bus station** is next to the Romkert, just ten minutes' walk west of Fő tér.

The Tourinform office is located on the southwestern corner of Fő tér at Kossuth utca 1–3 (Mon–Fri 9am–5pm; Ⓣ94/514-451, Ⓔszombathely@tourinform.hu). Train information and tickets are available from MÁV Tours at Király utca 8 (Mon–Fri 8.30am–4.30pm). The **post office** is at Kossuth utca 18 (Mon–Fri 8am–6pm, Sat 8am–noon) and there's **Internet access** at *Internet Pont* on the corner of Kossuth utca and Kiskar utca (Mon–Sat noon–midnight, Sun 6pm–midnight).

Accommodation

The cheapest form of accommodation is dormitory **beds** in one of the three centrally located colleges – available over summer and at weekends all year round through Ibusz at Fő tér 44 (Mon–Fri 8.30am–4.30pm, Sat 8.30am–noon; Ⓣ94/314-141, Ⓔi090@ibusz.hu), who can also book private rooms (❷). *Tópart* **camping** at Kenderesi utca 14 (Ⓣ94/509-039; May–Sept) has chalets sleeping two to three (❷) or four to five (❹); it's a ten-minute walk north of the *Hotel Claudius*, by the Anglers' Lake.

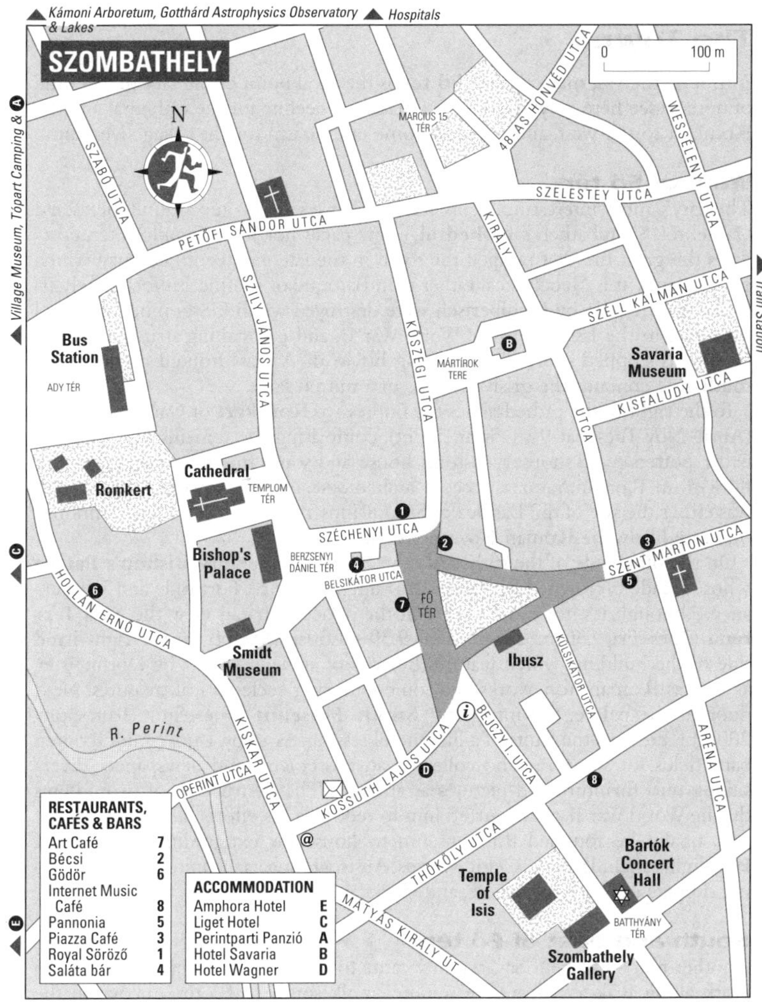

Amphora Hotel Dósza György utca 9 ⓣ94/512-712, ⓕ94/512-714. Elegant little hotel ten minutes' walk west of Fő tér across the river, with ultramodern, immaculately turned out, air-conditioned rooms. ❺

Liget Hotel Szent István park 15 ⓣ94/509-323, ⓦwww.hotels.hu/liget_szombathely. Motel-style place west of the centre by the lake. As imaginably dull as could be, with appallingly decorated rooms, but it is cheap. No extras in the rooms. ❸

Perintparti Panzió Kunos Endre utca 3 ⓣ94/339-265. Unfussy five-room place just 300m west of the bus station, across the river. Good value. ❸

Hotel Savaria Mártírok tere 4 ⓣ94/311-440, ⓦwww.savariahotel.hu. This hulk of a building dominating the ugly square has very dated but large and surprisingly comfortable rooms, with and without shower. ❹–❺

Hotel Wagner Kossuth Lajos utca 15 ⓣ94/322-208, ⓦwww.hotelwagner.hu. This small, compact hotel has class stamped all over it; beautifully styled, air-conditioned rooms with lush green carpets, desks with table lamps and safes. ❻

The Town

Although the vast main square, **Fő ter**, is the focal point of the city, there's little of note to see here, so you're best off making a beeline for the cathedral and the Romkert to the west, and conserve some enthusiasm for the Village Museum.

West of Fő tér

The city's most interesting sights lie to the west of Fő tér around Berzsenyi Dániel tér. Szombathely's **cathedral**, a few paces north on Templom tér, post-dates the great fire that ravaged the town in the late eighteenth century, which explains why it is Neoclassical rather than Baroque or Gothic. Unfortunately, its exuberant frescoes by Maulbertsch were destroyed when US bombers attacked the town in the last months of World War II, and painstaking structural restoration has stopped short of re-creating his work. A glass-fronted coffin in the south aisle contains the grisly remains of a mitred saint.

To the right of the cathedral lies the impressive **Romkert** or Garden of Ruins (April–Nov Tues–Sat 9am–5pm; 300Ft), comprising the remains of the public baths, potters' workshops, a customs house and some fine segments of mosaic floor from Roman Savaria. Recent archeological research would suggest this was either the site of the Basilica of St Quirinus, the largest church in Pannonia, or, more likely, the Roman Governor's Palace.

On the other side of the cathedral is an eighteenth-century **Bishop's Palace** whose facade is crowned by statues of Prudence, Justice, Fortitude and Temperance. Although it's not possible to visit the palace, you can view the **Sala Terrena** (Tues–Fri 9.30am–3.30pm, Sat 9.30–11.30am; 200Ft) on the right-hand side of the building, which features frescoes of ancient Savaria by Dorfmeister, as well as Roman stoneworks and some glittering ecclesiastical treasures. Next door to the palace, the intriguing **Smidt Museum** (Tues–Sun 10am–5pm; 200Ft) represents the fruits of a lifelong obsession. As a boy, Lajos Smidt scoured battlefields for souvenirs and collected advertisements and newspapers, diversifying into furniture and pictures as an adult. The destruction of many items during World War II only spurred him to redouble his efforts during retirement and, finally, he founded this museum to house his extraordinary collection. Highlights include huge Celtic swords, Austro-Hungarian uniforms, the dancing slippers of Széchenyi's wife, and clocks galore.

South and east of Fő tér

Another relic of ancient Savaria only came to light in 1955, when construction work along Rákóczi utca, five minutes' walk south of Fő tér, uncovered the **Temple of Isis**, dating from the second century AD, one of only three such temples extant in Europe. It's not possible to visit the ruins up close, but you can get good views from the balcony of the adjacent **Szombathely Gallery** (Tues–Sun 10am–5pm, till 7pm on Wed; 300Ft), which hosts an exhaustive display of modern art from the 1920s through to the present day, dominated by abstract and avant-garde works, and a stylish contemporary textile collection.

Across the road from the gallery stands Szombathely's former **synagogue**, a lovely piece of neo-Byzantine architecture, built in 1881 and now home to the **Bartók Concert Hall** and music college. Sadly, all that now remains of the town's Jewish presence is a plaque recording that "4228 of our Jewish brothers and sisters were deported from this place to Auschwitz on 4 June, 1944".

A five-minute walk to the northeast of Fő tér, at Kisfaludy utca 9, is the **Savaria Museum** (mid-April to mid-Oct Tues–Fri 10am–5pm, Sat & Sun 10am–4pm; mid-Oct to mid-April Tues–Fri 10am–5pm; 460Ft), which presents

Szombathely's history largely in the form of archeological and ethnographical displays, though it couldn't be duller if it tried.

Beyond the Belváros

Szombathely's northern suburbs harbour two more attractions which can be reached by bus #2 from Petőfi utca. The **Kámoni Arboretum** (April to mid-Oct Mon–Fri 8am–6pm, Sat & Sun 9am–6pm; mid-Oct to March daily 8am–4pm; 200Ft) contains 2500 different kinds of trees, shrubs and flowers, with an especially varied assortment of roses, while just up the road is the grandly named **Gotthárd Astrophysics Observatory** (Csillag Vizsgáló; Mon–Fri 9am–4pm; 300Ft), with an interesting exhibition on cosmology.

Northwest of the centre lie the **Rowing Lake** (Csónakázótó) and the **Anglers' Lake** (Horgásztó), two smallish ponds where locals fish and go boating near an outdoor **thermal bath** (mid-May to Sept Mon–Fri 9am–7pm, Sat & Sun 9am–5.30pm). Bus #7 takes you to both lakes and to the **Village Museum** (Skanzen) at Árpád utca 30, beyond the Anglers' Lake (April–Oct Tues–Sun 9am–5pm; 400Ft). Eighteenth- and nineteenth-century farmsteads are reconstructed here, culled from 27 villages in the Őrség region, and furnished with all the necessities and knick-knacks, making an architectural progression from log cabins to timber-framed wattle-and-daub dwellings. Every other month there are demonstrations of traditional folk crafts and dances of the region.

The green-belt district south of the lakes includes a small **game park** (Vadaszkert) with deer, pheasants and other wildlife – nothing to get too excited about, but a nice place for a picnic. The park is situated on Víztorony utca, southwest of the *Liget Hotel*; alight from bus #7 on Jókai utca and walk past the water tower, continuing for ten minutes.

Eating and drinking

Szombathely has a handful of terrific **restaurants**, the best of which can be found in the *Hotel Wagner*, where a beautifully appointed dining area is the setting for Hungarian cuisine of great distinction, including an above-average vegetarian menu (daily 9am–11pm, Sun till 4pm). Two other very accomplished places are the cool *Piazza Café* on Savaria tér (daily 8am–10pm), offering a delectable fusion of Mediterranean and Oriental food, and, just across the road next to *McDonald's*, the *Pannonia* which, with its thick wooden beams, bench seating and soothing lighting, is an ideal venue to indulge in the exceptional dishes of game, poultry and fish. In addition, the restaurant has a small wine shop (daily 10am–midnight). The *Gödör*, at Hollán Ernő utca 10–12 – sister restaurant to the *Jégverem* in Sopron (see p.271) – is a huge and immensely enjoyable cellar restaurant, serving roisteringly hearty meals (daily 11am–11pm, Fri & Sat till midnight, Sun till 3pm). A quick and cheap option is the *Saláta bár* at the end of Belsikátor utca, ideal for sit-down or takeaway salads (Mon–Fri 8am–6pm, Sat 8am–2pm).

During the summer, most people congregate in the pavement **cafés** on Fő tér, by far the most popular of which is the elegant *Art Café* (Mon–Sat 7.30am–midnight, Sun 9am–10pm) on the western side of the square. Alternatively, there's the *Royal Söröző* on the north side, which has draught beer and also serves meals, and the *Bécsi*, opposite. The *Internet Music Café*, at Thököly utca 32 (daily noon–2am), is a genuine, and very enjoyable, drinking den, secreted away down some stairs, with a dimly lit ambience and a good choice of beers – there are also a couple of terminals for Internet access.

Festivals

The town stages several major cultural events, the most important of which are the **Spring Days** in late March, the **International Dance Festival** in June, and, biggest and best of all, the **Savaria Historical Carnival** at the end of August, featuring medieval theatre, music and food, and a final, spectacular torch-lit procession. There is a strong musical tradition in Szombathely, and the town even has its own orchestra, the **Savaria Symphony**, and an early music ensemble, the Capella Savaria. The international **Bartók Festival** in mid-July is another highlight, with a two-week series of seminars and concerts. At other times of the year, check out what's happening at the Bartók Concert Hall, the hideous 1960s **Cultural Centre** on Március 15 tér, or the cultural hall on Ady tér, west of the bus station.

Ják

With hourly buses from Szombathely to the village of **JÁK**, 10km southwest, you can easily pay a visit to Hungary's most outstanding **Romanesque abbey church** (daily: April–Oct 8am–6pm; Nov–March 10am–2pm; free), which is far more impressive than the scaled-down replica in Budapest's Városliget. The church is sited on a hilltop overlooking the feudal domain of its founder Márton Nagy (1220–56), who personally checked that his serfs attended Sunday services – and whipped any who failed to do so.

The church is similar in plan to its ruined contemporaries at Lébény (see p.263), and likewise influenced by the Scottish Benedictine church in Regensburg, the point from which Norman architecture spread into Central Europe. It was restored in the 1890s by Frigyes Schulek, the architect of the Fishermen's Bastion in Budapest, who added the stumpy spires atop Ják's towers. The church's most striking feature is the magnificent **portal** on the western facade, where Christ and his apostles surmount a six-ordered Norman zigzag arch. Inside, the barely visible **frescoes**, and the exquisite medieval **altarpiece** in the north aisle (recently discovered in the nearby church of St James), can be viewed by depositing a 100Ft coin in the slot. Behind the church is the former **abbott's residence**, which displays a handful of locally excavated artefacts. Although there's no real reason to stay here, there is the *Jaki Turistaház* (Ⓣ94/321-436; ❷), just below the church on the main road, as well as several *Zimmer frei* signs around the village.

Sárvár

SÁRVÁR, 25km east of Szombathely on the River Rába, and accessible by hourly trains and buses, is the most recently developed **spa centre** in Hungary, following the discovery of hot springs over 25 years ago. The spas were developed to attract hard currency from German and Austrian tourists and still do a roaring trade, but aside from wallowing and quaffing, the town's only real attraction is the fortress that gives Sárvár its name – "**Mud Castle**".

Arrival and information

The **train station** is 800m to the north of town on Selyemgyár utca – take bus #1 or #1V, or it's a ten-minute walk along Hunyadi János utca and Batthyány utca towards the castle; the **bus station** is 500m west along Batthyány utca. Tourinform is located opposite the castle entrance at Várkerület 33 (July & Aug Mon–Fri 9am–5pm, Sat 9am–1pm, rest of year Mon–Fri 9am–4pm; Ⓣ95/520-178, Ⓔsarvar@tourinform.hu), while the main **post office** is next door at no. 32 (Mon–Fri 8am–7pm, Sat 8am–noon).

Accommodation

Thanks mainly to the baths, there's stacks of accommodation in town and even during the busiest period in August you shouldn't have a problem finding somewhere to stay. **Private rooms** (❷) are available through Savaria Tourist, next to Tourinform (May–Sept Mon–Fri 8am–5pm, Sat 8am–noon; Oct–April Mon–Fri 8.30am–4.30pm; Ⓣ95/320-578, Ⓦwww.savariatourist-sarvar.hu), or there's tent-space at the year-round *Sárvár* **campsite** behind the baths at Vadkert utca 1 (Ⓣ95/326-502, Ⓔinfo@sarvarfurdo.hu), which has chalets sleeping two (❸); the site can be reached by taking bus #1Y to the end of the line.

Hotel Arborétum Medgyessy Ferenc utca 20 Ⓣ95/520-630, Ⓦwww.hotelarboretum.hu. Tucked away on a quiet residential street behind the arboretum, this great-value place has cool, ultra-modern rooms. ❺

Platán Hotel Hunyadi János utca 23 Ⓣ95/326-484, Ⓦwww.platanhotel.hu. Between the train station and the centre, this delightful small hotel has generously sized rooms with pristine bathrooms, designer beds and minibar; also has a great café and restaurant (see p.286). ❺

Szieszta Panzió Rákóczi út 57a Ⓣ95/320-456, Ⓕ326-927. On the main road out towards the baths, this place has lounge-type rooms with sofa and small balcony; included in the price is use of the two pools and whirlpool – a water-lovers' paradise. ❺

Hotel Thermal Rákóczi út 1 Ⓣ95/888-400, Ⓦwww.danubiusgroup.com/sarvar. Supremely comfortable place with its own indoor and outdoor thermal pools, sauna, gym and curative facilities. ❽

Tinódi Panzió Hunyadi János utca 11 Ⓣ95/323-606, Ⓦwww.tinodifogado.hu. 200m up from the *Platán*, this place has minimal but colourful rooms, with small beds and small bathrooms. ❹

Wolf Panzió Rákóczi út 11 Ⓣ95/321-499, Ⓦwww.wolfhotel.hu. Big, blue-furnished rooms with more than ample cupboard space, TV and fridge. The same owners run the slightly smarter *Wolf Hotel* (❺) across the road at Alkotmány utca 4 (Ⓣ95/320-460). ❹

The Town

Though the term "Mud Castle" might have been appropriate in the Dark Ages, it hardly applies to **Sárvár Castle** today, which stands in the heart of the town encircled by the Várkerület. Modified by many owners over the centuries, its pentagonal layout and palatial interior are owed to the **Nádasdy family**, particularly Tamás Nádasdy, who hired Italian architects and made this a centre of Renaissance humanism. It was here that the first Hungarian translation of the New Testament was printed in 1541. The **Festival Hall** is decorated with Dorfmeister frescoes of biblical episodes, allegories of art and science, and murals depicting the "Black Knight" Ferenc Nádasdy routing the Turks. The **Ferenc Nádasdy Museum** (Tues–Sun 9am–5pm; 200Ft), inside the castle, displays a voluminous array of weapons, uniforms and memorabilia associated with Tamás and his son Ferenc, but barely a reference to the latter's wife, the infamous Countess Báthori (see box on p.286).

The former castle gardens across the Várkerület to the east are now a large **arboretum** (daily: April–Oct 9am–7pm, Nov–March till 5pm; 200Ft), which has been a protected reserve since 1952, though its oldest trees date from the eighteenth century. Now, these extensive gardens feature black pines, Japanese acacia, ash and yew trees, as well as a beautiful collection of azaleas and magnolias. From the arboretum it's nearly 1km along Rákóczi utca to the **thermal baths** (daily 8am–10pm; 1400Ft, 600Ft after 8pm) at Vadkert utca 1. The renovated complex includes three indoor pools and several outdoor pools (May–Sept), a sauna centre (900Ft), and numerous special treatment facilities. For something a little more animated, the owners of the *Vadkert Fogadó*, just behind the baths on Vadkert utca, run a **riding school** (daily 8am–4pm; 1500Ft per hour; Ⓣ95/320-045) and also have **tennis courts** for use.

Countess Erzsébet Báthori

Countess Erzsébet Báthori has gone down in history as *Die Blutgräfin* (The Blood Countess), who tortured to death over six hundred women and girls, sometimes biting chunks of flesh from their necks and breasts – the origin of legends that she bathed in the blood of virgins to keep her own skin white and translucent. Yet there's a strong case that the accusations arose from a conspiracy against her by the Palatine of Hungary, **Count Thurzó**, and her own son-in-law, Miklós Zrínyi, grandson of the hero of Szigetvár.

Born in 1560, the offspring of two branches of the Báthori family (whose intermarriage might explain several cases of lunacy in the dynasty), Erzsébet was married at the age of fifteen to Ferenc Nádasdy and assumed responsibility for their vast estates, which she inherited upon his death in 1604. To the chagrin of her sons-in-law and the Palatine, she refused to surrender any of them. Worse still from a Habsburg standpoint, the election of her nephew, "Crazy" Gábor Báthori, as Prince of Transylvania raised the prospect of a Báthori alliance that would upset the balance of power and border defences on which Habsburg rule depended.

In December 1610 Thurzó raided her residence at Aachtice, and claimed to have caught her literally red-handed. Under torture, her associates testified to scores of **secret burials** at Sárvár, Aachtice and elsewhere, and the Countess was immediately walled up in a room at Aachtice, where she died in 1614. Although Thurzó amassed nearly three hundred depositions, no trial was ever held, as the death of Gábor Báthori reduced her political significance to the point that it served nobody's interests to besmirch the Nádasdy and Báthori names.

While there's little doubt that there was a **conspiracy** against the Countess, it's hard to believe that she was totally innocent. There were accusations of her cruelty at Sárvár even before her widowhood, and the theory that the tortures were actually medical treatments doesn't explain the most atrocious cases. Probably the best one can say is that she was a victim of double standards in an era when brutality was rife and the power of nobles unbridled.

Eating, drinking and entertainment

There's a definite shortage of really good **restaurants** in town. The best one is the *Várkapu*, just west of the castle at Várkerület 5 (daily 8.30am–10pm), whose varied menu includes fish, rabbit, duck and that most rare of meats in Hungary, lamb; you can dine in its refined interior or on the stylish outdoor terrace. Otherwise, the restaurants in the *Platán Hotel* and *Tinódi Panzió* are worth trying, the former specializing in game dishes (daily 10am–10pm). The *Platán* also has the best **café** in town, while the *Tercia cukrászda*, in the baths complex, has some delicious pastries. For more serious drinking, with English beer on tap, head to *Club 63* at Batthyány utca 63 (daily 9am–11pm).

Sárvár's key event is the **International Folklore Festival**, celebrated in mid-August in the castle's courtyard, and in the same vein, but only every even-numbered year, there are the so-called **History Days**, with concerts, traditional dancing and singing. The **International Electro Acoustic Festival** at the end of July features various performers playing different instruments.

The Őrség

The forested **Őrség region**, some 30km south of Szombathely, has guarded Hungary's southwestern marches since the time of the Árpáds. Dotted with hilltop watchtowers and isolated hamlets, every man here was sworn to arms in lieu of paying tax. The people became used to their freedom and refused to be bound into serfdom by the Batthyány family, whose seat was at nearby Körmend. Moist winds from the Jura Mountains make this the rainiest, greenest part of Hungary, while the heavy clay soil allows no form of agriculture except raising cattle, but provides ample raw material for the local pottery industry. Until well into the twentieth century, when the Őrség declined as villagers migrated to Zalaegerszeg, houses were constructed of wooden beams plastered with clay. Today, the region's soft landscapes and folksy architecture are a powerful draw and village tourism is flourishing, with many homes offering a bed and food.

There are several approaches, depending on your starting point, although your best bet is to take one of the four daily buses from **Szentgotthárd** to **Őriszentpéter** via Szalafő – two of the nicest villages. Alternatively, you could head for Zalalövő by train from Körmend or Zalaegerszeg (7–10 daily) and travel on to Őriszentpéter (14km) via Pankasz, hitching or hiking if a bus doesn't materialize. Given the very limited bus services and quiet roads, **cycling** is the best way of getting around. Bikes can be rented at several villages, but it's wise to bring waterproof clothing for the inevitable drizzles.

Őriszentpéter

ŐRISZENTPÉTER is the obvious base for exploring the region, a straggling village made up of groups of houses (*szer*), built on nine separate ridges to escape flooding, each with one road bearing the same name – Városszer, Szikaszer, etc – and numbered round in a circle. During the last weekend of June the village hosts the **Őrség Fair**, with folk music, dancing and handicrafts. The village has bus connections to the nearby towns of Szentgotthárd and Körmend, and the village of Zalalövő, and boasts the best tourist facilities in the Őrség, including a tourist **information** office at Városszer 55 (April–Sept Mon–Fri 9am–noon & 1–4pm; ⓣ94/548-023, ⓦwww.orsegnet.hu), whose helpful staff can advise on **private accommodation** in the whole region. There are **rooms** advertised all along this street and along Kovácsszer. Alternatively, the *Centrum Panzió* at Városszer 17 (ⓣ & ⓕ94/350-319; ❸), by the crossroads in the centre of the village, has simple, cool rooms with TV and bathroom. You can get decent **meals** at the *Bognár Étterem*, 600m up the hill from the bus station at Kovácsszer 96 (daily 9am–9pm), where you can also try the local speciality *dödölle* (fried potato and onion dumplings served with soured cream). You can **rent bikes** from the house at Városszer 116 (ⓣ94/428-989; 1200Ft a day), and **horse-riding** can be arranged from the house at Szikaszer 18.

On the edge of the village, beside the road to Szalafő, stands a beautiful thirteenth-century **Romanesque church** with a finely carved portal and traces of frescoes inside, which can only be properly seen by attending Sunday Mass (9.30am; not the first Sun of the month), as the stairs up to the choir loft that provide access at other times (daily 10am–2pm; obtain the key from the priest next door) offer a poor view of the interior.

Szalafő

The village of **SZALAFŐ**, 6km up the road from Őriszentpéter, likewise consists of small separate settlements on adjacent ridges. From the church and bar that constitute the centre, it's 3km to Pityerszer, a mini **Village Museum** (mid-April to Oct Tues–Sun 10am–5pm; 300Ft) of heavy-timbered houses, typical of the region, which gives a good idea of life as it was five or six decades ago. Notice the little hen ladders that run up the sides of the houses. There are four buses a day between Monday and Friday and a couple on Saturday and Sunday from Őriszentpéter to Szalafő-felső, the end stop, and you'll find the museum a further kilometre's walk in the same direction. Tickets are sold at the *büfé* across the road from the museum, where you can also get refreshments.

If you happen to be here on **May 1**, look out for **dancing** around the tall, slender may tree. The origins of this ritual have long been lost, but many pine trees in the Őrség region are stripped of their lower branches as teenaged boys shin up to retrieve bottles of champagne suspended from the higher branches. Some even plant may trees in their girlfriends' gardens in the middle of the night.

Lots of houses advertise **rooms** for rent; try the *Csörgő Vendégház* at Csörgőszer 20 (☎94/428-623; ❷), run by the same people who run the bar in the centre of the village. They can also direct you to several houses selling delicious goat and cow cheese (*sajt*) and milk (*tej*). The *Hubertus Vendégház*, by the entrance to the village at Alsószer 20, serves hot **meals**.

Other villages in the region

Seven kilometres east of Őriszentpéter at **PANKASZ**, you can stop to admire the rustic **wooden bell-tower**; follow signs off the main road to the *Posta* for 200m. **Bikes** and **rooms** can be rented at **HEGYHÁTSZENTJAKAB**, 3km further north, off the road between Zalalövő and Pankasz, where you will find the comfortable *Trófea Panzió* (☎94/426-230; ❺) and a popular swimming **lake**, the Vadása-tó.

More appealing, though, are two villages along a minor road south of Őriszentpéter. In the hills along the Slovenian border, 12km away, the tiny village of **MAGYARSZOMBATFA**, with a population of three hundred, preserves the old tradition of **Habán pottery**, sold through the local Fazekasház (*fazekas* is the Hungarian for "potter"). The road continues 6km southeast to **VELEMÉR**, whose single-aisled Romanesque **church** contains beautiful frescoes from 1377. To view them, ask for the key at the house signposted *Templomkulcs*. The church lies across the fields, hidden in the trees, about 500m from the main road. There are daily buses to Velemér from Őriszentpéter via Magyarszombatfa.

Zalaegerszeg

The county capital **ZALAEGERSZEG**, just 37km west of Keszthely, and familiarly known as Zala, began to metamorphose after the discovery of oil in 1937, and is now the most industrialized town in southwestern Hungary, with a population of 70,000. Despite the futuristic television tower featured on tourist brochures and the bleak downtown area of housing estates and landscaped plazas, Zala hasn't totally forgotten its past; vestiges of folk culture from the surrounding region are preserved in two museums and an annual festival.

Into Slovenia

Hungary has two **border crossings into Slovenia**. Most traffic heads to the Rédics/Dolga Vas crossing, 30km south on Route 75, running down from Keszthely. The Hodos/Salovci crossing is quieter; the turn-off is midway between Őriszentpéter and Magyarszombatfa.

Arrival and information

The intercity **bus station** is on Balatoni út, a few minutes' walk to the east of the main thoroughfare, Széchenyi tér, while the **train station** is a fifteen-minute walk to the south of town (connected to the centre by buses #1, #7, #10 or #11). Tourinform, at Széchenyi tér 4–6 (June–Aug Mon–Fri 9am–6pm, Sat 9am–4pm; Sept–May Mon–Fri 10am–4pm; ⓣ92/316-160, Ⓔzalaegerszeg@tourinform.hu), can furnish you with maps and **information**. Zala's main **post office** is at Kossuth tér 6a (Mon–Fri 7.30am–7pm, Sat 8am–noon).

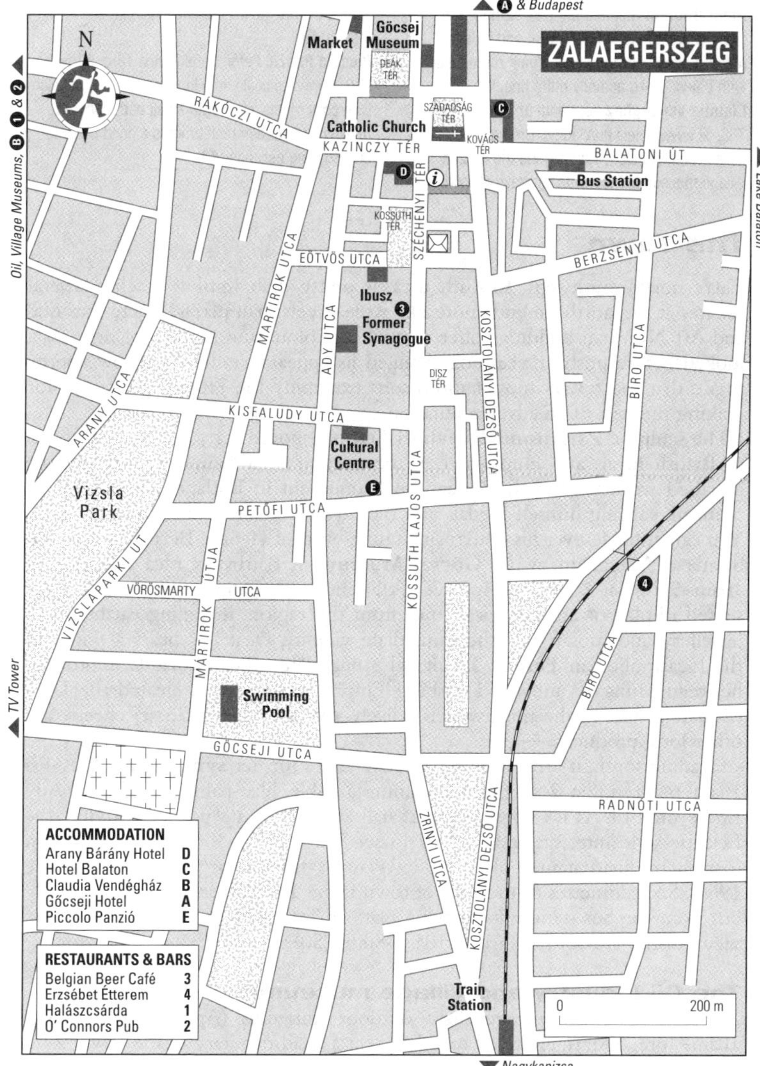

Accommodation

There's nothing particulary exciting about the sleeping possibilities in town, though you'll have little trouble finding somewhere should you decide to stop over. The cheapest accommodation is a **private room** (❷), available through Ibusz at Eötvös utca 6–10 (Mon–Fri 8am–5pm; ⓣ92/511-880, ⓔi094@ibusz.hu).

Arany Bárány Hotel Széchenyi tér 1 ⓣ92/550-040, ⓦwww.aranybarany.hu. The "Golden Lamb", in a fine old building in the centre, has smooth, decently furnished rooms, some with shower, some with bath. ❺–❻

Hotel Balaton Balatoni út 2a ⓣ92/550-870, ⓦwww.balatonhotel.hu. Central and hideous modern block, but the peachy/pink rooms, each with balcony, are actually quite fine. ❺

Claudia Vendégház Körmendi út 16 ⓣ92/596-738, ⓦwww.hotels.hu/claudia. Ordinary, but clean, seven-room pension, 1km beyond the Oil and Village museums. Discounts for stays of more than one night. ❷–❸

Gőcseji Hotel Kaszaházi utca 2 ⓣ92/511-924, ⓔgocsejhotel@zalatour.hu. Poorly located hotel with ageing rooms in the north of town, a ten-minute walk from the centre, past the stadium and across the bridge. It's the cheapest place in town though. ❷

Piccolo Panzió Petőfi Sándor utca 16 ⓣ92/510-055, ⓦwww.piccolo.hu. Eight-room family pension with cosy rooms, each with small bathroom and minibar; the garden restaurant is a good place to eat. Booking essential. ❸

The Town

Zala's north–south axis, Kossuth utca, is pretty drab until it reaches several squares at the northern end, more like wide streets than plazas, where Baroque and Art Nouveau buildings offer a touch of colour and an idea of how Zala looked before postwar planning changed its appearance. It's somehow appropriate that the town's most famous sons exemplify the Hungarian genius for making the best of an adverse situation.

The sculptor **Zsigmond Kisfaludi Strobl** enjoyed early success with busts of British royals and Hungarian aristocrats, and then switched to producing glorified workers (and the Liberation Monument in Budapest) under Communism, earning himself medals and the nickname "Step from Side to Side". You can chuckle over his oeuvre, including busts of George Bernard Shaw and Somerset Maugham, at the **Göcsej Museum** at Batthyány utca 2 (Mon–Fri 10am–5pm, Sat & Sun till 4pm; 300Ft), which also features a colourfully presented display of archeological finds from the region, including earthenware, jewellery and mosaics. In the immediate vicinity, Deák tér bears a statue of the local politician **Ferenc Deák**, who negotiated the historic Compromise between Hungary and the Habsburg Empire in 1867 that created the Dual Monarchy. Off to the northwest is a lively **market** selling Göcsej cheese and other local produce.

Heading south, it's five minutes' walk to Zala's former **synagogue** (Tues–Fri 10am–6.30pm, Sat 2–6.30pm), an unmistakeable, lilac-painted edifice at Ady Endre utca 14. As it's now a concert hall and gallery, it's possible to view the Eclectic-style interior, designed by József Stern in 1903, though it has been marred by lurid stained-glass windows and a massive organ, installed in the 1960s. Six kilometres to the west of town is the **TV Tower**, reached by hourly bus from the bus station; its viewing platform, complete with bar, affords fine views of the Göcsej Hills (daily 10am–8pm; 250Ft).

The Oil Industry and Village museums

Zala's main attractions are three outdoor museums (April–Sept Tues–Sun 10am–4pm; 300Ft), clustered together near a dead tributary of the River Zala,

2km to the northwest of town (bus #1, #1Y or #8Y). Giant pumps, drills and other hardware dominate the **Oil Industry Museum** (Olajipari Múzeum), which examines the history of the petroleum industry in Hungary. Unfortunately for the economy, exploratory drilling in the 1950s and 1960s discovered far more hot springs than oil, and the most promising field was found to straddle the Romanian border, so domestic production amounts to a fraction of Hungary's requirements.

Next door, the **Göcsej Village Museum** (Göcseji Falumúzeum) is the oldest of the *skanzen* in Hungary, and whilst it can't compare with the one in Szentendre (see p.163), it does hold nearly fifty original constructions. These include a watermill, a smithy, and several beautifully carved and painted gables, but the majority are dwellings from the late nineteenth century, complete with furniture and artefacts characteristic of the surrounding **Göcsej region**. Traditionally, this was so poor and squalid that no one would admit to being a part of it, and enquirers were always hastily assured that its boundaries began a few miles on, in the next village. The third, and smallest, of the museums is the **Finno-Ugrian Ethnographical Park**, still being constructed but currently comprising around half a dozen pine-log cabins typical of those inhabited by the Finno-Ugric peoples.

Eating and entertainment

The town has few decent **eating** options, but two places worth investigating are the *Belgian Beer Café* at Kossuth Lajos utca 5 (daily 11am–midnight), for its inventive meat-heavy dishes and delicious but pricey Belgian beer; and the *Erzsébet Étterem*, right by the tracks at Bíró utca 46 (daily 10am–11pm), which – if you don't mind eating with trains rumbling by – offers a good-value Hungarian menu. Midway between the Village Museum and the centre of town, you'll find *O'Connors Pub* at Ola utca 16 (daily 10am–midnight, Fri & Sat till 2am), which serves bar-style food and beers on tap, and, 200m further on at Rákóczi utca 47, the *Halászcsárda* fish restaurant (daily 10am–midnight). The pleasant garden restaurant at the *Piccolo Panzió* (see opposite) is also pretty good, either for a meal or a drink (daily 10am–midnight).

Local **entertainment** consists of whatever's on at the cultural centre on Kisfaludy utca, while for nightlife, try the wonderfully 1970s nightclub or 24-hour casino in the *Arany Bárány Hotel*. The major festival in town each year is the **Egerszeg Days**, a five-day event with concerts and folklore programmes held during the second week of May.

Southern Transdanubia

Bordered to the south by Croatia and to the north by Balaton, **Southern Transdanubia** is less built-up and more rural than the other Transdanubian regions and, bar a couple of isolated hilly areas, also much flatter – ideal for the agricultural industry which dominates the region. The outstanding draw is **Pécs**, the region's attractive capital, whose multitude of museums, fabulous nightlife and festivals can easily detain you for a few days. The hilly region south of Pécs should also appeal, particularly to wine lovers, with the marvellous **Villány–Siklós wine road** yielding some superlative reds, whilst a short trip west of Pécs is **Szigetvár**, renowned for its castle and Turkish ruins. Although the **Völgység**, the valley region between Lake Balaton and the **Mecsek Hills**, is pretty to drive through, none of the towns is really worth stopping for. Travelling from Balaton by train, however, you might have to change at **Nagykanizsa** or **Kaposvár**, and can take in their sights between connections; the latter is definitely worth taking time out to see for its fine museums and architecture. Express trains from Budapest to Pécs usually run via Dombóvár, while intercity buses are routed through **Szekszárd**, the most appealing small town in the region, within reach of the lovely **Forest of Gemenc**, part of the Duna-Drava National Park. In stark contrast, the steel town of **Dunaújváros**, on the way back to Budapest, will undoubtedly appeal to devotees of 1950s Socialist-Realist aesthetics.

Nagykanizsa

NAGYKANIZSA (pronounced "nodge-konizha"), 49km south of Zalaegerszeg, is a quiet backwater that makes a pleasant stopover, but isn't worth a special trip. In its day it was a proud fortress town straddling the River Principális, which together with Szigetvár and Siklós bore the brunt of Turkish assaults during the first decades of the occupation and finally succumbed. Unlike the others, the fortress at Nagykanizsa no longer exists, and the town is best known for its **brewery**, producing a brand named Kanizsai Kinizsi after the folk hero Pál Kinizsi, a miller's son of legendary strength who reputedly once used a millstone as a tray to serve a drink to a woman he admired.

The compact centre of Nagykanizsa consists of two leafy squares connected by Fő út. Coming in from the train station you'll pass a large, well-tended **Jewish cemetery** (Mon–Fri 8am–4.30pm, Sun 9am–4.30pm), attesting to the large community that once existed here; if it's closed, ask for the key from Sasvári Lajos at Őrház utca 6. The **synagogue**, in the courtyard of Fő út 6 (Tues–Sat 2–6pm; free), was built in 1821 with the support of Count Fülöp Batthyány, whose ancestors settled Jewish families on their estate. In April 1944, all three thousand Jews were deported to Auschwitz; only three hundred survived, of whom about 120 are still alive to meet in the prayer rooms in the courtyard opposite the synagogue, which was sold off to the municipality in 1982. Though sometimes used for concerts, it remains in a sorry state. Across the road at Fő út 5, the **Thury György Museum** (Wed–Sun 10am–4pm; 250Ft) mounts temporary exhibitions and displays a few Roman sarcophagi in its entrance way. You'd do better to go looking for the **parish church** on Zárda utca, built with masonry from the town's fortress, and originally a mosque where Nagykanizsa's last Turkish overlord, Mustafa Pasha, is buried in a tomb into which baptismal fonts have been cut. To get here, retrace your steps to Ady utca and turn left just beyond the post office at no. 10.

Alternatively, head up Fő út to reach Deák tér, a pleasant square with several café terraces overlooking a bizarre **statue** of the poet Petőfi urging a twentieth-century soldier to throw a grenade at the nearest row of shops. The monument honours the 48th Infantry Regiment in which he served in 1848–49, though it chiefly refers to their World War I campaigns, and was created in the Horthy era by Kisfaludi Strobl.

Practicalities

Arriving by bus you'll be dropped on the western side of Erzsébet tér, in the centre; coming from the **train station**, 1km south of town, you can walk to the centre in fifteen minutes or catch a bus (#18 or #23) along Ady utca, which runs down from Fő út. The Tourinform office is just off Fő utca at Csengery utca 3 (Mon–Fri 9am–5pm, Sat 9am–1pm; ⓣ93/313-322, ⓔnagykanizsa@tourinform.hu). Ibusz, at Erzsébet tér 2 (Mon–Fri 8am–5pm; ⓣ93/536-445, ⓔi071@ibusz.hu), can change money and book dormitory beds (in summer) and private rooms (❷). Other **accommodation** includes the polished *Hotel Central* at Erzsébet tér 23 (ⓣ93/314-000, ⓦwww.hotels.hu/central_nagykanizsa; ❺), and, to the west of town, two agreeable pensions: the *Király Panzió*, on the corner of Király utca and Kalmár utca (ⓣ93/325-480, ⓦwww.kiralypanzio.freeweb.hu; ❹), which has clean rooms with pine beds and chairs; and the neat *Hugi Panzió*, 150m further on at Király utca 7 (ⓣ93/336-100; ❸).

The most enjoyable **places to eat**, in a town seriously lacking any quality restaurants, are *Robinsons*, a cool cellar pizzeria (with an upstairs pub) at Deák tér 10 (daily 11am–11pm), and the nautically-themed *Nelsons*, at Fő utca 7 (daily 11am–10pm), whose menu is more wide-ranging but the atmosphere rather moribund. A reasonable third option is the *Kiskakas*, behind the Thury György Museum at Múzeum tér 6, which has a poultry-heavy menu (daily 11am–11pm, except Friday 11am–4pm). The *Amor Café* on Erzsébet tér (daily 7.30am–midnight) is great for an early-morning coffee or evening cocktail.

The **post office** is at Ady Endre utca 10 (Mon–Fri 7.30am–7pm, Sat 8am–noon). In summer you can go **rowing** on the Lower Town Wood Lake (*Alsovárosierdő-tó*), a few kilometres east of town on the Kaposvár road (bus #17 from the bus station). The nearest road **crossing into Croatia** is at **Letenye**, 26km west of town, where the *Arany Bárány*, Szabadság tér 1 (ⓣ93/343-047; ❷), has basic accommodation if needed.

Kaposvár and around

Capital of Somogy county, the industrial town of **KAPOSVÁR**, 76km east of Nagykanizsa and just 53km south of Lake Balaton, lies between the hilly slopes of the Zselic region and the valley of the River Kapos. The town is blessed with a fabulous stock of museums and, with an elegant centre stuffed with numerous Art Nouveau and classical buildings, it's well worth a visit. Apart from being famous for its theatre and as the birthplace of József Rippl-Rónai, the father of Hungarian Art Nouveau, Kaposvár is a stepping stone for walks in the **Zselic nature conservation area**. With frequent direct trains to Fonyód, Kaposvár is also a good place from which to head to or from Lake Balaton.

Arrival and information

Kaposvár's **stations** are close to each other, with local buses next to the train station on Budai Nagy Antal utca and long-distance services across the road on Petőfi Sándor tér. To reach the centre of town, head up Teleki utca or Dózsa György utca, both of which lead to Fő utca. Here, you can get **information** from the helpful Tourinform at no. 8 (Mon–Fri 9am–5pm, Sat 9am–1pm; ⓣ82/512-921, ⓔkaposvar@tourinform.hu). The **post office** is at Bajcsy-Zsilinszky utca 15 (Mon–Fri 7.30am–7pm, Sat 8am–noon).

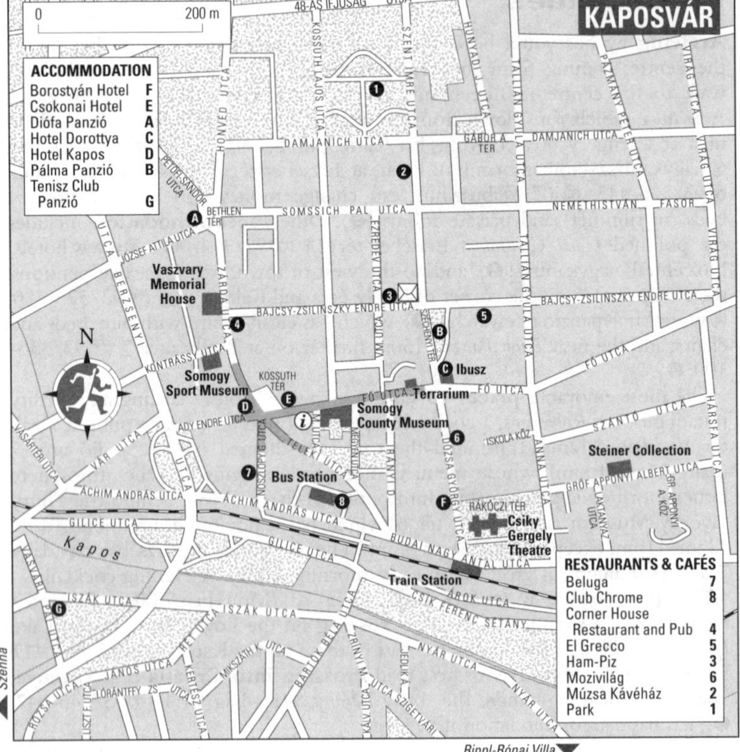

Accommodation

There's a good choice of accommodation in town, with a number of pensions offsetting the more expensive hotels. Ibusz, at Széchenyi tér 8 (Mon–Fri 5pm; ⓣ82/512-300, ⓔi058@ibusz.hu), can arrange a room in one of the centrally located colleges, or **private rooms** (❷) in the town and in the villages of the Zselic Hills; and Siotour, in the *Csokonai Hotel* at no. 1 (Mon–Fri 8am–4.30pm; ⓣ82/320-537), can also arrange private accommodation in town. The *Deseda* **campsite** (ⓣ82/312-030; June–Aug) is 6km northeast of town and can be reached by bus #8 or #18 from the station, or by alighting at the Toponár stop on the Siófok–Kaposvár branch line.

Borostyán Hotel Rákóczi tér 3 ⓣ82/320-735, ⓦwww.hotels.hu/borostyan_kaposvar. Art Nouveau building near the train station with disappointingly plain rooms. ❹–❺

Csokonai Hotel Fő utca 1 ⓣ82/312-011, ⓕ316-716. Renovated eighteenth-century building on the main street. Rooms come with or without shower, although the ubiquitous brown decor is a bit wearing. Breakfast not included. ❷–❸

Diófa Panzió József Attila utca 24 ⓣ & ⓕ82/422-504. Up the hill from Kossuth tér, this cheap pension has rooms with TV, phone and mini-bar but is ultimately rather bland. ❸

Hotel Dorottya Széchenyi tér 8 ⓣ82/315-055, ⓦwww.hoteldorottya.hu. Kaposvár's most characterful hotel, built in the nineteenth century, retains many of its original features, including thick wooden beams in most of the rooms. ❹–❺

Hotel Kapos Ady Endre utca 2 ⓣ82/316-022, ⓦwww.kaposhotel.hu. From the outside this place holds little promise but the variously sized rooms are reasonably modern, spacious and well equipped. Also has a coffee house. ❹–❺

Pálma Panzió Széchenyi tér 6 ⓣ & ⓕ82/420-227. Small, privately run pension just up from the *Dorrotya*, with standard rooms and bathrooms. ❸

Tenisz Club Panzió Iszák utca 37 ⓣ82/411-832. West of the stations and across the river, this good-value place has satisfying cucumber green-and-black coloured rooms, all neatly furnished and some with balcony. ❸

The Town

Most of Kaposvár's attractions are located along or just off the pretty, pedestrianized main street, Fő utca, and around Kossuth ter, the main square. Down in the cellar at Fő utca 31 is the **Terrarium** (Mon–Fri 9am–5pm, Sat 9am–noon, Sun 2–5pm; 400Ft), housing a collection of rare and exotic reptiles such as the Madagascar boa and Cuvier dwarf caiman. The **Somogy County Museum**, at no. 10 (Somogy Megyei Múzeum; Tues–Sun: April–Oct 10am–4pm; Nov–March 10am–3pm; 300Ft), contains the usual mix of local ethnographic and historical material, though you're best off heading straight to the top floor and the gallery of contemporary art, where you'll find a number of works by prominent Hungarians such as Egry, Kmetty and Vaszvary (see below). Confusingly, it is sometimes known as the Rippl-Rónai Museum, after the artist born on this street at no. 19 above the Golden Lion Pharmacy, though the museum doesn't contain any of his paintings. You'll find these at the **Rippl-Rónai Villa** on Fodor József utca, in the suburb of Rómahegy, 3km southeast of the centre (Emlekmúzeum; Tues–Sun: April–Oct 10am–6pm; Nov–March 10am–4pm; 300Ft); take bus #15 from the bus station. Born in 1861, Rippl-Rónai first studied in Munich and then under the academic painter Munkácsy before refining his own style in Paris, influenced by Postimpressionism and Art Nouveau. His return home in 1902 marked the end of his "black period", when some of his best-known works such as *Lady with a Black Veil* were produced, and the start of a "sunlit" one reflecting "the colours that surround me in my new house and garden". In his later years he abandoned oils and turned to crayon. The villa contains pictures from each phase, plus furniture, glassware and ceramics.

A couple of minutes' walk north of Kossuth tér past the *Kapos* hotel is the **Somogy Sports Museum** at Kontrössy utca 3 (Somogyi Sportmúzeum; Tues, Thurs & Fri 10am–5pm, Sun 9am–1pm; 250Ft), which is stuffed with memorabilia from every sport imaginable; naturally enough, the displays of trophies, photographs and sporting equipment focus on Hungarian sporting achievement, and a fair chunk of the museum is given over to Olympic mementoes, including the uniforms worn by athletes at the opening ceremonies. Five minutes up the road, at Zarda utca 9, the **Vaszvary Memorial House** (Tues–Sun 10am–4pm; free) has been converted into a lovely little gallery featuring paintings and sketches by János Vaszvary, who was born here in 1867.

One attraction not to be missed is the fabulous **Steiner Collection**, five minutes' walk east of Rákóczi tér at Gróf Apponyi utca 29 (Steiner Gyűjtemény; officially daily 9am–5pm, but best to check with Tourinform first; free), a private collection of cast-iron articles and ornaments from the nineteenth century. The owner, József Steiner, first started his unique collection in 1989 after purchasing an old iron stove, which inspired him to search for ever more unusual cast-iron objects. The collection now consists of an entire cellar of stoves and baths, a garden full of cast-iron grave markers and a house crammed with everything from kitchen utensils, table clocks and lamps, to chandeliers and a bust of Lajos Kossuth from 1848.

Eating and drinking

Kaposvár has a handful of pretty good **restaurants**, the best of which is the *Corner House Restaurant and Pub* at Bajcsy-Zsilinszky utca 2, a thoroughly modern outfit offering superb meat dishes including boar, deer and rabbit (daily 10am–11pm, Fri & Sat till midnight). Further along the same street, at no. 54, *El Grecco* is a colourful, cosy Mexican place also serving up paella and grills (daily 11.30am–midnight), and, if you don't mind dreadful kitsch, the film-themed *Mozivilág* at Dózsa György utca 3 has a particularly good steak menu. Simpler snacks are available at *Beluga*, a tiny pizzeria and grill café at Noszlopy G utca 10 (Mon–Sat 10am–11pm, Sun 11.30am–8pm), and *Ham-Piz*, at Bajcsy-Zsilinszky utca 13, serves pizzas, roasted meals and salads (daily 10am–11pm).

A delightful, out-of-the-way **coffee shop** is the *Múzsa Kávéház* at Szent Imre utca 21 – a serene, old-style place also serving teas, beers and cocktails (daily 7am–11pm). During the summer, cafés and bars spill out onto the pedestrianized stretch of Fő utca, but for more tub-thumping entertainment year-round, head to the *Park* at Szent Imre 29, a stereotypical **disco** venue with a glitzy bar which really cranks it up at the weekend (daily 5pm–2am); or the more sophisticated and full-on *Club Chrome*, at Petőfi tér 2 (Thurs, Fri & Sat 10pm–5am).

Entertainment

Kaposvár's distinctive **Csiky Gergely Theatre**, on Rákóczi tér, is one of the best in Hungary and has gained kudos abroad with its performances of *The Master and Margarita*; tickets are available from the ticket office (Színház Jegypéntzár), which shares the same building as Tourinform at Fő utca 8 (same opening times as Tourinform). To celebrate Mihály Csokonai's comic literary epic *Dorottya*, the first Saturday of February each year is given over to the **Dorottya Napok Fesztival** (Dorothy Day Festival), a day of carnival festivities and folk games along Fő utca. The day concludes with a mass ball at the *Hotel Dorottya* on Széchenyi tér, which is where most of the action in the book takes place. During the town's **Spring Festival** in late March, there are concerts in the **Liszt Concert Hall** at Kossuth utca 21.

The Zselic region

Nature lovers will enjoy **walking in the Zselic region** south of Kaposvár, with its watermeadows, woods and rolling hills. Maps (*Á Zselic*; 1:60,000) are available from Tourinform and bookshops in Kaposvár, showing marked trails; you can follow one from the village of **SZENNA**, 9km away (hourly buses from stand 9 of Kaposvár's bus terminal). Szenna harbours one of Hungary's smallest **skanzen** (Szabadtéri Néprajzi Gyűjtemény; Tues–Sun: April–Oct 10am–6pm; Nov–March 10am–4pm; 350Ft), consisting of five houses, complete with furnishings and personal belongings, three cellars and an eighteenth-century Calvinist church, transplanted from elsewhere in the region to a site opposite the main bus stop at Rákóczi utca 2. **Village tourism** is thriving here and you'll have little problem finding a **room** (either directly or through Ibusz in Kaposvár). One recommended place is the *Ágnes-Vendégház* at Kossuth utca 1 (Ⓣ82/712-273; ❷), who can also provide hot meals upon request.

Pécs and the Mecsek Hills

After Budapest, **PÉCS** (pronounced "paych"), 65km southeast of Kaposvár, is probably the finest town in Hungary. Its red-and-orange-tiled rooftops nestle against the slopes of the Mecsek Hills, and the sprawling modern housing estates can easily be forgotten once you are inside the old town. Pécs has a reputation for art and culture, boasting many excellent art galleries and museums, some fine examples of Islamic architecture, and the biggest market in western

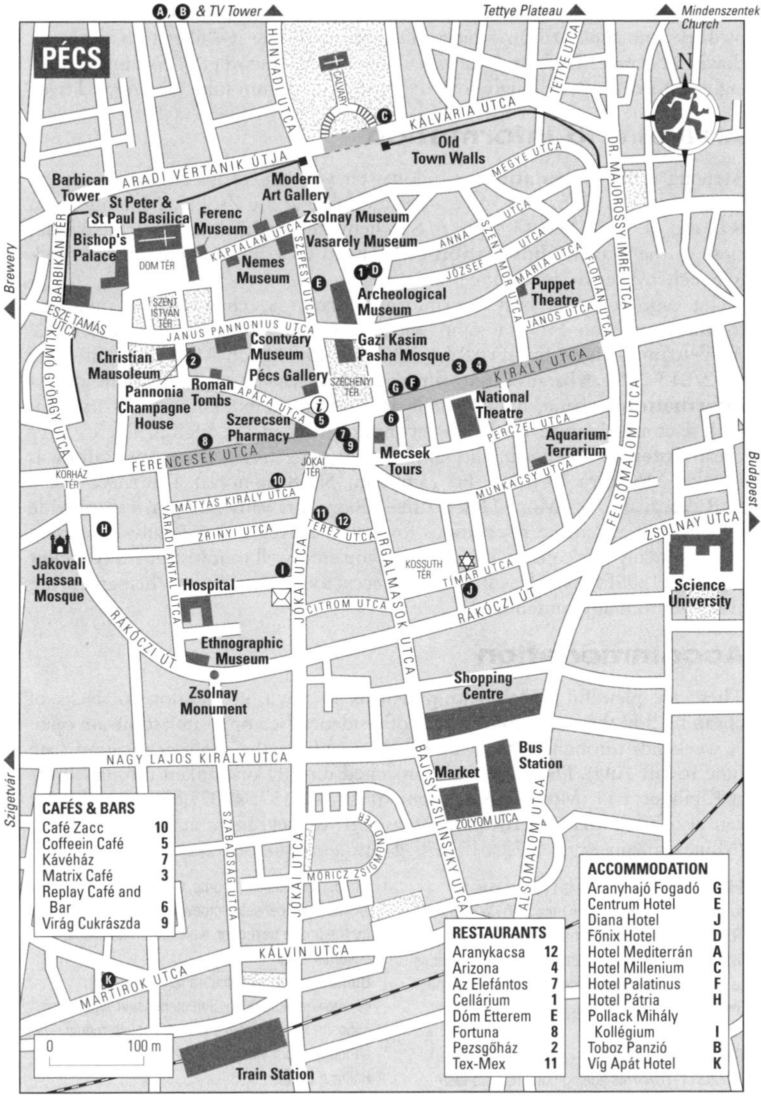

Hungary. Furthermore, it has one of the most diverse festival programmes in the country. As Transdanubia's leading centre of education, its population of 160,000 includes a high proportion of students, giving Pécs a youthful profile. The city is overlooked by the **Mecsek Hills**, where the Turks planted fig trees that still flourish, and where, until recently, uranium was mined.

Though prehistoric settlements existed here, the first town was Sopianae, settled first by the Celts and later by the Romans, who raised it to be the capital of the new province of Pannonia Valeria. Made an episcopal see by King Stephen, the town, known as Quinque Ecclesiae or Fünfkirchen (Five Churches), became a university centre in the Middle Ages. Under Turkish occupation (1543–1686) its character changed radically, its Magyar/German population being replaced by Turks and their Balkan subjects. Devastated during its "liberation", the city slowly recovered, thanks to local viticulture and the discovery of coal in the mid-eighteenth century, although both the coal and uranium mines are now closed.

Arrival and information

Arriving at the **train station** on Indóház tér, you can catch a bus north into the centre. Any bus up Szabadság utca can drop you at the Zsolnay Monument on Rákóczi út, while bus #30 runs to Széchenyi tér via Irgalmasok utcája, passing close to the intercity **bus station** on Zólyom utca, from where you can walk to Széchenyi tér in under fifteen minutes.

The large and very busy Tourinform office at Széchenyi tér 9 (mid-June to mid-Sept Mon–Fri 9am–6pm, Sat & Sun 9am–3pm; mid-Sept to Oct & April to mid-June Mon–Fri 8am–5.30pm, Nov–March Mon–Fri 8am–4pm; ⓣ72/213-315, ⓔbaranya-m@tourinform.hu) has a staggering amount of **information** to hand, and although it doesn't make bookings it can arm you with a comprehensive list of all accommodation in the region. There's very cheap **Internet access** in the same office (same times). The **post office** is at Jókai Mór utca 10 (Mon–Fri 7am–7pm, Sat 8am–noon). The MAV office at Rákóczi út 39c (Mon–Thurs 9am–4.30pm, Fri 9am–3.30pm) can provide information and make reservations for trains, as well as issue daily bus passes. With so many museums to choose from you'd do well to invest in a **day ticket** (*napijegy*; 1800Ft), which will gain you access to the majority of them; these are available from any museum.

Accommodation

There are plentiful **hotels** and **pensions** in town, in addition to stacks of cheap beds in the many college halls of residence (see opposite); some are open at weekends throughout term time, others only in the summer vacation (late June to late Aug). These can be approached directly or booked through Ibusz at Király utca 11 (Mon–Fri 9am–5pm; ⓣ72/212-157, ⓔi077@ibusz.hu). Ibusz can also book **private rooms** (❷), as can Mecsek Tours at Széchenyi tér 1 (Mon–Fri 8am–4pm; ⓣ72/513-370, ⓔutir@mecsektours.hu).

Hotels and pensions

Aranyhajó Fogadó Király utca 3 ⓣ72/310-263, ⓦwww.hotels.hu/aranyhajo_pecs. Housed in a listed medieval building, the "Golden Ship" claims to be one of Hungary's oldest hotels, and although the rooms are a little dated they retain a certain character. ❺

Centrum Hotel Szepesy Ignác utca 4 ⓣ & ⓕ72/311-707. This ageing hotel has old-fashioned, glum-looking rooms, though its price and location compensate somewhat. You could also try the house next door, which often has beds advertised. ❷

Diana Hotel Timár utca 4a ⓣ72/328-954, ⓦwww.hoteldiana.hu. Sweet, pension-type place opposite the synagogue with appealing rooms, although avoid those backing out onto noisy Rákóczi út. ❺

Főnix Hotel Hunyadi út 2 ⓣ72/311-680, ⓦwww.fonixhotel.hu. Rooms with and without shower in this reasonably modern, if a little colourless, place just off Széchenyi tér. ❸–❹

Hotel Mediterrán Hidegvólgyi utca 1 ⓣ72/514-110, ⓦwww.hotels.hu/mediterran_pecs. An ex-hostel gone upmarket, with comfortable rooms, and a view of the hills dominated by a quarry; take bus #35 to the end of the line, and follow signs downhill for 300m. ❺

Hotel Millenium Kálvária utca 58 ⓣ72/512-222, ⓦwww.hotelmillenium.hu. The city's most modern hotel, located on the south side of Calvary Hill just beyond the town walls; the rooms are immaculate, while those on the top floor offer splendid views across town. ❼

Hotel Palatinus Király utca 5 ⓣ72/889-400, ⓦwww.danubiusgroup.com/palatinus. Renovated *fin-de-siècle* pile right in the centre, with a magnificent lobby but rather ordinary rooms. ❽

Hotel Pátria Rákóczi út 3 ⓣ72/889-500, ⓦwww.danubiusgroup.com/patria. Sister hotel of the *Palatinus*, with a mix of older and newer rooms, the latter – with tea- and coffee-making facilities – are worth paying the extra for. ❻–❼

Toboz Panzió Fenyves sor 5 ⓣ72/510-555, ⓦwww.tobozpanzio.hu. A quiet pension with views of the woods and small comfy rooms with minibar and TV. Take bus #34 or #35 to Károlyi Mihály utca. ❹

Víg Apát Hotel Mártirok utca 14 ⓣ72/313-340, ⓦwww.hotels.hu/vig_apat_pecs. Located just 200m west of the train station, this well-run hotel has colourful, refreshing rooms and good service. ❹

Campsites, hostels and colleges

Familia Camping Gyöngyösi utca 6 ⓣ72/327-034. This year-round campsite, 2km from Pécs, also has rooms (❷). From the train station take bus #31 as far as the Gyárváros church – from here it's a short walk north.

Hunyadi Mátyás Kollégium Széchenyi tér 11 ⓣ72/310-875. A boys' hall of residence run by Cistercian monks. Open all summer and weekends during term time.

JPTE Kollégium Damjanich utca 30 ⓣ72/310-055. University hall of residence with four-bed rooms. Open June–Aug.

Kodály Zoltán Kollégium Kodály Zoltán utca 20 ⓣ72/326-968. College hostel located 500m west of the basilica. Open July & Aug.

Laterum Hotel/Youth Hostel Hajnóczy utca 37 ⓣ72/252-113, ⓕ252-131. A revamped workers' hostel on the road to Szigetvár, a few kilometres west of the centre; take bus #2, #4 or #27 to the MOL petrol station. Open all year. ❷

Mandulás Camping Ángyán János utca 2 ⓣ72/515-655, ⓕ515-657. Campsite in the woods below the TV tower. Rooms with showers and toilets (❷–❸). Bus #34 stops outside. Open mid-April to mid-Oct.

Pollack Mihály Kollégium Jókai Mór utca 8 ⓣ72/315-846. Brilliantly located college just along from the main post office. Open all summer and weekends during term time.

Around the Belváros

Most of Pécs' sights lie within the historic **Belváros**, encircled by a road marking the extent of the medieval town walls, and centred on Széchenyi tér. Passing Kossuth tér en route to the centre, don't miss one of the city's finest monuments, an elegant **synagogue** built in 1865 (Zsinagóga; May–Oct Mon–Fri & Sun 10am–5pm; 300Ft). Its carved and stuccoed interior is beautiful but haunting, emptied by the murder of over four thousand Jews now listed in a *Book of Remembrance* – ten times the number that live in Pécs today. Thanks to local efforts, state support and contributions from abroad, this was one of the first synagogues in Hungary to be restored, in the 1980s.

Further uphill, as Irgalmasok utcája nears Széchenyi tér, you'll spot the **Zsolnay Fountain** in front of a church to your right. Local Zsolnay ceramics are typified by polychromatic, metallic-looking glazes; the bulls' heads on the fountain are modelled on a gold drinking vessel from the "Treasure of Attila".

Before entering Széchenyi tér, take a look at pedestrianized **Király utca**, traditionally the *korzó* where townsfolk promenade. Among the buildings worth noting here are the Art Nouveau **Hotel Palatinus**; the **Nendtvich House** at no. 8, with its ceramic ornamentation; the **National Theatre**, surmounted by a statue of Genius; and the **Vasváry House** at no. 19, with its allegorical figurines.

Széchenyi tér

With its art galleries and tourist offices, modern-day **Széchenyi tér** is centuries removed from its Turkish predecessor, a dusty square crowded with "caravans of camels laden with merchandise from India and the Yemen". At its top end stands the Catholic church, whose ornate window grilles and scalloped niches denote its origins as the **Mosque of Gazi Kasim Pasha** (Belvárosi templom; April 15 to Oct 15 Mon–Sat 10am–4pm, Sun 11.30am–4pm; Oct 16 to April 14 Mon–Sat 10am–noon, Sun 11.30am–2pm; donations acccepted), which the Turks built from the stones of a medieval Gothic church. The vaulted interior and Islamic prayer niche (*mihrab*) are decorated with Arabic calligraphy.

Behind the mosque on the north side of the square, the **Archeological Museum** (Régészeti Múzeum; April–Oct Tues–Sun 10am–4pm; Nov to March Mon–Thurs 10am–3pm; 300Ft) covers the history of the region from prehistoric times to the Magyar conquest, but pales in comparison to the real Roman tombs a few streets over on Apáca utca (see p.302). Heading down the square, you'll find a selection of contemporary artwork in the **Pécs Gallery** at no. 10 (Mon & Wed–Fri noon–6pm, Sat 10am–6pm; 100Ft) – it's worth a quick look in case there's anything remarkable, but with so many art collections in Pécs it pays to be selective.

A few paces further down, just past the Tourinform office at Apáca utca 1, pop your head into the nineteenth-century **Szerecsen Pharmacy** (Patika Műzeum; Mon–Fri 10am–6pm; free), whose gorgeous wood-carved furnishings are inlaid with ceramic tiles from the Zsolnay factory, which is where the drinking fountain with the sculpture of the Black Saracen was also made. At this point, you have the option of three routes to the basilica – along Káptalan, Janus Pannonius or Apáca utca – via a clutch of museums.

Káptalan utca

Káptalan utca has no fewer than five museums virtually next to each other. The **Zsolnay Museum** at no. 2 (Zsolnay Kerámia Kiállítás; Tues–Sun: April–Oct 10am–6pm; Nov–March 10am–4pm; 700Ft) is a must for its vases, plaques and figurines from the Zsolnay Ceramics Factory, founded in 1868 by Vilmos Zsolnay and the chemist Vince Wartrha, the inventor of eosin glaze. Some pieces are exquisite, others totally kitsch. In the basement are sculptures by Amerigo Tot, whose *Erdély Family* with its clamped grave-posts symbolizes the plight of the ethnic Hungarians of Romania.

Across the road at no. 3, the **Vasarely Museum** (Tues–Sun: April–Oct 10am–6pm; Nov–March 10am–4pm; 600Ft) exhibits lurid Op Art canvases by Viktor Vasarely, who was born in this house in 1908, but made his name in Paris and New York. The **Modern Art Gallery**, next door to the Zsolnay Museum (Magyar Képtár; Tues–Sun: April–Oct 10am–6pm; Nov–March 10am–4pm; 400Ft), presents a *tour d'horizon* of Hungarian art, since the School of Szentendre, with a large section devoted to constructivist evocations of the proletarian struggle by Béla Uitz (1887–1972), who lived for fifty years in the Soviet Union. The **Endre Nemes Museum** at no. 5 (May–Oct Tues–Sun 10am–4pm; 400Ft) honours the surrealist Endre Nemes, who was born in nearby Pécsvárad in 1909, but spent most of his life in Sweden. In a separate building at the rear of the museum (same hours and ticket) is a curious exhibit by Erzsébet Schaár (1908–75); entitled *Utca* ("Street"), this enormous sculpted piece of work, featuring a series of delineating walls with rigid, haunting figures peering through doors and windows, is widely regarded as her finest piece of work. Diagonally across the street at no. 6, right by Dóm tér, the **Ferenc Martyn Museum** (April–Sept Tues–Sun 10am–4pm; 400Ft) showcases work by Ferenc Martyn, an early exponent of non-figurative painting, who died in 1986.

The Csontváry Museum

If you only visit one place in Pécs, make it the **Csontváry Museum** at Janus Pannonius utca 11–13 (Tues–Sun: April–Oct 10am–6pm; Nov–March 10am–4pm; 600Ft). Kosztka Tivadar Csontváry (1853–1919) was born in Slovakia in the same year as Van Gogh, and his artistic career was similarly affected by madness and the pursuit of "the path of the sun". His fascination with Hebrew lore and the Holy Land was expressed in huge canvases – *Baalbek, Mary's Well at Nazareth* and *Pilgrimage* – while his hallucinatory vision of nature produced *Tatra, Storm on the Great Hortobágy* and *Solitary Cedar*. One of his most poignant pieces of work is *Híd Mostárban* (1903), a gorgeous, richly coloured painting of the once elegant Mostar Bridge in Bosnia – subsequently blown up during the Bosnian war in 1993. By 1910, his psychosis had well and truly set in, as evinced by the series of schizoid drawings and sketches in the last room.

After his death, these works came close to being sold as tarpaulin, but at the last moment were purchased by an architect. When Picasso later saw an exhibition of Csontváry's work in Paris, he asked to be left alone in the room for an hour and then remarked, "I did not know there was another great painter in our century besides me", and later told Chagall, "There you are, old master, I bet even you could not paint something like this."

Dóm tér and around

Looming to the north on the large, cobbled main square is the huge, four-towered **St Peter and St Paul Basilica** (Székesegyház; April–Oct Mon–Sat 9am–5pm, Sun 1–5pm; Nov–March Mon–Sat 10am–4pm, Sun 1–4pm; 700Ft) that has been endlessly rebuilt since the first basilica was founded here in the eleventh century. Though a crypt and side chapels from eleventh- to fourteenth-century churches have been incorporated, its outward form is neo-Romanesque, the style chosen to replace Mihály Pollack's previous Baroque design. Its lavish blue and gold murals are by Lotz, Székely and other historicist painters of the 1890s.

The neo-Renaissance **Bishop's Palace** (Püspöki Palota; July to mid-Sept Thurs only 2–5pm; 1hr tour 1500Ft) to the west of the square is embellished with a modern statue of Liszt waving from the balcony, which might have amused its former bishops, Janus Pannonius, who was also a humanist poet, and György Klimó, founder of its library, who told borrowers: "You don't have to pay for anything. Depart enriched. Return more frequently." Around the corner to the south, a circular **barbican tower** punctuates the old town walls, giving access to Klimó György utca. Secreted away on the eastern side of the square is the so-called **Wine Pitcher Burial Chamber** (Korsos Sirkamra; daily 10am–6pm; 300Ft), on account of the existence of an almost complete fresco of a jug contained within a small niche in the chamber.

Szent István tér, the lower, park-like extension of Dóm tér, harbours ruins of what was once an early **Christian Mausoleum** from the fourth century (Ókeresztény Mauzoleum; Tues–Sun: mid-April to Oct 10am–6pm, Sun till 4pm; Nov to mid-April 10am–4pm; 300Ft). Discovered in 1975 during the demolition of an artificial waterfall, the mausoleum is decorated with frescoes of the Fall, Daniel in the Lions' Den and a scene of Adam and Eve. It also contains a white marble sarcophagus dating from the third century and some skeletal remains.

The necropolis of Sopianae lay more or less beneath Apáca utca (Nun Street), just south of Szent István tér, where several **Roman tombs** decorated with scenes of the Gates of Paradise have been excavated in the courtyard of no. 8. After the Romans went home and waves of migrating tribes swept across Hungary, the tombs were used as refuges and modified accordingly. At no. 14 are the remains of a **Burial Chapel** (Témetőkápolna Okeresztény), likewise dating from the third or fourth century AD. Tickets (350Ft) for both the tombs and the chapel must be obtained from the Christian Mausoleum – see p.301.

Around the periphery

From the barbican tower, just off Dóm tér, you can head uphill and on to Aradi Vértanuk útja to see a section of the **old town walls** – once a massive crenellated rampart 5500 paces long, buttressed by 87 bastions – erected after the Mongol invasion of the thirteenth century. Above the tunnel, 300m along, is a small garden with a decaying **Calvary Chapel**, offering a fine view of the Belváros.

Alternatively, head downhill around the peripheral boulevard – henceforth Rákóczi út – to find the inconspicuous **Jakovali Hassan Mosque** (Hasszán Pasa Dzsámija; April–Sept daily except Wed 10am–1pm & 2–6pm; 240Ft). Unlike its counterparts at Szigetvár (see p.306) and Eger (see p.341), this sixteenth-century mosque is still intact (though its minaret is closed), bearing traces of friezes and arabesque carving. The attractive *minbar* pulpit and kilims adorning its cool white interior are gifts from the Turkish Ministry of Culture. Around the corner on Ferencesek utca, you can see the ruins of a Turkish bath outside the *Minaret* restaurant.

At Rákóczi út 15, a small **Ethnographic Museum** (Néprajzi Múzeum; May–Oct Tues–Sat 10am–4pm; 300Ft) contains numerous folk costumes, ceramic vases and other household goods from the Baranya region, as well as a great set of masks, such as those worn at Mohács during the Busójárás Carnival. On the way back to the centre you can see the **Zsolnay Monument**, with an image of the factory's founder gazing benevolently over the junction with Szabadság utca; and the Romantic-style **post office** on Jókai utca, roofed with Zsolnay tiles. After digesting all these fine museums you may wish to turn your gaze to something more relaxing, in which case you should head for the **Aquarium-Terrarium** at Munkácsy utca 31 (daily 9am–5pm; 380Ft), whose sticky cellars house a colourful and substantial display of reptiles and fish.

Out of the centre

For a fresh perspective on Pécs, catch bus #33 from Kossuth tér up to the **Tettye plateau**, 2km from the centre, where a ruined sixteenth-century palace, later used as a Dervish monastery, stands in a park. Higher up and a further kilometre away, **Misina Hill** (534m) is crowned by a **TV tower** with an observation platform (TV Torony; daily 9am–7pm; 450Ft), and a café with a retro 1970s ambience, accessible by bus #35 from Kossuth tér or the train station. Should you care to walk back from the plateau, Havihegyi út offers a succession of views as it winds around the hillside, with several picturesque backstreets slinking down past the **All Saints' Church**, whose pastor supplements his income by selling poultry.

All kinds of livestock and farming paraphernalia appear at the monthly **Pécs Market**, a huge country fair held on the first Sunday of every month at a site 3km southwest of the Belváros; take bus #3 or #50 from outside the Konzum store on Rákóczi út and ask to be dropped off at the Vásártér market on Megyeri út. On other Sundays, there's a lively flea market on the same site.

Eating, drinking and entertainment

Pécs is one of the most sociable cities in Hungary, and with its tremendous array of fine **restaurants**, **cafés** and **bars** to choose from, you're almost guaranteed a good night out.

Restaurants

Aranykacsa Teréz utca 4. The upscale "Golden Duck" has goose, duck and turkey as the mainstays of its menu, plus good set menus (including cheaper vegetarian versions). Expensive. Mon–Thurs 11am–11pm, Fri & Sat till midnight, Sun till 4.30pm.

Arizona Király utca 21. Better than average American steak house, with a super grill garden; the only place to come for a cooked breakfast. Daily 8am–midnight, breakfast till 11am.

Az Elefántos Jókai tér 6. Informally stylish, and moderately priced, pizzeria restaurant, with a particularly good selection of pasta dishes. Daily 11.30am–midnight.

Cellárium Hunyadi út 2. Vast cellar restaurant beside the *Főnix Hotel*; the menu – written like a newspaper – takes some digesting, but once you've got past that, you'll enjoy the food and the atmosphere. Live music at weekends. Mon–Thurs 11am–midnight, Fri & Sun till 2am.

Dóm Étterem Király utca 3. You can choose to eat in the magnificently decorated section to the rear, or the cosy, vaulted section at the front; terrific house specialities include fish and venison, and it's the best place in town for vegetarians too. Daily 11am–11pm.

Fortuna Ferencesek utca 32. Posh, air-conditioned restaurant with a sophisticated international and Hungarian menu, heavily weighted towards seafood. Tues–Sat 10am–11.30pm.

Pezsgőház Szent István tér 12. Easily the classiest outfit in town, this beautifully lit, vaulted cellar offers an international menu of the highest quality, and a fine champagne and wine list. Mon–Sat 11am–11pm, Sun 11am–3pm.

Tex-Mex Teréz utca 10. Decent Mexican just along from the *Aranykacsa*, with the requisite enchiladas, burritos and tacos. Daily 11am–midnight, Fri & Sat till 1am.

Cafés, bars and cellars

With stacks of places to **drink** you'll have little problem in tracking down a place to suit you. Two of the most popular places for an evening beverage are the hip *Coffeein Café* at Széchenyi tér 9 (daily 8am–midnight, Fri & Sat till 2am), and the hectic *Replay Café and Bar* at Király utca 4 (daily 10am–2am) – both also offer a decent food menu. A couple of more low-key, but more characterful, places, are the splendidly relaxed *Café Dante*, in the same building as the Csontváry Museum at Janus Pannonius utca 11 (daily 10am–midnight), which stages live jazz on Friday and Saturday evenings; and *Café Zacc*, at Mátyás Király utca 2, a lovely, contemplative drinking hole offering teas, cocktails and beers (daily 10am–midnight).

For location and range of coffees, the classy, relaxing and no-smoking *Kávéház*, next to the *Az Elefántos* restaurant on Jókai tér, has no peers (daily 9am–midnight), although the *Virág Cukrászda*, opposite Mecsek Tours on Széchenyi tér, does offer some irresistible cakes (daily 8am–11pm). Two excellent cafés offering **Internet access** are the cool, orange-walled *Matrix Café*, set back from the street at Király utca 15 (daily 9am–11pm), which also has laptops on individual tables; and the mellow café adjoining the *Fortuna* restaurant, which also serves beer and coffee (daily 10am–11pm).

For a really late and infinitely sweatier evening, the *Magic City* **disco** at Szendrey Júlia utca 9 should satisfy (Mon–Thurs till 2am, Fri & Sat till 5am).

The Pécsi Sörfőzde or Pécs **brewery**, just off Rókusalja utca, produces some of Hungary's best beers – Szalonsör, Gilde, Goldfassl and the brown version of Szalon. As the brewery doesn't run tours, the *Rókus* beer cellar or the homely *Kiskorsó* restaurant on the same street are the nearest you can get to the source. One place that does run tours is the **Pannonia Champagne House** at Szent István tér 12, which has been producing sparkling wines since 1859; one-hour tours of the cellar, including tasting of five wines, are for groups only, but you should be able to hook up if you call in advance (☎72/214-490; 1600Ft).

Entertainment and festivals

Pécs's **opera** and **ballet** companies are highly regarded, and tickets for performances at the National Theatre on Király utca can be hard to obtain – ask about cancellations at the box office, next to the theatre, an hour before the show starts (Tues–Fri 10am–7pm, Sat & Sun 1hr before performance). Tickets for the **Pannon Philharmonic Orchestra** can be obtained from the box office just across from the theatre at Király utca 18 (Filharmónia Nemzeti; Mon–Thurs 9am–4pm, Fri till 3pm; on performance days it stays open until the beginning of the performance). Throughout the year there are regular **concerts** in many of the city's churches, including organ concerts in the basilica. For children (and adults), the Bóbita **puppet theatre** is at Mária utca 18.

The highlights of a packed festival programme are the **Spring Festival**, a two-week programme of classical concerts, dance and film events from mid- to late March; and the **Pécs Weeks of Art and Gastronomy** in mid-June and early July, three weeks of joyously eclectic open-air musical, theatrical and literary events – essentially mini-festivals such as the International Romany Music Festival, the International Adult Puppet Festival and Festival of Fine Arts. In addition, many of the town's restaurants have tasting sessions on the main squares. The **Pécs Cultural Festival** in September incorporates a male-voice choir festival and a wine procession.

The dedicated **festival information office**, next to Mecsek Tours at Széchenyi tér 1 (Fesztivál Információs Iroda; Mon 8am–4pm, Tues–Fri 9am–5pm, Sat 9am–3pm; ☎72/336-622), can fill you in on what's happening in the city and also book tickets for concerts in the basilica.

The Mecsek Hills

The karstic **Mecsek Hills** north of Pécs offer panoramic views and trails fanning out from the television tower through groves of sweet chestnuts and almond trees. If you fancy some **hiking**, buy a 1:40,000 map of the hills, available from most bookshops or tourist offices in town. Alternatively, you can catch a bus (every 1hr–1hr 30min) from the intercity depot out to Orfű or Abaliget, two popular resorts forty minutes' ride from town, where **accommodation** can be pre-booked through Mecsek Tours in Pécs (see p.298).

The widely dispersed village of **ORFŰ**, 16km northwest of Pécs, features four artificial **lakes** surrounded by sports facilities, restaurants and accommodation, with an antique **mill** (Malommúzeum; Tues–Sun May–Sept 10am–6pm; Oct–April 10am–4pm; 400Ft) to the east of the smallest lake. The complex actually comprises two mills – the Water Mill and the Horse-Driven Mill, both of which were operational until the early 1950s, before they were made redundant. Both were renovated in the 1970s. **Information** can be obtained from the small Tourinform office at Széchenyi tér 1 (Mon–Fri 8am–5pm; ☎72/598-

116, Ⓔorfu@tourinform.hu), the main square in the northern part of the village. There's loads of **accommodation**, including many private rooms, in Orfű, much of it clustered around Széchenyi tér; three good places are the very comfortable *Arkádos Panzió*, opposite Tourinform at no. 4 (Ⓣ72/598-020, Ⓦwww.nexus.hu/arkados; ❸); the similar *Atrium Panzio* at no. 17 (Ⓣ72/498-288; ❸); and the *Molnár Panzió*, at no. 18 (Ⓣ72/498-363; March–Nov; ❷). There's also the large *Panoráma* **campsite** at Dollár utca 1 (Ⓣ72/378-501; mid-April to mid-Oct), with bungalows with baths (❸), and bikes and windsurfing boards for rent. The *Muskátli*, near the last of these at no. 13 (daily noon–10pm), is the best **restaurant** in the resort.

A few kilometres further west, the larger settlement of **ABALIGET** has an outdoor **thermal pool** and a 640-metre-long **stalactite cave** (Cseppkőbarlang; Tues–Sun: April–Sept 9am–6pm; Oct–March 10am–3pm; 750Ft) beside one of its lakes. The cave, whose main branch was discovered in 1819, has relatively few stalactites and stalagmites but does have a series of interesting rock formations, resulting largely from the active brook within and frequent flooding. The cave is inhabited by blind crabs and also shelters a large colony of Greater Horseshoe Bats during the winter, one of three species that can be found in the Western Mecsek region – there's a curious little exhibition on bats, including lots of dead ones, in the **Bat Museum** (same times; 300Ft), in the small building just across from the cave. Should you wish to stay, try the *Hotel Abaliget*, near the caves (Ⓣ30/9943-790; ❹); the *Abaliget Barlang* campsite by the lake (Ⓣ & Ⓕ72/498-730; mid-April to mid-Oct), with a pension (❸), a motel (❷), chalets (❷) and a restaurant; or one of the many **rooms** for rent on Kossuth utca.

Szigetvár

SZIGETVÁR, 33km west of Pécs, rivals Kőszeg for its heroic resistance to the Turkish invasion. Every Hungarian child is taught the story (see p.306), which is enshrined in poetry and music, and is the subject of a colossal painting in the Hungarian National Gallery in Budapest. Although a striking new community centre designed by Imre Makovecz has aroused some attention, and the local **thermal baths** are as agreeable as any, it is the **castle** and **relics of the Turkish occupation** that are still the main attractions of this dusty town.

The Town

Szigetvár's sights can all be easily explored on foot. On the way to the castle from the bus station, it's worth stopping off at the sixteenth-century **Turkish House** at Bástya utca 3 (Török Ház; June–Sept daily 10am–noon & 1–3pm; 200Ft), a simple brick building across the road from the market near the bus station. Originally a caravanserai, it now displays a modest collection of Turkish artefacts.

Turn left along Szecsődi Máté utca and up Rákóczi utca, where you'll come to a shoe factory at no. 7, festooned with awards won in the 1950s, their red stars now crudely effaced. This presages a grander act of revisionism on **Zrínyi tér**, where what was built as the **Mosque of Ali Pasha** in 1596 was converted into a Baroque church in the late eighteenth century; only the Turkish-style windows around the back betray its origins. The frescoes inside date from 1788 (daily 8am–noon). At this point your eyes will be drawn by the twin towers of Makovecz's **Cultural Centre**, a typically bizarre structure by the eccentric Hungarian architect (see box p.172), resembling an alien spacecraft come to earth. During its construction the town council ran out of money and refused to trim other budgets to fulfil Makovecz's conception of the project, to his outrage, resulting in the fact that the inside of the theatre wasn't finished. You can inspect it at close quarters on József Attila utca, not far away.

Returning to Zrinyi tér and turning right past a snarling lion statue on to Vár utca, you'll pass the *Török Kávéház* at no. 1, a café decorated with Turkish motifs that maintains a **local history museum** in a vaulted room out back (Tues–Sun 10am–4pm; 150Ft), exhibiting Habsburg-era shop signs, folk carvings, embroidery, weaponry and old photos of Szigetvár. From here it's a straight, 200-metre walk up the road to the castle.

The Castle

As the town's name, Island Castle, suggests, this quadrilateral fortress was once surrounded by lakes and marshes. Under local strong man Bálint Török, it resisted sieges by the Turks in 1541 and 1554, but its finest hour came in 1566, when 2400 soldiers under **Miklós Zrínyi**, governor of Croatia, resisted the onslaught of 100,000 Turks for 33 days. Enraged by the loss of 20,000 troops and the failure of his seventh attempt to march on Vienna, **Sultan Süleyman** died of apoplexy before the siege finally wore down the defenders. Spurning offers of surrender, Zrínyi donned his court dress before leading a final, suicidal sally when they could no longer hold out.

A **mosque** was erected after the castle's capture, which you'll find past a typically dour Soviet war memorial at the foot of the massive brick ramparts and through a gateway. Its minaret has long since disappeared, but the interior survives, complete with ornamental grilles, Koranic inscriptions, and frescoes depicting the deaths of Zrínyi and Süleyman (added later by the Hungarians). At no time, however, was the sultan buried here – though his viscera once reposed in another mosque in town (see below).

In an adjacent **museum** (Vár Zrínyi Miklós Múzeum; Tues–Sun: May–Sept 9am–6pm; April & Oct 9am–3pm; 250Ft), built as the summer house of Count Andrássy, coloured miniatures of Turkish life are counterpointed by praise for Magyar heroism. Copies of the epic *Szózat* (Appeal) are on display, penned by Zrínyi's grandson, himself a general. A cry for liberty and a call for endurance, this seventeenth-century poem was adapted as a chorale by Kodály in 1956. Its single performance at the Budapest Academy turned into an emotional symbolic protest against the Rákosi regime. Chanting crowds took up the refrain, *Ne Bántsd a Magyart!* ("Let the Magyars alone!"), causing government members who were there to walk out.

The Hungarian-Turkish Friendship Park

One of those ideas that appeal to politicians but leave the public cold, the **Hungarian-Turkish Friendship Park** (Magyar-Török Barátság Emlékpark) was opened in 1994 by Turkey's prime minister, as a token apology and symbol of reconciliation. While a stone commemorating the death of Süleyman on the spot where his tent once stood (and he presumably expired) was acceptable, local people objected to a larger-than-life statue of the sultan until the Turks commissioned one of Zrínyi, whereupon it was agreed to place them side by side rather than confronting one another.

For the record, Süleyman's heart and innards were buried by his son, Selim II, in a **mosque** built nearby shortly after his death, and taken back to Constantinople when campaigning ceased. After the Turks were finally driven out, the mosque was turned into a church, though its past was acknowledged by a plaque.

The park is 3km north of Szigetvár on the left-hand side of the road to Kaposvár, so it's accessible by bus – unlike the mosque, which is 3km down the road towards Zsibót.

Practicalities

Szigetvár's **bus** and **train stations** are about 500m down Rákóczi utca from the main square, Zrínyi tér, from where it's a short walk north along Vár utca to the castle. There's no tourist office in Szigetvár, but the Tourinform in Pécs (see p.298) can supply **information** on the town. For comfort, price and location, by far the best place to **stay** is the new and very smart *Szeráj Panzió* at Kossuth tér 8 (Ⓣ & Ⓕ73/414-145; ❹). The three other places are much of a muchness: the *Kumilla Hotel* at Olay Lajos utca 6, behind the Makovecz building (Ⓣ73/510-288, Ⓦwww.hotels.hu/kumilla; ❹), is just about the best and guests get free use of the **thermal baths** 150m away at Tinódi Sebestyén utca 23 (Tues–Sun 9am–6pm; 500Ft); the *Hotel Oroszlán* on Zrínyi tér (Ⓣ73/310-116, Ⓕ510-382; ❸), whose rooms are better than the grubby building suggests; and the *Lenzl Panzió*, at József Attila utca 63 (Ⓣ73/413-045, Ⓔlenzis@dravanet.hu; ❹), which has fairly cluttered rooms but is otherwise fine.

The *Szeráj Panzió* also has the best **restaurant** in town, or, beyond the *Lenzl Panzió* on József Attila utca, there's the *Kisváros*, at no. 81, and the *Florián*, opposite at no. 58 (both open till 10pm) – all serve stock Hungarian fare. The *Vigadó*, in the cultural centre, is good for a lunchtime snack, but no more (daily 9am–10pm). The **post office** is at József Attila utca 27–31 (Mon–Fri 8am–5pm, Sat 8am–noon).

Harkány, Villány and Siklós

The area south of Pécs offers several attractions. Those in search of a therapeutic wallow in yet another thermal bath should visit the spa town of **Harkány**, but perhaps a greater draw is the thirty-kilometre-long **Villány-Siklós wine road**, Hungary's first wine route. **Siklós**, a short ride east of Harkány and Hungary's southernmost town, is the white wine centre of the region and also boasts a fabulous fifteenth-century castle. **Villány** is an absolute must for the wine aficionado, with its extensive vineyards and cellars producing some of the country's finest red wines.

Harkány

Twenty-four kilometres south of Pécs, **HARKÁNY**'s main draws are its enormous open-air **thermal baths** (Gyógyfürdő; daily 9am–6pm; 1800Ft, 1100Ft after 2pm) and indoor **pools** (Strandfürdő; June–Aug daily 9am–10pm; Sept–May Mon–Thurs & Sun 9am–6pm, Fri & Sat till 8pm; 840Ft, 640Ft after 2pm), with a section for wallowing in **hot mud**, therapeutically rich in sulphur and fluoride. The open-air *strand* can be entered from Kossuth utca, the main thoroughfare, to the west or Bajcsy-Zsilinszky utca to the east, while the entrance to the spa is on Zsigmond sétány on the south side of the compound, in the middle of town. Aside from this, there's not much else to visit except a small **market** near the bus station and an early nineteenth-century **Calvinist Church** on Kossuth utca.

Arriving by train, a fifteen-minute walk up Táncsics Mihály and then Arany János utca will bring you close to the Kossuth utca entrance to the *strand*; the bus station is at the southern end of Bajcsy-Zsilinszky utca, on the far side of the baths. **Information** is available from Tourinform in the small cultural house at Kossuth utca 2 (June–Sept Mon–Fri 9am–6pm, Sat & Sun 9am–5pm; Oct–May Mon–Fri 9am–4pm; Ⓣ72/479-624, Ⓔharkany@tourinform.hu), and **private rooms** (❷) can be arranged through Mecsek Tours at Bajcsy-Zsilinszky ucta 2, by the pools' entrance (May–Sept Mon–Fri 8am–6.30pm, Sat 8.30am–noon; Oct–April Mon–Fri 8.30am–4.30pm; Ⓣ72/480-322, Ⓔharkany@mecsektours.hu). Harkány is swarming with **hotels**, the best of which are those along Kossuth utca, including the very classy *Xavin* at no. 43 (Ⓣ72/580-158, Ⓦwww.xavin.hu; ❺), with its own lovely indoor pool, and the equally fine *Atrium*, 500m further along at no. 10 (Ⓣ72/580-880, Ⓦwww.atriumharkany.hu; ❹). More modestly, there's the *Kokó Panzió,* just off Kossuth utca at Arany János utca 7b (Ⓣ & Ⓕ72/480-326; ❸). Of the hotels by the baths, the only one of any real quality is the immaculate *Korona* at Bajcsy-Zsilinszky utca 3 (Ⓣ72/580-830, Ⓕ480-808; ❺). The *Thermal* **campsite**, at Bajcsy-Zsilinszky utca 6 (Ⓣ72/480-117; mid-April to mid-Oct), has a basic hotel (❸), motel (❶), and four-bed chalets (❹). The excellent **restaurants** in the *Atrium* and *Xavin* hotels aside, there is a string of pizzerias and pubs along Kossuth utca and a good wine shop at no. 44 (Mon–Fri 10am–1pm & 2–6pm, Sat 10am–1pm).

Siklós

Most buses plough on from Harkány a further 5km across the dusty plain to **SIKLÓS**, a small compact town huddled around a medieval castle – the town's star attraction. The town is also a favoured destination with shoppers from **Croatia**, where goods are much more expensive due to high tariffs and VAT; as a result the local market is a cornucopia of goods, and every shop advertises its wares in Croatian.

From the **bus station** follow the main street, Felszabadulás utca, past the post office on Flórián tér and on up to Kossuth tér just below the castle, which is located on Vajda János tér. Arriving by **train**, it's a ten-minute walk up Táncsics Mihály utca to the bottom of Kossuth tér. Opposite the bright, peach-coloured Baroque town hall on **Kossuth tér**, no. 12 was the **birthplace of George Mikes**, the émigré writer known for his parodies of British life in the 1960s. A couple of steps down the road to the right stands the sixteenth-century **Malkocs Bej Mosque** (Malkocs Bej Dzsámija; mid-April to mid-Oct Tues–Sun 9am–4pm; mid-Oct to mid-April Sat & Sun 9am–4pm; 200Ft), recently restored and stuffed with Turkish carpets and other knick-knacks.

Siklós Castle (daily: mid-April to mid-Oct 9am–6pm; mid-Oct to mid-April 9am–4pm; 660Ft) remained in private hands from its foundation in the fifteenth century up until 1943, when it was confiscated by the state. Bastions and rondellas form an impressive girdle around a mansion once occupied by the enlightened Casimir Batthyány, who freed his serfs in 1847. His tomb is in the Gothic chapel, located (with no sense of incongruity according to medieval values) within whipping distance of a dungeon filled with instruments of torture. Next to the dungeon, a small **museum** contains cabinets stuffed with gloves, fans and umbrellas, illustrating the period between the late eighteenth and early nineteenth centuries when these manufacturing industries were thriving – indeed, the factories of Pécs were renowned throughout Europe for the quality of the gloves produced. The museum cellar holds archeological remains and some rather large cannonballs. From the ramparts – where you'll also find a small coffee shop – you can enjoy tremendous views of the surrounding Villány Hills. The **Castle Festival** takes place in the last weekend in June and has international brass bands performing in the courtyard as its highlight.

The Villány-Siklós wine road

Running along the sunny southern slopes of the Villány Hills, the **Villány-Siklós wine road** was the first wine route to be set up in Hungary, in 1994. Named after the villages of Villány and Siklós, located 13km apart, the thirty-kilometre-long route runs through one of the largest concentrations of cellars in the country, winding its way past eleven settlements and vineyards.

It is believed that wine making in the region started during Roman times and continued through the Middle Ages. The industry collapsed as the Ottoman Empire swept all before it, leaving many villages abandoned, but production quickly resumed following their retreat. However, it is only since the end of Communism that the wider world has been alerted to the region's propensity for producing top-quality wines.

Thanks to its favourable geographical location and Mediterranean climate and soil, the region consistently yields a superb range of red and white wines. Generally speaking, **white wines** emanate from the more westerly district around Siklós, whilst the more famous **reds** are produced in Villány and surrounding vineyards. Some of the local vintners, such as Attila Gere and József Bock (see below), are internationally renowned and have recently produced some of the country's most distinctive and finest reds.

Siklós's Tourinform office is at Felszabadulás utca 3 (Mon–Fri 9am–5pm; ⓣ72/579-090, ⓔsiklos@tourinform.hu), just a few steps away from the town's sole **hotel**, the very bland *Központi* at Kossuth Lajos tér 5 (ⓣ72/352-513, ⓦwww.kozponti.hu; ❸), which also has a very ordinary **restaurant** (daily 8am–11pm).

Alternatively, you can book a local **room** through Mecsek Tours in Harkány (see opposite) or Pécs (see p.298). There's excellent strudel at the oddly named *Hamburger Cukrászda* by the entrance to the market at Felszabadulás utca 22 (daily 8am–7pm).

Villány

Fifteen kilometres east of Siklós, acres of vineyards lap the slopes of Mount Szársomlyó, producing red wine under the appellation Villányi. The village of **VILLÁNY** is of Swabian (German) origin, as you might guess from its neatness and uniformity, with pots of geraniums outside all the houses and everything signposted for the benefit of visitors.

The local viticultural tradition goes back two thousand years, though you won't find anything that ancient in the **Wine Museum**, in a 200-year-old cellar at Bem József utca 8, just off Baross Gábor utca (Borműzeum; Tues–Sun 9am–5pm; free). You can sample local **wine** at many places on Baross Gábor utca, Batthyány utca, and Diófas tér – the names to look out for are Gere (see p.310) and Bock (see p.310), whose wines have an international reputation; both charge around 1500Ft for five wines, or 2000Ft for seven wines, including snacks. Bock's are labelled *Jammertal* (German for "Valley of Lamentation"), after a battle in 1687 where the Turks were hacked to death amid the Drava bogs. Wine lovers should also investigate the Polgár, Blum and Tiffán cellars in Villánykövesd, 2.5km northwest of town towards Pécs.

Arriving at the **train station**, exit left and it's a dull fifteen-minute walk past crumbling warehouses and grubby wasteland to the centre of the village, which is essentially the main street, Baross Gábor utca – the majority of cellars are located at the upper end of this street. Turning right out of the station will lead you towards Villánykövesd. **Buses** stop in the centre by the town hall.

Just as you enter the village, at Deák Ferenc utca 22, is a small **information office** (Borút Iroda; Mon–Fri 8am–4pm; ⓣ72/492-181, ⓔiroda@borut.hu), which can advise on visiting cellars in the region. The *Oportó Panzió* at Baross Gábor utca 33 (ⓣ72/492-582, ⓦwww.oporto,hu; ❺) has first-class **rooms** with polished wooden flooring and pretty pictures gracing the walls. Otherwise, there is the very comfortable *Gere Panzió* at Diófás tér 4 (ⓣ72/492-195; ⓦwww.gere.hu; ❸), which has a lovely Mediterranean-style garden and the most renowned **wine cellar** in the village; or the *Bock Panzió* at Batthyány utca 15 (ⓣ72/492-919, ⓦwww.bock.hu; ❹), where József Bock has his cellar. There are also many houses in the village advertising beds (*falusi szálláshely*). The best **meals** in the village are served in the *Oportó*'s beautifully appointed restaurant, and the *Júlia Vendéglő* at Baross Gábor utca 41 (daily 11am–10pm), while if you're heading towards Villánykövesd, stop off at the peaceful *Fülemüle Csárda* (daily 11am–11pm).

Mohács

The small town of **MOHÁCS**, 41km east of Pécs by the River Danube, is a synonym for defeat. As a consequence of a single **battle** here in 1526, Hungary was divided and war-torn for 150 years and lost its independence for centuries thereafter. The state was tottering before Mohács, however: its treasury depleted, and with an indecisive teenager on the throne. Only after Süleyman "the Magnificent" had taken Belgrade and was nearing the Drava did the Hungarians muster an army, which headed south without waiting for reinforcements from Transylvania, engaging the Turks on August 29.

Legend has it that an olive tree planted two hundred years earlier by Louis the Great suddenly became barren on that day, while the king's scribe records how the young Louis II gave orders for the care of his hounds before riding out to meet his fate. Attacking first, the Magyars broke ranks to loot the fallen and suffered a crushing counterattack by Turkish janissaries and cavalry, which caused a rout. Louis was crushed to death by his horse when trying to ford a stream, and the twenty thousand Hungarian dead included five hundred nobles and scores of prelates, leaving the country unable to organize resistance as the Turks advanced on Buda.

The battlefield and town

The battle occurred 7km south of Mohács, at a site thenceforth known as Sátorhely (Place of the Tent), which in 1976 was declared a **memorial park** (Mohácsi Történelmi Emlékpark; May–Sept daily 9am–6pm; Oct–April Sat & Sun 10am–4pm; 600Ft) to mark the 450th anniversary of the battle. By coincidence, it was also the site of a later battle in 1687 between Habsburg and Turkish forces, in which the latter were defeated. Though easily reached by Route 56 (buses heading from Mohács towards Nagynyárád, Majs, Lippó, Bezedek or Magyarbóly run past), there's little to see but a bunker-like edifice containing maps of each side's deployments and endless texts in Hungarian – bar a wreath-laying ceremony on Mohács Memorial Day (August 29).

In Mohács itself, the **Kanizsai Dorottya Museum**, just off Szabadszág utca at Városház utca 1 (April–Oct Tues–Sat 10am–5pm, Sun 10am–noon & 2–4pm; Nov–March Tues–Sat 10am–4pm; 200Ft), commemorates the battle, in addition to hosting an exhibition on the diverse ethnic groups that repopulated Mohács in the late seventeenth century, with national costumes from the Croatian, Serbian and Slovenian communities. On Széchenyi tér stands an impressively ugly **Votive Church**, built to commemorate the 400th anniversary of the battle; and the **Town Hall**, where the Sultan's calligraphic signature is engraved on one of the windows. The town's only other sight is the eighteenth-century **Serbian Orthodox Church**, down towards the river at Szerb utca 2, whose magnificent iconostasis was painted by the Hungarian Csóka Mór.

Each spring, exactly seven weeks before Easter, the streets of Mohács come alive with the annual **Busójárás Carnival**. At night the carnival assumes a macabre appearance, with a procession of grotesquely masked figures waving flaming torches, who cross the River Danube – which rolls through the town disconcertingly near street level – in wooden boats to chase away the winter. Originally, it was probably a spring ritual intended to appease the gods, but over time participants also began to practise ritualistic abomination of the Turks to magically draw the sting of reality. Similar carnivals are held in Serbia, Slovenia and Croatia, where many of the revellers at Mohács travel from.

Practicalities

While the **train station** is half an hour's walk north of the centre, the **bus station** is on Rákóczi utca, close to Szabadság utca, the main street running eastwards across Széchenyi tér and on to the Danube embankment near the ferry landing stage on Szent Mihály tér. From here the **car ferry** crosses the river to the residential area of Újmohács (and the Great Plain) every half an hour between 5.20am and 6pm (420Ft for a car, plus 120Ft for each passenger, 230Ft for a bike). **Information** is available from Tourinform at Széchenyi tér 1 (mid-June to mid-Sept Mon–Fri 7.30am–5pm, Sat 10am–3pm; mid-Sept to mid-June Mon–Fri 7.30am–4pm; Ⓣ69/505-515, Ⓔmohacs@tourinform.hu), while the **post office** is next door (Mon–Fri 8am–5pm, Sat 8–11am).

There's scant choice when it comes to **accommodation**, your options being limited to two places either side of the landing stage: the bargain-value *Révkapu Panzió* (Ⓣ69/311-129; ❸), and the rather dismal *Hotel Csele* (Ⓣ69/511-020; ❹), where the best rooms are on the river-facing side of the second floor – note that it's essential to reserve rooms at carnival time. Alternatively, there's the year-round *Aréna Camping* at Dunaszekcső, 12km north along Route 56 (Ⓣ69/335-161), which has a menagerie of animals, lovely views of the river, a restaurant, rooms (❷) and bungalows (❷).

For **eating**, you can choose between the posh *Halászcsárda* beside the hotel, with fish soups and stews and a terrace overlooking the river (Tues–Sun 11am–midnight), or the *Veli Aga Vendéglő* at Szentháromság utca 7, just along from the Holy Trinity statue, whose cuisine has a distinct Serbian and Turkish flavour (Mon–Thurs 11am–10pm, Fri & Sat till midnight). Moving on, there are **buses** to Szekszárd and Budapest, and to Baja and Kecskemét or Szeged on the Great Plain, which are far more convenient than the train. There is a **border crossing** into Croatia at Udvar, 11km south of town.

Szekszárd and the Forest of Gemenc

The chance to sample red wine produced in vineyards dating from Roman times and to buy inexpensive black pottery makes **SZEKSZÁRD** the prime stopover between Pécs and Budapest. Baroque squares, leafy streets and ancient wine cellars make this an ideal base to explore the wild, marshy **Forest of Gemenc** – while in June, early August and mid-September several festivals are held.

The Town

Szekszárd's centre fans out from the intersection of two main axes: the park-like Szent Istvàn tér that eventually leads uphill to Béla tér, via cobbled Garay tér, and the busy Széchenyi utca, crossing it at right angles. In a neo-Renaissance pile at the eastern end of Szent Istvàn tér, the **Wosinsky Museum** (Wosinsky Mór Megyei Múzeum; April–Sept Tues–Sun 10am–6pm; Oct–March Tues–Sat 10am–4pm; 200Ft, free on Tues) has a rich, but wearily presented, collection of Roman artefacts and peasants' costumes, as well as workshops and replicas of the shops that existed about a century ago. Behind the museum is an old **synagogue** (Tues–Sun 10am–6pm; 150Ft), whose interior and exterior have both been beautifully and tastefully restored, the former having incorporated the original iron columns into the new design. Outside, the Triumphal Arch is flanked by four more columns, protected by concrete. The synagogue is now used as a concert hall and a venue for temporary art exhibitions.

The final uphill stretch beyond Széchenyi utca leads to Béla tér, where porticoed buildings tilt perceptibly around a statue marking the plague of 1730. The Neoclassical palace on the south side was built in 1828 by Mihály Pollack, on the site of an abbey church from the time of the Árpáds – the foundations are visible in the courtyard. Inside, a small **Liszt Memorial Exhibition** (Liszt Emlék kiallitás; April–Sept Tues–Sun 9am–5pm; Oct–March Tues–Sat 9am–3pm; 200Ft) commemorates Liszt's four visits to Szekszárd, and displays the piano that he played and a few of his scrawls.

At the top end of the square, Babits utca runs off towards the **House of Mihály Babits**, across the bridge at no. 13 (Babits Mihály Emlékház; April–Sept Tues–Sun 9am–3pm; Oct–March Tues–Sat 9am–5pm; 200Ft), a homely residence exhibiting photos and manuscripts related to the journal *Nyugat* (West). This avant-garde publication was edited by Babits and included the Village Explorers' exposés of rural life in interwar Hungary, launching the literary careers of Endre Ady and Gyula Illyés. Alas for Attila József, the finest poet of that era, Babits refused to publish his work in *Nyugat*, earning József's eternal hostility. Babits went to his graveside to ask his forgiveness.

Szekszárd's dark, rich "ox-blood" wine (Szekszárdi Vörös) was exported as far afield as Britain and Turkey in the 1700s, and Franz Liszt, Pope Pius IX and Emperor Haile Selassie are all said to have been admirers. Today, wine lovers can visit the numerous surrounding **vineyards**, or several excellent private **vintners** in town such as the Vesztergombi family, which has a shop at Béla tér 7 (Mon–Fri 10am–noon & 1–5pm, Sat 9am–noon) selling Vida and Sárosdi, as well as their own wines, and a cellar on Kadarka utca, uphill behind the square. The Garay Winery, just below the palace at Béla tér 1, offers wine and cheese tasting in its cellar (Mon–Fri 9am–6pm, Sat 8am–5pm; around 1200Ft for tour and tasting). Many other private cellars open their doors during the Alisca Wine Days (Bornapok) at the end of May (see opposite).

Practicalities

Arriving at the bus or train station on Pollack Mihály utca, it's a ten-minute walk up pedestrianized Bajcsy-Zsilinszky utca to Szent István tér. **Information** can be obtained from Tourinform just below Béla tér at Garay tér 18 (Mon–Fri 9am–5pm, also June–Aug Sat & Sun 10am–6pm; ⓣ74/511-263, ⓔszekszard@tourinform.hu). The main **post office** is at Széchenyi utca 11–13 (Mon–Fri 7.30am–7pm, Sat 8am–noon), and there's **Internet access** available just around the corner in the Matav shop.

The cheapest accommodation is a room at the *Illyés Gyula Pedagógiai Főiskola kollégium*, ten minutes' walk north of the centre at Mötyös kiröly utca 3 (ⓣ74/412-133;❶), or **private rooms** bookable through Ibusz at Széchenyi utca 20 (Mon–Fri 8am–5pm, Sat 8am–noon; ⓣ74/319-822, ⓔi086@tourinform.hu). The best of the few **hotels** here is the *Zodiaco* at Szent László utca 19, five minutes' walk north of Béla tér (ⓣ74/511-150, ⓦwww.hotelzodiaco.hu; ❺), a joy of a place with minimally but coolly furnished air-conditioned rooms, each named after a star sign or planet. Other accommodation options boil down to the horrible 1970s *Hotel Gemenc*, behind the Wosinsky Museum at Mészáros Lázár utca 4 (ⓣ74/311-722, ⓦwww.hotels.hu_gemenc; ❹), which has small, stuffy rooms; and the *Alisca Hotel* at Kálvária utca 1, up a steep path above Béla tér (ⓣ & ⓕ74/511-242; ❺), which has fine views over town, but little else to commend it. There's a **campsite** 5km north of the centre, at the junction of Route 6 in the Gemenc Szabadidőpark (ⓣ74/410-151; April–Oct).

Though Szekszárd's gastronomic efforts are less remarkable than its wine, you can take in a hugely enjoyable **meal** at the *Szász Söröző*, Garay tér 18, a medieval-themed place with particularly delicious soups and some fantastic vegetarian options – it's equally great for a beer (daily 10am–midnight, Sun till 10pm). The *Főispán*, tucked away to the left of the town hall on Béla tér, is a more polished restaurant with seductive, overhanging lamps under which you can enjoy fine Hungarian cuisine (daily 11.30am–midnight, Sun till 10pm), while the *Gilde Söröző* at Kossuth Lajos utca 16, just off Szent László utca, has a reasonably varied, if rather beef-heavy, menu (daily 11.30am–midnight). Cheap, hot lunches, washed down with good wine, can be consumed at *Papa's Winehouse* (Mon–Fri 9am–8pm, Sat 7am–8pm, Sun 9am–6pm), at the bottom of Garay tér at no. 6. For coffee, cakes and ice cream head to the *Belvárosi Kávéház* next to the *Szász Söröző*, with a pleasant terrace looking down the square. For **entertainment**, check out the alternative arts centre, Zug, at Béla tér 6, which hosts concerts, films and other events and has a bar open until 10pm.

The town's two major wine-related events are the **Alisca Wine Days** (Bornapok) at the end of May, which sees tastings and craft fairs, and the **Grape and Wine Harvest**, a three-day festival in the third week of September where the whole town is in a festive mood, with visitors welcome to participate in picking and pressing the grapes, and enjoy the music, wine and song. Another event worth attending is the **folklore festival at Decs** at the beginning of August. Though only 8km from Szekszárd, this village was traditionally isolated by marshes yet remained *au courant*, as its menfolk worked as bargees, bringing home the latest news and fabrics from Budapest. Their wives wore beribboned silk skirts and cambric blouses with lace inserts, and later acquired a taste for lime green and yellow metallic thread, making their **costumes** as lurid as rave attire.

The Forest of Gemenc

Part of the Danube-Drava National Park since 1996, the **Forest of Gemenc**, 12km east of Szekszárd, is a remnant of the wilderness of woods, reeds and mudland that once covered the Danube's shifting, flood-prone banks. Only at the beginning of the twentieth century was the river tamed and shortened by 60km, thus helping to stem the annual flooding of its backwaters and the Sárköz (Mud Region). However, marshes and ponds remained to provide habitats for boar, wildcats, otters, deer, ospreys, falcons, bald eagles, black storks and other **wildlife**. Nowadays, the forest is a nature reserve of sorts, although the deer and wild boar are fair game for Western hunters.

The gateway to the forest is the Gemenc **excursion centre** (May–Oct daily 9.30–11am & noon–4pm; ☎72/312-552) in **Bárányfok**, a popular recreation spot on the northwestern edge of the forest; to get there from Szekszárd, take any bus heading for Keselyűs (4–5 daily). A short walk from the entrance is the red-pine **Trophy Museum** (Tues–Sun 10am–5pm; 500Ft), built in 1896 for the Millennium exhibition and which was later used to house Archduke Franz Ferdinand's hunting trophies. It now has exhibits on the forest's flora and fauna and displays on the difficulties that the park's inhabitants have traditionally faced, such as in 1956, when a major flood forced the evacuation of some forty settlements and more than five thousand homes were destroyed. Also located here is the *Trófea* restaurant, a typically rustic *csárda* serving predominantly game and fish (daily till 9pm). The excursion centre has information on **boat trips** on the forest's backwaters, and on the **miniature train**, which runs between May and October from the terminal at Bárányfok down through the forest to **Pörböly** (on the main line between Bátaszék and Baja), 30km to the south; there are only three trains a day (leaving Bárányfok at 10.30am, 1.35pm & 3.35pm; Pörböly at 8am, 9.20am & 1.15pm), and tickets (920Ft return, 600Ft single) can be purchased from the excursion centre at Bárányfok.

Szekszárd to Budapest

The road and train line between Szekszárd and Budapest pass through dreary countryside punctuated by three towns that, although not worth a special visit in themselves, might tempt you to make a stopover – **Paks**, **Dunaföldvár** and **Dunaújváros**. If not, and you're driving, consider a **scenic detour** along minor roads through the pretty villages of Högyész, Gyonk and Cece, before rejoining the trunk route at Dunaföldvár, which – aside from Baja – has the only bridge across the Danube. Irregular **car ferries** from Fadd-Dombori, Gerjen, Paks and Dunaújváros also enable motorists to cross over to the Great Plain.

Paks

PAKS, 27km north of Szekszárd, is the site of Hungary's only **nuclear power station**, four Soviet-designed pressurized water reactors which supply up to forty percent of the country's electricity. Bar some anxiety in the aftermath of Chernobyl, the issue of nuclear power has never aroused much public concern in Hungary except among communities living near the site of proposed nuclear waste dumps, and in Paks itself people are quick to point out that the plant gets good marks from international safety inspectors.

From the main train station south of downtown Paks, bus #1 takes you past the remarkable **Catholic Church** on Hősök tere, built by Imre Makovecz (see p.172) in 1988. A strikingly organic structure made of wood, its separate bell-tower has three spires topped by a cross, a crescent and a sun sign – which provoked letters to the press condemning the "Satanic forces" behind it, despite Makovecz's claim that they were early Christian symbols. You can get the key to the church at Hősök tere 19.

The remaining sights are on Szent István tér, the main square in the north of town, where a small **City Museum** (Tues 10am–4pm, Wed–Sun 10am–6pm; 200Ft) displays the usual Bronze Age, Roman, Celtic and Magyar artefacts, plus a table used by the statesman Deák. More excitingly, there's the **Paks Gallery** at Szent István tér 4 (Tues–Sun 10am–6pm; free), set up by local artist Károly Halász, whose stimulating exhibition of contemporary Hungarian works is

▲ Catholic Church, Paks

hung within a cool white conversion of a grand classical building that was only the third casino in the country when it was built in 1844 – later it became a hotel.

If you're **arriving** by train it's better to get off at the Paks Duna-part station near Szent István tér rather than the main station over a kilometre south of the centre, where the bus station is located near the bottom of Dózsa György út. Both are connected to the centre by regular buses. While Tourinform at Szent István tér 2 (Mon–Fri 9am–5pm; ⓣ75/421-575, ⓔpaks@tourinform.hu) can supply **information**, Viking Tours at Kossuth utca 1–3 (Mon–Fri 9am–5pm; ⓣ75/310-475) are responsible for booking private rooms – which are the only alternative **accommodation** to the modern *Duna Hotel* at Dózsa György út 75 (ⓣ75/310-891; ❸).

The *Halászcsárda* fish **restaurant** at Dunaföldvár utca 5a, fifteen minutes' walk upriver from the main square, has a terrace with fine views of the river, and a good reputation, despite the reactor being a mile downstream.

Dunaföldvár

DUNAFÖLDVÁR, 24km north of Paks, is by far the prettiest and smallest of the three towns en route to Budapest. Arriving by **bus**, it's a two-minute walk north to the main square, Béke tér, while the **train station** is located 2km south of town on Batthàny utca. The town's name derives from the sixteenth-century fortress that was hastily erected to guard the Danube after Belgrade fell to Süleyman's army, of which only the keep – known as the **Turkish Tower** – has survived. The tower, up on Rátkai köz (Tues–Sun 10am–6pm; 160Ft), is now a small museum containing bits and bobs from the twelfth century, and an assortment of items representing various local trades such as blue-dyers and bootmakers. A better reason to visit is for the fantastic views of the Danube below and the puffing chimneys of the Dunaújváros ironworks away in the distance. Across the courtyard, the **Fafaragó Gallery** (same ticket and times) has a small ethnographic collection as well as paintings and handiwork by local artists. After the Turks were finally driven out, the town was repopulated by outsiders, as its Baroque **Serbian Orthodox Church** at Kossuth Lajos utca 18 attests; the small, white church is likely to remain closed for some time whilst its icons undergo restoration work in Szentendre. Besides some elegant **Art Nouveau buildings** in the centre, it's possible to inspect **craft workshops** such as that of the blue-dyer (*kékfestő*) Vadász Istvánné, at Duna utca 6 (Mon–Fri 8am–4pm).

Visits can be arranged through Tourinform, Rákóczi utca 2 (June to mid-Sept Mon–Fri 9am–5pm, Sat 9am–1pm; mid-Sept to May Mon–Fri 9am–5pm; ⓣ75/341-176, ⓔdunafoldvar@tourinform.hu), which can provide other **information** and book **private rooms** (❷) if required. Two central, and good-value, pensions close to each other are the *Prajda Panzió*, Kossuth Lajos utca 22 (ⓣ75/342-182), and the *Varró Panzió*, Petőfi utca 20 (ⓣ75/341-810; ❷). The Kék-Duna **campsite**, at Hősök tere 26, occupies a wonderful grassy spot on the river bank (ⓣ75/541-107), and has rooms in chalets (❶). For **eating**, the red-and-black rustically styled *Vár Étterem*, up by the Turkish Tower, is worth a visit as much for the views as for the food (daily 9am–10pm), while the *Halászcsárda* fish restaurant, next to the campsite on Hősök tere, also has resplendent views across the Danube – the Földvári fish soup is highly recommended (daily 11am–10pm). There's good coffee, cakes and ices at the quaint *Marcipán Cukrászda* at Béke tér 3.

Dunaújváros

In total contrast, **DUNAÚJVÁROS** (Danube New Town), 20km upriver, is a monument to Stalinist economics, created around a vast ironworks which the Party saw as the lynchpin of its industrialization strategy for the 1950s. The construction of Sztálinváros (as the town was originally called) was trumpeted as a feat by Stakhanovites, though much of the heavy work was performed by peasants and "reformed" prostitutes living under appalling conditions. Yet, at the same time, it embodied a striving for a brighter future for the working classes – a paradox that has assumed a new form today, as this incarnation of the planned economy has weathered the transition to capitalism better than "traditional" industrial towns such as Ózd in northeastern Hungary.

The town's appeal lies in its **Bauhaus and Socialist-Realist aesthetic**, though its uniform rows of blocks make orientation difficult. A tall redbrick block on Városháza tér serves as the main landmark in the centre, whence Vasmű út runs to the Iron Works. On Városháza tér, at no. 4, the former Party headquarters now houses the **Intercisa Museum** (Tues–Sun 2–6pm; 260Ft), which relates the history of this site from Roman times – mainly in the form of urns and grave goods – before advancing abrubtly to the twentieth century and the Stalinist era. The latter is epitomized by a book of 14,800 signatures presented to Party Secretary Rákosi "demanding" that Sztálinváros be built – although it doesn't go into much detail about the suffering involved. A few minutes' walk towards the river brings you to a **sculpture park** of rusting iron supplied by the works.

The **Institute of Contemporary Art**, just round the corner at Vasmű út 12 (Tues–Sun 10am–6pm; free), is worth a visit for its temporary exhibitions of Hungarian and foreign works, and also has a pleasant little coffee bar (Mon–Sat 7am–10pm). Further along Vasmű út, a right turning down Babits utca leads onto **Bartók tér**, featuring a store with mosaics depicting workers and peasants building the town. On the same square, the **Bartók Cultural Centre** combines classical, Egyptian and Bauhaus motifs, while through the archway a school of the same era has separate doors for boys and girls, topped by reliefs of idealized children at study. Leading away from the square is Majus 1 út, one of the first streets to be built in 1950, and a must for lovers of the Bauhaus style. For real fanatics, the tourist office (see below) has produced a leaflet detailing a two-hour walk around the town's many other socialist monuments.

Continuing along Vasmű út you'll pass a **statue of a foundry worker** relaxing, which Party officials complained should show the worker working, not resting, and was consequently not erected until 1961. Another twenty minutes' walk, past the football stadium, brings you to the entrance of the **Iron Works**, like something out of a Cecil B. De Mille set, with enormous frescoes of joyous workers above a Neoclassical portico. The works cover a huge area, almost as big as the town itself, and employ some eight thousand people, both from the town and the region.

Practicalities

There are regular bus services into the centre from the **train station**, 2km south of town, while the **bus terminal**, on Béke tér, is within easy walking distance; buses into town often stop at Városháza tér. As you might expect, Dunaújváros is hardly geared up for tourists, though there is a Tourinform office at Vasmű út 10a (Mon–Fri 8am–4pm; Ⓣ25/500-148, Ⓔdunaujvaros@tourinform.hu) dispensing **information**. Ibusz, at Devecseri utca 8 (Mon–Fri 8am–5pm, Sat 9am–noon Ⓣ25/409-960, Ⓔi046@ibusz.hu), can book private rooms (❷) or beds in the *Kerpely Antal kollégium* at Dózsa György út 33 (ⓣ25/551-123; 2500Ft; July & Aug), while **hotel** options are limited to the very smart and business-like *Klub Hotel* at Epítők útja 2 (ⓣ25/581-045, ⓦwww.klubhotel@ber.dunaferr.hu; ❻), 400m east of the bus station, and the quite awful *Dunaferr Hotel* next door (ⓣ25/581-225, ⓕ412-030; ❸). There is also a **campsite** (ⓣ25/310-285; May–Sept), with an open-air bathing area, on a small island 3km north of the centre, accessible by bus #24 or #26.

Dunaújváros has a few reasonably good **eating** options, the best of which are the *Topo Pizzeria and Salad Bar*, behind the cinema at Kőműves utca 5 (daily 10am–11pm), and *Geronimo*, to the side of the cinema on Ságvári tér, which has juicy steaks and ribs plus some Mexican dishes thrown in for good measure (noon–midnight). There's also the *Aranysárkány*, a fairly authentic Chinese place at Vasmű út 9–11 (daily 9am–midnight). The *City Café* and *Caribian Bar*, both a few paces along from the *Topo Pizzeria*, are the obvious choices for a daytime or evening drink, while the *Buszor Café*, alongside the Bartók Cultural Centre, is not a bad place either (daily 2pm–midnight).

Travel details

Trains

Fertőboz to: Nagycenk (April–Oct 5 departures Sat & Sun; 30min).
Győr to: Budapest (hourly; 1hr 30min–2hr); Mosonmagyaróvár (hourly; 30min); Pápa (12 daily; 40min–1hr); Sopron (9 daily; 1hr–1hr 30min); Szombathely (2 daily; 1hr 50min); Veszprém (6 daily; 2hr–2hr 30min).
Kaposvár to: Fonyód (8 daily; 1hr); Pécs (4 daily; 1hr 30min–2hr).
Kőszeg to: Szombathely (every 1hr–1hr 30min; 30min).
Mohács to: Pécs (3 daily; 1hr 30min); Villány (6 daily; 30min).
Nagycenk to: Fertőboz (April–Oct 4 departures Sat & Sun; 30min).
Nagykanizsa to: Balatonszentgyörgy (every 1–2hr; 30–40min); Budapest (every 1–2hr; 3–4hr); Pécs (5 daily; 2hr 30min–3hr); Szombathely (6 daily; 1hr 30min–2hr).
Pécs to: Budapest (9 daily; 2hr 45min–3hr 30min); Kaposvár (3 daily; 1hr 30min–2hr); Mohács (4 daily; 1hr 30min); Nagykanizsa (2 daily; 2hr 30min–3hr); Szigetvár (7 daily; 30-50min); Szombathely (2 daily; 4hr 30min); Villány (10 daily; 50min).
Sopron to: Budapest (7 daily; 2hr 30min–3hr); Győr (8 daily; 1hr–1hr 30min); Szombathely (7 daily; 1hr 30min).
Szekszárd to: Budapest (3 daily; 3hr).
Szombathely to: Budapest (5 daily; 2hr 45min–3hr 30min); Kőszeg (every 1hr–1hr 30min; 30min); Nagykanizsa (7 daily; 1hr 30min–2hr 30min); Pécs (3 daily; 4hr 30min); Sárvár (every 40–60min; 15–25min); Sopron (6 daily; 1hr 30min); Székesfehérvár (7 daily; 2hr 15min–2hr 45min); Szentgotthárd (every 1–2hr; 1hr); Tapolca (4 daily; 1hr 45min–2hr 15min).
Villány to: Mohács (7 daily; 30min); Pécs (11 daily; 50min).
Zalaegerszeg to: Budapest (3 daily; 3hr 30min); Szombathely (3 daily; 1hr 25min); Zalalövő (10 daily; 35min).
Zalalövő to: Körmend (6 daily; 35min); Zalaegerszeg (10 daily; 35min).

Buses

Dunaföldvár to: Dunaújváros (every 40–60min; 25min); Kecskemét (6 daily; 1hr 10min); Szekszárd (hourly; 50min).
Dunaújváros to: Budapest (hourly; 1hr 30min); Dunaföldvár (every 40–60min; 25min); Kecskemét (5 daily; 1hr 40min); Székesfehérvár (every 1hr–1hr 30min; 1hr).
Győr to: Balatonfüred (7 daily; 2hr); Budapest (hourly; 1hr 15min–2hr); Pannonhalma Monastery (every 30–90min; 30min); Pápa (1hr–1hr 30min; 50min); Sopron (every 40min; 1hr 30min); Sümeg (5 daily; 2hr 15min); Székesfehérvár (8 daily; 2hr); Szombathely (6 daily; 2hr 30min); Tapolca (4 daily; 4hr); Tata (3 daily; 1hr); Veszprém (hourly; 2hr); Zalaegerszeg (5 daily; 4hr 30min).
Harkány to: Budapest (4 daily; 4hr 15min); Mohacs (5 daily; 1hr 10min); Pécs (every 40–60min; 45min); Siklós (every 30min–1hr; 15min); Szekszárd (1 daily; 2hr 15min).
Kaposvár to: Hévíz (1 daily; 2hr 30min); Pécs (every 1hr–1hr 30min; 2hr); Siófok (5 daily; 2hr);

Szekszárd (2 daily; 2hr 15min); Szigetvár (4 daily; 45min); Zalaegerszeg (1 daily; 3hr).
Komárom to: Budapest (3 daily; 2hr); Esztergom (3–5 daily; 1hr 30min); Győr (2–4 daily; 1hr); Sopron (1 daily; 2hr 45min); Tata (7 daily; 1hr).
Kőszeg to: Bozsok (6 daily; 45min); Sárvár (6 daily; 50min); Sopron (6 daily; 1hr 15min); Szombathely (every 40min–1hr; 30min); Velem (10 daily; 30min); Zalaegerszeg (2 daily; 1hr 15min).
Mohács to: Baja (11 daily; 1hr 30min); Budapest (4 daily; 4hr); Kecskemét (2 daily; 4hr); Pécs (hourly; 1hr); Szeged (7 daily; 4hr); Szekszárd (6 daily; 1hr).
Paks to: Baja (2 daily; 1hr 30min); Budapest (hourly; 2hr); Pécs (6 daily; 2hr); Szekszárd (every 30min; 45min).
Pécs to: Abaliget (5 daily; 1hr); Budapest (5 daily; 4hr); Harkány (every 30min–1hr; 45min); Hévíz (2 daily; 4hr 30min); Kaposvár (every 1hr–1hr 30min; 2hr); Keszthely (4 daily; 4hr); Mohács (every 40–60min; 1hr 20min); Orfű (every 1hr–1hr 30min; 1hr); Siklós (every 1hr–1hr 30min; 1hr); Siófok (5 daily; 3hr); Székesfehérvár (4 daily; 4hr 30min); Szekszárd (every 1–2hr; 1hr 15min); Szigetvár (every 45min–1hr 30min; 1hr); Zalaegerszeg (6 daily; 4hr 15min).
Sárvár to: Sopron (2 daily; 1hr 15min); Sümeg (2 daily; 1hr); Szombathely (7 daily; 1hr).
Siklós to: Budapest (1 daily; 5hr); Harkány (every 30min–1hr; 15min); Pécs (every 40min–1hr; 1hr); Villány (6 daily; 30min).
Sopron to: Balatonfüred (2 daily; 4hr); Budapest (4 daily; 3hr 45min); Fertőd (every 30min–1hr; 45min); Fertőrákos (every 40min–1hr; 30min); Győr (hourly; 2hr); Hévíz (2 daily; 3hr); Keszthely (2 daily; 3hr 15min); Komárom (2 daily; 2hr 45min); Kőszeg (6 daily; 1hr 15min); Nagycenk (every 30–40min; 20min); Pápa (4 daily; 2hr 30min); Sárvár (3 daily; 1hr 15min); Sümeg (3 daily; 2hr 15min); Szombathely (7 daily; 1hr 45min); Zalaegerszeg (2 daily; 3hr).
Szekszárd to: Baja (12 daily; 1hr); Budapest (hourly; 2hr 30min); Mohács (6 daily; 1hr); Paks (every 30min; 45min); Pécs (8 daily; 1hr 15min); Siófok (6 daily; 2hr); Szeged (3 daily; 3hr); Székesfehérvár (4 daily; 2hr); Veszprém (2 daily; 3hr 45min).
Szigetvár to: Kaposvár (8 daily; 45min); Nagykanizsa (3 daily; 2hr 30min); Pécs (every 1hr–1hr 30min; 1hr).
Szombathely to: Budapest (3 daily; 3hr 45min); Ják (hourly; 30min); Keszthely (2 daily; 2hr 30min); Nagykanizsa (4 daily; 2hr 45min); Körmend (hourly; 1hr); Kőszeg (every 40min–1hr; 30min); Sárvár (every 45min–1hr 30min; 1hr); Sopron (5 daily; 1hr 45min); Zalaegerszeg (8 daily; 1hr 30min).
Tata to: Esztergom (every 1hr–1hr 30min; 1hr 30min); Komárom (9 daily; 1hr).
Zalaegerszeg to: Budapest (6 daily; 4hr 45min); Győr (4 daily; 4hr 30min); Kaposvár (4 daily; 3hr); Keszthely (hourly; 1hr); Körmend (5 daily; 1hr); Nagykanizsa (hourly; 1hr); Pécs (5 daily; 4hr 15min); Sopron (2 daily; 3hr 15min); Sümeg (6 daily; 1hr 10min); Szombathely (10 daily; 1hr 20min).

5

The Northern Uplands

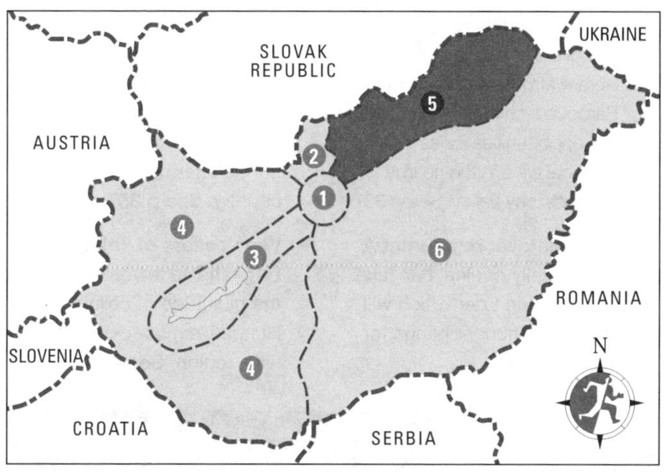

CHAPTER 5 Highlights

* **Hollókő** Extraordinary two-street village where traditional customs remain strong. See p.330
* **Narrow-gauge trains** Take a trip on one of the Uplands' delightful narrow-gauge lines. See p.333, p.345, p.349 and p.370
* **Eger** One of the most enchanting towns in Hungary, with a vibrant atmosphere, fantastic Baroque architecture and plentiful opportunities for sampling the local wine in the nearby Szépasszony Valley. See p.337
* **Palacsintavár restaurant** A fantastically original pancake restaurant in Eger which will knock any hunger pangs for six. See p.343
* **Bükk National Park** Hungary's greenest region is also the best in the country for cycling and hiking. See p.345
* **Aggtelek Stalactite Caves** The largest, and one of the most spectacular, stalactite systems in Europe. See p.355
* **Zemplén villages** Beautiful, tranquil villages dotted around the attractive Zemplén range in the remote northeastern corner of the country. See p.357
* **Wine cellars of Tokaj-Hegyalja** Take your pick from the multitude of cellars in Hungary's most celebrated wine region. See p.361

▲ Vineyards, Tokaj

5

The Northern Uplands

Hungary's **Northern Uplands** boast beautiful wooded hills, karstic rock formations, ruined castles and tranquil villages, as well as three major wine-producing regions, offering some of the best wines in the world. With few major centres of population in the region, it makes for an ideal retreat after a few hectic days in Budapest, with opportunities aplenty for hiking, cycling and other relaxing pursuits.

Historically, the Uplands were more important than they are today, both strategically and economically. Most of the fortresses here saw active service against the Turks and the Habsburgs, particularly during the War of Independence (1703–11), led by Ferenc Rákóczi II. In between times, commerce and culture thrived in tandem with highland Slovakia, until the Treaty of Trianon in 1920 severed the links that sustained old market towns like **Balassagyarmat**, while industrialization gave rise to utilitarian towns that did well under Communism but have since become Hungary's "Rust Belt". **Miskolc**, the largest city in the Uplands, is symptomatic of the industrial decline to ravage the region, but it's not without its attractions, and is further redeemed by its proximity to the scenic **Bükk Hills** and the *fin-de-siècle* spa of **Lillafüred**. To the north of Miskolc, the remote Aggtelek National Park, bordering Slovakia, is home to the Upland's greatest natural attraction – the amazing **Aggtelek Stalactite Caves**.

Another appealing aspect of the region is its Jewish heritage, which draws many Jewish-Americans to places like **Sátoraljaújhely**, **Gyöngyös** and **Verpelét** in search of their ancestors. The old synagogues and cemeteries here are even more neglected than the former aristocratic mansions that also languished under Communism, though these are now slowly being restored – most impressively at **Gödöllő**, a short ride away from Budapest. In the Cserhát Hills north of Gödöllő, the outstanding draw is the delightful museum village of **Hollókő**, a UNESCO World Heritage Site. Moving eastwards, beyond the forested **Mátra Hills**, you'll arrive at **Eger**, the most appealing town in the region, if not in Hungary itself, which combines a fabulous castle and Baroque town centre with a viticultural pedigree that's only surpassed by **Tokaj**, a small, sleepy town in the foothills of the **Zemplén Hills**. The Zemplén, in the far northwestern corner of the country, harbour some of Hungary's finest vineyards and prettiest villages, such as **Füzér** and **Boldogkőváralja**, both of which have an impressive **ruined castle**, although the best preserved is at **Sárospatak**, on the eastern lowlands bordering the Great Plain.

The western approaches

Although the westerly Cserhát Hills are accessible by train from Vác on the Danube Bend, the commonest **approaches** are **from Budapest** or the Great Plain. Several trains leave the capital's Keleti Station daily, passing through Hatvan and Füzesabony en route to Miskolc and Szerencs, from where branch lines head further north. Buses from the Stadion terminal run directly to Hollókő and Eger, and the HÉV line makes Gödöllő an easy day excursion from the capital. Driving to Eger or Miskolc, the fastest route is via the M3 motorway, which runs close to both towns.

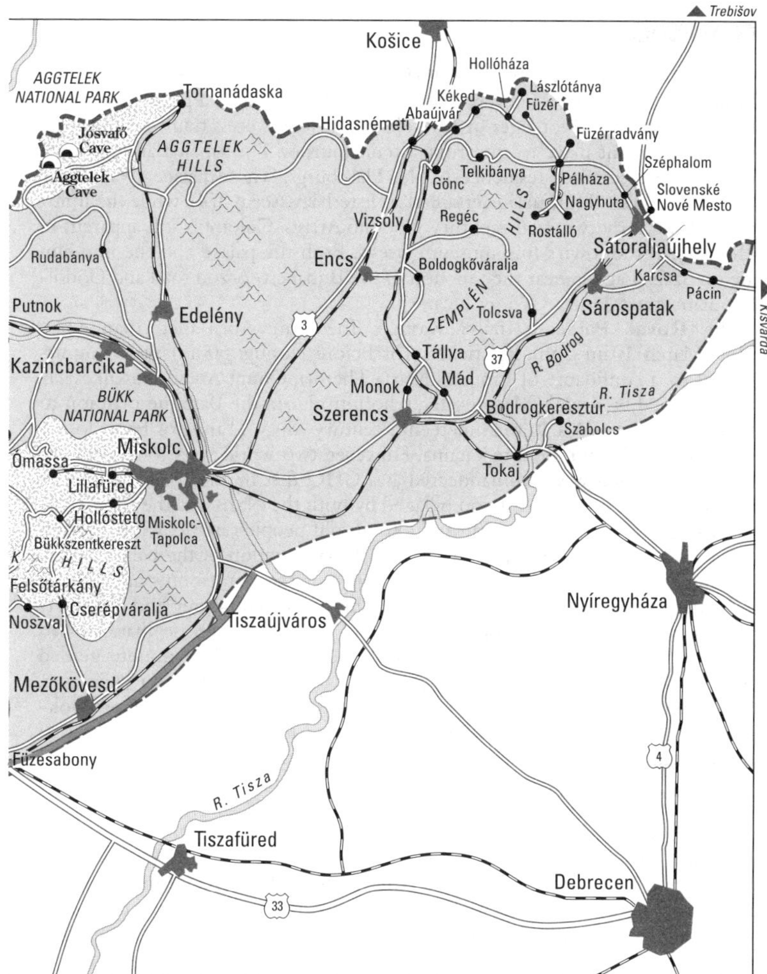

Gödöllő and Aszód

The rolling countryside between Budapest and Eger is given over to extensive vineyards that eventually become rather monotonous, so that the onset of the Mátra Hills at Gyöngyös and the scenic route via Feldebrő are a welcome diversion for travellers. There are also a few places worth visiting as you head eastwards out of Budapest along the M3 motorway – notably **Gödöllő**, whose Royal Palace and artistic legacy are impressive enough to rate a trip from Budapest. Though the same can't be said about **Aszód**, a brief stopover is probably justified for a visit to the Podmaniczky Mansion and the interesting Petőfi Museum.

Gödöllő

Only 30km from Budapest, **GÖDÖLLŐ** is readily accessible by HÉV train from the capital's Örs Vezér tere Station (45min) and makes a pleasant stopover for motorists bound for Eger or Miskolc, but as few express trains stop here it's not a convenient place to interrupt a train journey. This small Baroque town used to be a summer residence of the Habsburgs, whose palace rivalled the splendour of the "Hungarian Versailles" at Esterházy (see p.274), while the influence of the early twentieth-century Gödöllő Artists' Colony is still apparent in Hungary, as the town's fine museum attests. Both the palace and the museum are on Szabadság tér, near the junction of the Budapest–Aszód road and Gödöllő's main street, Dózsa György utca.

The **Royal Palace** (Királyi Kastély; Tues–Sun: April–Oct 10am–6pm; Nov–March 10am–5pm; last tickets 1hr before closing; 600Ft) was commissioned by a confidante of Empress Maria Theresa, Count Antal Grassalkovich, and designed by András Mayerhoffer, who introduced the Baroque mansion to Hungary in the 1740s. In the nineteenth century, "Sissy", Emperor Franz Josef's wife, preferred living here to Vienna. However, two world wars took a toll on the palace, which was commandeered as a GHQ first by the "Reds" and then by the "Whites" in 1919–20, and pillaged by both the Nazis and the Red Army in 1944. One wing was later turned into an old people's home, while the rest was left to rot until a few years ago, when the restoration of the palace began. Though this is far from complete, you can visit the state rooms and private apartments used by Franz Josef and Sissy – his decorated in grey and gold, hers draped in her favourite colour, violet – and the secret staircase that she had installed for some privacy in a relentlessly public life. A fifty-minute guided **tour** in English costs 2000Ft per person, or you could explore on your own, armed with the English-language *Guide to Gödöllő*, sold at the palace bookshop. Regular musical and cultural programmes are staged within the palace throughout the year, including open-air classical concerts in the Ornamental Yard during the summer – check with the Tourinform office inside the palace (see opposite) for details.

Winner of the Hungarian museum of the year in 2000, the delightful **Town Museum of Gödöllő** at Szabadság tér 5 (Gödöllői Városi Múzeum; Tues–Sun 10am–6pm; 300Ft) focuses heavily on the **Gödöllő Artists' Colony**. Founded in 1901, the colony was inspired by the English Pre-Raphaelites and the Arts and Crafts movement of William Morris and John Ruskin, whose communal, rural ethos it took a stage further. Members included Aladár Körösfői Kriesch, who wrote a book about Ruskin and Morris, Sándor Nagy, whose home and workshop may eventually become a separate museum, and the architect Károly Kós. Though the colony dispersed in 1920, its stamp on the decorative arts persisted until the 1950s, while Kós's work has been a major influence on Imre Makovecz and his protégés, who dominate today's architectural scene. The museum also has a terrific exhibition of regional history, including mock-up rooms illustrating the life of the Gödöllő estate, and a room of exhibits from New Guinea donated by the local naturalist and explorer Ferenc Ignácz. The museum has English captions throughout. For the really keen, there is a **workshop** at Körösfői utca 15–17, where local artists work on and display their projects (enquire at the museum for opening times).

If you have the time and inclination for a stroll, there's a huge **arboretum** on the road to Isaszeg, 3.5km south of the junction (Sat & Sun 9am–dusk; free). Along this road you'll find several stately old trees and buildings, since this whole area on the edge of town used to be part of the palace grounds.

If you head 3km down the road towards Aszód, you'll see a Transylvanian-style wooden gateway fronting a **Capuchin Church** that has been a place of pilgrimage ever since workmen dug up an ivory statue of the Virgin in 1759. The Grassalkovich family vault is situated here, and you can also see the grave of Pál Teleki, the wartime prime minister who committed suicide in protest at Hungary's participation in the Nazi invasion of Yugoslavia.

Practicalities

Arriving by HÉV train, get off before the terminal at the Szabadság tér stop, which is bang in the centre of town opposite the palace; the bus station is a couple of minutes' walk east of the HÉV station by the cultural centre. You can get **information** from the extremely well-informed Tourinform booth inside the palace near the ticket office (same hours as palace; ⓣ28/415-402, ⓦwww.gkrte.hu), who can also book **private rooms**, although with Budapest so close there's little chance that you'll want, or need, to stay. If you do, however, there are cheap rooms at the *Szent István Egyetem* on Páter Károly utca, just east of the main train station (ⓣ28/522-971; ❷), or five more expensive ones at the *Galéria Panzió*, Szabadság tér 8 (ⓣ & ⓕ28/418-691; ❹). The *Galéria* also has a sublime **restaurant** offering over a hundred moderately priced dishes, with exotic choices such as deer stew and shark on the menu (daily 11am–11pm; reservations advisable). Alternatively, the *Yellow* pub and restaurant at Dózsa György utca 64 is well worth the fifteen-minute walk for its grilled meats or fish and a beer (daily 11am–midnight).

Aszód and Hatvan

In **ASZÓD**, 10km further east, the main Szabadság tér is likewise dominated by a gorgeous, decrepit Baroque pile in faded Maria Theresa yellow. The former **Podmaniczky Mansion** also dates from the eighteenth century and was damaged during the war; unlike the Royal Palace, it was promptly restored, but then stood empty for forty years, typifying the Communists' ambivalent attitude to the national heritage. It functions as an archive now, as well as a student dormitory, and the staff of the *kollégium* section along the left-hand side can guide visitors to the former ballroom, whose ceiling fresco by János Kracker is in bizarre contrast to the dreary corridors leading to the *díszterem* (ceremonial hall). The **war memorial** outside the mansion is unusual for bearing a menorah as well as a cross, in remembrance of those who died in the Holocaust – about a quarter of Aszód's prewar population was Jewish.

A few minutes' walk to the right of the mansion, the small, two-storey **Petőfi Museum**, in an erstwhile Lutheran grammar school at Szontágh lépscő 2 (Tues–Sun: March–Nov 9am–5pm; Dec–Feb 10am–4pm; 300Ft), contains material about the poet-revolutionary Sándor Petőfi – largely in the form of books and reports from his school years – who studied here for three years, as well as the usual mix of local archeological, ethnographic and historical exhibits. Although all captions are in Hungarian, there is an English leaflet detailing the contents of each room. In the building to the right of the museum there's a small, rotating exhibition of paintings by local artists (same hours and ticket). Some of Hungary's earliest biplanes were produced at the local airplane factory (now a detention centre), whose militant workers earned the town the name "Red Aszód" for their role in the 1919 revolution.

Regular **buses** between Aszód and Hatvan run right past Szabadság tér. From the train station, east of the centre, you can board main-line services to Budapest and Miskolc, or local ones to Balassagyarmat (see p.328). To reach the centre of town from the station, head up the steep, narrow path in front of the station and turn left at the top.

Hatvan

HATVAN, whose name (meaning "sixty") refers to its distance from Budapest in kilometres, straddles a crossroads between the Northern Uplands, the Great Plain and the capital, and was a market town until its wholesale industrialization last century, since when any incentive to linger has been hard to find. Given its pivotal role in the **transport** system, however, you might have an hour to kill between changing buses or trains. While the train station is 2km away down Grassalkovich út, the bus terminal is on Kossuth tér in the old town centre, east of the River Zagyva, alongside a **museum** (Tues–Sun 10am–4pm; 60Ft) featuring temporary exhibitions of local art and history, and another, forlornly empty, **Grassalkovich mansion**. **Buses** fan out from Hatvan to Szolnok, Gyöngyös, the Mátra settlements, and as far afield as Eger.

The Cserhát Hills

The **Cserhát Hills**, like their loftier neighbours, the Mátra and the Börzsöny, were once continuously forested, with a chain of fortresses guarding the valleys and passes into Slovakia, which formed part of Hungary until 1920. The Treaty of Trianon not only sundered economic ties, but stranded ethnic minorities on both sides of the redrawn border – Magyars in Slovakia, and **the Palóc** in Hungary. The Palóc, though probably of Slovak origin, are noted for their antiquated Hungarian dialect and fantastic costumes that are still worn (with an eye for the tourist trade) at the museum village of **Hollókő**, though you'll learn more about their traditions from the Palóc museum in **Balassagyarmat**.

Elsewhere, you can glimpse the region's feudal past as you pass picturesquely **ruined castles** dotted around the countryside. Taking a closer look inside the Forgách mansion at **Szécsény** gives an insight into the world of the warlords and counts who held sway before industrialization.

Balassagyarmat

After losing its medieval fortress and most of its inhabitants to the Turks, **BALASSAGYARMAT** (pronounced "bolosho-dyarmot"), 90km north of Budapest close to the Slovakian border, was repopulated by Germans, Slovaks and Czechs in the eighteenth century, when its prosperity was reflected in the Baroque edifices along its main street. This archetypal provincial town produced two of Hungary's leading nineteenth-century writers: Imre Madach, whose play *The Tragedy of Man* is widely held to be Hungary's greatest classical drama, and Kálmán Mikszáth, whose short stories satirized the landed gentry.

Today, the town has little to show for its status as the "Palóc capital" except for an imposing nineteenth-century **county hall** on Köztársaság tér, the main square, and the **Palóc Ethnographical Museum** in a grand, eclectic-style building in Palóc Park, a few minutes' walk down Bajcsy-Zsilinszky út (Tues–Sun 9am–5pm; 300Ft). The exhibition covers every aspect of Palóc life from the cradle to the grave, with all kinds of home-made artefacts and a fantastic collection of folk costumes. Another **exhibition** housed in two thatched cottages behind the museum presents the traditional Palóc way of life *in situ* (Palóc Ház; May–Oct Tues–Sun 10am–4pm; 200Ft). En route to Palóc Park from Köztársaság tér, you'll pass the small **City Gallery** on the corner of Bajcsy-Zsilinszky út (Tues–Sun 9am–5pm; 100Ft), exhibiting work by local artists.

Practicalities

Balassagyarmat's **bus station** lies a block or so north of the central Köztársaság tér, while the **train station** is fifteen minutes' walk south along Kossuth utca. Almost everything else is located on the main Rákóczi fejedelem utca, which runs across Köztársaság tér, namely: Tourinform in the town hall at no. 6, which has a wealth of **information** (Mon–Sat 8am–4.30pm; ⓣ35/500-640, ⓔbalassagyarmat@tourinform.hu); the post office at no. 24 (Mon–Fri 8am–8pm, Sat 8am–1pm); and all the eateries in town – the *Zorba Háza*, a uniquely Greek-themed pizzeria in the courtyard at no. 28, the cheap and pile-it-high Hungarian *Balassa* restaurant at no. 34, and the agreeable *Orchidea* coffee house, further down at no. 48.

Aside from **private rooms** (❷), bookable through Tourinform, there is the hugely average *Club Panzió* at Teleki út 14, a few minutes' walk from the post office (ⓣ & ⓕ35/301-824, ⓦwww.nyirjes.hu; ❹), and a small campsite on the edge of town on the Budapest road, at Kóvári út 13 (ⓣ35/300-965; June–Aug).

Szécsény

Just 17km east of Balassagyarmat, the small town of **SZÉCSÉNY** is ennobled by the **Forgách Mansion**, a vivid yellow Baroque pile occupying the site of a medieval fortress that was blown up by the Habsburgs during the War of Independence. As the Forgáchs were previously noted for their Habsburg sympathies, it's ironic that their mansion was the site of the Hungarian Diet's election of Ferenc Rákóczi II as ruling prince and commander-in-chief of the Magyar forces, and the declaration of the union of Hungary and Transylvania in 1705. Today it houses the **Kubinyi Ferenc Museum** (Tues–Sun 10am–4pm; 230Ft), which was closed for renovation at the time of writing but due to reopen in September 2005. The museum contains various hunting and local archeology exhibits in a splendid setting, while the gatekeeper's lodge holds a collection of religious artefacts collected by Sándor Csoma Körösi, who travelled widely in Asia and compiled the first Tibetan–English dictionary. Down the road, to the right of the mansion, stands a **bastion** from the old fortress (same hours and price as museum), exhibiting instruments of torture and engravings showing their use, which staff at the museum or at Tourinform will open on request; other remnants of the old **town walls** can be seen in the vicinity.

The mansion is situated on Ady Endre utca, a few minutes' walk from Fő tér, where you'll find an eighteenth-century **Firewatch Tower** (Tűztorony) that has listed three degrees since the town was bombed in 1944. Initially built on the site of a wooden bell-tower to commemorate the passing of the plague, it's not exactly the Leaning Tower of Pisa, but from mid-May to mid-September you can ascend it to enjoy a bird's-eye view of town. The keys can be obtained from the Tourinform office. More intriguingly, you can visit a **Franciscan church and monastery** (Ferences templom & kolostor) on Erzsébet tér, to the west of the Tourinform office on Rákóczi út, which dates back to the Middle Ages. There are guided **tours** of the church and the dining hall, library and monks' cells in the monastery (Tues–Sat 10am, 11am, 2pm, 3pm & 4pm; free), but unless you understand Hungarian, they raise more questions than they answer. You can also enter from the far end of Ady Endre utca, beyond the Forgách mansion.

Practicalities

Buses stop on Király utca, just east of the main square Fő tér; the **train station** is located 1.5km north of town. Tourinform, Ady Endre utca 12, just north of Fő tér (Mon–Fri 8am–4.30pm; Ⓣ & Ⓕ32/370-777, Ⓔszecseny@tourinform.hu), can supply limited **information**. In the same building as Tourinform, the *Agro Hotel*, Rákóczi út 90B (Ⓣ & Ⓕ32/370-382; ❶), has the most basic rooms in town, with bathroom, but book ahead or arrive before 4pm when they close their doors. The alternative is the somewhat lacklustre *Bástya Panzió*, in the attractive servants' quarters of the Forgách Mansion at Ady Endre utca 14 (Ⓣ & Ⓕ32/372-427, Ⓔbastyapanzio@profinter.hu; ❸), which has serviceable rooms with TV and small bathrooms. The *Paradiso*'s very agreeable **restaurant** serves regional specialities like *tócsni* (potato pancake), and its Saturday-night **disco** is usually pepped up by erotic shows. Alternatively, the *Frédi Cukrászda* at Rákóczi út 85 is a good spot for coffees and beers but closes at 7pm.

Hollókő

From Szécsény there are hourly buses to **HOLLÓKŐ** (Raven Rock), 16km further south, where a ruined fortress overlooks a **museum village** on UNESCO's World Heritage list. Following a fire in 1909, Hollókő's white-washed Palóc houses were rebuilt in traditional style with broad eaves and carved gables. The old dwellings may now be largely owned by Budapest intellectuals who can better afford the upkeep – their original owners having long since installed themselves in flats on the outskirts – but the village has lost none of its striking appearance. Hollókő's apotheosis comes on the last Sunday in July, when local dance groups and international folk troupes in gorgeous costumes perform at the **Palóc Festival** (Palóc szőttés fesztivál).

At other times, traditional Palóc dress is chiefly worn by old ladies attending vespers at Hollókő's wooden-towered **church** – outwardly austere, but decorated inside in vibrant colours and with flowers. Once, each village had its own style of homespun attire: in Őrhalom in the Börzsöny Hills, for example, the Hollókő-style cap was transformed into a bonnet by the insertion of a stiff cardboard lining. Fine examples from various localities are displayed in the **Village Museum** at Kossuth utca 82 (Falumúzeum; daily 10am–4pm; 100Ft). This Palóc house follows the Magyar peasant custom of having one room where the family lived and slept, and a parlour solely used for storing bedding and entertaining guests, with a jug and basin serving as a bathroom for the whole family. Three wells served the whole village until 1959, when piped water and electricity arrived on the same day.

To delve further into Palóc crafts, visit the **Weaving House** at no. 94 (Szövőház; daily 10am–4pm; 150Ft), which contains a workshop and sells local textiles, or the **Táj és a nép** exhibition at no. 99 (Tájház; Tues & Thurs–Sun

10am–4pm; 200Ft), featuring photos of the village over the years. The **Pottery** (Fazekasműhely), at Petőfi utca 7, sells ceramics, gives demonstrations and may even let you have a go at the wheel yourself. Lastly, walk up to the ruined **Hollókő castle** (Vár; April–Oct daily 10am–5.30pm; 400Ft) on the hilltop, which is signposted down past the church (10min), and also accessible by a steeper path through the woods, seldom used by visitors, which you can reach by carrying on down to the edge of the village and turning left uphill. Although the tumbled ramparts and single surviving tower are a far cry from their former glory as the original seat of the Illés family, the views over the village and the lush, green hills are wonderful. The small museum within the castle contains a few unspectacular items, such as cannonballs and tiles, many of which were unearthed during the castle's recent restoration programme.

Practicalities

Hollókő is directly **accessible by bus** from Budapest's Stadion terminal (1 daily; 2hr), and connected by hourly services to Szécsény, plus four a day to Pásztó – the jumping-off point for the Mátra Hills – and Salgótarján. Buses run through the modern part of Hollókő before dropping visitors at the top of Kossuth utca, the main street running down to the church.

Information is available from Kossuth utca 68, which houses both the the Foundation for Hollókő (Hollókőért Közalapítvány) and Tourinform (June–Oct Mon–Fri 8am–6pm, Sat & Sun 10am–4pm; Nov–May Mon–Fri 8am–6pm, Sat & Sun 9am–2pm; Ⓣ & Ⓕ32/579-011, Ⓦwww.holloko.hu), who can reserve **rooms**, or even whole houses (❹), furnished with Palóc wardrobes, embroidered bolsters, and traditional outdoor grills. If you want to **eat** in Hollókő, bear in mind that things close early. The main eatery in town is the *Vár* restaurant at Kossuth utca 95 (daily 11am–7pm), which has homestyle roasts in suitably cosy surrounds, or there's the *Muskátli* at Kossuth utca 61 (daily 11am–5pm), a coffee shop that also cooks up a few simple dishes.

Hollókő puts on some great **festivals**, and two of the best times to visit are in late March or mid-April for the **Easter Festival** (Hollókői Húsvéti Fesztivál), when egg-painting and dancing groups form just part of the two-day jollities, or in mid-August for the **Castle Tournament** (Hollókői Várjátékok), a day of medieval tournaments and folklore events.

The Mátra Hills

Hungarians make the most of their highlands, and the **Mátra Hills**, where Mount Kékes just tops 1000m, are heavily geared to domestic tourism. Mount Kékes itself is a popular place for winter sports, despite the relatively lacklustre resort facilities at Mátraháza. In the summer, families ramble the paths between picnic sites and beer gardens, unaware of the wild boar and deer that live deeper in the thickets of oak and beech. The major settlement here is the town of **Gyöngyös** on the southern rim, while the many villages scattered amongst the hills are principally of interest for their amenities. In any case, it's the hills and forests that are the main attraction.

Gyöngyös

Most visitors approach the Mátra via **GYÖNGYÖS** (pronounced "dyurn-dyursh"), the centre of the Gyöngyös-Visonta **wine** region, where white wine grapes predominate. Gyöngyös itself is a mellow town with enough museums and Baroque monuments to rate an hour or two of sightseeing before pushing on into the hills.

The town's central **Fő tér** is a long, thin square surrounded by Baroque and Art Nouveau buildings, reconstructed after a fire in 1917. On the northeast corner stands **St Bartholomew's Church** (daily 9am–noon), originally Gothic but heavily remodelled in the eighteenth century, when the small building behind it was a music school. Across the road at Szent Bertalan utca 3, the Baroque **House of the Holy Crown** (Szent Korona-ház) is so named because the Crown of St Stephen was brought here three times for safekeeping between 1806 and 1809. By ringing the bell you can gain admission to a splendid **Ecclesiastical Treasury** of vestments, books and medieval chalices (Egyházi Kincstár; Tues–Sun 9am–noon & 2–5pm; 100Ft), and view a ceiling fresco that includes a picture of Hungary's last monarch painted in the 1920s, whose final legislative action was to approve the rebuilding of the town after the 1917 fire. The anti-monarchist regime of the time condemned the fresco as illegal, as it depicted a king.

Five minutes' walk east along Kossuth utca brings you to the former Orczy mansion at no. 40, housing the **Mátra Museum** (Tues–Sun: April–Oct 9am–5pm; Nov–March 10am–2pm; 500Ft), whose local archeology and history section, including photos of the great fire, has some English explanations. The wildlife section upstairs includes tableaux on hunting, and a dazzling collection of minerals, butterflies and other Mátra wildlife, while downstairs, live lizards, snakes and birds from around the world appear in a **Mikroárium** (same hours; 100Ft).

By heading south from the museum, past the bus station, and turning right, you come to a **Franciscan Church** endowed by the Báthori family (see box on p.286), whose coat of arms – three dragon's teeth surrounded by a dragon biting its own tail – appears in the chancel. The Franciscan **Memorial Library** on the first floor (Műemlék Konytára; Tues–Fri 2–4pm, Sat 10am–1pm; free) has a wonderful stock of over 15,000 volumes, including 210 incunabula and five codices, plus other beautiful leather-bound works from European printing houses and exhibitions of illuminated manuscripts.

Before the Holocaust Gyöngyös had a considerable Jewish population, as evinced by the **Great Synagogue** on Vármegye tér, west of Fő tér, a Moorish-Gothic hybrid designed in 1929 by Lipót Baumhorn that once belonged to the Reform community, but now sadly serves as a carpet warehouse. Their Orthodox co-religionists used the older **Memorial Synagogue**, a Neoclassical edifice next door, built in 1816, that nowadays houses a local TV station.

Practicalities

Arriving at the **train station** on Vasút utca, simply follow Kossuth utca past the terminal for the narrow-gauge line, the Mátra Museum and the main crossroads until you come to central Fő tér. The **bus station** is 100m south of the crossroads, on Koháry út. Tourinform at Fő tér 10 (mid-June to mid-Sept Mon–Fri 9am–5pm, Sat 9am–1pm; mid-Sept to mid-June Mon–Thurs 8.30am–4pm, Fri 8.30am–2.30pm; Ⓣ & Ⓕ37/311-155, Ⓔgyongyos@tourinform.hu) can provide **information** on both the town and the hills, and also sells **maps** of the Mátra and Bükk hills. They can also arrange **private rooms** (❷) in Gyöngyös and in the villages of the Mátra hills (see opposite).

The only **hotel** in town is the *Hotel Opál*, Könyves Kálmán tér 12 (Ⓣ37/505-400, Ⓦwwwhotelopal.hu; ❺); shiny and new but a little characterless, it's just east of the bus station. Better to head for either the *Viktória Panzió*, on a small side street off Török Ignác utca (Ⓣ37/301-107; ❷), or the *Vincellér Panzió*, 400m north of the bus station at Erzsébet királyné utca 22 (Ⓣ & Ⓕ37/311-691, Ⓦwww.hotels.hu/vinceller_panzio; ❸), both of which have clean, simple rooms and cheery **restaurants** (both daily 10am–10pm). Other eating possibilities include the more sophisticated, and hence pricier, *Kékes Étterem* on Fő tér, opposite Tourinform (daily 11am–11pm); the dowdy but strangely popular *Kulács Vendéglő* on Pater Kis Szalész út 10, just across from the post office (Mon–Fri 9am–8.30pm, Sat till 3pm); and *Giardinetto d'Italia*, which has affordable pizzas in stylish surroundings, set in a pretty location on Rózsa utca 8, just south of Fő ter (daily 11am–11pm). The *Mephisto Rock Café*, at Kossuth Lajos 16, is a bit of a hippy dive frequented by young bloods, but will do for a beer (daily 11am–2am). You can access the **Internet** at *Internet Klub* (Mon–Fri 9am–5pm, Sat 9am–noon) on the parallel side street to *Viktoria Panzió*.

To quit town in style, head for the terminus of the Mátravasút, a **narrow-gauge train line** on Kossuth utca, just beyond the Mátra Museum. One line runs to Mátrafüred, 7km to the north (daily: roughly hourly departures; 230Ft one-way), while the other breaks off after 2km and heads to Lajosháza, 11km away in roughly the same direction (May–Sept Sat & Sun 4 departures; mid-June to Aug also Wed & Fri 4 departures; 245Ft one-way).

The Mátra villages

Though most tourists head straight for Mátrafüred, there are several picturesque **villages** at the foot of the Mátras that are relatively undiscovered, and right in the heart of the **wine country**. With your own transport it's feasible to explore the region thoroughly, but travellers dependent on local buses may have to settle for the village of **GYÖNGYÖSPATA**, 12km west of Gyöngyös. This has a fifteenth-century **Gothic church** with a fine doorway and an imposingly high Baroque "Tree of Jesse" altar (showing the family tree of Jesus), the only one of its kind in Europe. Keys are held in the house just uphill or at the addresses listed on the door. If you feel like staying, try the *Patavár Panzió* at Fő út 47 (Ⓣ & Ⓕ37/364-486; ❸). Alternatively, you can follow a minor road for 20km in the direction of Eger to reach **KISNÁNA** and view a **ruined castle** destroyed by Ottomans in the sixteenth century, before carrying on to Verpelét (see p.336). Once a flourishing court, all that remains of the castle are the tower of the inner gate, parts of the wall and a Gothic church tower. There's also a small museum inside the ruins, with a lapidarium (Vármúzeum; Tues–Sun: May–Sept 9am–5pm; Oct–April 10am–4pm; 60Ft).

From Gyöngyös, **buses** run every half hour or so to Mátrafüred and Mátraháza, and four or five buses a day pass through Parád, Recsk and Sirok on their way to Eger. Recsk and Sirok are also accessible via the branch train line down from **Kál-Kápolna** (the station before Füzesabony on the Budapest–Miskolc line). Anyone intending to visit Sirok or Feldebrő, or go walking in the hills, should buy a large-scale **hiking map** beforehand (*A Mátra turistatérképe* – available from Tourinform in Gyöngyös). Egertourist in Eger (see p.339) and Gyöngyös Tourinform can help find **accommodation** in the villages.

Mátrafüred and Sás-tó

The Mátravasút narrow-gauge train line is the fun way to get from Gyöngyös to **MÁTRAFÜRED**, and takes no longer than the bus, dropping passengers off at the centre of this sloping, popular spa settlement. Although local walks are the main attraction, there is a small **Ethnographical Museum** at Pálosvörösmarti utca 2 (Palóc Néprajzi Magányűjtemény; daily 9am–5pm; 200Ft), displaying sumptuous folk headdresses as well as the usual dolls and other folkcraft. Aside from private **rooms**, there's the enormous three-star *Hotel Avar* at Páradi út 24 (ⓣ37/320-131, ⓦwww.hotels.hu/avarhotel_matrafured; ❻), which has a swimming pool and sauna and can organize tennis and horse-riding, or you could try the less expensive *Hegyalja Panzió*, a well-presented former trade union resort at Béke út 7 (ⓣ37/320-027, ⓦwww.hotels.hu/hegyalja; ❹). For **eating**, there are endless buffets and snack stands in the centre of the village, but if you need something a little more refined you can rely on the restaurant at the *Hegyalja*.

Four kilometres uphill from Mátrafüred, on the bus route between Gyöngyös and Mátraháza, lies **Sás-tó** (Sedge Lake). More of a large pond than a lake, it's a friendly place full of Hungarians boating and fishing amid the usual snack stands. If you feel like **staying**, *Sas-tó Camping* (ⓣ & ⓕ37/374-025, ⓦwww.sasto.elpack.hu; mid-April to mid-Oct) is an attractive complex with a 28-room motel and chalets of varying size and luxury (❷–❹). At 8pm the bustling resort restaurant closes and action shifts down to the bars in Mátrafüred. Heading on, you can easily walk from Sás-tó to Mátraháza along the footpath through the forest, where **wild boars** reputedly lurk.

Mátraháza and Mount Kékes

MÁTRAHÁZA, 9km north of Mátrafüred, is a small village consisting mainly of ex-trade union hostels converted into tourist facilities, plus a few bars, though there are plenty of enjoyable walks in the vicinity. Just outside the village is the chalet-style *Bérc Hotel* (ⓣ37/374-102, ⓕ374-095; ❹), a clean and pleasant place to stay and a great base for hiking; the friendly *Pagoda Panzió*, set back amongst the trees in the centre of the village (ⓣ37/374-023, ⓦwww.hotels.hu/pagoda; ❹), is also well situated. The village's most reliable restaurant, *Borostyán* (daily noon–10pm), is furnished throughout in wood, and dishes up well-executed traditional food to hungry hikers.

From Mátraháza, you can easily make the quick hourly bus trip to **Mount Kékes**, the highest point (1015m) in the Mátra range. Two **ski runs** (*sípálya*) descend from the summit (you can rent skiing equipment at the slope and the car park during the November–March ski season), which is crowned by a nine-storey telecommunications **tower** offering an impressive view of the highlands (Kilátótorony; Tues–Sun: April–Oct 9am–5pm; Nov–March 8am–4pm; 350Ft). The *Hotel Hegycsúcs* (ⓣ & ⓕ37/367-086; ❷) may be only half the height of its neighbouring tower, but its views are still stunning, and it also houses a sauna and gym.

Parádsasvár, Parád and Parádfürdő

About 10km to the northeast, a group of similarly named villages gathers around Parád, where Count Károlyi tried to set an example to other nobles in 1919 by distributing land to his serfs. **PARÁDSASVÁR** is home to one of the grandest castle hotels in Hungary, the *Kastély Hotel Sasvár* (ⓣ36/444-444, ⓦwww.sasvar.hu; ❽). Once the hunting seat of the Károlyi and Rákóczi family, the Miklós Ybl-designed Neoclassical pile sits in its own large private parkland, has an elegant spa, opulent rooms and a selection of excellent restaurants. The village also boasts a large **glassworks** that has been producing Parád crystal since the 1800s; it's open for guided tours (Mon–Fri 8am–3pm, Sat & Sun book in advance ⓣ36/364-353), where you can watch the glass-blowers at work, and end your visit in the factory shop. Signposted from the village, 1km up the hill is **Fényes Major Equestrian Farmstead** (Wed–Sun 8am–6pm; 500Ft), which stables the famous **Lippizaner** horses (see box, p.345; horse-riding 3000Ft per hour, carriage rides 8000Ft per hour; ⓣ36/444-444), as well as keeping a variety of other animals including buffalo and goats; the restaurant serves up hearty Hungarian fare on its open range.

Three kilometres further east lies **PARÁD**, where at Sziget utca 10, an old **Palóc House** (Palóc Ház; March–Oct Tues–Sun 9am–5pm; Nov–Feb 10am–2pm; 140Ft), and accompanying pigsty, is fully kitted out with peasant costumes and artefacts, and at Hársfa utca 6, there is an intriguing exhibition of **woodcarving**, signposted *Fafaragó Kiállitása* (daily 9am–6pm; 150Ft), by the master craftsman Joachim Asztalos. His life-size Palóc peasant figures are particularly touching. Inexpensive **accommodation** is available at the well cared for *Parádi Kisvendéglo* (ⓣ30/364-831; ❷) at Kossuth utca 234, which has a small garden restaurant serving good home-cooked food.

In the 1880s, local quarry workers discovered that drinking the shaft water seemed to cure a range of illnesses; today, the popular **thermal spa** of **PARÁDFÜRDŐ** still boasts the sulphurous, fizzy water that is said to mainly benefit digestive complaints. Such are the curative powers of the local water, a **sanitarium**, Kossuth utca 221 (ⓣ36/364-104), now stands over the village. It holds a unique collection of over 300 mineral waters from 25 countries, which can be viewed and sampled on request. But the village really deserves a visit for its **Coach Museum** at Kossuth utca 217 (Kocsimúzeum; April–Oct daily 9am–5pm; Nov–March Tues–Sun 10am–4pm; 350Ft). The splendid collection includes vehicles for state occasions, hunting and gallivanting around in. For the record, the coach, which superseded the cumbersome wagon throughout Europe, was actually invented in the Hungarian village of Kocs, west of Budapest. Some beautiful horses can be seen in adjacent stables, which were designed for the Károlyi family by Miklós Ybl. You'll find cheap **places to stay** along Peres utca, a quiet country lane, which turns left off the main road at the eastern end of the village. The *Boroka Mini Hotel* (ⓣ36/364-527; ❹) has plain rooms at no. 18, and the *Izabella Panziò* at no. 43 (ⓣT36/364-221; ❸) is much cosier.

Recsk

Mention **RECSK**, a village 2km east of Parádfürdő, and many older Hungarians will share recollections of terror. During the late 1940s and early 1950s, thousands of the tens of thousands of citizens arrested by the ÁVO were sentenced to labour in the quarries southwest of here. Half-starved and frequently beaten by their jailers, prisoners died of exhaustion or in rockfalls, or more usually while sleeping in muddy pits open to the sky. The operation, modelled on the Soviet Gulag, was highly secretive and few knew what was being carried out until it was eventually closed by Imre Nagy in 1953. **Recsk concentration camp** was effaced by a tree plantation during the Kádár years, and not until 1991 were its victims commemorated. A stone **monument** symbolizing repression, and a bronze model of the camp, stand near the still-working quarry, 4.5km up from the village (look for the *Kőbánya* signs). Before heading up here, you may want to check out the **Mining Museum** (Mon–Fri: June–Sept 10am–5pm; Oct–May 2–5pm; 200Ft) for a healthy dose of hulking machinery. There's also a **Palóc House** at Kossuth utca 116, if you feel like dropping in to view its typical furnishings (Mon–Fri 8am–noon; free).

Sirok, Verpelét, Feldebrő and Egerszalók

The bus from Parádfürdő to Eger stops at **SIROK**, 8km further east of Recsk, and is a great place to visit if you're wild about romantic views. On a mountain top above the village, 1.5km northeast of the train station, there's a ruined thirteenth-century **castle** from which you can admire the mingled peaks of the Mátra, the Bükk and Slovakia. The village itself is also lovely, its old houses nestling among cliffs and crags; some ancient dwellings are carved out of the rock itself – head for Széchenyi utca to see some examples. The village has a **campsite** at Dobó utca 30, at the end of the road towards the castle (ⓣ36/361-558; May–Sept).

Antiquity buffs with their own transport should head 11km south to **VERPELÉT**, where the **Jewish cemetery** on the far side of the village has gravestones from as long ago as 1628, many richly carved or tilting at crazy angles. The cemetery is tended by a Roma Gypsy family living nearby, who can help you climb into the grounds. Alternatively, you can ask for the key from the town hall in the centre of the village (Tues, Thurs & Fri 10am–noon & 1–4pm). Opposite the town hall is the blink-and-you'll-miss-it **Palóc forge-shop**, Kossuth utca 60 (Tues–Sun 9am–1pm; 60Ft), where, so legend has it, Hungarian kings have had their horses shod. Ask at the house behind the shop to see its small array of old tools and blacksmith apparel.

Hiking in the Mátra and Bükk hills

Taken together, the Mátra and Bükk hills boast over 1000km of walking trails, with hikes to suit all abilities. The **Mátra** range contains the highest peak in Hungary and accompanying panoramic vistas over the surrounding countryside, while the swathes of beech forests that make up the sparsely populated **Bükk** Hills provide unparalleled tranquility and some marvellous caves.

The most beautiful and diverse hike in the Mátra Hills is the thirty-kilometre **Rákóczi Trail**, which traverses the whole of the range, from Gyöngyös to Parádfürdő. It takes about three days to complete but you can also do a shortened version covering just the last section in one day. This starts in Páradsasvár, from where the trail passes through beech forests with a halfway resting point at Farkas kút ("Wolf Well"), before crossing the Kis-Hidas-Folyás creek and emerging at Sás-tó; the route then winds up to Matrafűred along the Muzsla Valley. Another hike that affords fantastic views is the nine-kilometre round tour of **Mount Kékes**. Starting from the car park at the top of the mountain, the path heads south towards Sirok before veering left to cross the small creek next to the rocks of Gabi Halála ("Gabi's Death", named after a local woodsman's son who fell to his death here). Pisztrángos-tó makes a peaceful resting point midway, where you can take a drink from the spring or make use of a rain shelter. From here, the trail leads down through the beech groves into Mátraháza and back up the southern ski run to Mount Kékes.

A dramatic but leisurely Bükk Hills trail leads you from Bánkút, at the foot of Mount Bálvány to Bélapátfalva, an eleven-kilometre marked hike running along the **Bükk Plateau**. The first part of the walk heads south along narrow ravines towards Tar-kő, from which you head west across the plateau. Magnificent cliffs run along its south side affording breathtaking views, before the craggy peaks of Istallós-kő and Vőrős-kő rise up either side of you as you continue westwards. Eventually you make the steep descent into Bélapátfalva where you can explore a Romanesque church which nestles at the foot of the Bélkő rocks.

Getting hold of a hiking **map** is a good idea before you attempt any walk in either range, even though many of the trails are clearly marked on the ground. Maps for the Mátra Hills (*Mátra Turistatérképe*) are available from Tourinform in Győngyős, and those for the Bükk Hills (*Bükk Turistatérképe*) can be found at the Tourinform in Eger.

Four kilometres further down the road, **FELDEBRŰ** boasts one of the oldest church crypts in Hungary, containing twelfth-century **frescoes** influenced by Byzantine art, and the **grave of King Aba** (1041–44), one of the ephemeral monarchs between the Árpád and Angevin dynasties. Keys for the crypt (Tues–Sat 9am–noon & 1–6pm, Sun & holidays 1–6pm) are held at Szabadság tér 19, nearby. The local **linden leaf wine** (Debrői hárslevelű) is good for refreshing weary travellers, as you can discover in **wine cellars** such as the one at Árpád út 2, just off the road beside the church.

If you're still feeling weary, then head for **EGERSZALÓK**, 16km from Feldebrő, home to a stunning **hot spring**, which is worth a look even if you aren't planning a dip, due to its huge crystallized crust of salt deposits that have formed around the pool. The spring is set amongst trees, signposted from the village.

The Bükk Hills and the Aggtelek National Park

The largest, and most beautiful, of the Uplands' hilly regions is the **Bükk** range, named after the beech trees (*bükk*) that blanket these modestly sized peaks. For those with time to spare, this is fine walking country, while there are also possibilities to participate in more relaxing activities, such as horse-riding, boating or riding a narrow-gauge train. The Bükk Hills can easily be reached from either of the region's two major settlements – the gorgeous Baroque town of **Eger**, with its abundance of historical monuments and wine, and the city of **Miskolc**, which conceals a handful of worthwhile attractions underneath its hard-nosed and gritty industrial appearance. Further north, scraping the Slovakian border, the **Aggtelek National Park** contains arguably Hungary's greatest natural wonder, the fabulous **Aggtelek Caves**.

Eger and around

Situated in its own sunny valley between the Mátra and the Bükk, **EGER** is famed for its wine, its minaret, and the heroic legend attached to its castle, which overlooks a florid Baroque town centre. In terms of tourist popularity, this enchanting town is a serious rival to Szentendre and Tihany, and with by far the liveliest atmosphere of anywhere in the Northern Uplands, it is a must on anyone's itinerary.

From Eger, buses and local trains head to various villages bordering the Bükk National Park, notably **Szilvásvárad**, near the **Szalajka Valley** to the north, and **Cserépváralja** to the northeast.

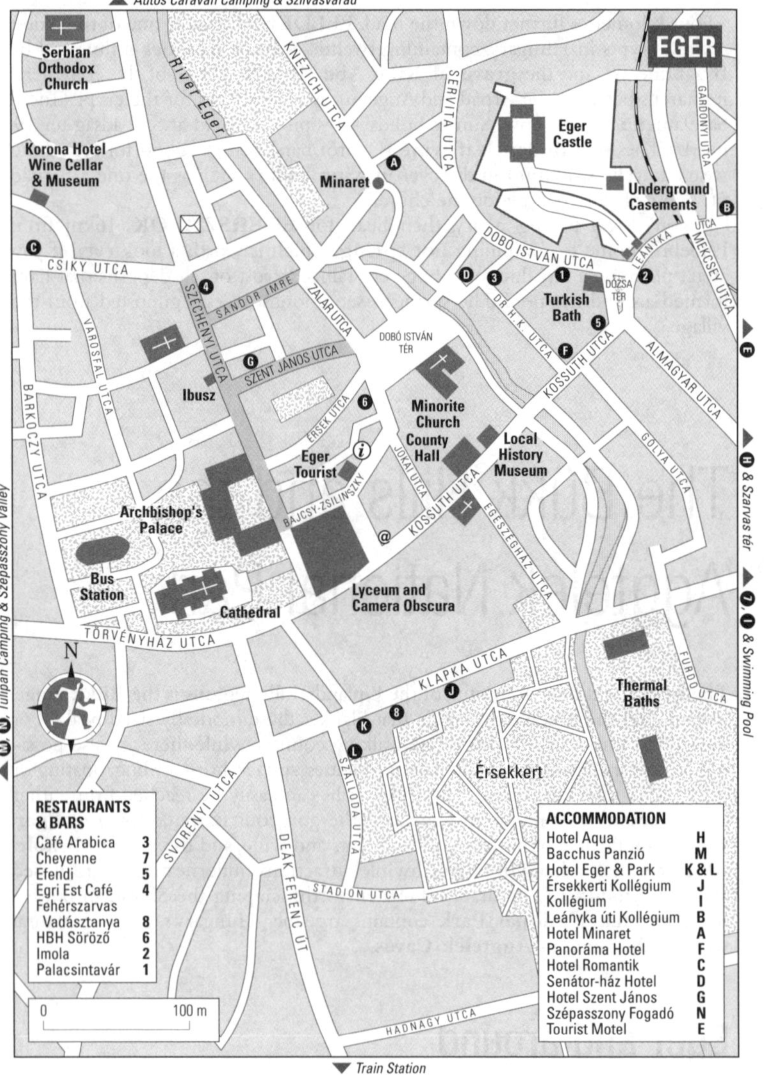

Arrival and information

Travellers arriving at the **bus station**, near the cathedral, can stroll into the centre. Coming from the **train station** on Állomás tér, walk up the road to Deák Ferenc út, catch bus #10, #11 or #12 and get off just before the cathedral. Within the centre of the town, orientation is simple and everything is within walking distance.

The super-helpful Tourinform are located in the centre at Bajcsy-Zsilinsky út 9 (mid-June to mid-Sept Mon–Fri 9am–7pm, Sat & Sun 9am–6pm; mid-Sept to mid-June Mon–Fri 9am–5pm, Sat & Sun 9am–1pm; ⓣ36/517-715, ⓦwww.

tourinform.hu/eger), and can provide **information** on both the town and activities on offer in the region. The **post office** is at Széchenyi utca 20–22 (Mon–Fri 8am–8pm, Sat 8am–1pm). **Internet access** is available at Matáv Pont, at the corner of Kossuth utca and Fellnér J utca (Mon–Fri 8am–6pm, Sat 8am–1pm).

Accommodation

Eger is a hugely popular destination, and although the town is blessed with a healthy stock of terrific hotels and pensions, it's advisable to **book ahead** to get the place of your choice – though there are usually **private rooms** (❷) available beyond the centre. Tourinform has a comprehensive list of private rooms, but don't do bookings; these are handled by Egertourist at Bajcsy-Zsilinszky utca 9 (Mon–Fri 9am–5pm, also July & Aug Sat 9am–noon; ⓣ36/510-277, ⓦwww.egertourist.hu), and Ibusz at Széchenyi utca 9 (June–Aug 20 Mon–Fri 8am–5pm, Sat 9am–1pm; Aug 21–May Mon–Fri 8am–4pm; ⓣ36/321-652, ⓔeger@ibusz.hu).

The cheapest option is a bed in one of the town's **student hostels** (*kollégium*), which you can book either direct or through Ibusz. The most centrally located is the *Érsekkerti Kollégium* at Klapka György utca 12 (ⓣ36/413-661, ⓦwww.ektf.hu; dorm bed 1600Ft; July to mid-Sept). Otherwise, there is the *Leányka úti Kollégium*, east of the castle at Leányka utca 6 (ⓣ36/520-430, ⓦwww.uktf.hu; dorm bed 1500Ft; July & Aug), and the *Kollégium* at Pozsonyi utca 4–6 (ⓣ36/424-202; dorm bed 1500Ft; mid-June to Aug). Another, perhaps less enticing, option is a bed in one of the four-bedded rooms in the MÁV Turista Szálló (the train station building) at Állomás tér 2 (ⓣ36/410-132; dorm bed 1700Ft).

Hotels and pensions

Hotel Aqua Maklári út 9 ⓣ36/512-510, ⓦwww.hotelaqua-eger.hu. A very stylish place south of Szarvas tér, with designer-furnished, air-conditioned rooms which have been given some neat touches with bedside rugs, wall pictures and pot plants. Attractive grill terrace and pub, too (see p.343). ❺

Bacchus Panzió Szépasszonyvölgy 29 ⓣ & ⓕ36/428-950, ⓦwww.bacchuspanzio.hu. Smoothly run and very comfortable place at the entrance to the valley. Some of the lovely rooms have small terraces. Decent restaurant, billiard room and secure parking. ❺

Hotel Eger & Park Szálloda utca 1–3 ⓣ36/413-233, ⓦwww.hotelegerpark.hu. A three-star establishment made up of the modern *Eger*, which has bigger, slick rooms, and the older *Park*, which is awaiting a refit, just around the corner. Both are identically priced. Facilities include a swimming pool, tennis courts, sauna and even a bowling alley. ❻

Hotel Minaret Knézich utca 4 ⓣ36/410-233, ⓦwww.hotels.hu/minaret. The fine building and great location opposite the minaret promise much, but the rooms come as a bit of a letdown. A small swimming pool in the delightful yard and the jazz club downstairs somewhat make up for it. ❺

Panoráma Hotel Dr Hibay Károly utca 2 ⓣ36/412-886, ⓦwww.panorama.guards.hu. The sole four-star hotel in town and it shows: spotless and enormous air-conditioned rooms with minibar and fantastic beds, plus impeccable service. ❻

Hotel Romantik Csiky Sándor utca 26 ⓣ36/310-456, ⓦwww.hotels.hu/romantik. You're sure of a jovial welcome at this compact and perky little hotel a short walk west of the centre, complete with a verdant, romantic rock garden. ❺

Senátor-ház Hotel Dobó István tér 11 ⓣ & ⓕ36/320-466, ⓦwww.hotels.hu/senatorhaz. Despite its location in the heart of tourist territory, this lovely eighteenth-century inn is quite wonderful, with fully-equipped, air-conditioned rooms. Reservations essential. ❻

Hotel Szent János Szent János utca 3 ⓣ36/510-350, ⓦwww.hotels.hu/st_janos. Ultramodern ten-room hotel just off Széchenyi utca with gorgeous pastel-coloured rooms fitted out with minibar, safe and phone. Fitness and aerobics room and sauna. ❺

Szépasszony Fogadó Szépasszonyvölgy ⓣ & ⓕ36/310-777. A simple guesthouse with just four rooms out in the heart of the valley. Breakfast not included. ❸

Tourist Motel Mekcsey utca 2 ⓣ36/429-014. Just off Szarvas tér, this very simple place has rooms sleeping two to four people. Shared bathrooms and no breakfast, but it's clean and centrally located. ❸

Campsites

Autós Caraván Camping Rákóczi ferenc út 79 ⓣ36/428-593, ⓔcarcamp@enternet.hu. Huge site 3km north of the centre by bus #10 or #11. Two-person bungalows (❷) and huts (❶), tent space, a restaurant and snack bar. Open mid-April to mid-Oct.

Tulipán Camping Szépasszonyvölgy 71 ⓣ & ⓕ36/410-580, ⓦwww.hotels.hu/freddy. Across the road from the riding centre, this site at the entrance to the Szépasszony Valley has four-bed chalets (❷). Open all year.

The Town

One of the oldest Magyar settlements in Hungary, Eger was a flourishing Renaissance centre at the time of the Turkish invasion, when it found itself on the front line after the occupation of Buda. To general amazement, its castle withstood the **siege of 1552**, when two thousand soldiers and Eger's **women** (who hurled rocks, hot soup and fat), under the command of **István Dobó**, repulsed a Turkish force six times their number – a victory immortalized in Géza Gárdonyi's novel *Egri Csillagok* (*Eclipse of the Crescent Moon*). During the siege of 1596, however, the castle was held by foreign mercenaries who surrendered after a week, whereupon the Turks sacked Eger, leaving only "blackened walls and buildings razed to the ground" and "the naked bodies of Christians baking in the sun, in some places four yards high".

By the time the Turks were driven out in 1687, Eger had only 3500 inhabitants, including 600 Muslims who subsequently converted to Christianity. Its **revival** in the eighteenth century was directed by the episcopal see, which commissioned much of the Baroque architecture that gives Eger its characteristic appearance. This was largely financed by the local vineyards, whose robust red Egri Bikavér – known abroad as **Bull's Blood** – is still a major money-earner, from both direct sales and the tourism that it generates. Under Communism, local co-ops had little incentive to aim for quality and a lot of fairly rough stuff was produced (which is still on sale), but in recent years, independent producers such as Thummerer have done much to raise standards.

The Cathedral, Lyceum and Serbian Orthodox Church

Eger Cathedral, on Eszterházy tér, occupies a site hallowed since the eleventh century, and looms large above a flight of steps flanked by statues of saints Stephen, László, Peter and Paul, by the Italian sculptor Casagrande. Constructed between 1831 and 1836, this ponderous Neoclassical edifice was architect József Hild's rehearsal for the still larger basilica at Esztergom. Its interior was largely decorated by J.L. Kracker, who spent his last years working in Eger. Particularly impressive is the frescoed cupola, where the City of God arises in triumph as evildoers flee the sword. Between mid-May and mid-October, at around noon, you can hear organ presentations in the basilica. Close by, at Széchenyi utca 5, stands the **Archbishop's Palace** (Éseki palota), a U-shaped Baroque pile with fancy wrought-iron gates. In the right wing of the palace you'll find the treasury and a history of the bishopric of Eger (Egyházi Gyűtemény; April–Oct Tues–Sat 9am–5pm; Nov–March Mon–Fri 8am–4pm; 120Ft). Items on display, largely from the eighteenth and nineteenth centuries, include chalices, reliquaries and robes, including one worn by Maria Theresa when she was crowned queen.

The florid, Zopf-style **Lyceum**, opposite the cathedral, was founded in the late eighteenth century by two enlightened bishops whose proposal for a university was rejected by Maria Theresa. Now a teacher training college (named after Ho Chi Minh during the Communist era), the building is worth visiting for its **library** (April–Sept Tues–Sun 9.30am–3.30pm; Oct–March Sat & Sun 9.30am–1.30pm, closed Dec 22–Jan 6; 450Ft), whose beautiful floor and fittings are made of polished oak. There is also a huge trompe l'oeil ceiling fresco of the Council of Trent by Kracker and his son-in-law. The lightning bolt and book in one corner symbolize the Council's decision to establish an Index of forbidden books and suppress all heretical ideas. The library also contains the only original letter by Mozart in the country. While in the building, it's definitely worth checking out the **observatory**, at the top of the tower in the east wing (same hours as the library; 450Ft), where a nineteenth-century **camera obscura** projects a view of the entire town from a bird's-eye perspective.

North of the Lyceum up Széchenyi utca lies the eighteenth-century **Serbian Orthodox Church** (Rác templom; Tues–Sun 10am–4pm; 300Ft), whose elaborate, gold-braided iconostasis (1789–91) is strikingly similar to the one in the Greek Orthodox Church in Miskolc, and, at 13m high, is just 3m shorter. The former parsonage next to the church now houses a memorial room containing various works of the Serbian poet Mihály Vitkovics and an exhibition of the Hungarian painter and photographer **György Kepes** (Mon–Sat 10am–4pm; 350Ft).

Kossuth utca and Dobó István tér

From the Lyceum and Provost House across the way, **Kossuth utca** leads past a Franciscan church, where a mosque stood in Turkish times, and the **County Hall**, whose magnificent gates were wrought by Henrik Fazola – notice the stork with a snake in its beak and a vine in its claws, on the county coat of arms. The same man who designed the gates was also responsible for the prison bars in the old Eger jail at Kossuth utca 9, now a small **local history museum** (April–Oct Tues–Sun 9am–5pm; 140Ft), displaying artefacts from Eger and Heves county. It also houses a few sporting exhibits but focuses predominantly on the achievements of the local swimming team and water polo club, whose members regularly form the basis of Hungary's Olympic team. Printed information is available in English detailing the exhibits of each room.

Continuing along Kossuth utca across the bridge, you pass on your right the deserted "Buttler House" that featured in Mikszáth's novel, *A Strange Marriage*, and on your left a synagogue now transformed into a shop. Alternatively, follow Bajcsy-Zsilinszky or Érsek utca into **Dobó István tér**, the starting point for further sightseeing. On the southern side of the square stands the former **Minorite Church**, a twin-towered Baroque edifice completed in 1771, and one of the most stunning in Central Europe. The altarpiece of the Virgin Mary and St Anthony – the church patron – was completed by the ubiquitous Kracker, whilst the Latin inscription above its entrance asserts that "Nothing is Enough for God". The small exhibition of Palóc folk art next door (April–Oct Tues–Sun 9am–5pm; 100Ft) is also worth a visit. More striking, however, are the square's action-packed **statues of warriors** commemorating the siege of 1552, including several women wreaking havoc on Turkish assailants.

A short distance from Dobó István tér are two relics of the Turkish occupation. A slender, fourteen-sided **minaret**, rising 40m above Knézich utca, is Eger's most photographed structure, and, despite looking rather forlorn since its mosque was demolished in 1841, it offers fine views from its balcony, 97 steps up (April–Oct daily 10am–5pm; 140Ft). If the door is locked, the reception desk of the adjacent *Hotel Minaret* will loan you a key. A passing glance suffices for the unimpressive remains of a **Turkish bath** nearby, en route to Eger Castle.

Eger Castle

With every approach covered by batteries of cannons, you can easily appreciate why **Eger Castle** (daily: March–Oct 9am–5pm; Nov–Feb 9am–3pm; 800Ft, grounds only 300Ft, discounted admission Mon as exhibitions closed except the underground galleries) was so formidable. Ascending from its lower gate past the Gergely Bastion, the ticket office on your left offers a historical video and English-language cassette for a do-it-yourself tour if you feel so inclined. On entering the inner section of the castle through the Várkoch Bastion, you are also passing underneath the **tomb of Géza Gárdonyi**, on which is inscribed "Only his body lies here".

One of the few Gothic structures left in northeastern Hungary, the **Bishop's Palace** harbours a **museum** containing tapestries, Turkish handicrafts and weaponry. On the ground floor are temporary exhibits and a "**Hall of Heroes**" *(*Hősök terme), where István Dobó is buried amid a bodyguard of siege heroes carved in best Stakhanovite style. The adjacent **art gallery** boasts several fine Munkácsys and three romantic Transylvanian landscapes by Antal Ligeti.

To the east of this complex lies a jumble of medieval foundations signposted as a "Romkert" – **Garden of Ruins**. Here stood Eger's Gothic cathedral, which was damaged by fire in 1506 and used by the Turks as a gunpowder magazine during the first siege "to spite the Christians". To the south, tour groups gather outside the concrete tunnel entrance to the Kazamata or **underground galleries**, a labyrinth of sloping passages, gun emplacements, deep-cut observation shafts and mysterious chambers.

Out from the centre: the Szépasszony Valley

Although the **Wine Cellar and Museum** at the *Korona Hotel*, Tündérpart utca 5 (Tues–Sat 2–9pm; free), offers a display of viticultural implements and some simple wine tasting to whet your palate, it's more fun to go drinking in the **Szépasszony Valley**, a pleasant twenty-minute walk west of town. The "Valley of the Beautiful Women" is surrounded by dozens of vineyards producing four types of **wine** – Muskotály (Muscatel), Bikavér (the famous Bull's Blood), Leányka (medium dry white with a hint of herbs) and Médoc Noir (rich, dark red and sweet – coating your tongue black). The valley has suffered at the hands of mass tourism, and can be slightly underwhelming if you are expecting lush, cellar-studded countryside (the cellars somewhat resemble a clutch of concrete bunkers), but the compact and friendly neighbourhood is still fun to visit, particularly outside peak season.

Finding the right **wine cellar** is a matter of luck and taste – some are dank and gloomy, some serve wines of ambrosial quality and others will pour you a trickle of vinegar. Certain cellars also have their own **musicians**, who appear only when tourist numbers have reached critical volume. Most cellars are open daily until at least 8pm, although many do close later depending on custom. Head down to the far end of the horseshoe-shaped scattering of establishments for the more appealing and livelier drinking cellars, including those of Sándor Árvai at no. 31 (try his excellent Médoc Noir), and János Birincsik at no. 32, who stocks some fine old wines, including a vintage Bikavér. Tourinform can also advise you on other good cellars to try. Although there are several very touristy and almost identical **restaurants** in the valley, you're better off ordering some nibbles at one of the cellars, or taking a packed lunch.

Your best bet, if you really don't want to walk, is to arrange before you go for a **taxi** to come and pick you up (try City Taxi; ⓣ36/555-555; around 800Ft one-way), or swallow your pride and take the miniature tourist "train" (May–Aug 9am–6pm; 400ft one-way), which shuttles back and forth between the valley and Dobó István tér.

Eating and drinking

With more than a dozen restaurants and takeaways around the centre, particularly along Széchenyi utca, **eating out** in Eger is never a problem. However, you'll find the better eateries on the periphery of town.

Restaurants

Efendi Kossuth Lajos utca 19. Decent, if overly fancy, place serving some of the better Hungarian cuisine in town, although strangely lacking in atmosphere.

Fehérszarvas Vadásztanya Klapka György utca 8. If you don't mind being surrounded by stuffed animals' heads, the "White Deer Hunters' Farm", a glamorous-looking place next to the *Park Hotel*, should satisfy. Very affordable range of game dishes complemented by swift service. Daily noon–midnight.

HBH Söröző Bajcsy-Zsilinszky utca 9. Steady place just off the main square offering the requisite Hungarian meals. Daily 10am–11pm.

Imola Dózsa tér 4. Just down from the castle on a picturesque little square, the *Imola* is the smartest restaurant in town, with a varied menu featuring fish and – unusually in Hungary – lamb. Good vegetarian options too.

Palacsintavár Dobó utca 9, entrance on Fazola Henrick utca. This magnificently original restaurant offers every pancake imaginable – salty, sweet, vegetarian and many more. In addition to the fine food, the dim hanging lamps, wicker chairs and amiable staff make this place a must. Daily noon–11pm.

Cafés and bars

Eger has some elegant **patisseries** such as the *Dobos Cukrászda* at Széchenyi utca 6 (daily 9.30am–9pm), which has a fabulous, classy hall at the rear (good when the weather gets chilly), and the *Marján Cukrászda* at Kossuth utca 28 (daily 9am–10pm), famous for its parfaits and cakes iced with marzipan in the style of Palóc and Matyó embroidery. *Café Arabica*, on the corner of Dobó and Hibay Király utcas, is a fine old tea house with dark wooden tables and stools, and huge bowls of confectionery awaiting the sweet-toothed (daily 8am–8pm).

Eger has several sprightly **drinking** spots: *Egri Est Café*, at Széchenyi utca 16, manages to be one of the slightly more unique venues that line the street, with a neon-lit bar and occasional live music (daily 11am–midnight, Fri & Sat till 2am). The most authentic pub-type places are *Champs*, at the *Hotel Aqua*, whose enormous grill terrace gives it a real summery feel, and *Cheyenne*, 100m down from *Champs* on Kertész utca, an easy-going, round-the-clock place with African-styled decor and a casino out back. The alternative is to head out to the cellars of the Szépasszony Valley to sample the local wines (see opposite).

Activities and festivals

Contact Tourinform if you're interested in **horse-riding** in the Szépasszony or Szalajka valleys, or **aeroplane tours** over town (May–Aug, weather permitting; 4000Ft per person). A very good riding school is the Egedhegyi Lipicai Farm at Vécsey völgy 6, 2km northeast of town on the road to Noszvaj, where the saddle-shy can enjoy carriage rides (May–Sept; horse-riding 1600Ft per hour; Ⓣ36/517-937). You can also get simple accommodation at the stud itself, in the *Mátyás Udvarház* (same telephone; ❷). Alternatively, head for the **thermal baths** on Petőfi tér (May–Sept Mon–Fri 6am–7.30pm, Sat & Sun 8am–7pm; Oct–April daily 9am–6pm; Turkish baths Sat (women) & Sun (men) only; 700Ft) or the **swimming pool**, close by on Frank Tivadar utca (Mon–Fri 6am–9pm, Sat & Sun 8am–6pm; 660Ft), where half the town comes to wallow and splash at weekends during summertime. Folk or rock **concerts** are sometimes held in the open-air theatre at the end of the Szépasszony Valley. Contact Tourinform for details.

The town's cultural traditions are celebrated by a series of immensely enjoyable festivals, including the **International Festival of Military Bands** at the end of June, a jamboree of brass and woodwind bands; the **Baroque Festival** (Barokk Hetek) in late July and early August, three weeks of dance and classical music concerts in the basilica, Minorite Church and Lyceum; and the **Vintage Days Festival** (Szüreti Napok) in September, a weekend of predominantly wine-related events, but which also includes folk dancing and a parade of floats. Though finding somewhere to stay could be a bit problematic, this is the best time to visit – particularly if you enjoy drinking wine. In the Szépasszony Valley, the **Szépasszony Festival Mátra** in mid-August is a weekend of wine, food and song, taking place in a huge tent.

Up to Szilvásvárad and the Szalajka Valley

The road and rail line skirt the western foothills of the Bükk as they wiggle northwards towards Putnok. Twelve kilometres out from Eger the scenery is promisingly lush around **SZARVASKŐ** (Stag Rock), a pretty village with a **ruined castle**, a basic **hotel** – the functional *Turistaszálló* at Rózsa utca 8 (ⓣ36/352-085; ❶) – and *Őko-Park* (ⓣ & ⓕ36/352-201, ⓦwww.oko-park.hu; ❹), a super little campsite and guesthouse occupying a pretty site next to a stream, in the shadow of the rock itself. Six kilometres further on, quarries and an ugly cement factory spoil the view at **BÉLAPÁTFALVA**, where the sole reason to stop is a well-preserved Romanesque **abbey church** (Tues–Sun 10am–4pm; 200Ft), founded by French Cistercian monks in 1232. Next to the church are the remains of a monastery. To get to the church, follow the signpost off the main road for 2km. On chilly days, the caretaker can be found at Rózsa utca 42 – look for the *apátság gondnok* (abbey wardens) sign on the right shortly after leaving the main road.

Szilvásvárad

Eight kilometres further north, **SZILVÁSVÁRAD** occupies a dell beside wooded hills rising to the east. Once the private estate of the pro-Fascist Pallavicini family, and then a workers' resort after 1945, nowadays it is chiefly known as a breeding centre for **Lippizaner horses** (see box opposite). It's also the site of Hungary's annual coach-driving championship, the **Bükk Trophy**, usually held the last weekend in August. Those who feel inspired to go **horse-riding** themselves should head for the Péter Kovács stables, just out of town on the main highway to Eger at Egri utca 16 (2200Ft per hour in German, 1500Ft per hour in Hungarian; ⓣ36/355-319).

You don't have to be mad on horses to enjoy the **Horsebreeding Exhibition** at Park utca 8 (9am–noon & 1–5pm: April–Oct Tues–Sun; Nov & Dec Sat & Sun only; 200Ft), which includes a collection of coaches and a stable of beautiful white Lippizaners. The totemic columns in the park around the stud farm are dedicated to the memory of the farm director's beloved mount, Zánka, who died in harness of a heart attack – evoking the time of the Magyar conquest, when favourite horses were buried in graves.

Except during the coach-driving championships, there shouldn't be any problem finding **accommodation**. On the road in from Eger you'll find the *Kalebas Panzió*, with views from its neat rooms over the lovely garden at Egri utca 48 (ⓣ36/355-319; ❸), and the welcoming and relaxing *Szalajka Fogadó* at no. 2 (ⓣ & ⓕ36/564-020, ⓔszalajka.fogado@axelro.hu; ❺), while up the hill at Park utca 6 is the reasonably priced *Szilvás Kastély Hotel* (ⓣ36/355-159, ⓦwww.hunguesthotels.hu; ❹), which is rather grand despite being hopelessly dated. *Hegyi Camping* at Egri út 36 (ⓣ36/355-207, ⓦwww.hegyicamping.com; mid-April to mid-Oct) has small chalets (❷), and there are private rooms (❷)

Lippizaner horses

Descended from Spanish, Arabian and Berber stock, **Lippizaner horses** are bred at six European stud farms. The original stud was founded at Lipica in Slovenia in 1580 by the Habsburg archduke Karl, but when Napoleon's troops invaded Italy its horses were brought to Mezőhegyes in southern Hungary for safekeeping. During the recent wars in former Yugoslavia, a similar rescue mission was carried out by the Austrians. Lippizaner horses are comparatively small in stature – 14.3 to 15.2 hands – with a long back, a short, thick neck and a powerful build. They are usually white or grey. Like their counterparts at the famous Spanish Riding School in Vienna, Szilvásvárad's horses are trained to perform bows, provettes and other manoeuvres that delight dressage cognoscenti.

available too – look for the *Zimmer frei* signs. If you fancy exploring the area by **bike**, rentals are organized by Mountain Bike Rental at Szalajka-völgy (800Ft per hour; ⓣ60/352-695).

The Szalajka Valley

If walking doesn't appeal, it's possible to take the five-kilometre-long narrow-gauge train from Szilvásvárad – the station is at Szalajka-völgy 6 – into the **Szalajka Valley** (May–Sept 7 daily; April & Oct 4 daily). The valley really begins at Szikla-Forrás, a gushing rock cleft beyond the food stalls and captive **stags** that guard its approaches. Signposted just off the main path is an outdoor **Forestry Museum** (Erdészeti Múzeum; May–Oct Tues–Sun 8.30am–4.30pm; Nov–April daily 9am–2.30pm; 150Ft) exhibiting weathered huts and tools, including an ingenious water-powered forge, once used by the charcoal-burners and foresters of the Bükk. Trout is on every restaurant's menu round here, freshly caught from the streams of the Szalajka Valley.

Higher up, the valley is boxed in by hills, with paths snaking 5km through the woods to the triangular **Istállóskői cave** (*barlang*) and the barefaced **Mount Istállóskő**, which at 959m is the highest in the Bükk range. The second-highest, Bálvány, can be reached by footpath from Istállóskő (8km) or from Nagyvisnyó (9km), the next settlement after Szilvásvárad and on the same branch train line.

The Bükk Hills

Unlike most of the northern hills, the **Bükk** were formed from sedimentary limestone, clay slate and dolomite, and are riddled with sinkholes and caves that were home to the earliest tribes of *homo sapiens*, hunters of mammoths and reindeer. As civilization developed elsewhere, the Bükk declined in importance, except as a source of timber, until the start of the nineteenth century, when Henrik Fazola built a blast furnace in the Garadna Valley, exploiting the iron ore which spurred the industrialization of Miskolc and Ózd. Despite this, almost four hundred square kilometres have been declared a **national park and wildlife refuge**, which can be explored superficially by train and bus, or more thoroughly if you're prepared to do some hiking.

If you are planning to **walk**, a hiking map (*Bükk hegység*) is essential. Since paths are well marked and settlements are rarely more than 15km apart, it's hard to go far astray on foot, but a few **preparations** are advisable (including taking

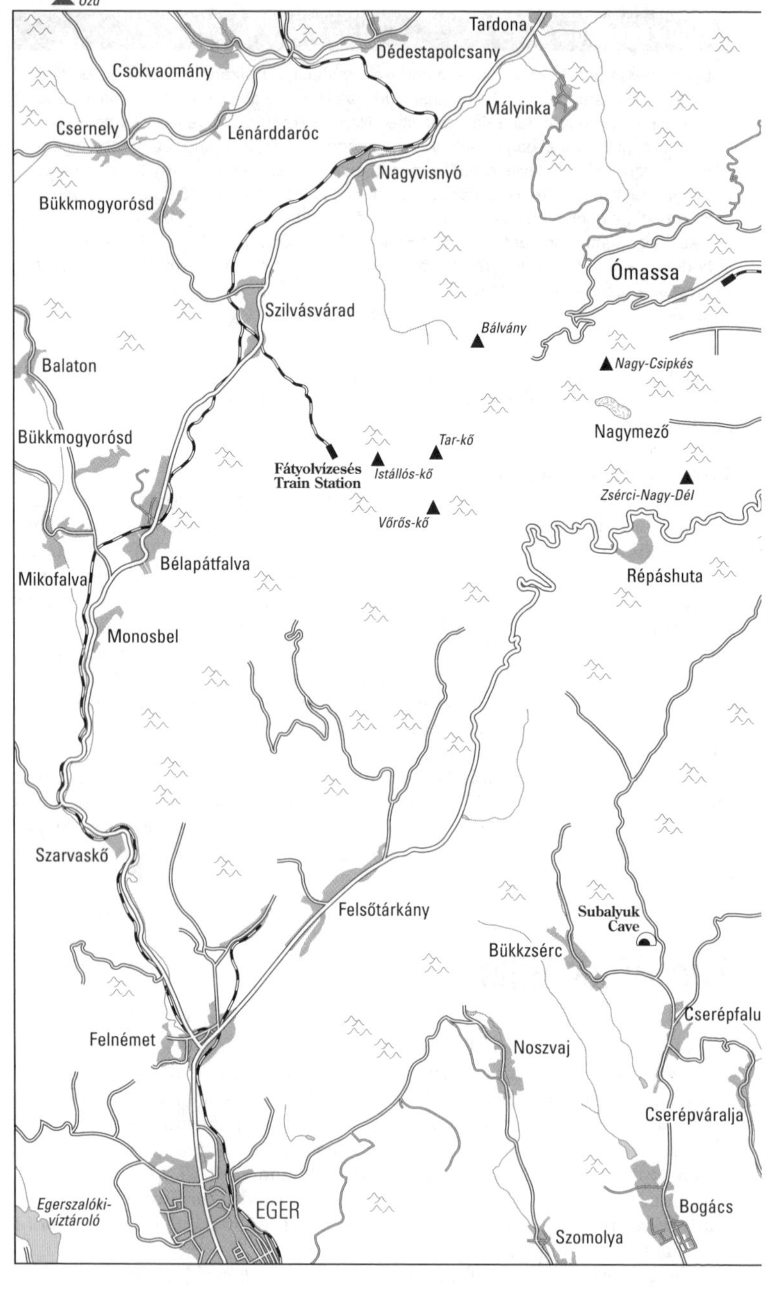

Ózd
Tardona
Dédestapolcsany
Csokvaomány
Mályinka
Csernely
Lénárddaróc
Nagyvisnyó
Bükkmogyorósd
Ómassa
Szilvásvárad
Bálvány
Nagy-Csipkés
Balaton
Nagymező
Bükkmogyorósd
Tar-kő
Fátyolvízesés Train Station
Istállós-kő
Zsérci-Nagy-Dél
Vőrős-kő
Bélapátfalva
Mikofalva
Répáshuta
Monosbel
Szarvaskő
Felsőtárkány
Subalyuk Cave
Bükkzsérc
Cserépfalu
Felnémet
Noszvaj
Cserépváralja
Egerszalóki-víztároló
EGER
Bogács
Szomolya

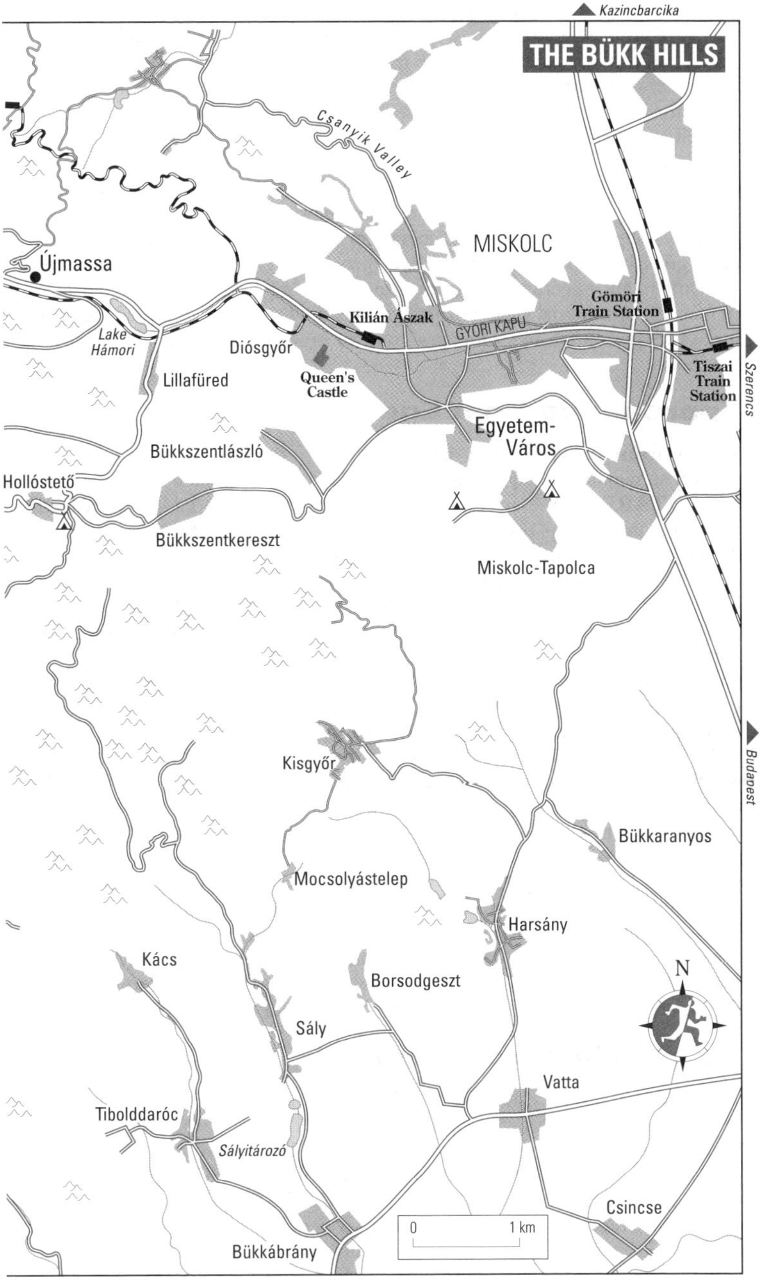

THE BÜKK HILLS

Kazincbarcika
Csanyik Valley
MISKOLC
Újmassa
Gömöri Train Station
Kilián Ászak
GYORI KAPU
Lake Hámori
Diósgyőr
Lillafüred
Queen's Castle
Tiszai Train Station
Szerencs
Egyetem-Város
Bükkszentlászló
Hollóstető
Bükkszentkereszt
Miskolc-Tapolca
Kisgyőr
Budapest
Bükkaranyos
Mocsolyástelep
Harsány
Kács
Borsodgeszt
N
Sály
Vatta
Tibolddaróc
Sályitározó
Csincse
0
1 km
Bükkábrány

plenty of food and water, as well as some insect repellent). Drinking water (*ivóvíz*) isn't always available, though many of the springs are pure and delicious. To be sure of **accommodation**, make reservations through Egertourist in Eger, or ask for help from Tourinform there (see p.338). If need be, you can also sleep in shelters (*esőház*) dotted around the hills.

The Bükk is particularly lovely in autumn, when its foliage turns bright orange and yellow, contrasting with the silvery tree trunks. Among the mountain flora are violet-blue monkshood which blooms at the end of summer, yellow lady's-slipper, an endangered species in Europe, and the Turk's-cap lily. The undergrowth is home to badgers, beech martens, ermines and other animals, and you might encounter rock thrushes and other birds in abandoned quarries, or see an imperial eagle cruising overhead. The seldom glimpsed "smooth" snake isn't poisonous. In spring, look out for limekilns and charcoal-burners in the forests.

Approaches from Eger

Starting **from Eger**, the most direct approach to the hills is to take a bus, getting off somewhere along the route to Miskolc, or the branch train line up to **FELSŐTÁRKÁNY** – an ideal starting point for walks and a lovely village in its own right, with parks, ponds and vine-laden gardens. Paths also lead into the Bükk from Bélapátfalva, Szilvásvárad and Nagyvisnyó, north of the range (see p.344), and from villages to the south, accessible by bus from Eger. On the south side, arrowheads and other remains were found in the **Subalyuk Cave**, a Paleolithic dwelling 1km east of **Bükkzsérc** and north of **Cserépfalu**, at the start of one of the footpaths. Further east, "rocking stones" and hollowed-out pillars, used by medieval beekeepers and known as "hive rocks", line the rocky **Felső-szoros ravine** north of **Cserépváralja**.

Accommodation is offered by two villages on this side of the hills. In Felsőtárkány are the *Park-Hotel Táltos*, tucked away up the hill at Ifjuság út 1, where you'll also find hostel-style accommodation from May–Sept (Ⓣ36/534-071, Ⓦwww.parkhotel-taltos.info.hu; ❹; dorm bed 1900Ft), and the cheaper, smoky *Szikla Fogadó*, Fő utca 313 (Ⓣ36/434-604; ❸). Alternatively, **NOSZVAJ**, 13km from Eger, has a clutch of guesthouses, plus a Baroque mansion converted into the *De La Motte Kastély Hotel* at Dobó utca 10 (Ⓣ36/463-090; ❹–❺), which has rooms in the annexe and more expensive apartments in the main house. The 200-year-old **mansion** can also be visited by non-guests (Tues–Sun 10am–noon & 1–3pm; 240Ft), who can admire the bizarrely decorated rooms with rather kitsch frescoes. Allegedly there were once some voluptuous nudes in the master bedroom, until a new mistress of the house had them painted over.

Approaches from Miskolc

The Bükk can also be visited **from Miskolc** (see p.350), which offers a number of approaches. From Újgyőri főtér in the western part of the city (bus #101 from Tiszai Station), a #68 bus will take you to **Bükkszentlászló**. From here you can either walk or hitch via **BÜKKSZENTKERESZT**, a small village with a quaint glass-blowing museum, to **HOLLÓSTETŐ**, 6km on, which is on the Miskolc–Eger bus route, though services are infrequent. Bükkszentkereszt offers **private rooms** as well as the *Bükk Fogadó* (Ⓣ46/390-165; ❹), while Hollóstető has a **campsite** with **chalets** (Ⓣ46/390-183; ❷; May–Sept).

The easiest approach, however, is to aim for **Lillafüred** (see opposite), a small resort that's accessible by **bus** #5 or #15 (every 30min) from the end stop, Diósgyőr Villamos, in the western part of the city (bus or tram #1 from Tiszai

Station), or by **narrow-gauge train** from Miskolc's Kilián Észak terminal (served by bus or tram #1 – alight at the LÁÉV stop, two before the last one). Trains make the delightful thirty-minute trip from Miskolc four times daily year-round with extra trains at the weekend. Both the train, and bus #15, continue via Újmassa to Ómassa, further up the valley.

Lillafüred and its caves

LILLAFÜRED ("Lilla Bath"), 12km west of Miskolc, was named after Lilla, the wife of Count András Bethlen, who established the place as a resort in 1892. Despite its weekend popularity, Lillafüred can still be peaceful and romantic, with its lake and grand hotel set amidst wooded hills. Out of season, the whole place seems rather forgotten.

The village's principal attractions are three **stalactite caves** (*barlang*), two of which can be visited on short guided tours, starting every hour or so from each cave entrance. The only cave which can't be visited is the **Szeleta Cave**, tucked away above the Miskolc road, and found to contain Ice Age spearheads and tools. The **Anna Cave** (mid-April to mid-Oct daily 10am–3pm; 600Ft), at the bottom of the path that runs down beside the *Palota Hotel*, has a long entrance passage and six chambers linked by stairs formed from limestone. If your appetite for stalactites is still unsatiated, walk 1km up the road towards Eger to find the **Szent István Cave** (daily: mid-April to mid-Oct 9am–5pm; mid-Oct to mid-April 9am–4pm; 600Ft), which is longer and less convoluted, with a "cupola hall" of stalactites, various pools and chambers. Bats can usually be seen roosting above your head.

Two hundred metres beyond this at Erzsébet sétány 33 stands the wooden **house of Ottó Herman** (Fri–Sun 10am–4pm; 250Ft), where the naturalist and ethnographer spent many years trapping and mounting local wildlife until his death in 1914. Stuffed boars, birds and rodents, plus an extraordinary collection of giant beetles, are the main attraction, but you can also see Ottó's top hat and butterfly nets, and a letter from Kossuth. A few minutes' walk north of Lillafüred is **Lake Hámori**, used for **boating** during the summer and **ice-skating** in winter.

Practicalities

Dominating the resort is the grand *Palota Hotel* at Erzsébet sétány 1 (Ⓣ46/331-411, Ⓦwww.hunguesthotels.hu; ❼), a nostalgic creation built in 1927 in the style of a medieval hunting lodge; it is, as you might expect, pretty classy, with a fitness centre, pool, sauna and games room – ask for a room with a balcony overlooking the park. Just across from the *Palota*, the *Tókert Panzió* at no. 3 (Ⓣ & Ⓕ46/379-028; ❺) offers seven far more modest, and more modestly priced, rooms. Three hundred metres up the hill from here, at no. 19, is the *Ózon Szálló* (Ⓣ46/532-594, Ⓦwww.hotels.hu/ozon_lillafured; ❸), where the compact rooms have balconies. All the above have very reasonable **restaurants**, the most glamorous of which is the *Mátyás Terem* (daily noon–11pm) in the *Palota Hotel*, although it takes the medieval theme a touch too far and the waiters look a little daft in their get-up. The windows in the restaurant represent towns from the former Hungarian territories lost in the Treaty of Trianon. Second best is the restaurant at the *Tókert*, a multi-terraced affair with idyllic views of the lake and a buzzy atmosphere.

Újmassa and beyond

Narrow-gauge trains continue from Lillafüred up the Garadna Valley, which cleaves the Bükk plateau. At **ÚJMASSA**, the next stop 4km further west, a nineteenth-century foundry and metallurgy museum (mid-April to Oct Tues–Sun 9am–5pm; 100Ft) attests to the work of **Henrik Fazola**, a Bavarian-born Eger locksmith, and his son Frigyes, who first exploited the iron ore deposits of the Bükk. Nearby are the sooty camps of **charcoal-burners**, who still live for part of the year in the forest.

ÓMASSA, further up the valley, is the last stop on the train and bus routes. From here it's a few hours' walk up a well-marked path to **Mount Bálvány**, southeast of which lies the "Great Meadow" (Nagymező), where wild horses graze. A ski chalet and the summits of **Nagy-Csipkés** (822m) and **Zsérci-Nagy-Dél** (875m) can be reached to the southeast, but more impressive crags lie to the southwest, namely **Tár-kő** (950m) and **Istállós-kő** (959m). The land drops rapidly south of Tár-kő, and water from the plateau descends through sinkholes, bursting forth in a spring at **Vörös-kő** (Red Rock). During winter, when the plateau is covered with snow, the entrances to these **sinkholes** are marked by rising steam.

Miskolc and the Aggtelek Range

The area to the north and east of Bükk National Park is Hungary's "Rust Belt", a region afflicted by the collapse of its heavy industry in the 1990s. **Miskolc**, straddling the transport network, is hard to avoid but holds far more promise than you'd imagine, with a bustling downtown, an impressive castle and "thrashing" cave baths in the nearby resort of Miskolc-Tapolca – plus some tremendous summer festivals to enjoy. The wonderful **Aggtelek Stalactite Caves**, north of Miskolc near the Slovak border, are easily the main draw of the region and the reason why most visitors end up in Miskolc.

Miskolc

Due to the closure of its steel factory and other industries, **MISKOLC** (pronounced "**mish**-koltz"), 61km northeast of Eger and the third largest city in Hungary, has long suffered from high unemployment and problems with racist attacks on its Roma minority, to which the city council responded at one point by proposing that they all be moved to an outlying housing estate, until dissuaded by a national outcry. However, the city puts a brave face on its woes, at least around the centre, whose oddly appealing main street retains much of its prewar charm, surrounded by relics of the city's Greek and Jewish communities, and nineteenth-century artisans' dwellings with gardens dwarfed by concrete high-rises. Aside from the Queen's Castle and the spa resort of Miskolc-Tapolca, everything of interest is in the city centre.

Arrival and information

The main **points of arrival** are the Tiszai **train station**, 1km east of the centre (tram #1 or #2; bus #1 or #101 for the castle or Majális Park, aiming for Lillafüred or the Bükk Hills), and the intercity **bus station** on Búza tér, from where you can either walk into the centre, or head straight for Miskolc-Tapolca by bus #2 from the adjacent local bus station. Should you arrive at the Gömöri train station instead, walk down to Zsolcai kapu, catch any bus heading west and alight near Ady utca.

As ever, a wealth of **information** can be obtained from Tourinform at Széchenyi út 35 (mid-June to mid-Sept Mon–Fri 9am–7pm, Sat & Sun 9am–6pm; mid-Sept to mid-June Mon–Fri 9am–5pm, Sat 9am–1pm; ⓣ46/350-425, ⓔmiskolc@tourinform.hu). The MÁV office at Szemere utca 1 (Mon–

Sat 7.30am–6.30pm) can supply train information and book tickets, while the **post office** is opposite Hősök tere at Kazinczy utca 16 (Mon–Fri 8am–7pm, Sat 8am–12pm). X café at Széchenyi út 8 (Mon–Fri 8.30am–9.30pm Sat 12am–9.30pm) will cater to all your **Internet** needs.

Accommodation

For such a large city there is precious little hotel accommodation, so you might wish to head for **Miskolc-Tapolca** (see p.354) instead, or opt for a **private room** (❷) – although most of these tend to be in outlying housing estates. Ibusz at Széchenyi út 14 (Mon–Fri 8am–4pm; Ⓣ46/518-210, Ⓔi069@ibusz.hu) have the best stock but you could also try Borsod Tourist at Széchenyi út 35 (Mon–Fri 8am–4.30pm, July & Aug also Sat 9am–1pm; Ⓣ & Ⓕ46/350-645, Ⓔutaztatas@borsodtourist.hu), or Express at no. 56 (Mon–Thurs 8am–4pm, Fri 8am–3.30pm; Ⓣ46/349-530). Private rooms in Miskolc-Tapolca can be arranged through Borsod Tourist at the *Éden* campsite (see p.352; April–Oct daily 9am–4pm; Ⓣ46/561-510).

As usual, student **hostels** are the cheapest option, the best of which is the *Karács Teréz Kollégium* (Ⓣ46/370-495) at Győri kapu 156 (bus #1 or tram #1

or #2), open from late June to late August. Alternatively, there is the *Bólyai Kollégium* at Egyetem út 17, in the hilly Egyetemváros district south of town (ⓣ46/365-111), which is open the same times as the *Karács*; take bus #12 from Hősök tere to the last stop. There are two **campsites** in Miskolc-Tapolca, both with chalets (❸): *Éden Camping* at Károly Mihály utca 1, 300m west of the *Hotel Junó* (ⓣ46/368-917; mid-April to mid-Oct), resembles a manicured parking lot; while *Autós Camping*, 2km along Iglói utca (ⓣ46/367-171; May to mid-Sept), is a leafier site popular with motorists.

Miskolc

Britannia Hotel Hunyadi utca 3 ⓣ & ⓕ46/351-066, ⓦwww.hotels.hu/britannia. Great location opposite Városház tér, but rather austere, with stark split-level rooms. ❺

Gösser Udvar Déryné utca 7 ⓣ & ⓕ46/505-045, ⓦwww.hotels.hu/gosser_miskolc. Just along from the National Theatre, a small and cosy pension, albeit with tired-looking rooms. ❹

Korona Panzió Kis Avas 18 ⓣ46/506-882, ⓔkorona7@axelro.hu. At the foot of the Avas Hill, this is a pleasing, if unspectacular, place. A good alternative if *Székelykert* is full (see below). Breakfast not included. ❹

Hotel Pannonia Kossuth utca 2 ⓣ46/504-980, ⓦwww.hotelpannonia-miskolc.hu. Facing the main pedestrianized street, this overpriced three-star has neat little rooms, some air-conditioned, and a sauna. ❽

Székelykert Panzió Földes utca 4 ⓣ & ⓕ46/411-222, ⓦwww.hotels.hu/szekelykert. Occupying an old town house just down from the *Korona Panzió*, this pension has a few small single rooms as well as doubles, all with TV and bathroom. Enjoyable restaurant attached (see p.354). ❹

Miskolc-Tapolca

Bástya Hotel Miskolctapolcai utca 2 ⓣ & ⓕ46/369-154, ⓦwww.bastyahotel.hu. Only a couple of minutes' walk from the cave baths, this great hotel keeps with the theme by having its own "wellness centre". Facilities include indoor and outdoor pools, water massage facilities and Jacuzzis. ❺

Pallaz Panzió Bencések utca 3 ⓣ & ⓕ46/368-770. Round the corner from the *Bástya*, the furnishings are wearing thin at this pension, but it remains pretty good value. ❸

Zenit Panzió Miskolctapolcai utca 25 ⓣ46/561-561, ⓦwww.bokit.hu/zenit. Large rooms with TV, phone and balcony. Triples and quads available. ❺

The City

The main downtown thoroughfare, **Széchenyi út**, is characterized by an eclectic mix of boutiques and restaurants interspersed with Baroque facades painted pea green and sky blue or in the last stages of decrepitude, which gives the impression of a boom and slump happening simultaneously. Here you'll find the recently restored **National Theatre** (Nemzeti Színház), which apart from musicals like *Fiddler on the Roof* also stages some good straight drama, and has an alternative theatre run by the ex-rock star Péter Müller. Opened in 1823, it was the first Hungarian-language theatre in the country, fourteen years before Budapest acquired one. Miskolc's thespian tradition is celebrated in the **Theatre Museum**, just around the corner at Déryné utca 3 (Színészmúzeum; Tues–Sun 9am–5pm; 115Ft). At the far western end of Széchenyi út, a new statue of its namesake, Count Széchenyi, appears to be doing a painful form of yoga on **Városház tér**, which looks especially atmospheric with its town hall spotlit at night.

North of Széchenyi út

A century ago, Miskolc was distinguished by its Greek and Jewish communities – the former descended from refugees from the Turks, who fled here during the seventeenth century, and the latter migrating from Sub-Carpathian Ruthenia after it was incorporated within the Austro-Hungarian Empire. Though both are now a shadow of their former size and significance, their places of worship are among the finest monuments in the region.

On the south side of **Hősök tere** is an **Orthodox Synagogue** designed by Ludwig Förster, the architect of the Dohány utca Synagogue in Budapest, whose magnificent but crumbling interior seems painfully empty on major feast days – little over 300 Jews now live in Miskolc, whereas the prewar Jewish population numbered 16,000, of whom 14,000 were sent to the death camps; ask at the office behind the synagogue for the keys. On the far side of the square stands a former **Minorite Church** and monastery, dating from 1729–40.

Heading left onto Deák tér you'll encounter a splendid, newly restored neo-Renaissance pile designed by György Lehóczky in 1927 for the **Forestry Commission** (Erdőigazgatoság), an important institution in this region of wooded hills. Next door stands the **Feledy Museum** (Tues–Sat 9am–5pm; 115Ft), devoted to the work of local artist Gyula Feledy, which reflects his preoccupation with the world of Orthodox Christianity. Greek Orthodox and Uniate religious art from all over Hungary is exhibited in the **Orthodox Ecclesiastical Museum** further along at no. 7 (Magyar Orthodox Egyházi Múzeum; Tues–Sat: April–Oct 10am–6pm; Nov–March 10am–4pm; 200Ft).

The finest sight in the town is the eighteenth-century **Greek Orthodox Church**, screened by trees, which contains an extraordinary sixteen-metre-high **iconostasis**, dating from 1793. The iconostasis incorporates some one hundred icons painted by Greek and Serbian masters and represents revered Orthodox saints and important Orthodox holidays. To the left of this is the *Black Mary of Kazan*, an icon presented by Catherine the Great of Russia, hung with tokens representing prayers for children, health and marriage. There is also a jewelled cross from Mount Áthos, brought by the first Greek settlers. Originally there were about 250 Greek families in Miskolc, who traded in wine and lived around Búza tér, but the quarter was pulled down in the 1960s, and only a handful of families remain from the community.

Further north on the slope above Petőfi tér, the wonderful Gothic-style **Plank Church** (Deszka templom; May–Sept daily 9am–5pm; free) has been completely rebuilt following an arson attack in 1997. There has been a wooden church on this spot since 1698, although it has been torn down and rebuilt several times since. The interior's finely varnished and freshly smelling pine pews are testament to the latest reincarnation. This kind of wooden church is rare in Hungary but common in northern Romania, where architecture of this type, particularly in the northern Maramureş region, reached its zenith in the eighteenth century. The Székely gate at the entrance to the church is typical of the type found in Romania.

Visitors who go **mushroom hunting** in the Bükk can have their fungi checked at the *Gomba Vizsgálat* hut on Búza tér, near the #2 bus stop (mid-May to mid-Nov Sat, Sun & holidays 1–5pm).

Avas Hill

South of Széchenyi út, a once beautiful domed *fin-de-siècle* **bathhouse**, currently being slowly restored, presages the **Ottó Herman Museum** at the foot of Avas Hill (Tues–Sun 10am–4pm; 250Ft), exhibiting a collection of folk costumes, minerals and pottery. The pile of broken mugs is a result of the tradition at wakes of drinking and then smashing your mug. Just uphill stands a Gothic **Calvinist Church** dating from 1560, which features a detached **wooden belfry** (as required by Counter-Reformation ordinances) and Baroque pews decorated with flower motifs, added later.

From here, a maze of paths snakes upwards to the **TV Tower** and observation platform on the summit. The right-hand paths climb through an extraordinary shantytown of miniature villas and rock-hewn **wine cellars**, some up to 50m deep, some of which may be visited. In the summer and early autumn you can roam all over the hill sampling local wine, and even food at some of the bigger cellars. Ten minutes' walk down Mendikás dülő past the TV Tower is a **Jewish Cemetery** with beautifully carved gravestones dating back to the eighteenth century, and memorials to those killed during the war. On weekdays until late afternoon a caretaker will let you in if you ring the bell.

Out of the centre

The oldest building in Miskolc is the **Queen's Castle**, located 7km west of the centre in the suburb of Diósgyőr, beyond the steelworks (Diósgyőr vár; daily 10am–5pm; 600Ft). Built for King Louis between 1350 and 1375, the castle marked the introduction of the southern Italian type of fortress to Hungary. Though eminently defendable, it served chiefly as a royal holiday home and a residence for dowager queens. Today it is the main site for summer concerts, festivals and events in the city. Blown up in the Rákóczi wars, it has been crudely restored with breeze blocks and poured concrete, but the views from its towers of Miskolc and the Bükk Hills are as splendid as ever. To get there, catch a #1 bus to the *Ady Endre Művelődési Ház* and walk towards the four stone towers poking above the rooftops.

If you feel like a relaxing bath, head out to **MISKOLC-TAPOLCA**, a resort suburb twenty minutes' ride from Búza tér (bus #2). Crammed with holiday homes and school parties, its main attractions are an outdoor **pool** (May–Sept daily 9am–6pm; 700Ft), complete with rowing boats, water slides, electronic cars and rides; and the **cave baths** (Barlangfürdő; July–Sept daily 9am–7pm; Oct–June daily 9am–6pm; 1600Ft), a series of dimly lit warm-water grottoes discovered in the 1920s, culminating in a twelve-metre-high waterfall known as the "pounding shower", which should get your circulation going if nothing else (take bus #2 to the end stop). There are snack stands aplenty and a **disco** in the *Hotel Junó*, as well as a wide range of pensions and private rooms (see p.352).

Eating, drinking and entertainment

Beyond the hotels and pensions, there are few really enticing options for **eating**, although the city does buzz with some original drinking venues and fairly sparky **nightlife**.

Restaurants

Avas Beer House Meggyesalja utca 1. Elegant Austrian-styled place with specialities from Tyrol plus a promising Hungarian menu. Also houses a dispiriting-looking pub. Daily 11am–11pm.

Café du Boucher Görgey utca 42. This top-quality Belgian restaurant also happens to be the best in town; the food is superb, albeit pricey, and the service brisk. The Belgian beers are a treat. Daily 11am–midnight.

Dionysos Mélyvölgy utca 212. Situated on the slope of the Avas Hill, this delightful Greek restaurant has a rich menu – including fish, lamb and game. Great views from the polished upstairs section. Tues–Sat 11am–10pm.

Gösser Udvar Déryné utca 7. Varied menu in this average-looking restaurant in the pension of the same name. Next door you can get simple pizzas served up on plastic trays and paper plates. Daily noon–10pm.

Pannonia Kossuth utca 2. The *Hotel Pannonia*'s old-fashioned restaurant, with its compartmentalized seating areas, has a good reputation for its high-standard Hungarian food. Daily noon–11pm.

Székelykert Földes utca 4. In the pension of the same name, this cosy restaurant specializes in dishes from Transylvania, with occasional Gypsy music to enliven things somewhat. Daily 11am–10pm.

Bars and clubs

You can down fancy cocktails, to the background of pumping music, at the groovy *Mona Lisa* next to the Theatre Museum (daily 1pm–midnight), or at the marginally more sophisticated *Club Havanna* on Városház tér (daily 8am–

2am). For a beer, head to the relaxing *Big Ben Caffe* at Kossuth utca 8, which also serves hot food (Mon–Sat 11am–11pm), or the marvellous *Liky Pera*, at Széchenyi út 94, a fun-filled three-floored tea house and bar which occasionally puts on live music; you can also access the **Internet** here (daily 10am–10pm, Fri & Sat till midnight). Nightlife of a weightier kind revolves around the *Bahnhof Music Club* at Csaba vezér út 91/93, and the *Vian Klub*, a massively popular live music venue at Győri kapu 57. Look out for flyers for Saturday-night raves in the TV Tower, too. In Miskolc-Tapolca over summer, there are regular raves and parties in the *Hotel Junó*, and visiting DJs and groups appear at other venues, as advertised.

Festivals and events

The city's most prestigious event is the **Bartók and International Opera Festival** (Miskolci Nemzetközi Operafesztivál) in mid-June, a week of high-quality concerts starring some of the finest operatic singers in Europe. Each year the works of a different composer are run alongside works of the great Hungarian Béla Bartók. Otherwise, the city is at its liveliest during the **Miskolc Summer Festival** (Miskolci Nyár; June–Aug), when jazz, classical music and opera are performed at the Queen's Castle and in Miskolc-Tapolca. Among its highlights is the **Kaláka Folklore Festival** in mid-July, one of the largest folk gatherings in the region, attended by musicians and dancers from all over Hungary and abroad. The national holiday on **August 20** is marked by equestrian displays and a folk fair in the Queen's Castle. Tickets for all the above can be obtained from Tourinform. Tickets for operatic, ballet and theatrical performances are available from the National Theatre ticket office at Széchenyi út 23 (Mon–Fri 10am–7pm, Sat & Sun 3–7pm; ⓣ46/344-862), while for classical concerts head to the Philharmonic ticket office at Kossuth utca 4 (Mon–Fri 9am–1pm & 2–4pm).

Aggtelek National Park

Declared a UNESCO World Heritage Site in 1995, the **Aggtelek National Park**, bordering Slovakia, comprises an area of 20,000 hectares. Like the Bükk, the Aggtelek range displays typical **karstic** features such as gullies, sinkholes and caves, caused by a mixture of water and carbon dioxide dissolving the limestone. The **Baradla caves**, between the villages of Aggtelek and Jósvafő, and the **Béke caves** to the southeast, are the park's real treasures, constituting an amazing subterranean world with Stygian lakes and rivers, waterfalls, countless stalactites and nearly three hundred species of wildlife. Set in remote countryside that's ideal for walking, cycling, and bird-watching, the caves are deservedly popular with tourists.

Getting to the Aggtelek entails catching an early bus from Budapest, Miskolc or Eger, or travelling later in the day, starting from the industrial town of Ózd, northwest of Miskolc, which has daily services around 8am, noon & 3pm, less frequently at weekends, or Putnok, northeast of Ózd, where there are **buses** to Aggtelek and Jósvafő every ninety minutes. Alternatively, catch one of the six daily (Sunday 1 only) **trains** from Miskolc, which take an hour and drop you at the Jósvafő-Aggtelek station, 10km east of Jósvafő, from where regular buses run to both villages (less frequently on Sundays).

Jósvafő and Aggtelek

Aside from the fortified church with its picturesque cemetery in **JÓSVAFŐ**, and the algae-green lake outside **AGGTELEK**, both villages are fairly unremarkable. Shops are few and social life centres around the church and a few "drinks shops". **Information** is available from Tourinform at Baradla oldal 1, by the entrance to the caves in Aggtelek (daily: April–Sept 8am–6pm; Oct–March 8am–4pm; Ⓣ48/503-000, Ⓦwww.anp.hu), who can also arrange guided walks and ecotours of the region. There is plenty of **accommodation** in both villages, largely in the form of guest and tourist houses. In Jósvafő, you'll find the *Tengerszem Hotel* at Tengerszem oldal 2 (Ⓣ48/506-005, Ⓦwww.hotels.hu/josvafo; ❺), tucked away at the end of a lush valley, which is pretty well equipped with TV, minibar and phone in each room. Accommodation in Aggtelek consists of the seventy-room *Hotel Cseppkő* at Gyömrői út 2, picturesquely situated on a hill by the entrance to the caves (Ⓣ48/343-075; ❸), and the more intimate *Karszt Üdülő* at Deák utca 11 in the village (Ⓣ46/382-181; ❸). You might also try the *Baradla Camping* complex right by the cave entrance in Aggtelek (Ⓣ & Ⓕ48/343-073), which has four-bed chalets studded around the hill above the cave (❷) and a hostel (1300Ft); the camping ground is open between mid-April and mid-October. Both the *Tengerszem* and the *Cseppkő* have **restaurants** and display local bus schedules in their lobbies.

The region is replete with opportunities for leisure activities. Aside from hiking (see opposite), there are **cycling** trails aplenty, including a 51-kilometre circular route heading up towards the Slovakian border and taking in the major villages; you can **rent bikes** in Jósvafő at Fenyves utca 11 (Ⓣ48/350-128). There's also **horse-riding** available at the Hucul stud in Jósvafő (Ⓣ48/350-052; 1200Ft per hour, or 2000Ft for carriage rides; book in advance).

The tourist office or hotels can tell you about the classical music **concerts** that are held in the caves between June and September and at New Year. The main event in the region each year is the **Gömör-Torna Festival**, a week-long affair at the end of July featuring folk and art camps, sporting events, jazz bands and various ensembles from around the country.

Visiting the caves

Both sets of caves are open daily from 8am to 6pm (Oct–March until 5pm), and hourly guided tours leave at 10am, 1pm, 3pm and 5pm (Oct–March last tour 3pm) from the cave entrances (*bejárat*).

The main **Baradla cave passage** twists underground for 22km, and there is a range of **tours** you can take. There are one-hour tours from both ends (1400Ft), or you can do a combined tour (1800Ft). The **Aggtelek** end of the passage is more convoluted and thus more rewarding for shorter tours. No description can do justice to the variety and profusion of **stalactites and stalagmites**, whose nicknames can only hint at the fantastic formations, glittering with calcite crystals or stained ochre by iron oxides. Among them is the world's tallest stalagmite, a full 25m high. In the "Concert Hall", boats sway on the "River Styx", and the guide activates a tape of Bach's *Toccata in D minor* to create a *Phantom of the Opera* type ambience. **Long tours** (3000Ft) last four hours, take in 4.5km of cave, much of which is unlit, and require some stamina: it's a long time to clamber around dank, muddy caves, however beautiful they are. You need to book in advance for these longer tours (Ⓣ & Ⓕ48/503-003).

Three-hour guided tours around the **Béke caves** (6000Ft) are also fairly demanding. Although they contain a sanatorium, the underground air being judged beneficial to asthmatics, most of the caves are, in fact, untamed, even unexplored, and as recently as 1973 a new passage was found when cavers penetrated a thirty-metre waterfall. You'll need boots and warm, waterproof clothing, and visitors are issued with helmets.

Excursions in the vicinity

The surrounding countryside is riddled with smaller caves and rock formations, clearly marked on the hiking **map** (*Aggtelek és Jósvafő környéke*) sold at the Tourinform office in Aggtelek. This also shows the **border zone** – it's always a good idea to carry your passport when hiking. For those with a car or bike, lots of attractive **villages** are within reach in this part of the highlands, for example **RUDABÁNYA**, where the ten-million-year-old jawbone of *Rudapithecus hungaricus*, an ancient primate, can be seen at the mine where it was excavated. The mine is now closed but there is an exhibition of various mining implements and artefacts in the **Museum of Mining and Minerals** at Petőfi utca 24 (Ásványbányászafi múzeum; Mon–Fri 8am–5pm, Sat & Sun 9am–5pm; 200Ft). There is also a delightful fifteenth-century Gothic church with a painted panelled ceiling, dating from the seventeenth century.

The Zemplén Hills and around

The northeasternmost corner of the Uplands is consumed by the **Zemplén range**, a region largely unspoiled by industry and tourism, and richly textured by nature and history. Its volcanic soil and microclimates provide a favourable environment for diverse wildlife, particularly snakes and birds of prey, while the architecture reflects a tradition of trade and cultural exchange between the Great Plain and the Slovakian highlands. The small town of **Tokaj**, home to Hungary's most famous wine, absorbs most of the region's tourists, surprisingly few of whom make it up to **Sárospatak**, site of the superb Rákóczi castle, or to the smaller **Zemplén villages** such as Füzér and Boldogkőváralja, and the castles that loom over them.

Tokaj

TOKAJ is to Hungary what Champagne is to France, and this small town, 54km east of Miskolc, has become a minor Mecca for wine lovers. Squeezed onto a narrow strip of land between Tokaj Hill and the confluence of the rivers Bodrog and Tisza, its sloping streets and pastel-painted dwellings are rife with wine cellars and nesting storks, overlooked by lush vineyards climbing the hillside towards the "Bald Peak" and the inevitable TV Tower. Though it looks prosperous and laid-back, Tokaj is far from rich, and most people have to work hard to get any kind of living from the vineyards. For those with money to invest, however, there are exciting prospects for exports. In Tokaj, you can sample local wines in the famous Rákóczi cellar, or countless other, humbler places. To see a working winery, take a trip to Tarcal, Mád or Tolcsva in the Tokaj-Hegyalja (see p.361).

▲ Tokaj

Arrival and information

Arriving at the **train station**, south of town on Baross Gábor utca, take your bearings from the large map posted outside before heading down to the main road, Bajcsy-Zsilinszky utca, and into the old centre of Tokaj – a fifteen-minute walk. The main **bus stop** (there is no station here) is on Serház utca, just south of the synagogue. For **information** on wine tours and the Tokaj-Hegyalja villages, drop into Tourinform at Serház utca 1 (June–Sept daily 9am–6pm; Oct–May Mon–Fri 9am–4pm; ⓣ47/352-259, ⓔtokaj@tourinform.hu). The **post office** is at Rákóczi út 24 (Mon–Fri 8am–5pm, Sat 8am–noon).

Accommodation

There is an abundance of private **accommodation** in Tokaj, and the streets are awash with *Zimmer frei* signs. If you have any problems, however, Activ Tours, Rákóczi út 6 (July–Oct Mon–Sat 10am–5.30pm; Nov–June closed Sat; ⓣ47/552-187, ⓕ47/552188) can help to locate rooms and also organize wine-tasting trips. Cheap doubles with bathrooms, and quadruples without, can be found at the *Széchenyi Kollégium*, Bajcsy-Zsilinszky utca 15–17 (ⓣ47/352-355; ❶), from late June till late August, and at weekends the rest of the year. The busy and noisy *Vízisport Turistaház* (ⓣ & ⓕ47/352-645, ⓦwww.tokaj-hostel.hu), across the Tisza bridge and immediately to your left by the river, has rooms in a hostel building (❶) as well as a small **campsite**. There are two other campsites close by, both of which have chalets (❷): behind the *Vízisport* is the peaceful

Pelsőczy (ⓣ47/352-626; May to mid-Sept), and across the road lies the very large *Tisza* (ⓣ47/352-927; April–Oct).

Lux Panzió Serház utca 14 ⓣ & ⓕ47/352-145. The best value-for-money place in town, with colourful, intimately-styled rooms, although breakfast is not included. ❸

Millennium Hotel Bajcsy-Zsilinszky utca 34 ⓣ47/352-247, ⓦwww.tokajmillennium.hu. Spacious, attractive rooms in this sleek building on the way to the old town. ❺

Tokaj Hotel Rákóczi út 5 ⓣ & ⓕ47/352-344. The biggest hotel in town, just by the riverfront, has largely uninspiring rooms, but it's reasonable value and very central. ❹

Toldi Fogadó Hajdú köz 2 ⓣ47/353-403, ⓦwww.hotels.hu/toldi. Just up from the *Makk Marci* restaurant, this central pension is the star turn in town, with sparkling, air-conditioned rooms and very obliging staff. Good restaurant too (see p.361). ❺

Torkolat Panzió Vasvári utca 26 ⓣ & ⓕ47/352-827, ⓦwww.torkolat.uw.hu In the northern part of the old town, this efficiently run place has nine, very homely rooms, each with an individualistic touch. Bikes and canoes are available to guests free of charge; bikes cost 1000Ft a day for non-residents. ❹

Vaskó Panzió Rákóczi út 12 ⓣ & ⓕ47/352-107. Tokaj's cheapest pension, this place is above a bar, so can be noisy, but the comfortable rooms are well worth the price. ❸

The Town

Wine is omnipresent in Tokaj, with cellars at every step, all kinds of wine-making equipment displayed in shop windows, and barrel staves piled in people's backyards. The main street that runs northwards through the centre, Rákóczi út, has recently been spruced up and pedestrianized, so you can admire its Baroque facades at leisure. At no. 54 you'll pass the grand-looking, Zopf-style **Town Hall**, just short of the main square, **Kossuth tér**. To the left of the church on the main square you'll find the venerable **Rákóczi cellar** at Kossuth tér 15, the most famous in Tokaj and a place of pilgrimage where 20,000 hectolitres of wine repose in 24 cobwebbed, chandelier-lit passages (mid-March to mid-Oct daily 10am–6pm; 2200Ft for tasting of six wines; ⓣ47/352-009, ⓔrakoczi@axelro.hu). On the outside wall is a plaque commemorating Máté Szepsi Lackó (1567–1633), a Calvinist minister who invented *Aszú* wine. The cellar now belongs to a foreign firm, but functions much as it previously did. However, you'll get more personal service in smaller **private cellars** in the backstreets above Rákóczi út, such as the excellent Hímesudvar at Bem utca 2, five minutes up from Kossuth tér. Once a hunting lodge owned by the eighteenth-century nobleman János Szapolyai, it now houses the cellars of the Várhelyi family, where you can taste wines and nibble *pogácsa* (savoury pastries); (daily: March–Nov 10am–8pm; Dec–Feb 10am–7pm; 2000Ft for tasting of six wines; ⓣ47/352/416, ⓦwww.himesudvar.hu).

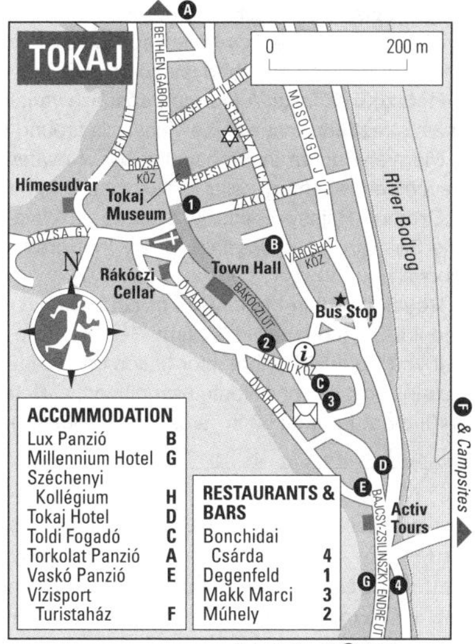

Tokaji wines

Tokaji wines derive their character from the special soil, the prolonged sunlight and the wine-making techniques developed here. Heat is trapped by the volcanic loess soil, allowing a delayed **harvest** in October, by which time many of the grapes are overripe and botrytized (attacked by a rot that shrivels them and makes them incredibly sweet). It is these **Aszú grapes** that make the difference between regular *Hárslevelű* (linden leaf) and *Furmint* wine, and the special wines sold in short, stubby bottles under the names *Szamorodni* and *Aszú*, whose qualities depend on the number of hods (*puttony*) of *Aszú* added to 136-litre barrels of ordinary grapes. *Szamorodni* is a word of Polish origin meaning "as it comes". It is typically golden in colour and can be dry or sweet, but never as sweet as *Aszú*. Another crucial factor is the ageing of the wine in cellars encrusted with a black odourless **mould** called *penész*, which interacts with the fermentation process.

Tokaj wine has collected some notable **accolades** since the late Middle Ages. Beethoven and Schubert dedicated songs to it; Louis XVI declared it "the wine of kings, the king of wines"; Goethe, Voltaire, Heine and Browning all praised it; and Sherlock Holmes used it to toast the downfall of von Bork, after troubling Watson to "open the window, for chloroform vapour does not help the palate".

In the Communist era, collective wineries tended to level standards down to the lowest common denominator, but also produced such gems as a 1972 6-*puttonyos*, that has a prize-winning chocolate and almond taste. During the 1990s foreign investors fell over themselves to get involved, resulting in what was known as the **Tokaji Renaissance**. Tokajis from the old days tend to be a richer brown-red in colour due to oxidization, which doesn't occur in the state-of-the-art stainless steel tanks used by foreign wineries. Some like the new style, others prefer the old. You can decide for yourself on **tours and tastings** (expect to pay around 2000Ft for the tasting of six wines) at wineries in the region, of which the following are recommended:

Degenfeld Terézia kert 9, Tarcal ⓣ47/380-357, ⓦwww.grofdegenfeld.com. Bought by a German sewing-machine magnate for his Hungarian wife, this winery has cellars fronted by a pretty house set among chestnut trees, and an adjoining plush four-star hotel (ⓣ47/580-400; ❽).

Disznókő Mezőzombor, outside Tarcal ⓣ47/569-410. This place's French owners began by scrubbing all the mildew off the cellar walls, to the horror of the locals. The winery was designed by Makovecz (note the circular tractor shed) and has a restaurant and pension attached (same phone).

Hétszőlő in Tokaj. A Franco-Japanese venture that owns the Rákóczi cellar on the main street and most of the vineyards around town. See p.359 for details.

Megyer-Pajzos in Sárospatak. Now owned by a French company, this famous seventeenth-century cellar is associated with Prince Rákóczi. See p.367 for details.

Oremus Bajcsy-Zsilinszky utca 45, Tolcsva ⓣ47/384-520. A wise investment by the Spanish, as it was this winery that produced the 1972 6-*puttonyos* mentioned above.

Royal Tokaji in Mád. Miles of old cellars lined with oak barrels and smothered in mould. Owned by a British firm. See opposite for details.

If you would like more information on wineries and cellars in the region contact the Tokaj-Hegyalja Wine Route Association, at Bethlen-Gábor utca 11 in Tokaj (ⓣ47/580-440), or at Fő utca 57 in Tarcal (ⓣ47/380-261).

Just past Kossuth tér at Bethlen Gábor utca 7, the **Tokaj Museum** (Tues–Sun 10am–4pm; 400Ft), in a lovely building with an old wooden staircase, has an excellent local history exhibition, including a re-creation of a drawing room from a Greek wine-trader's house, and Judaica from the former **synagogue** behind the museum on Serház utca – now almost entirely boarded up and in a terrible state. Prewar Tokaj had a large Jewish population, which handled most of the wine trade in conjunction with a smaller number of Greek families – hence the **Jewish cemetery** 6km north along the main road, the keys for which are available from the house just beyond it.

If you fancy a longer walk, follow the road behind Kossuth tér uphill to the summit of Tokaj's 516-metre-high "**Bald Peak**", topped by a TV Tower. The four-kilometre round-trip takes you past dozens of vineyards, each labelled with its owner's name. The TV tower is accessible by road too, but you have to drive round the hill via the village of Tarcal. From the summit you can scan the distant Great Plain and the lush green Tokaj-Hegyalja – the hilly wine-producing region.

Eating, drinking and activities

There's little to get excited about when it comes to **eating** in town, and you may well spend more time in the wine cellars than you initially thought. The best option if you do want a meal is *Degenfeld* (daily 11.30am–10pm), Kossuth tér 1, whose creative menu includes some great fish dishes. The neatly laid out restaurant in the *Toldi Fogadó* is also enjoyable, with a reasonably ambitious Hungarian menu, although the service is a little slack – they've got a pleasant beer garden too (daily 11am–10pm). Otherwise, the very ordinary options include the touristy *Bonchidai Csárda* at Bajcsy-Zsilinszky utca 21 (daily 11am–11pm), with its enormous riverside terrace, and *Makk Marci* (daily noon–10pm, a fail-safe pizzeria option. If you're looking for somewhere to drink something other than wine, you can grab a cool, crisp beer at *Műhely*, Rákóczi út 42 (daily noon–10pm).

Activities available in Tokaj include cycling and canoeing, both of which can be arranged through *Vízisport Turistaház* (see p.358). Swimming in the Tisza may be tempting, but is not advised due to the dirtiness of the water and its unpredictable whirlpools. The major festivals in town each year are the **Wine Festival** (Tokaj-Hegyaljai Borfesztivál) at the beginning of August, and the **Grapes Harvest Festival** (Szüreti Napok Tokaj) at the beginning of October, both of which involve, naturally enough, much consumption of wine.

The Tokaj-Hegyalja

The southern slopes of the Zemplén form the distinctive region known as the **Tokaj-Hegyalja**, which is largely devoted to producing wine. Most of its beautifully sited villages are accessible by bus from Tokaj or Szerencs, a drab little town 18km west of Tokaj (many are also served by the train line from Szerencs to Hidasnémeti), but the paucity of tourist accommodation may oblige you to stick to day-trips – you can stop off at one or two villages a day, depending on schedules.

In **MÁD**, 11km east of Szerencs, it's worth enquiring about **tasting tours** at the British-owned **Royal Tokaji cellars** at Rákóczi utca 35 (Ⓣ47/348-601), in the centre of the village, which is also home to the renowned vintner István Szepsy (allegedly descended from the inventor of Aszú), who can be found at Táncsics utca 57 (Ⓣ47/348-349). While the train station lies ten minutes' walk down Bányász utca, visitors arriving by bus will pass a folk Baroque-style **synagogue**, built in 1765, whose ornate ceilings are rotting with damp while pigeons desecrate its pews. The talisman-sized key is held at Kossuth út 73, below the former **Rabbi's house** and arcaded **Yeshiva** (religious school), long

Lajos Kossuth

Lajos Kossuth was the incarnation of post-Napoleonic bourgeois nationalism. Born into landless gentry in 1802, he began his political career as a lawyer, representing absentee magnates in Parliament. His parliamentary reports, advocating greater liberalism than the Habsburgs would tolerate, were widely influential during the Reform Era. While in jail for sedition, Kossuth taught himself English by reading Shakespeare. Released in 1840, he became editor of the radical *Pesti Hírlap*, was elected to Parliament and took the helm during the 1848 Revolution, whereupon his eloquent idealism tragically fulfilled its latent demagogic chauvinism.

After Serbs, Croats and Romanians rebelled against Magyar rule and the Habsburgs invaded Hungary, the Debrecen Parliament proclaimed a republic with Kossuth as de facto dictator. Having escaped to Turkey after the Hungarians surrendered in August 1849, he toured Britain and America, espousing liberty. So eloquent were his denunciations of Habsburg tyranny that London brewery workers attacked General Haynau, the "Butcher of Vienna", when he visited the city. Karl Marx loathed Kossuth as a bourgeois radical, and tried to undermine his reputation with articles published in the New York *Herald Tribune* and the London *Times*. As a friend of the Italian patriot Mazzini, Kossuth spent his last years in Turin, where he died in 1894.

divided into flats and sunk into disrepair. On the northern edge of Mád lies an old **Jewish Cemetery**, which is also locked; ask around for the key.

TÁLLYA, 9km further north, is another wine-producing village with hundreds of barrels maturing in seventeenth-century **cellars** near a former Rákóczi mansion. In the village **church** you can view the font where Lajos Kossuth was baptized, while on the road up to the TV tower, the former synagaogue has been been turned into an art gallery where exhibitions and **concerts** are held during the Zemplén Days in late August; Tourinform in Sárospatak has details. The only pension in the village is the *Kisház Panzió* at Rákóczi utca 49 (☎47/398-028; ❷).

MONOK, 10km northwest of Szerencs, was the **birthplace of Kossuth**, whose childhood home at Kossuth utca 18 is now a **museum** (Kossuth emlékek; March–Oct Tues–Sun 9am–5pm; rest of the year by appointment; 150Ft) that casts his career (see box above) in the most favourable light. Monok's other famous son is Miklós Németh, Hungary's Prime Minister during the transition from Communism to democracy in 1989.

Some 30km north of Tokaj and 2km off the road to Sárospatak, **TOLCSVA** can be reached by the hourly bus from Tokaj to Komlóska. Its erstwhile Rákóczi manor at Kossuth Lajos utca 55 beyond the two churches in the centre is now a **Wine Museum** (Tues–Sun 10am–5pm; 100Ft), while the hillside is honeycombed with 2.5km of cellars full of local **linden leaf wine** (Tolcsvai Hárslevelű). Tolcsva's Spanish-owned **winery** produces some of the finest modern Tokajis (see box on p.360). The *Király Panzió*, at Kossuth utca 61 (☎47/384-555; ❸), is a well-facilitated pension with restaurant and bar.

The village of **SZABOLCS**, 10km southeast, on the far side of the River Tisza, was once important enough to lend its name to a county in northeastern Hungary. Here you'll find the only surviving earthworks fortress (*földvár*) in Central Europe, dating from the ninth century; the eighteenth-century **Mudrány Mansion** at Petőfi utca 38 (May–Sept Tues–Sun 10am–6pm); and a **Calvinist Church** with fifteenth-century frescoes that was built as a Catholic church in the eleventh century.

The western Zemplén

The western flank of the Zemplén is dotted with **villages** whose remote and sleepy existence today belies their historic significance. Unlike the other parts of Hungary with medieval churches and ruined castles, there's rarely another tourist in sight here, even though the **scenery** everywhere is great. In contrast to the rounded sedimentary hills on the western side of the valley, the volcanically formed Zemplén often resemble truncated cones called *sátor* (tent). If all of this appeals, and you don't mind the lack of bright lights and facilities, the region is well worth exploring.

Though private **transport** is definitely advantageous, most places are accessible by local buses or trains up the Szerencs–Hidasnémeti branch line. The scarcity of **accommodation** could be more of a problem unless you bring a tent, or encounter sympathetic locals. Try to buy a hiking **map** (*Zempléni hegység*) from the Tourinform in Tokaj or Miskolc, which is useful even if you don't intend to go **hiking**. There are two maps: *északi*, covering the northern part, and *déli* the south, showing all the villages mentioned below.

The route described below approximately follows the **Hernád Valley** up towards the river's source in the Slovakian highlands, and the **border crossing** into Slovakia at Tornyosnémeti (by road) and Hidasnémeti (by rail).

Boldogkőváralja and Vizsoly

Best reached by road, since the village lies 2.5km from its train stop, **BOLDOGKŐVÁRALJA** is dominated by a massive **castle** (mid-April to mid-Oct Mon 10am–6pm, Tues–Sun 9am–6pm; 250Ft) upon a volcanic mound. Erected in the thirteenth century to discourage a return visit by the Mongols, it commands a spectacular view of the Zemplén Hills, and the surrounding woods are rife with red squirrels. You can **stay** at the clean and bright *Bodóvár Panzio* (Ⓣ46/306-062, Ⓦwww.castles.hu/bodovar ❸) at the foot of the road leading up to the castle.

At **VIZSOLY**, 2km from its train station, Korlát-Vizsoly, a thirteenth-century **Calvinist Church** (daily 9am–11.30am & 12.30pm–5pm; 250Ft) harbours fantastic frescoes of Jesus's Ascension (leaving his footprints behind) and St George and the dragon, which were only discovered in 1940 after being lost for many centuries. A Latin inscription on the chancel wall reads "If you did not come to pray in this place then leave as you have come." The church also contains an original edition of the **Vizsoly Bible**, the first Hungarian translation of the Bible by Gáspár Károlyi, dean of Gönc, in 1590, which was printed in the house across the road and played a formative role in the development of Hungarian as a written language. In summertime, it's possible to **stay** at the priest's house (*református lelkesz*; known as *Károlyi Gáspár Ifjúsági Tábor*; Ⓣ46/387-187; ❷) at Szent János út 123, where you'll get a warm welcome. There are regular **buses** to Abaújszantó and a daily service to Miskolc and Szikszó.

Gönc and Regéc

Thirteen kilometres further up the valley, amid ravishing countryside, the village of **GÖNC**, accessible by buses from Hidasnémeti as well as by train, was a thriving trade centre in the Middle Ages. It was here that Dean Károlyi was born and translated the Vizsoly Bible, and Sárospatak's Calvinist College took refuge during the Counter-Reformation. Subsequently, the village became famous for making the 136-litre oak **barrels** (*Gönci hordok*) used to store Tokaj wine – sadly no longer made here.

The most tangible relic of this history is the white **Hussite House** at Kossuth utca 85 (Huszita Ház; mid-April to mid-Oct Tues–Sun 10am–6pm; 250Ft), whose Calvinist inhabitants could escape into the maze of cellars beneath the village via a door in the cellar of the house. Notice the Gönc barrel, and the weird bed that pulls out from a table upstairs. If it's shut, the old woman at Rákóczi utca 115, across the stream and off to the right, can let you in; she was born in the Hussite House.

Gönc is very picturesque but facilities are minimal, with nowhere to eat except a cake shop and a single bar, where locals get stuck into *pálinka* at 10am – you can even buy alcohol at the flower shop. However, there is pleasant year-round **accommodation** at Arany János utca 1B at the far end of Kossuth utca (Ⓣ46/388-477; ❷), plus the *Diákotthon*, a school building behind the Hussite House at Károlyi Gáspár utca 33 (Ⓣ46/388-052; ❶) over the summer.

Some might enjoy a hard day's **hiking to REGÉC**, along an eight-kilometre ill-marked path skirting the 787-metre-high Gergely-hegy (bring a compass, food and water). Regéc is the site of another **ruined castle**, which is also accessible by two buses a day from Encs, on the Miskolc–Hidasnémeti line, leaving around noon and 2pm.

Telkibánya, Abaújvár and Kéked

Buses from Hidasnémeti to Gönc carry on to **TELKIBÁNYA**, 9km to the east (also served by two buses from Sátoraljaújhely, on the other side of the hills), whose **museum** at Múzeum utca 15 (Ipartőrténeti Gyűjtemény; daily 10am–5pm; 180Ft) has a fine collection of Zemplén crystals, pottery and carved heads. The *Gyermektábor* (Children's Camp) at Fürdő utca 17 offers self-catering **accommodation** during summer, and also out of season if you book ahead (Ⓣ46/325-766, Ⓦwww.gyermektabor.hu; ❷), and there are private rooms at Múzeum utca 3 (Ⓣ46/388-665; ❶) and on the same street at no. 10 (Ⓣ46/388-463; ❷).

Buses from Gönc and a limited service (2 daily on weekdays) from Hidasnémeti, 4km away, to Hollóháza (see p.371) can get you to **ABAÚJVÁR**, 9km to the north of Gönc. This pretty village has a picturesque **Calvinist Church** with battered frescoes from 1332; ask for the key on Rákóczi utca, below the church. Another 4km along the way to Hollóháza, buses call at **KÉKED**, which boasts a **fortified manor** (Tues–Sun 10am–4pm; 200Ft) containing rustic knick-knacks and antiques that belonged to the present mayor's grandmother prior to its expropriation in 1947. The manor now houses a very posh hotel with an extensive range of facilities (Ⓣ46/588-566, Ⓔkeked@axelro.hu; ❻). Otherwise, you can **stay** at the *Kéked Fogadó* at Fürdő utca 13 (Ⓣ46/388-077; ❷; May–Sept), near an **outdoor bath** in the forest (May–Aug Tues–Sun 10am–6pm), fed by a cold-water spring.

Sárospatak

Half an hour's train journey from Szerencs, **SÁROSPATAK** ("Muddy Stream") basks on the banks of the River Bodrog – a graceful, serene spot with almost unlimited expanses of green. The town once enjoyed a significant role in Hungarian intellectual life, thanks to its **Calvinist College**: Magyars given to hyperbole used to describe Sárospatak as the "Athens on the Bodrog". In the last twenty years, some fine examples of **Makovecz architecture** have drawn attention to the town, but Sárospatak's main claim to fame is still its historic

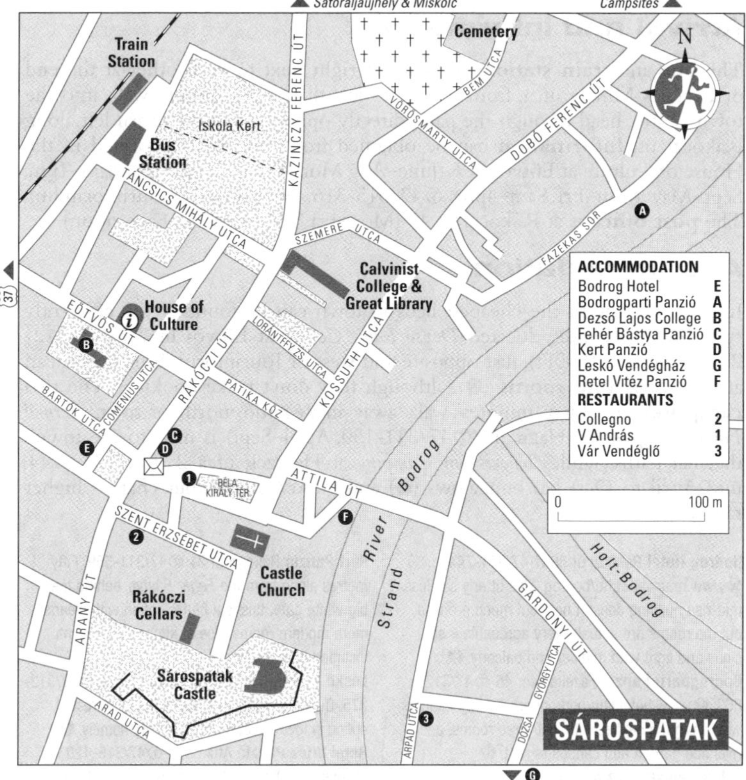

association with the **Rákóczi family**, whose **castle** is one of the main sights in town.

The Rákóczi family played a major role in Transylvania and Hungary during a turbulent era. Shortly after **György I Rákóczi** acquired Sárospatak Castle in 1616, his Transylvanian estates – and political influence – were augmented by marriage to the immensely wealthy **Zsuzsanna Lorántffy**. In 1630 the nobility elected him Prince of Transylvania, hoping that György would restore the stability enjoyed under Gábor Bethlen – which he did.

Alas, **György II** was as rash as his father was cautious, managing to antagonize both Poland and Vizier Mehmet, whose invasion of Transylvania forced the clan to flee to Habsburg-controlled Hungary in 1658. Here the Counter-Reformation was in full swing, and Magyar landlords and peasants reacted against Habsburg confiscations by sporadically staging ferocious revolts of "dissenters" (*kuruc*). Though the original revolt, led by Imre Thököly, was bloodily crushed, conspirators gathered around György's son **Ferenc I**.

By 1703, the insurgency had become a full-scale **War of Independence**, led by **Ferenc II**, whose irregular cavalry and peasant foot soldiers initially triumphed. By 1711, however, the Magyars were exhausted and divided, abandoned by their half-hearted ally Louis XIV of France, and Ferenc fled abroad as his armies collapsed under the weight of Habsburg power, to die in exile (in Tekirdag, Turkey) in 1735.

Arrival and information

The **bus** and **train stations** are located right next to each other at the end of Táncsics Mihály utca, from where it's less than a ten-minute walk into the town centre; head through the park, directly opposite, and then turn left along Rákóczi út. **Information** can be obtained from Tourinform, located in the House of Culture at Eötvös út 6 (June–Aug Mon–Fri 8am–6pm, Sat 8am–1pm; Sept–May Mon–Fri 8am–4pm; ⓣ47/315-316, ⓔsarospatak@tourinform.hu). The **post office** is at Rákóczi út 45 (Mon–Fri 8am–6pm, Sat 8am–noon).

Accommodation

In July and August the cheapest beds in town can be found at the efficiently run and very handily located *Dezső Lajos College* at Eötvös út 7 (ⓣ47/312-211; dorm bed 1500Ft), just opposite and west of Tourinform. Tourinform can advise on **private rooms** (❷), although they don't make bookings. The two **campsites** are thirty minutes' walk away in Végardó, north of town: *Termál Fürdő Camping* on Határ út (ⓣ47/311-150; April–Sept) is next to the town's thermal baths, while *Tengerszem Camping* at Herczeg utca 2 (ⓣ47/312-744; mid-April to Oct) has bungalows (❷) and good facilities, but charges higher rates all round.

Bodrog Hotel Rákóczi út 58 ⓣ47/311-744, ⓦwww.matavanet.hu/bodrog. This utterly soulless mid-rise building doesn't hold out much promise, but the rooms are actually very agreeable – spacious and light with minibar and balcony. ❺

Bodrogparti Panzió Fazekas sor 46 ⓣ47/312-663, ⓦwww.hotels.hu/bodrogpart. Twenty minutes' walk from the centre, with just three rooms, a riverside garden and canoes to rent. ❺

Fehér Bástya Panzió Rákóczi út 39 ⓣ47/312-400, ⓦwww.hotels.hu/feher_bastya. Five very ordinary rooms, each with bathroom and TV. ❸

Kert Panzió Rákóczi út 31 ⓣ47/311-559. Fifty metres along from the *Fehér Bástya*, behind the big white gate, this is a better option with cleaner, more modern rooms. Use of kitchen and sauna included in price. ❸

Leskó Vendégház Dózsa György út 30/b ⓣ47/312-375. Out across the river, this is the most restful option in town; neat rooms and very homely. ❸

Retel Vitéz Panzió Attila út 2 ⓣ47/315-428, ⓔretelvitez@freemail.hu. The newest addition in Sárospatak, situated by the bridge, hence some of the quiet, clean rooms overlook the river. ❸

The Town

As good a place as any to start your exploration of the town is the **Iskola Kert** (School Garden), full of statues of alumni from the **Calvinist College** across the park (Mon–Sat 9am–5pm, Sun 9am–1pm; closed Easter, Whitsun & Oct 31; 400Ft). Founded in 1531, the college achieved renown under the rectorship (1650–54) of the great Czech humanist **Jan Comenius**, who published several textbooks with the support of György Rákóczi. During the Counter-Reformation, it was forced to move to Gönc, and then to Slovakia, before returning home in 1703. Illustrious graduates include Kossuth, Gárdonyi, the writer Zsigmond Móricz and the language reformer Ferenc Kazinczy. Like the Calvinist College in Debrecen, it has long-standing ties with England and runs an international **summer language school**. Since regaining control in 1990, the church has striven to make the college an educational powerhouse once again. Hour-long **tours** take in the Neoclassical **Great Library** (Nagykönyvtár), to the right of the main entrance, and a **museum** of college history. The modern building in the courtyard was designed by Makovecz (see box on p.172).

The Makovecz buildings

Passing through the centre of town you can see a succession of buildings by the visionary architect Imre Makovecz, whose association with Sárospatak dates back to 1972, when Makovecz was on the Party's blacklist. His first project for the council was the **department store** on the corner of Rákóczi út and Bartók utca, quite anodyne by Western standards, but far removed from the then prevailing brutalist style. Next came the **House of Culture** on Eötvös utca, whose silvery, insectile facade conceals an amazing wooden auditorium; followed by an **apartment building** on the corner with Rákóczi út, manifesting his passion for asymmetry and organic forms, rooted in a fascination with ancient Celtic and Magyar culture. In the 1990s Makovecz returned to Sárospatak to embellish the Calvinist College and build a delightful **school** on Arany út, just past the castle.

Sárospatak Castle

In a park outside the centre, **Sárospatak Castle** (Tues–Sun: March–Oct 10am–6pm; Nov–Feb 10am–5pm; free) is a handsome mélange of Gothic, Renaissance and Baroque architecture, both doughty and palatial. Grouped around a courtyard in the Renaissance wings, the **Rákóczi Museum** dotes upon the dynasty, even down to a series of watercolours depicting the stages of Ferenc II's exile. Heavy inlaid furniture, jewellery, monstrous stoves, and a banqueting hall complete with piped court music re-create domestic life, while other rooms contain life-size paintings of fearsome cavalry and the moustachioed portrait of Ferenc II that is much reproduced.

A romantic loggia, like a set from *Romeo and Juliet*, links the residential wings to the fifteenth-century keep, known as the **Red Tower**. Guided tours (in Hungarian only) take you around the dungeons and underground wells, the labyrinth of galleries used by gunners and a series of impressive halls. The **Knights' Hall**, remaining somehow austere despite its throne and stained-glass windows, hosted sessions of Parliament during the Independence War. Plots were hatched by Ferenc I in the adjoining circular balcony room, beneath a ceiling decorated with a stucco rose – the rose being a cryptic warning to guests to be discreet (hence the expression "sub rosa", meaning conspiratorial). Beyond the courtyard is a sloping grass bank, now a **nature conservation area**, running down to the river.

The Rákóczi Cellars and Castle Church

Founded in 1531, the **Rákóczi Cellars**, just outside the castle gates at Szent Erzsébet utca tér 26, are the most impressive in the Zemplén. Hewn out by prisoners from the castle dungeons in the seventeenth century, they are thickly coated in a black *penész*, the "noble mould", whose presence is considered vital to the flavour of local **wine**. The one-kilometre-long cellars consist of three parallel tunnels lined with some one thousand oak barrels through which the wine breathes in humidity exceeding ninety percent. Between the two chilly tasting rooms, there is a famous niche with a bench in it where Ferenc Rákóczi himself used to come and smoke a pipe and plot the overthrow of the Habsburgs. The cellar is now owned by **Megyer-Pajzos**, a French company with a Hungarian name. **Tours and wine-tasting** take place every 45 minutes – book in advance or just show up and wait your turn (Mon–Fri 10am–5pm, also May–Sept Sat & Sun 10am–6pm; 1400Ft for tasting of six wines; ⓣ47/311-902, ⓔpajzosmegyer@axelro.hu).

A minute's walk away, further up Szent Erzsébet utca, stands Sárospatak's **Castle Church** (Tues–Sat 9am–5pm, Sun 11.30am–4pm; 140Ft). Though much remodelled since the fourteenth century, with painted-on rather than genuine vaulting, it remains one of the largest Gothic hall churches in eastern Hungary. Its huge Baroque altar was brought here from the Carmelite church in Buda Castle after their order was banned in 1784. Look out for posters outside advertising **organ recitals**.

Eating, drinking and entertainment

There are two outstanding Hungarian **restaurants** in town: the stylish *V András* restaurant and coffee house at Béla Király tér 3, a delightfully mellow place with model aeroplanes and airships dangling from the ceiling (daily 10am–10pm, Fri & Sat till midnight); and the *Vár Vendéglő*, across the river at Árpád utca 35 (daily noon–10pm), a serene little spot with a fantastic wooden-roofed terrace and some interesting variations on Hungarian dishes – turn right upon crossing the bridge and walk straight on for 200m. Simpler alternatives include the *Collegno* restaurant at Szent Erzsébet utca 22, a cellar pizzeria with a beer garden (daily 11am–midnight), and the none too cheery restaurant in the *Fehér Bástya Panzió* (daily 8am–9pm). The **café** at the entrance to the castle is a good place to settle down with a coffee and a pastry but is invariably quite busy (Tues–Sun 10am–5pm), while the popular café on the first floor of the House of Culture is a good spot for a beer (daily 1pm–midnight) and has **Internet** access. There are often various forms of entertainment going on at the cultural house, too.

Tourinform can supply a detailed list of **concerts**, plays and other events happening in town, the most popular of which is the **Zémplen Music Days** (Zempléni Művészeti Napok) in mid-August – a series of fairly highbrow classical concerts in town and the surrounding villages (tickets can be bought at the National Philharmonic box office in Budapest – see p.141 – or at Tourinform in Sárospatak; 800–1800Ft). During the last weekend of June a **Jazz and Blues Festival** takes place in the castle gardens. Should you wish to wallow in the **thermal baths**, then head to the recreational complex 2km north of town in Végardó (daily 8am–6pm; 600Ft, 400Ft after 2pm).

Sátoraljaújhely and around

Easier to reach than it is to pronounce ("**shah**-tor-oll-yah-oowee-hay"), **SÁTORALJAÚJHELY**, 13km northeast from Sárospatak, is the last Zemplén town before the border crossing to Slovenské Nové Mesto in Slovakia. Formerly a thriving county town, it was relegated to a backwater by the Treaty of Trianon and the provincial mergers which made Sárospatak the Zemplén "capital", while its once prosperous Jewish wine-trading community was wiped out in the war. Unless you happen to be searching for an ancestor, the reason for coming is to catch buses to the villages around, rather than to see the town itself – unless your visit happens to coincide with its **international folk dancing festival** in mid-August, which alternates every year between being for children or adults; odd-numbered years are for the adults.

From the bus and train stations 1km south of the centre, follow Fasor utca until it joins Kossuth utca, beside the striking red and yellow Reynolds tobacco factory. Across the main road lies a direly neglected **Jewish cemetery**, one of two in Sátoraljaújhely, where Jews amounted to forty percent of the population at the turn of the twentieth century. Further uphill, past a Gothic parish church, one reaches a cluster of Baroque edifices around Kossuth tér. It was from the balcony of the **Town Hall** at no. 5 that Kossuth first demonstrated his talent for oratory, during the Zemplén cholera epidemic and riots of 1830. In the middle of the square stands an almost unrecognizable Soviet war memorial covered with ivy. Rounding off the air of desolation, there's a dull local history exhibition in the **Kazinczy Museum** on Dózsa utca, down to the right past Kossuth tér (Mon–Sat 8am–4pm; 400Ft).

If you fancy some walking, the wild ravines and forested slopes of **Mount Magas** (509m) loom just outside town to the west. These heights saw bitter fighting between Magyars and Slovaks in 1919, and between partisans and Nazis in 1944.

Practicalities

Sátoraljaújhely's Tourinform, in the Town Hall at Kossuth tér 5 (May–Sept Mon–Fri 9am–6pm, Sat & Sun 9am–5pm; Oct–April Mon–Fri 8am–4pm; Ⓣ & Ⓕ47/321-458, Ⓔsatoraljaujhely@tourinform.hu), can supply **information** and also has a list of **private rooms** in the Zemplén. If you want to actually book a room however, you'll need to head to Ibusz at Kossuth tér 26 (Mon–Fri 8am–5pm; Ⓣ & Ⓕ47/321-757).

Accommodation in town is limited to two very reasonable choices: spacious rooms are available at *Hotel Henriette*, 50m down from the museum at Vasvári Pál utca 16 (Ⓣ47/323-118; ❸), while west of Kazinczy út is the brighter, air-conditioned *Csillagféhy Panzio* at Mártírok útja 29 (Ⓣ47/322-619, Ⓔcsillagfenypanzio@axelro.hu; ❸). There is also a budget option, *Kossuth Tourist Hotel*, a hostel with a wide veranda ten minutes' walk south at Török utca 1 (Ⓣ47/321-164, Ⓔberecsiek@freemail.hu; dorm bed 2300Ft). Hunting down a place to **eat** will yield little joy, with options restricted to the *Halászcsárda* at Kossuth tér 10 (daily 7am–10pm), one of the least inspiring fish restaurants around (although you may care to try the "Hungover" fish soup); and your safest bet, a pizza at *Zempléni Casino*, Kazinczy út 1. For coffee and cakes the *Sarokház Cukrasda* at Táncsics tér 2 should assuage any sugar pangs.

Around Sátoraljaújhely

In the highlands beyond Sátoraljaújhely there are more villages that are just as lovely as those on the western side of the Zemplén. With a car, you can visit half a dozen of them in a day and not feel cheated if a couple are less appealing than expected. Relying on local buses, you'll have to go for a simpler itinerary and be more selective.You can reach Füzér (2 daily Mon–Fri, 1 daily Sat & Sun), Pálháza (8 daily Mon–Fri, 7 daily Sat & Sun), Hollóháza (5 daily Mon–Fri, 3 daily Sat & Sun), Karcsa and Pácin (6 daily Mon–Fri, 4 daily Sat & Sun), and Telkibánya (2 daily Mon–Fri). **Village tourism** is flourishing in this region, and should you wish to stay there are plenty of houses advertising **rooms** (❶). Ibusz in Sátoraljaújhely have information and can make bookings in lodgings in local houses (see above). The following itineraries are basically structured around bus routes.

Towards Pálháza and Rostállo

This route can be a long excursion, or even a prelude to hiking over the Zemplén, depending on your inclinations. There are eight buses daily (seven at weekends) from Sátoraljaújhely via Széphalom and Füzérradvány to Pálháza, from where you can reach Rostállo in the hills.

At **SZÉPHALOM** ("Beautiful Mill"), 5km from Sátoraljaújhely, a park beside the road contains the elaborate **mausoleum of Ferenc Kazinczy** (May–Oct Tues–Sun 9.30am–5pm; 200Ft). It was largely thanks to Kazinczy and his associates that Hungarian was restored as a literary language in the nineteenth century rather than succumbing entirely to German, as the Habsburgs would have preferred. The *Múzeumkert Panzió*, at Kazinczy utca 273 (Ⓣ & Ⓕ47/324-172, Ⓔmuzeumkert@freemail.hu; ❸), has three- and four-bed rooms, as well as doubles, and also sports a gym, sauna and accomplished restaurant.

Six kilometres later, buses stop by an avenue of pines leading to the **Castle Garden** (Kastély Kert) surrounding a derelict manor house on the edge of **FÜZÉRRADVÁNY**, whose arboretum of variegated oaks and pines provides a haven for vipers and other wildlife (daily dawn till dusk; free). If the main gates are closed, follow the road round to the left and ask at the lodge. Work continues on converting the manor house into a hotel and museum. In the village there's a youth camp, the *Ifjúsági Tábor*, at Táncsics Mihály utca 14 (Ⓣ47/370-123; ❶), that lets **rooms** from April to October, bookable through Ibusz in Sátoraljaújhely, or you can stay at the *Nagytanya Fogadó* across the road at Fenyvesalja utca 1 (Ⓣ47/370-550; ❶) – there is also a small **campsite** here.

Another kilometre or so on up the main road lies **PÁLHÁZA**, the place to board the **narrow-gauge train** that runs 9km up to Rostalló. This *erdei vasút* (forest railway) runs three times daily (departing 8.30am, 11.40am & 3.10pm, returning at 9.35am, 12.45pm & 4.15pm; 45min; 210Ft) between mid-April and mid-October, to coincide with buses for Sátoraljaújhely. Lászlóné Ulicska offers **rooms** with a sauna and a pretty garden at Vörösmarty utca 10, at the eastern end of the village (Ⓣ47/370-278, Ⓔulicskalaca@freemail.hu; ❸), or there are clean, basic rooms at the *Megálló Turistaház* at Dózsa György utca 160 (Ⓣ47/370-121; ❶). To really get away from it all, you can stay at the *Kőkapui Vadákastély* in Pálháza-Kőkapu (Ⓣ47/370-032, Ⓦwww.kokapu.hu; ❸–❺), an old hunting lodge, 8km from Pálháza, deep in the woods. The best rooms are in the lodge itself, rather than in the annexe, as they overlook the lake. You can rent bikes and boats, and the **restaurant** is quite a hub of activity in the summer months, serving decent post-hike nourishment.

ROSTALLÓ, the train terminus 1km further on, is the starting point for **hikes** in various directions – mostly ambitious ones for which you need proper equipment and a map. A good objective is **István kut** (Stephen's Well), a silver birch wood between Rostalló, Háromhuta and Regéc, noted for its special flora and diverse butterflies.

Füzér, Hollóháza and Lászlótanya

If one excursion is your limit, the village to aim for is **FÜZÉR**, a stopover for buses between Sátoraljaújhely and Hollóháza, only 9km from Pálháza. An idyllic place of vine-swathed cottages, dignified elders and wandering animals, Füzér enjoys an exceptionally temperate climate and maintains its traditional ways less self-consciously than museum villages like Hollókő – though a single old dwelling at Szabadság út 11 has been preserved as a *tájház* for visitors to poke around (Tues–Sun 9am–4pm; free).

The ruined **Perényi Castle** is almost directly overhead, although screened by trees and the precipitous angle of the hill. Erected in case the Mongols should return, it served as a repository for the Hungarian crown from 1301 to 1310, while foreign rivals squabbled over the throne. At a later date it was owned by Countess Báthori, who is said to have murdered several victims here (see box on p.286). From the huge Gothic arches of its ruined chapel there's a magnificent view of the sleepy village below, the blue-green hills along the border and the distant plain beyond – the whole scene enlivened by flocks of swifts swooping and soaring on the powerful thermals. Due to the microclimate, the hillsides abound in **wildlife**, with special flora, vipers, birds of prey and – sometimes

– wolves and wildcats. You'll find plenty of houses advertising **rooms**, particularly along Kossuth utca and Árpád utca – just look out for the signs.

The village of **HOLLÓHÁZA**, 5km east of Füzér, is most notable for its **Porcelain Museum** at Károlyi út 11 (Porcelanmúzeum; April–Oct Tues–Sun 9.30am–4.30pm; 500Ft). As well as relating the history of the factory, established in 1831, the museum also documents industrial activity in the region, which began in 1777 with glass production. When the factory shop is closed, an outlet selling seconds is open round the corner (Tues–Sat 10am–4pm). At the top end of the village is a small modern **church**, one wall bearing the stations of the cross by the ceramicist Margit Kovács. There are three clean double **rooms** at the *Éva Panzió* (ⓣ47/305-038; ❷), set up amongst trees just off Szent László utca, the main street running through the village. Also in the centre, at Miki Nándor utca 12, is *Csini Camping* (ⓣ47/305-111; May–Sept), which also has a few double-room apartments (❸). You can enjoy a hearty meal at the *Nagymilic Étterem* at Károlyi utca 46 (daily noon–10pm), before pushing on to Lászlótanya, or catching one of the **buses** across the hills to Kéked and Abaújvár (see p.364).

About 6km by road from Hollóháza or a four-kilometre hike from Füzér, the tiny hamlet of **LÁSZLÓTÁNYA** gets its name from the former **hunting lodge** of Count László Károlyi, which stands only 400m from the Slovak border. During the early 1950s, the lodge served as a holiday resort for top Communist officials, notably the then Party leader Mátyás Rákosi, the route being lined by ÁVO guards during his visits. This mock-Tudor folly is currently closed for refurbishment, but it's worth checking with Tourinform in Sátoraljaújhely whether work has finished, as there are plans to reopen it as a hotel. Rákosi slept in the suite at the top of the stairs, if you're curious to know.

Karcsa and Pácin

Heading east from Sátoraljaújhely or Sárospatak (from which there are also buses) brings you to two villages of note, Karcsa and Pácin. On the edge of **KARCSA**, 15km east of Sátoraljaújhely, stands a tenth-century **Romanesque Church** with a Gothic nave and a freestanding belfry. The keys are next door, at the house with the *Belyegzés* sign. In **PÁCIN**, 4km further on, there's a fifteenth- to sixteenth-century **Renaissance manor** exhibiting peasant furniture (mid-April to mid-Oct Tues–Sun 10am–6pm; 200Ft). The kitchen cupboard carries a picture of a woman slaving over the stove, shouting "Hurry up, it's eleven o'clock!" to her husband who sits by the fire.

Travel details

Trains

Aszód to: Balassagyarmat (8 daily; 1hr 30min).
Balassagyarmat to: Aszód (9 daily; 1hr 30min); Diósjenő and Vác (7 daily; 1–2hr).
Budapest (Keleti Station) to: Eger (4 daily; 2hr); Miskolc (hourly; 2hr–2hr 30min); Sárospatak and Sátoraljaújhely (2 daily; 3hr 45min–4hr).
Eger to: Budapest (5 daily; 2hr); Füzesabony (every 1hr–1hr 30min; 25min); Szilvásvárad (7 daily; 1hr).
Füzesabőny to: Debrecen (7 daily; 2hr); Eger (hourly; 25min); Hortobágy (6 daily; 1hr); Tiszafüred (7 daily; 30min).
Miskolc to: Budapest (hourly; 2hr–2hr 30min); Kazincbarcika (every 2hr; 30min); Nyíregyháza (every 1hr–1hr 30min; 2hr); Ózd (every 2hr; 1hr 30min); Putnok (every 2hr; 1hr); Sárospatak (hourly; 1hr 15min–1hr 45min); Sátoraljaújhely (9 daily; 1hr 25min–1hr 55min); Szerencs (hourly; 30min); Tornanádaska (8 daily; 1hr 40min).
Sárospatak to: Budapest (3 daily; 3hr 45min–4hr); Miskolc (8 daily; 1hr 15min–1hr 45min); Sátoral-

jaújhely (every 1hr–1hr 30min; 10min).
Szerencs to: Boldogkőváralja (1 daily; 1hr); Gönc (1 daily; 1hr 15min); Mád (8 daily; 10min); Sárospatak (hourly; 1hr); Tállya (8 daily; 25min); Tokaj (hourly; 15–25min).

Buses

Budapest (Népstadion) to: Aggtelek (2 daily; 5hr); Balassagyarmat (every 1–2hr; 2hr 10min); Eger (hourly; 2hr); Gödöllő (every 1hr–1hr 30min; 45min); Gyöngyös (hourly; 1hr 35min): Mátraháza (every 2–3hr; 1hr 50min); Miskolc (1 daily; 4hr 30min); Salgótarján (every 1hr–1hr 30min; 2hr 30min).
Aggtelek to: Budapest (1 daily; 5hr); Eger (1 daily; 3hr); Miskolc (2 daily; 2hr).
Balassagyarmat to: Budapest (every 1–2hr; 2hr); Salgótarján (hourly; 1hr); Szécsény (hourly; 1hr).
Eger to: Aggtelek (1 daily; 4hr); Békéscsaba (2 daily; 5hr); Budapest (hourly; 3hr); Debrecen (4 daily; 2hr 45min); Gyöngyös (every 40min–1hr; 1hr 30min); Gyula (1 daily; 5hr 30min); Hajdúszoboszló (1 daily; 3hr 15min); Jászberény (2 daily; 2hr); Kecskemét (1 daily; 4hr); Mátraháza (4 daily; 2hr); Miskolc (1 daily; 2hr 30min); Recsk (hourly; 1hr 45min); Salgótarján (5 daily; 2hr); Sirok (every 40min; 1hr 30min); Szeged (2 daily; 5hr); Szilvásvárad (hourly; 1hr); Szolnok (5 daily; 2hr 30min); Tiszafüred (5 daily; 1hr 15min).
Gyöngyös to: Abádszálok (3 daily; 2hr); Debrecen (2 daily; 4hr 30min); Eger (every 40min–1hr; 1hr 30min); Mátrafüred (every 20–40min; 30min); Mátraháza (every 20–40min; 45min); Miskolc (2 daily; 3hr 15min); Salgótarján (5 daily; 1hr 30min).
Hollókő to: Salgótarján (6 daily; 1hr); Szécsény (hourly; 45min).
Mátraháza to: Eger (3 daily; 2hr); Gyöngyös (every 20–40min; 45min); Miskolc (1 daily; 4hr).
Miskolc to: Aggtelek (2 daily; 3hr); Békéscsaba (1 daily; 5hr); Bükkszentkereszt (10 daily; 1hr); Debrecen (hourly; 2hr); Eger (9 daily; 2hr 30min); Gyöngyös (3 daily; 3hr); Jászberény (2 daily; 3hr); Kecskemét (1 daily; 5hr); Lillafüred (every 30min; 30min); Mátraháza (2 daily; 4hr); Miskolc-Tapolca (every 10min; 15min); Nyíregyháza (2 daily; 2hr); Ómassa (every 30min; 45min).
Ózd to: Aggtelek (1 daily; 1hr 30min); Debrecen (2 daily; 3hr 45min); Miskolc (2 daily; 3hr 30min).
Putnok to: Aggtelek (7 daily; 30min).
Salgótarján to: Balassagyarmat (7 daily; 1hr); Budapest (hourly; 2hr 30min); Gyöngyös (3 daily; 1hr 30min); Hatvan (2 daily; 1hr 30min); Hollókő (4 daily; 1hr); Ipolytarnóc (hourly; 30min); Kecskemét (1 daily; 3hr); Miskolc (2 daily; 3hr); Pásztó (8 daily; 1hr); Szécsény (every 1hr–1hr 30min; 45min).
Sárospatak to: Debrecen (2 daily; 3hr 30min); Sátoraljaújhely (hourly; 20min); Tokaj (2 daily; 1hr 30min).
Sátoraljaújhely to: Debrecen (2 daily; 4hr); Sárospatak (hourly; 20min); Tokaj (2 daily; 2hr).
Szécsény to: Balassagyarmat (every 1hr–1hr 30min; 1hr); Budapest (8 daily; 2hr 15min); Hollókő (hourly; 45min); Salgótarján (every 1hr–1hr 30min; 45min).
Tokaj to: Debrecen (3 daily; 2hr).

6

The Great Plain

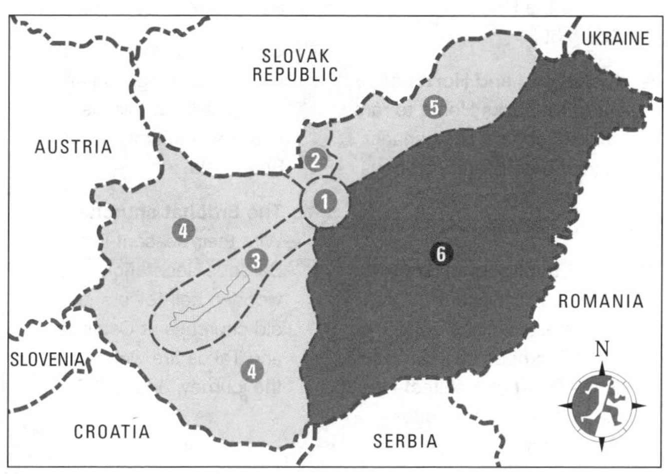

CHAPTER 6

Highlights

* **Cifra Palace, Kecskemét** Splendid Art Nouveau gallery housing an excellent art collection. See p.389

* **Horse-riding** The countryside around Kecskemét is a great place to saddle up and go for a gallop across the Plain. See p.393

* **Kiskunság and Hortobágy national parks** Home to rare wildlife, special Hungarian animal breeds and cowboys cracking their whips. See p.395 and p.426

* **Great Synagogue, Szeged** With its magnificent blue-stained-glass dome and cavernous interior, this is the finest of architect Lipót Baumhorn's synagogues. See p.404

* **Fish Soup Festival, Baja** All the fish you could wish for at this colourful open-air festival on Baja's main square. See p.384

* **Wine Tasting, Hajós Pincék** Take your pick from hundreds of cellars in this isolated countryside village. See p.382

* **Debrecen Jazz Festival** Catch top Hungarian and foreign acts at this well-established summer festival. See p.425

* **The Erdőhát churches** With their peasant-Baroque decoration and wooden bell-towers, the old churches at Csaroda and Tákos are well worth the journey. See p.439

▲ Horses in Hortobágy National Park

6

The Great Plain

Covering half of Hungary, the **Great Plain** (Nagyalföld) is awesome in its flatness. It can be as drab as a farmworker's boots or it can shimmer like the mirages of **Hortobágy National Park**, which, along with **Kiskunság National Park**, preserves the traditional *puszta* landscape – the name used to describe the arid grasslands that once covered almost the entire Plain – and wildlife of the region. In the villages, often with names prefixed by *Nagy-* or *Kis-* (Big or Little), the most characteristic sight is an isolated whitewashed farmstead (*tanya*) with a rustic artesian well, surrounded by flocks of geese and strings of paprika hanging out to dry. Marcell Iványi's short film *The Wind*, which won an award at Cannes in 1996, wonderfully captures the visual and emotional impact of this landscape.

With its often monotonous vistas and widely spaced towns, the Plain is something most people cross as much as visit and, if you're pressed for time, large areas can be skipped with a clear conscience. The Kiskunság National Park aside, the region between the Danube and the Tisza is chiefly notable for the towns of **Szeged** and **Kecskemét**, both flush with some marvellous architecture, though Kecskemét is just ahead when it comes to museums and culture. Of the smaller towns, both **Hódmezovásárhely** and **Gyula**, close to the Romanian border, merit a visit, the latter on account of its fine medieval fortress. Further beyond the River Tisza, the beguiling Hortobágy National Park offers the quintessential *puszta* experience, while **Lake Tisza** is ideal for those seeking more leisurely pursuits. **Debrecen**, Hungary's second largest town, retains a large student presence and has a high cultural profile, making it a worthwhile place to stop over for a day or two. Heading further east, towards the Ukranian border, the pace of life slows somewhat with the onset of the **Nyírség** and **Erdőhát** regions, whose gentle rolling landscapes, spotted with pretty little villages and churches with wooden bell-towers, are perfect for visitors keen on experiencing Hungarian rural life.

The Plain has more than its fair share of **festivals**, the best, and most diverse, of which are the Flower Carnival in Debrecen, the equestrian Bridge Fair at Hortobágy, the folk camp/festival at **Nagykálló**, and, for foodies, the wonderful Sausage Festival in **Békéscsaba**. Meanwhile, the pilgrimages to **Máriapócs** and the tomb of the "miracle rabbi" in **Nagykálló** cast a fascinating light on religious life.

From Budapest, **InterCity trains** are the fastest way of reaching the larger towns of Debrecen and Nyíregyháza to the east and Kecskemét and Szeged to the south. **Buses** from Budapest's Népstadion terminal are the best way of reaching towns such as Kalocsa and Baja, which are awkward or impossible to reach by train. All these services are covered under "Travel Details" at the end of the Budapest chapter.

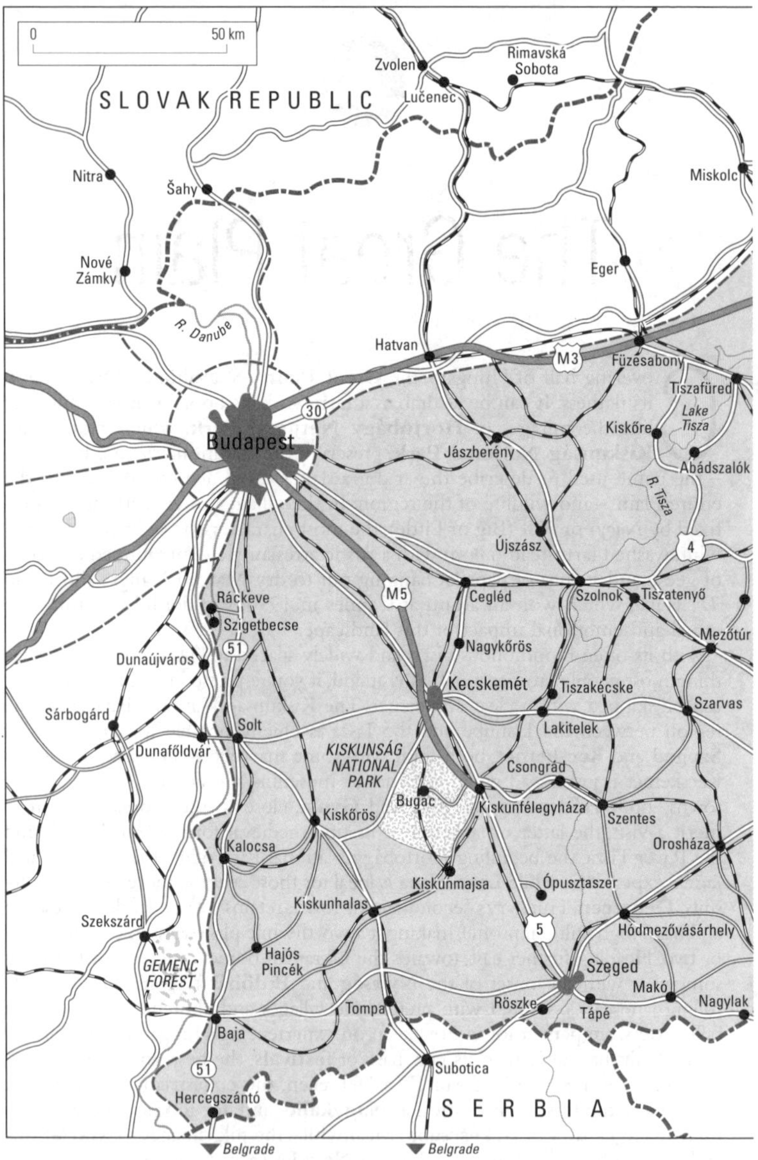

For **drivers**, the best route south is the M5, which runs as far as Kiskunfélegyháza en route to Szeged, while the M3 heads east in the direction of Miskolc (eventually to reach Nyiregyháza), though at present it only runs to Polgár, near Tiszaűjváros. The best non-toll alternative is Route 30 via Hatvan; Route 4 via Szolnok can be slow with lots of heavy trucks on the road.

Although **hitchhiking** is feasible along the trunk routes to Baja, Szeged and

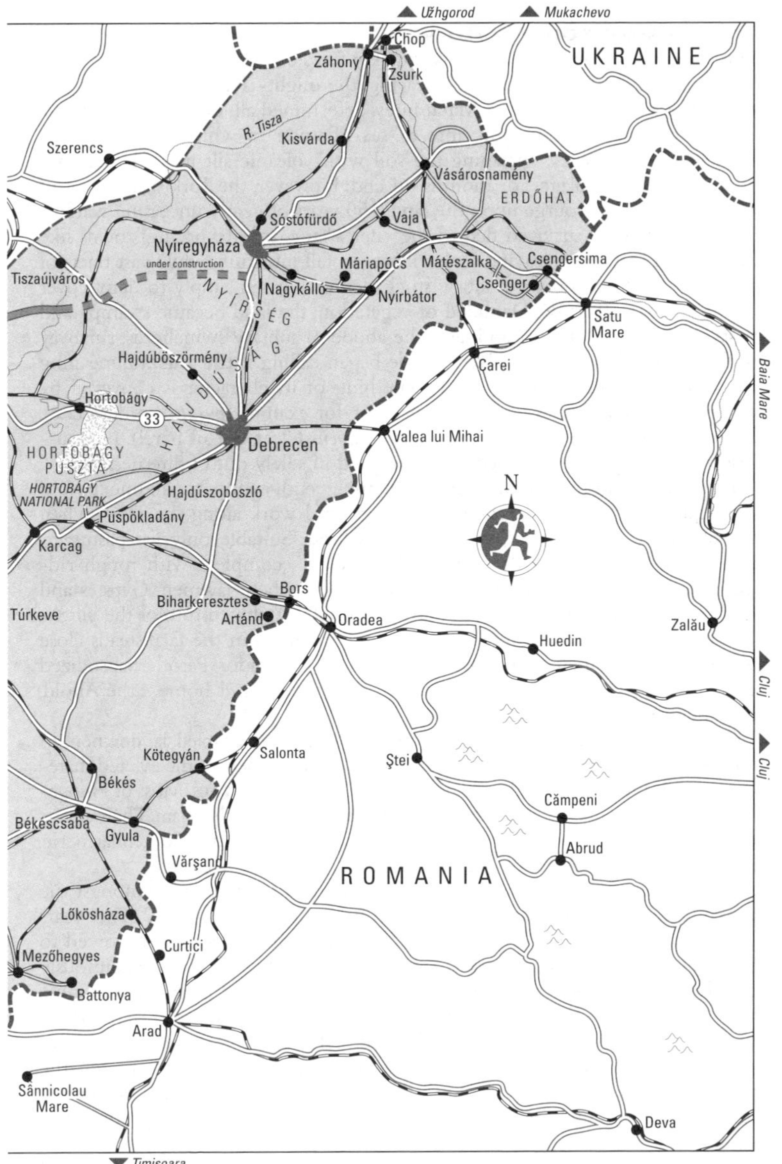

Debrecen, it's not worth attempting it elsewhere unless there's no alternative. Conversely, **cyclists** are banned from major (single-digit) roads, but should find minor ones delightful. Carts and animals are more common than cars, and wild flowers bloom along the verges.

The Puszta: some history

During medieval times the Plain was thickly forested, with hundreds of villages living off agriculture and livestock-rearing; the mighty **River Tisza**, fed by its tributaries in Transylvania and Maramureş, determined all. Each year it flooded, its hundreds of loops merging into a "sea of water in which the trees were sunk to their crowns", enriching the soil with volcanic silt from the uplands and isolating the villages for months on end. However, the Turkish invasion of 1526 unleashed a scourge upon the land: 150 years of nearly unceasing warfare. The peasants who survived fled to the safer *khasse* (tribute-paying) towns like Szeged and Debrecen, leaving their villages to fall into ruin, while vast tracts of forest were felled to build military stockades, or burned simply to deny cover to the partisans (*hajdúk*). Denuded of vegetation, the land became swampy and pestilent with mosquitoes, and later the abode of solitary swineherds, runaway serfs, outlaws (*betyár*) and wolves. People began calling it **the puszta**, meaning "abandoned, deserted, bleak", and something of its character is conveyed by other words and phrases with the same root; for example *pusztít* (to devastate), *pusztul* (to perish, be ruined), and *pusztulj innen* (Clear out of here!). Not surprisingly, most people shunned it, or ventured in solely out of dire necessity.

Yet another transformation began in the nineteenth century, as an unexpected consequence of Count Széchenyi's flood-control work along the Tisza, when soil alkalinity increased the spread of **grassland**. Suitable only for pasturage, in time this became the "Hungarian Wild West", complete with rough-riding *csikósok* (cowboys) and wayside *csárdák* (inns), where lawmen, Gypsies and outlaws shared the same tables, bound not to fight by the custom of the *puszta*. It was a man's world – women and children remained in the farmsteads close to town – and nineteenth-century romantics like Sándor Petőfi rhapsodized over it as the incarnation of Magyardom: "My world and home... the Alföld, the open sea".

By the 1920s reality had crushed romance. Irrigation enabled landowners to enclose common pasture for crops, while mechanization denied the evicted sharecroppers and herders even the chance of work on the big estates. Most of Hungary's landless peasants, or "**three million beggars**", lived on the Plain. Their efforts to form agrarian leagues were violently opposed by the gentry and gendarmerie, particularly in the Viharsarok region, meaning the "Stormy Corner".

True to their promises, the Communists distributed big estates amongst the peasantry and **nationalized land** "for those who till it" in 1947. Two years later, however, following the dictates of Stalinism, the peasants were forced to join state-run cooperative farms. Treated as socialist serfs, they unanimously dissolved "their" cooperatives in 1956 and reverted to subsistence production, vowing to prevent the landlords from returning. In response to this, the Party pursued a subtler **agricultural policy** from the 1960s onwards, investing in ever larger cooperative and state farms, while allowing peasants to sell the produce of their "household plots" (limited to 1.5 acres), which accounted for half the meat and seventy percent of the fruit and vegetables produced in Hungary.

The coalition government elected after the collapse of Communism in 1989 rejected calls for the return of land to its pre-1947 owners, but as a compromise gave cooperative members the option of leasing or buying the land, which provided more continuity in agriculture than in other East European countries. But even in Hungary agricultural production was badly hit, as those that became **independent farmers** often lacked the capital for modern equipment, while the emphasis on export crops meant that in 1994–95, Hungary even had to import potatoes, traditionally the poor man's food.

The subsequent upturn in the economy, however, has improved the agricultural situation and brought an increase in investment, too, though production levels remain far below those of the 1980s. The largest shadow hanging over agriculture is what will happen now that Hungary has joined the EU: there are widespread fears that this will allow large foreign concerns to buy up the best land, and that meeting EU demands on hygiene and quality will require the kind of money that Hungarian farmers can only dream about.

Between the Danube and the Tisza

Approaching from the direction of Budapest or Transdanubia, your first experience of the Plain will be the region **between the Danube and the Tisza**. Its chief attractions lie along two main routes from Budapest: **Kalocsa** and **Baja**, on the road following the Danube southwards; and **Kecskemét** and **Szeged**, on the trunk road towards Romania. If you're short of time and want to see something of the *puszta* grasslands at **Kiskunság National Park**, the second itinerary has a lot more to offer.

South to Kalocsa and Baja

The route south from Budapest leads eventually to laid-back **Baja**, on the lower reaches of the Danube. On the way you pass **Ráckeve**, close to Budapest – an ideal place to break your journey if you are in a car. If not, it is most easily reached by suburban train from Budapest (HÉV), making a good day-trip from the city. About halfway between Ráckeve and Baja lies the quaint little town of **Kalocsa**, which despite its sleepy atmosphere is actually one of the three archbishoprics in Hungary.

Ráckeve and Szigetbecse

The town of **RÁCKEVE**, 46km south of Budapest, is a diminutive counterpart to Szentendre on the Danube Bend, likewise founded by Serbian (Rác) refugees and rich in Baroque architecture, but far less touristy, despite being easily accessible from Budapest – hourly HÉV trains run from Budapest's Vágóhíd terminal on Soroksári út. Motorists should turn off the Route 51 just beyond Kiskunlacháza, and cross the bridge onto Csepel Island, where the town is situated.

Arriving at the HÉV station, it's a pleasant twenty-minute walk along Kossuth utca, the main street running parallel to the Danube, into the centre of town. Along the way, you'll pass the **Savoy Mansion**, a grandiose fusion of Italian and French Baroque with a Neoclassical dome and other nineteenth-century additions. The original building was commissioned by Prince Eugene of Savoy, shortly after his armies drove the Turks from Hungary, and was constructed between 1702 and 1722 according to the designs of J.L. Hildebrandt. Restored in the 1970s after decades of neglect, it is now a hotel (see below). Continuing down Kossuth utca, at no. 34 the small **Árpád Museum** (daily 9am–5pm; 400Ft) exhibits a bog-standard collection of archeological finds, ethnographic goods and ecclesiastical treasures.

The town's main draw, however, is the magnificent **Serbian Orthodox Church** at Viola utca 1 (Szerb Orthodox Templom; April–Oct Tues–Sat 10am–noon & 2–4pm, Sun 2–5pm, Nov–March Sat 10am–noon & 1–4pm, Sun 1–4pm; 200Ft), whose blue and white tower, topped by a gilded cross, rises above the rooftops to the west of the town centre. The oldest Orthodox church in Hungary, dating from 1487, it has a Baroque iconostasis – with icons of the apostles and scenes from the life of Christ – and frescoes painted by Teodor Gruntovich between 1765 and 1771, using traces of the original fifteenth-century ones as a guide. The most impressive, and the best-preserved, frescoes are those on the west wall, depicting scenes from the Last Judgement and revered Orthodox saints. The oldest part of the church is the nave, while the narthex and freestanding bell-tower are sixteenth-century additions. Mass is still celebrated on important Orthodox holidays, though the congregation mainly comes from neighbouring villages like Lórév, which have preserved their Serb character.

Ráckeve practicalities

The friendly Tourinform office, in the small cultural centre at Kossuth utca 51 (Mon–Fri 8am–4pm; ⓣ24/429-747, ⓦwww.rackeve@tourinform.hu), has plenty of **information** to hand. If stopping the night appeals, there are several good **accommodation** possibilities: the fabulously stylish *Kék-Duna Hotel*, at Dömsödi utca 1a (ⓣ24/523-230, ⓦwww.wellnesshotel.hu; ❼), is a cut above anything else in town and also has a beautiful thermal pool in the basement, while the *Savoyai Kastély Hotel* (ⓣ24/485-253, ⓦwww.hotels.hu/savoyai; ❺), at Kossuth utca 95, looks great but has hugely disappointing rooms. Considerably cheaper, but perfectly fine, is the *Bálványos Panzió*, 500m along from the *Kék-Duna Hotel* at Dömsödi utca 34 (ⓣ24/422-585; ❸), and the *Laguna Panzió*, conveniently sited near the HÉV station at Kossuth utca 108 (ⓣ & ⓕ24/422-939; ❸). Otherwise, the Sophia Utazási Iroda at Kossuth utca 12 (Mon–Fri 8am–5pm, Sat 8–11am; ⓣ24/424-855, ⓦwww.sophia.ini.hu) can help with private **accommodation** (❸), or there is *Hidláb Camping*, near the *Kék-Duna Hotel* at Dömsödi utca 2 (ⓣ24/385-501), which also has chalets sleeping four (❷).

For **eating**, there's first-class international cuisine at the glittering restaurant in the *Kék-Duna Hotel*, while the vaulted cellar restaurant at the *Savoyai* hotel has excellent Hungarian food. Less fancily, there's the *Csöni* at Szent János tér, offering Hungarian standards, or the cosy *Cadran Pizzeria and Pub* by the bridge on Hősök tere.

Szigetbecse

From Ráckeve you can catch a local bus or taxi 4km to the village of **SZIGETBECSE**, where the renowned Hungarian-born photographer **André Kertész** spent much of his childhood. A small **museum** at Makádi út 40 (April–Sept Sat & Sun 10am–4pm; donations accepted) exhibits over sixty of his early works, ranging from pictures of Szigetbecse to scenes from World War I, including one of troops sitting on a collective latrine. On weekdays throughout the year you can get the key from the mayor's office (polgármesteri hivatal) at Petőfi utca 34, ten minutes' walk away.

Kalocsa

Around 120km south of the capital, **KALOCSA** makes a pleasant and convenient stopover, with regular buses passing through en route to Baja further south. The town is promoted for its flowery **embroidery** and "**painting women**", who made it their business to decorate everything in sight, and also as Hungary's "**paprika capital**". If you happen to be here around September 8, when the harvest season officially begins, head out to the surrounding countryside to see the paprika fields transformed into a sea of red.

Nearly all of Kalocsa's sights are located along Szent István király út, the town's main street running from the bus station through to the cathedral and archbishop's palace at the other end. Starting at the bus station, you can't miss the 22-metre-high **Chronos 8 light tower**, a bequest from the locally born Parisian conceptual sculptor Nicolas Schöffer, some of whose smaller kinetic works are exhibited in the **Nicolas Schöffer Museum** at Szent István király út 76 (Tues–Sun 10am–5pm; 300Ft). Continuing five minutes up the road, to the pedestrianized stretch of the street, you pass a row of seven small statues commemorating the town's famous archbishops – starting with Asztrik, who brought Pope Sylvester II's gift of a crown to King Stephen in 1000 AD, thereby setting the seal on the deal between the new king and the Christian West. A couple of minutes further along on the left, at no. 25, is the **Viski Károly Museum** (April–Oct Tues–Sun 9am–5pm; 300Ft), which has a dazzling collection of nineteenth-century Magyar, Swabian (*Sváb*) and Slovak (*Tót*) folk costumes. The overstuffed bolsters and quilts on display were mandatory for a bride's dowry. Fifty metres on at no. 6, the **Paprika Museum** (April–Oct daily except Tues 10am–5pm; 200Ft) is an exhaustive presentation of the nation's favourite powder (see box below), with piles of the stuff filling the building with its pungent smell.

Carrying on to the old main square, Szentharomság tér, you'll find Kalocsa's Baroque **Cathedral**, designed by the prolific András Mayerhoffer in the early eighteenth century. Don't miss the richly attired embalmed bishop that adds a bizarre touch to its pink and white interior, nor the ornate gold pulpit. Across

Paprika

Hungary is one of the world's biggest suppliers of **paprika**, and more of the spicy stuff is grown around Kalocsa and Szeged than anywhere else in the country. Revered as "red gold" (*piros arany*), no one really knows when this member of the *Capsicum* genus was first introduced. Some theories ascribe its introduction to the Age of Migration via the Balkans, while others even credit Christopher Columbus. Its consumption received an important boost during the Napoleonic Wars thanks to continental blockades, which compelled Europeans to find a substitute for pepper.

The nineteenth-century preference for milder paprika spurred cross-fertilization experiments, which led to the discovery of capsaicin, produced by the plant in response to drought and sunlight and responsible for its piquancy. Inventions such as the Pálffy roller frame eased the laborious task of chopping and grinding, while the plant's nutritional qualities were investigated by **Dr Albert Szent-Györgyi** of Szeged University, who won the 1933 Nobel Prize for synthesizing vitamin C (paprika is also rich in vitamin A).

More recently, there was national outrage over the **paprika scandal** of 1994, when it was discovered that powdered paprika was being laced with red lead to look extra ruddy. To protect the public and the reputation of the national condiment, all supplies were withdrawn from shops until the source of the contamination had been identified and fresh, certifiably pure, paprika became available.

the road from the cathedral, at Hunyadi utca 2, is the **Treasury** (Érseki Kincstár; April–Oct daily 9am–5pm; 500Ft), which keeps a dazzling assortment of vestments and monstrances, including a beautifully embroidered, three-inch high reliquary from the sixteenth century. The most important item on display, however, is a twelfth-century processional bronze cross with traces of gold. On the other side of the cathedral, and dating from the same period, is the **Archbishop's Palace** (April–Oct Tues–Sun; Hungarian-only tours begin at noon, 2pm & 4pm; 500Ft), whose grandeur recalls the medieval heyday of Kalocsa's bishopric, when local prelates led armies and advised monarchs. Its 120,000-volume **library** contains medieval illuminated manuscripts, a Bible signed by Luther, and impressive frescoes by Maulbertsch. The library was founded by Archbishop Patachich, who was transferred to Kalocsa from his previous post as a punishment for founding a theatre there, and henceforth stuck to books. His apartments were lodged between his chapel and his library, with a door connecting the two, as can still be seen.

Following Kossuth utca off to the right as far as the hospital, you'll see a signpost for the thatched **Folk Art House** at Tompa utca 5–7 (Népművészetek Háza or Tájház; April–Oct daily except Tues 10am–4.30pm; 250Ft). Several of its rooms are decorated with exuberant floral murals, traditionally found in the *tiszta szoba* or "clean room" of peasant households, where guests were entertained. In Kalocsa, almost uniquely, these were painted by groups of women who were respected artisans. Also displayed is a host of Kalocsa embroidery. This has changed considerably over the decades, with embroiderers working entirely in white in the nineteenth century, until blue and red slowly crept into the designs; then, in the 1920s, when the Kalocsa folk dance troupe became more widely known, it was decided to brighten up the costumes so that they would be more startling on stage – hence the present multicoloured, rather twee, designs.

Practicalities

Arriving by bus, you might be allowed to jump off on Kossuth utca near Szentháromság tér, rather than alighting at the **bus station** at the junction of Szent István király út and Route 51. Kalocsa's **train station** is on Mártírok tere, a fifteen-minute walk along Kossuth utca from the Archbishop's Palace.

In the absence of a Tourinform office, you can get (very limited) **information** from Ibusz at Szent István király utca 37 (Mon–Fri 8am–4pm; ⓣ78/462-012, ⓔi057@ibusz.hu), who also book private **rooms** (❹). Next door to Ibusz, there's the effortlessly dull *Hotel Piros Arany* (ⓣ78/462-220; ❹), though far better options exist in the form of the simple, but clean and bright, *Club Hotel* at Szent István király utca 64 (ⓣ78/562-804, ⓦwww.clubhotel.ini.hu; ❹), and the beautifully restored 200-year-old *Beta Hotel Kalocsa* on Szentháromság tér (ⓣ78/461-244, ⓦwww.danubiusgroup.com; ❹), which has polished rooms, pool and sauna, and a **restaurant** that's the best in town. Cheaper eating options are the *Barokk Kávéház* (daily 8am–9pm, Fri & Sat till 11pm) by the cathedral, which serves pizzas and has pool tables, and the *Muzeum*, attached to the Paprika Museum at Szent István király utca 6 (daily 11am–10pm), not surprisingly offering all manner of paprika-enhanced dishes. The **post office** is at Szent István király utca 44 (Mon–Fri 8am–6pm, Sat 8am–noon).

Hajós Pincék

Hajós Pincék, 24km southeast of Kalocsa on Route 54 (and 3km beyond the village of Hajós itself), is an extraordinary village: no one actually lives here, the entire settlement being devoted to **wine cellars** – 1260 of them in all. The

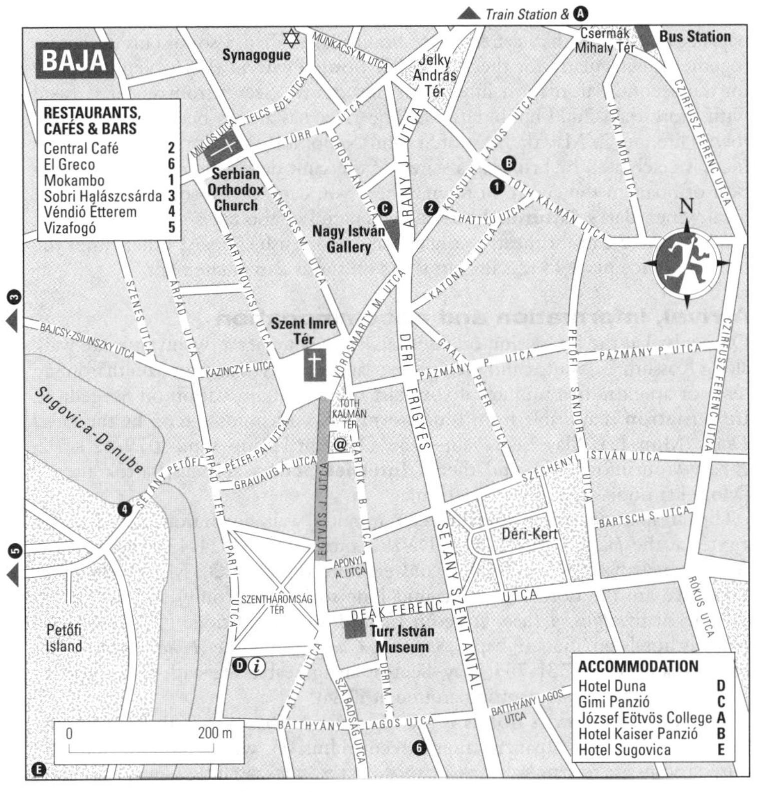

mainly Swabian population of the surrounding area has been storing and fermenting wine here for centuries, and you can sample it to your heart's content in the cellars along every street. St Orbán's day on May 25 (or the nearest weekend) is when all the vintners come out in force to celebrate the coming harvests with folk dancing and the like. Though there are visitors here all year round, summer is the best time to visit, as you are more likely to find someone in the labyrinth of cellars who will invite you to sample and buy their wine. Although catering mainly to groups, you could also check out the Kovács Wine House (Ⓣ78/404-947) at the end of the village on the main road (Route 54), which has wines to taste and buy. There are a couple of places to **stay** if you want to hang around: the gaily-coloured *Kellermotel* (Ⓣ78/504-010, Ⓦwww.kellermotel.com; ❹) at the entrance to the village, and the more basic *Judit Panzió*, 200m on from the Kovács Wine House, opposite the petrol station at Borbiró sor 1 (Ⓣ78/404-832; ❸), which also has a very ordinary restaurant. There are regular daily **buses** from Kalocsa, and four from Baja on weekdays.

Baja

BAJA, 41km south of Kalocsa on the shady banks of the Sugovica-Danube, is a restful town with an almost Mediterranean climate, whose culinary pride is manifest in its **fish soup** (halászlé) – a rich mix of carp, catfish, pike-perch and paprika that's more like a freshwater bouillabaisse than a soup. This all comes together spectacularly for the **Baja Fish Soup Festival** (Bajai Népünnepély) on the second Saturday in July, when the massive Szentháromság tér is filled with more than 2000 bubbling pots. The river has always been central to the town's life, and in May the feast of St John Nepomuk, the patron saint of fishermen, is celebrated by bringing a statue of the saint down the river in a procession of boats to the centre of town, where you can eat fish soup and taste the local wines. Baja's **Autumn Festival** in September also takes place in the main square – three days of theatre, concerts and more fish soup. At other times the town is a nice place to rest up, but short on sights and excitement.

Arrival, information and accommodation

On **arrival** at the bus station on Csermák Mihály tér, it's a twenty-minute walk along Kossuth Lajos utca and then pedestrianized Eötvös utca to Szentháromság tér – or an extra five minutes if you start from the train station on Szegedi út. **Information** is available from Tourinform at Szentháromság tér 5 by the *Hotel Duna* (Mon–Fri: May–Sept 9am–5pm, Oct–April 8am–4pm; ⓣ79/420-792, ⓔbaja@tourinform.hu), and there's **Internet access** at Bela Bartók utca 7 (Mon–Fri noon–9pm, Sat 9am–1pm).

The cheapest **accommodation** is ten minutes' walk north from Szentháromság tér at the *József Eötvös College*, Deszkás utca 2 (ⓣ79/324-451; mid-June to Aug), which has dorms (1000Ft) and en-suite doubles (❷). Marginally more expensive are the dorms (1300Ft; mid-June to late Aug only) and rooms (❷; all year) at the *Ifjusági Tábor* at Petőfi Island 5 near the bridge (ⓣ79/324-022, ⓦwww.hotels.hu/ifjusagi_baja). *Sugovica Camping* by the *Hotel Sugovica* on Petőfi Island (ⓣ79/321-755; May–Sept) is an agreeable site with huts and chalets (❷), and pheasants strutting around at dawn.

The best of the town's **hotels** is the *Hotel Kaiser Panzió* at Tóth Kálmán utca 12 (ⓣ79/520-450, ⓔpanziokaiser@freemail.hu; ❹), whose smooth, red-coloured rooms are terrific value, as are those in the cracking little *Gimi Panzió*, just behind the Nagy István Gallery at Oroszlán utca 2a (ⓣ79/428-485, ⓦwww.gimicafe.uw.hu; ❸). Alternatives consist of the comfortable and secluded *Hotel Sugovica* on Petőfi Island (ⓣ79/321-755, ⓦwww.hotelsugovica.hu; ❹), and the old-fashioned and weary-looking *Hotel Duna* at Szentháromság tér 6 (ⓣ79/323-224, ⓦwww.hotelduna.hu; ❹).

The last of the Habsburgs

Although the Habsburg Empire ended with the abdication of **Karl IV** and the establishment of republics in Austria and Hungary in 1918, the dynasty refused to die. In October 1921, Karl attempted to regain the Hungarian throne by flying into Baja, where a royalist force awaited him with trucks supplied by Major Lehár (cousin of Franz, composer of *The Merry Widow*). However, their advance on Budapest was swiftly halted by regular troops, and a British gunboat transported Karl into exile in Madeira. His widow **Zita** was barred from Austria until 1982 for refusing to renounce her claim, and only returned thereafter to be buried in Vienna.

Meanwhile, their son **Otto** had become a Euro MP and roving ambassador to the former Habsburg territories. An apocryphal story has it that when asked if he would be watching the Austria–Hungary football match, Otto replied, "Who are we playing?" More recently, his son **György** has been given the role of travelling ambassador for Hungary (notwithstanding his Austrian citizenship), and in 1997 married Eilika von Oldenburg in Budapest's St Stephen's Basilica – an event covered live on Hungarian television.

The Town

In the heart of town, imposing civic edifices and the massive **Szentháromság tér** – compared rather optimistically in a local leaflet to St Mark's Square in Venice, but really just a huge cobbled car park – overlook the Sugovica River and Petőfi Island, recalling Baja's importance before the Treaty of Trianon relegated it to a minor border town in 1920. At Deák Ferenc utca 1, off the main square's southeast corner, the **Turr István Museum** (mid-March to Nov Wed–Sat 10am–6pm; 300Ft) is named after a Hungarian general who fought alongside Garibaldi in Italy, just as many Poles and Italians fought with Hungary against the Habsburgs. An exhibition on fishing illustrates the vital role that water and the Danube have played in the city's history, and there's also an excellent ethnographic and natural history section upstairs. The museum's local history display – covering 300 years of local events, including the farcical attempt by Karl IV to regain the Habsburg throne (see box opposite) – is in the same block but accessed via a separate entrance on the other side of the building on Roosevelt tér.

Icon buffs should try to visit the late eighteenth-century **Serbian Orthodox Church** on Táncsics utca (Wed 9am–noon; contact Tourinform to view the church at other times), one of two ministering to locals of Serbian descent. Otherwise crudely bare, it contains a magnificent, ten-metre-high iconostasis incorporating some fifty icons representing scenes from the Bible. There is also a German high school catering to a smaller community of Swabians, whom the Habsburgs encouraged to settle here after the Turks were evicted. From the church, a short walk down Telcs Ede utca brings you to Munkácsy Mihály utca and a fabulous Neoclassical **Synagogue** (now serving as a library; Mon–Thurs 1–6pm, Fri 10am–6pm, Sat 8am–noon), with a monument to the town's 5705 victims of Fascism. The building has been sensitively restored, and visitors are welcome to admire what was once the spiritual base of a proud and thriving community. Heading back towards Szentháromság tér, you pass the **Nagy István Gallery** on Arany János utca (mid-March to Nov Wed–Sat 10am–6pm; 250Ft), where a collection of paintings by the Alföld School is displayed – Nagy himself being the group's best-known proponent – along with shows by contemporary artists.

Across the river from the main square lies the green **Petőfi Island**, where the locals like to go boating, swimming and fishing. It was from here that the last Habsburg emperor was ignominiously deported by a British gunboat, after the failure of his putsch in 1921.

Eating and drinking

The town's two best **restaurants**, both of which have superb fish menus, are on Petőfi Island: the upmarket *Véndió Étterem* (daily 10am–10pm, Fri & Sat till 11pm) down by the bridge, and the more sociable *Vizafogó* (daily 11am–10pm), fifteen minutes' walk west on the northwestern corner of the island. The *Sobri Halászcsárda*, fifteen minutes' walk west of the main square at Bajcsy-Zsilinszky utca 8 (daily 11am–10pm), is also renowned for its fish soup – it was founded by the champion *halászlé* chef Jószef "Sobri" Farkas. For a change from Hungarian cuisine, and fish in particular, there's halfway decent Greek food at *El Greco* on Babits Mihály utca (Tues–Sun 11am–10pm). Three popular cafés in the vicinity of Vőrősmarty tér are *Mokambo* (Mon–Sat 7.30am–8pm), a cool, cheery place with bright orange walls and squishy chairs opposite the *Hotel Kaiser Panzió*; *Central Café* at Kossuth utca 1 (daily 7am–9pm), which is also good for tea; and the café in the *Gimi Panzió* (Mon–Sat 7am–8pm, Sun 2–8pm). For evening **drinking**, the place to head to is the Halászpart ("Fisherman's Beach"), the river bank opposite the *Véndió*, where a dozen or so cafés and bars do roaring summer trade.

Jászberény

JÁSZBERÉNY, 50km east of Budapest, merits a mention for its historic links to the **Jász** (Jazygians), an Iranian-speaking people who migrated here from around the Caspian Sea at the beginning of the thirteenth century. Granted feudal privileges by Béla III, they prospered as cattle-breeders, tanners and furriers, each extended family owning several farms and a town house. A dozen settlements with names prefixed by "Jász-" denotes the extent of the Jászság region, which remained semi-autonomous until the 1890s, by which time the people had become totally assimilated. As Patrick Leigh Fermor wrote, "this entire nation seems to have vanished like a will o' the wisp, and only these place-names mark the points of their evaporation". Today, Jászberény celebrates the folk traditions of another small ethnic group – the Csángó of eastern Transylvania – with an annual festival.

The Town

Leafy **Lehel vezér tér** is more like a street than a square, but indisputably the heart of town, flush with Baroque piles and festooned with plaques and other memorials to local worthies and 1956 martyrs. The Déryné Cultural Centre at no. 33 (Ⓣ57/406-639) is the venue for the annual **Csángó Festival** in the first week in August, a chance to hear haunting music from the eastern Carpathians, where the ancestors of the Csángó (literally, "wanderer") fled to during the fifteenth, eighteenth and nineteenth centuries. The festival also provides an opportunity to buy embroidered quilts, tablecloths, jackets and other Csángó handicrafts in the fair (kirakodó vásár), usually held in the park by the baths.

To delve into the town's Jazygian heritage, cross the square and visit the **Jász Museum** at Táncsics Mihály utca 5 (May–Sept Tues–Sun 9am–5pm; Oct–April Tues–Fri 9am–4pm, Sat & Sun 9am–1pm; 200Ft). Although it has some interesting archeological finds – beaded jewellery, buckles, vases and statuettes – and ethnographic goods, the museum's star exhibit (and the only one to have notes in English) is the beautiful ivory **Lehel Horn**, intricately carved with hunting scenes. According to Jász tradition this belonged to a Magyar general, Lehel, whom the German emperor Otto I defeated near Augsburg in 955. Legend has it that Lehel begged to be allowed to blow his horn before being executed and, when the last notes had faded, suddenly stabbed Otto to death with it; alas for legend, the horn is reckoned to be of eleventh- or twelfth-century Byzantine origin, and it was Lehel, not Otto, who perished at Augsburg.

The town's **thermal baths**, at Hatvani út 5, just west of the centre, have an outdoor *strand* (May to mid-Sept daily 9am–6pm; 500Ft), and a sauna and indoor pool (open all year Tues–Sun 9am–7pm; 450Ft).

Practicalities

The **bus station** on Petőfi tér is five minutes' walk from Szentháromság tér, which opens off Lehel vezér tér; the **train station** lies 1km further out past the bus station, on Rákóczi út. Tourinform, in the Cultural Centre (mid-June to mid-Sept Mon–Fri 8am–5pm, Sat & Sun 8am–2pm; mid-Sept to mid-June Mon–Fri 8am–4.30pm; Ⓣ57/406-439, Ⓔjaszbereny@tourinform.hu), can supply all the necessary local **information**.

Accommodation possibilities are limited to private rooms (❷) bookable through Ibusz at Szövetkezet utca 7/a, the road south of Lehel vezér tér (Mon–Fri 8am–4.30pm; Ⓣ57/412-143, Ⓔi056@ibusz.hu); the poor-value *Hotel Tour-*

ing at Serház út 3 near the bus station (Ⓣ57/412-051; ❹), and the reasonable *Sólyom Panzió*, a ten-minute walk east of Lehel vezér tér, along Táncsics utca and Ady Endre utca at Sólyom utca 8 (Ⓣ57/401-267, Ⓦwww/hotels.hu/solyom; ❸). During July and August, the cheapest beds (❶) are in local *kollégium* such as the one at Rákóczi út 55 (Ⓣ57/502-405). **Eating** options are similarly stark, the best place being the *Viktoria* restaurant behind the cultural centre on Holló András utca, which is actually a fairly decent pizzeria. Otherwise, there's the *Kohid*, by the bridge near the bus station, which suffices for nothing more than a lunch snack (Mon–Fri 10am–3pm), and you can also get a toasted sandwich and a coffee in the Cultural Centre's buffet (Mon–Fri 8am–4pm).

Kecskemét and around

Hungarians associate **KECSKEMÉT** with *barackpálinka* (the local apricot brandy) and the composer Kodály (who was born in what is now the train station), but its cultural significance doesn't end there. Ranking just behind Szeged and Debrecen as a centre of higher education and the arts, Kecskemét rivals both cities in terms of festivals and museums, and surpasses them architecturally. Given this sophistication, you would never imagine that its name derives from the Hungarian word for "goat" (*kecske*).

Besides being one of the most attractive towns on the Plain, Kecskemét is readily **accessible** from Budapest (by train from Nyugati Station or bus from Népstadion), and there are equally regular services from Szeged (plus less frequent buses from Baja and Cegléd), making it an ideal day excursion from either city, and the prime stopover between them. The town is also a good base for **excursions** to the Kiskunság National Park, with the option of relaxing along the River Tisza, or getting right back to nature by horse-riding or renting a farmhouse in the surrounding countryside. There's also the Lakitelek-Tőserdő nature reserve close by, where you can swim or go boating.

Arrival, information and accommodation

Kecskemét's **bus and train stations** are situated close to each other a ten-minute walk north of the centre; follow Nagykőrösi utca or Rákóczi út to Szabadság tér, where the monumental architecture begins. Tourinform, on the corner of the town hall (Mon–Fri 8am–5pm, May–June & Sept also open Sat 9am–1pm, July & Aug also open Sun 9am–1pm; Ⓣ76/481-065, Ⓦwww.kecskemet.hu), can provide all the necessary **information** on the town and the Kiskunság National Park. The main **post office** is at Kálvin tér 10–12 (Mon–Fri 8am–7pm, Sat 8am–noon), and there is **Internet access** at the Piramis Internet Café on the first floor of the modern precinct at Csányi utca 1–3 (Mon–Fri 10am–8pm, Sat & Sun 1–8pm).

Accommodation

Kecskemét is packed with some quality **hotels** and pensions, and finding a room at any time of year shouldn't be a problem. During the summer holidays you can get cheap rooms (❷) in the **colleges** at Jókai tér 4 (Ⓣ76/486-977) or Izsáki utca 10 (Ⓣ76/506-526). **Private rooms** are hard to find in the town, but you can book flats through Ibusz on the ground floor of the *Hotel Aranyhomok* (Mon–Fri 8am–5pm, Sat 9am–1pm; Ⓣ76/481-529, Ⓔi061@ibusz.hu) (minimum three nights, sleeping four people; ❹), or there's the *Autós* **campsite** (Ⓣ76/329-398; mid-April to mid-Oct) with chalets (❶) at Sport utca 5 (past

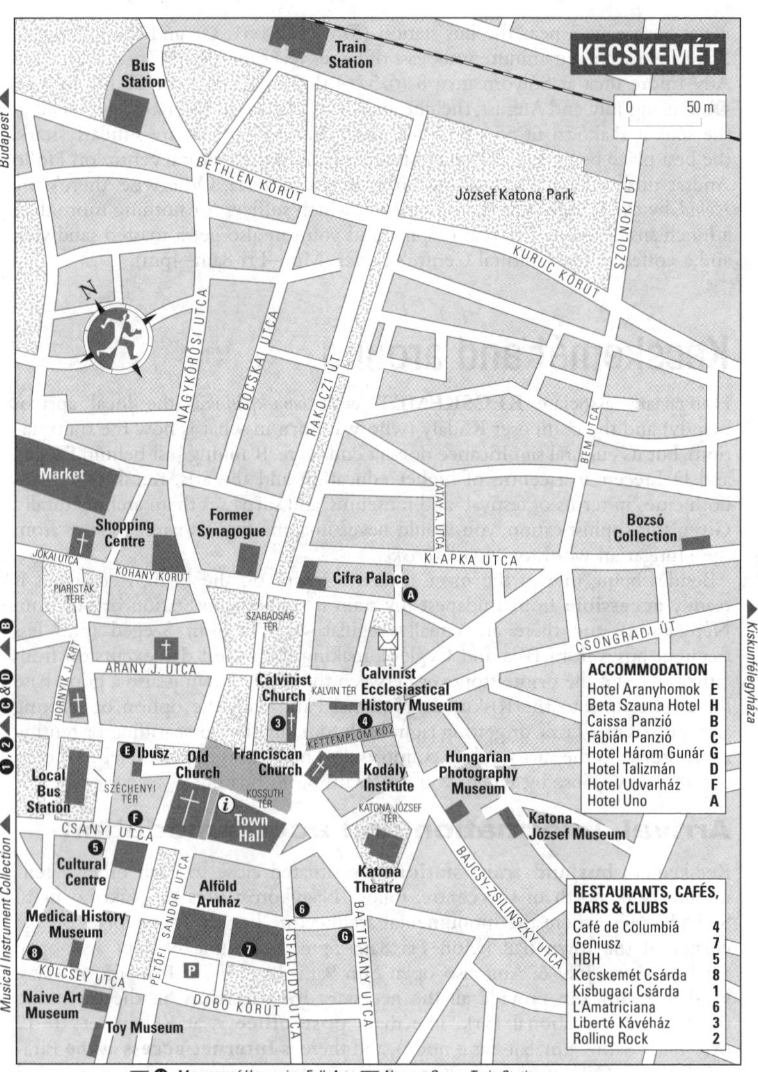

the *Beta Szauna Hotel*), which is accessible by bus #22. Tourinform can also inform about lodgings on one of the old isolated peasant farms (*tanya*) in the countryside around Kecskemét.

Hotel Aranyhomok Kossuth tér 3 ⓣ76/503-730, ⓦwww.hotels.hu/aranyhomok. Named after the "golden sands" of the *puszta*, this ugly looking building actually conceals very modern and comfy rooms – those facing the park are larger and more expensive than those on the other side, though the furnishings are the same. ❻

Beta Szauna Hotel Csabay Géza körút 2 ⓣ76/501-190, ⓦwww.danubiusgroup.com. Well-equipped hotel with a sauna and gym, beside the thermal baths, 2.5km south of the centre; buses #1 and #11 stop nearby. ❹

Caissa Panzió Gyenes tér 18 ⓣ76/481-685, ⓔcaissa@axelero.hu. Unusual location on the fifth floor of an apartment block, ten minutes northwest of Kossuth tér, this friendly and tidy pension has rooms sleeping two- to five- people, with and without bathroom. Caissa is the patron saint of chess, and the owner, an avid fan of the game, organizes tournaments in the pension. ❷–❹

Fábián Panzió Kápolna utca 14 ⓣ76/477-677, ⓦwww.hotels.hu/fabian. Sweet, family-run pension with ten lovely, lilac-coloured rooms overlooking a lush garden. Bikes for rent too. Terrific value. ❹

Hotel Három Gunár Batthyány utca 1–7 ⓣ76/505-785, ⓦwww.hotelharomgunar.hu. Centrally located but rather dated hotel, with rooms and furniture straight from the 70s, though the bathrooms are modern enough. ❹

Hotel Talizmán Kápolna utca 2 ⓣ76/504-856, ⓦwww.hotels.hu/talizman. Bright, business-like place a short walk west of the Town Hall, with immaculately prepared, a/c rooms. Best-value hotel in town. ❺

Hotel Udvarház Csányi utca 1–3 ⓣ76/413-912, ⓦwww.hotels.hu/udvarhaz. Odd location on the first floor of a shopping complex just off Kossuth tér, this is a calm little hotel with smart, nicely lit rooms, all with a/c. ❺

Hotel Uno Beniczky F utca 4 ⓣ76/480-046, ⓦwww.hoteluno.hu. Quiet, friendly hotel with neat, tidy rooms in a great location just 200m from Szabadság tér. ❺

The Town

Although nothing remains of medieval Kecskemét, its size can be judged from the ring boulevard (körút), which follows the old moat. Unlike most towns in the region, it was spared devastation by the Turks, as the Sultan took a liking to it. Waves of refugees settled here, and Kecskemét became the third-largest town in Hungary, its various religious groups co-existing in harmony. This fortunate history, underpinned by agricultural wealth, explains its air of confidence and the flamboyant, eclectic **architecture**, skilfully integrated with modern buildings by town planner József Kerényi. To enhance its charms, the centre of town consists of two open squares that merge into a single verdant expanse, with traffic diverted several blocks away.

Szabadság tér

The northern end of Szabadság tér is characterized by three strikingly different buildings. On one corner of Rákóczi út stands a white, onion-domed former **synagogue** built between 1862 and 1871 in the Moorish style, which was sacked by the Nazis when they deported Kecskemét's Jews in 1944, and transformed in 1970 into a conference centre (Technika és Tudomány Háza), with a hideous interior – there's also a lounge-style café on the ground floor. Across the road, the **Cifra Palace** resembles a scene from *Hansel and Gretel* on acid, with ceramic mushrooms sprouting from psychedelic tiles above a gingerbread-like facade. Designed by Géza Markus in 1902, this wonderful example of Art Nouveau (termed the "Secessionist style" in Hungary) now houses the **Kecskemét Art Gallery** (Tues–Sat 10am–5pm, Sun 1.30–5pm; 450Ft), whose collection includes work by the Jewish painter István Farkas, who died in Auschwitz. Upstairs is a splendid peacock ballroom with enamel tiles and Art Nouveau motifs that was once a casino. Carry on up the stairs and you'll emerge onto a terrace affording a close-up view of the palace's Art Nouveau chimneys and gables. Originally built to house small shops and flats, the building is one of the architectural gems of Kecskemét, though it has been sadly neglected over the last fifty years.

The Transylvanian-Gothic hulk diagonally opposite the Cifra Palace is one of two buildings in Kecskemét in the Art Nouveau style known as **National Romanticism**. Built between 1911 and 1913 as a Calvinist college, its steeply pitched roofs and intimidating tower hark back to the vernacular architecture of rural Hungary and Transylvania. It now houses a library and a Calvinist high school. Across the road, at Kalvin tér 1, is the **Museum of Calvinist Ecclesiastical History** (Református Egyházművészeti Műzeum; Tues–Sun 10am–6pm; 300Ft), a marvellous collection of seventeenth- and eighteenth- century ecclesiastical art that includes beautifully embroidered communion cloths, baptismal jugs and wine pitchers, and a rustic painted wooden ceiling saved from a church near Lake Balaton just before the whole edifice collapsed. The second part of the museum is a horologists' delight, with two rooms stuffed with clocks, watches and all manner of other nineteenth-century timepieces.

Kossuth tér and around

To the south, across Kossuth tér, is the building that started the whole National Romanticism movement: the **Town Hall**, designed by Ödön Lechner and Gyula Pártos in 1893. Like Lechner's later works in Budapest, it is richly ornamented with Zsolnay tiles inspired by the decorative traditions of Magyar folk art and nomadic Turkic cultures. However, the building itself is a Renaissance-Baroque pastiche, whose lack of "authentic form" was criticized by later National Romanticists such as Károly Kós. Its Grand Hall contains gilded murals by Bertalan Székely, who decorated the interior of the Mátyás Church in Budapest. Unfortunately there are no regular hours for visits – ask at reception about access. The bells outside play snatches of Kódaly, Handel, Beethoven, Mozart and Erkel on the hour.

With five churches in the vicinity you can afford to be selective; the three most interesting are on Kossuth tér. Next to the town hall stands the so-called **Old Church**, which is Catholic and Baroque. Designed by Oszwald Gáspár, an eighteenth-century Piarist father, its facade is decorated with reliefs commemorating the Seventh Wilhem Hussars and local heroes of the War of Independence. In the summer months you may be able to climb the church tower, which gives you an excellent view of the city (200Ft, when the tower is open). The **Calvinist Church** was founded in 1683 and enlarged in the 1790s, when its "Red Tower" was added. Its meeting hall contains frescoes similar to those in the town hall. The **Franciscan Church** to the east is really the oldest one, but Baroque restoration has obscured its medieval features. Around the corner on Kéttemplom köz (Two Churches Lane) stands the former Franciscan monastery, which now houses the **Kodály Institute** (see box opposite).

Kecskemét's museums

The diversity of Kecskemét's architecture is matched by that of its museums. One not to miss is the **Hungarian Photography Museum** at Katona József tér 12 (Magyar Fotográfiai Múzeum; Wed–Sun 10am–5pm; 200Ft; Ⓦwww.fotomuzeum.hu), one of only two such museums in the country, the other being in Budapest (see p.117). Originally a dance hall, the building was converted into a synagogue in 1918 and sold off by the decimated Jewish community after the last war. Beautifully restored, it retains such original features as the female gallery and the painted ceiling on which Rabbi Loewe's sacred animals appear. The collection itself features rotating exhibitions of the best of Hungarian photography, as well as occasional exhibitions by international photographers. In addition there is a permanent display of vintage cameras and other apparatus. For real photography buffs, it is possible to see the museum's archives, though you should call a day or two in advance.

Just south of the centre there is a cluster of museums beyond the large modern Erdei Ferenc Cultural Centre. Housed in an old pharmacy at Kölcsey utca 3, the **Medical and Pharmaceutical History Museum** (Orvos és Gyógyszerészetörténeti Múzeum; May–Sept daily 10am–2pm; 200Ft) won't detain you

Zoltán Kodály and Jósef Katona

For a small town, Kecskemét has made a not inconsiderable contribution to national culture, and its Spring Days festival features the work of its two famous sons.

Through his researches into the folk roots of Hungarian music, **Zoltán Kodály** (1882–1967) was inspired to write compositions that eschewed the Baroque and Western strains his colleague Bartók termed "New Style". He also revolutionized the teaching of music, inventing the "Kodály method" that is now applied throughout Hungary and around the world. Kodály's belief that music can only be understood by actively participating in it remains the guiding principle of Kecskemét's **Institute of Music Teaching** (Zenepedagógiai Intézet). Students on the **one-year course** are exhorted to approach music through the human voice, "the most easily accessible instrument for all", and build upon their national folk traditions when teaching children – a task Kodály considered supremely important, claiming "No one is too great to write for the little ones. In fact one has to strive to be great enough." For those who want to know more, there's an exhibition in the institute itself, at Kéttemplom köz 1–3 (daily 10am–6pm; 100Ft).

The town can also boast of **József Katona** (1791–1830), the "father" of Hungarian romantic drama, who was born and died in Kecskemét. His masterpiece, *Bánk Bán* (later made into an opera by Erkel), revolves around the murder of Gertrude, the German-born queen of King Andrew II, by his vassal Bánk. Katona himself expired of a heart attack outside the town hall, the spot now marked by a cloven block. The fallible organ was preserved in a jewelled casket, and his name was bestowed upon Kecskemét's playhouse. Designed by the Viennese architects who built the Vígszínház in Budapest, it is a smaller version of the same and was erected in 1896. During the 1980s, the **Katona Theatre** was directed by film-maker Miklós Jancsó, whose avant-garde productions scandalized many townsfolk. There is now a **museum** (Tues–Sat 10am–2pm; 200Ft) dedicated to the playwright at Katona József utca 5, near the Hungarian Photography Museum, though its literary exhibits lack any explanation in English, and the period furniture isn't actually Katona's own.

for long, with a collection that consists mostly of old pharmacy bottles, although it does have some fancy old medical instruments and an old weighing chair. More appealing is the nearby **Toy Museum** (Szórakaténusz Játékmúzeum; mid-March to Dec Tues–Sun 10am–12.30pm & 1–5pm; 300Ft), which occupies an airy wooden building especially designed by Kerényi. It contains a delightful collection of nineteenth- and twentieth-century toys with notes in English, and its helpful English-speaking staff also organize children's workshops. In the run-down house adjacent, the **Naive Art Museum** (Naiv Művészeti Múzeum; mid-March to Oct Tues–Sun 10am–5pm; 300Ft) provides a fascinating insight into the colourful world of the pre-World War I naïve artists. This delightful little collection includes wood-carved sculptures of farmers and shepherds, and a series of bright paintings representing indigenous peasant culture.

Fans of Magyar folk art should head 500m south towards the junction of Petőfi utca and the ring boulevard (bus #1, #11 or #22). One block on and to the right, at Serfőző utca 19A, the **Museum of Hungarian Folk Craft** (Népi Iparművészeti Múzeum; Feb to mid-Dec Tues–Sat 10am–5pm; 200Ft) exhibits a wealth of textiles, pottery and embroidery from the 1950s onwards in a seemingly endless succession of rooms. Besides the names of the artists, there is little guidance to the exhibits, and the most striking items – embroidered jackets and waistcoats – are saved for the very last room, if you make it that far.

The extensive **Bozsó Collection** (Bozsó Gyüjtemény; Fri–Sun 10am–6pm; 200Ft) of antique furniture and other artefacts, assembled by a local artist, is housed at Klapka utca 34, 500m east of the Cifra Palace, in a Baroque residence that once belonged to György Klapka, a general in the 1848 Hungarian War of Independence. Finally, just north of Széchenyi tér at Zimay utca 6, is the fascinating **Leskowsky Musical Instrument Collection** (Leskowsky Hangszergyüjtemény; Mon–Sat 9am–5pm all year, or by appointment; 500Ft; book visits on ⓣ76/486-616), which has more than 1500 instruments from all over the world. Musician Albert Leskowsky takes you on a very personal tour, playing everything from zithers, guitars and washboards to bizarre experimental percussion, giving explanations in excellent English.

Eating, drinking and entertainment

Aside from two or three very good **restaurants**, you'll have your work cut out finding decent places to eat in town. There are some good bakeries in the vicinity of the local bus station and the outdoor **market** should do the trick for cheap snacks and fresh produce. **Drinking** possibilities are easier to find, with a good spread of cafés, pubs and bars spotted around the centre.

Eating

The cosy, inn-style *Kecskemét Csárda* at Kőlcsey utca 7 (daily 11am–11pm; ⓣ76/488-686) offers expensive, but genuinely superb, Hungarian food, with waiters scuttling around purposefully, though its popularity is such that reservations are advisable. No less excellent, and only slightly less pricey, is the warm and classy *Geniusz* at Kisfaludy utca 5 (daily 9am–11pm), which specializes in delicious tasting and beautifully presented international food, albeit with a slight French twist. Nearby, on the corner of Kisfaludy utca and Festo utca, *L'Amatriciana* (daily 10am–11pm) is a bristling pizzeria that also does a decent line in traditional Hungarian meals. For more Magyar nosh try the *Kisbugaci Csárda* a little further out, beyond Széchenyi tér at Munkácsy utca 10, in a quarter that is full of tree-lined older streets (daily noon–midnight).

Drinking

The best daytime **drinking** spots are *Café de Columbia* at Kéttemplomkőz 4 (daily 8am–11pm), and the tiny *Semiramis Tea House* (Mon–Fri 8am–6pm, Sat & Sun 8am–2pm), underneath the *Hotel Udvarház,* which has a great selection of teas. Two agreeable **patisseries** are the *Fodor Cukrászda* by the *Liberté Kávéház*, and the *Delicatesse Cukrászda* in an arcade on the corner of Kossuth and Széchenyi tér.

The *HBH*, on Csányi utca, near the local bus station, and the *Liberté Kávéház* are worthwhile **drinking** spots too, as is the *Rolling Rock* bar at Jókai ut 44. When it comes to dancing, Kecskemét's students prefer places like *Xtreme Music Club* at Kisfaludy utca 4 and the *Silver Club* on Izsaki út – you can find more **nightlife** places listed in the freebie listings magazine *Kecskeméti Est.*

Entertainment

Kecskemét is at its liveliest during the **Spring Festival** in late March, a feast of music and drama coinciding with Spring Festival in Budapest, and the **Hiros Hét**, a week-long local festival in late August featuring street theatre, pageants, wine tasting and craft fairs on Szabadság tér and Petőfi utca. The town's key musical event is the **Kodály Festival**, a two-month-long series of concerts in July and August in the Erdei Ferenc Cultural House on Deák Ferenc tér, and other cultural institutions around town. There are other summertime concerts and fairs on Kossuth tér and Szabadság tér, and shows at the **Ciróka Puppet Theatre**, Budai utca 15. Details of all these events are available from Tourinform.

Into Romania and Serbia

Besides numerous destinations on the Plain and Eger in the Northern Uplands, the intercity bus station is also the point of departure for **buses to Romania and Serbia**. These are used by ethnic Hungarians returning to Miercurea Ciuc, Oradea, Cluj and Târgu Mureş in Romania (designated by their Hungarian names as Csíkszereda, Nagyvárad, Kolozsvár and Marosvásárhely), or Subotica (Szabadka) in the Voivodina region of Serbia. At present, most foreigners are not obliged to have visas for either country if staying less than 90 days. If you do require a visa, however, you should get these in advance, and not attempt to do so at the border.

Excursions around Kecskemét

The countryside around Kecskemét is ideal for **horse-riding**, with numerous riding schools and stables known to Tourinform. There are also scores of **farmsteads** that welcome tourists who enjoy riding, walking, fishing or simply relaxing in rural surroundings. For details and bookings, contact Mrs Ferenc Palásti of the Kiskunsági Vendégvárók Egyesűlet at Csongrádi utca 25 (☎76/486-230).

The town also makes a good base for **excursions** to the Kiskunság region (see below) and the Tisza resorts. Bus #2 from Széchenyi tér can drop you at the *Átrakó állomás* on Halasi út, the terminal for narrow-gauge trains to Kiskunság National Park.

Thirty kilometres east of Kecskemét are several low-key **resorts** where you can swim in the Tisza or wander beside it as it meanders through woodlands and meadows. Lakitelek and Tőserdő make for a relaxed excursion from Kecskemét or Kiskunfélegyháza, while Tiszakécske is more of a family holiday centre. **From Kecskemét**, six trains daily stop at Lakitelek en route to Kunszentmárton; to reach Tőserdő you can take the same trains from Kecskemét, alighting at the Szikra station, or catch the bus. **From Kiskunfélegyháza**, the five daily Szolnok trains call at Lakitelek, Tiszakécske and Tőserdő.

The big local attraction is the lovely **Lakitelek-Tőserdő**, a sylvan nature reserve 4km away. Turning off the main road beside the **thermal baths** (Tősfürdő; May–Aug daily 9am–5pm; 600Ft), a path runs 1km down to the *Holtág*, a dead branch of the river that's nice for swimming and boating, with cheap **restaurants** and a campsite (mid-May to mid-Sept). Every year on August 20, St Stephen's Day celebrations are held here with concerts and fireworks. Up the road there is **accommodation** at the *Tölgyfa Fogadó* at Napsugár utca 6 (☎76/449-037; ❷), and there's another campsite, *Autóscamping*, also with chalets (❷), up by the thermal baths (☎76/449-012; May–Aug). The Tőserdő train station is a couple of kilometres south, on the main road.

TISZAKÉCSKE, 8km further north, has more of a tourist industry outside town. Hourly buses run from the train station to the centre, passing by several rooms for rent, before heading to the riverside resort area (Üdülő telep), which has horse-drawn carts and a **children's railway** (May–Sept; 600Ft), **thermal baths** (daily 9am–5pm; 700Ft), and both free and paying **campsites**.

The Kiskunság

The **Kiskunság** region, to the south of Kecskemét, is called "Little Cumania" after the Cumanian (*Kun*) tribes that settled here in the Middle Ages. This sandy tableland was unfit for anything but raising sheep until, in the nineteenth century, it was laboriously transformed by afforestation and soil husbandry to yield grapes and other fruit. While Magyars esteem this as "Petőfi country", where their national poet was born, its prime attractions for visitors are Kiskunság National Park and the exhibition complex at Ópusztaszer.

Kiskunfélegyháza

To Hungarian ears, **KISKUNFÉLEGYHÁZA** suggests people and paths converging on the "House of Cumania". The present town was actually created by Jazygian settlers in the 1740s, but the name is nevertheless appropriate as the Cumanian original was wiped out by the Turks. As regional capital, it is a rural foil to urbane Kecskemét, a town that lives by geese-breeding and market gardening, with storks' nests on the chimneys and draw-wells in the courtyards.

Like many small towns on the Plain, Kiskunfélegyháza's main street follows the primary trade route of old, and its main square, Petőfi tér, is sited at the crossroads with the secondary route. On one side of the square is the majolica-encrusted **town hall** in the National Romantic style; built by József Vass and Nándor Morbitzer in 1912, its facade is adorned with embroidery motifs typical of the region, as are the staircase and main hall. Diagonally opposite is the white **Swan House** (Hattyuház), where Petőfi's father had a butcher's shop and the poet spent his childhood (it's now the town library), while his statue stands opposite. His life is documented with newspaper articles, maps and suchlike at the **Petőfi Ház**, just past the bus station, behind the church, at Petőfi utca 7 (March–Oct Wed–Fri 9am–noon; 120Ft). Five minutes' walk south, at Móra utca 19, is a museum with exhibits on **Ferenc Móra**, writer, journalist and antiquarian, who was born in this house in 1879 (March–Oct Wed–Fri 9am–noon; 150Ft).

However, it's better to walk 300m up the main road in the direction of Kecskemét to visit the **Kiskun Museum** (March–Oct Wed–Sun 9am–5pm; 250Ft), in an eighteenth-century manor house at Holló Lajos utca 9. Exhibits on the Cumanians and Jazygians and modern paintings of rural life by László Holló pale before a section devoted to the **history of prisons**, in the very cell where the famous *betyár* Sándor Rózsa languished in 1860. Amongst the many fascinating exhibits on display are some fiendish-looking torture implements, and several items made by prisoners, including musical instruments, toys, and a beautifully crafted chess set – look out, too, for the carefully preserved etchings on the walls of the cells. Down in the prison chapel, where inmates were allowed to worship each Saturday, there's a lovely collection of ecclesiastical treasures and folk art, such as chalices, vestments, scriptures and icons. The nineteenth-century wooden **windmill** in the courtyard was transported here from the village of Mindszent by the River Tisza, where Cardinal Mindszenty was born (see p.175). For a break from museums, you could go for a soak in the outdoor **thermal baths** at Blaha Lujza tér 1, down towards the train station (daily 9am–8pm, Fri & Sat until 11pm; 450Ft).

Practicalities

The **bus station** is on the eastern side of Petőfi tér, and the **train station** twenty minutes' walk in the opposite direction at the end of Kossuth utca. You can get limited **information** from Kiskun Tours at Martirok utca 1 (Mon–Fri 9am–6pm, Sat 9am–noon; ☎76/433-243) and **accommodation** at the rather old-fashioned, but homely and cheerful, *Hotel Oázis,* 500m south of the centre at Szegedi út 13 (☎76/461-913; ❹), or the fairly basic *Mónika* (☎76/466-022;

❷) and *Borostyán* (Ⓣ76/466-785; ❷) pensions at Szőlő utca 1. Choices for **eating** boil down to the uninspiring sounding, but actually rather decent, *Irish pub and restaurant* on Móra tér (diagonally across from Petőfi tér), and *Caffe pub and pizzeria* at Kossuth utca 8.

Kiskunság National Park

The 300 square kilometres of **Kiskunság National Park** (May–Sept daily 10am–5pm; 1400Ft, includes entry to equestrian display and museum) consist of several tracts of classic *puszta* landscape, the largest of which starts 3km beyond the village of **BUGAC**. Buses from Kiskunfélegyháza and Kecskemét can drop you near the entrance to the park, where you'll find the **park office** – which can supply maps and English-language information – and the *Bugaci Karikás Csárda*, a traditional-style restaurant catering for coach parties.

From the entrance a sandy track runs 1km past flower-speckled meadows and lounging shepherds, to the **museum**, **farm** and **stables**, where *csikósok* (cowboys) in white pantaloons stage equestrian displays (May–Sept daily 1.15pm; June–Aug extra show at 3.15pm), riding bareback and standing up with much cracking of whips. On a hot day it is worth paying the extra 1000Ft for a **horse-drawn carriage ride** from the entrance, which also includes a short ride out into the park. In the wooden **Shepherds' Museum** (same hours as park), you can see felted cloaks, hand-carved pipes and a grotesque tobacco pouch made from a ram's scrotum. Among the animals bred at the **farm** are old protected species of Hungarian livestock, such as grey long-horned cattle, Merino sheep and Mangalica pigs (said to make the finest bacon). The surrounding reedy marshes that extend far beyond Bugac support diverse birdlife and flora – including rare blue globe-thistles in August – and serve as baths for water buffalo, which plod back to their barns at sunset. The office at the park entrance can give information about marked **trails** round the park.

There are two ways of getting here: the narrow-gauge **train** from Kecskemét's *Átrakó állomás* (see p.393; 3 daily; 1hr) would be the most enjoyable method but for the two-kilometre walk from the Bugac felső terminal to the park entrance – not pleasant on a hot day – whereas **buses** from Kecskemét and Kiskunfélegyháza (5 daily, 2 at weekends; 1hr 30min from Kecskemét) drop you close to the entrance of the park – ask the driver to let you off at the nearest point. To catch the 1.15pm horse show you'll need to get the first train (leaving 7.50am) or the 11am bus from Kecskemét; bus times do change, however, and it's worth checking bus timetables and park details with Tourinform in Kecskemét. You can **stay** near the park at the countrified *Táltos Lovas Panzió* (Ⓣ76/372-633; ❸), 500m from the entrance, or the modern *Bucka Hotel* (Ⓣ76/372-511, Ⓦwww.hotels.hu/bucka; ❹), about 1km beyond the rail terminal, which also offers smart wooden chalets (❻).

Kiskőrös

KISKŐRÖS deserves a mention as the **birthplace of Sándor Petőfi** (see box on p.396), and this small town flogs this connection for all it can. Built at the end of the eighteenth century, the simple, three-roomed thatched **Petőfi House** at Petőfi tér 5 is reputedly where the poet was born, and is now preserved as a museum decked out with furniture that belonged to the family. Next door the **Petőfi Museum** (both museums Tues–Sun 9am–5pm; 200Ft for both) houses local history displays, with the final room devoted to the poet's life and death – when local history effectively stopped, it seems. Between the two is **Translators' Park**, with busts of those who have translated Petőfi's verse into other languages (there is no English representative – yet). Nearby stands the first Petőfi **statue** in a country where every town has at least one feature named after him. Such is the cult of the poet (which the Communists tried to appropriate, but which Hungarian youth reclaimed as a symbol of rebellion) that in 1972, to mark the 150th anniversary of Petőfi's birth, Kiskőrös was re-elevated to the rank of a town, a standing it had lost in the nineteenth century.

Five minutes' walk away to the northeast at Szent István utca 23, the **Slovak Nationality House** (Szlovák tájház; Tues–Sun 9am–noon & 1–4pm), covered by the same ticket as the Petőfi museums, preserves the memory of the 700 Slovaks who settled here in 1718 as the countryside was repopulated after the retreat of the Ottomans. The colourfully decorated interior of this neat thatched cottage has displays on how the Slovaks lived, worked and dressed at the end of the nineteenth century, and also shows how houses were furnished then, including a large open fireplace in the kitchen. For a spot of relaxation, head for the town's **thermal baths**, just west of the Road Museum, where the temperature is a constant 38°C (Mon–Thurs & Sun 9am–7pm, Fri & Sat till 10pm; 700Ft), or to the small **park** 50m behind the Petőfi Museum, a small grassy space centred around a small bridge – a bizarre sight given the lack of any water – inscribed with a corny Eric Clapton quote: "Love can build a bridge". On the far side of the park there's a small **Internet café** on Martini utca (Mon–Fri 9am–6pm, Sat 9am–noon).

From the **bus station**, it's a short two-minute walk to central Petőfi tér, and from the **train station** it's a fifteen-minute walk along Kossuth utca to the centre. **Information** is available from Tourinform, housed in the ugly concrete building near the Petőfi House at Petőfi tér 4 (Mon–Fri 9am–4pm; ⓣ78/514-850, ⓔkiskoros@tourinform.hu). The *Hotel Imperial*, out by the thermal baths at Erdőtelki utca 21 (ⓣ78/514-400; ⓦwww.hotelimperial.hu; ❹), is the most comfortable place to **stay**, though the *Hotel Szarvas*, in the centre at Petőfi Sándor tér 17 (ⓣ78/511-500, ⓔszarvasfogado@emitelnet.hu; ❺), has tasteful rooms befitting a grand old building, as well as a restaurant, fitness room

Sándor Petőfi

Born on New Year's Eve 1822, of a Slovak mother and a Southern Slav butcher-innkeeper father, **Sándor Petőfi** was to become obsessed with acting and poetry, which he started to write at the age of fifteen. As a strolling player, soldier and labourer, he absorbed the language of working people, writing lyrical poetry in the vernacular, to the outrage of critics. Moving to Budapest in 1844, Petőfi fell in with the young radical intellectuals who met at the *Pilvax Café*; from this time on, poetry and action were inseparable. His *Nemzeti Dal* (National Song) was declaimed from the steps of the National Museum on the first day of the 1848 Revolution ("Some noisy mob had their hurly-burly outside so I left for home," complained the director). Mindful of the thousands of landless peasants encamped outside the city, Parliament bowed to the demands of the radicals and voted for the abolition of serfdom.

During the War of Independence, Petőfi fought alongside General Bem in Transylvania, and disappeared at the battle of Segesvár (Sighişoara, Romania) in July 1849. Though he was most likely trampled beyond recognition by the Cossacks' horses (as foreseen in one of his poems), Petőfi was rumoured to have survived. In 1990, entrepreneur Ferenc Morvai announced that Petőfi had been carted off to Siberia by the Russians, married a peasant woman and later died there. The Hungarian Academy refused to support Morvai's expedition to uncover the putative grave, and it was subsequently reported that forensic analysis had proved the corpse to be that of a Jewish woman.

and solarium. Otherwise, there's the large, unappealing motel-like *Vinum* and *Kiskőrös* hotels out on the edge of town towards Soltvadkert at Petőfi utca 106 (Ⓣ78/511-050; ❹) and Petőfi utca 112 (Ⓣ78/312-788, Ⓦwww.hotels.hu/kiskoros; ❸) respectively, or the **campsite** (May–Sept) by the thermal baths. Aside from the restaurant at the *Hotel Szarvas*, simple **meals** are served in the *Kurta kocsma* on József Attila utca.

Kiskunhalas

KISKUNHALAS has more going for it than Kiskőrös, especially if you happen to be around for the **Grape Harvest Festival** in September, when folk dancing and other celebrations enliven the squares around its Art Nouveau town hall. Another more specialized attraction of Kiskunhalas is its tradition of **lace making**, a medieval industry whose revival in the 1890s owed much to local schoolteacher Maria Markovits, who studied patterns and samples from before the Turkish occupation.

A statue of Maria Markovits stands outside the **Lace House** (Csipkemúzeum), ten minutes' walk from the centre towards the train station at Kossuth utca 37A (daily 9am–noon & 1–4pm; 200Ft). The house features a treasury of tablecloths, ruffs and petticoats and other trimmings – some composed of 56 different types of stitches – as well as a workshop. The **Thorma János Museum**, opposite the town hall at Kőztársaság utca 2 (March–Nov Tues–Sat 9am–5pm; 250Ft), features local history and the artistic oeuvre of the eponymous impressionist painter, including two enormous canvases dedicated to the 1848 Revolution, *Rise Up Magyar!* and *Arad Blood Witness* – the former stars key Hungarian revolutionaries Sándor Petőfi and Jókai Mór. Other sights in town include an old **windmill** on Kölcsey utca, 1km north of the centre to the right of the main road (April–Oct Sat & Sun 10am–6pm; 150Ft), and a lovely classical **synagogue** at Petőfi utca 1 (Raáb András has the key at Semmelweis tér 24, Ⓣ77/423-489). Aside from lace making, the craft of saddlemaking is also pursued here, and **saddlemaker** Balázs Abonyi Tóth welcomes visitors to his workshop at Vas utca 1, out past the bus station.

At weekends, people make for the **thermal baths** on Dr. Monszpart László utca, ten minutes west of the centre (daily 7am–7pm; 650Ft), or go **fishing** at Sóstó pond, 3km north of town.

Practicalities

Kiskunhalas is accessible by train or bus from Baja or Kiskunfélegyháza. Its **train station** lies 1km east of the centre on Kossuth utca, while the **bus station** is located just west of the centre on Május 1 tér. Proko Travel at Hősök tere 1 (Mon–Fri 9am–5pm, Sat 9am–noon; Ⓣ77/421-984) can supply **information** and arrange private rooms. The town's sole **hotel** is the dowdy *Hotel Csipke*, a ten-minute walk west of the bus station on Semmelweis tér near the baths (Ⓣ77/421-455, Ⓦwww.csipkehotel.hu ❹). Kiskunhalas has two **campsites**: one by the baths and the other at Sóstó; the latter has wooden chalets, open all year round (Ⓣ77/422-222; ❷).

Ópusztaszer Historical Park

The **Ópusztaszer National Historical Memorial Park** (Ópusztaszeri Nemzeti Tőrténeti Emlékpark; daily: May–Sept 9am–6pm, Oct–April 9am–4pm; 1600Ft, 800Ft park only; Ⓦwww.opusztaszer.hu), just outside the village of the same name, commemorates the conquest of the seven Magyar tribes who crossed into the Carpathian Basin and spread out across the plains, each claiming a territory – an event known in Hungarian history as the *honfoglalás*, or "land-taking". The park supposedly marks the site of their first tribal "parliament" after the land-taking, in about 896 AD, although the only evidence for this comes from an anonymous writer from 300 years later. A huge memorial was erected here for the millennial anniversary celebrations of 1896, and in 1945 the Communists symbolically chose Ópusztaszer for the first distribution of land amongst the peasants.

Today, the park, 55 hectares in size, has some excellent displays, but reeks of nationalism, stressing the links between those early tribes and today's Hungary – the place is littered with maps of pre-World War I Hungary, which similarly covered the Carpathian Basin, as if that were the natural Hungarian "homeland". The park's most touted attraction is housed in the large round building 200m down from the entrance: the **Cyclorama**, entitled "Arrival of the Conquering Hungarians", by Árpád Feszty, is a monumental canvas 15m high and 120m long that depicts Prince Árpád leading the tribes into the Verecke pass in the Ukraine as they enter the Carpathian basin. Taking just two years to complete, it was first exhibited in 1894 in Budapest's City Park, but was badly damaged during World War II when more than half of the painting was destroyed. This most recent restoration, by a team of Polish experts, was completed in 1995. Inside the same building is a pathetically small and easily missable waxworks exhibition (Panoptikum; 350Ft), and a Tourinform office (same times as park; ⓣ62/275-257, ⓔinfo@opusztaszer.hu) which can give the usual **information** about accommodation as well as help with horse-riding and hiring sports equipment in the park.

Heading up the slope from the Cyclorama past the **Árpád Memorial**, a grand Classical-style stone memorial to the leader of the Magyars set up in 1896, you reach the ruins of the thirteenth-century **Szer Monastery** – although the layers of brick covering the old remains make the place look like a modern fabrication. Excavations here have revealed a cemetery containing the remains of the first Hungarian settlers. Peeping over the trees 50m away is a series of yurta-like structures – supposedly inspired by early Hungarian architecture and crowned with symbols said to come from the early tribes – housing the **Men and Forests exhibition** (Erdő és Ember), a small set of displays on forestry and wildlife with English notes. The best section of the park, however, is the **Village Museum** (Skanzen; closed in winter), which re-creates buildings from villages in southern Hungary, including a school, post office and bakery – the last two still functional. The park is the focus for craft fairs and demonstrations throughout the year, including Easter, Whitsun, August 20 and the **Hunnia**, a festival on the last Saturday of June celebrating the arrival of the all-conquering Hungarian tribes. There are also Nomadic shows during the summer (11.30am & 2.30pm; 500Ft), featuring horse-riding, archery displays and the like.

Practicalities

ÓPUSZTASZER itself lies 10km east of Kistelek on the Kecskemét–Szeged road, and is linked by regular buses from Szeged. Buses stop at the top of the road that leads down to the park. Alternatively, you could try hitching from Kistelek, a stop for buses along the highway. Note that if you are travelling by train from anywhere in Hungary to Szeged or Kistelek and buy a single ticket, you can return to the same station free of charge if you get your ticket stamped at the park ticket office. On the way to the park on Árpád liget you'll find the *Szeri Csárda* restaurant and next door the basic *Szeri Camping* (ⓣ62/275-123; April–Oct).

The legend of Attila the Hun

The lower reaches of the Tisza are associated with the **legend of Attila the Hun**, who died in 453 AD of a nasal haemorrhage following a night of passion with his new bride, Kriemhild. The body of the "Scourge of God" was reputedly buried in a triple-layered coffin of gold, silver and lead, and then submerged in the Tisza at an unknown spot – unknown because the pallbearers were slain before the Huns departed. Archeologists have yet to find it, but the legend gains credence from the "treasure of Attila". Thought to have belonged to a Hun general, the treasure was discovered at Nagyszentmiklós (in what is now Romania) and is currently held by Vienna's Kunsthistorisches Museum.

Szeged

SZEGED straddles the River Tisza like a provincial Budapest, as cosmopolitan a city as you'll find on the Great Plain, with a friendly atmosphere that's mainly thanks to the students from the university. The old city's eclectic good looks have been saved by placing the ugly modern housing and industry over the river, in the suburb of Újszeged. Though Kőrös folk settled here four to five thousand years ago, and the town flourished after 1225 because of its royal monopoly over the salt mines of Transylvania, Szeged's present layout dates from after the **great flood** of March 1879, which washed away all but 300 homes and compelled the population to start again from scratch. With aid from foreign capitals (after whom sections of the outer boulevard are named), the city bounced back, trumpeting its revival with huge buildings and squares where every type of architectural style made an appearance.

During Communist times **Szeged University** was at the forefront of student protests in 1956, and one of the seedbeds of the peace movement and punk rock scene in the 1980s. More recently, the wars in the former Yugoslavia led to a boom in cross-border **smuggling** and Mafia activity, which made Szeged notorious in Hungary and enriched the local economy at a time when other cities were feeling the pinch.

Arrival, information and accommodation

To get to the old city (Belváros) from the **train station**, take tram #1, while from the intercity **bus terminal** on Mars tér it's a five-minute walk. The Belváros, on the west bank of the Tisza, is encircled by Tisza Lajos körút and an outer ring boulevard, with radial avenues (*sugárút*) emanating from the centre. For a map and **information**, drop into the helpful Tourinform at Dugonics tér 2 (mid-May to mid-Sept daily 9am–6pm; mid-Sept to mid-May Mon–Fri 9am–4pm; Ⓣ62/488-690, Ⓔszeged@tourinform.hu), which also operates a stall in the square (daily May–Sept 9am–9pm). There's **Internet access** at Datanet, Dugonics tér 11 (daily 8am–11pm); Internet Virus, Kígyó utca 7 (Mon–Sat 10am–midnight); and Cyber Arena at Hid utca 1 near the bridge (open 24hr). The **post office** is at Hid utca 3 (Mon–Fri 8am–7pm, Sat 8am–noon).

Accommodation

There's a reasonable spread of accommodation in Szeged, and you should be able to get some form of **accommodation** at any time of the year, though the city's resources can be strained during the Festival Weeks in July and August. **Private rooms** (❷), from Szeged Tourist at Klauzál tér 7 (Mon–Fri 9am–5pm;

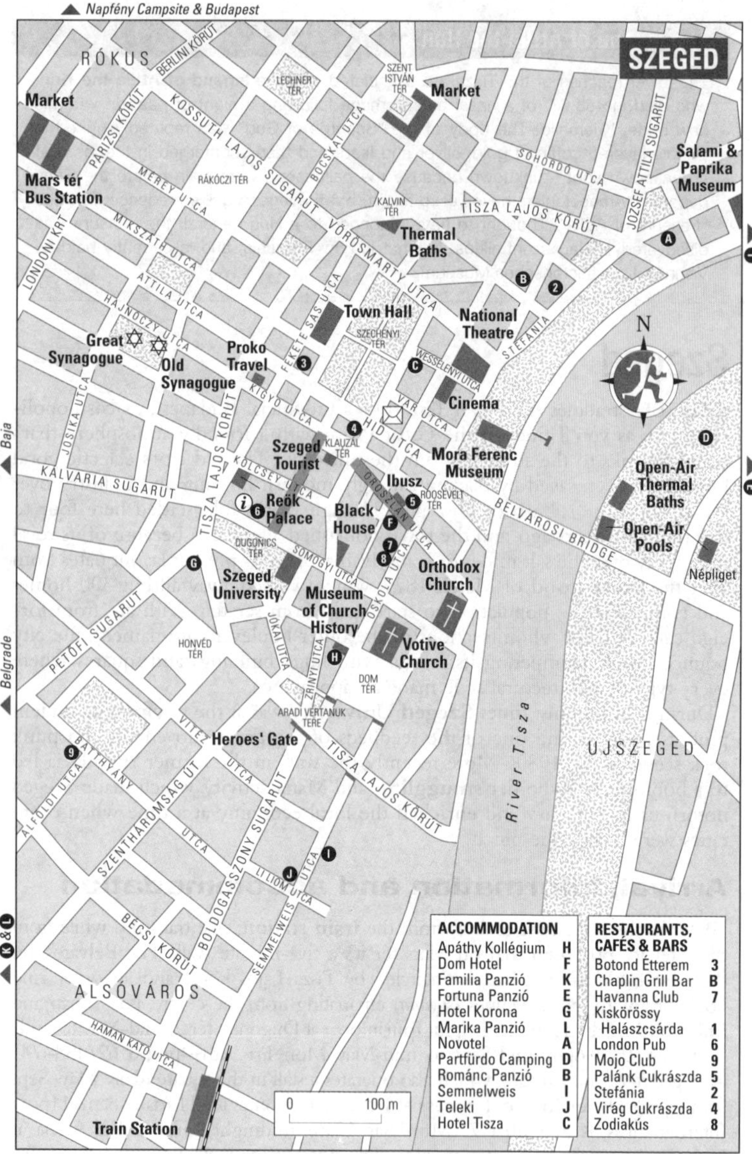

☎62/420-428, ⓔszegedtourist@mail.tiszanet.hu), and Ibusz at Oroszlán utca 3 (Mon–Fri 9am–6pm, Sat 9am–1pm; ☎62/471-177, ⓔi085@ibusz.hu), are the best value for money if you can get somewhere in the centre. Double rooms in **colleges** in the vicinity of Dóm tér – such as the *Apáthy Kollégium* at Apáthy István utca 4 (☎62/545-896; ❸) or the *Semmelweis* at Semmelweis utca 4 (☎62/545-042; ❷) – are more expensive, though the *Teleki* just further out at

Semmelweis utca 5 (ⓣ62/546-088; ❶) is cheaper. These all function during July and August only, and are bookable through Proko Travel at Kígyó utca 3 (Mon–Fri 9am–5pm; ⓣ62/450-367). In addition to the campsites listed below, there is a **nudist camp**, *FKK Naturista Camping & Strand*, 10km northwest of the city in Kiskundorozsma (ⓣ62/463-988).

Hotels and pensions

Dóm Hotel Bajza utca 3-6 ⓣ62/423-750, ⓦwww.domhotel.hu. A real gem of a hotel secreted away on a closed-off street behind the Black House. Sophisticated, business-like rooms, with big TVs, Internet access and large wooden desks. ❻

Familia Panzió Szentháromság utca 71 ⓣ62/441-122, ⓦwww.familiapanzio.hu. Large, hospitable pension south of the town centre and ten minutes' walk west of the train station. Two- to four-bed rooms, some with a/c. Protected parking available. ❸–❹

Hotel Korona Petőfi sgt 4 ⓣ62/555-787, ⓦwww.szallasinfo.hu/hotelkorona. Cracking hotel just a stone's throw from the centre, with large, decently furnished and good-looking rooms. ❺

Marika Panzió Nyíl utca 45 ⓣ62/443-861, ⓔmarika@tiszanet.hu. Well-equipped pension in a charming old peasant house in the Alsóváros, 600m south of the train station, complete with a/c, minibars, protected parking and a swimming pool. ❸–❹

Novotel Maros utca 1 ⓣ62/562-200, ⓦwww.novotel.com. Polished chain hotel offering bright, spacious and smoothly furnished rooms, most of which have computer phone lines. Also has a sauna and fitness room. ❼

Románc Panzió Arany János utca 5 ⓣ62/543-330, ⓔromanchotel@invitel.hu. Fabulous new pension incorporated within a slender, corner tower. The gorgeous, light blue-coloured rooms come with designer furnishings and a/c. Best value for money place in town. ❺

Hotel Tisza Széchenyi tér 3 ⓣ62/478-278, ⓦwww.tiszahotel.hu. A hotel of sorts since 1886, this fine old building overlooking the square now harbours rooms with parquet flooring and lovely wood-finished furnishings, though there's a rather hollow atmosphere about the place. ❺–❻

Campsites

Napfény Camping Dorozsmai út 4 ⓣ62/421-800. In the western suburbs of the city near the start of the Budapest highway (bus #78), with wooden chalets (❷). Open May–Sept.

Partfürdő Camping Középkikötő sor ⓣ62/430-843. On the river bank just across the bridge in Újszeged near the *strand* and thermal baths. Has wooden chalets (❷). Open May (later if the Tisza is in flood) to Sept.

The Town

Dóm tér is the most impressive feature of the inner city. Flanked by arcades with twisted columns and busts of illustrious Hungarians, this 12,000-square-metre expanse (approximately the same size as St Mark's Square in Venice) was created in 1920 by demolishing a network of backstreets to accommodate a gigantic **Votive Church** (Mon–Sat 9am–6pm, Sun 9.30–10am, 11–11.30am & 1–6pm; 400Ft), which the townsfolk had pledged to erect after the flood. Built of brown brick in the neo-Romanesque style, its portal is surmounted by a statue of the Virgin whose image recurs inside the church in peasant costume, wearing embroidered "Szeged slippers". Visitors are dwarfed by the white, blue and gold interior, where the organ, with its 10,180 pipes and five manuals, benefits from superb acoustics.

The eight-sided **Demetrius Tower** out in front dates from the eleventh century, but was largely rebuilt by Béla Rerrich, who designed the square. A chiming clock plays the folk song "Szeged, a famous town" at midday. Across from the tower, at no. 5, is a small **Museum of Church History** (Tues–Sun 10am–6pm; 100Ft), which holds a fine hoard of church treasures, including bejewelled chalices, reliquaries and vestments. On the south side of the square crowds gather every day at 12.15pm and 5.45pm (and at 8.15pm during the summer festival) to watch the **Musical Clock** (Zenélő óra), whose figures move round to the rich sound of the bells.

In the summer rows of seats are banked opposite the Votive Church for Szeged's festival, where local operas are performed. When performances (which start with everyone standing for the national anthem) finish, the crowds flood out towards the **Heroes' Gate** (Hősök Kapuja), which links Aradi vértanúk tere with Boldogasszony sugárút. The gate was raised to honour Admiral Horthy's henchmen, the "Whites", who gathered here in 1919, waiting for the Romanian army to defeat the Republic of Councils before they fanned out across Hungary to persecute Jews and "Reds" in the "White Terror". The mural inside the gate, by Aba Novak Vilmos, one of Hungary's leading interwar artists, was painted over by the Communists, who hated its glorification of Horthy and its nationalist references. A few years ago the Aba Novak Society raised funds to remove the paint, though the figure of Horthy itself remained covered until recently. The mural itself is a rather simplistic militaristic affair, but the local people are very proud of it. Behind the Votive Church to the northeast of Dóm tér stands an eighteenth-century **Serbian Orthodox Church** (Szerb Templom; 150Ft), worth a look for its magnificent iconostasis framed in pear wood.

Szeged University and around

Many of the buildings to the west of Dóm tér are part of **Szeged University**, whose main building overlooks Dugonics tér and a **Water Music Fountain** where students congregate during breaks. Locally known by its Hungarian initials, JATE (pronounced "yohteh"), the university is named after the poet **Attila József**, whom it expelled in 1924 for a poem which began "I have no father, I have no mother, I have no god and I have no country" and continued "with a pure heart, I'll burn and loot, and if I have to, even shoot". Attila's bitterness was rooted in his childhood, when his mother, a poor washerwoman, died of starvation. Later he was expelled from the Communist Party for trying to reconcile Marx and Freudian pyschology and, rejected by the woman he loved, finally jumped under a train at Lake Balaton (see p.209). Though unappreciated during his lifetime, Attila's poetry is now recognized as some of the best in the language. Elderly Hungarians weep upon hearing his sentimental "Mama", while anarcho-punks relish lines such as "Culture drops off me, like clothes off a happy lover".

Across from the university, on the corner of Somogyi and Kelemen utca, is the so-called **Black House** (Fekete-Ház). This Romantic-style edifice, now badly crumbling, is actually painted brown and white, but the ironmonger who lived here in the nineteenth century always told peasants "You can find me in the Black House". It now houses a very missable local history exhibition, though there are occasionally some good temporary exhibitions staged here (Tues–Sun 10am–5pm; 200Ft). If you carry on up Somogyi utca and bear right onto Fekete sas utca you'll find the fabulous **Reök Palace** (Reök palota) on the corner of Kölcsey utca. Built for Iván Reök, a nephew of the painter Munkácsy, this Art Nouveau masterpiece by Ede Oszadszki Magyar is now owned by a bank, which has restored its facade and retained some of its interior features too. Look out for the siren over the entrance with her Medusa-like coils of hair.

Around the waterfront and Széchenyi tér

Heading northwards from Dóm tér towards Roosevelt tér, you can't miss the enormous Neoclassical façade of the **Móra Ferenc Museum** (daily 10am–5pm; 400Ft), named after the eponymous local excavator. The museum conceals a typical mix of *objets d'art* and artefacts of local significance, notably a huge painting of the great flood by Pál Vágó. More fascinating is the display on the Avars, the people displaced by the arriving Magyars – the highlights

▲ Town Hall, Szeged

of a memorable collection include jewellery, pottery and weapons, exquisitely embossed artwork, and a double grave excavated by Ferenc himself. Behind the museum stand the **remains of a castle** that later served as a prison for the outlaw Sándor Rózsa and for convicts who laboured on the river towpaths during the eighteenth century. As in Debrecen, this was a time of mass witch trials organized by the church elders, when victims were tortured to make them confess. The castle museum is currently closed for rebuilding work – ask at Tourinform for the latest.

From here you can walk away from the river up Wesselényi utca between the **National Theatre** (Nemzeti Szinház) and the **City Cinema** (Belvárosi Mozi) – both stunning buildings in very different styles – to spacious, verdant **Széchenyi tér**, Szeged's inner-city park. On the far side stands the neo-Baroque **Town Hall**, rebuilt in 1883 following the great flood and likened by the poet Mihály Babits to "a lace-covered young woman dancing in the moonlight". The town hall is linked to the neighbouring council house – built at the same time on account of the visit of Franz Joseph – by a charming "Bridge of Sighs", modelled on the one in Venice. In front of the town hall stand two allegorical **fountains**, known as "The Blessed" and "the Angry", symbolizing the benevolent and destructive aspects of the River Tisza. Among the many other statues scattered throughout the park is one of Pál Vásárhelyi, underneath which is a marble plaque denoting the high-water mark in the city during the more recent flood of June 2, 1970.

A short walk south is **Klauzál tér**, a bright, Mediterranean-style piazza fringed by some fine pastel-coloured Neoclassical buildings, and setting for some of the town's most inviting cafés (see opposite). In the centre of the square stands a statue of Lajos Kossuth, who gave his last speech before his exile in 1849 from the balcony of the building at no. 5, which is now a bank. Opposite is the attractive Well of Kings, featuring four winged lions, from whence water spouts. Heading northwards from Széchenyi tér on Tisza Lajos körút are the magnificent **thermal baths** (daily 8am–8pm; 700Ft), indoor steam baths built at the end of the nineteenth century and recently completely restored – the complex now comprises some ten different pools.

Back on the riverside, a ten-minute walk north of the castle brings you to the **Salami and Paprika Museum**, situated within the Pick Salami Factory at Felső-Tisza-part 10 (Fri 3–6pm, Sat 1–4pm; 250Ft). The display on salami downstairs could put you off the stuff forever, but there are some good historical photos to look at, and the paprika exhibition upstairs – complete with lots of information on the healthy properties of the plant – smells marvellous. The entrance ticket has two halves: a token that entitles you to some salami samples in the restaurant at the end of your visit, and a postcard that you can send anywhere in the world for free – you just have to write it and put it in the museum postbox.

The Jewish quarter and beyond

Beyond Tisza Lajos körút, Szeged is shabbier and more utilitarian, but not devoid of sights, especially in the former **Jewish quarter** around Hajnóczy utca. The classical **Old Synagogue**, dating from 1843, bears a plaque showing the height of the water during the flood; it is now a contemporary arts centre, Alterra (events are advertised in the weekly *Szegedi Est*). Far grander and more alluring is the Secession-style **Great Synagogue** (Új Zsinagóga) with its entrance on Jósika utca (Mon–Fri & Sun: April–Sept 10am–noon & 1–5pm; Oct–March 10am–2pm; 400Ft). One of the largest synagogues in Europe, it was built between 1900 and 1903 by Lipót Baumhorn, who designed 22 synagogues throughout Hungary; this one is regarded as the finest example of his work. Its magnificent dome, executed in blue stained glass, represents the world, with 24 columns for the hours of day and night, white flowers for faith, and blue stars for the infinity of the cosmos. The stained-glass windows illustrate texts from *The Flora of the Jews*, by Rabbi Immanuel Löw, who was the Chief Rabbi here in the early part of the century.

Around the outer boulevard (bus #11 or #21), to the south, parts of the **Alsóváros** or "lower town" resemble a village, with ochre-painted cottages and rutted streets. This quarter was traditionally inhabited by paprika-growers, and centres around the **Alsóvárosi Church** on Mátyás király tér, begun in the late fifteenth century. Its reworked Baroque interior contains the *Black Madonna*, a copy of the famous Madonna of Czistochowa, and the focus of attention during the reconsecration ceremonies at the annual melon harvest festival.

Two busy outdoor **markets**, on Mars tér in the Rókus quarter, and Szent István tér between the inner and outer boulevards, are well worth a visit, while the town's **flea market** (Használtcikk piac), with a strong Serbian presence, lies on Cserepes Sor on the Belgrade road (tram #4 or buses #22 and #13 from the centre). To the west of the centre (tram #3 from Dugonics tér), there's a **wildlife park** (Vadaspark; daily 9am–dusk; 300Ft) with a large collection of small monkeys, parrots and South American animals.

Eating and drinking

Szeged has a decent, though not exceptional, range of **restaurants** (see below), and is famous for its sausages and for dishes such as *halászlé* (fish soup) and *halpaprikás* (fish in paprika sauce). For **coffee and cakes**, most people congregate at the large and sociable *Virág* and *A Capella Cukrászdas*, opposite each other on Klauzál tér, both of which have bustling summer terraces. Less conspicuous are the *Palánk Cukrászda* on the corner of Viktor Hugó utca and Oskola utca (daily 9am–10pm), and the cosy *Stefánia* at Stefánia 9 by the riverside park (8am–9pm).

Restaurants

Botond Étterem Széchenyi tér 13. Housed in an old printing works, this is an agreeably simple place with inexpensive dishes and an enjoyable terrace looking across to the square. Daily 9am–midnight.

Chaplin Grill Bar Arany János utca 5. Attached to the *Románc Panzió*, this no-fuss gaff has large, simple and cheap portions of grilled meats, and is also open round the clock.

Kiskörössy Halászcsárda Felső Tisza-part 336. Fish lovers should make a pilgrimage to this place on the banks of the Tisza where the Prince of Wales (later Edward VII) often came in the 1890s. Bus #73 or #73Y from Mars tér (ask the driver to tell you when to get off), then walk along the dyke and follow a road down to the right, where there are two restaurants and holiday houses amongst the trees. Daily 11am–midnight, Fri & Sat till 2am.

London Pub Dugonics tér 2. This heavily-wooded restaurant doesn't do a bad job of apeing a typical English pub, and offers good food, including lots of grill and steak dishes. Daily 10am-midnight.

Mojo Club Alföld utca 1. Just south of the centre, this ordinary-looking place offers typically meaty and super-tasty Serb specialities. Daily 11am–2am, Sun till midnight.

Zodiákus Oskola utca 13. Beautifully but subtely decorated, this is the classiest place in town, offering fish dishes and grilled meats in the main. Mon–Thurs 11am–midnight, Fri & Sat till 1am.

Nightlife

Although it's a large university town, Szeged can be quiet at weekends, when many students head home; the big student night out is Thursday, known as *kis péntek* – "little Friday". A popular student hangout is the *Mojo Club* (see p.405), which is highly recommended for its very mellow feel and live music on Tuesdays (Sept–June only), while the *Nem Egri Borozó* at József Attila utca 6 (closed Sun) attracts a mix of locals and students. A couple of cool spots are the laid-back *Havanna Club*, next door to the *Zodiákus* restaurant at Oskola utca 13, and the *Bounty Bar* at Wesselényi utca 2, across from the National Theatre, with excellent service and amusingly kitsch furnishings. There are regular **raves and parties** at the *JATE Klub* at Toldi utca 2 behind the university, and at the *SZOTE Klub* (the medical university club) at Dom ter 13 – in July and August the music only starts after the open-air stage (see below) has finished. The weekly freebie *Szegedi Est* carries information about what's on in town.

Entertainment

Szeged's **concert season** runs from September to May, with events held in the National Theatre, while in July and August Dóm tér is filled with a huge stage hosting a festival of drama and music known as the **Szeged Open-Air Theatre Festival** (Szegedi Szabadtéri Játékok). Events are advertised around town, and **tickets** are available from the Szabadtéri jegyiroda ticket agency at Deák utca 28–30 (Mon–Fri 10am–5pm, Sat 10am–1pm; ⓣ62/554-713). Szeged also boasts a series of **beer festivals** in June and July, when pubs and restaurants put up tents in town and the beer flows.

Outdoor activities

On hot summer weekends people flock to the grassy **open-air pools** in Újszeged across the river: the *Partfürdő* on the river bank (May–Sept Mon–Fri 9am–7pm, Sat & Sun 8am–6pm; 800Ft), and the *Ligetfürdő* (May–Sept daily 6am–8pm; 800Ft) across the road, both of which also have thermal pools. In winter, wallowing in the neighbouring outdoor **thermal baths** (Termálfürdő: Oct–April daily 7am–6pm; 900Ft) becomes the favoured pastime. There are indoor thermal baths just north of Széchenyi tér (see p.404). A less crowded place to get some fresh air is the **botanical garden** (Fűvészkert; April–Oct 10am–6pm, Nov–March 9am–4pm; 300Ft) at the end of the #70 bus line.

There are various opportunities for **excursions** from the city, using buses leaving from Mars tér. Tourinform has information about **bird-watching** expeditions to the Fehér-tó Nature Reserve, a haven for 250 kinds of migratory birds, as well as **horse-riding** trips, **angling**, **boating**, **hiking** and **cycling** tours, and even an **archery course** at Ópusztaszer (see p.398).

The Southern Plain beyond the Tisza

The **Southern Plain** east of the Tisza is sunbaked and dusty, with small towns that bore the brunt of the Turkish occupation and often suffered from droughts, giving rise to such paranoia that "witches" were burned for "blowing the clouds away" or "selling the rain to the Turks". Resettled by diverse ethnic groups under Habsburg auspices, they later attracted dispossessed Magyars from Transylvania, who displaced the existing communities of Swabians, Serbs, Slovaks and Romanians. In the 1950s, geologists scoured the region for oil, but almost every borehole struck thermal springs instead, hence the numerous **spas** in this region. The most attractive towns are **Hódmezővásárhely**, **Gyula** and **Szarvas**, while the famous stud farm at **Mezőhegyes** is another attraction.

Approaches to the region are largely determined by where you cross the river. Crossing at Szeged, the main trunk route heads towards Békéscsaba. Csongrád, further upriver, marks the start of a less clear-cut itinerary which might include Szarvas. The more northerly route from Szolnok to Debrecen is covered under the Northern Plain (see p.416).

East from Szeged

Heading on from Szeged there are two basic routes: northeast towards Békéscsaba via **Hódmezővásárhely**, or southeast through **Makó** to the Romanian border. Counting the lovely park at nearby **Mártely**, Hódmezővásárhely is better endowed with sights than Makó, but the latter is closer to the stud farm at **Mezőhegyes**, with its horse-riding opportunities.

Hódmezővásárhely

HÓDMEZŐVÁSÁRHELY's tongue-twisting name can be translated as "marketplace of the beaver's field", though it's disputed whether the *hód-* prefix really derives from the Magyar word for "beaver". That aside, this long-established market town has the distinction of being the second-largest municipality in Hungary, incorporating several distant settlements. It's an appealing little town, with some worthwhile museums and plenty of fine architecture to admire. Otherwise the best time to visit is the **St Stephen celebrations** around August 20, four days of events, including a craft market and fireworks. The other major annual event is the **Shepherd Contest** (Juhászverseny), a four-day animal fair held in April on the northeast edge of town, which is more than just a farming get-together, with horse displays, crafts fairs and entertainments.

The Town

Most of the town's sights are located around the grand main square, Kossuth tér, and the street leading north, Szántó Kovács János utca. Kossuth tér is dignified by an eighteenth-century **Calvinist Church** and an imposing **town hall** (Mon–Fri 8am–3pm), whose magnificent banqueting hall is hung with pictures of local heroes and historical figures; ask the porter who will let you visit if the hall is free. On the other side of the square is a huge bank topped with a four-metre statue of Mercury, and the **Fekete Sas ("Black Eagle") Hotel**, a grand, vanilla-coloured edifice where merchants once gathered to trade agricultural products from all over the Balkans, storing their money in the bank and gambling the profits in the former casino opposite. It is not actually a hotel at all, but is a venue for important functions – you can, though, pop your head in and have a look.

On Szőnyi utca around the side of the town hall, the **Alföldi Gallery** (Tues & Wed 10am–4pm, Thurs–Sun 10am–5pm; 200Ft) exhibits scenes of *puszta* life by local artist János Tornyai, an oeuvre recently enhanced by the discovery of 700 canvases in a Budapest attic. Work by other local artists hangs in the **Tornyai János Museum** at Szántó Kovács János utca 16, north of Kossuth tér (Tues & Wed 10am–4pm, Thurs–Sun 10am–5pm; 150Ft); its archeological collection includes a 5000-year-old statue of a fertility goddess known as "the Venus of Kökénydomb". Across the street stands a fine Baroque **Greek Orthodox Church**, whose "Nahum iconostasis" from Mount Athos is named after an obscure seventh-century prophet – unfortunately, however, it's currently not possible to enter, such is its poor state. Still more impressive is the florid Art Nouveau **synagogue** (daily 9am–2pm) on Szent István tér, east of Kossuth tér, both the interior and exterior of which have been beautifully restored to the 1906 design of Gyula Müller. To the rear of the synagogue is a small exhibition commemorating those from Hódmezővásárhely who died in the Holocaust.

Hódmezővásárhely is renowned for its **pottery**, and each district of the town has a different style. The most distinctive is the black pottery based on Turkish designs, fired in a manner dating back to Neolithic times. Examples are displayed in the **Csúcs Potter's House** (Tues–Sun 1–5pm; 150Ft), twenty minutes' walk north of the centre at Rákóczi utca 101, and in the **Folk Culture House**, two thatched cottages at Árpád utca 21, near the levee (Tájház; Tues–Sat 10am–5pm; 150Ft), which also displays peasant costumes and furniture. To buy pottery or watch it being made, visit the **workshop** of Sándor Ambrus, close to the centre at Lánc utca 3 (Fazekasház; Mon–Fri 10am–6pm, Sat 10am–2pm) – to get there walk east from Kossuth tér along Andrássy utca for around 500m. The town's **thermal baths** complex, south of Kossuth tér at Ady Endre utca 1, includes an outdoor thermal pool and an Olympic-size indoor pool (daily 8am–8pm; 650Ft).

Practicalities

All **trains** to Hódmezővásárhely stop at two stations: Népkert, south of the centre, and the main station to the east, both of which are connected to the centre by local buses. **Buses** from Szeged run right through the centre before terminating at the main train station rather than the intercity bus terminal, in Bocskai út, where buses from elsewhere wind up.

Tourinform at Szegfű utca 3 (entrance on Szántó Kovács János utca, 100m up the main street from Kossuth tér) has lots of good **information** (Mon–Fri 8am–4pm; ⓣ62/249-350, ⓔhodmezovasarhely@tourinform.hu), while Szeged Tourist at Szőnyi utca 1 (Mon–Fri 9am–5pm; ⓣ62/534-915, ⓔhmvhely@szegedtourist.hu) by the town hall can organize private **rooms** (❶). The best option for other **accommodation**, in a town with few possibilities, is the homely *Kenguru Panzió*, just under a kilometre north of the centre at Szántó Kovács János utca 78, opposite the watertower (ⓣ62/534-841, ⓦwww.hotels.hu/kenguru; ❷), which has lovely little rooms, as well as a sauna, solarium, heated outdoor pool and off-street parking. The alternatives are the extremely dull *Hotel Fáma*, behind the synagogue at Szeremlei utca 7 (ⓣ62/222-231; ❹), and the similarly colourless *Hotel Pelikán* next to the thermal baths at Ady Endre utca 1 (ⓣ62/245-072, ⓦwww.pelikanhotel.hu; ❹). There are dorm beds in the *Kollégium* at Hóvirág utca 1 (ⓣ62/242-011; 1500Ft per person), while another option for those with transport is the *Vándorsólyom Fogadó* (ⓣ62/535-150; ❸), a country inn 2km out along the road to Orosháza, where guests can go horse-riding. The town's **campsite** (ⓣ62/245-033; March–Oct; wooden chalets ❷) is next to the *Hotel Pelikán* by the thermal baths. The **post office** is on Kossuth tér (Mon–Fri 8am–5pm, Sat 8am–noon).

The best **restaurant** in town is the posh-looking, but inexpensive, *Bandula* at Pálffy utca 2, north of the centre near the watertower, which has an unusually varied Hungarian menu, while the vegetarian choices are better then average. A respectable second choice is the *Bagólyvár*, near the Folk Art centre at Kaszap utca 31, offering similarly bright Hungarian dishes. Hősök tere, south of Kossuth tér, is a popular place to hang out in the summer, with two **bars** that both have terraces running under the trees: the *Hordó Pub*, where you can also get pizza; and the *Casino Söröző*, which offers beer, food, pool tables and darts. If you're coming from Szeged, check out the Hódmezővásárhely section of the *Szegedi Est* listings magazine for nightlife.

Mártély

From Hódmezővásárhely regular buses run 10km northwest to the village of **Mártély** beside a backwater of the Tisza, with boats for rent, hand-woven baskets for sale and a gorgeous **bird reserve** nearby. Ideal for picnics and **horse-riding**, it's a nice spot in which to relax and unwind, featuring a **campsite** (Ⓣ62/228-057; ❶), with chalets (❷) and apartments (❸). In the first weekend of August the village's peace is disturbed by the *Mártélyi Kavalkád* festival, when there's a fair, music and other events.

Makó and Mezőhegyes

Aside from being the "onion capital" of Hungary, the faded town of **MAKÓ**, 32km south of Hódmezővásárhely on the Romanian border, is notable for its **therapeutic baths** in radioactive Maros mud, and for being the birthplace of Joseph Pulitzer, who won fame as a journalist and publisher in America in the nineteenth century and founded the Pulitzer Prize. It was here, too, that the poet Attila József was sent to school after his mother died, had his first verses published, and made several attempts to commit suicide between 1912 and 1913 – he finally succeeded in 1937 when he threw himself under a train (see p.402). His former domicile is now the **Attila Memorial House** at Kazinczy utca 6 (Epersit Ház; daily 9am–4pm; 150Ft), while his name graces the **Attila József Museum** on the corner of Kazinczy and Megyeház utca (daily 9am–4pm; 200Ft); a typical collection of local paintings and artefacts, this museum also documents the history of Makó's onion trade. More interesting is the handful of dwellings in the yard, containing various agricultural implements and wooden contraptions used for onion harvesting. Two buildings worth tracking down are the crenellated **Orthodox Synagogue**, near the bus station at Eötvös utca 15, and the **Onion House**, hidden away on Posta utca, just behind Széchenyi tér. Built in 1998, it's a typically outlandish structure by Imre Makovecz (see p.172), the dome indeed resembling the top half of an onion, and flanked by four gherkin-shaped glass pillars. The inside, which is a theatre, is no less unusual, the roof resembling something like an upturned hull of a ship – ask at reception if you want to have a look. The **thermal baths** are a five-minute walk west of Széchenyi tér on Szép utca (Mon–Fri 8am–7pm, Sat & Sun 11am–7pm; 600Ft). The town's largest annual event is, naturally enough, the **Onion Festival** in mid-September, with a procession and various events on a stage at the western end of town.

From the **bus station** it's a ten-minute walk south to the main square, Széchenyi tér, while the **train station** lies about 500m in the opposite direction, on Lonovics sugár út. There's lots of **information** available from Tourinform, located inside the town hall at Széchenyi tér 22 (June–Aug daily 8am–6pm, Sept–May Mon–Fri 8am–4pm; Ⓣ62/210-708, Ⓔmako@tourinform.hu). The uninspiring **accommodation** possibilities boil down to the very basic, and not particularly good-value, *Bástya Hotel* at Szegedi utca 2 (Ⓣ & Ⓕ62/214-224; ❸); the friendly *Karaván Panzió* in an old town house ten minutes' walk further west at Szegedi utca 16 (Ⓣ62/219-912; ❸); and the *Kerekes Pension*, beyond the museums east of the centre at Megyeház utca 37 (Ⓣ62/216-687; ❸). There's also a pleasant **campsite** (Ⓣ62/211-914; May–Sept) beside the River Maros, 500m out towards Szeged, which has a pool and chalets charmingly equipped with old peasant furniture (❷). The old Korona Hotel building in the centre of Széchenyi tér now houses a fine **restaurant** and coffee house.

From Makó regular buses make the thirty-kilometre journey northeast to **MEZŐHEGYES**, home to a stud farm for breeding Lippizaner horses, founded in 1785. Today the **stud farm** breeds **Gidrán and Nonius horses**, the latter having been introduced from Normandy in 1810 to produce resilient cavalry chargers. There is a covered **riding school** offering horse or carriage rides (1800Ft/3000Ft per hour respectively), and you can stay at the *Hotel Nónius* in the same complex (Ⓣ68/467-321, Ⓦwww.hotels.hu/nonius; ❹), which also organizes visits to the stables. A tour of the buildings and coach museum costs 2000Ft, and has to be booked in advance though the hotel.

Békéscsaba and around

Travelling by road from Szeged to Debrecen, you're almost bound to pass through **BÉKÉSCSABA**, the "sausage capital" of Hungary. While carnivores might be attracted by its Kolbász Sausage Festival, a more compelling reason for a stopover is to visit the old border fortress town of **Gyula**, a far livelier place, with one of the hottest baths in Hungary. As Gyula is only 20km from Békéscsaba, you can easily get there and back by bus in a day.

Settled by the Magyars at the time of the land-taking, the region around Békéscsaba was left virtually devoid of life by the Turkish wars and the War of Independence, until it was revived by settlers from all over the Habsburg Empire, making it the most ethnically diverse town in eighteenth-century Hungary. The town itself was rebuilt by Slovaks, whose characteristic folk costumes and handicrafts are exhibited in an ornate **Slovak House** at Garay utca 21 (Szlovák Tájház; Tues–Sun 10am–noon & 2–4pm; 150Ft), which you can find by bearing off the main Szent István tér along Baross utca, and turning right.

Other oddments relating to the Slovaks can be found in the **Munkácsy Mihály Museum** at Széchenyi utca 9, a short way off the square along the Gyula road (Tues–Sun: April–Nov 10am–6pm; Dec–March 10am–4pm; 200Ft). The museum is named after the nineteenth-century Romantic painter Mihály Munkácsy (1844–1900), several of whose dark landscapes and historical pictures are displayed here. Better still is a fine ethnographic collection representing the multifarious settlers in the region, with German furniture, Slovak embroidery and clothing, Romanian and Serbian Orthodox icons, and some jewellery and woodcarvings courtesy of the Roma, all on display. Munkácsy actually spent much of his time as a teenager at Gyulai út 5, 100m along the road, in what is now the **Munkácsy Memorial House**, (Tues–Fri 9am–4pm, Sat 10am–4pm; 150Ft). This fine whitewashed porticoed domicile contains a far more representative sample of Munkácsy's work, in addition to some splendid period furniture. If you feel like a wallow, the **Árpád thermal baths** are on the east bank of the canal at Árpád Sor 3 (daily 6am–6pm; mid-June to mid-Aug till 9pm; 850Ft); bus #8 runs fairly close by.

If you're here in late October and have a strong stomach you could take in the **Kolbász Sausage Festival**, which celebrates *kolbász* – a crude but tasty salami-style sausage – as well as Békéscsaba's role in the meat-processing industry. Folk music and dancing events are accompanied by demonstrations of pig-slaughtering and sausage-making.

Practicalities

From the **train and bus stations** on the southern edge of town, bus #1, #1G, #2 or #7 can get you to the start of the pedestrian stretch of Andrássy út, from where it's fifteen minutes' walk to Szent István Tér. Here you'll find Tourinform at no. 9 (Mon–Fri 9am–5pm; ⓣ66/441-261, ⓔbekescsaba@tourinform.hu), and Ibusz next door (Mon–Fri 8am–4pm; ⓣ66/328-428, ⓔi043@ibusz.hu), who can help with private rooms (❷). The **post office** is across the road at Szabadság tér 1–3 (Mon–Fri 8am–6pm, Sat 8am–noon).

Aside from private rooms, dormitory beds at weekends and in the summer (900–1500Ft per person, booked through Ibusz) are the cheapest **accommodation**. The choice of hotels is limited to the *Fiume*, a restored prewar hotel across from Tourinform at Szent István tér 2 (ⓣ66/443-243, ⓦwww.hotelfiume.hu; ❺), and the appreciably more modern, and much better value, *Szlovák Hotel* (ⓣ66/441-750, ⓔszlovakhaz@mail.globonet.hu; ❹), five minutes' walk north of Szent István tér at Kossuth tér 10. For **eating**, try your luck at the canalside *Halászcsárda* fish restaurant, 200m east of Szent István tér at Árpád Sor 1, or there's more simple fare at the *Speed Pizzeria*, just off Szent István tér on Hunyadi tér, which also has a good choice of sweet and savoury pancakes. For drinks, the *Mozart café* is a quiet little bolt hole at Andrássy út 4, while the *Narancs Klub*, across the square from the *Fiume*, is a hangout for young people, with occasional live music.

Gyula

GYULA, en route to the Romanian border, is one of the prettiest towns in the Southern Great Plain region, strong in Art Nouveau buildings and with the most to show for its history. Named after a Hungarian tribal chieftain, the town was heavily fortified by the Angevins but quickly succumbed to the Turks, who held its castle for nearly 130 years. After the Turks were evicted, Gyula was rebuilt as a twin town, with Hungarian Magyargyula on one side of the Élővíz Canal, and German–Romanian Németgyula on the other. Though this distinction ceased long ago, you'll still hear German and Romanian spoken in town: Germans come here for the thermal baths and Romanians to trade. Gyula's lively character, however, is largely due to its sizeable student population, rather than its tourists.

Arrival, information and accommodation

The **bus station** is a five-minute walk south of the centre on Vásárhelyi Pál utca, while the **train station** is a fifteen-minute walk north of the centre at the end of Béke sugárút. Tourinform is located at Kossuth utca 7 (mid-June to mid-Sept daily 9am–5pm; mid-Sept to mid-June Mon–Fri 9am–5pm; ⓣ66/561-680, ⓔbekes-m@tourinform.hu). The **post office** is on Eszperantó tér (Mon–Fri 8am–7pm, Sat 8am–noon), and there's **Internet access** at Fókusz Pont (Mon–Fri 9am–noon & 1–6pm, Sat 9am–noon), at the end of Várfürdő utca near the baths.

Accommodation abounds in Gyula, with a large number of modern and unappealing hotels (❹) near the baths. Private rooms (❷) are available through Békéstourist at Vásárhelyi Pál utca 2 (Mon–Thurs 8am–4.30pm, Fri 8am–3.30pm; ⓣ66/463-028), and Gyulatourist, just across the bridge at Eszperantó tér 1 (June–Aug Mon–Fri 8am–5pm, Sat 9am–noon; Sept–May Mon–Fri 8am–5pm; ⓣ66/463-026, ⓔgytour@gyula.hungary.net), who also handle beds in colleges during the summer.

Best of the town-centre **hotels** is the *Hotel Corvin* at Jókai utca 9–11 (ⓣ66/362-044; ⓦwww.hotels.hu/corvin_hotel; ❺), a neat, compact place with shiny, green-coloured rooms. Slighty cheaper is the *Hotel Aranykereszt*, Eszperantó tér 2 (Ⓣ66/463-194; ❸), which is a bit dated but retains a modicum of character, and the canalside *Halászcsárda Panzió*, out towards the baths at Part utca 3 (Ⓣ & Ⓕ66/466-303; ❹), which has elementary furnishings but is homely. *Termál Camping* at Szélső utca 16 (Ⓣ66/463-551) has chalets (❶) and a motel (❷), but is almost 1km from the castle, so you might prefer the closer *Mark Camping* at Vár utca 5 (Ⓣ66/463-380). Both are open year round.

The Town

All the town's sights are within fifteen minutes' walk of the small squares that comprise downtown Gyula, either side of the canal. West of Erkel tér, the **Ladics House** at Jókai utca 4 (Ladics ház; Tues 1–5pm, Wed–Sat 9am–5pm, Sun 9am–1pm; 200Ft) is a fascinating nineteenth-century bourgeois home preserved down to the last antimacassar, though, unfortunately, lacking any information in English. Further out in the same direction, the **Erkel Museum** at Ápor Vilmos tér 7 (Erkel Ferenc Emlékház; Tues 1–5pm, Wed–Sat 9am–5pm, Sun 9am–1pm; 200Ft) pays homage to Ferenc Erkel, composer of two of Hungary's most famous operas, *Hunyadi László* (1844) and *Bánk bán* (1861), and the Hungarian national anthem; exhibits in this, Erkel's birthplace, include musical scores, personal effects, and his piano. The **György Kohán Museum** at Béke sugárút 35, just north of the centre (Kohán Képtár; Tues 1–5pm, Wed–Sat 9am–5pm, Sun 9am–1pm; 200Ft), exhibits some of the 3000 works that its namesake bequeathed to his home town – mostly bold depictions of horses, women and houses.

Two further attractions lie out along Kossuth utca, to the east. At no. 17 is an exhibition hall called the **Dürer Terem** (Tues 1–5pm, Wed–Sat 9am–5pm, Sun 9am–1pm; 150Ft), named after the German artist Albrecht Dürer, whose jeweller father migrated from Gyula to Germany. (Their original surname was Ajtossy, from the Hungarian for "door"; Dürer has an identical root in the German word *Tür*.) Strangely, though, there is nothing related to its namesake, just a hoard of medieval weaponry. Close by stands Gyula's fourteenth-century **Castle** (Vár), an imposing rectangular bulk and the only brick fortress to have survived in Hungary; its walls are 3m thick and originally incorporated every defensive feature known in Europe at that time. Ongoing renovation of the interior will eventually result in a museum exhibiting the castle's history. For the time being you can visit the Powder Tower, which is now a wine bar, while in July and August the courtyard provides a stage for the **Castle Theatre** (Várszinház; Ⓦwww.c3.hu/~casteatr), which presents historical dramas, opera, jazz and classical and folk music – there is a second stage by the lake outside the castle walls. Erkel used to compose in the park beside the castle under the shade of an oak known as "**Erkel's Tree**", which still stands. On the north side of the castle is a **memorial to the Arad Martyrs**, commemorating the thirteen Hungarian generals executed by Austrian troops in Arad, just across the border in Romania, on October 6, 1849. Nearby are the popular **Castle Baths** (Várfürdő; daily 8am–8pm, 950Ft), a complex of 22 thermal pools ranging in temperature from 46°C to 75°C – the latter can only be endured after you've acclimatized yourself, and then only for a very short time. There is also a large outdoor pool, likewise full of peaty-coloured water, where people lark about.

Eating and drinking

For a relatively small town, there's a decent range of places to **eat and drink** in Gyula. Pick of the **restaurants** is the *Kisködmön* at Városház utca 15 (daily noon–midnight), a genuinely enjoyable place where you can tuck in to tasty and beautifully presented Hungarian food amidst a very folksy interior design, with waitresses suitably attired in peasant garb. The *Sörpince* beer cellar at Kossuth ter 1 has good grilled meats alongside big jugs of beer, or there's the decent *Skorpió Pizzeria* at Jókai utca 17 (Mon–Sat 11am–midnight, Sun 4pm–midnight), and the *Maestro* at Kossuth utca 3, which has fairly standard Hungarian offerings down in its cosy cellar surrounds.

Don't miss the gorgeous *Százéves Cukrászda* at Erkel tér 1 (daily 10am–6pm, Fri & Sat till 7pm), which is the **oldest patisserie** in Hungary after *Ruszwurm*'s in Budapest, open since 1840. Furnished in the Biedermeier style and painted in shades of crème de menthe and chocolate, the "Old Lady", as it is locally known, includes a small museum of pastry-chef's utensils. Run by the same management is the excellent *Kézműves* coffee house at Városház utca 21 (Mon–Fri 7am–8pm, Sat & Sun 10am–8pm). There are several loud drinking spots along Kossuth utca, including *Bols Café* at no. 1 and *Bacardi* at no. 3, while the *Macho Pub*, close by at Városház utca 1, has a more party-like atmosphere. For information on nightlife, check out the freebie **listings** publication *Békési Est*, which has a section on Gyula.

Csongrád and Szarvas

An alternative route across the Tisza is via Csongrád, east of Kiskunfélegyháza, a good base for visiting Szarvas before joining the main route to Debrecen at Kisújszállás. Although neither town will set the pulse racing, both have a couple of worthwhile sights, and frequent **buses** mean that you needn't stay long if they don't appeal. Trains, on the other hand, are not much use here unless you strike lucky or juggle timetables. The country roads around here are excellent for **cycling**, especially in the late summer when the verges are awash with purple sea lavender.

Csongrád

The town of **CSONGRÁD** derives its name from the "Black Castle" (Czernigrad) erected at the confluence of the Tisza and Körös by the Bulgar princes who conquered this region in the early ninth century, before the coming of the Magyars. Though long since vanished, it lends its name to the Öregvár (Old Castle) district, a protected folk architecture area some twenty minutes' walk east of the modern centre (or bus #2). Its narrow winding streets are lined with black-and-white 200-year-old thatched **fishermen's houses**, restored to a state that their original owners would scarcely recognize. Many are still fully equipped and are rent out as guesthouses (see p.414), while one **Tájház**, at Gyökér utca 1, displays vintage domestic artefacts *in situ* (May–Oct Tues–Sun 1–5pm; free).

In the 1840s Count Széchenyi organized an association of riparian landowners with the aim of making the Tisza navigable, curtailing its floods, and reclaiming nearly 4000 square kilometres of swampland. The embankments were thrown up by thousands of day-labourers who wandered from site to site with their barrows. Their lives are commemorated in the **Tari László Museum** at Iskola utca 2, just off Kossuth tér in the centre of town (Tues–Fri 1–5pm, Sat 8am–noon, Sun 8am–5pm; 200Ft). Across from the museum, in the centre of Kossuth tér, stands the Baroque **Church of the Virgin Mary**, worth a look for its richly adorned interior. Most notable is the high altar, with a painting of the Assumption and statues of saints Stephen and László either side, and some

Suicides

Csongrád county has the unenviable distinction of the highest **suicide** rate in Hungary, fifty percent higher than the national average. This is impressive in a country that for many years topped the world rankings, although its suicide rate has fallen from its 1980s peak and Hungary has now been knocked off top position by Lithuania, Russia, Estonia and Belarus. Nobody is sure why the suicide rate is so high, but theories are legion. Many Hungarians believe it's in their genes, citing the old saying that "the Magyar takes his pleasures sadly" and the fact that their ethnic cousins, the Finns, are also high up in the suicide charts. Both countries have many isolated dwellings and a high incidence of alcoholism, and winter on the Great Plain can be as harsh as in Finland, with the *puszta* as monotonous as the Karelian forests. Yet while both countries share a prevalence of suicide in rural areas, other factors are specific to Hungary. Besides the local custom of parading the deceased through the streets in an open coffin – thought to encourage attention-seekers – Hungarian history and culture is full of suicides, from military heroes like Zrínyi to the poet Attila József (whose death under a train at Lake Balaton is emulated by several people every year), and 17-year-old Csilla Molnár, who killed herself shortly after becoming Miss Hungary in 1986. Some cases are simply known for their oddity: for one woman in Kaposvár, the final straw was the death of Bobby in the TV series *Dallas*.

splendid ceiling frescoes of the Annunciation, the Nativity, and St Stephen offering the crown to Mary. Like most towns on the Plain, Csongrád has its own outdoor **thermal baths**, located on Dob utca around the corner from the *Hotel Tisza* (Mon–Thurs & Sun 7am–8pm, Fri & Sat till 10pm; 450Ft).

Practicalities

Whereas it's a twenty-minute walk along Zrínyi utca from the **train station** to the centre (which has shifted from the Öregvár since Széchenyi's day), the **bus terminal** lies only a couple of blocks from Fő utca and Szentháromság tér. Tourinform is located on the ground floor of the cultural centre (Művelődési központ) at Szentháromság tér 8 (Mon–Fri: mid-June to mid-Sept 9am–5pm, mid-Sept to mid-June 8am–4pm; ⓣ63/570-325, ⓔcsongrad@tourinform.hu), and can supply all the **information** you need. For **accommodation** there's the very ordinary and overpriced *Hotel Tisza* at Fő utca 23 (ⓣ63/483-594, ⓔhoteltisza@vnet.hu; ❺), or the older but fairly priced *Hotel Erzsébet* at no. 3 (ⓣ63/483-960, ⓕ570-120; ❷–❸), which has a mix of rooms with and without television and shower. More appealingly, between May and September, you can rent fishermen's cottages (❹) sleeping two or four people; a couple have heating and are available in winter too – contact reception in the *Hotel Erzsébet* for details. The pleasant *Köröstoroki* **campsite** (ⓣ63/483-631) is near the *strand* on the river 3km away, and is accessible by bus.

For **meals**, the best of an average bunch is the *Golden Horse Irish Pub*, on the way down to the Öregvár at Gróf Andrássy Gyula utca 17/a, which has a surprisingly varied menu and large portions, and the *Bohém Kávéház*, at Fő utca 20–24, whose pub-style interior is reflected in its simple food. Otherwise, there's the *Kert Vendéglő*, through the archway at Dózsa György tér 6, whose pleasant terrace backs on to the baths, or the *Csuka Csárda* at Szentesi út 1, overlooking the backwater of the Tisza.

Szarvas

SZARVAS ("Stag") feels peculiarly spacious, with a broad main street intersected by wide roads. The town was laid out like a chessboard in the eighteenth century by the enlightened thinker Samuel Tessedik, who served as a Lutheran priest in the town until his death in 1820. The **Tessedik Samuel Museum**, to the west of town near the bridge at Vajda Péter utca 1 (Tues–Sun 10am–4pm; 200Ft), features a better than average display of local archeological finds, agricultural implements and ceramics, though, predictably, it's all in Hungarian. Like Békéscsaba and Kiskőrös, Szarvas was populated by Slovak settlers after the withdrawal of the Turks in 1722, athough the domestic items and folk costumes on show in the **Slovak House** at Hoffmann utca 1 (Szlovák Tájház; April–Oct Tues–Sun 11am–5pm; 200Ft) date from the late nineteenth century. Devotees of national tat shouldn't miss the sculpture fountain by the bridge at the western end of town, which has St Stephen's crown resting on top of what looks like a leaking pipe. A new attraction in the town – and one that brings in hordes of school parties – is the kilometre-long **Historical Memorial Way** (Történelmi Emlékút), yet another piece of Trianon nostalgia: starting from a Transylvanian-style gateway in Szent István park down by the backwater of the Kőrös, eighteen wooden sculptures, symbolizing the stations of Hungarian history up to the present day, lead up to a small windmill marking the very centre of pre-World War I Hungary.

The town's principal draw, however, is the **Arboretum**, a couple of kilometres out along the road to Mezőtúr, beside a backwater of the River Körös (daily mid-March to mid-Nov 8am–6pm, mid-Nov to mid-March 8am–3pm; closed Dec 15 to Jan 5; 300Ft). This 82-hectare park contains 1600 different plants in its five arboreal collections. The oldest of the five is the *Pepikert* (Pepi Garden), laid out by Count Pál "Pepi" Bolza in emulation of the grounds of Schönbrunn Palace in Vienna. You can try your hand at catching jumping fish on excellent **boat trips** (40min; 300Ft per person) along the Körös backwater past the sights of the park and the Memorial Way; ask at the entrance of the Arboretum for departure times.

Practicalities

Tourinform at Kossuth tér 3 – the entrance is actually on Szabadság utca (June–Sept Mon–Fri 9am–6pm, Sat 9am–1pm; Oct–May Mon–Fri 9am–4pm; Ⓣ66/311-140, Ⓔszarvas@tourinform.hu) – can furnish you with any **information** about the town. If you wish to **stay**, there's the very comfortably furnished *Lux Panzió* down the road from Tourinform at Szabadság utca 35 (Ⓣ66/313-417, Ⓦwww.aqua-lux.hu; ❹), while in the park to the west of town on the banks of the backwater is the relaxing *Liget Panzió and Camping* (Ⓣ66/311-954, Ⓦwww.ligetpanzio.hu; ❺), with chalets sleeping four (❺), and its own swimming pool. For **meals**, the *Lux Panzió* has a good restaurant, while across the bridge west of town both the *Halászcsárda* and the *Ciprus Fogadó*, facing each other, have terraces looking onto the water. The *Kiszely Cukrászda* next to Tourinform serves coffee, cakes and ice cream.

The biggest events in the year are the **National Pastor Meeting and Piper Festival** held in Erzsébet liget in July, which brings together a lot of animals and music, and **Plum Day** (Szilvanap) in mid-September, when Fő tér is awash with *pálinka* and *szilvagombóc* (plum dumplings).

The Northern Plain beyond the Tisza

The **Northern Plain** has more to offer than the south, with **Hortobágy National Park**, the friendly city of **Debrecen** and picturesque villages around the headwaters of the River Tisza. In July and August, you can catch colourful **festivals** at Nagykálló, Hortobágy and Debrecen, while in September there's a carnival at Nyíregyháza. The region is also noted for its **pilgrimages**, and long history of religious fervour. Debrecen is the centre of Hungarian Protestantism, dubbed "the Calvinist Rome", the village of Máriapócs is a focus for Greek Catholics and Roma believers, while the tomb of the "miracle rabbi" at Nagykálló is a vestige of the rich Hasidic culture that existed here before the Holocaust.

Szolnok

Sited at the confluence of the Zagyva and Tisza rivers, **SZOLNOK** has never been allowed to forget its importance as a bridgehead. Once the Mongols had stormed its castle in the thirteenth century, there was nothing to stop them riding on to Buda. In the last century, the town's seizure by the Red Army foretold its inexorable advance in 1944 and again in 1956, when it crushed the Uprising. Given this history, it's not surprising that most of Szolnok consists of unsightly postwar blocks, or that the population turned out to jeer the Soviets goodbye in 1990.

Along the main axis through the centre, the **János Damjanich Museum** at Kossuth tér 4 (Tues–Sun: April–Oct 10am–6pm; Nov–March 10am–4pm; 700Ft for the whole museum, or 200Ft for each section, free on Tues) bears the name of the general who trounced the Habsburg army just up the road in 1849. Of the four separate sections located within, two stand out: the archeological section, displaying some fabulous grave goods, including colourful beaded jewellery, statuettes and ceramic jugs and vases; while the no less impressive ethnographic section features some splendid folk art, such as regional peasant attire, viticultural and agricultural implements, and cottage furnishings, many of which are painted a striking "kunkék" blue, a colour peculiar to this region. The two remaining sections focus on nineteenth-century interiors and work by the Szolnok Artists' Colony, whose leading members were László Mednyánsky (1852–1919) and Adolf Fényes (1867–1945).

Heading south from the centre towards the banks of the Tisza, several Art Nouveau buildings on Szapáry utca presage Szolnok's former **synagogue**, a magnificent creation by Lipót Baumhorn in the last years of the nineteenth century. Gutted during the war like so many others, it was turned into an art gallery in the 1960s, and retains some original features (Tues–Sun 9am–5pm). On Templom út nearby stands a handsome Baroque Franciscan church (Belvárosi Nagytemplom), where **organ concerts** are held in August. Heading in the opposite direction along Sóház út you come to Szolnok's striking modern **theatre** in Tisza park.

With more time to kill, it's worth investigating the **Tabán district** beside the Zagyva, a twenty-minute walk east along the main street and off to the left. One of the oldest parts of Szolnok, it used to be a poor quarter of fishermen and bargees, but is now a quiet residential area. As a reminder of the past, one thatched house on the river side, at Tabán utca 24, has been preserved as a **Tájház** (May–Sept Thurs–Sun 1–5pm; 150Ft), with its interior as it would have looked in the 1930s, when fisherman Sándor Kovács and his family lived here; the adults slept on the bed and their six children on the dirt floor.

Practicalities

Szolnok's **bus station** is on Ady Endre utca, the street running parallel to the main thoroughfare, Baross Gábor út, and its **train station** is west of the city centre on Jubileumi tér (bus #24, #8, #7, #6 or #15). The city is sited along the main road and rail line from Budapest to Debrecen, and serves as a terminus for trains to Kiskunfélegyháza via Lakitelek, and a nexus for buses to Jászberény, Cegléd, Tiszafüred and other towns on the Plain.

You can get **maps** and **information** from the ever-helpful Tourinform, across from the bus station at Ságvári körút 4 (mid-June to mid-Sept Mon–Fri 8am–4pm, Sat & Sun 9am–5pm; mid-Sept to mid-June Mon–Thurs 8am–4pm, Fri 8am–3pm; ⓣ56/424-803, ⓔszolnok-m@tourinform.hu). **Internet access** is available at Matávpont at Baross utca 16.

There's a decent spread of **accommodation** in town, with the three best hotels located down near the banks of the Tisza. The *Tisza Hotel* at Verseghy park 2 (ⓣ56/371-155; ❻) is a wonderfully old-fashioned place with its own thermal bath and a fine patio overlooking the river. A little further along at Sóház ut 4, the cracking *Hotel Sóház* (ⓣ56/516-560, ⓦwww.sohazhotel.hu; ❺–❻) has ultra-modern air conditioned rooms equipped with a small kitchen area. Continuing west, at Mária utca 25, is the very pricey *Hozam Hotel* (ⓣ56/510-530, ⓦwww.hozamhotel.hu; ❼), a plush four-star apartment hotel in a quiet, leafy street with off-street parking, pool and sauna. A more affordable alternative to these three is the *Pelikán Hotel*, smack bang in the centre at Jászkürt út 1 (ⓣ56/423-855, ⓦwww.hotel-pelikan.hu; ❹) – the ghastly looking exterior actually conceals pleasantly refurbished rooms. Szolnok's **campsite** (ⓣ56/424-403) is on Tiszaligeti sétány in the neglected resort area across the river (accessible by bus #15), where you'll also find the open-air **thermal baths**. Ibusz at Szapáry utca 24 (Mon–Fri 8am–5pm, Sat 9am–1pm; ⓣ56/423-602) handles private rooms (❶).

For Hungarian **food**, the restaurant in the *Tisza Hotel* has a grand ambience and a riverside summer garden, while the fairly formal *Galéria*, at the end of Szapáry utca by the synagogue, offers arguably the best food in town. There's more atmosphere, however, at the *Caffé Alexander Pizzeria* (Mon–Thurs & Sun 9am–10pm, Fri & Sat 9am–midnight), at Táncsics utca 15 opposite the theatre, and the lively *Bajnok* at Hősök tere 3. The *Irish Pub* at Szapáry utca 24 is a lively **drinking** place, and you can get coffee and cakes at the *Tünde Cukrászda* (Mon–Thurs & Sun 9am–10pm, Fri & Sat 9am–midnight), housed in a building a few doors along with fine floral Art Nouveau decorations on its upper floors. For **nightlife**, try the *Matróz Disco* down by the river on Tiszaparti sétány 7 (Wed, Fri & Sat 9pm–5am), or the studenty *Moment Klub* (Tues & Thurs–Sat from 8pm) across the river in Tiszaliget. The *könnyű* section of the free weekly *Szolnoki Est* has **listings** information on events in town. One of the region's more intriguing festivals is the **Szolnok Goulash Festival** (gulyasfesztival) during the first or second weekend of September, when the town is taken over by food and wine to celebrate the nation's most famous dish.

Debrecen

Once upon a time, **DEBRECEN** was the site of Hungary's greatest livestock fair, and foreigners tended to be snooty about "this vast town of unsightly buildings", with its thatched cottages and a main street that became "one liquid mass of mud" when it rained, "so that officers quartered on one side were obliged to mount their horses and ride across to have dinner on the other". Even so, none denied the significance of Debrecen (pronounced "*Deb*-ret-zen"), both economically and as the fount of **Hungarian Calvinism**. From the sixteenth century onwards there wasn't a generation of lawyers, doctors or theologians that didn't include graduates from its Calvinist College.

Now the second most populous city in Hungary (around 200,000), Debrecen is still renowned for its university and teacher-training colleges, but for all its past grandeur there's a strong sense that the region is missing out on incoming Western investment. However, using his good connections with central government, the Fidesz mayor has in recent years arranged huge grants for beautifying the city, and is pressing for the completion of the M3 motorway to nearby Nyiregyháza, which would open up the region.

More pertinently for visitors, Debrecen hosts two major **festivals**, plus a mega Flower Carnival on August 20; its restaurants, pubs and nightlife are as good as any on the Plain; and the city makes an ideal base for **excursions** to Hortobágy National Park and the Hajdúság and Nyírség regions.

Arrival, information and accommodation

The **train station** is on Wesselényi tér, at the bottom of the main street Piac utca, while the **bus station** is west of the centre off Széchenyi utca, from where it's a ten-minute walk into the centre. There's stacks of **information** available from the two Tourinform offices, the main one at Piac utca 20 (mid-May to mid-Sept daily 8am–8pm; mid-Sept to mid-May Mon–Fri 9am–5pm; ⓣ52/412-250, ⓦwww.debrecen.hu), and a smaller one at Kálvin tér 2a (Mon–Fri 9am–6pm, Sat 9am–1pm). The helpful Mezon youth/student office and centre at Batthyány utca 2b (Mon–Fri 10am–6pm, Sat 10am–1pm; ⓣ52/415-498, ⓦwww.c3.hu/~mezon) can also assist with queries and accommodation. The **post office** is on Hatvan utca 5–9 (Mon–Fri 7am–7pm, Sat 8am–1pm) and there's **Internet access** at Datanet, Kossuth utca 8 (daily 8am–midnight).

Accommodation

Given the size of the city, Debrecen's choice of hotels is not brilliant. It's wise to make **reservations** during the annual festivals (many hotels are booked a year ahead of the Flower Carnival), though you should be able to find something at short notice the rest of the time. Ibusz, at Révész tér 2 (mid-May to mid-Sept Mon–Fri 8am–4pm, Sat 8am–noon; mid-Sept to mid-May Mon–Thurs 8am–5pm, Fri 9am–noon; ⓣ52/415-555, ⓔi045@ibusz.hu), can arrange accommodation in **college dormitories**, charging by the room, with places available on Friday and Saturday throughout the year and daily throughout July and August, and **private rooms** (❷) and flats (❹). Convenient it may be for the train station, but the very cheap and seedy *Hotel Debrecen* (❶) on Wesselényi tér is best avoided.

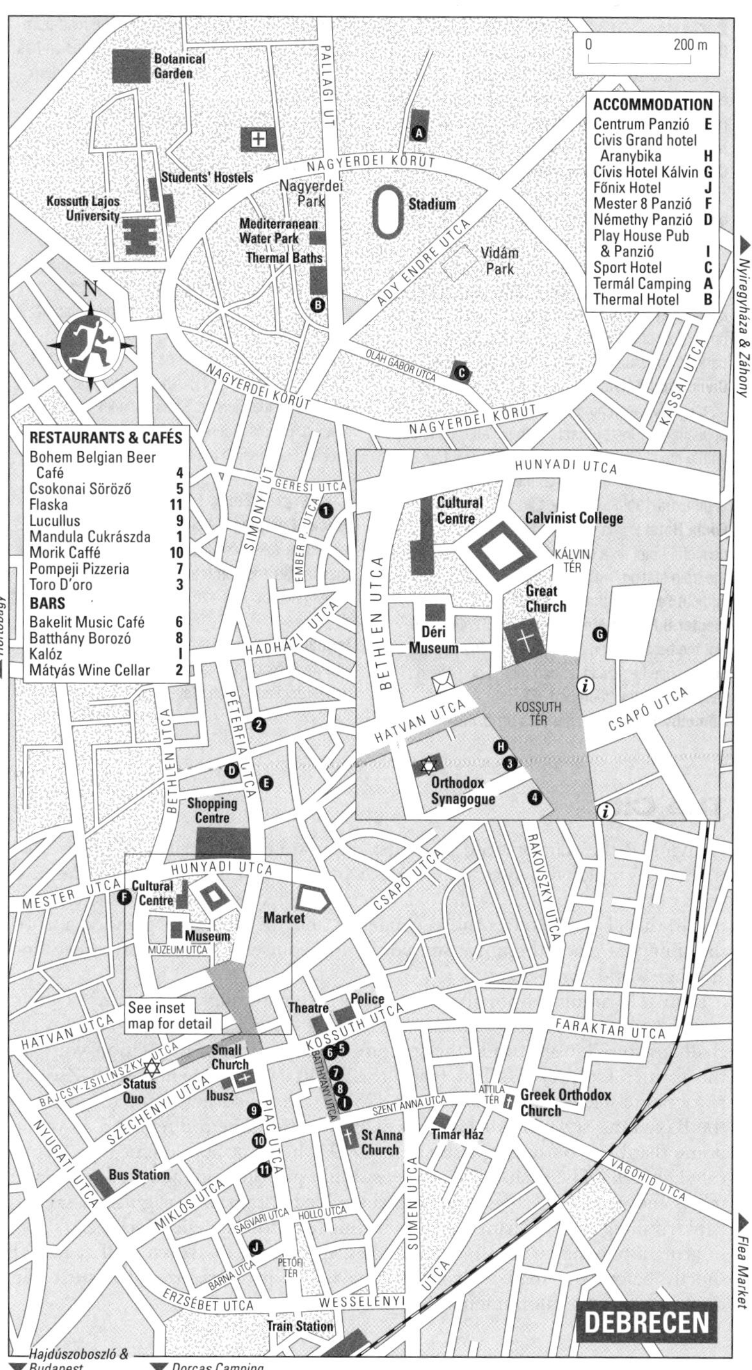

0
200 m
ACCOMMODATION
Centrum Panzió E
Civis Grand hotel Aranybika H
Cívis Hotel Kálvin G
Főnix Hotel J
Mester 8 Panzió F
Némethy Panzió D
Play House Pub & Panzió I
Sport Hotel C
Termál Camping A
Thermal Hotel B
RESTAURANTS & CAFÉS
Bohem Belgian Beer Café 4
Csokonai Söröző 5
Flaska 11
Lucullus 9
Mandula Cukrászda 1
Morik Caffé 10
Pompeji Pizzeria 7
Toro D'oro 3
BARS
Bakelit Music Café 6
Batthány Borozó 8
Kalóz I
Mátyás Wine Cellar 2
Botanical Garden
Students' Hostels
Kossuth Lajos University
Nagyerdei Park
Mediterranean Water Park
Thermal Baths
Stadium
Vidám Park
PALLAGI ÚT
NAGYERDEI KÖRÚT
ADY ENDRE UTCA
OLÁH GÁBOR UTCA
KASSAI UTCA
HUNYADI UTCA
Cultural Centre
Calvinist College
KÁLVIN TÉR
Great Church
Déri Museum
BETHLEN UTCA
HATVAN UTCA
KOSSUTH TÉR
CSAPÓ UTCA
Orthodox Synagogue
GERESI UTCA
SIMONYI ÚT
EMBER P. UTCA
HADHÁZI UTCA
PÉTERFIA UTCA
Shopping Centre
MESTER UTCA
Museum
MÚZEUM UTCA
Market
RAKOVSZKY UTCA
See inset map for detail
Theatre
Police
KOSSUTH UTCA
FARAKTAR UTCA
Small Church
BAJCSY-ZSILINSZKY UTCA
Status Quo
SZÉCHENYI UTCA
Ibusz
BATTHYÁNY UTCA
PIAC UTCA
SZENT ANNA UTCA
ATTILA TÉR
Greek Orthodox Church
St Anna Church
Timár Ház
NYUGATI UTCA
Bus Station
MIKLÓS UTCA
SÁGVÁRI UTCA
HOLLÓ UTCA
SUMEN UTCA
VÁGÓHÍD UTCA
PETŐFI TÉR
BARNA UTCA
ERZSÉBET UTCA
WESSELÉNYI UTCA
Train Station
DEBRECEN
Nyíregyháza & Záhony
Hortobágy
Flea Market
Hajdúszoboszló & Budapest
Dorcas Camping

Hotels and pensions

Centrum Panzió Péterfia utca 37A ⓣ52/416-193, ⓦwww.axelero.hu/centrum. Comfortable pension a few blocks north of the Great Church, though the rooms are rather cluttered and the decor leaves something to be desired. ❹

Civis Grand Hotel Aranybika Piac utca 11–15 ⓣ52/508-600, ⓦwww.civishotels.hu. Hungary's oldest hotel, established in 1690 (though most of today's building dates from the early twentieth century), has over 200 rooms, with those in the older wing far classier (and considerably more expensive) than those in the modern part of the hotel. Pool and sauna for guests. Protected car-parking costs an extra 1700Ft per day. ❻–❼

Cívis Hotel Kálvin Kálvin tér 4 ⓣ52/418-522, ⓦwww.civishotel.hu. Business-like establishment opposite the Great Church, with sullen rooms, each with a small kitchen area. Guests receive free use of the sauna and the pool at the Aranybika. Parking is an extra 1300Ft per day. ❻

Főnix Hotel Barna utca 17 ⓣ & ⓕ52/413-054. A peaceful hotel on a quiet street a few blocks from the train station, with old but clean rooms, with and without TV and bathroom. ❸–❹

Mester 8 Panzió Mester utca 8 ⓣ52/447-146. Not the best location going, but this friendly little guesthouse has clean, cheap rooms and a good restaurant in the courtyard. ❸

Némethy Panzió Péterfia utca 50 ⓣ52/444-480, ⓦwww.hotels.hu/nemethy. Just up the road from the *Centrum Panzió*, this terrific-value pension has bright, orange-walled rooms with smart, modern furniture. ❹

Play House Pub and Panzió Batthány utca 24–26 ⓣ52/411-252, ⓕ452-738. Pleasant guest-house with a dozen modern rooms, and which is surprisingly quiet given that it's located on the top floor of a pub. ❹

Sport Hotel Oláh Gábor utca 5 ⓣ52/514-444, ⓦwww.dbsporthotel.hu. Stylishly renovated hotel in Nagyerdei park with well-equipped rooms; guests get one free entry to the sauna, solarium and excellent gym. ❺

Thermal Hotel Nagyerdei park 1 ⓣ52/514-111, ⓦwww.aquaticum.hu. Plush four-star spa hotel attached to the thermal baths complex to the north of town. Guests receive free use of the thermal pool and swimming pool. ❼

Campsites

Dorcas Camping Vekeri tó, 6km south of town near Lake Vekeri ⓣ52/541-119. Tent-space and chalets (❶) and can organize horse-riding and angling nearby. Bus #26 from the bus station. Open all year.

Termál Camping Nagyerdei körút 102 ⓣ52/412-456. Tent-space and chalets (❷) northeast of Nagyerdei Park. Open May–Sept.

The City

Arriving at the train station, your first impressions of the city – with its busy traffic and huddled masses – may make you want to get straight on the next train out, but as you follow the old, much maligned **Piac utca** (Market Street) north, the place becomes more congenial and the buildings grander, and by the time you reach the university you'll find yourself in quiet leafy streets and another world completely.

Tram #1, running from the train station right through the centre of town to the baths and university, makes sightseeing a cinch (tickets 140Ft from the Bauhaus-style kiosk outside the station). Setting off from the station you pass the former **County Hall** at Piac utca 54, its facade crawling with Zsolnay pyrogranite statues of Haiduks (see p.425); an ornate corner house (no. 51) and the Romantic-style **Small Church**, whose bastion-like top replaced an onion dome that blew off during a storm in 1909 – hence its local name, the "Truncated church". The flesh-coloured Secessionist pile opposite, adorned with swan reliefs and statues of eagles (note, too, the gilded portal), was originally a savings bank rivalling the Gresham Building in Budapest for opulence. Debrecen's coat of arms, a phoenix arising from the ashes, appears on the **town hall** at no. 20, shortly before the road widens into the newly pedestrianized **Kossuth tér**, dominated by the monumental Great Church.

Around the Great Church

The **Great Church** (Nagytemplom; April–Nov Mon–Fri 9am–4pm, Sat 9am–noon, Sun noon–4pm; 200Ft) is an appropriately huge monument to the *Református* faith that swept through Hungary during the sixteenth century and still commands the allegiance of roughly one third of the population. Calvinism took root more strongly in Debrecen than elsewhere, as local Calvinists struck a deal with the Turks to ensure their security and forbade Catholics to settle here after 1552. In 1673, the Catholic Habsburgs deported 41 Calvinist priests (who ended up as galley slaves), but failed to shake the faith's hold on Debrecen. A reconciliation of sorts was achieved during the pope's visit in 1991, when he laid a wreath at their memorial.

The church is a dignified Neoclassical building designed by Mihály Pollack. Its typically austere interior, completely bare, accommodated the Diet of 1849 that declared Hungary's secession from the Habsburg Empire. The *Rákóczi-harang* – forged from cannons used in the Rákóczi War of Independence – is the largest **bell** in Hungary. From the tower you can get an excellent view of the city (same times; 150Ft).

Southwest of the church on the same square stands the **Grand Hotel Arany-bika** (The Golden Bull), reputedly the oldest hotel in Hungary. Although its grandeur has faded somewhat, it's worth a peek inside to see the kitschy stained glass around the walls of the potentially magnificent glass-roofed restaurant, though a better reason to visit is the old casino, now turned into the very upbeat *Génius Bar* (see p.424). In front of the hotel is an exuberant new 18-metre-wide glass and ceramic **fountain**, part of an effort to spruce up the square. Two days before its unveiling it was embroiled in controversy when a nymph representing the city of Debrecen was apparently stolen. It turned out that the council had removed it without consulting the artist, claiming that it was responding to popular outrage at the figure – though popular gossip has it that the figure offended the mayor's wife.

Around the back of the church on Kálvin tér stands the **Calvinist College** (Református Kollégium), where students were compelled to rise at 3am and be in bed by 9pm until the end of the eighteenth century. The college motto, inscribed over the entrance, is *orando et laborando* ("praying and working"). Though venerable in appearance, this is not the original college founded in 1538, but an enlarged nineteenth-century version. It was here that the Provisional National Assembly of left-wing and centre parties met under Soviet auspices late in 1944, unwittingly conferring legitimacy on the Soviet occupation. You can learn plenty about Calvinist Debrecen in the worthwhile **Calvinist College Museum** (Református Kollégium Múzeuma; Tues–Sat 9am–5pm, Sun 9am–1pm; 200Ft) located within the college. The first part of the museum offers a useful insight into the activities of those that lived and studied here, as well as a few items belonging to some of the college's most distinguished former members, such as Endre, Csokonai and Zsigmond. The second part is given over to the college's rich ecclesiastical history, comprising a sublime collection of goodies including Turkish embroidery, Renaissance-era communion jugs and vessels, and boat-shaped wooden grave markers particular to this region. There's also a beautiful painted ceiling panel from Mezőcát, typical of the kind found in churches in villages and smaller market towns of the region. You can also view the **Library**, which keeps a splendid, and voluminous, collection of fifteenth- to eighteenth-century books, copper-engraved incunabula and hand-painted atlases.

Witchcraft

The early Calvinists' hatred of popery was only exceeded by their animus towards pagan beliefs among the peasantry of the Great Plain, who regarded *táltos* (village wise men) with benevolence, while fearing *boszorkány*, their female counterparts. Until the eighteenth century, women accused of **witchcraft** were able to plead that they were beneficent *táltos* (for example Frau Bártha, who claimed to have learned *táltos* skills from her brother), but as the Calvinists' grip tightened this defence became untenable. Midwives were particularly vulnerable as it was popularly believed that the murder of a relative or newborn child was a prerequisite for acquiring their "magical" skills, but women in general suffered from the Calvinists' witch-hunting zeal, which also found scapegoats in herbalists, beggars and vagabonds.

Witch trials were finally banned by Maria Theresa in 1768 after some scandalous trials in Szeged when "witches" had confessions tortured out of them. By the nineteenth century the bloody deeds of Debrecen's forefathers were buried beneath platitudes eulogizing the "Calvinist Rome".

The Déri Museum

The beguiling **Déri Museum** (Tues–Sun: April–Oct 10am–6pm; Nov–March 10am–4pm; 600Ft, or 350Ft just for the ethnographic section and 250Ft just for the Munkácsy exhibition – see below) is fronted by statues by Ferenc Medgyessy that won a prize at the 1937 Paris Expo. Its superb ethnographic collection includes the richly embroidered shepherds' cloaks (*szűr*) which played a significant role in local courtship rituals. A herdsman would "forget" to remove his finest *szűr* from the porch when he left the house of the woman he was courting, and if it was taken inside within an hour a formal proposal could be made. Otherwise, the cloak was hung prominently on the veranda, giving rise to the expression *kitették a szűrét* ("his cloak was put out"), meaning to reject an unwanted suitor. Amongst the other must-see exhibits is a fine collection of agricultural and viticultural implements, and various items related to the many branches of industry prominent in Debrecen during the eighteenth century, the most important of which were tanners, boot-makers and furriers.

A separate gallery in the same building contains painter **Mihály Munkácsy**'s monumental Christ trilogy. The three works, *Ecce Homo*, *Christ before Pilate* and *Golgota*, were reunited only a few years ago, but already there is a danger they will be split up again if desperate attempts to keep *Golgota* in the country come to nothing. *Ecce Homo*, an allegorical representation of good and evil, truth and falsehood, toured the world in the 1890s. Having viewed it in Dublin, James Joyce commented: "It is a mistake to limit drama to the stage; a drama can be painted as well as sung or acted, and *Ecce Homo* is a drama." There's more artwork in the gallery of Old Masters, featuring sixteenth- to nineteenth-century paintings by some of Hungary's foremost artists, such as Kiss, Lotz and Paál.

Other sights in the centre

Given the focus on Calvinism, it's easy to overlook the existence of other faiths in Debrecen. Before the war there were over 9000 Jews (there are now around 1200) and eight synagogues, of which only two remain in the backstreets west of Kossuth tér. The Eclectic-style **Orthodox Synagogue** on Pásti utca is so derelict that the Jewish community is negotiating with the council to turn it into a cultural centre. The nearby **Status Quo Synagogue** on Kápolnási utca, built to serve the Status Quo Jews in 1909, has been restored and may be visited (daily 7am–1pm, or call ⓣ52/415-861 if the door is locked). Its pale pastel decor and *bemah* are as austere as a Calvinist church, unlike the rich interiors of the synagogues of Szeged and Budapest.

If ecclesiastical architecture is your thing, consider tracking down **St Anna's Church**, a couple of blocks east of Piac utca, which is Catholic and Baroque and originally belonged to the Piarist order. It's worth a peek inside to view the fanciful Rococco decor and medallion-shaped ceiling frescoes representing venerable saints from the Árpád dynasty. Above the portal you can discern the coat of arms of its founder, Cardinal Csáky. The street on which it stands was previously called Béke útja (Avenue of Peace), which raised a mordant chuckle amongst the townsfolk, as it leads to a slaughterhouse beyond the **Greek Orthodox Church** on Attila tér. Built in 1910, this, too, has some impressive frescoes, depicting the bombing of the city in 1914. Just before you reach the church, on the right at Nagy Gál István utca 6, is the **Timár Ház** (Tues–Fri 10am–6pm, Sat 10am–4pm; 200Ft), a small crafts centre where pottery, basketweaving and other skills are on display – you can buy the finished product.

Nagyerdei Park and Kossuth Lajos University

North of Kálvin tér the city turns greener and quieter, with stylish residences lining the roads to **Nagyerdei Park**. In the western section you'll find the **thermal baths** (daily: April–Oct 8am–8pm; Nov–March 8am–6pm; 840Ft 1–8pm and at weekends, 560Ft 8am–1pm), an indoor complex fed by springs of sulphurous "brown water" (bárna-víz) rising up from beneath the park. The large dome just behind the baths is the **Mediterranean Water Park** (daily 10am–10pm; 3300Ft per day, 1500Ft for 2hr), a new water complex with dozens of chutes, slides and jets. Elsewhere you may notice hemp growing wild; the plants are so low in THC that they're not worth smoking, but the local *táltos* have been known to boil bushels in cauldrons, to some effect.

Beyond the reedy lake and wooden footbridge rises the columned bulk of **Kossuth Lajos University**, fronted by fountains where newlyweds pose for photos. The university's **Hungarian language courses** in mid-January, late May and mid-July draw students from all over the world (ⓣ52/489-117, ⓦwww.nyariegyetem.hu). Beyond the campus lies a **Botanical Garden** (daily April–Oct 8am–6pm; Nov–March 8am–4pm; 200Ft).

Markets

Though the great bi-monthly fairs "held here since time immemorial" no longer take place, Debrecen's **fruit and vegetable market** is a pungent, compulsive affair. The indoor market (vásárcsarnok), next to the supermarket on Csapó utca (Mon–Sat 4am–3pm, Sun 4–11am), is awash with kerchiefed grannies hawking pickles, meat, soft cheese and strange herbs, the air filled with smells and Magyar interrogatives ("*Hogy a… ?*" is slang for "how much is the… ?").

Debrecen's **flea market**, known as the **Noisy Market** (Zsibogó Piac), is held in an industrial quarter of the city (daily except Wed 8am–noon or 1pm). Take a #30 bus from the train station and get off where everybody else does, just past the cigarette factory (Dohánygyár). The market is across the road and through a portal, its 800-odd stalls selling clothes, tools, loads of junk and a few antiques.

Eating, drinking and entertainment

Debrecen has a handful of great **cafés** and distinguished **restaurants**, though most menus stick to Hungarian standards.

Cafés and restaurants

Bohem Belgian Beer Café Piac utca 29. Simple, pub-style place serving pricey, but tasty, well-cooked and nicely presented food, and the beer is the best in town. Mon–Fri 10am–midnight, Sat & Sun noon–midnight.

Csokonai Söröző Kossuth utca 21. Romantic cellar establishment with wall lamps and candle-topped tables, offering an upscale take on Hungarian favourites. Roll four dice at the end of the meal, and if the right symbols come up you receive a 2000Ft credit towards your next meal here (daily noon–11pm).

Flaska Vendéglő Miklós utca 4. Homely basement restaurant with peasant-style decor, serving inexpensive regional specialities such as Hortobágy pancakes, stuffed cabbage and steamed lamb with pasta. Daily 11.30am–11pm.

Lucullus Ȩtterem Piac utca 41. The Medieval-themed interior is a bit over the top, but the food is genuinely first class – fish, game and grilled meats, alongside the best veggie options in town. Daily 11.30am–11pm.

Mandula Cukrászda Ember Pál utca 6. Although awkwardly located on a side street up towards Nagyerdei Park, this sweet little café has great cakes and ices (daily 9am–7pm).

Morik Caffé Miklós utca 1. The best coffee in town is to be had in the gorgeous, mock-eighteenth-century café – the best time to visit is after dark, when oil lamps adorn the tables and it becomes very atmospheric. No smoking. Mon–Sat 7am–11pm, Sun 10am–10pm.

Pompeji Pizzeria Batthány utca 4. Colourful, labryinthine cellar joint (non-smokers can eat upstairs) offering standard pizza and pasta dishes, plus a good sideline in steaks. Daily 11am–11pm, Fri & Sat till midnight.

Toro D'oro Piac utca 11–15. Thoroughly modern and cool place in the *Hotel Aranybika*, dishing up the best pizzas in town, deliciously creamy pasta dishes, and some extremely appetizing desserts. Daily 10am–11pm.

Nightlife

With a large student and local population, Debrecen does well for **nightlife**, and you can find many little bolt holes in and around Kossuth tér and Piac utca. Still the coolest place is the *Génius Bar* in the old casino inside the *Hotel Aranybika*; a relaxed café during the day, by night this turns into a hip bar, with a varied programme of club and party nights, DJs and live music (Mon & Thurs 11am–11pm, Tues, Wed & Fri till 3am, Sat till 5am; ⓦwww.geniusbar.hu). After 10pm the entrance is from the terrace around the side of the hotel on Bajcsy-Zsilinszky utca. Three reliable **drinking** spots near each other on Batthány utca include the *Play House Pub* and *Kalóz Pub*, both at no. 24, and the *Battháný Borozó*, a smaller cellar den at no. 14. Another is the *Bakelit Music Café*, next to the *Csokonai* restaurant, which is loud, smoky and usually crammed (Mon–Thurs 9am–11pm, Fri 9am–2am, Sat 6pm–2am). The *Mátyás Pince* on the corner of Bem tér and Péterfia utca (Mon–Sat noon–midnight) has a quieter ambience, and still employs the enjoyable rigmarole of serving wine from glass spigots.

For up-to-date information on nightlife and events, get hold of *Debreceni Est*, the free weekly **listings** guide. The *Klinika Mozi* at Nagyerdei körút 98 hosts **concerts** and raves with visiting DJs, as does the *El Tornádó* at Pallagi út 2 which attracts foreign students. The *Lovarda*, out at Kassai út 24, is another popular bar which also hosts regular concerts.

Festivals and events

Debrecen endeavours to dispel its austere image with several big annual events. In late March, the **Spring Festival** (Tavaszi Fesztivál) of music and drama coincides with events in Budapest, though Debrecen claims to have originated the custom. There's a riot of colour on August 20, when the **Flower Carnival** trundles north from Petőfi tér, along Kossuth utca and round towards the stadium by the university (the route can change) – thirty floats laden with flowers, bands and operatically dressed soldiers. People hang from windows en route, cheer wildly when the band plays tunes from *István a király* (*Stephen the King* – a patriotic rock opera) and surge behind the last float to the stadium, where the show continues into the late afternoon. In the evening there's a **fireworks** display outside the Great Church. The carnival also incorporates supporting programmes, such as the **Borsodi Beer Carnival**, which takes place near the City Hall. The four-day **Jazz Festival** (Dzsessz Napok or Jazzfeszt) in mid-September is Hungary's principal such festival, featuring top Hungarian musicians and some big-name foreign acts. Finally, the **Autumn Festival** in October has classical music concerts, films and theatrical performances as the key events.

There's often something worth watching at the **Csokonai Theatre** on Kossuth utca, an exotic-looking Moorish structure named after the locally born poet, Mihály Csokonai Vitez (1773–1805). In early July, the week-long **Bartók International Choir Competition**, held in odd-numbered years, alternates with the biennial **International Military Bands** festival.

The Hajdúság

The **Hajdúság** region around Debrecen takes its name from the **Haiduk** communities who occupied eight derelict villages here during the early seventeenth century. Originally Balkan cattle drovers-cum-bandits who fought as mercenaries against the Turks, they were unfettered by feudal servitude and infamous for their ferocity and bisexuality. Their ranks were swollen by runaway serfs and homeless peasants, and they formed a guerrilla army, led by István Bocskai, which turned against the Habsburgs in the winter of 1604–5. After Bocskai achieved his ambition to be Prince of Transylvania, the Haiduk were pensioned off with land to avert further disturbance. The result was a string of settlements with names prefixed *Hajdú-*, where the Haiduk farmed, enjoyed the status of "nobles" (*natio*) and, if necessary, were mustered to fight. Chief amongst these settlements is **Hajdúszoboszló**, a rapidly expanding spa resort, which also features one of the country's largest water theme parks and a sprinkling of small museums.

Hajdúszoboszló

A spa since 1927, **HAJDÚSZOBOSZLÓ** gets about one and a half million visitors – the majority of them Poles and Germans – each year, far more than anywhere else in the Hajdúság. Surveying the wallowing, guzzling crowds in the steaming brown waters of its **thermal baths** (daily 7am–7pm; 800Ft), you might try the old Haiduk war cry, *Huj, huj, hajrá!*, to clear some space before jumping in yourself. A new development inside the massive pool complex, the **Aquapark** (May–Sept daily 8am–7pm; 3500Ft) contains the largest water slide in Hungary, with six chutes arranged round a twelve-metre tower. Away from the baths, things are more relaxed, with tennis courts for hire in the park, and cafés and quaint old buildings around Hősök tere, guarded by a comically fierce statue of Bocskai.

Twenty metres of **fortress wall**, part of the fifteenth-century defences, lurk behind the inevitable Calvinist church on Hősök tere. Around the corner at Bocskai utca 12, the **Bocskai Museum** (Tues–Sun 9am–1pm & 2–5pm; 150Ft) exhibits photos of nineteenth-century Haiduk villagers, and assorted military relics – among them Bocskai's embroidered silk banner, given pride of place alongside the town's charter. Although Bocskai comes across as a benevolent leader, he didn't balk at betraying another group who fought for him: the Székely of Transylvania, who were butchered when they had outlived their usefulness during the so-called "Bloody Carnival". Another building at no. 21

houses a folklore and ethnographic display, and there are temporary exhibitions at no. 11 (350Ft for all three museums).

On the edge of town, around the train station, the atmosphere is more rural. Chunky whitewashed cottages, their vegetable gardens fringed with sunflowers, shimmer in the heat, passed by errant cows and wagon-loads of pigs.

Practicalities

Buses #1, #4 and #6 run from the **train station**, 2km southeast of town, into the centre, terminating at the **bus station** near the baths. Most things are on or just off the main street, Szilfákalja út, which is also Route 4 between Budapest and Debrecen. Tourinform at Szilfákalja út 2 (Mon–Fri 9am–6pm, Sat & Sun 9am–noon; mid-June to mid-Sept open till 5pm at weekends; ⓣ52/361-612, ⓔhajduszoboszlo@tourinform.hu) can supply **information**.

Spa tourism is big business in Hajdúszoboszló, as the huge number of **hotels** testifies. At the top end of the scale is the super-luxurious *Hotel Silver* (ⓣ52/363-811, ⓦwww.silverhotel.hu; ❼) at Mátyás király sétány 25, and the *Aqua Sol* right next to the baths (ⓣ52/273-310, ⓦwww.hunguesthotels.hu; ❼), both with their own thermal spas. Cheaper, less glamorous, options by the baths include the *Start Panzió* at József Attila utca 22 (ⓣ52/365-981; ❸) and the *Admirális Panzió*, across Debreceni ut at Hőforrás utca 2 (ⓣ52/364-198; ❷). Back in the centre of town, on Hősök tere, is the modern and friendly *Puskás Panzió* (ⓣ52/362-158; ⓦwww.puskaspanzio.hu; ❹). On the same square, opposite the *Puskás*, the *Nelson* **restaurant** is as good a place as any to eat, and preferable to the cluster of touristy places by the baths. The **campsite** beside Debreceni út (ⓣ52/557-851; May–Sept) has a hotel (❸), four-bed chalets (❸) and apartments (❻).

Hortobágy National Park

Petőfi compared the **Hortobágy puszta** of the central Plain to "the sea, boundless and green". In his day, this "glorious steppe" resounded to the pounding hooves of countless horses and cattle being driven from well to waterhole by mounted *csikósok* (horse-herds) and *gulyások* (cowboys), while Racka sheep grazed under the surveillance of Puli dogs. Medieval tales of cities in the clouds and nineteenth-century accounts of phantom woods, or the "extensive lake half enveloped in grey mist" which fooled John Paget, testify to the occurrence of **mirages** during the hot, dry Hortobágy summers. Caused by the diffusion of light when layers of humid air at differing temperatures meet, these *délibáb* sporadically appear at certain locations – for example north of Máta, south of Kónya, and along the road between Cserepes and the *Kis-Hortobágyi Csárda*.

Over the ages tribes have raised burial mounds (*kurgán*), some dating back 4000–5000 years. One of them served as the site of a duel between Frau Bártha of Debrecen and two rival *táltos*. Nowadays, the grasslands have receded and mirages are the closest that Hortobágy gets to witchcraft, but the classic *puszta* landscape can still pass for Big Sky country, its low horizons casting every copse and hillock into high relief. Now a UNESCO World Heritage Site, the 730-square-kilometre **Hortobágy National Park** is a living heritage museum, with roaming animals and cowboys demonstrating their skills. You should, however, be prepared for a relatively costly touristic experience – the *puszta* comes packaged at Hortobágy.

Hortobágy village and around

The park's main settlement, situated about halfway between Debrecen and Tiszafüred, is **HORTOBÁGY** village. Approaching from Tiszafüred, you'll enter the village via the lovely **nine-arched stone bridge**, depicted in a famous painting by Tivadar Csontváry. Beyond here stands the much-restored **Great Inn** (Nagycsárda), or *Hortobágyi Csárda*, a rambling thatched edifice dating from 1871 that's now a touristy restaurant (see p.428). Across the road you'll find the **Herdsmen's Museum** (Pástor múzeum; daily: May–Sept 9am–6pm, mid-March to April & Oct 10am–4pm; during the rest of the year contact Tourinform; 250Ft), whose embroidered *szűr* (cloaks), carved powder horns and other objects were fashioned by plainsmen to while away solitary hours. Status had great significance within their world: horse-herds outranked shepherds and cowherds, who, in turn, felt superior to the *kondás* or swineherd. Beneath the stars, however, all slept equally, only building crude huts (*kunyhó*) or sharing the protection of a reed screen (*szárnyék*) with their animals in bad weather.

Across the bridge from the village and 800m down to the left, the **Hortobágy Rare Breeds Park** (Pusztai Állatpark; mid-April to mid-Nov daily 9am–6pm; 250Ft) is devoted to the distinctive breeds of the Great Plain: hairy Mangalica pigs, corkscrew-horned Racka sheep, grey horned cattle, water buffalo and kuvasz sheepdogs, with information on each in English. Exploring further afield is getting easier as the park becomes more visitor-friendly, and **visitor passes** (1000Ft a day) for four protected areas are available from Tourinform.

You can witness equestrian displays and go riding in horse-drawn carriages in the **Szálkahalom nature reserve** 7km to the east, which is more secluded, and in the *Hortobágy Club Hotel* at **Máta**, a large tourist development tacked onto the Máta stud farm. Both have displays from April till October, while the Rare Breeds Park (see above) also has displays in July and August – you can get information and tickets (2000Ft for 90min) for all programmes from Tourinform.

The summer's main events are the **Village Days** (Falunap) at the end of May, an excuse for folk music and dancing, a craft fair and general merriment; the **Hortobágy Goulash Competition** at the beginning of June; an **Interna-**

Bird-watching and other wildlife

The Hortobágyi-halastó lakes (head 6km west of Hortobágy village and turn right) are great for **bird-watching** – especially storks, buzzards, mallards, cranes, terns and curlews – with lodgings at the lakeside *Öregtavi Vendégház* (☎52/589-321; ❹), bookable through Tourinform. The *Hortobágy Club Hotel* in Mata (see p.428) also arranges bird-watching excursions (15,000Ft per person for 4hr). Most trains stop at the Halastó halt, the next station west of Hortobágy. Elsewhere in the park, little ringed plovers, stone curlews and pratincoles favour dry sheep-runs, while red-footed falcons behave unusually for their species, forming loose groups in abandoned rooks' nests. Millions of migratory birds pass through in spring and autumn – the thousands of cranes that fill the skies in late September make an incredible sight and sound. There's less to see at the bird reservation southwest of Nagyiván, although large colonies of storks nest in the villages of Nagyiván and Tiszacsege till the end of August.

Wild **mammals** can be found all over the park – boars near Kecskéses in marshy thickets, otters at Árkus and by the canals and fishponds, ground squirrels near Kónya in the northern grasslands, and roe deer in the reeds, meadows and copses between Óhat and Tiszaszőlős.

tional Horse Show (Nemzetközi Lovas Napok) on the first weekend of July, held in Máta and – the biggest event of the year – the annual **Bridge Fair** on August 19–20, a Magyar rodeo occasioning the sale of leatherwork, knives and roast beef, which is staged by the bridge near Hortobágy.

Practicalities

A succession of small tourist inns gives advance notice of the park to drivers approaching via the Debrecen–Füzesabony road, but **getting there** by train offers a subtler transition from farmland to *puszta*. Services from Debrecen (towards Tiszafüred and Füzesabony) are better than trains from Nyíregyháza, which leave you stranded at Óhat-Pusztakócs, several kilometres west of Hortobágy village. During summer there might even be a "nostalgia" steam train from Debrecen. Buses, calling at Hortobágy en route between Eger and Hajdúszoboszló (or direct from the latter during high season), are another option. Although cycling is the best way of getting around (see below), some of the sites are within walking distance of train halts along the Debrecen–Tiszafüred, Tiszafüred–Karcag and Nyíregyháza–Óhat-Pusztakócs lines. **Bike rental** (2000Ft per day) is available from the *Hortobágy Club Hotel* (see below) – though you've got to get there first – or you can get the addresses of locals renting bikes from Tourinform.

Most amenities are concentrated at the western end of Hortobágy village, including Tourinform in the same building as the Herdsmen's Museum, who can supply all sorts of **information** about the park, including details on **permits** and **programmes** (March–Nov Mon–Fri 8am–6pm, Sat & Sun 9am–4pm; ⓣ52/589-369, ⓔhortobagy@tourinform.hu); out of season (Dec–Feb) it moves premises to Czinege utca 1 in the centre of the village (Mon–Fri 8am–4pm; ⓣ52/589-110). They can also organize private rooms (❷) and point you in the direction of *Puszta Kemping*, just down the river bank from the museum (ⓣ52/369-300; May–Oct; ❶). Other, rather limited, **accommodation** options include the very basic and run-down *Hortobágy Fogadó* at Kossuth utca 1, in the centre of the village (ⓣ52/369-137; ❸); the grubby *Hortobágy Hotel* 2km to the east at Borsós utca 12 (ⓣ52/369-071; ❸); and the *Pásztortanya Vendégfogadó* 5km west of the village by the main road (ⓣ52/369-127, ⓔpasztortanya@freemail.hu; ❷), which has a good restaurant (daily 8am–9pm) and also offers expensive fifteen-minute **flying trips** over the park (15,000Ft for three passengers). Considerably more upmarket, the *Hortobágy Club Hotel* in Máta (ⓣ52/369-020, ⓦwww.hortobagyhotel.hu; ❼) is a lavish resort complex with its own swimming pool, fitness centre, tennis courts and **riding school** – the room rate includes everything but the riding. Despite its obvious tourist trappings, the *Hortobágyi Csárda*, across the road from Tourinform, has some excellent local specialities, such as guinea fowl soup, mangalica pork and kettle goulash (daily 8am–10pm).

Lake Tisza

Created by damming the upper reaches of the river, **Lake Tisza** has become a new centre for tourism, though it's nowhere near as developed as Lake Balaton – its very charm for many visitors. It has three main areas: the southern end around Kisköre and Abádszalók, where motorboats are permitted; the middle section around Tiszafüred, which is reserved for ecotourism and is slightly quieter, with fishing and bird-watching, swimming and canoeing (motorboats are banned here); and the area north of Route 33, which is a nature reserve with restricted access. If you plan to spend any length of time exploring the environs of the lake, then you might consider buying the 1:35,000 *Tisza-Tó* map (700Ft), available from Tourinform.

Tiszafüred

Thirty-four kilometres west of Hortobágy, the faceless town of **TISZAFÜRED** is the largest of the Lake Tisza resorts, and a transport junction between the Plain and the Northern Uplands. Its bus and train stations are ten minutes' walk from the centre; head up Vasút út to Kossuth tér and follow the main street, Fő út. The only "sights" are the **Kis Pál Museum** on Tariczky sétány near Kossuth tér (Tues–Sun 9am–noon & 1–5pm; 150Ft), where fishing features prominently in the local history display; and the **Pottery House** (Fazekasház; Tues–Sun 9am–noon & 1–5pm; free) at Malom utca 12 up the far end of the main street, turning right opposite the Calvinist church. The real lure, however, is swimming and sunbathing, either in a backwater of the Tisza twenty minutes' walk down Ady Endre út towards the lake, where you can hire canoes, or on the river itself at Tiszaörvény, accessible by regular buses from Tiszafüred. There are also **thermal baths** (daily: April–Oct 8am–7pm; Nov–March 9am–5pm; 350Ft), a few minutes' walk up Fürdő út from Tourinform.

Tourinform, at Fürdő út 21, south of Kossuth tér along the Debrecen road (mid-June to mid-Sept Mon–Fri 8am–6pm, Sat 9am–4pm; mid-Sept to mid-June Mon–Fri 8am–4pm; Ⓣ59/353-000, Ⓔtiszafured@tourinform.hu), can furnish you with **information** you might need on the lake and surrounding areas. Ibusz, in the centre at Fő út 30 (Mon–Fri 9am–4pm, Sat 9am–noon; Ⓣ59/511-005), can supply **private rooms**, though it's advisable to book ahead in high season. The most comfortable place to **stay** in town is the delightful, thatched-roofed *Nádas Panzió*, south of Tourinform at Kismuhi utca 2 (Ⓣ59/511-401, Ⓦwww.nadaspanzio.hu; ❺), which has cool, beautifully furnished rooms. Two less exciting, though cheaper, options are the *Füzes Panzió* on the corner of Ady Endre út and Húszőles út (Ⓣ59/351-854; ❸), and the *Aurum Panzió*, 50m further along at Ady Endre út 29 (Ⓣ59/351-338; ❹). Three kilometres west of town, in Tiszaörvény, the pleasant *Hableány Hotel* at Hunyadi utca 2 (Ⓣ59/353-333, Ⓦwww.hotels.hu/hableany; April–Dec; ❺) offers fishing and boat hire. Tiszafüred has three **campsites** (all open April–Oct): *Tóparti Kemping* (Ⓣ59/351-132) and *Fortuna Camping* (Ⓣ59/352-424) by the lake, and *Termál Camping* opposite Tourinform (Ⓣ59/542-210; cabins ❹).

Abádszalók

Twenty-four kilometres southwest of Tiszafüred is the small and busy, though not particularly exciting, resort of **ABÁDSZALÓK**. If you fancy staying here there's the noisy and crowded *Füzes Panzió* at Strand út 2 (Ⓣ59/355-408; ❹), near a beach (daytime entry 400Ft) that rents boats. The attached campsite holds a branch of Tourinform (May–Sept daily 24hr; Oct–April Mon–Fri 8am–4pm; Ⓣ59/535-346, Ⓔabadszalok@tourinform.hu). A quieter alternative is the small campsite 8km north near Tiszaderzs, or you can even camp rough further along the shore – though you'll never escape other holidaymakers entirely.

Szabolcs-Szatmár-Bereg county

North of Debrecen, the Plain ripples with low ridges of wind-blown sand, anchored by birches, apple groves and tobacco fields. The soft landscape of the *Nyírség* (Birch Region) makes a pleasant introduction to **Szabolcs-Szatmár-Bereg**, an area scorned by many Magyars as the "black country", mainly a disparaging reference to the region's large Roma population. More densely settled than other parts of the Plain, Szabolcs would be wholly agricultural if not for industrialized Nyíregyháza, straddling the main routes to the Northern Uplands, the Erdőhát villages and Ukraine. Historically isolated by swamps, and then severed from Transylvania and Ruthenia in 1920, the region has remained poor and backward in comparison with the rest of Hungary and was badly hit by recession in the 1990s, with unemployment levels in this region up to five times higher than in Budapest.

If your interest in **rural life** is limited, stick to **Nyíregyháza**, with its Village Museum, or **Nyírbátor**, with its striking churches – both conveying something of the character of the region. For anyone seeking the challenge of remote areas, encounters with rural Roma, or the folk customs and architecture of old Hungary, though, the county has much to offer, particularly in the **Erdőhat** region. Though sufficient accommodation and transport exists to make independent travel feasible, the only **tourist offices** are in Nyíregyháza and Vásárosnamény, both of which can supply information on the whole region, including private accommodation.

Nyíregyháza

NYÍREGYHÁZA grew into the "Big Apple" of Szabolcs county thanks to the food-processing industry developed to feed the Soviet market during the 1960s and 1970s, and the collapse of this market has hit the region badly. The town itself (population 125,000) has a core of old buildings which have recently been smartened up, girdled by factories and housing estates, with an attractive garden suburb, **Sóstófürdő**, to the north. The best time to come is the first Saturday in September, when a **carnival** inaugurates the month-long Nyírség autumn arts festival.

Arrival, information and accommodation

Arriving at the **bus or train station** on Petőfi tér, 1km south of the centre, you can catch bus #8 or #8A downtown, riding on to Sóstófürdő at the end of the line if you prefer. It is also accessible by a narrow-gauge line from Nyíregyháza's main station, the Balsa-Dombrád line. Most other buses leave from Jókai tér, in the centre. Tourinform, at Országzászló tér 6 (Mon–Fri 9am–5pm; Ⓣ42/504-647, Ⓦwww.tourinform.szabolcs.net), can supply **information** on both the town and the county as a whole. During the summer there's also a branch in the old water tower in Sóstófürdo (mid-June to Sept Mon–Fri 9am–6pm, Sat & Sun 10am–4pm; Ⓣ42/411-193, Ⓔsostofurdo@tourinform.hu).

Ibusz, next to Tourinform (Mon–Fri 8am–5pm, Sat 8am–noon; Ⓣ42/311-817, Ⓔi072@ibusz.hu), can arrange private accommodation, while, in July and August and at weekends throughout the year, you may also be able to get beds (1600Ft) or rooms (❷) in the *Tanárképző Főiskola*, 3km from the centre of town at Sóstó út 31/b (Ⓣ42/441-276). Otherwise, the town's **accommodation** is pretty limited, and you might prefer to find a place out in the more civilized Sóstófürdo district (see opposite). The best downtown option is the business-like *Hotel Európa* at Hunyadi utca 2 (Ⓣ42/508-677), with the alternatives

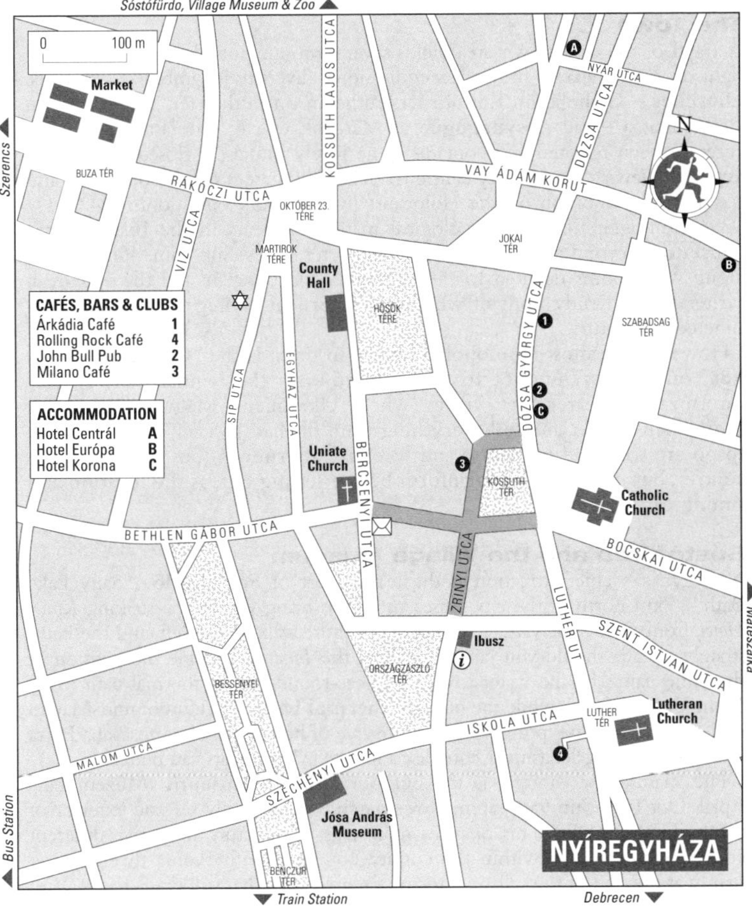

consisting of the quirkily designed, but overpriced, *Hotel Centrál* at Nyár utca 2–4 (Ⓣ42/411-330, Ⓦwww.centralhotel.hu; ❺), and the grand-looking but disappointing *Hotel Korona* at Dózsa György utca 1–3 (Ⓣ42/409-300, Ⓦwww.korona.cs.hu; ❺).

If a more restful alternative appeals then head to **Sóstófürdő**, where there's plenty of decent accommodation. Just past the Village Museum turn-off, you'll find *Fenyves Camping* and its hostel (Ⓣ42/501-360; May to mid-Sept; ❶); and *Igrice Camping* and the *Summer Village* near the outdoor baths (Ⓣ42/479-711; mid-May to mid-Sept), the latter offering both fancy and humbler chalets (❶–❺). Guests of the comfortable *Fürdőház Panzió* (Ⓣ42/411-191, Ⓦwww.furdohaz.hu; ❹) by the water tower receive free use of the indoor thermal pool, as do guests of the nearby *Svájci Lak* (Swiss Chalet), a charismatic place that boasts of having once accommodated Gyula Krúdy and the singer, Lujza Blaha (Ⓣ42/405-793; ❺) – it also has a very good restaurant (see p.432).

The Town

A trawl of the downtown area yields several monuments that cast a bit more light on Nyíregyháza's history. Its confessional diversity is symbolized by three **churches** – Catholic on Kossuth tér, Lutheran on Luther tér, and Uniate on Bethlen utca – plus a **synagogue** at Mártirok tere 6. The last of these has recently been restored and contains some lovely murals; if closed, ask for the key at the Jewish community centre (Izraelita Hitközség) next door, which also has a small exhibition on the Holocaust (Mon–Thurs 9am–noon; ⓣ42/417-939). Ethnographic and archeological material appears in the **Jósa András Museum**, beyond pastel-hued Országzászló tér (Tues–Sun 8am–4pm; 200Ft), along with rooms devoted to the painter Gyula Benczúr and the epicurean writer Gyula Krúdy, both of whom were born in Nyíregyháza in the mid-nineteenth century.

However, the most cosmopolitan place in town is the "**Comecon Market**" on Rákóczi út (not to be confused with the regular daily market on Búza tér nearer the centre), where Ukrainians, Magyars, Poles and Romanians barter and sell everything from fur hats to cars. The best times to go are weekend mornings and weekday afternoons (bus #1A from the centre), but check with Tourinform before setting out, as the location and timing can change.

Sóstófürdő and the Village Museum

Nyíregyháza's chief attraction is the leafy resort of **Sóstófürdő** ("Salty Lake Bath"), 7km north of the city. Buses and trains bring you to the striking *Krudy Hotel*, from where the Village Museum is a short walk to the left, and the baths straight ahead. Should you fancy a wallow, the *Fürdőház*, inside the pension of the same name, by the water tower, is a year-round indoor thermal bath (daily 10am–8pm; 1700Ft), while the outdoor **thermal baths** (Parkfürdő; mid-May to mid-Sept daily 9am–7pm; 550Ft) are a couple of hundred metres up Blaha Lujza sétány, near the Igrice tourist complex and lake, where boats can be rented.

The main draw, though, is the outdoor **Village Museum** (Műzeumfalu; April–Oct Tues–Sun 9am–5pm; Nov–March, you can only see the exterior of the buildings; 400Ft). This *Skanzen* represents architecture from five different ethnographic regions within the county, complete with Roma dwellings set firmly at the end of the village, a form of segregation that still exists today. With clothes hanging on the washing line, tables laid and boots by the hearth, the farmsteads appear to have been abandoned by their occupants only yesterday, leaving mute testimony to their lives in a nineteenth-century Szabolcs village. In this world, the size of the barns and stables denoted a family's wealth, as did the presence of a Beam Gate opening onto the street: "A gate on a hinge, the dog is big, the farmer is great", runs an old proverb. Other clues to social standing are the knick-knacks beloved of the "sandled nobility" or petty gentry, and the placing of a bench between two windows in Orthodox households. A single communal bowl speaks volumes about life in the poorest dwellings, but it's worth buying the excellent guidebook (1200Ft), in English, to learn more. If you fancy some refreshments, there's a typical *kocsma* (pub) in the centre of the museum. If animals are your thing, the town **zoo** (daily 9am–4pm; 700Ft), 300m down from the Village Museum, is one of Hungary's better ones.

Eating and drinking

Decent culinary possibilities in Nyíregyháza are few and far between, and you'll have to head to the high-class, though not overly expensive, *Krűdy Vigadó* in Sóstófürdo for the best, and most traditional, Hungarian food – the enormous canopied terrace is a lovely spot to dine in the summer (daily noon–10pm). Back in town the most reliable **restaurant** is the one in the *Hotel Central*, while the *Rolling Rock Café* at Luther tér 5 (daily 10am–midnight, Fri & Sat till 3am) serves up steaks, grilled meats and the like, and also doubles up as the town's liveliest **bar**. Alternatively there's the *Bahnhof Music Club* at Bethlen Gábor utca 24, which has regular concerts and visiting DJs (Thurs–Sat 8pm), and the *Shamrock Irish Pub* on Korányi Frigyes utca, featuring every beer you can imagine, and 1970s sounds (daily 10am–midnight). The *John Bull Pub* at Dózsa György utca 1–3 (easily spotted because of the British red phone box outside) is a straightforward drinking den, and a few paces up the road at no. 5, the *Árkádia Café* does the job for both a quiet daytime coffee or an evening drink, and also has **Internet access** (Mon–Sat 8am–midnight, Sun 2–10pm). The freebie **listings** publication *Nyíregyházai Est* has information about local events and raves.

Nagykálló and Máriapócs

"Go to **NAGYKÁLLÓ**!" used to be a popular insult east of the Tisza, referring to the large mental asylum in this small town of converging houses painted a flaky ochre. The asylum still stands at one end of the long and eerily empty main square, but such visitors as the town receives come for quite different reasons. The big attraction is the annual *Művészeti Tábor*, a **festival of Hungarian folk arts** held in a weird "barn" shaped like a Viking's helmet, amid a cluster of other buildings designed by Imre Makovecz, 2km north of the centre. The event occurs in late June and lasts about ten days; you can obtain the exact dates from the Nagykálló Cultural Centre at Báthori utca 1 (Ⓣ42/263-141), or from Tourinform in Nyíregyháza or Vásárosnamény.

For Hasidic Jews, however, Nagykálló is a cradle of the Satmar sect, one of the largest in the diaspora (see box below). Two reminders of Nagykálló's once size-

The Satmar Hasids

The pilgrims who come and pray at Rabbi Taub's tomb are members of the **Satmar sect**, which originated in the town of Satu Mare (Szatmár in Hungarian) in what is now Romania. Like the better-known Lubavitchers, the Satmars follow **Hasidism**, a form of Judaism founded by Jewish mystics in southern Poland in the mid-eighteenth century as a movement of spiritual renewal. The rabbinical authorities of the day denounced the Hasidim, or "pious ones", on the grounds that "they conduct themselves like madmen... and turn over like wheels with the head below and the legs above". Their ecstatic worship and emphasis on song and dance as an expression of joy, their strict laws on dress, diet and everyday life, and their use of Yiddish appealed to the poor village communities of Jews, and the movement won millions of adherents in Poland, Romania, Hungary and the Ukraine.

It was only because so many Hasids emigrated to the US, Canada, Britain and Australia between the 1890s and 1930s that Hasidism survives today. In Central and Eastern Europe, the distinctively dressed Yiddish-speaking Hasid communities were easy targets for the Fascists, and there was little opposition to the Holocaust from local Gentiles. With frightening ease a whole way of life was cleaned out of the region, leaving only vandalized synagogues and cemeteries. In Hungary ninety percent of provincial Jews perished, whereas about half of the Jews of Budapest survived (few of whom were Hasids). The traditions of the old country are now preserved by the descendants of emigrants, who now return to visit the tombs of the great rabbis in Nagykálló, Bodrogkeresztúr and Sátoraljaújhely.

able Jewish population can be found on Nagybalkáni út, running off the other end of the main square from the asylum. A plaque at the top of the street on the right indicates the former Jewish school, while the Jewish cemetery further down harbours the **tomb of Rabbi Isaac Taub**, one of the most revered of the Hungarian Hasidic rabbis, who was called "the miracle rabbi" and credited with writing the plaintive folk tune *Szól a kakás már* ("The cock has crowed"). Hundreds of pilgrims come in early spring (7th of Adar by the Jewish calendar) to ask for his help. To get the key to his shrine (in the red and yellow building behind the wall) try ringing Gábor Blajer (☎42/262-947) and someone will bring the key to the grave.

MÁRIAPÓCS, off the road between Nagykálló and Nyírbátor, is a place of pilgrimage for the Orthodox and Catholic faithful, and especially for the Roma. Its **Orthodox Church** contains an icon of the Virgin that has been seen to shed tears since 1696 – though this is a replica of the original, which is now in Venice. The beautiful (though incomplete) iconostasis features some thirty icons representing scenes from the Old and New Testaments. Now that old identities are reasserting themselves across the Carpathians, Máriapócs has become a spiritual focus for ethnic Magyars and Uniate Christians in Romania, Slovakia, Ukraine and the Voivodina – in 1991, 200,000 worshippers from all round the region attended an open-air papal Mass here. **Pilgrimages** occur on August 15 (the Feast of the Assumption), and the Saturday closest to September 8, which is particularly holy to Roma. The train station is at least 3km from the village, making buses a better bet.

Nyírbátor and around

The tangled history of Trans-Carpathia has also left its mark on **NYÍRBÁTOR**, an attractive small town whose name recalls the **Báthori family**, a Transylvanian dynasty which veered between psychopathic sadism and enlightened tolerance. Both attributes are subtly manifest in Nyírbátor's two churches, which were equally funded by the Báthoris in an age when religious strife was the norm. The churches are a superb venue for **concerts** of choral and chamber music from mid-July to early September, the high point being the **Music Days** in August.

The Calvinist Church

Sited on a grassy hillock above Báthori utca, the **Calvinist Church** was originally founded as a Catholic church in the 1480s, complete with a fourteen-seat pew that's now in the National Museum in Budapest. At the back of its web-vaulted Gothic nave lies the **tomb of István Báthori**, whose sleeping figure indicates that he died in bed, but reveals nothing of the character of this Transylvanian Prince. Hungarian history judges him a shrewd ruler, forgiving his machinations against the Transylvanian Saxons, and the bouts of orgiastic cruelty for which István atoned by endowing churches. Scholars are less willing, however, to dismiss the tales about his cousin, the "Blood Countess" Báthori. It's possible that she, too, is buried here, as her body was reputedly removed from Aachtice after relatives of her victims protested, and it might well have been reburied in the Báthori crypt at Nyírbátor.

When the church turned *Református* in the late sixteenth century, it was obliged to erect a freestanding **wooden bell-tower**, since only Catholic churches were permitted stone belfries during the Counter-Reformation. From its wide-skirted base, the tower rises to a defiant height of 30m, with a spire like a wizard's hat sprouting four mini-towers known as *fiatorony* ("sons of the tower"), symbolizing a civic authority's right to execute criminals. Its hand-cut shingling and oak-pegged joists and beams can be inspected from the crooked stairway up to the balcony and bell chamber.

The Minorite Church and Báthori Museum

István Báthori's other legacy to Nyírbátor is located on Károlyi Mihály utca, and signposted from the main square. Paid for by the spoils of war against the Turks (who, perhaps appropriately, gutted it in 1587), the **Minorite Church** contains fantastic Baroque woodcarvings from Eperjes in Slovakia. The altars swarm with figures wearing disquieting expressions, suggestive of István's soul but actually commissioned by János Krucsay around 1730. To gain admission, ring at the side door marked *plébánia csengője*, which leads to an exhibition of photos of ancient Szabolcs churches.

Next door you'll find the **Báthori Museum** (April–Sept Tues–Sun 9am–5pm, Oct–March Mon–Fri 8am–4pm; 300Ft), where various relics with unintelligible captions trace the history of the dynasty, whose estates included most of Szatmár. Though predominantly inhabited by Hungarians, this region was bisected as a result of the Treaty of Trianon, which allotted the provincial capital (now Satu Mare) and its surroundings to Romania. Relations have been awkward, if not hostile, ever since, which partly explains the small number of border crossings in these parts.

Practicalities

Arriving at the **bus and train stations** on Ady Endre utca, it's a fifteen-minute walk down Kossuth utca to the main square, Szabadság tér. **Accommodation** in Nyírbátor boils down to the colourful and engaging *Hotel Hódi*, in a beautiful old town house just off Szabadság tér at Báthory utca 11 (Ⓣ42/283-556, Ⓕ281-012; ❺); the down-at-heel *Bástya Hotel* at Hunyadi utca 10, south of the main square (Ⓣ42/281-657; ❹); and the similarly rudimentary *Napsugár Panzió*, en route to the museum at Zrinyi Ilona út 15 (Ⓣ42/283-878; ❹). The small *Holdfény Camping* is on Széna tér (Ⓣ42/281-494; May–Aug).

The best **meals** can be had at the restaurant in the *Hotel Hódi* (daily 6–10pm), or there's the cheaper *Kakukk* at Szabadság tér 21 (daily 11.30am–10pm), and the *Csekő* pizzeria and patisserie, 300m west of the *Napsugár Panzió* at Bajcsy-Zsilinszky út 62 (daily 10am–8pm). There's an outdoor **market** on the corner of Váci and Fürst utcas.

Mátészalka, Nagyecsed and Vaja

A shabby fusion of flaking estates and low yellow houses, **MÁTÉSZALKA**'s main claim to fame is that it's the birthplace of the parents of the actor **Tony Curtis**. It was also the first town in provincial Hungary to be lit by electricity – though as the carts, woodcarvings and ceramics in the **Szatmár Museum**, ten minutes' walk east of Hősök tere at Kossuth út 5 (Tues–Fri 8am–4pm, Sat & Sun 10am–3pm; 350Ft) attest, its urbanity was merely a veneer on what was, and still is, an extended village. More impressive is the outdoor display of carriages, carts and sledges – some 100 in all, making it one of the largest such collections in Europe. On the same street at no. 30 stands Mátészalka's old **synagogue**, recently restored but still closed, a sad reminder of the now minute Jewish population of the town.

The museum and synagogue can be found by turning right off Bajcsy-Zsilinszky utca, leading east off the main square, Hősök tere, which is ten minutes' walk from the bus and train stations. If you need **to stay**, both the *Bianco Panzió*, near the stations at Kölcsey utca 27 (Ⓣ44/502-628; 3), and the Swiss-chalet-style *Kristály Panzió* at Eötvös utca 17 (Ⓣ44/312-036; 3), are preferable to the

Szatmár Hotel on Hősök tere (☎44/311-429; 3) – the *Bianco* also has a reasonable **restaurant**. More likely, though, you'll want **transport** to somewhere else. There are regular buses to Nagyecsed and Vaja (see below), and both buses (8 on weekdays, 2 at weekends) and trains (3–4 daily) to Csenger and Fehérgyarmat in the Erdőhát region. Other slow trains (5 daily) run up to Vásárosnamény and Záhony, and across the border to Carei in Romania.

The small town of **NAGYECSED**, 15km south, deserves a mention as the birthplace of the **"Blood Countess" Báthori**, the most notorious of the Báthori clan (see p.286). In the 1560s Ecsed was a palatial Renaissance court surrounded by mires and quicksands, where the family's ancestor Vid Báthori reputedly slew a dragon (hence the Báthori coat of arms, a dragon coiled around three dragon's teeth). It was here that Erzsébet Báthori spent her childhood till she was sent to marry Ferenc Nádasdy at Sárvár. Alas for sensation-seekers, nothing remains of the palace but a few stones.

A tangible relic of the past is the splendidly restored **fortified manor** (April–Oct Tues–Sun 10am–6pm; Nov–March Mon–Fri 8am–4pm; 300Ft) 14km northwest of Mátészalka in **VAJA**, the feudal seat of Ádám Vaj, an early supporter of Rákóczi's campaign against the Habsburgs. Once within the thick-set walls, and having donned a pair of felt slippers, there's plenty to see, including lots of painted furniture – trousseau chests, inlaid tables and carved wardrobes – portraits of the Vaj dynasty, the grand meeting hall (the *Rákóczi-terem*), and an exhibition on the Hungarian War of Independence. The school next door can sometimes provide **accommodation** (☎44/385-317).

The Erdőhát

The **Erdőhát** is Hungary's most isolated region, a state imposed by nature and confirmed by history. Meandering and flooding over centuries, the headwaters of the Tisza and its tributaries carved out scores of enclaves beneath the flanks of the Subcarpathians, where dense oak forests provided acorns for pig-rearing and ample timber for building. Though invaders were generally deterred by Escedi Swamp and similar obstacles, scattered communities maintained contact with one another through their intricate knowledge of local tracks and waterways. When the borders came down like shutters in the twentieth century, people were suddenly restricted to three tightly controlled frontier crossings into the Ukraine, which have been only partially relaxed since the demise of Communism.

If you're interested in rural customs and architecture that's almost extinct elsewhere in Hungary, the Erdőhát **villages** are well worth the effort. Although neither is particularly enticing, the two small towns of Fehérgyarmat and Vásárosnamény serve as jumping-off points for the region, while public transport links are surprisingly good in these parts, with fairly frequent bus services on weekdays.

Fehérgyarmat and Vásárosnamény

Much of the southern Erdőhát is accessible from **FEHÉRGYARMAT**, a small town whose main street is one long park. The train station is ten minutes' walk south of the centre, while the bus station is at the foot of the main street along Móricz Zsigmond út. Its only sights are a Calvinist church with a **medieval tower** topped by a Transylvanian wooden spire, and, 300m beyond here at Vörösmarty utca 1, the **Szatmár-Bereg National Conservation Museum** (Mon–Fri 9am–2pm; 250Ft), with a collection of paintings and photos of the local flora and fauna. The only **accommodation** is the grotty *Hotel Szamos* (☎44/362-211; ❷) by the bus station and the *Szarkafészek Panzió* 400m away

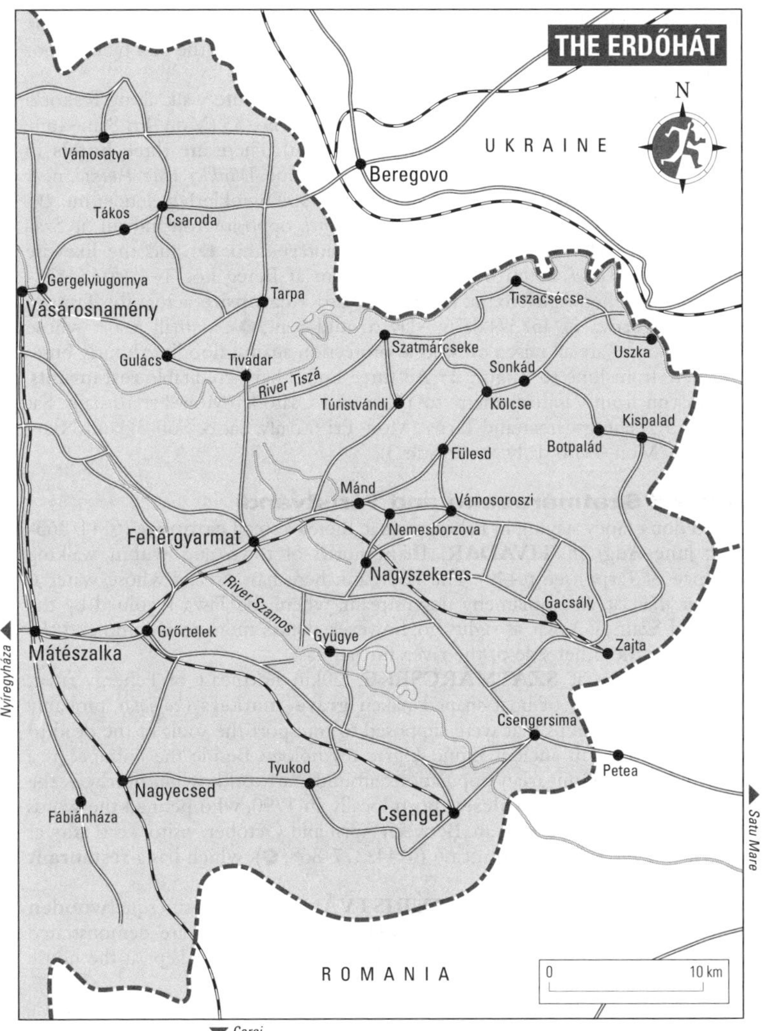

at Rákóczi utca 40 (☎44/362-300; ❷), so you'd do better staying in one of the villages. **Buses** fan out to Tivadar (Mon–Fri 7 daily, Sat & Sun 4), Gyügye (Mon–Fri 8 daily, Sat & Sun 3), Tűristvándi & Szatmárcseke (Mon–Fri 7 daily, Sat & Sun 2), Tiszacéscse (Mon–Fri 5 daily, Sat & Sun 2), Vásárosnamény (Mon–Fri 6 daily, Sat & Sun 3) and Csengersima (Mon–Fri 3 daily, Sat & Sun 2), while **trains** to Zajta (2–3 daily) can drop you at Nagyszekeres or Gacsály.

Villages in the northern Erdőhát are generally easier to reach by bus from **VÁSÁROSNAMÉNY**, an erstwhile trading post on the "salt road" from Transylvania, whose **Beregi Museum** at Rákóczi utca 13 (Tues–Fri 8.30am–4.30pm, Sat & Sun 8am–4pm; 200Ft) displays local embroidery and cast-iron stoves from Munkachevo, with a room devoted to Erdőhát funerary customs; you'll need to wear slippers over your shoes, available from the box by the door saying *papucs kötelező*.

From the **bus and train stations**, it's a twenty-minute walk along Rákóczi utca to Szabadság tér and the Tourinform office at no. 33 (Mon–Fri 8am–4pm; ⓣ45/570-206, ⓔvasarosnameny@tourinform.hu). There are three **hotels** in town, the best of which is the tidy and good-value *Winkler Ház Panzió*, near the museum at Rákóczi utca 5 (ⓣ45/470-945, ⓔwinklerh@elender.hu; ❸). The alternatives are the *Marianna Center Hotel*, opposite Tourinform at Szabadság tér 19 (ⓣ45/470-401, ⓔmarianc@enternet.hu; ❸) and the likewise decent *Fehér Hotel*, 200m beyond Tourinform at Bereg köz 1–4 (ⓣ45/471-073, ⓔhotelfeher@axelero.hu; ❸). There's also a **campsite** across the Tisza in Gergelyiugornya (ⓣ45/371-076; May to mid-Sept; ❶), a small resort whose holiday homes are all raised on stilts as protection against flooding; hourly buses run here from June to August 25. All three hotels have creditable **restaurants**. **Buses** run from Vásárosnamény to Tákos and Csaroda (Mon–Fri 10 daily, Sat & Sun 3), Fehérgyarmat and Tarpa (Mon–Fri 6 daily, Sat & Sun 3), and Nyiregyháza (Mon–Fri 8 daily, Sat & Sun 3).

Around Szatmárcseke and Túristvándi

If you don't fancy staying in Fehérgyarmat, there's a small **campsite** (ⓣ44/363-859; June–Aug) in **TIVADAR**, 10km north of town and within walking distance of Tarpa (see p.440). The riverbank here has a *strand* whose water is cleaner than at Vásárosnamény downstream, where the Tisza is joined by the polluted Szamos. As far as sights go, however, there's more to recommend the villages on the other side of the river, further east.

The cemetery at **SZATMÁRCSEKE**, 20km northeast of Fehérgyarmat, contains a number of boat-shaped oaken **grave markers** (*kopjafa*), probably representing the ships that were supposed to transport the souls of the dead to the other world in ancient Finno-Ugric mythology. Beside the entrance is a map indicating Hungarian populations around the world, while nearby is the mausoleum of **Ferenc Kölcsey**, born locally in 1790, who penned the words to Hungary's national anthem. Between April and October, visitors can **stay** at the *Kölcsey Fogadó*, Honvéd utca 6 (ⓣ44/377-868; ❶), which has a **restaurant** attached.

A few kilometres to the south, **TÚRISTVÁNDI** has a picturesque **wooden watermill** (Mon–Fri 10am–6pm; 100Ft), whose workings are demonstrated should a group of tourists materialize. The key to the mill is kept at the house on the corner, across the main road.

Other fine examples of wooden architecture used to grace Nemesborzova, Vámosoroszi and Botpálad, until they were removed to Szentendre's Village Museum in the 1970s. However, **TISZACSÉCSE** retains the thatched cottage where the novelist and critic **Zsigmond Móricz** was born in 1879, and also affords fine views across the plain towards the Carpathian mountains.

The southern Erdőhát

The southern Erdőhát is notable for its beautiful churches, folksy adaptations of Gothic or Baroque architecture. Slow trains bound for Zajta can drop you off at **NAGYSZEKERES** or **GACSÁLY**, whose churches feature striking wooden **bell-towers**. The tiny **church** in **GYÜGYE** has a coffered ceiling decorated with astrological symbols (illuminated in turn by a sunbeam during the course of the year, so the priest says), but it has been closed for repair for a while, and no one knows when it will open again. If you want to take the chance, Gyügye is easily reached by bus from Fehérgyarmat, or you can walk there in an hour from Nagyszekeres.

Committed church buffs might also visit **CSENGER**, where the **Catholic Church** dates from the Middle Ages. Built of red and black brick, it similarly features a superb coffered ceiling with folk Baroque paintings; ask at the parish office next door for the key if it is closed. Csenger used to be in the centre of Szatmár county until the 1920 Trianon Treaty put a border between the village and the old county seat, now Satu Mare in Romania. The road and the railway now end abruptly, and the place is served by a branch line down from Mátészalka; the last train back leaves at 6.30pm. By rights, Csenger should be a dead-end sort of village, but a few years ago the town's mayor started a local revival by calling in the architect Imre Makovecz and giving him a free hand with a sweep of land in the centre; today the school, church, sports hall, library and numerous other buildings all display the distinctive Makovecz exuberance. Csenger's history is captured in the enchanting **Local History Museum** opposite the church at Hősök tere 3 (Helytörténeti Múzeum; Tues–Sun 9am–5pm; 200Ft), a very personal collection of the museum director, which re-creates a typical room of a wealthy peasant household using his grandparents' furniture and photographs; don't miss the wooden ice skates. Should you need **accommodation**, there's the *Barcsay Panzió* at Hősök tere 11 (Ⓣ44/341-335; ❷) and there are also camping facilities in the museum's garden.

Although **CSENGERSIMA**, a few kilometres north, has been designated a 24-hour **crossing into Romania** – it also happens to be one of the least crowded – the Romanian officials at Petea may refuse to admit travellers after dark. There are five **buses** daily (1 on Sun) between Csengersima and Fehérgyarmat, but none across the border.

North of the Tisza

Another clutch of villages lies north of the Tisza, in the region known as *Bereg*. While some are only accessible from Vásárosnamény, others, such as Csaroda and Tákos, can also be reached from Fehérgyarmat.

Nine kilometres east of Vásárosnamény, **TÁKOS** harbours a tiny wattle-and-daub **Protestant church** (100Ft), dubbed the "bare-footed Notre Dame". Not much bigger than the size of a house, the church's quaint interior features bold floral designs on its gallery, pews and walls and a coffered ceiling painted by Ferenc Asztalos in 1766. As in most village churches, the men sit up front and the women at the back. The church is usually closed, but you can get the key from the lady living at Bajcsy-Zsilinszky utca 29, 200m down the road; she might also be able to help with **accommodation**. She herself needed it in the big floods of 2001, which severely damaged her house and threatened to cause lasting damage to the church too.

One of the oldest, and loveliest, churches in the region lies 2km to the east in **CSARODA**. Sited on a small rise, and surrounded by trees and thatched cottages, the shingled, thirteenth-century **Gothic Church** was originally built as a Catholic church in the eleventh century, and later decorated with frescoes of various "smiling saints", although not all of them look very cheerful. In 1552 the building was turned into a Calvinist church, and red and blue floral designs similar to those found on shepherds' cloaks were added. These were later painted over, remaining hidden from view until the 1960s when, so the story goes, restorers brought them back to life by covering them overnight with raw minced meat. The church is normally open from 10am to 6pm daily (100Ft), but ask in the village if it's closed. If you want to **stay** here, the *Székely Panzió*, close to the church at József Attila utca 54 (Ⓣ45/484-830;

Troubled waters

The Tisza is esteemed the most fishy river in Europe, if not the whole world; they have a common saying that it consisteth of two parts of water and one part of fish.

English traveller Edward Brown, 1670.

Hungary's second largest waterway – after the Danube – has always played an important role in the economy of the country, but on the flat plain the river has also been a frequent source of woe in the form of floods. In the words of Hungarian poet Sándor Petőfi: "Like a madman breaking his bonds, the Tisza runs across the plains. Raging and wailing it breaks its dykes, wanting to swallow the world".

The new millennium started badly for the river. On January 30, 2000, 100,000 cubic metres of waste water with a very high concentration of cyanide was released into the River Samos from a gold mine in Baia Mare, Romania. The Samos, a highly polluted river at the best of times, joins the Tisza by Vásárosnamény, and for twelve days a "plume of poison" swept down the Tisza through Hungary killing everything in its path and devastating the local economy, which relies heavily on fishing and tourism for its survival. Over 100,000 kilos of dead fish were hauled from the river, and just 1500 tourists – instead of the usual 20,000 – came to holiday by the Tisza in the summer of 2000.

Hardly had the river recovered from the cyanide, when heavy rains brought a renewed threat of disaster. After reaching record-breaking levels in 1998 and 1999, the river rose even higher to break new records in April 2000, and twelve million sandbags were used to strengthen the dykes around Szolnok and the surrounding countryside. Worse followed in March 2001 when the water level of the upper Tisza rose over 10m in just 52 hours, breaking through the river defences in Bereg county. It destroyed 200 houses and forced the evacuation of 20,000 people, once again badly hitting the local economy – though in the Ukraine the damage was far worse. Some blame tree-felling in the Ukraine and the subsequent soil erosion for the recurrence of flooding, others point to global climate change. Whatever the cause, the government has embarked on a massive dyke-building programme, but official sources admit they cannot ensure safety.

❷), is a lovely three-room guesthouse – two rooms with a shared bathroom and the other en suite.

The restorers have also been at work in **TARPA**, some 10km to the southeast, where a large horizontal "dry" **mill** (száraz-malom) with an intricate conical roof stands amongst the cottages. The **Protestant church**, a short walk away at Kossuth utca 13, retains some interesting features, notably some recently discovered frescoes on the north wall (including one of St George and the Dragon), and the original six-hundred-year-old wooden door, carved from a single piece of wood. There's **accommodation** here at the very pleasant *Pálma Panzió* (Ⓣ45/488-124; ❷), in the centre of the village at Kossuth utca 25, and the *Kuruc Vendéglő* (Ⓣ45/488-121; ❷) immediately next door, where you can also get a decent lunch. Another formidable-looking **wooden bell-tower** can be found in **VÁMOSATYA**, 8km northwest of Csaroda.

Around Kisvárda and Záhony

The fruit-growing area northeast of Nyíregyháza is called the *Rétköz* (Meadow Land) or *Tiszakanyár* (Tisza Bend). Though pretty to drive through, there is little to attract visitors beyond Kisvárda, midway along the road and train line to Záhony, the only border crossing into Ukraine.

Kisvárda

KISVÁRDA is a backwater **spa** with a **ruined castle** used for staging plays in the summer. The **theatre festival** in early June (Határontúli Magyar Színházak Fesztiválja), for Hungarian minorities living in the neighbouring countries and further afield, attracts some very good companies. Despite being undamaged in the war, a random selection of buildings along the main street has been replaced by ugly modern structures, spoiling the look of Fő utca, which leads to the main square. Just off Fő tér at Csillag utca 5 stands an old **synagogue** with an ornamental ceiling and stained-glass windows, housing the **Rétköz Museum** of local history (April–Oct Tues–Sun 9am–noon & 1–4pm; 100Ft). For **accommodation** there is the *Bástya Panzió* at Krucsay Marton út 2, in the centre of town (Ⓣ45/421-100; ❷), with en-suite bathrooms.

Záhony and Zsurk

ZÁHONY is the "front line" between relatively prosperous, westernized Hungary and the impoverished masses of the former Soviet Union. When travel restrictions were eased in 1990, people flooded in from Ukraine and Russia to trade goods for foodstuffs at the "**free**" **market** on the edge of town, until controls were reimposed the following year. Since then, spivs and dealers from Hungary and Poland drive across the border to do business in Uzhgorod, using Záhony as a base. Unless you relish hobnobbing with such characters, however, the only reason to come here is another picturesque **church** with a wooden belfry, in the nearby village of **ZSURK**.

Should either prospect appeal, it's possible to stay at the *Európa Panzió* at Ady Endre út 4, near the station in Záhony (Ⓣ45/425-835; ❷). There are **trains** from here down to Nyíregyháza and Debrecen, but you are not allowed to board international expresses running in either direction.

Into the Ukraine

Obtaining **Ukrainian visas** is an uncertain business, best done at the Ukrainian Embassy in Budapest or elsewhere – leave several days for the process – and *not* at the border. The **road crossing** is a narrow bridge, easily found by following the traffic, but notorious for robberies and car thefts. Even **customs** at Chop on the Ukrainian side may be out to extort cash or confiscate desirable items. The reason for this becomes apparent once you enter Trans-Carpathia, the mountainous region traditionally known as **Ruthenia**, control of which has passed from Hungary to Czechoslovakia to the USSR to the Ukraine within the last eighty years. This forgotten corner of Central Europe is as poor and backward as Albania, with a tradition of emigration that took Andy Warhol and Robert Maxwell to their adoptive countries. Its ethnic mix includes Hungarians, Slovaks, Roma and Romanians, not to mention a large number of Ruthenians (*Rusyns*), who cling to their Uniate faith.

The main road and rail line run through **Uzhgorod** (also a border crossing into Slovakia), known as *Ungvár* to its Hungarian-speaking inhabitants. Another road heads east to **Mukachevo** (*Munkács*), the site of a last-ditch battle against the Habsburgs during the Kuruc War. From here, the road continues across the mountains towards the Ukrainian city of Lvov, via the **Verecke Pass** through which Árpád led the Magyar tribes into the Carpathian Basin.

Travel details

Trains

Baja to: Bátaszék (12 daily; 20min); Budapest (2 daily; 4hr); Kiskunhalas (8 daily; 2hr).
Békéscsaba to: Budapest (every 1–2hr; 3hr); Szeged (11 daily; 2hr).
Debrecen to: Budapest (hourly; 2hr 30min–3hr 30min); Hortobágy (9 daily; 1hr); Mátészalka (8 daily; 1hr 20min); Nyírbátor (8 daily; 1hr); Nyíregyháza (every 30–45min; 30–45min).
Kalocsa to: Kiskőrös (4 daily; 1hr).
Kecskemét to: Budapest (10 daily; 1hr 30min); Bugac (3 daily; 1hr); Kiskunfélegyháza (every 1–2hr; 20min); Szeged (12 daily; 1–2hr).
Kiskőrös to: Kalocsa (4 daily; 1hr).
Kiskunfélegyháza to: Budapest (10 daily; 1hr 45min); Kecskemét (every 1–2hr; 20min); Szeged (every 1–2hr; 45min–1hr).
Kiskunhalas to: Baja (8 daily; 1hr 30min).
Mátészalka to: Csenger (5 daily; 1hr); Vásárosnamény (6 daily; 30min); Záhony (6 daily; 1hr 30min).
Nyírbátor to: Záhony (5 daily; 45min).
Nyíregyháza to: Budapest (every 1–2hr; 3hr–3hr 30min); Debrecen (every 30–45min; 30–45min); Mátészalka (8 daily; 1hr 15min); Nagykálló (8 daily; 15min); Nyírbátor (7 daily; 1hr).
Szeged to: Békéscsaba (11 daily; 2hr); Budapest (10 daily; 1–2hr); Hódmezővásárhely (12 daily; 30–45min); Kiskunfélegyháza (every 30–45min; 45min–1hr).

Buses

Baja to: Budapest (10 daily; 3hr 15min); Hajos (4 Mon–Fri; 40min); Kalocsa (hourly; 1hr); Kecskemét (8 daily; 2hr 40min); Kiskőrös (6 daily; 1hr 15min); Mohács (10 daily; 40min); Pécs (11 daily; 2hr); Szeged (every 1–2hr; 2hr 15min); Szekszárd (11 daily; 40min).
Békéscsaba to: Budapest (3 daily; 4hr); Debrecen (9 daily; 3hr); Eger (2 daily; 5hr); Gyula (every 30–60min; 1hr); Kecskemét (5 daily; 2hr 30min); Miskolc (1 daily; 5hr); Pécs (1 daily; 6hr 30min); Szeged (8 daily; 1hr 45min).
Csongrád to: Baja (2 daily; 3hr); Budapest (8 daily; 3hr); Gyula (1 daily; 2hr); Hódmezővásárhely (8 daily; 45min); Kecskemét (10 daily; 50min); Kiskunfélegyháza (every 45–90min; 30min); Őpusztaszer (10 daily; 45min); Szeged (12 daily; 1hr 15min).
Debrecen to: Békéscsaba (8 daily; 3hr 30min); Eger (4 daily; 3hr); Gyöngyös (2 daily; 4hr 45min); Gyula (3 daily; 3hr); Hajdúszoboszló (hourly; 45min); Hortobágy (4 daily; 1hr); Jászberény (1 daily; 2hr 30min); Miskolc (every 30–90min; 2hr); Nyíregyháza (5 daily, 3 at weekends; 1hr); Szeged (3 daily; 5hr); Tiszafüred (2 daily; 1hr 45min); Tokaj (2 daily; 1hr 30min).
Gyula to: Békéscsaba (every 30–60min; 1hr); Debrecen (3 daily; 2hr); Eger (1 daily; 5hr 30min); Mako (6 daily; 2hr); Mezohegyes (4 daily; 1hr 30min); Miskolc (1 daily; 5hr 15min); Szarvas (Mon–Fri 6 daily; 1hr 15min); Szeged (7 daily; 2hr).
Hajdúszoboszló to: Debrecen (hourly; 45min); Eger (1 daily; 3hr 15min); Hajdúböszörmény (2 daily; 1hr); Miskolc (5 daily; 2hr 45min).
Hódmezővásárhely to: Békéscsaba (8 daily; 1hr 20min); Csongrad (8 daily; 45min); Kecskemét (5 daily; 1hr 45min); Kiskunfélegyháza (5 daily; 1hr 15min); Mako (1–2hr; 45min); Mártely (every 60–90min; 20min); Szeged (every 40–60min; 30min).
Hortobágy to: Debrecen (1 daily; 45min); Eger (1 daily; 2hr 15min); Hajdúszoboszló (1 daily; 1hr 15min); Tiszafüred (1 daily; 1hr).
Jászberény to: Cegléd (6 daily; 1hr 15min); Debrecen (1 daily; 4hr 30min); Kecskemét (6 daily; 2hr); Miskolc (2 daily; 4hr 45min); Parádfürdő (3 daily; 2hr 15min); Szolnok (6 daily; 50min).
Kalocsa to Baja (every 40–90min; 1hr); Budapest (12 daily; 2hr 30min); Hajos (8 daily; 30min); Szeged (4 daily; 2hr 30min); Székesfehérvár (2 daily; 3hr); Szekszárd (6 daily; 1hr).
Kecskemét to: Budapest (every 60–90min; 1hr 45min); Bugac (Mon–Fri 5 daily, Sat & Sun 2 daily; 45min); Dunafoldvár (8 daily; 1hr 10min); Eger (3 daily; 4hr); Gyöngyös (5 daily; 3hr); Jászberény (7 daily; 2hr); Kiskőrös (4 daily; 1hr); Kiskunfélegyháza (every 40–60min; 45min); Szeged (10 daily; 1hr 30min).
Kiskunfélegyháza to: Bugac (Mon–Fri 9 daily Sat & Sun 4 daily; 30min); Kecskemét (hourly; 45min); Kiskunhalas (5 daily; 1hr 20min); Szeged (11 daily; 1hr).
Nyírbátor to: Máriapócs (7 daily; 25min); Mátészalka (2 daily; 30min); Nagykálló (4 daily; 40min); Nyíregyháza (Mon–Fri 3 daily; 1hr).
Nyíregyháza to: Debrecen (5 daily, 3 at weekends; 1hr); Miskolc (3 daily except Sun; 2hr); Szeged (2 weekly; 6hr); Tokaj (2 daily; 1hr 15 min).
Szeged to: Baja (8 daily; 2hr 15min); Békéscsaba (7 daily; 2hr); Budapest (7 daily; 3hr); Csongrád (8

daily; 1hr 30min); Debrecen (2 daily; 5hr); Gyula (5 daily; 2hr); Hódmezővásárhely (hourly; 1hr 30min); Kecskemét (10 daily; 1hr 30min); Miskolc (2 daily; 6hr 30min); Őpusztaszer (10 daily; 45min); Pécs (7 daily; 3hr 15min); Tiszafüred (2 daily; 5hr).
Szolnok to: Eger (2–3 daily; 2hr 30min); Jászberény (8 daily; 1hr 15min); Tiszafüred (6 daily; 1hr 30min).
Tiszafüred to: Hodmezővásárhely (1 daily; 4hr 30min); Miskolc (2 daily except Sat & Sun; 1hr 30min); Szeged (1 daily; 5hr); Szentes (1 daily; 3hr 45min).

Contexts

Contexts

History

The region of the Carpathian basin known as Hungary (Magyarország) changed hands many times before the Magyars arrived here at the end of the ninth century, and its history is marked by migrations, invasions and drastic changes, as Asia and Europe have clashed and blended. Over the centuries, borders have shifted considerably, so geographical limits as well as historical epochs are somewhat arbitrary. Transylvania, an integral part of Hungary for hundreds of years, was lost to Romania in 1920, and the plight of its Magyar minority remains a contentious issue, while the situation of ethnic Hungarians in Serbia and Slovakia is also a cause for national concern.

Prehistory

Although recorded history of the area now covered by Hungary begins with the arrival of the Romans, archeological evidence of **Stone Age** (30,000–8000 BC) humans has been found in the Istállóskő and Pilisszántó caves in northern Hungary, suggesting that the earliest inhabitants lived by gathering fruit and hunting reindeer and mammoths. The end of the Ice Age created favourable conditions for the development of agriculture and the domestication of animals, which spread up through the Balkans in the Neolithic era, and was characteristic of the **Kőrös culture** (5500–3400 BC): clans living alongside the River Tisza, herding sheep and goats and worshipping fertility goddesses. As humans became more settled and spread into Transdanubia, evidence survives of mounds (*tell*) full of artefacts, apparently leading towards the rise of the **Lengyel culture** around Lake Balaton.

During the **Bronze Age** (2000–800 BC), warlike tribes arrived from the Balkans and steppes, introducing cattle and horses. Subsequent migrants brought new technology – iron came with the Cimmerians, and the Asiatic Scythians (500–250 BC) brought the potter's wheel and manufactured goods from Greek traders on the Black Sea coast – while the **Celts**, who superseded them in the early third century BC, introduced glassblowing and left mournful sculptures and superb jewellery (most notably the gold treasures of Szárazd-Regöly), before being subdued by the Romans.

The Romans

The **Roman conquest** was initiated by Augustus at the beginning of the Christian era, primarily to create a buffer zone in **Pannonia** between the empire and the barbarians to the east. By the middle of the first century AD, Roman rule extended throughout Transdanubia, from the Sava to the Danube; fortified with *castra*, the river formed the *limes* or military frontier. Trade, administration and culture grew up around the garrison towns and spread along the roads constructed to link the imperial heartland with the far-flung colonies in Dacia (Romania) and Dalmatia (Yugoslavia). Pécs, Sopron, Szombathely and Buda were all Roman towns, as archeological finds have revealed. Some of the best-preserved Roman remains are found in these towns, including Buda's amphitheatre and baths, the ruins of Gorsium near Székesfehérvár, and Szombathely's Temple of Isis.

During the fourth century the Romans began to withdraw from Pannonia, handing over its defence to the Vandals and Jazygians who lived beyond the Danube. In 430 these people fell under the invading **Huns**, whose empire reached its zenith and then fragmented with the death of Attila in 453. Other warring tribes – Ostrogoths, Gepidae and Langobards – occupied the region for the next 150 years, before being swept aside by the **Avars**, whose empire survived until the beginning of the eighth century, when the region once again came up for grabs for any determined invader.

The Magyars

The **Magyars**' origins lie in the Finno-Ugric peoples who dwelt in the snowy forests between the Baltic and the middle Urals. Around the first century AD, some of these tribes migrated south across the Bashkiran steppes and fell under the influence of Turkic and Persian culture, gradually becoming tent-dwelling nomadic herders who lived on a diet of mare's milk, horse flesh, fish and berries. Some archeologists believe that they mingled with the ancient Bulgars north of the Caspian Sea (in a land known as "Magna Bulgaria"), before the majority fled from marauding Petchenegs in about 750 and moved westwards to settle on the far bank of the River Don in the so-called Etelköz region, around the year 830. Ties with the Huns and Avars have been postulated, including a common language, but there's more evidence to link the seven original Magyar tribes with three Kavar tribes, known collectively as the Onogur, or "Ten Arrows".

Overpopulation and Petcheneg attacks forced the Onogur to move westwards in 889, and tradition has it that the seven Magyar chieftains elected **Árpád** as their leader, pledging fealty to his heirs with a blood oath. Accompanied by smaller Kun (or Cuman) tribes, the Onogur entered the Carpathian basin in 896, and began the "**land-taking**" (*honfoglalás*) or conquest of the region. Six Magyar tribes settled west of the Danube and in the upper Tisza region, the seventh took the approaches to Transylvania, while the lower Tisza and the northern fringes of the Plain went to the Kuns and Kavars. The Magyars continued to raid for the next seventy years, striking terror as far afield as Constantinople and Orleans (where people thought them to be Huns), until a series of defeats persuaded them to settle for assimilating their gains.

Civilization developed gradually, after Árpád's great-grandson **Prince Géza** established links with Bavaria and invited Catholic missionaries to Hungary. His son **Stephen (István)** took the decisive step of applying to Pope Sylvester for recognition, and on Christmas Day in the year 1000 was crowned as a Christian king and began **converting** his pagan subjects with the help of Bishop Gellért. Royal authority was extended over the non-tribal lands by means of the *megye* (county) system, and defended by fortified *vár* (castles); artisans and priests were imported to spread skills and the new religion; and tribal rebellions were crushed. Stephen was subsequently credited with the foundation of Hungary and canonized after his death in 1038. His mummified hand and the Crown of St Stephen have since been revered as both holy and national relics.

The Middle Ages

Succession struggles raged for decades following Stephen's death, and of the sixteen kings who preceded Andrew II (1205–35) only the humane László I (also canonized), Kálmán "the Booklover" and Béla III contributed anything significant to Hungary's development. Fortunately, invasions were few during the eleventh and twelfth centuries, and **German and Slovak immigrants** helped double the population to about two million by 1200. Parts of **Transylvania** were settled by the Magyars and Székely, perhaps before the second half of the eleventh century, when the "lands of St Stephen" were extended to include **Slavonia** (between the Sava and Drava rivers) and the unwillingly "associated" state of **Croatia**. The growth in royal power caused tribal leaders to rebel in 1222, when Andrew II was forced to recognize the "noble" status and rights of **the Natio** – landed freemen exempt from taxation – in the "Golden Bull", a kind of Hungarian Magna Carta.

Andrew's son **Béla IV** was trying to restore royal authority when disaster struck from the east – the **Mongol invasion** of 1241, which devastated Hungary. Hundreds of towns and villages were sacked; refugees fled to the swamps and forests; crops were burned or left unharvested; and famine and plague followed. Population losses ranged from sixty to one hundred percent on the Plain and twenty percent in Transdanubia, and after the Mongol withdrawal a year later (prompted by the timely death of the Khan) Hungary faced a mammoth task of **reconstruction** – the chief achievement of Béla's reign, to which foreign settlers made a large contribution. Renewed domestic feuding (complicated by foreign intervention and the arrival of more Cuman tribes) dogged the reign of Andrew III, and worsened when he died heirless in 1301, marking the **end of the Árpád dynasty**.

Foreign rule

Foreign powers advanced their own claimants, and for a while there were three competing kings, all duly crowned. **Charles Robert** of the French Angevin (or Anjou) dynasty eventually triumphed in 1310, when his rivals went home in disgust; and despite colonial skirmishes with Venice, Serbia and Wallachia, Hungary itself enjoyed a period of peace, while the Mongols and other great powers were occupied elsewhere. Gold mines in Transylvania and northern Hungary – the richest in Europe – stabilized state finances and the currency. Charles's son **Louis the Great** reigned (1342–82) during a period of expansion, when the population rose to three million; and by war and dynastic aggrandizement crown territory grew to include Dalmatia, the Banat, Galicia and (in theory) Poland. Louis, however, sired only daughters, so that after his demise another foreigner ascended the throne in 1395 – **Sigismund of Luxembourg**, Prince of Bohemia, whom the nobles despised as the "Czech swine". His extravagant follies and campaigns abroad were notorious, and while Sigismund recognized the growing threat of the Turks he failed to prevent their advance up through the Balkans.

During the fourteenth century, the realm contained 49 boroughs, about 500 market towns and 26,000 villages. Everyone benefited from peace and expanded trade, but the rewards weren't shared evenly, for the Angevins favoured towns and guilds, and, most of all, the top stratum of the Natio, on whom they depended for troops (*banderia*) when war posed a threat. The burden fell upon the **peasantry**, who lacked "free" status and were compelled to pay *porta* (gate tax) to the state, tithes to the church, and one ninth of their produce to the landlords – plus extra taxes and obligations during times of war, or to finance new royal palaces.

Sigismund died in 1447 leaving one daughter, Elizabeth, just as **the Turks** were poised to invade and succession struggles seemed inevitable. The Turks might have taken Hungary then, but for a series of stunning defeats inflicted upon them by **János Hunyadi**, a Transylvanian warlord of Vlach (Romanian) origin. The lifting of the siege of Nándorfehérervár (Belgrade) in 1456 checked the Turkish advance and caused rejoicing throughout Christendom – the ringing of church bells at noon was decreed by the pope to mark this victory – while Hunyadi rose to be Voivode or Prince of Transylvania, and later regent for the boy king László. Following Hunyadi's death, László's early demise, and much skulduggery, Mihály Szilágyi staged a coup and put his nephew Mátyás (Matthias), Hunyadi's son, on the throne in 1458.

Renaissance and decline

Mátyás Corvinus is remembered as the "**Renaissance King**" for his statecraft and multiple talents (including astrology), while his second wife **Beatrice** of Naples lured humanists and artists from Italy to add lustre to their palaces at Buda and Visegrád (of which some remains survive). Mátyás was an enlightened despot renowned for his fairness: "King Mátyás is dead, justice is departed", people mourned. By taxing the nobles (against every precedent) he raised a standing force of 30,000 mercenaries called the Black Army, which secured the realm and made Hungary one of Central Europe's leading powers. However, when he died in 1490 leaving no legitimate heir, the nobles looked for a king "whose plaits they could hold in their fists".

Such a man was Ulászló II (whose habit of assenting to any proposal earned him the nickname "King Okay"). Under his rule the Black Army and its tax base were whittled away by the Diet, which met to approve royal decrees and taxes, while the nobility filched common land and otherwise increased their exploitation of the peasantry. Impelled by poverty, many joined the crusade of 1514, which, under the leadership of **György Dózsa**, turned into an **uprising against the landlords**. Its savage repression (over 70,000 peasants were killed and Dózsa was roasted alive) was followed by the **Werbőczy Code** of 1517, binding the peasants to "perpetual **serfdom**" on their masters' land and 52 days of *robot* (unpaid labour) in the year.

Hungary's decline accelerated as corruption and incompetence bankrupted the treasury, forts along the border crumbled and the revived banderia system of mobilization disintegrated. Ulászló's son Louis II was only nine when crowned, and by 1520 the Turks, under Sultan Süleyman "the Magnificent", had resumed their advance northwards, capturing the run-down forts in Serbia. In August 1526 the Turks crossed the Drava and Louis hastened south to confront them at the **battle of Mohács** – a catastrophic defeat for the Magyars, whose army was wiped out together with its monarch and commanders.

Turkish conquest: Hungary divided

After sacking Buda and the south, the Turks withdrew in 1526 to muster forces for their real objective, Vienna, the "Red Apple". To forestall this, Ferdinand of Habsburg proclaimed himself king and occupied western Hungary, while in Buda the nobility put **János Zápolyai** on the throne. Following Zápolyai's death in 1541 Ferdinand claimed full sovereignty, but the Sultan occupied Buda and central Hungary, and made Zápolyai's young son ruler of Transylvania. Thereafter Transylvania became a semi-autonomous principality, nominally loyal to the Sultan and jealously coveted by the Habsburgs. The tripartite **division of Hungary** was formally recognized in 1568. Despite various official or localized truces, warfare became a feature of everyday life for the next 150 years, and national independence was not recovered for centuries.

Royal Hungary – basically western Transdanubia and the north – served as a "human moat" against the Turkish forces that threatened to storm Austria and Western Europe, who were kept at bay by Hungarian sacrifices at Szigetvár, Kőszeg and other fortresses. Notwithstanding constitutional arrangements to safeguard the Natio's privileges, real power passed to the Habsburg chancellery and war council, where the liberation of Hungary took second place to Austria's defence and aggrandizement, and the subjugation of Transylvania.

Turkish-occupied Hungary – Eyalet-i Budin – was ruled by a Pasha in Buda, with much of the land either deeded to the Sultan's soldiers and officials, or run directly as a state fief (*khasse*). The peasants were brutally exploited, for many had to pay rent to both their absentee Magyar landlords and the occupying Turks. Their plight is evident from a letter to a Hungarian lord by the villagers of Batthyán: "Verily, it is better to be Your Lordship's slaves, bag and baggage, than those of an alien people." Peasants fled their villages on the Alföld to the safer fields around the expanding "agro-towns" of Debrecen and Szeged, the nexus of the cattle trade which gradually supplanted agriculture, while neglect and wanton tree-felling transformed the Plain into a swampy wasteland – the *puszta*.

The Voivodes of **Transylvania** endeavoured to provoke war between the Habsburgs and Turks, in order to increase their independence from both and satisfy the feudal Nationes. The latter, representing the elite of the region's Magyars, Saxons and Székely, combined to deny the indigenous Vlachs political power, while competing amongst themselves and extending the borders of Transylvania (then much bigger than today). István Bocskai's Hajdúk forces secured the Szatmár region and Gábor Bethlen promoted economic and social development, but Prince György Rákóczi II aimed too high and brought the wrath of the Sultan down on Transylvania.

Religion was an additional complicating factor. The Protestant Reformation gained many adherents in Hungary during the sixteenth century, and, while religious toleration was decreed in Transylvania in 1572, in Royal Hungary the Counter-Reformation gathered force under Habsburg rule. The Turks, ironically, were indifferent to the issue and treated all their Christian subjects (Rayah) with equal disdain. After the expulsion of the Turks, Protestant landowners were dispossessed in favour of foreign servants of the crown – a major cause of subsequent anti-Habsburg revolts.

Habsburg rule

After heavy fighting between 1683 and 1699, a multinational army evicted the Ottomans, and the Turks relinquished all claims by signing the **Peace of Karlowitz**. Yet for many years peace remained a mirage, for the Hungarians now bitterly resented Habsburg policy and their plundering armies. The **Kuruc revolt** (1677–85) led by **Imre Thököly** was but a prelude to the full-scale **War of Independence** of 1703–11, when peasants and nobles banded together under **Ferenc Rákóczi II**, György's grandson, and initially routed the enemy. Ultimately, however, they were defeated by superior Habsburg power and the desertion of their ally, Louis XIV of France, and peace born of utter exhaustion came at last to Hungary.

Habsburg rule combined force with paternalism, especially during the reign of Empress **Maria Theresa** (1740–80), who believed the Hungarians to be "fundamentally a good people, with whom one can do anything if one takes them the right way". The policy of "*impopulatio*" settled thousands of Swabians, Slovaks, Serbs and Romanians in the deserted regions of Hungary, so that, in areas such as the "Military Border" along the Sava, Magyars became a minority. By the end of the eighteenth century they formed only 35 percent of the population of the huge kingdom. For the aristocrats it was an age of glory: the Esterházy, Grassalkovich and Batthyány families and their lesser imitators commissioned over 200 palaces, and Baroque town centres flourished. Yet the masses were virtually serfs, using medieval methods that impoverished the soil, and mired in isolated villages. Cattle, grain and wine – Hungary's main exports – went cheap to Austria, which tried to monopolize industry.

The **Germanization** of culture, education and administration was another feature of Habsburg policy. Yet, though the richest nobles and most of the urban bourgeoisie chose the Habsburg style, the petty gentry and peasantry clung stubbornly to their Magyar identity. The ideals of the **Enlightenment** found growing support among intellectuals, and the revival of the **Magyar language** became inseparable from nationalist politics. **Ferenc Kazinczy**, who refashioned Hungarian as a literary language and translated foreign classics, was associated with the seven **Jacobin conspirators**, executed for plotting treason against the Habsburgs in 1795.

The nineteenth century: nationalism and reform

Magyar nationalism, espoused by sections of the Natio, became increasingly vocal during the early nineteenth century. Hungary's backwardness was a matter for patriotic shame and self-interested concern, especially after the occurrence of peasant riots in the impoverished, cholera-ridden Zempléni, and the publication of *Hitel* ("Credit"), written by Count István Széchenyi, which scathingly indicted the country's semi-feudal economy. However, most nobles were determined to preserve their privileges. One wrote that "God himself has differentiated between us, assigning to the peasant labour and need, to the lord abundance and a merry life". Moreover, national liberation was seen in exclusively Magyar terms – the idea that non-Magyars within the multinational state might wish to assert their own identity was regarded as subversive.

The **Reform Era** (roughly 1825–48) saw many changes. Business, the arts, and technology were in ferment, with Jews playing a major role in creating wealth and ideas (although they remained second-class citizens). The **Diet** became increasingly defiant in its dealings with Vienna over finances and laws, and parliamentarians like Ferenc Deák, Count Batthyány and Baron Eötvös acted in the shadow of the "giants" of the time, Széchenyi and Kossuth, who expounded rival programmes for change. Count **István Széchenyi**, the land-owning, Anglophile author of *Hitel*, was a tireless practical innovator, introducing silkworms, steamboats and the Academy, as well as an unprecedented tax on the Natio to pay for the construction of his life's monument, the Chain Bridge (Lánchíd) linking Buda and Pest. His arch rival was **Lajos Kossuth**, small-town lawyer turned Member of Parliament and editor of the radical *Pesti Hirlap*, which scandalized and delighted citizens. Kossuth detested the Habsburgs, revered "universal liberty", and demanded an end to serfdom and censorship. Magyar chauvinism was his blind spot, however, and the law of 1840, his greatest pre-revolutionary achievement, inflamed dormant nationalist feelings among Croats, Slovaks and Romanians by making Magyar the sole official language – an act for which his ambitions would later suffer.

Revolution

The fall of the French monarchy precipitated a crisis within the Habsburg Empire, which Kossuth exploited to bring about the **1848 Revolution** in Hungary. The emperor yielded to demands for a constitutional monarchy, universal taxation, wider voting rights and the union of Transylvania with Hungary; while in Budapest the nobles took fright and abolished serfdom when the poet **Sándor Petőfi** threatened them with thousands of peasants camped out in the suburbs. However, the slighted nationalities rallied against the Magyars in Croatia and Transylvania, and the reassertion of Habsburg control over Italy and Czechoslovakia closed the noose. The new emperor Franz Josef declared that Hungary would be partitioned after its defeat, in reaction to which the Debrecen Diet declared **Hungarian independence** – a state crushed by August 1849, when Tsar Nicholas of Russia sent armies to support the Habsburgs, who instituted a reign of terror.

Gradually, brute force was replaced by a **policy of compromise**, by which Hungary was economically integrated with Austria and given a major shareholding in the Habsburg Empire, henceforth known as the "Dual Monarchy". The compromise (*Ausgleich*) of 1867, engineered by **Ferenc Deák**, brought Hungary prosperity and status, but tied the country inextricably to the empire's fortunes. Simmering nationalist passions would henceforth be focused against Hungary as much as Austria, and diplomatic treaties between Austria and Germany would bind Hungary to them in the event of war. In 1896, however, such dangers seemed remote, and people celebrated **Hungary's millennial anniversary** with enthusiasm.

World War I and its aftermath

Dragged into **World War I** by its allegiance to the Central Powers, Hungary was facing defeat by the autumn of 1918. The Western or Entente powers decided to dismantle the Habsburg Empire in favour of the "**Successor States**" – Romania, Czechoslovakia and Yugoslavia – which would acquire much of their territory at Hungary's expense. In Budapest, the October 30 "Michaelmas Daisy Revolution" put the Social Democratic party of **Mihály Károly** in power, but his government avoided the issue of land reform, attempted unsuccessfully to negotiate peace with the Entente, and finally resigned when France backed further demands by the Successor States.

On March 21, 1919, the Social Democrats agreed on cooperation with the **Communists**, who proclaimed a **Republic of Councils** (Tanácsköztársaság) led by **Béla Kun**, which ruled through local Soviets. Hoping for radical change and believing that "Russia will save us", many people initially supported the new regime, but enforced nationalization of land and capital, and attacks on religion, soon alienated the majority. Beset by the Czech Legion in Slovakia and by internal unrest, the regime collapsed in August before the advancing Romanian army, which occupied Budapest.

The rise of fascism

Then came the **White Terror**, as right-wing gangs spread out from Szeged, killing "Reds" and Jews, who were made scapegoats for the earlier Communist "Red Terror". **Admiral Miklós Horthy** appointed himself regent and ordered a return to "traditional values" with a vengeance. Meanwhile, at the Paris Conference, Hungary was obliged to sign the **Treaty of Trianon** (July 4, 1920), surrendering two-thirds of its historic territory and three-fifths of its total population (three million in all) to the Successor States. The bitterest loss was **Transylvania**, whose 103,093 square kilometres and 1.7 million Magyars went to Romania – a devastating blow to national pride.

During the **1920s and 1930s**, campaigning for the overturn of the Trianon diktat was the "acceptable" outlet for politics, while workers' unions were tightly controlled and peasants struggled to form associations against the landlords and the gendarmerie, who rigged ballots and gerrymandered as in the old days. Politics were dominated by the Kormánypárt (Government Party) led by Count Bethlen, representing the Catholic Church and the landed gentry, which resisted any changes that would threaten their power. Social hardships increased, particularly in the countryside where the landless **peasantry** constituted "three million beggars" whose misery concerned the **Village Explorers** (Falukutató), a movement of the literary intelligentsia ranging across the political spectrum. With the Social Democrats co-opted by conservatism and the Communist Party illegal, many workers and disgruntled petits bourgeois turned to the **radical right** to voice their grievances, and were easily turned against Jews and the "Trianon Powers".

Resentment against France, Britain and Romania predisposed many Hungarians to admire **Nazi Germany**'s defiance of the Versailles Treaty – a sentiment nurtured by the Reich's grant of credits for **industrialization**, and Nazi sympathizers within Volksdeutsche communities, commerce, the civil service and the officer corps. The rise of **anti-Semitism** gave power to nationalist politicians like **Gyula Gömbös**. At the same time, Hungary's belated industrial growth was partly due to the acquisition of territory from Czechoslovakia, following Germany's dismemberment of the latter. The annexation of Austria made the Reich militarily supreme in Central Europe, and Hungary's submission to German hegemony almost inevitable.

World War II

With the outbreak of **World War II**, the government's pro-Nazi policy initially paid dividends. Romania was compelled to return **northern Transylvania** in July 1940, and Hungary gained additional territory from the invasion of Yugoslavia a year later. Hoping for more, Premier Bárdossy committed Hungary to the Nazi invasion of the USSR in June 1941 – an act condemned by the former prime minister, Teleki (who had engineered the recovery of Transylvania), as the "policy of vultures". The Hungarian Second Army perished covering the retreat from Stalingrad, while at home, Germany demanded ever more foodstuffs and forced labour. As Axis fortunes waned Horthy prepared to declare neutrality, but Hitler forestalled him with "Operation Margarethe" – the outright **Nazi occupation of Hungary** in March 1944.

Under Sztójay's puppet government, Hungarian **Jews** were forced into ghettos to await their deportation to Auschwitz and Belsen, a fate hindered only by the heroism of the underground, a handful of people organized by the Swedish diplomat Raoul Wallenberg, and by the manoeuvring of some Horthyite politicians. Mindful of Romania's successful escape from the Axis in August, Horthy declared a surprise armistice on October 15, just as the Red Army crossed Hungary's eastern border. In response, Germany installed a government of the native **Arrow Cross Fascists**, or Nyilas, led by Ferenc Szálasi, whose gangs roamed Budapest extorting valuables and murdering people, while the Nazis systematically plundered Hungary. They blew up the Danube bridges and compelled the Russians to take Budapest by storm – a siege that reduced much of Buda to ruins. Meanwhile in Debrecen, an assembly of anti-Fascist parties met under Soviet auspices to nominate a **provisional government**, which took power after the Germans fled Hungary in April 1945.

The Rákosi era

In the November 1945 **elections** the Smallholders' Party won an outright majority, but the Soviet military insisted that the Communists and Social Democrats (with seventeen percent of the vote) remain in government. **Land reform** and limited **nationalization** were enacted, while the Communists tightened their grip over the Ministry of the Interior (which controlled the police) and elections became increasingly fraudulent. **Mátyás Rákosi**, Stalin's man in Hungary, gradually undermined and fragmented the "bourgeois" parties with what he called "salami tactics" (chopping his opponents into small groups and then swallowing them), and by 1948, officially called the "**Year of Change**", the Communists were strong enough to coerce the Social Democrats to join them in a single **Workers' Party**, and neutralize the Smallholders. Church schools were seized, Cardinal Mindszenty was jailed for "espionage" and the peasants were forced into collective farms. More than 500,000 Hungarians were imprisoned, tortured or shot in native concentration camps like Recsk, or as deportees in the Soviet Union – victims of the **ÁVO** secret police (renamed the ÁVH in 1949), who spread terror throughout society.

Soviet culture and the personality cults of Rákosi (known as "Baldhead" or "Asshole" to his subjects) and Stalin were imposed on the country, and Hungarian classics such as the *Tragedy of Man* were banned for failing to meet the standards of Socialist Realism. Under the 1949 **Five Year Plan**, heavy industry took absolute priority over agriculture and consumer production. To fill the new factories, peasants streamed into towns and women were dragooned into the labour force. Living standards plummeted, and the whole of society was subjected to the laws and dictates of the Party. "Class conscious" workers and peasants were raised to high positions and "class enemies" were discriminated against, while Party officials enjoyed luxuries unavailable to the populace, who suffered hunger and squalor.

Although the Smallholders retained nominal positions in government, real power lay with Rákosi's clique, known as the "Jewish Quartet". As elsewhere in Eastern Europe at this time, Hungary saw bitter **feuds within the Communist Party**. In October 1949, the "Muscovites" purged the more independently minded "national" Communists on the pretext of "Titoism". The former Interior Minister **László Rajk** was executed, and his friend and successor (and, later, betrayer), **János Kádár**, was jailed and tortured with others during a second wave of purges. Two years later, following Stalin's death in March 1953, Kremlin power struggles resulted in a more moderate Soviet leadership and the abrupt replacement of Rákosi by **Imre Nagy**. His "**New Course**", announced in July, promised a more balanced industrial strategy and eased pressure on the peasants to collectivize, besides curbing the ÁVH terror. Nagy, however, had few allies within the Kremlin, and in 1955 Rákosi was able to strike back, expelling Nagy from the Party for "deviationism", and declaring a **return to Stalinist policies**. This brief interlude, however, had encouraged murmurings of resistance.

1956: the Uprising

The first act of opposition came from the official Writers' Union, who, in their November Memorandum, objected to the rule of force. The Party clamped down, but also began to rehabilitate the Rajk purge victims. During June **1956** the intellectuals' **Petőfi circle** held increasingly outspoken public debates, and **Júlia Rajk** denounced "the men who have ruined this country, corrupted the Party, liquidated thousands and driven millions to despair". Moscow responded to the unrest by replacing Rákosi with **Ernő Gerő**, another hardliner – a move which merely stoked public resentment. The mood came to a head in October, when 200,000 people attended Rajk's reburial, Nagy was readmitted to the Party, and **students** in Szeged and Budapest organized to demand greater national independence and freedom.

In Poland, Gomulka's reform Communists had just won concessions from the Kremlin, and Budapest students decided to march on October 23 to the General Bem statue, a symbol of Polish-Hungarian solidarity. Patriotic feelings rose as about 50,000 people assembled, the procession swelling as it approached Parliament. A hesitant speech there by Nagy failed to satisfy them, and students besieged the Radio Building on Bródy utca, demanding to voice their grievances on the airwaves. In response, the ÁVH guards opened fire, killing many. Almost immediately, this triggered a city-wide **Uprising** against the ÁVH. The regular police did little to control it, and when Soviet tanks intervened units of the Hungarian army began to side with the insurgents.

Over the next five days fighting spread throughout Hungary, despite Nagy's reinstatement as premier and pleas for order. **Revolutionary councils** sprang up in towns and factories and free newspapers appeared, demanding "*Ruszkik* *haza*" (Russians go home), free elections, civil liberties, industrial democracy and neutrality. Intellectuals who had led the first protests now found themselves left behind by uncontrollable dynamism on the streets. The Party leadership temporized, reshuffled the cabinet and struggled to stay in control, as all the "old" parties reappeared and the newly liberated Cardinal Mindszenty provided a focus for the resurgent Right.

The negotiated **Soviet withdrawal**, beginning on October 29, was merely a delaying tactic, while the Russians regrouped in the countryside before bringing in fresh troops from Romania and the USSR. On November 1, Nagy announced Hungary's withdrawal from the Warsaw Pact and asked the UN to support **Hungarian neutrality**; that night, Kádár and Ferenc Münnich slipped away from Parliament to join the Russians, who were preparing to crush the "counter-revolution". America downplayed Hungary in the United Nations while the Suez crisis preoccupied world attention, but the CIA-sponsored **Radio Free Europe** encouraged the Magyars to expect Western aid. At dawn on November 4, once Budapest and other centres had been surrounded with tanks under cover of a snowstorm, the **Soviet attack** began.

Armed resistance was crushed within days, but the workers occupied their factories and proclaimed a **general strike**, maintained for months despite **mass arrests**. Deprived of physical power, the people continued to make symbolic protests like the "Mothers' March" in December. Inexorably, however, the Party and ÁVH apparatus reasserted its control. Over 200,000 **refugees** fled to the West, while at home thousands were jailed or executed, including Nagy and other leading "revisionists", shot in 1958 after a secret trial.

Kádár's Hungary

In the aftermath of the Uprising, the new Party leader **János Kádár** ruthlessly suppressed the last vestiges of opposition. After the mid-1960s, however, his name came to be associated with the **gradual reform** of Hungary's social and economic system from a totalitarian regime to one based, at least in part, on **compromise**. Kádár's famous phrase, "Whoever is not against us is with us" (a reversal of the Stalinist slogan), invited a tacit compact between Party and people. Both had been shaken by the events of 1956, and realized that bold changes – as happened in Czechoslovakia in 1967 and 1968 – only invited Soviet intervention, justified by the Brezhnev doctrine of "limited sovereignty".

Having stimulated the economy by cautious reforms in the structure of pricing and management, and overcome opposition within the Politburo, Kádár and Resző Nyers announced the **New Economic Mechanism** (NEM) in 1968. Though its impact on centralized planning was slight, the NEM was accompanied by measures to promote "socialist legality" and make merit, rather than class background and Party standing, the criterion for promotion and higher education.

While generally welcomed by the populace, these reforms angered "New Left" supporters of either Dubček's "Socialism with a human face" in Czechoslovakia or the Chinese Cultural Revolution, and also, more seriously, conservatives within the Party. With backing from Moscow, they watered down the NEM and ousted Nyers, its leading advocate, from the Politburo in 1973, expelling Hegedüs and other "revisionist sociologists" from the Party later.

Following a power struggle, Kádár was able to reverse the reactionary tide, and reduce constraints on the so-called "second economy". While structural reforms were extremely limited, consumerism, a private sector and even "forint millionaires" emerged during the **1970s**, when Hungary became a byword for **affluence** within the Socialist bloc – the "happiest barracks in the camp", as the joke had it. Mechanics and other artisans with marketable skills were able to moonlight profitably, as demonstrated by the boom in private home-building; and workers and unions acquired some say in the management of their enterprises. This "**market socialism**" attracted the favours of Western politicians and bankers, and before *perestroika* the "Hungarian model" seemed to offer the best hope for reform within Eastern Europe.

In the **1980s**, however, economic and social problems became increasingly obvious, ranging from thirty percent **inflation**, whose effect was felt hardest by the "**new poor**" living on low, fixed incomes, to Hungary's $14.7 billion **foreign debt** (per capita, the largest in Eastern Europe). Despite reformist rhetoric, vested interests successfully resisted the logic of the market, whose rigorous application would entail drastic lay-offs and mass **unemployment** in towns dominated by the unprofitable mining and steel industries. Although frank analyses of Hungary's economic plight started appearing in the media during the mid-1980s, other issues ran up against the limits of state tolerance. These included fears for **the environment** in the wake of Chernobyl and the decision to build a dam at Nagymaros (see p.185); an unofficial **peace movement** that was quickly driven back underground; and any discussion of the Party's "leading role" or Hungary's alliance with the Soviet Union. Discussion of such topics could only be found in **samizdat** (underground) magazines such as *Beszélő*, whose publishers were harassed as dissidents. Although in 1983 the Party announced that "independents" could contest elections, it proved unwilling to let them enter Parliament, as demonstrated by the gerrymandering used against László Rajk in 1986.

Yet the need for change was becoming evident even within the Party, where the caution of the "old guard" – Kádár, Horváth and Gáspár – caused increasing frustration among **reformists**, who believed that Hungarians would only accept income tax and economic austerity if greater liberalization seemed a realistic prospect. Happily, this coincided with the advent of **Gorbachev**, whose interest in the Hungarian model of socialism and desire to bring a new generation into power was an open secret.

The end of Communism

The **end of Communism in Hungary** was so orderly that it can hardly be termed a revolution, but it did set in motion the collapse of hardline regimes in East Germany and Czechoslovakia. Prefiguring the fate of Gorbachev, the politicians who created an opening for change hoped to preserve Communism by reforming it, but were swept away by the forces which they had unleashed.

At the **May 1988 Party Congress**, Kádár and seven colleagues were ousted from power by a coalition of radical reformers and conservative technocrats. The latter backed **Karóly Grósz** as Kádár's successor, but his lacklustre performance as Party leader enabled the reformists to shunt him aside in July 1989, forcing conservatives and hardliners onto the defensive. As the ascendancy of **Imre Pozsgay**, **Rezső Nyers**, **Miklós Németh** and **Gyula Horn** became apparent there was a "traffic jam on the road to Damascus" as lesser figures hastened to pledge support for reforms.

In mid-October 1989, the Communist Party formally reconstituted itself as the **Hungarian Socialist Party** (MSzP), dissolved its private militia and announced the **legalization of opposition parties** as a prelude to free elections. To symbolize this watershed, the People's Republic was renamed the **Republic of Hungary** in a ceremony broadcast live on national television, on the thirty-third anniversary of the Uprising.

Meanwhile, the Iron Curtain was unravelling with astonishing speed. In May, Hungary began dismantling the barbed wire and minefields along its **border** with Austria, and thousands of **East Germans** seized their chance to escape to the West, crossing over via Hungary at a rate of two hundred every day. Despite protests from the Honecker regime, Hungary refused to close the border or deport would-be escapees back to the DDR, and allowed 20,000 refugees encamped in the West German embassy in Budapest to leave the country. After the DDR sealed its own borders, frustration spilled over onto the streets of Leipzig and Dresden, where mass demonstrations led to the **fall of the Berlin Wall** (November 9, 1989) and the ousting of Erich Honecker. A week later, the brutal repression of a pro-democracy demonstration in Prague's Wenceslas Square set in motion the "**Velvet Revolution**" in Czechoslovakia, which overturned forty years of Communist rule in ten days. The *annus mirabilis* of 1989 climaxed with the **overthrow of Ceaušescu** in Romania on December 22.

The 1990s

After such events Hungary's first **free elections** since 1945, in 1990, seemed an anticlimax. During the first round of voting on March 6, Pozsgay and the Socialist Party were obliterated, while two parties emerged as frontrunners. The **Hungarian Democratic Forum** (MDF), founded at the Lakitelek Conference of 1987, articulated populist, conservative nationalism, encapsulated in the idea of "Hungarianness", whereas the rival Alliance of **Free Democrats** (SzDSz) espoused a neo-liberal, internationalist outlook, similar to that of the **Federation of Young Democrats** (Fidesz). Two prewar parties revived under octogenarian leaders also participated, namely the **Smallholders' Party** (under the slogan "God, Home, Family, Wine, Wheat and Independence") and the **Christian Democrats**.

Despite being diminished by voter apathy, the **1990 elections** unceremoniously swept the reformist Communists out of power. Their place was taken by a centre-right coalition dominated by the Hungarian Democratic Forum (MDF) and its prime minister **Jozsef Antall**. A born politician with a schoolmasterly style, Antall relished the opportunity to take a role he had longed for but never expected to get during the Communist years. The model for his Hungary was its prewar state, with the restoration of the **traditions** and the **social hierarchies** that had prevailed at that time. Very much a moderate, his policies rested on the belief that over forty years of Communism had destroyed the true values of Hungarian society. However, not everyone wanted the **Catholic Church** to return to the dominant social position it had enjoyed before the war, and his party's proud belief in restoring the Hungarian nation to its former position sounded to Hungary's neighbours like a revanchist claim on the lost lands of Trianon – an interpretation that was strengthened by Antall's failure to distance himself from the ultra-right-wing nationalism advocated by **István Csurka**.

After Antall's death in 1993, his successor Peter Boross was unable to turn the economy around, and the **1994 elections** saw the **return to power** of the Socialists (reform Communists), assisted by sympathetic media that presented the outgoing government as amateurish and arrogant. To guard against accusations of abusing power as their Communist predecessors had done, the Socialists also brought the Free Democrats into the government. The government's **corruption** became blatant, however, and, though their austerity policies succeeded in bringing an economic upturn, living standards did not improve for most people.

Despite this, the government still rode high in the opinion polls, helped by the fact that the opposition was in disarray. After its poor showing in the 1994 elections, Fidesz had been repositioned by its leader **Viktor Orbán** to the right of centre, bidding to become the focus of opposition to the Socialist-led government. Orbán adopted phrases about the need to revive national culture that would appeal to the right, and renamed the party Fidesz-Hungarian **Civic Party** (the word for civic – **polgári** – also evokes notions of bourgeois middle-class values). It still seemed, however, that Orbán needed more time to mature as a potential prime minister.

Then, in early 1998, the Socialists committed their biggest blunder, announcing that Hungary would go ahead with building the controversial **Nagymaros dam** (see box on p.185). It was the revenge of Gyula Horn: as a leading figure in the old Communist Party he had given full support to the dam, but it had been condemned as undemocratic; now as prime minister of a democratically elected government he could give the go-ahead. At first it looked as if he had got away with it, but as the May **1998 elections** approached, public disillusionment mounted. **Fidesz's win** by a narrow margin came as a surprise to many people – though it was not as unexpected as Csurka's extreme right-wing Hungarian Justice and Life Party (MIÉP) breaking the four percent threshold to get into Parliament. Orbán, given the chance to be the youngest premier in Hungarian history, set about talks with the MDF and Smallholders with alacrity in order to form a **coalition** – despite the fact that the prospect of government with the unpredictable Torgyán and his Smallholders worried many Fidesz supporters. Orbán, however, bit the bullet.

Hungary's first major step into the wider European arena came the following year on March 12, 1999 when, just twelve days before NATO allies were due to begin a bombing campaign against Yugoslavia, Hungary was formally **admitted into NATO**. Whilst delighted at receiving the recognition it had long coveted, the timing was awkward to say the least. With the country now a fully-fledged member, it was placed in the rather dubious position of having to play an active role in the campaign, if only as a base from which allied aircraft could fly from – convenient for the allies, not so for Hungarians who were distinctly nervous at the prospect. Not only was Hungary a neighbouring country – one of the few with which Serbia was on good terms – but there was also the very delicate question of the large Hungarian minority living in the Serbian province of Vojvodina, which borders southern Hungary. However, despite very real fears of a backlash against Hungarians living there, it turned out that most Serbs were far too concerned with surviving the bombs to be bothered about stirring up further trouble. In the event, the bombing lasted eleven weeks, and aside from the odd stray cruise missile, Hungarians were not too troubled.

Europe and the new millennium

Back on the domestic front, few predicted anything other than another Orbán victory in the **2002 parliamentary elections**, thanks to an upwardly mobile economy, steadily falling inflation and low unemployment levels. However, in what was the most spitefully contested election since the end of Communism, the Orbán-led Fidesz-MDF coalition was surprisingly ousted by a centre-left alliance – comprising a combination of the Hungarian Socialist Party (MSzP) and the Alliance of Free Democrats (SzDSz) – whose margin of victory was just ten seats. Rejecting Orbán's media-savvy, aggressive style and attendant nationalist overtures, the Hungarian electorate – in an unprecedented post-Communist turnout of more than 70 percent – instead opted for a return to the same coalition that had governed, albeit largely ineffectively, between 1994 and 1998. The new premier was **Peter Medgyessy**, a former banker and an altogether less charismatic figure than Orbán. Medgyessy's past, however, was discovered to be rather more colourful when it was revealed just a few months later that he had, alongside ten other government ministers, worked as an agent for the country's Moscow-linked secret service, though he was quick to deny any links to the KGB.

Internationally, at the tail end of the same year, Hungary saw final accession negotiations to the European Union wrapped up, with referendums held the following April. Although the turnout was disappointingly low, support was more or less unequivocal, with 84 percent of voters in favour. A little over a year later, on May 1, 2004, Hungary, alongside nine other former Eastern bloc countries, was **admitted to the EU**. While most Hungarians remain fervently committed to membership, believing that they will benefit under Europe's protective mantle, there are several areas of deep concern, such as the desire of most Hungarians to limit foreign ownership, which goes against EU directives, and apprehension over the distribution of agricultural subsidies.

With the euphoria surrounding the country's accession having barely died down, domestic problems were brewing. A poor showing in the European elections, combined with bitter party infighting and barely disguised dissatisfaction at Medgyessy's performance as prime minister, resulted in the premier's **shock resignation** in August 2004. His successor was sports minister and millionaire businessman, **Ferenc Gyurcsány**, who now faces an uphill task to revive the party's ailing fortunes in time for the elections in 2006.

Books

Publishers are detailed below in the form of British publisher/American publisher, where both exist. Where books are published in one country only, UK or US follows the publisher's name. Out of print books are designated o/p; University Press is abbreviated UP. Books tagged with the ★ symbol are particularly recommended. For a gentle introduction to current affairs and literature, look for the Budapest-published *The Hungarian Quarterly* (Ⓦwww.hungarianquarterly.com). Most of Budapest's better bookshops have a good range of books and can take orders (see Budapest "Listings").

Travel writing

★ **Patrick Leigh Fermor** *A Time of Gifts* and *Between the Woods and the Water* (both Penguin). In 1934 the young Leigh Fermor started walking from Holland to Turkey, reaching Hungary in the closing chapter of *A Time of Gifts*. In *Between the Woods and the Water* the Gypsies and rusticated aristocrats of the Great Plain and Transylvania are superbly evoked. Lyrical and erudite.

Ruth Gruber *Jewish Heritage Travel: A Guide to Central and Eastern Europe* (Jason Aronson). The most comprehensive guide to Jewish sights in Hungary (amongst other countries), as well as lively historical accounts of pre-World War II Jewish communities and cultures.

Brian Hall *Stealing from a Deep Place* (Heinemann). In 1982 Hall cycled through Hungary, Romania and Bulgaria and came up with this engaging portrayal of rural life in southeastern Europe. The account of the several months he spent in Budapest is particularly absorbing.

★ **Gyula Illyés** *People of the Puszta* (Corvina, UK o/p). An unsentimental, sometimes horrifying immersion in the life of the landless peasantry of prewar Hungary, mainly in Transdanubia. Illyés, one of Hungary's greatest twentieth-century writers, was born into such a background, and the book breathes authenticity.

★ **Claudio Magris** *Danube* (Collins Harvill). Magris undertakes an epic voyage along the course of Europe's most romantic river, blending travel narrative, history and anecdote to wonderful effect. Rightly proclaimed as one of the great travel books of recent years.

Walter Starkie *Raggle-Taggle* (John Murray/Transatlantic Arts o/p). The wanderings of a Dublin professor with a fiddle, who bummed around Budapest and the Plain in search of Gypsy music in the 1920s. First published in 1933 and last issued in 1973; a secondhand bookshop perennial.

History, politics and society

As well as the more specific titles below, there are quite a number of books on the changes of 1989 across Eastern Europe, well worth dipping into if you're travelling around the region. Two of the best are Misha Glenny's *The Rebirth of History* (Penguin) and Timothy Garton-Ash's *History of the Present* (Penguin), both of which have very readable chapters on Hungary post-1989.

Judit Frigyesi *Béla Bartók and Turn-of-the-century Budapest* (University of California Press). Placing Bartók in his cultural milieu, this is an excellent account of the Hungarian intellectual world at the beginning of the century.

András Gero *Modern Hungarian Society in the Making: The Unfinished Experience* (Central European UP, Hungary). A good collection of essays setting Hungary in the context of the Eastern European environment.

Jörg K Hoensch *A History of Modern Hungary 1867–1994* (Longman/Addison-Wesley). A good history of the country on its way from tragedy to tragedy, but with a happy(ish) outcome.

László Kontler *Millennium in Central Europe: A History of Hungary* (Atlantisz). Another very thorough and reliable history of the country, although its slightly archaic wording lets it down somewhat.

★ **Paul Lendvai** *The Hungarians: 1000 Years of Victory in Defeat* (Hurst & Co). Refreshing and authoritative book on Hungary's complex and often tragic history, with particularly stimulating accounts of the Treaty of Trianon and the subsequent Nazi and Communist tyrannies – there are some fascinating pictures, too.

★ **Bill Lomax** *Hungary 1956* (Allison & Busby/St Martin's Press o/p). Still probably the best – and shortest – book on the Uprising, by an acknowledged expert on modern Hungary. Lomax also edited *Eyewitness in Hungary* (Spokesman, UK), an anthology of accounts by foreign Communists (most of whom were sympathetic to the Uprising) that vividly depicts the elation, confusion and tragedy of the events of October 1956.

John Lukács *Budapest 1900* (Weidenfeld/Grove Press). Excellent and very readable account of the politics and society of Budapest at the turn of the twentieth century, during a golden age that was shortly to come to an end.

George Mikes *A Study in Infamy* (Andre Deutsch o/p). Better known in the West for his humorous writings, Mikes here exposes the activities of the secret police during the Rákosi era. Based on captured documents which explain their methods of surveillance and use of terror as a political weapon.

Miklós Molnár *A Concise History of Hungary* (Cambridge UP). Comprehensive thousand-year history of Hungarian land, people, culture and economy, right up until the 1998 elections.

John Paget *Hungary and Transylvania* (Ayer, US). Paget's massive book, published in 1971, attempted to explain nineteenth-century Hungary to the English middle class, and, within its aristocratic limitations, succeeded.

★ **Michael Stewart** *The Time of the Gypsies* (Westview Press). Based on anthropological research in a Gypsy community in Hungary, this superb book presents Gypsy culture as a culture, and not as a parasitic body on society, as it is widely perceived in Hungary and elsewhere.

Peter Sugar (ed) *A History of Hungary* (L B Tauris). A useful, not too academic, survey of Hungarian history from pre-Conquest times to the close of the Kádár era, with a brief epilogue on the transition to democracy.

Rudolf L. Tőkés *Hungary's Negotiated Revolution: Economic Reform, Social Change, and Political Succession, 1957–1990* (Cambridge UP). Very sound and comprehensive account of the Communist regime's survival, decline and fall.

Literature

Hungary has a fabulously rich literary heritage, and approach to the genre has greatly improved in recent years, thanks in no small part to the success of authors such as the Nobel-prize-winning Imre Kertész. Writers such as Péter Nádas and Péter Esterházy, whose dense and very Hungarian style had long been inaccessible to English readers, are now also appearing in translation. A useful starting point is *Hungarian Literature* (Babel Guides), an informative guide to the best Hungarian fiction, drama and poetry in translation, with selected excerpts. There are also numerous collections of short stories published in Budapest, though the quality of translations varies from the sublime to the ridiculous. Works by nineteenth-century authors such as Mór Jókai are most likely found in secondhand bookshops (see p.149).

Anthologies

Loránt Czigány (ed) *The Oxford History of Hungarian Literature from the Earliest Times to the Present* (Oxford UP). Probably the most comprehensive collection in print to date. In chronological order, with good coverage of the political and social background.

György Gömöri (ed) *Colonnade of Teeth* (Bloodaxe/Dufour). In spite of its strange title, this is a good introduction to the work of young Hungarian poets.

Michael March (ed) *Description of a Struggle* (Picador/Vintage). A collection of contemporary Eastern European prose, featuring four pieces by Hungarian writers including Nádas and Esterházy.

George Szirtes (ed) *Leopard V: An Island of Sound* (Harvill). Superbly compiled anthology featuring the cream of Hungarian prose and poetry from the end of World War II through to 1989, including Márai, Esterházy and Nagy.

Poetry

★ **Endre Ady** *Poems of Endre Ady* (University Press of America). Regarded by many as the finest Hungarian poet of the twentieth century, Ady's allusive verses are notoriously difficult to translate. *Explosive Country* (Corvina) is a collection of essays about his homeland.

George Faludy *Selected Poems, 1933–80* (McClelland & Stewart/University of Georgia Press o/p). Fiery, lyrical poetry by a victim of both Nazi and Soviet repression. Themes of political defiance, the nobility of the human spirit, and the struggle to preserve human values in the face of oppression predominate. The author's cheerfully resigned biographical account of the 1940s and 1950s and the prison camps of the period, *My Happy Days in Hell*, is also worth reading.

Ágnes Nemes Nagy *Selected Poems* (o/p). Nagy is a major postwar poet, who often speculates on knowledge and the role of poetry in trying to impose order on the world.

János Pilzinsky *Selected Poems* (o/p). Themes of humanity's suffering and sacrifice by a major poet.

Miklós Radnóti *Under Gemini: the Selected Poems of Miklós Radnóti, with a Prose Memoir* (Ohio UP, US); *Foamy Sky: the Major Poems* (Princeton UP, US). The two best collections of Radnóti's sparse, anguished poetry. His final poems, found in his coat pocket after he had been shot on a forced march to a labour camp, are especially moving.

Zsuzsa Rákovsky *New Life* (Oxford UP, UK). Well-received volume translated by the Hungarian-born English poet George Szirtes.

Sándor Weöres *Eternal Moment* (Anvil Press Poetry, UK). The collected poetry of a major Hungarian poet of the postwar period.

Fiction

★ **Miklós Bánffy** *The Transylvanian Trilogy* (Arcadia). Vivid portrayal of the vanished world of pre-World War I Hungary as seen through the eyes of a pair of aristocratic Transylvanian cousins. Fans of Leigh Fermor should love this.

Géza Csáth *The Magician's Garden and Other Stories* (Penguin/Columbia UP o/p) and *Opium and Other Stories* (Penguin o/p). Disturbing stories written in the magic realist genre. The author was tormented by insanity and opium addiction, finally killing his wife and then himself in 1918.

Tibor Dery *The Portuguese Princess* (Calder/Northwestern UP o/p). Short stories by a once-committed Communist, who was jailed for three years after the Uprising and died in 1977.

Péter Esterházy *Celestial Harmonies* (Flamingo). This most recent novel, by a descendant of the famous aristocratic family, is a dense and demanding novel chronicling the rise of the Esterházys during the Austro-Hungarian empire, and their subsequent downfall under Communism. Other works by this playful wordsmith include *The Glance of Countess Hahn-Hahn*, *Down the Danube* (both Quartet/Grove), *Helping Verbs of the Heart* (Grove), *A Little Hungarian Pornography* and *She Loves Me* (both Quartet/Northwestern UP).

Tibor Fischer *Under the Frog, A Black Comedy* (Penguin/New Press). A fictional account of the 1956 Uprising by the son of Hungarian survivor émigrés. Witty and enjoyable.

Agnes Hankiss *A Hungarian Romance* (Readers International). A lyrical first novel by "Hungary's new feminist voice", dealing with a woman's quest for self-identity during the sixteenth century and the timeless conflict between personal and public interests.

★ **Imre Kertész** *Fateless* (Northwestern). Drawing from his own experiences as an Auschwitz survivor, this Nobel-prize-winning book tells the tale of a young boy's deportation to, and survival in, a concentration camp. A very worthwhile read.

Dezso Kosztolányi *Skylark* (Central European UP, Budapest). A short and tragic story of an old couple and their beloved child by one of Hungary's top writers of the twentieth century, in a masterly translation by Richard Aczél and Anna Édes.

Gyula Krúdy *Adventures of Sinbad*

(Central European UP, Budapest/ Random House). Stories about a gourmand and womanizer by a popular Hungarian author with similar interests to his hero. Good translation.

★ **Sándor Márai** *Embers* (Penguin). Atmospheric and moving tale about friendship, love and betrayal by one of Hungary's most respected pre-World War II writers. A beautiful read.

Zsigmond Móricz *Be Faithful Unto Death* (Penguin). This book, by a major figure in late nineteenth-century Hungarian literature, is helpful in understanding the way Hungarians see themselves – both then and now.

Péter Nádas *A Book of Memories* (Vintage/Overlook Press). This novel about a novelist writing about a novel caused a sensation when it appeared in 1998. A Proustian account of bisexual relationships, Stalinist repression and modern-day Hungary in a brilliant translation by Iván Sanders, which captures the flavour of the original without losing any readability.

Giorgio and Nicola Pressburger *Homage to the Eighth District* (Readers International). Evocative tales of Jewish life in Budapest, before, during and after World War II, by twin brothers who fled Hungary in 1956.

Erno Szép *The Smell of Humans* (Central European UP, Budapest/ Arrow, UK). Another superb and harrowing memoir of the Holocaust in Hungary.

★ **Antal Szerb** *Journey by Moonlight* (Pushkin Press). This recently translated Hungarian classic, written in 1937, tells the story of a Hungarian businessman on honeymoon in Italy who embarks upon a mystical and dazzling journey through the country. The superb translation by Len Rix ensures that the atmosphere of the original is beautifully retained.

Biography and autobiography

John Bierman *The Secret Life of Laszlo Almasy: the Real English Patient* (Viking). Engaging, if somewhat dry, portrayal of Laszlo Almasy, the enigmatic Hungarian explorer, soldier and spy. For most people, Almasy first came to light as the fictional character in Michael Ondaatje's Booker-winning novel (and later an Oscar-winning film), *The English Patient.*

Magda Dénes *Castles Burning: A Child's Life in War* (Anchor/Touchstone Books). A moving biographical account of the Budapest ghetto and postwar escape to France, Cuba and the United States, seen through the eyes of a Jewish girl. The author died in December 1966, shortly before the book she always wanted to write was published.

Charles Fenyvesi *When the World was Whole: Three Centuries of Memories* (Viking, US o/p). A very readable account of Jewish life in eastern Hungary up until the Holocaust.

Paul Hoffmann *The Man Who Loved Only Numbers: the Story of Paul Erdöss and the Search for Mathematical Truth* (Fourth Estate/Hyperion). The amazing story of a Hungarian-born mathematician who became a legend. Totally dedicated to his goal, he wandered from friend to friend with his possessions in a few carrier bags, concerned with nothing but mathematics. Affectionate, engaging account of this genius and his world.

★ **Béla Zsolt** *Nine Suitcases* (Jonathan Cape). Originally published in serial form in 1946, this recently translated English version of the author's experiences in the ghetto of Nagyvárad and as a forced labourer in the Ukraine is one of the most powerful accounts of the Holocaust.

Foreign writers on Hungary

Heinrich Böll *And Where Were You, Adam* in *Adam and the Train* (Penguin/Northwestern UP o/p). A superb short novel by one of the major postwar German novelists, consisting of loosely connected and semi-autobiographical short stories describing the panic-stricken retreat of Hitler's forces from the *puszta* before the Red Army in 1944. Told through both Hungarian and German eyes, these stories are a haunting evocation of the chaos, cruelty and horror of the retreat, but also of a rural culture that seems to resist everything thrown at it.

Hans Habe *Black Earth* (NEL o/p). The story of a peasant's commitment to the Communist underground and his disillusionment with the Party in power; a good read, and by no means as crude as the artwork and blurb suggest.

Cecilia Holland *Rakossy* (Hodder/Atheneum o/p) and *The Death of Attila* (Hodder/Pocket Books o/p). Two well-crafted historical romances: *Rakossy* is a bodice-ripping tale of a shy Austrian princess wed to an uncouth Magyar baron, braving the Turkish hordes on the Hungarian marches; while *The Death of Attila* evokes the Huns, Romans and Goths of the Dark Ages, pillaging around the Danube.

Ken Smith *Wild Root* (Bloodaxe, UK). A collection of poetry that includes sharp, sympathetic observations on travels in Hungary and elsewhere.

Art, folk traditions and architecture

Irén Ács *Hungary at Home* (Jövendő, Hungary). Excellent collection of photos covering all walks of life in postwar Hungary.

Val Biro *Hungarian Folk Tales* (Oxford UP). Children's tales of dragons and the like in a crisp, colloquial translation.

Tekla Dömötör *Hungarian Folk Beliefs* (Corvina/Indiana UP o/p). A superb collection of social history, folk beliefs and customs.

Györgyi Éri et al *A Golden Age: Art and Society in Hungary 1896–1914* (Corvina). Hungary's Art Nouveau age captured in a beautifully illustrated coffee-table volume.

János Gerle et al *Budapest: An Architectural Guide* (6 BT, Budapest). The best of the new guides to the city's twentieth-century architecture, covering almost 300 buildings with brief descriptions in Hungarian and English.

Tamás Hofer et al *Hungarian Peasant Art* (Constable/International Publications Service o/p). An excellently produced examination of Hungarian folk art, with lots of good photos.

Dora Wieberson et al *The Architecture of Historic Hungary* (MIT Press, US). Comprehensive and invaluable survey of Hungarian architecture through the ages, placing it in its historical context.

Food and drink

Lesley Chamberlain *The Food and Cooking of Eastern Europe* (Penguin o/p). A great compendium of recipes, nostrums and gastronomical history, guaranteed to have you experimenting in the kitchen.
Susan Derecskey *The Hungarian Cookbook* (HarperCollins, US). A good, easy-to-follow selection of traditional and modern recipes.
Stephen Kirkland *The Wines and Vines of Hungary* (New World Publishing). The definitive book on Hungarian wine, covering its history, the varied regions and the myriad wines produced.
George Lang *The Cuisine of Hungary* (Penguin/Random House). A well-written and beautifully illustrated work, telling you everything you need to know about Hungarian cooking, its history and how to do it yourself.

Miscellaneous

Bird's-eye view of Hungary (MTI). Stunning aerial views of the country, including pictures of the countryside in flood.
Gerald Gorman *Birds of Hungary* (C Helm, UK). The best book available on the ornithological world of the country by a resident expert.
★ **Rogan Taylor & Klára Jamrich (eds)** *Puskás on Puskás* (Robson Books Ltd). Not only does this marvellous book depict the life of Hungary's, and one of the world's, greatest footballers, it also provides an intriguing insight into postwar Communist Hungary.
Ray Keenoy *Eminent Hungarians* (Boulevard). Everything you always wanted to know about Hungary's most renowned historical and contemporary figures – from Lajos Kossuth and Attila József, to Harry Houdini and Ernő Rubik, creator of the Rubik's cube.

Music

Hungarian classical **music** enshrines the trinity of Liszt, Bartók and Kodály: Liszt was the founding father, Bartók one of the greatest composers of the twentieth century, and Kodály (himself no slouch at composition) created a widely imitated system of musical education. When you also take into account talented Hungarian soloists like Perényi, it's clear that this small nation has made an outstanding contribution to the world of classical music. After classical, the musical genres most readily associated with Hungary are Gypsy and folk, both of which have some excellent exponents, most notably the supreme Gypsy violinist Roby Lakatos and the wonderful folk singer Márta Sebestyén. The increasing popularity of jazz is manifest in the growing number of clubs in Budapest and other larger cities, as well as several terrific summer jazz festivals held around the country. Meanwhile, Hungarian popular music, whilst not exactly cutting-edge, is becoming more adventurous as a new generation of DJs and bands soaks up the influence of Western European and American artists.

Classical music

Franz Liszt (1811–86), who described himself as a "mixture of Gypsy and Franciscan", cut a flamboyant figure in the salons of Europe as a virtuoso pianist and womanizer. His *Hungarian Rhapsodies* and other similar pieces reflected the "Gypsy" side to his character and the rising nationalism of his era, while later work like the *Transcendental Studies* (whose originality has only recently been recognized) invoked a visionary "Franciscan" mood. Despite his patriotic stance, however, Liszt's first language was German (he never fully mastered Hungarian), and his expressed wish to roam the villages of Hungary with a knapsack on his back was a Romantic fantasy.

That was left to **Béla Bartók** (1881–1945) and **Zoltán Kodály** (1882–1967), who began exploring the remoter districts of Hungary and Transylvania in 1906, collecting peasant music. Despite many hardships and local suspicion of their "monster" (a cutting stylus and phonograph cylinders), they managed to record and catalogue thousands of melodies, laying down high standards of musical ethnography, still maintained in Hungary today, while discovering a rich source of inspiration for their own compositions. Bartók believed that a genuine peasant melody was "quite as much a masterpiece in miniature as a Bach fugue or a Mozart sonata . . . a classic example of the expression of a musical thought in its most conceivably concise form, with the avoidance of all that is superfluous".

Bartók created a personal but universal musical language by reworking the raw essence of Magyar and Finno-Ugric folk music in a modern context – in particular his six String Quartets – although Hungarian public opinion was originally hostile. Feeling misunderstood and out of step with his country's increasingly pro-Nazi policies, Bartók left Hungary in 1940, dying poor and embittered in the United States. Since then, however, his reputation has soared, and the return of his body in 1988 occasioned national celebrations, shrewdly sponsored by the state.

Kodály's music is more consciously national: Bartók called it "a real profession

Discography

Many of the recordings listed below can be bought from Passion Music in the UK (☎01256/770 747; Ⓦwww.passion-discs.co.uk). In Hungary, good quality **records and CDs** produced by Hungaroton (Ⓦwww.hungaroton.hu) retail for half or a third of what you'd pay abroad, which makes it well worth rooting through record shops (*lemezbolt*). After Western and Hungarian **pop**, the bulk of their stock consists of **classical music**. A full discography of the works of Liszt, Bartók and Kodály, directors like Dohnányi and Doráti, and contemporary Hungarian soloists and singers would fill a catalogue, but look out for the following names: pianists András Schiff, Zoltán Kocsis (who also conducts) and Dezső Ránki; the cellist Miklós Perényi; the Liszt Ferenc Chamber Orchestra, the Budapest Festival Orchestra and the Hungarian Radio and TV Symphony; conductors Iván Fischer and Tamás Vasáry; and singers Mária Zádori, Ingrid Kertesi, Andrea Rost, Adrienne Csengery, József Gregor, Kolos Kovats and László Polgar, the last two excellent bass singers.

For those who like contemporary music, the grand old man of the modern Hungarian scene is György Kurtág, while Tibor Szemző produces meditative works, one of which, *Tractatus*, inspired by German philosopher Ludwig Wittgenstein, is quite extraordinary. If you're into ethnomusic, then László Hortobágyi's "Gaia" music is worth listening to.

Folk and Gypsy music can be bought at all record stores, though you should be warned that a CD with a picture of a Gypsy orchestra all dressed up in red waistcoats is of the "*nóta*" variety – it's worth asking to listen before you buy. As well as the artists listed below, there are hundreds of great recordings in the above fields. The following simply offer an introduction.

Individual artists

Kálmán Balogh *Roma Vándor* (MWCD 4009). On this live recording, the virtuoso of the cimbalom turns this staple of Hungarian Gypsy restaurant bands into something much more than entertainment for eating. Recorded with artistic director Romano Kokalo, *Gipsy Colours* (FA 061 2) is a fabulous selection of Balkan-inspired dance tunes.

Félix Lajkó *Lajkó Félix és zenekara* (FA-056-2) and *Félix* (CDA02). The best recordings so far of this Hungarian virtuoso violinist from Subotica in northern Serbia – the latter is a collection of his work from various projects and festivals between 1997 and 2002. He also features with the Boban Markovic Orchestra, the fantastic Serbian Gypsy ensemble, on the CD *Srce Cigansko*, which combines typically rumbustious Serbian brass with Lajkó's violin to marvellous effect.

Roby Lakatos *Lakatos* (DG 457 879-2). Recording featuring new workouts of favourites by the likes of Brahms alongside traditional Hungarian folk songs. *Lakatos: Live from Budapest* (DG 459 642-2) is one of his homecoming concerts in Budapest's Thália Theatre in 1999. His latest album, *As Time Goes By* (DG 471 562-2), is a recording of popular soundtracks from the movies, including the gorgeous "Djelem, Djelem" from Emir Kusturica's memorable *Time of the Gypsies*.

Márta Sebestyén *Kismet*. Hungary's leading Táncház singer, who made many recordings with the folk group Muzsikás (see below), has now developed well beyond those horizons to become an international star, thanks first to the Canadian duo Deep Forest, who used her voice in a recording (although they were rather slow to acknowledge their debt) and later to the film *The English Patient*, where she contributed to the soundtrack.

Groups

Di Naye Kapelye The band's two albums to date are the eponymous *Di Naye Kapelye* (RIEN CD17) and *A Mazeldiker Yid* (RIEN CD37), both terrific, and typically exuberant, Klezmer recordings, which make for immensely enjoyable listening.

Jánosi Ensemble *Jánosi Együttes*. A young group performing "authentic" versions of some of the folk tunes that Bartók borrowed in his compositions. A record that makes a bridge between classical and folk music (Hungaroton SPLX 18103).

The Kalamajka Ensemble *Bonchidától Bonchidáig*. Another leading Táncház group, plays Transylvanian and Csángó ballads and dances (Hungaroton MK 18135).

Muzsikás *The Bartók Album*. Featuring Márta Sebestyén and the violinist Alexander Balanescu, this manages to set the music of Bartók in its original context. Three of Bartók's violin duos are presented alongside original field recordings and recordings of his transcriptions by Muzsikás (HNCD 1439). *Morning Star* is another fine Muzsikás volume – interestingly, their record company recommended slight changes and a softening of edges for this foreign edition of *Hazafelé*, the original Hungarian recording (Gong HCD 37874). Their latest release, 2004's *Live at the Liszt Academy of Music*, which again stars Sebestyén, is a compilation of recordings taken from successive appearances at the Budapest Spring Festival.

Transylvanians *Denevér* (Mega 758 00672) and *Igen!* (Westpark 698 437621). On these two recent albums, this exceptional group of young musicians showcase their full range of talents – the latter features the wonderful voice and terrific bass playing of the front woman, Isabel Nagy.

Vízöntő *New Wave*. The traditional Hungarian folk band Vízöntő combines its roots with other music (FY 80042).

Vujicsics Ensemble *Serbian Music from South Hungary*. More complex tunes than most Magyar folk music, with a distinct Balkan influence (Hannibal HNBL 1310). Two more recent albums, both featuring Márta Sebestyén, are *25 – Live at the Academy of Music* (R-E-Disc 005), a concert in Budapest celebrating the group's twenty-fifth anniversary, and *Podravina* (R-E-Disc 004), a selection of Croatian dance melodies.

János Zerkula and Regina Fikó *Este a Gyimesbe Jártam*. Music from the Csángó region; sparser, sadder and more discordant than other Transylvanian music (Hungaroton MK 18130).

Compilation albums

Magyar népzene 3 (Hungarian folk music). A four-disc set of field recordings covering the whole range of folk music, including Old and New Style songs, instrumental and occasional music, that's probably the best overall introduction. In the West, the discs are marketed as "Folk Music of Hungary Vol.1".

Magyar hangszeres népzene (Hungarian Instrumental Folk Music; Hungaroton LPX 18045-47). A very good three-disc set of field recordings of village and Gypsy bands, including lots of solos.

VII. Magyarországi Táncház Találkozó. One of a series, the *Seventh Dance House Festival* (MK 18152) features a great mixture of dances, ballads and instrumental pieces from all over Hungary. The *Tenth Dance House Festival* collection (MK 18205) is also especially good.

Rough Guide to Hungarian Music (RGNET 1092). Despite one or two obvious omissions, this is an otherwise excellent introduction to the many wildly differing sounds of Hungarian music.

Rough Guide to the Music of Eastern Europe (RGNET 1024). Although most of the songs on this CD are from the Balkans, there is a healthy representation from Hungary, featuring songs by Márta Sebestyén, Vízöntő and Kálmán Balogh and the Gypsy Cimbalom Band.

Rough Guide Music of the Gypsies (RGNET 1034). From India to Spain, this is a fantastic introduction to gypsy music worldwide. Hungary is represented by Kálmán Balogh and the Joszef Lacatos Orchestra.

Táncházi muzsika (Music from the Táncház; Hungaroton SPLX 18031-32). A double album of the Sebö Ensemble playing Táncház music from various regions of Hungary. Wild and exciting rhythms.

of faith in the Hungarian soul". His *Peacock Variations* are based on a typical Old Style pentatonic tune and the *Dances of Galanta* on the popular music played by Gypsy bands. Old Style tunes also form the core of Kodály's work in musical education: the "Kodály method" employs group singing to develop musical skill at an early age. His ideas have made Hungarian music teaching among the best in the world, and Kodály himself a paternal figure to generations of children.

For others Kodály was a voice of conscience during the Rákosi era, writing the *Hymn of Zrínyi* to a seventeenth-century text whose call to arms against the Turkish invasion – "I perceive a ghastly dragon, full of venom and fury, snatching the crown of Hungary. . ." – was tumultuously acclaimed as an anti-Stalinist allegory. Its first performance was closely followed by the Uprising, and the *Hymn* was not performed again for many years; nor were any recordings made available until 1982.

Gypsy music

In recent years **Gypsy or Roma music** has really made a mark on the Hungarian music scene. Played on anything from spoons and milk jugs to guitars, Roma music ranges from haunting laments to playful wedding songs – as can be seen in French director Tony Gatliff's excellent film *Latcho Drom*, which explores Roma music from India to Spain. The most exciting artist around in the field of Gypsy music is the wizard violinist **Roby Lakatos**. A seventh-generation descendant of János Bihari (aka "King of the Gypsy Violinists"), Lakatos began playing the violin aged 5, graduated from Budapest with a First in classical violin and then, at the age of 18, formed his own orchestra in Brussels. He has since become one of the foremost violinists in the world. Fusing traditional Hungarian Gypsy sounds with elements of classical and jazz, the charismatic Lakatos and his band – which, unusually for a gypsy band, includes piano and guitar – are an extraordinary proposition live, rarely failing to dazzle with their electric, often improvised performances. At one stage a regular at Les Ateliers in Brussels, Lakatos now tours extensively around the world and was a huge hit at the London Proms.

Although not Roma, another major star, and the one musician who could justifiably claim to be in the same league as Lakatos, is **Félix Lajkó**, a Hungarian virtuoso violinist from Vojvodina in Serbia, whose eccentric fusion of Gypsy, jazz and folk inspires a devout following. Other well-established Roma artists in Hungary include Kálmán Balogh, one of the world's foremost exponents of the cimbalom (a stringed instrument played with little hammers), Romano Drom, Andro Drom, the Szilvási Folk Band, and Kalyi Jag – all these groups tour extensively and are the focal point of most Roma festivals in Hungary and abroad.

None of the above, however, has much in common with the "Gypsy music" which you will see advertised at touristy restaurants, known in Hungarian as **Magyar nóta** – although that is not to say it should be avoided. Consisting of a series of mid-nineteenth-century Hungarian ballads traditionally played by Roma musicians, Magyar nóta is usually performed by one or two violinists, a bass player and a guy on the cimbalom. The more famous restaurants boast their own musical dynasties, such as the Lakatos family, who have been performing this sort of music for over a century. In the past, wandering self-taught artists like János Bihari, Czinka Panna and Czermak (a nobleman turned vagabond) were legendary figures. Hungarian diners are usually keen to make requests or sing along when the *prímás* (band leader) comes to the table, soliciting tips. If approached yourself, it is acceptable (though rather awkward) to decline with a "*nem köszönöm*", but if you signal a request to the band, you have to pay for it.

Folk music

Hungarian folk music (*Magyar népzene*) originated around the Urals and the Turkic steppes over a millennium ago, and is different again from Gypsy or Roma music. The haunting rhythms and pentatonic scale of this "Old Style" music (to use Bartók's terminology) were subsequently overlaid by "New Style" European influences – which have been discarded by more modern enthusiasts in the folk revival centred around Táncház. These "Dance Houses" encourage people to learn traditional dances – with much shouting, whistling, and slapping of boots and thighs. The two biggest names to emerge from the Táncház movement were Muzsikás and Márta Sebestyén, who have been regular collaborators for years. Unquestionably Hungary's finest folk singer, and one of the best in Europe, Sebestyén's gorgeous and distinctive voice has seen her become firmly established on the world music scene in recent years, a reputation that was sealed after she featured on the soundtrack to the film *The English Patient*. Sebestyén has also guested with Vujicsics, a marvellous seven-strong ensemble from Pomáz near Szentendre who specialize in Serbian and Croatian folk melodies. A somewhat more unorthodox outfit are the Transylvanians, a group of four young German-based Hungarians whose frenetic blend of folk, classical, rock and techno (termed speedfolk) pretty much defies any standard form of categorization. Other folk artists to watch out for include the Őkrős Ensemble, who play folk music from Transylvania, the Slovakian-based Hungarian group Ghymes, and the superb Budapest Klezmer outfit Da Naye Kapelye.

Popular music and jazz

Budapest has undergone a **popular music** revival in the last few years: radio stations and music magazines have taken off and the city has become part of the international tour circuit. This has all had a knock-on effect on local music, which ranges from instrumental groups (Korai Öröm and Másfél) to techno-inspired performers like Anima Sound System. Heaven Street Seven call their version of guitar pop Dunabeat, while Quimby is the Hungarian equivalent of Tom Waits. The controversial, and one-time underground, local radio station **Tilos Rádió** has done much to promote **DJs**, and there are now a host of them around the country. Some like Tommy Boy and Schultz play run-of-the-mill **techno**, while others like Palotai and Mango do a lot of wild mixing using a mass of sources and sounds. Bestiák are a sort of Magyar Spice Girls and Ganszta Zoli looks to LA gangster rap for his inspiration. A rather more unlikely figure on the Hungarian pop scene is Uhrin Benedek, a septuagenarian, wig-enhanced, former warehouse worker who, since an appearance at the Sziget Festival, has gained a cult following for his extremely bizarre, and somewhat less than tuneful, songsmithery.

Jazz has always had a devout, but small, following in the country and more and more clubs and bars offer live jazz. There are excellent summer jazz **festi-**

vals in Miskolc, Salgótarján and Sárospatak, but the biggest and best is in Debrecen. Dés, Mihály Dresch, Aladár Pege and the Benkó Dixieland Band have all achieved success outside Hungary, as has György Szabados, who works on the interface between jazz and classical music. Another name worth checking out is Béla Szakcsi Lakatos, a jazz pianist who frequently plays in Budapest clubs.

Language

Language

Hungarian

Hungarian is a unique, complex and subtle tongue, classified as belonging to the Finno-Ugric linguistic group, which includes Finnish and Estonian. If you happen to know those languages, however, don't expect it to be a help – there are some structural similarities, but lexically they are totally different. In fact, some scholars think the connection is completely bogus, and have linked Hungarian to the Siberian Chuvash language and a whole host of other pretty obscure tongues. Basically the origins of Hungarian remain a total mystery, and though a few words from Turkish have crept in, together with some German, English and (a few) Russian neologisms, there is not much that the beginner will recognize.

Consequently, foreigners aren't really expected to speak Hungarian, and natives are used to being addressed in German, the lingua franca of tourism. It's understood by older people, particularly in Transdanubia, and by many students and business people, besides virtually everyone around Balaton or in tourist offices. For a brief visit it's probably easier to brush up on some German for your means of communication. A few basic Magyar phrases can make all the difference, though. Hungarians are intensely proud of their language, and as a nation are surprisingly bad at learning anyone else's. However, English is gaining ground rapidly, and is increasingly widely understood.

The Rough Guides' *Hungarian phrasebook* is handy, while if you're prepared to study the language seriously, the best available book is *Colloquial Hungarian* (Routledge). As a supplement, invest in the handy little *Angol–Magyar/Magyar–Angol* Kisszótár dictionaries, available from bookshops in Hungary.

Basic grammar

Although its rules are complicated, it's worth describing a few features of **Hungarian grammar**, albeit imperfectly. Hungarian is an agglutinative language – in other words, its vocabulary is built upon **root-words**, which are modified in various ways to express different ideas and nuances. Instead of prepositions – "to", "from", "in", etc – Hungarian uses **suffixes**, or tags added to the ends of genderless **nouns**. The change in suffix is largely determined by the noun's context: for example the noun "book" (*könyv*) will take a final "*et*" in the accusative (*könyvet*); "in the book" = *könyvben*; "from the book" = *könyvből*. It is also affected by the rules of vowel harmony (which take a while to get used to, but don't alter meaning, so don't worry about getting them wrong). Most of the nouns in the vocabulary section below are in the nominative or subject form – that is, without suffixes. In Hungarian, "**the**" is *a* (before a word beginning with a consonant) or *az* (preceding a vowel); the word for "**a/an**" is *egy* (which also means "one").

Plurals are indicated by adding a final "k", with a link vowel if necessary, giving *-ek*, *-ok* or *-ak*. Nouns preceded by a number or other indication of quantity (eg: many, several) do *not* appear as plural: eg *könyvek* means "books", but "two books" is *két könyv* (using the singular form of the noun).

Adjectives precede the noun (*a piros ház* = the red house), adopting suffixes to form the comparative (*jó* = good; *jobb* = better), plus the prefix *leg* to signify the superlative (*legjobb* = the best).

Negatives are usually formed by placing the word *nem* before the verb or adjective. *Ez* (this), *ezek* (these), *az* (that) and *azok* (those) are the **demonstratives**.

Pronunciation

Achieving passably good **pronunciation**, rather than grammar, is the first priority (see below for general guidelines). **Stress** almost invariably falls on the first syllable of a word and all letters are spoken, although in sentences the tendency is to slur words together. Vowel sounds are greatly affected by the bristling **accents** (that actually distinguish separate letters) which, together with the "double letters" *cs*, *gy*, *ly*, *ny*, *sz*, *ty*, and *zs*, give the Hungarian **alphabet** its formidable appearance.

A o as in hot
Á a as in father
B b as in best
C ts as in bats
CS ch as in church
D d as in dust
E e as in yet
É ay as in say
F f as in fed
G g as in go
GY a soft dy as in due
H h as in hat
I i as in bit, but slightly longer
Í ee as in see
J y as in yes
K k as in sick
L l as in leap
LY y as in yes
M m as in mud
N n as in not
NY ny as in onion
O aw as in saw, with the tongue kept high
Ó aw as in saw, as above but longer
Ö ur as in fur, with the lips tightly rounded but without any "r" sound
Ő ur as in fur, as above but longer
P p as in sip
R r pronounced with the tip of the tongue like a Scottish "r"
S sh as in shop
SZ s as in so
T t as in sit
TY ty as in Tuesday or prettier, said quickly
U u as in pull
Ú oo as in food
Ü u as in the German "über" with the lips tightly rounded
Ű u as above, but longer
V v as in vat
W v as in "Valkman," "vhiskey" or "WC" (vait-say)
Z z as in zero
ZS zh as in measure

Words and phrases

Basics

Do you speak. . .?	. . . beszél . . .	**yes**	igen
English	angolul	**OK**	jó
German	németül	**no/not**	nem
French	franciául	**I (don't) understand**	(nem) Értem

please	kérem
excuse me	bocsánat
Two beers, please	Két sört kérek.
thank you (very much)	köszönöm (szépen)
you're welcome	szívesen
hello/goodbye (informal)	szia
goodbye	viszontlátásra
see you later (informal)	viszlát
good morning	jó reggelt
good day	jó napot
good evening	jó estét
good night	jó éjszakát
How are you? (informal)	Hogy vagy?
(more formal)	Hogy van?
Could you speak more slowly?	Elmondaná lassabban?
What do you call this?	Mi a neve ennek?
Please write it down	Kérem, írja le.
today	ma
tomorrow	holnap
the day after tomorrow	holnapután
yesterday	tegnap
the day before yesterday	tegnapelőtt
in the morning	reggel
in the evening	este
at noon	délben
at midnight	éjfélkor

Questions and requests

Legyen szíves ("Would you be so kind") is the polite formula for attracting someone's attention. Hungarian has numerous interrogative modes whose subtleties elude foreigners, so it's best to use the simple *van?* ("is there?"), to which the reply might be *nincs* or *nincsen* ("there isn't"/"there aren't any"). In shops or restaurants you will immediately be addressed with the one-word *tessék,* meaning "Can I help you?", "What would you like?" or "Next!". To order in restaurants, shops and markets, use *kérek* ("I'd like. . .") plus accusative noun; *Kérem, adjon azt* ("Please give me that"); *Egy ilyet kérek* ("I'll have one of those").

I'd like/we'd like	Szeretnék/szeretnénk
Where is/are . . . ?	Hol van/vannak . . ?
Hurry up!	Siessen!
How much is it?	Mennyibe kerül?
per night	egy éjszakára
per week	egy hétre
a single room	egyágyas szoba
a double room	kétágyas szoba
hot (cold) water	meleg (hideg) víz
a shower	egy zuhany
It's very expensive	Ez nagyon drága
Do you have anything cheaper?	Van valami olcsóbb?
Do you have a student discount?	Van diák kedvezmény?
Is everything included?	Ebben minden szerepel?
I asked for . . .	Én . . . .-t rendeltem
The bill please	Fizetni szeretnék
We're paying separately	Külön-külön fizetünk
what?	mi?
why?	miert?
when?	mikor?
who?	ki?

Some signs

bejárat	entrance
kijárat	exit
érkezés	arrival
indulás	departure

nyitva	open	**szoba kiadó** or **Zimmer frei**	room for rent
zárva	closed	**kórház**	hospital
szabad belépés	free admission	**gyógyszertár**	pharmacy
női (or **WC** – "vait-say")	women's toilet	**(kerületi) Rendőrség**	(local) police
férfi mosdó (or **WC** – "vait-say")	men's toilet	**vigyázat!/vigyázz!**	caution/beware
bolt	shop	**tilos a dohányzás/ dohányozni tilos**	no smoking
piac	market	**tilos a fürdés/füredni tilos**	no bathing

Directions

Where's the . . . ?	Hol van a . . . ?	**towards**	felé
campsite	kemping	**on the right (left)**	jobbra (balra)
hotel	szálloda/ hotel	**straight ahead**	egyenesen előre
railway station	vasútállomás	**(over) there/here**	ott/itt
bus station	buszállomás	**Where are you going?**	Hova megy?
bus-stand	kocsiállás	**Is that on the way to . . . ?**	Az a . . . úton?
(bus or train) stop	megálló	**I want to get out at . . .**	Le akarok szállni . . .-on/en
inland	belföldi	**Please stop here!**	Itt álljon meg!
international	külföldi	**I'm lost!**	Eltévedtem!
Is it near (far)?	Közel (messze) van?	**arrivals**	érkező járatok (or érkezés)
Which bus goes to . . . ?	Melyik busz megy . . .-ra/re?	**departures**	induló járatok (or indulás)
A one-way ticket to . . .please	Egy jegyet kérek . . -ra/re csak oda.	**to/from**	hova/honnan
A return ticket to . . .	Egy retur jegyet . . .-ra/re	**change**	átszállás
Do I have to change trains?	Át kell szállnom?	**via**	át

Descriptions and reactions

and	és	**small**	kicsi
or	vagy	**quick**	gyors
nothing	semmi	**slow**	lassú
perhaps	talán	**now**	most
very	nagyon	**later**	később
good	jó	**beautiful**	szép
bad	rossz	**ugly**	csúnya
better	jobb	**Help!**	Segítség!
big	nagy	**I'm ill**	beteg vagyok

Numbers

1	egy	**40**	negyven
2	kettő	**50**	ötven
3	három	**60**	hatvan
4	négy	**70**	hetven
5	öt	**80**	nyolcvan
6	hat	**90**	kilencven
7	hét	**100**	száz
8	nyolc	**101**	százegy
9	kilenc	**150**	százötven
10	tíz	**200**	kettőszáz
11	tizenegy	**300**	háromszáz
12	tizenkettő	**400**	négyszáz
13	tizenhárom	**500**	ötszáz
14	tizennégy	**600**	hatszáz
15	tizenöt	**700**	hétszáz
16	tizenhat	**800**	nyolcszáz
17	tizenhét	**900**	kilencszáz
18	tizennyolc	**1000**	egyezer
19	tizenkilenc	**half**	fél
20	húsz	**a quarter**	negyed
21	huszonegy	**each/piece**	darab
30	harminc		

Time, days and dates

Luckily, the 24-hour clock is used for timetables, but on cinema programmes you may see notations like 1/4, 3/4, etc. These derive from the spoken expression of time which, as in German, makes reference to the hour approaching completion. For example 3.30 is expressed as *fél négy* – "half (on the way to) four"; 3.45 – *háromnegyed négy* ("three quarters on the way to four"); 6.15 – "*negyed hét*" ("one quarter towards seven"), etc. However, ". . . o'clock" is . . . *óra*, rather than referring to the hour ahead. Duration is expressed by the suffixes *-től* ("from") and *-ig* ("to"); minutes are *perc*; to ask the time, say "*Hány óra?*".

Sunday	vasárnap	**on Monday**	hetfő
Monday	héttő	**on Tuesday**	kedden etc.
Tuesday	kedd	**day**	nap
Wednesday	szerda	**week**	hét
Thursday	csütörtök	**month**	hónap
Friday	péntek	**year**	év
Saturday	szombat		

Hungarian food and drink terms

The food categories below refer to the general divisions used in menus. In cheaper places you will also find a further division of meat dishes: ready-made dishes like stews (*készételek*) and freshly cooked (in theory) dishes such as those cooked in breadcrumbs or grilled (*frissensültek*).

Tészták is a rogue pasta-doughy category that includes savoury dishes such as *turoscsusza* (pasta served with cottage cheese and a sprinkling of bacon), as well as sweet ones like *somlói galuska* (cream and chocolate covered sponge).

Basics

bors	pepper
cukor	sugar
ecet	vinegar
Egészségedre!	Cheers!
Jó étvágyat!	Bon appétit!
kenyér	bread
kifli	croissant-shaped roll
méz	honey
mustár	mustard
rizs	rice
só	salt
tejföl	sour cream
tejszín	cream
vaj	butter
zsemle or péksütemeny	bread rolls

Cooking terms

comb	leg
mell	breast
angolosan	(English-style) underdone/rare
főtt	boiled
főzelék	basic vegetable stews
jól megsütve	well done (fried)
jól megfőzve	well done (boiled)
pörkölt	stewed slowly
rántott	deep fried in breadcrumbs
roston sütve	grilled
sülve	roasted
sült/sütve	fried

Soups (levesek)

bakonyi betyárleves	"Outlaw soup" of chicken, beef, noodles and vegetables, richly spiced
csirke-aprólék leves	mixed vegetable and giblet soup
erőleves	meat consommé often served with noodles (*tésztával* or *metélttel*), liver dumplings (*májgombóccal*), or an egg placed raw into the soup (*tojással*)
gombaleves	mushroom soup
gulyásleves	goulash in its original Hungarian form as a soup, sometimes served in a small kettle pot (*bográcsgulyás*)
halászlé	a rich paprika fish soup often served with hot paprika
húsleves	meat consommé
jókai bableves	bean soup flavoured with smoked meat
kunsági pandúrleves	chicken soup seasoned with nutmeg, paprika and garlic
lencseleves	lentil soup

hideg meggyleves delicious chilled sour cherry soup

palócleves mutton, bean and sour cream soup

paradicsomleves tomato soup

tarkonyos borjúraguleves lamb soup flavoured with tarragon

ujházi tyúkleves chicken soup with noodles, vegetables and meat

zöldségleves vegetable soup

Appetizers (előételek)

These can be served cold (*hideg*) or hot (*meleg*).

füstölt csülök tormával smoked knuckle of pork with horseradish

hortobágyi palacsinta pancake stuffed with minced meat and served with creamy paprika sauce

körözött a paprika-flavoured spread made with sheep's cheese and served with toast

libamáj goose liver

rakott krumpli layered potato casserole with sausage and eggs

rántott gomba mushrooms fried in breadcrumbs, sometimes stuffed with sheep's cheese (*juhtúróval töltött*)

rántott sajt, Camembert, karfiol Camembert or cauliflower fried in breadcrumbs

tatárbeefsteak raw mince that you mix with an egg, salt, pepper, butter, paprika and mustard and spread on toast

velőcsont fokhagymás pirítóssal bone marrow spread on toast rubbed with garlic, a special delicacy associated with the gourmet Gyula Krúdy

Salads (saláták)

Salads are often served in a vinegary dressing, although other dressings include blue cheese (*rokfortos*), yogurt (*joghurtos*) or French (*francia*).

csalamádé mixed pickled salad

fejes saláta lettuce

idénysaláta fresh salad of whatever is in season

jércesaláta chicken salad

paradicsom saláta tomato salad

uborka saláta cucumber which can be gherkins (*csemege* or *kovászos*) or the fresh variety (*friss*)

Fish dishes (halételek)

csuka tejfölben sütve fried pike with sour cream

fogas a local fish of the pike-perch family

fogasszeletek Gundel modra breaded fillet of *fogas*

harcsa catfish

kecsege sterlet (small sturgeon)

nyelvhal sole

paprikás ponty carp in paprika sauce

pisztráng trout

pisztráng tejszínes mártásban trout baked in cream

ponty carp

ponty filé gombával carp fillet in mushroom sauce

rántott pontyfilé	carp fillet fried in breadcrumbs
rostélyos töltött ponty	carp stuffed with bread, egg, herbs and fish liver or roe
süllő	another pike-perch relative
sült hal	fried fish
tonhal	tuna

Meat dishes (húsételek)

baromfi	poultry
bécsi szelet	Wiener schnitzel
bélszin	sirloin
bélszinjava	tenderloin
csirke	chicken
fácán	pheasant
fasírt	meatballs
hátszin	rumpsteak
kacsa	duck
kolbász	spicy sausage
liba	goose
máj	liver
marha	beef
nyúl	rabbit
őz	venison
pulyka	turkey
sertés	pork
sonka	ham
vaddisznó	wild boar
vadételek	game
virsli	frankfurter
borjúpörkölt	closer to what foreigners mean by "goulash", veal stew seasoned with garlic
cigányrostélyos	"Gypsy-style" steak with brown sauce
csikós tokány	strips of beef braised in bacon, onion rings, sour and tomato sauce
csülök Pékné módra	knuckle of pork
erdélyi rakott-káposzta	layers of cabbage, rice and ground pork baked in sour cream (a Transylvanian speciality)
hagymás rostélyos	braised steak piled high with fried onions
pacal	tripe in a paprika sauce
paprikás csirke	chicken in paprika sauce
rablóhús nyárson	kebab of pork, veal and bacon
sertésborda	pork chop
sült libacomb tört burgonyával és párolt káposztával	grilled goose leg with potatoes, onions and steamed cabbage
töltött-káposzta	cabbage stuffed with meat and rice, in a tomato sauce
töltött-paprika	peppers stuffed with meat and rice, in a tomato sauce
vaddisznó borók amártással	wild boar in juniper sauce
vasi pecsenye	fried pork marinated in milk and garlic

Sauces (mártásban)

bormártásban	in a wine sauce
ecetes tormával	with horseradish
fokhagymás mártásban	in a garlic sauce
gombamártásban	in a mushroom sauce
kapormártásban	in a dill sauce
meggymártásban	in a morello cherry sauce
paprikás mártásban	in a paprika sauce
tárkonyos mártásban	in a tarragon sauce
tejszínes paprikás mártásban	in a cream and paprika sauce
vadasmártásban	in a brown sauce (made of mushrooms, almonds, herbs and brandy)

zöldborsós	in a green pea sauce
zöldborsosmártásba	in a green peppercorn sauce

Accompaniments (köretek)

galuska	noodles
hasábburgonya	chips/French fries
krokett	potato croquettes
petrezselymes burgonya	boiled potatoes served with parsley
rizs	rice
zöldköret	mixed vegetables (often of frozen origin)

Vegetables (zöldségek)

bab	beans
borsó	peas
burgonya/krumpli	potatoes
fokhagyma	garlic
gomba	mushrooms
hagyma	onions
káposzta	cabbage
karfiol	cauliflower
kelkáposzta	savoy cabbage
kukorica	sweetcorn
lecsó	a tomato-green pepper stew, a popular ingredient in Hungarian cooking
padlizsán	aubergine/eggplant
paprika (édes/erős)	peppers (sweet/hot)
paradicsom	tomatoes
sárgarépa	carrots
spárga	asparagus
spenot	spinach
uborka	cucumber
zöldbab	green beans
zöldborsó	peas
zukkini	courgette

Fruit (gyümölcs)

alma	apple
bodza	elderflower
citrom	lemon
dió	walnut
eper	strawberry
füge	fig
(görög) dinnye	(water) melon
körte	pear
málna	raspberry
mandula	almond
meggy	morello cherry
mogyoró	hazelnut
narancs	orange
őszibarack	peach
sárgabarack	apricot
szilva	plum
szőlő	grape
tök	marrow or pumpkin/squash

Cheese (sajt)

füstölt sajt	smoked cheese
juhtúró	sheep's cheese
márvány	Danish blue cheese
trappista	rubbery, Edam-type cheese
túró	curd cheese

Glossary

ÁFA Goods tax, equivalent to VAT

alföld Plain; usually refers to the Great Plain (*Nagyalföld*) rather than the Little Plain (*Kisalföld*) in northwestern Hungary

állatkert zoo

áruház department store

autóbuszállomás bus station

ÁVO The dreaded secret police of the Rákosi era, renamed the ÁVH in 1949

barlang cave

Belváros Inner town or city, typically characterized by Baroque or Neoclassical architecture

borkostoló wine tasting

borozó wine bar

botanikuskert botanical garden

büfé snack bar

castrum (Latin) a Roman fortification

cigány Gypsy (can be abusive); hence *cigánytelep*, a Gypsy settlement; and *cigányzene*, Gypsy music

csárda inn; nowadays, a restaurant with rustic decor

csárdás traditional wild dance to violin music

csikós (plural *csikósok*) *puszta* horse herdsman; a much romanticized figure of the nineteenth century

cukrászda cake shop

diszterem ceremonial hall

djami or **dzami** mosque

domb hill; *Rózsadomb*, "Rose Hill" in Budapest

Duna River Danube

Erdély Transylvania; for centuries a part of the Hungarian territories, its loss to Romania in 1920 still rankles

erdő forest, wood

erőd fortification

étterem restaurant

falu village

falusi turizmus tourist network for accommodation in villages

fogadó inn

folyó river

forrás natural spring

fő tér main square

fő utca main street

fürdő public baths, often fed by thermal springs

gyógyfürdő mineral baths with therapeutic properties

hajdúk cattle-drovers turned outlaws, who later settled near Debrecen in the Hajdúság Region

hajó boat

hajóállomás boat landing stage

halászcsárda/halászkert fish restaurants

ház house

hegy hill or low mountain (**hegység** = range of hills)

HÉV commuter train running between Budapest and Szentendre, Gödöllő, Csepel and Ráckeve

híd bridge; Lánchíd, the Chain Bridge in Budapest

honvéd Hungarian army

ifjúsági szálló youth hostel

iskola school

italbolt "drink shop", or a village bar

kápolna chapel

kapu gate

kastély manor house or stately home, country seat of noble families

kávéház coffee house

kert garden, park

kerület (ker.) district

kiállítás exhibition

kincstár treasury

kirakodó vásár fair, craft or flea market

kollégium student hostel

komp ferry

körút (krt.) literally, ring; normally a boulevard around the city centre. Some cities have semi-circular "Great" and "Small" boulevards (Nagykörút and Kiskörút) surrounding their Belváros

kőtár lapidarium

köz alley, lane; also used to define geographical regions, eg the "Mud strip" (*Sárköz*) bordering the Danube

kulcs key

kút well or fountain

lakótelep high-rise apartment buildings

lépcső flight of steps, often in place of a road

liget park, grove or wood

limes (Latin) fortifications along the Danube, marking the limit of Roman territory

lovarda riding school

Magyar Hungarian (pronounced "*mod*-yor")

Magyarország Hungary

Malév Hungarian national airline

MÁV Hungarian national railways

megálló a railway station or bus stop

megye county; originally established by King Stephen to extend his authority over the Magyar tribes

mihrab prayer niche in a mosque, indicating the direction of Mecca

műemlék historic monument, protected building

művelődési ház/központ arts centre

Nyilas "Arrow Cross", Hungarian Fascist movement

Ottomans Founders of the Turkish empire, which included central Hungary during the sixteenth and seventeenth centuries

palota palace; *Püspök-palota,* a Bishop's residence

pályaudvar (pu.) rail terminus

panzió pension

patak stream

pénz money

piac outdoor market

pince cellar; a **Bor-Pince** contains and serves wine

plébánia Catholic priest's house

polgármesteri hivatal mayor's office

puszta another name for the Great Plain, coined when the region was a wilderness

rakpart embankment or quay

Református The reformed church, which in Hungary means the Calvinist faith; *Református lélkész hivatal* is the church office

rév ferry

rom ruined building; sometimes set in a garden with stonework finds, a *Romkert*

Roma The Romany word for Gypsy, preferred by many Roma in Hungary

sétány "walk" or promenade

skanzen outdoor ethnographic museum

söröző beer hall

strand beach, or any area for sunbathing or swimming

szabadtér open-air; as in *színház* (theatre) or *múzeum* (museum)

szálló or **szálloda** hotel

szent saint

sziget island

szoba kiadó room to let

szüret grape harvest

tájház old peasant house turned into a museum, often illustrating the folk traditions of a region or ethnic group

Tanácsköztársaság the "Republic of Councils" or Soviets, which ruled Hungary in 1919

táncház venue for Hungarian folk music and dance

temető cemetery

templom church

tér square; *tere* in the possessive case, as in Hősök tere, "Heroes' Square"

terem hall

tó lake

torony tower; as in *Tv-Torony*, television tower, and *Víztorony*, water tower

türbe tomb or mausoleum of a Muslim dignitary

túristaház tourist hotel

turista térkép hiking map

üdülőház holiday home or workers' hostel

udvar courtyard

út road; in the possessive case, *útja*, eg *Mártírok útja*, "Road of the Martyrs"

utca (u.) street

vár castle; *várrom*, castle ruin

város town; may be divided into an inner *Belváros*, a lower-lying *Alsóváros* and a modern *Újváros* section

városháza town hall

városközpont the town centre

vásár market
vásárcsarnok market hall
vasútállomás train station
vendéglő a type of restaurant
völgy valley; *Hűvösvölgy*, "Cool Valley"
Zsidó Jew or Jewish
zsinagóga synagogu

Rough Guides

advertiser

...music & reference

Mexico
Peru
St Lucia
South America
Trinidad & Tobago

Africa & Middle East

Cape Town
Egypt
The Gambia
Jordan
Kenya
Marrakesh DIRECTIONS
Morocco
South Africa, Lesotho & Swaziland
Syria
Tanzania
Tunisia
West Africa
Zanzibar

Travel Theme guides

First-Time Around the World
First-Time Asia
First-Time Europe
First-Time Latin America
Skiing & Snowboarding in North America
Travel Online
Travel Health
Walks in London & SE England
Women Travel

Restaurant guides

French Hotels & Restaurants
London Restaurants

Maps

Algarve
Amsterdam
Andalucia & Costa del Sol
Argentina
Athens
Australia
Baja California
Barcelona
Berlin
Boston
Brittany
Brussels
Chicago
California
Corsica
Costa Rica & Panama
Crete
Croatia
Cuba
Cyprus
Czech Republic
Dominican Republic
Dubai & UAE
Dublin
Egypt
Florence & Siena
Florida
Frankfurt
Greece
Guatemala & Belize
Iceland
Ireland
Kenya
Lisbon
London
Los Angeles
Madrid
Mallorca
Marrakesh
Mexico
Miami & Key West
Morocco
New York City
New Zealand
Northern Spain
Paris
Peru
Portugal
Prague
Rome
San Francisco
Sicily
South Africa
South India
Sri Lanka
Tenerife
Thailand
Toronto
Trinidad & Tobago
Tuscany
Venice
Washington DC
Yucatán Peninsula

Dictionary Phrasebooks

Czech
Dutch
Egyptian Arabic
European Languages (Czech, French, German, Greek, Italian, Portuguese, Spanish)
French
German
Greek
Hindi & Urdu
Hungarian
Indonesian
Italian
Japanese
Mandarin Chinese
Mexican Spanish
Polish
Portuguese
Russian
Spanish
Swahili
Thai
Turkish
Vietnamese

Music Guides

The Beatles
Bob Dylan
Cult Pop
Classical Music
Elvis
Hip-Hop
Irish Music
Jazz
Music USA
Opera
Reggae
Rock
World Music (2 vols)

Reference Guides

Books for Teenagers
Children's Books, 0–5
Children's Books, 5–11
Cult Fiction
Cult Football
Cult Movies
Cult TV
The Da Vinci Code
Ethical Shopping
iPods, iTunes & Music Online
The Internet
James Bond
Kids' Movies
Lord of the Rings
Muhammad Ali
PCs and Windows
Pregnancy & Birth
Shakespeare
Superheroes
Unexplained Phenomena
The Universe
Weather
Website Directory

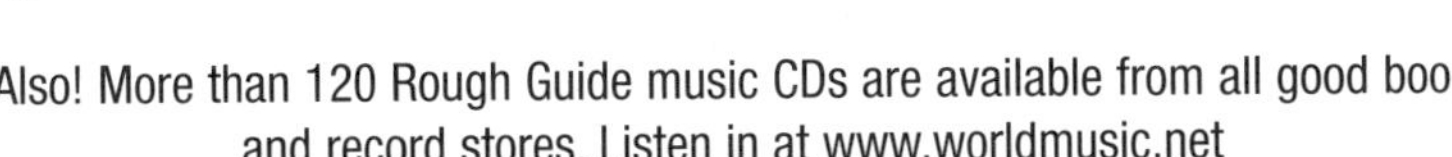

Absolutely everything you need to plan your trip, stay in touch and share your experiences.
CS
INCLUDES
• Planning tools
• Personal website
• Email account
• Digital photo storage
ROUGH GUIDES
intouch
THE ALL-IN-ONE SOFTWARE PACKAGE FOR TRAVEL COMMUNICATIONS AND PLANNING

ROUGH GUIDES

A NEW CONCEPT IN TRAVEL

WHSmith

W

PC WORLD
The Computer Superstore

NOTES

small print and

Index

A Rough Guide to Rough Guides

In the summer of 1981, Mark Ellingham, a recent graduate from Bristol University, was travelling round Greece and couldn't find a guidebook that really met his needs. On the one hand there were the student guides, insistent on saving every last cent, and on the other the heavyweight cultural tomes whose authors seemed to have spent more time in a research library than lounging away the afternoon at a taverna or on the beach.

In a bid to avoid getting a job, Mark and a small group of writers set about creating their own guidebook. It was a guide to Greece that aimed to combine a journalistic approach to description with a thoroughly practical approach to travellers' needs – a guide that would incorporate culture, history and contemporary insights with a critical edge, together with up-to-date, value-for-money listings. Back in London, Mark and the team finished their Rough Guide, as they called it, and talked Routledge into publishing the book.

That first *Rough Guide to Greece*, published in 1982, was a student scheme that became a publishing phenomenon. The immediate success of the book – with numerous reprints and a Thomas Cook prize shortlisting – spawned a series that rapidly covered dozens of destinations. Rough Guides had a ready market among low-budget backpackers, but soon also acquired a much broader and older readership that relished Rough Guides' wit and inquisitiveness as much as their enthusiastic, critical approach. Everyone wants value for money, but not at any price.

Rough Guides soon began supplementing the "rougher" information about hostels and low-budget listings with the kind of detail on restaurants and quality hotels that independent-minded visitors on any budget might expect, whether on business in New York or trekking in Thailand.

These days the guides – distributed worldwide by the Penguin group – offer recommendations from shoestring to luxury and cover more than 200 destinations around the globe, including almost every country in the Americas and Europe, more than half of Africa and most of Asia and Australasia. Our ever-growing team of authors and photographers is spread all over the world, particularly in Europe, the USA and Australia.

In 1994, we published the *Rough Guide to World Music* and *Rough Guide to Classical Music*; and a year later the *Rough Guide to the Internet*. All three books have become benchmark titles in their fields – which encouraged us to expand into other areas of publishing, mainly around popular culture. Rough Guides now publish:

- Travel guides to more than 200 worldwide destinations
- Dictionary phrasebooks to 22 major languages
- History guides ranging from Ireland to Islam
- Maps printed on rip-proof and waterproof Polyart™ paper
- Music guides running the gamut from Opera to Elvis
- Restaurant guides to London, New York and San Francisco
- Reference books on topics as diverse as the Weather and Shakespeare
- Sports guides from Formula 1 to Man Utd
- Pop culture books from *Lord of the Rings* to Cult TV
- World Music CDs in association with World Music Network

Visit **www.roughguides.com** to see our latest publications.

Rough Guide credits

Text editors: Sally Schafer, Andy Turner
Layout: Diana Jarvis, Dan May
Cartography: Ashutosh Bharti
Picture research: Jj Luck
Proofreader: Jan Wilshire

....

Editorial: **London** Martin Dunford, Kate Berens, Claire Saunders, Geoff Howard, Ruth Blackmore, Gavin Thomas, Polly Thomas, Richard Lim, Clifton Wilkinson, Alison Murchie, Sally Schafer, Karoline Densley, Andy Turner, Ella O'Donnell, Keith Drew, Edward Aves, Nikki Birrell, Chloë Thomson, Helen Marsden, Andrew Lockett, Joe Staines, Duncan Clark, Peter Buckley, Matthew Milton, Daniel Crewe; **New York** Andrew Rosenberg, Richard Koss, Chris Barsanti, Steven Horak, AnneLise Sorensen, Amy Hegarty
Design & Pictures: **London** Simon Bracken, Dan May, Diana Jarvis, Mark Thomas, Jj Luck, Harriet Mills, Chloë Roberts; **Delhi** Madhulita Mohapatra, Umesh Aggarwal, Ajay Verma, Jessica Subramanian, Amit Verma
Production: Julia Bovis, Sophie Hewat, Katherine Owers
Cartography: **London** Maxine Repath, Ed Wright, Katie Lloyd-Jones; **Delhi** Manish Chandra, Rajesh Chhibber, Jai Prakash Mishra, Ashutosh Bharti, Rajesh Mishra, Animesh Pathak, Jasbir Sandhu, Karobi Gogoi
Online: **New York** Jennifer Gold, Cree Lawson, Suzanne Welles, Benjamin Ross; **Delhi** Manik Chauhan, Narender Kumar, Shekhar Jha, Rakesh Kumar
Marketing & Publicity: **London** Richard Trillo, Niki Hanmer, David Wearn, Demelza Dallow; **New York** Geoff Colquitt, Megan Kennedy
Custom publishing and foreign rights: Philippa Hopkins
Finance: Gary Singh
Manager India: Punita Singh
Series editor: Mark Ellingham
PA to Managing Director: Megan McIntyre
Managing Director: Kevin Fitzgerald

Publishing information

This sixth edition published August 2005 by
Rough Guides Ltd,
80 Strand, London WC2R 0RL.
345 Hudson St, 4th Floor,
New York, NY 10014, USA.
Distributed by the Penguin Group
Penguin Books Ltd,
80 Strand, London WC2R 0RL
Penguin Putnam, Inc.
375 Hudson Street, NY 10014, USA
Penguin Group (Australia)
250 Camberwell Road, Camberwell
Victoria 3124, Australia
Penguin Books Canada Ltd,
10 Alcorn Avenue, Toronto, Ontario,
Canada M4V 1E4
Penguin Group (New Zealand)
Cnr Rosedale and Airborne roads
Albany, Auckland, New Zealand
Typeset in Bembo and Helvetica to an original design by Henry Iles.

Printed and bound in China

512pp includes index
A catalogue record for this book is available from the British Library

ISBN 1-84353-480-0

The publishers and authors have done their best to ensure the accuracy and currency of all the information in **The Rough Guide to Hungary**, however, they can accept no responsibility for any loss, injury, or inconvenience sustained by any traveller as a result of information or advice contained in the guide.

1 3 5 7 9 8 6 4 2

Help us update

We've gone to a lot of effort to ensure that the sixth edition of **The Rough Guide to Hungary** is accurate and up-to-date. However, things change – places get "discovered", opening hours are notoriously fickle, restaurants and rooms raise prices or lower standards. If you feel we've got it wrong or left something out, we'd like to know, and if you can remember the address, the price, the time, the phone number, so much the better.

We'll credit all contributions, and send a copy of the next edition (or any other Rough Guide if you prefer) for the best letters. Everyone who writes to us and isn't already a subscriber will receive a copy of our full-colour thrice-yearly newsletter. Please mark letters: "**Rough Guide Hungary Update**" and send to: Rough Guides, 80 Strand, London WC2R 0RL, or Rough Guides, 4th Floor, 345 Hudson St, New York, NY 10014. Or send an email to **mail@roughguides.com**

Have your questions answered and tell others about your trip at **www.roughguides.atinfopop.com**

Acknowledgements

Norm Longley: A very special thanks to Elizabeth Courage, Magdolna and Gabor Tarr, and Tsvia Vorley. Thanks are also due to Andrea Rádóczy, Maria Pap, Edit Árki, Ilona Katona, Fruszina Szép, Péter Brózik, Michael Felsch, Bob Cohen and Szilvia Kenessey. Last, but by no means least, my colleague Charles, and my inordinately patient editor, Sally.

Charles Hebbert: Thank you to Caroline Hebbert, Rachel Appleby, Balogh Ildiko, Biber Krisztina, Eileen GP Brown, Farkas Lilla, Fenyő Krisztina, Sean Harvey, Kosa Judit, Lőrincz Anna, Meriel and Bill, Mihalcsik Judit, Nadori Peter and Duncan Shiels.

Readers' letters

Thanks to all the readers who have taken the time to write in with comments and suggestions (and apologies if we've inadvertently omitted or misspelt anyone's name):

John and Hilda Allen, Ruth Colclough, Jonathan Heppell, Bill Hosker and Kate Winter, Dr. Ryan James, Davida Jordan, Peter Lord, Brian McMahon, Marius Møllerson, Dwight Newman, Rohan Oberoi, Nick Robinson, Anthony Rosen, Sheila Rowell, Joyce Simson, Alexa Spiller, Ronelle Ward, Schy Willmore, Mel Ziino.

Photo credits

Cover
Main front: Opera House, Budapest © Getty
Small front top: Applied Arts Museum, Budapest © Alamy
Small front lower: Old street, Buda © Alamy
Back top: Abbey church, Tihany © Alamy
Back lower: Gellért Baths, Budapest © Alamy

Introduction
Esztergom Basilica, Esztergom, Danube Bend © jonarnoldimages
Chain Bridge, Budapest © David Mark Soulsby/arcaid.co.uk/Alamy
Countryside in Kecskemét © Sandro Vannini/Corbis
Esterházy Palace, Fertőd © T.Bognar/Trip
Sailing on Lake Balaton © Péter Korniss
Trams in Budapest © Peter Wilson
Statue Park, Budapest © Tony Waltham/Robert Harding
Souvenirs, Szentendre © jonarnoldimages
Cifra palace, Kecskemét © Dave Bartruff/Corbis
Grapes, Tokaj region © Peter Wilson
Chess at Széchenyi Baths, Budapest © Catherine Karnow/Corbis
Countryside in Kecskemét © Sandro Vannini/Corbis

Things not to miss
1. Hollókő © Peter Wilson
2. Thermal baths, Budapest © Kleb Attila
3. View over the vineyards of Mt Badacsony © CEPHAS/Mick Rock/Alamy
4. Pécs © Gregory Wrona
5. Tihany peninsula © John Miller/Robert Harding
6. Aggtelek Caves © Peter Wilson
7. Szentendre © Hungarian National Tourist Office
8. Statue Park, Budapest © Tony Waltham/Robert Harding
9. Sailing on Lake Balaton © Péter Korniss
10. Rákóczi wine cellar, Tokaj © Péter Korniss
11. Eger © R.H. Productions/Robert Harding
12. Paprika © Charles Hebbert
13. Esterházy Palace, Fertőd © T.Bognar/Trip
14. Corkscrew-horned sheep, Hortobágy National Park © Péter Korniss
15. Budapest Spring Festival, Chain Bridge © Courtesy of Budapest Spring Festival
16. Pannonhalma Monastery © Péter Korniss
17. Sopron © jonarnoldimages
18. Budapest at night © Péter Korniss
19. Busójárás Carnival, Mohács © Péter Korniss
20. Solomon's Tower, Visegrád, Danube Bend © Robert Harding
21. Bükk Hills © Péter Korniss
22. Folk musicians © Charles Hebbert

Black and white photos
Gellért Baths © Péter Korniss p.64
Chain Bridge and Parliament building at night © Simon Reddy/Alamy p.96
Central Kávéház © jonarnoldimages p.130
Esztergom Basilica © Peter Wilson p.154
Hungarian Open-Air Museum © mediacolors/Alamy p.164
Festetics Palace, Keszthely © Peter Wilson p.192
Gyógy-tó, Hévíz © jonarnoldimages p.204
St Peter and St Paul Basilica, Pécs © jonarnoldimages p.246
Catholic Church, Paks © Charles Hebbert p.315
Vineyards, Tokaj © Péter Korniss p.322
Tokaj © jonarnoldimages p.358
Horses in Hortobágy National Park © Péter Korniss p.374
Town Hall, Szeged © jonarnoldimages p.403

Index

Map entries are in colour.

INDEX

C

D

E

F

INDEX

G

H

I

J

K

L

M

N

O

W

Z

Map symbols

maps are listed in the full index using coloured text

- Chapter division boundary
- International boundary
- Motorway
- Major road
- Minor road
- Pedestrianized street
- Steps
- Railway
- Footpath
- River
- Ferry
- Wall
- Gate
- Bridge
- Level crossing
- Mountain range
- Mountain peak
- Swamp
- Airport
- Metro station
- Bus stop
- Parking
- Point of interest
- Internet café
- Tourist office/information point
- Post office
- Museum
- Campsite
- Cave
- Ruin
- Arch
- Lighthouse
- Synagogue
- Mosque
- Church (regional maps)
- Church (town maps)
- Building
- Market
- Stadium
- Cemetery
- Park
- Forest